Rethinking the Education of Multilingual Learners

with best wishes

Jim Cummins

LINGUISTIC DIVERSITY AND LANGUAGE RIGHTS

Series Editor: Dr Tove Skutnabb-Kangas, *Åbo Akademi University, Finland*

Consulting Advisory Board:
François Grin, *Université de Genève, Switzerland*
Miklós Kontra, *Károli Gáspár University, Hungary*
Robert Phillipson, *Copenhagen Business School, Denmark*
Reetta Toivanen, *University of Helsinki, Finland*

The series seeks to promote multilingualism as a resource, the maintenance of linguistic diversity, and development of and respect for linguistic human rights worldwide through the dissemination of theoretical and empirical research. The series encourages interdisciplinary approaches to language policy, drawing on sociolinguistics, education, sociology, economics, human rights law, political science, as well as anthropology, psychology, and applied language studies.

All books in this series are externally peer-reviewed.

Full details of all the books in this series and of all our other publications can be found on http://www.multilingual-matters.com, or by writing to Multilingual Matters, St Nicholas House, 31-34 High Street, Bristol BS1 2AW, UK.

LINGUISTIC DIVERSITY AND LANGUAGE RIGHTS: 19

Rethinking the Education of Multilingual Learners

A Critical Analysis of Theoretical Concepts

Jim Cummins

MULTILINGUAL MATTERS
Bristol • Blue Ridge Summit

DOI https://doi.org/10.21832/CUMMIN3580
Library of Congress Cataloging in Publication Data
Names: Cummins, Jim, author.
Title: Rethinking the Education of Multilingual Learners: A Critical Analysis of
  Theoretical Concepts/Jim Cummins.
Description: Bristol, UK; Blue Ridge Summit, PA: Multilingual Matters, 2021. | Series:
  Linguistic Diversity and Language Rights: 19 | Includes bibliographical references
  and index. | Summary: "Over the past 40 years, Jim Cummins has originated
  theories which have had a profound effect on the education of multilingual learners
  across the world. In this book he traces the development of these theories, and
  addresses the critiques they have received and their subsequent impact on his
  thinking and the application of his theories in schools"— Provided by publisher.
Identifiers: LCCN 2021015598 (print) | LCCN 2021015599 (ebook) |
  ISBN 9781800413580 (hardback) | ISBN 9781800413573 (paperback) |
  ISBN 9781800413597 (pdf) | ISBN 9781800413603 (epub)
Subjects: LCSH: Multilingual education. | Language and education. | Linguistic
  minorities—Education.
Classification: LCC LC3715 .C86 2021 (print) | LCC LC3715 (ebook) |
  DDC 370.117/5—dc23 LC record available at https://lccn.loc.gov/2021015598
LC ebook record available at https://lccn.loc.gov/2021015599

A catalog record for this book is available from the Library of Congress.

British Library Cataloguing in Publication Data
A catalogue entry for this book is available from the British Library.

ISBN-13: 978-1-80041-358-0 (hbk)
ISBN-13: 978-1-80041-357-3 (pbk)

Multilingual Matters
UK: St Nicholas House, 31-34 High Street, Bristol BS1 2AW, UK.
USA: NBN, Blue Ridge Summit, PA, USA.

Website: www.multilingual-matters.com
Twitter: Multi_Ling_Mat
Facebook: https://www.facebook.com/multilingualmatters
Blog: www.channelviewpublications.wordpress.com

The policy of Multilingual Matters/Channel View Publications is to use papers that
are natural, renewable and recyclable products, made from wood grown in
sustainable forests. In the manufacturing process of our books, and to further
support our policy, preference is given to printers that have FSC and PEFC Chain of
Custody certification. The FSC and/or PEFC logos will appear on those books
where full certification has been granted to the printer concerned.

Typeset by Nova Techset Private Limited, Bengaluru and Chennai, India.
Printed and bound in the UK by Short Run Press Ltd.
Printed and bound in the US by NBN.

Contents

Acknowledgements

A book that attempts to synthesise almost half a century of research and academic work owes a debt of gratitude to many, many, people without whom it would not have been written. First, I want to acknowledge my parents whose love and support created a foundation which remains solid today. My partner of 34 years, Ioana, shared psychological and physical space with these ideas, with only occasional complaints about the laden bookshelves gathering dust in basement, garage, attic and bedrooms. Thank you for your patience, love, support, and wonderful sense of humour. My children, Holly, Daniel, Josiane, Stephen, Thomas and Julisa, knew that their Dad worked at the university and did something related to education; despite their vague sense of how people in universities spend their days, each in his or her own way contributed to my understanding of possibility and lightened my step as I trudged home on a daily basis from the university where I was 'doing something'.

My early academic work was strongly influenced by four colleagues who have continued their guidance and encouragement over many years and with whom I have published and/or presented on many occasions. My long-term colleague, Merrill Swain, first suggested the possibility of joining the Modern Language Centre (MLC) of the Ontario Institute for Studies in Education (OISE) and was instrumental in making that happen in the late 1970s. Colleagues and graduate students in the MLC and in the Language and Literacies Education programme at OISE have supported and sustained my research and scholarly work for almost my entire academic career. Merrill and I attempted to integrate our research and theoretical perspectives in the 1986 book *Bilingualism in Education*, and we also collaborated with other colleagues during the 1980s on a major research project entitled 'The Development of Bilingual Proficiency' funded by the Social Sciences and Humanities Research Council of Canada.

Tove Skutnabb-Kangas was reckless enough to invite me to give a series of lectures and seminars in Finland and Sweden in early 1979, long before I had the academic knowledge, personal experience, or communication skills to discuss the issues coherently. Needless to say, it was a learning experience, but it did eventually help me learn how to swim in the deep end of academic debate. The collaboration and friendship that took root during that trip resulted in our edited volume *Minority Education: From Shame to Struggle* and has culminated in the appearance of this current book in Tove's Multilingual Matters book series 'Linguistic Diversity and Language Rights'.

Lily Wong Fillmore has also been a close friend and mentor, both to me and my family, since the late 1970s and we have presented together at many conferences, professional development workshops, and university courses over a period of almost 40 years. I am truly grateful to Lily for the Foreword she has written to this volume which draws on her immense experience of working with teachers, families, policymakers, and curriculum developers to frame, and situate in the real world, the theoretical ideas I discuss in these pages. Lily's razor-sharp intellect, her passion for equity, and her infectious humour have guided the professional practice of countless educators. Her work has also enriched the lives of minoritised students and their families throughout the United States and beyond.

Finally, I owe a major debt of gratitude to Margaret Early of the University of British Columbia with whom I have worked closely since the late 1980s. Margaret was instrumental in obtaining funding for our 4-year 'Multiliteracies' project which we led between 2002 and 2006. The inspirational instructional initiatives implemented by teachers in the context of this project helped generate the notion of 'identity texts' and resulted in our jointly edited volume entitled *Identity Texts: The Collaborative Creation of Power in Multilingual Schools* (2011). The ideas I have tried to synthesise in the present volume have been shaped by the insightful and critically constructive feedback that Margaret has offered on many occasions.

I would also like to acknowledge the influence of many other colleagues with whom I have worked over the years. For example, in the late 1990s, Sandra Schecter of York University in Toronto invited me to participate in a collaborative project with teachers in Thornwood and Floradale elementary schools in the Peel District Board of Education near Toronto. This project generated many significant instructional initiatives including the Dual Language Showcase, which was the brainchild of Grade 1 teacher, Patricia Chow (see Chapter 11). This was one of the first examples of how teachers could mobilize multilingual students' language and cultural knowledge for learning. The outcomes of the project were described in the 2003 book that Sandra and I edited entitled *Multilingual Education in Practice: Using Diversity as a Resource*.

I have also had the privilege of collaborating with Professor Kazuko Nakajima (University of Toronto) over many years, initially during the early and mid-1980s with a focus on investigating L1/L2 interdependence among Japanese-speaking students in the Toronto area. Our ongoing collaboration, facilitated by former OISE doctoral student Hitomi Oketani (University of Michigan), has explored ways in which educational policies and instructional practices in Japan can become more evidence-based and equitable in relation to the children of migrant workers.

Pedagogical innovation in the context of changing demographics and emerging technologies was the focus of my collaboration with my late friend and colleague, Dennis Sayers, who together with Kristin Brown were pioneers during the early 1980s and beyond in exploring the potential of new communication technologies for multilingual and intercultural exchange. Dennis and I co-authored the 1995 book *Brave New Schools: Challenging Cultural Illiteracy through Global Learning Networks*, and Kristin, Dennis and I wrote *Literacy, Technology, and Diversity: Teaching for Success in Changing Times* (2007).

I have benefitted greatly from the opportunity to spend time in several European countries where issues related to diversity and the education of immigrant and minoritised students have frequently been the subject of volatile debate. In the mid-1990s, Eleni Skourtou of the University of the Aegean in Rhodes, Greece, invited me to spend some time working with faculty, students, and the multilingual community in that magical city. We have continued to meet and collaborate over the past 25 years on both sides of the Atlantic. Eleni was instrumental in arranging for a Greek translation of my 1996 book *Negotiating Identities: Education for Empowerment in a Diverse Society*. The many intense and fruitful discussions I have had with both Eleni and Vasilia Kourtis-Kazoullis, also from the University of the Aegean, were instrumental in helping to formulate the notions of *nested pedagogical orientations* and *identity texts* that are discussed in Chapter 5. Vasilia graciously agreed to contribute a Foreword to the second edition (2001) of my *Negotiating Identities* book.

Starting in the mid-2000s, Lars Anders Kulbrandstad and colleagues at Høgskolen i Innlandet (formerly Høgskolen i Hedmark – Hedmark University College) invited me (and other Toronto-based educators) on multiple occasions to participate in conferences and seminars in Hamar, Norway, focused on issues of diversity and teacher education. The exchange was two-way, with extended visits to Toronto from Norwegian university faculty and educators. During a similar time period, several reciprocal visits and exchange of experiences and perspectives also took place with educators and university faculty from Falun, Sweden, with Åsa Wedin from Dalarna University as the main organizer. I also had the opportunity over a three-year period (2016–2019) to serve as an Adjunct Professor at Åbo Akademi University, in Vaasa, Finland. My understanding of the complexities of linguistic diversity in education was deepened through various forms of collaboration with Liselott Forsman, Siv Björklund, Mikaela Björklund and other colleagues. Finally, I would like to thank Jenni Alisaari of Turku University for the opportunity to contribute to and learn from the Diversity in Education project that she led. One of the significant outcomes of this project has been the publication of a rich tapestry of 'language-friendly' instructional strategies for use in Finnish schools.

It is important to acknowledge one other collaboration with Swedish colleagues Päivi Juvonen and Marie Källkvist who edited the book *Pedagogical Translanguaging: Theoretical, Methodological and Empirical Perspectives* (Multilingual Matters, 2021). My paper in their edited book addresses similar issues related to the concept of 'Translanguaging' to those discussed in Chapter 10. The decision to name two opposing conceptions of translanguaging theory (Unitary versus Crosslinguistic), rather than just critique some current problematic conceptions of translanguaging, was based on editorial feedback provided by Päivi and Marie, and I am grateful for their insightful suggestion which clarifies discussion of the issues.

In recent years, I have benefitted from joint projects and theoretical discussion with Rahat Zaidi (University of Calgary) whose research has explored issues related to early multilingual literacy interventions and bilingual education in the Alberta context. I am also indebted to Judith Bernhard (Ryerson University) who invited me to co-author one of the research papers on identity texts that emerged from her innovative large-scale family literacy project entitled the *Early Authors Project*. The *Songide'ewin: Aboriginal Narratives* project initiated by Kristiina Montero (Wilfred Laurier University) deepened my knowledge of what could be achieved in concrete terms through a decolonizing educational approach. I am grateful to Kristiina for her generous invitation to participate in exploring students' insights and reflections regarding the identity affirmation they experienced as a result of their individual and collective 'identity text' work.

The ideas and insights of former OISE graduate students, with whom I worked over the past 30 years, are also reflected in this volume. Roma Chumak-Horbatsch of Ryerson University in Toronto, Shelley Taylor of Western University in London Ontario, Fiona Walton and Sandy McAuley of the University of Prince Edward Island, Antoinette Gagné of OISE, and Jia Li of the Ontario University of Technology have all contributed significantly to our collective understanding of multilingual learning, intercultural teaching, and teacher education in contexts of diversity and unequal power relations. The evolution of my own ideas relating to these issues continues to be shaped through ongoing exchange with these friends and colleagues.

With the advent of the new millennium, significant insights were generated by several graduate or postdoctoral students who participated in the Multiliteracies project. The research of Vicki Bismilla (formerly Centennial College), Sarah Cohen (Loyola University Chicago), Frances Giampapa (University of Bristol), and Kristin Snoddon (Ryerson University), documented in concrete ways the central role that dual language identity texts could play in generating collaborative relations of power between teachers and students.

In early January 2021, 11 former graduate students with whom I worked either as thesis supervisor or committee member read an early draft of the present volume and provided useful feedback and suggestions in the course of a Zoom meeting. These former graduate students are all making important contributions in the fields of bilingual education, plurilingual pedagogy, critical literacy, and the education of marginalised multilingual students. I am grateful to the following friends and colleagues for their important feedback which has been incorporated into the book: Stephen Bahry, Bapujee Biswabandan, James Corcoran, Angelica Galante, Amir Kalan, Sunny Man Chu Lau, Mario López-Gopar, Brian Morgan, Burcu Yaman Ntelioglou, Gail Prasad and Saskia Van Viegen. The influence of these scholars on my own thinking obviously goes far beyond a simple collective Zoom meeting and I continue to follow and learn from their impressive research and theoretical insights.

A major theme running through this book is that of *educators as knowledge generators* and I would like to acknowledge and express my appreciation to the many teachers and school administrators who have shared their creativity and wisdom with me over the past 40 years. Two school principals with whom I have worked stand out as inspirational leaders and champions of equity. Raymond Isola served for 13 years as principal of Sanchez School in the heart of San Francisco's Mission district. The innovative structures of shared leadership, community engagement, and biliteracy instruction at both preschool and elementary school levels that Raymond initiated transformed Sanchez from a failing dysfunctional school to one that significantly outperformed a large majority of schools with similar demographic characteristics. Raymond and I co-authored a book entitled *Transforming Sanchez School: Shared Leadership, Equity, and Evidence* (2020) that documented this journey and its broader significance for educational policy.

Another inspirational leader from whom I have learned is Roberto Di Prospero ('Mr. Di' to his students) who was principal of Thornwood Public School in the Peel District School Board when I was involved with the school in a collaborative project entitled 'Pushing the Boundaries' (2009–2011). Roberto strongly promoted collective leadership among his teaching staff and encouraged them to innovate instructionally in pursuit of the 'big ideas' and shared vision of the school, which had been generated collectively by the teachers themselves. One interaction with Roberto stands out for me. Some of the teachers had expressed the fact that they were not at all concerned about how their students would do on the grade 3 provincially mandated standardised math and literacy tests. Their perspective was the test will take care of itself, and they felt no need to spend any instructional time preparing students for the test. They knew that their students were engaged in such powerful learning that they were not at risk of performing poorly. 'And even if what they are capable of doing doesn't show up on the test, so what? We know what they can do, and they know what they can do'. Roberto's response to hearing this was: 'I've got goosebumps right now, Jim. I am so happy they answered like that'. The school where Roberto is currently principal, Silver Creek Public School, is the first Canadian school to formally become a 'Language Friendly School' (see Chapter 11 and languagefriendlyschool.org).

Teachers who have played prominent roles as knowledge generators in the various collaborative projects I have been involved in over the past 20+ years include Patricia Chow, Sukayna Dewji, Hina Kauser-Ahmad, Lisa Leoni, Rania Mirza, Robin Persad, Perminder Sandhu, Padma Sastri and Tobin Zikmanis among others. The inspirational work of many of these teachers is outlined in Chapter 11 and elsewhere (e.g. Cummins & Early, 2011, 2015).

Educators within the International Schools community have also been leaders in challenging monolingual approaches to teaching multilingual students and have pioneered the implementation of innovative multilingual instructional strategies. These strategies have gradually evolved and have been shared among colleagues during regular conferences in which I have been fortunate to participate since the 1980s. This change in orientation from a deficit view of children's multilingual experience to a vibrantly multilingual/plurilingual approach is very clearly expressed in Eithne Gallagher's (2008) book entitled *Equal Rights to the Curriculum: Many Languages, One Message*. Eithne and I have presented workshops together on multiple occasions and I am grateful to her and her International Schools colleagues for the opportunity to participate in many discussions about how change can be enacted at the level of the individual school. I particularly appreciate the ongoing dialogues about these issues I have had with Mindy McCracken and Lara Rikers of the International School of The Hague (ISH) who, together with Pascale Hertay, the ISH primary school vice-principal at the time, and other ISH colleagues, have been at the forefront of integrating powerful multilingual instructional perspectives across the entire school curriculum.

It has been surprising and humbling to realize how lengthy this minimal sketch of the many people who have contributed to 'my' academic work has turned out to be. It remains for me to thank three additional people who do not fit easily into any of the superficial categories outlined above. First, I want to thank Robert Phillipson, partner and academic collaborator over many years with Tove Skutnabb-Kangas, who has shared incisive and thought-provoking insights on issues related to this book. Robert's ground-breaking work on linguistic imperialism highlighted the intersection of societal power relations and educational policy, themes that are reflected, from a somewhat different perspective, in this volume.

Second, I want to acknowledge my recent collaboration with my OISE colleague, Emmanuelle Le Pichon Vorstman, on a variety of issues ranging from the *Language Friendly Schools* project, initiated by Emmanuelle and Ellen-Rose Kambel in the Netherlands, to our current research on exploring the potential of *Binogi*, an online instructional resource developed initially in Sweden about 10 years ago that includes the presentation of academic content in multiple languages spoken by immigrant students. Emmanuelle's intellectual energy and personal charisma has made it easy to stay engaged in working with teachers who are opening up classroom spaces that enable multilingual students to use their full linguistic repertoire.

Finally, I want to thank Christine Hélot (Université de Strasbourg) who provided sage feedback on initial drafts of papers that explored the issues discussed in the present volume. It was Christine who initially introduced me to language policy and pedagogical issues in France and its overseas territories. We had the opportunity to present at the same conference in Tahiti in November 2011 where the challenges of decolonising educational systems were intensely discussed. Christine invited me to spend a month at the University of Strasbourg in early 2015, an opportunity that significantly extended my understanding of possibilities and constraints in educating multilingual students. During this period, I also had the opportunity to discuss with Andrea Young and Latisha Mary the illuminating research on classroom translanguaging they were undertaking at the time. This research is outlined in Chapter 11.

Ideas are germinated, grow, and take flight through engaged and affirming dialogue. I have been fortunate that many friends and colleagues have helped the ideas in this book not only take flight but also come safely back to earth where they have the possibility of being infused into new dialogues. I am reminded of what one elementary school student who participated in the Multiliteracies project said when asked about the use of home languages in the school: *I feel that when I speak my first language I will be accepted, not rejected. If I had the permission to speak my first language, I will feel confident, free, feel like I can catch a dream and run with it*. Thank you to everybody who, over many years, has helped me to catch a dream and run with it.

Foreword

In the world of bilingual education research and practice, Jim Cummins stands out as the leading theorist and major influencer on educational policy, assessment and classroom practice. This book is both a critical analysis of current takes on various theoretical constructs that have come from or are relevant to Cummins' work, and an intellectual history of the evolution of his major theories and their transformation into frameworks for action: on the nature of language proficiency and how judgments of proficiency can affect educational treatment of students, on cognitive consequences of bilingual development, and on power relations between groups and how they can affect student academic performance and the development of identity. Grounded in research, tempered by criticism (constructive and otherwise), Cummins' theories have stood the test of time and influenced instruction in ways that the work of few others in the field have. Bilingual education, despite its obvious suitability for schools in a linguistically diverse society, is an educational approach that has been politicised, polarised, and freighted with controversy from its inception. The pushback to this instructional approach lays bare the long-standing underlying problem of power relations and allocation that exists between groups in American society, and the distrust of groups that are perceived as outsiders.

The overarching framework in this book is that the poor educational outcomes for minoritised students in a society like the US are directly related to power relations that operate in schools and the society, and evidence of that relationship can be seen in the disparities in school facilities and educational opportunities provided students depending on where they live, and student characteristics such race, ethnicity, language background, and parental economic status. What Cummins offers us is a cogent framework for understanding how that happens, and consequently for how that relationship can be altered or ameliorated. The fraught relations between groups were magnified in the 1980s when sizeable influxes of immigrants and refugees from Central America and Southeast Asia entered the US, which aroused a resurgence of long- standing nativist and anti-immigrant sentiments in states and communities where they settled. The hostility towards immigrants and minoritised groups in the society would eventually expand into restrictive legislation aimed at banning the use of languages other than English in schools and in public life and designating English as the official language in many states. US schools have become increasingly segregated in recent decades, with English learners concentrated in schools with high proportions of racial minorities and high poverty background students, and English is the only language of instruction in most schools beyond the early elementary years.

When Cummins' work began in the late 1970s, bilingual instruction was being adopted in schools across the US in response to the Office of Civil Rights' enforcement of the Supreme Court's decision in the *Lau* v. *Nichols* case, and opposition to the approach was becoming vocal. Why, it was asked, if the goal of bilingual education is to help children learn English and to succeed in school, are they being taught in Spanish, or whatever language it is they already speak? How is teaching children to read in Spanish helping them learn to read in English? Among mainstream educators especially, there was a suspicion that instructing students in their primary language any longer than necessary would impede their educational progress. Would the use of students' L1s in school any longer than necessary delay their learning of English? How long should students remain in bilingual programmes? Schools were required to assess students' developing proficiency in English – how proficient must students be in English and how long does that take before they can be 'exited' from bilingual instruction, and placed in the mainstream school programme?

For educators and supporters of bilingual programmes, Cummins' research and theories of linguistic and educational development in bilingual children were lifelines – foundational works, not only for understanding the complexities of bilingual development and to counter the arguments being made against the approach, but also as guides for improving instructional practice. How a second language develops in relation to a first language, and how that process might affect children's performance in school were issues for which bilingual educators needed clarity. Among the most important findings from his early research was evidence that language proficiency was markedly more complex than recognised at the time. For schools, the assessment of language proficiency was a key to determining which students required bilingual instructional support and for how long, but the few instruments then available for making such important decisions were mostly assessments of oral language. Children were asked to respond to questions, provide simple descriptions of pictures, distinguish between words that were read to them, and the like. Such assessments had the advantage of being easy to administer and to score, but they revealed little about how children might perform in literacy or the learning of school subjects.

Bilingual educators took notice when Cummins argued that the assessments in use at that time were based on an inadequate understanding of language proficiency and how it figures in academic development. His argument that language proficiency comprised two more or less specialised

components – what he initially characterised as basic interpersonal communication skills (BICS) and cognitive academic language proficiency (CALP),
which required different types of experiences and time to develop – may have
been controversial for armchair bilingual theorists who subjected it to acer-
bic criticism, but practitioners who were working most directly with learners recognised the usefulness of this distinction for understanding children's
language learning behavior, which they could observe in school. Children
were indeed able to learn enough English in a year or two to communicate
with peers and to function socially in the classroom but were nevertheless
unable to participate with much understanding in literacy or subject matter
learning. Equally persuasive and relevant for policy was Cummins'
research finding that it could take from five to seven years for children to
attain the level of proficiency in a second language equivalent to that of
native speakers and would no longer require special linguistic consideration. Cummins' research and framework on bilingual proficiency helped
bilingual educators build the case for additive bilingual programmes which
provide children time enough to develop their academic and linguistic
capabilities in both languages. There has been a near universal acceptance
of the finding that it takes from five to seven years for children to achieve
proficiency in a second language, although that depends on the instructional support they are provided in school.

Over the past couple of decades, however, there have been numerous
reports of students who do not achieve the level of English proficiency
required for reclassification well beyond the five to seven years that have
been established as the norm. In some places, students are reported as
taking as long as eight to ten years to pass an English proficiency test.
Indeed, a review of the research on the time it takes for children to achieve
proficiency in a second language that was included in the 2017 consensus
study on *Promoting the Educational Success of Children and Youth
Learning English* by the National Academies of Sciences, Engineering and
Mathematics (NASEM, 215-257), concluded that although 5 to 7 years is
the standard, the time it actually takes for ELs to be reclassified as fluent
English speakers may vary by group, it depends on the quality of instruction students are provided in school, and it can also vary, depending on
teachers' beliefs about ELs' ability to meet high educational standards,
and on their attitudes about the role they should play in supporting students' language and learning efforts in school.

Students who have difficulty passing English proficiency tests that ELs
are required to take each year are eventually categorized by their schools
as 'long-term English learners' (LTELs) which includes any student who
has been classified as an English learner longer than 6 years.[1] In a statewide
study of the phenomenon, 59% of English learners in California high
schools were identified as LTELs, with some having been classified as ELs
since they first entered elementary school.[2] For many such students, difficulty in school can be traced to early problems with literacy development,

which in turn can be traced to their initial lack of proficiency in the language of literacy.[3] By high school, the programmes of studies in which they find themselves tend to be low-tracked classes designed for underachieving students that do not prepare them for college or the world of work beyond high school. This often comes as surprise to the students themselves, who aspire to attend college and believe they have done well enough in school; they report being puzzled that they are regarded as English learners since English is what they speak at school, and at home as well by the time they are in high school. According to the California study, many such students are unaware that they are stuck at the 'intermediate level' on the test of English proficiency used by the state and believe that they are doing fine academically. So, what accounts for this discrepancy in perceptions in what counts as language and learning?

Again, Cummins' framework points us to places to look at what has gone awry in the education of these students. Many if not most such students have had difficulty attaining the English literacy skills required for academic progress. Had they received literacy development in their primary languages, or had they received the attention to developing the academic register of English, they might have had a quite different experience. How indeed is the aspect of language Cummins long ago characterised as 'academic language proficiency' acquired, in contrast to socially supported spoken language? What role does instruction play in its development?

For researchers like me, Cummins' distinction was a revelation. As a researcher studying second language acquisition among young school age children in the 1970s and 80s, I was concerned with the process and progress of their efforts to learn the language for interactional and communicative purposes at school, but had not paid much attention to the language demands of the materials they were working on. The texts used in school did not seem particularly difficult or interesting at the time. Textbook publishers had been gradually simplifying the language and informational load of texts in response to pressure by educators for materials that were easier to read and understand by all students, not just for English learners. This process of text and content simplification resulted in many students unprepared to meet the literacy demands of college and careers at the end of high school, a situation that eventually led to major reforms of educational standards across the United States.

It took me a while to take a deep dive into the relationship between the materials used in school and language development, but the distinction drawn by Cummins was what caused me to take a look initially. Were there notable grammatical and lexical differences between the language used in social discourse and the language of cognitively demanding discourse? How is the language Cummins subsequently described as 'context reduced, cognitively demanding language' learned – is it just a matter of additional time and engagement in the use of such language in school? I pored through grammars and studies of language learning in school age students.[4] If the language of social discourse and functioning is learned in the context of face-to-face interactions with speakers of that language, what is the context in which learners might encounter the grammatical structures, devices and forms that are characteristic of CALP? The power of any theoretical framework is in its ability to highlight critical connections. For the most part, language development is considered in terms of the role it plays in literacy development, while the role literacy plays in language development except perhaps in the learning of vocabulary, is given less attention.

Studies comparing the linguistic characteristics of various forms of oral and written language[5] suggest that the relationship may be more complex than assumed, however. There are grammatical structures, forms, and devices that are features of written academic and literary language which are rarely used in spoken language,[6] for example. How are such aspects of language learned then, except through literacy? Considered from that perspective, language and literacy can be recognized as reciprocal developments. Where children are concerned, this relationship can also be a bottleneck in learning. In many US schools, children who are deemed to be lacking in language skills for literacy are provided texts that avoid the use of the forms and structures of academic language they need to acquire to make progress in literacy and learning in school. And this is where Cummins' theoretical framework has led me and other researchers who have found his academic language distinction a compelling one to look into. This is but one way in which Cummins' larger theoretical framework allows us to sleuth out the many ways in which power relations within the school and society affects student performance. How much more effectively can groups be held down than by denying them the means for advancement? The construct of academic language has been subjected to critique and discussion, with recent challenges focused on whether it is just another way to discriminate against racialized students, whose language is judged as 'inherently non-academic'.[7] And yet, when the great disparities in educational outcome between student groups are examined closely, literacy development is a key to school performance, and that depends on mastery of, or at least a familiarity with, the language of written language discourse. Educational and text linguists who have delved into the grammatical, lexical and pragmatic aspects of the language of academic discourse have documented qualitative and quantifiable differences between it and the language children might ordinarily expect to encounter in the communicative situations in which they are likely to find themselves. The challenge for educators has been what to do about this observation. Can or should its forms and structures be taught as a subject in school?

Aside from the pedagogical considerations, there are sociopolitical considerations raised by some scholars and theorists whose concerns and arguments Cummins addresses in some detail in Chapter 8 on the legitimacy of 'academic language' as a theoretical construct. As an educational linguist who has spent several decades looking at language in literacy development, academic language and more importantly academic language proficiency are more than theoretical constructs. They are realities that children and teachers confront as soon as they have dealt with the most basic levels of reading and writing instruction. To get meaning from the texts they are to learn from, to communicate their thoughts effectively in writing, students must work with a form of language which is learned primarily through the process of literacy itself. This is true whether the students are English learners or native speakers of English. Those who have had the most exposure to the language of written discourse, whether through prior literacy in another language or vicarious literacy through participation in read-alouds of storybooks by parents or caregivers, have an advantage over those who have not had such prior experiences. Their familiarity with the language of written texts allows them to assume that the words are meaningful and may convey information or ideas that may be interesting even if they do not make immediate sense. That expectation and belief, along with instructional support, is what it takes for young readers to figure out what the text is saying, and ultimately to learn how such language works. Children who have not had such prior experience with literacy will require extra instructional support to discover how the language of written discourse works, and how it is deployed for communicating ideas and information, and for communicative effect. Literacy is recognized as foundational to academic performance in all other aspects of the school's curriculum, but literacy is dependent on language.

In the third part of this book, which one might be tempted to regard as its tail rather than its heart, coming as it does right at the end, Cummins discusses the implication for instructional practice of the prior discussions of theoretical concepts from his own research and from that of others. Since the theme of how transformative pedagogy can empower students and change schools runs throughout this work, it is hardly an afterthought. Cummins' concern with improving educational outcomes for minoritised students has been a continuous motif in his work from early on. His work with educators in Canadian, European and US schools began when his research began. The practical implications of his work have been an integral part of his agenda, and never just an addendum as is sometimes the case with theoreticians and researchers. How schools have dealt with children from immigrant backgrounds who speak languages other than the one ordinarily used in school has given Cummins the opportunity both to influence practice and to learn from practitioners, which gives his work an applicability and practicality not ordinarily found in the writings of theoreticians.

Learning from practitioners – teachers who have developed and tested pedagogical solutions to the myriad problems that confront schools in educating multilingual and minoritized students in the sociopolitical context of societies that are sometimes indifferent to their needs and situation – can be done only at ground level, embedded as it were in schools where the work is going on. Cummins has been deeply invested in learning from practitioners, and in celebrating their efforts and successes. We recognise in the descriptions of instructional practices that are listed in this chapter, the many ways which teachers have found to give voice to students who may speak various languages in a classroom. Teachers have found creative solutions to communicating with students with whom they do not share a common language; they have found innovative ways to support the students' efforts to learn, to share what they know with one another, and to build on what they already know and can do. And they have found strategies for engaging parents and communities in support of their efforts to provide students with a meaningful infusion of their language, culture and history into the school's curricular offerings. In all this, it is clear that the secret to creating schools where linguistic, cultural and social differences are assets on which students can flourish and be successful learners is not a grand and innovative pedagogy, but is instead many interlocking activities and inclusive practices that begin by respecting the students and their experiences, assume that they are not only willing but are ready to learn, and which provide students the support they need to participate fully in the educational enterprise of the school.

This book draws together the multiple components of Cummins' work on language and learning and responds not only to recent critiques and analyses of various constructs from his theoretical frameworks, but also provides a synthesis of, and his responses to, earlier critiques and commentary. As valuable as such an exposition is, I am tempted to suggest especially to educators who have more than a theoretical interest in what Cummins has to say about these weighty matters, to skip ahead to the final chapter if they want to know what works. They will find a trove of ideas there on how to deal with seemingly insuperable problems in schools, descriptions of practices that thoughtful and skillful teachers have devised for addressing problems in communicating with and making learning possible for students in situations like theirs. And then, because it is crucial that educators know what they are doing and why, they should circle back and read about the many critical components of the theoretical framework that will help them see how it all hangs together.

Lily Wong Fillmore

Notes

(1) Menken, K. and Kleyn, T. (2009) Supporting English Language Learners; The Difficult Road for Long-Term English Learners. *Educational Leadership* 66 (7). 'LTELs are defined as English-language learners who have not yet reached a minimum threshold of English-language proficiency after five to seven years in a U.S. school.' Wisconsin Center for Educational Research—Ryan, 2019.
(2) Olsen, L. (2010) *Reparable Harm: Fulfilling the Unkept Promise of Educational Opportunity for California's Long Term English Learners.* Long Beach, CA: Californians Together.

(3) The high school students in the 2010 Californians Together study would have entered school around 1998–9, soon after the passage of California's voter referendum, Proposition 227, which banned bilingual education in the state's schools. Some students may have received initial literacy development in their primary languages since parents were nonetheless able to opt for bilingual instruction, but for more than 18 years when California's voters repealed the ban on bilingual education in 2016 English learners were instructed in English only. Even before then, the state had adopted the seal of biliteracy for students who could demonstrate the bilingual language and literacy skills at graduation from high school.

(4) Walter Loban's 1976 study of *Language Development: Kindergarten through Grade Twelve* (National Council of Teachers of English Committee on Research, Report No. 18, was especially useful. <https://eric.ed.gov/?id=ED128818>

(5) Biber, D. (1986) Spoken and Written Textual Dimensions in English: Resolving the Contradictory Findings. *Language* 62 (2), 384–414. Halliday, M.A.K. (1989) *Spoken and Written Language*. Oxford University Press, USA. Halliday, M.A.K. (1989) Some grammatical problems in scientific English. *Australian Review of Applied Linguistics*. Supplement Series 6 (1), 13–37.

(6) Biber, D., Johansson, S., Leech, G., Conrad, S., Finnegan, E. (1999) *Longman Grammar of Spoken and Written English*. London: Longman Educational Ltd.

(7) García, O. and Solorza, C.R. (2020) Academic language and the minoritization of U.S. bilingual Latinx students *Language and Education*. doi:10.1080/09500782.2020.1825476

Series Editor's Preface

The first book in the Multilingual Matters series *Linguistic Diversity and Language Rights* was published in 2004. Jim Cummins' book is the last and corresponds to a large extent to most of the wishes and goals that the series had from the very beginning. This is how the series was described in 2004:

> The series seeks to promote multilingualism as a resource, the maintenance of linguistic diversity, and development of and respect for linguistic human rights worldwide through the dissemination of theoretical and empirical research. The series encourages interdisciplinary approaches to language policy, drawing on sociolinguistics, education, sociology, economics, human rights law, political science, as well as anthropology, psychology, and applied language studies. Publications analysing successful attempts to promote linguistic diversity and theoretical analyses of alternative paradigms in conceptualising and implementing change in language policy are welcomed. (see (https://www.multilingual-matters.com/page/series-results/linguistic-diversity-and-language-rights/for the books in the series)

As the editor of the series I could not wish for a more magnificent book as the last book in 'my' series. What a book! Not only does it, just in one book, touch upon most of the areas that the description above sets as goals for the whole series. This book sums up a life-time of research and engagement by a giant in the area. Having followed the literature about multilingualism and education worldwide for almost 60 years, I cannot think of many researchers, in fact hardly anybody else who has developed the research as consistently and as much as Jim has. Lily Wong Fillmore describes the content of the book in great detail in her fascinating and competent Foreword, so I will not repeat it here. Instead, I will add a few personal remarks.

Jim started writing the book you are about to read in 2017, but in a way he has been 'writing' it at least since 1976 when he was a young and promising scholar. (That was also the year when Jim (born in 1949), Pertti Toukomaa (born in 1934) and I (born in 1940) started a cooperation and friendship that Jim and I have continued for 45 years). There are few people in the world that I have learned so much from. Jim is one of the few who has always developed and anchored high-level theory with meticulous empirical work, with students, teachers, parents and classrooms in mind. He has really been listening, and worked WITH them, not 'on' them or even 'for' them. At the same time he has also always been available for presenting his and other researchers' results to educational administrators and for discussing various alternative ways to improve schools for not only minority children but also linguistic majority children. Even if most of his empirical studies have been in the Western world, I have heard countless Asian and African colleagues telling me how reading Jim has made them see things in their own environments in a completely new way. Even when Jim emphasises the fact that situations and power relations are always context-dependent, many researchers in other parts of the world recognise the universality of much of Jim's work and see its relevance for their own part of the world.

But being true and thorough (and beloved), has also evoked counter-forces (and even envy, as I see it). Jim has also taken criticism (even unfounded attacks) seriously, and in this book he also patiently shows in detail how untenable some of it is. His argumentation about the require-ments for solid research (even if some of it requires the reader's full atten-tion – some of this book is hard-going for the reader) will unmask many of the currently fashionable critiques of Jim's work as invalid, and thus also support all those people who are confronted with the now trendy attacks.

Sometimes I have been hoping that Jim would present (and start demanding) more radical solutions, such as complete mother-tongue medium education, K-12 (OF COURSE with a dominant language as a second language subject). But in most contexts this would be impossible in practice, whereas what Jim has suggested has been and is doable. Likewise, when I have been moving towards looking at the extent to which much of Indigenous and minority education today all over the world fits several of the definitions of genocide in the United Nations 1948 Convention on the Prevention and Punishment of the Crime of Genocide (and it does), it has so far not helped much in practice to limit or eliminate linguistic and cul-tural genocide, even if many people now have to admit that such education IS genocidal. Claiming this makes many people defensive, or angry, and some also feel guilt. This is not a good starting point for achieving change.

But the assimilatory, genocidal principles in much of this education permeate today's societies not only at the individual level but also at the structural, institutional level, covertly or overtly. That means that the discriminatory and often racist control has become so thoroughly insti-tutionalised that the individual, for instance a teacher or a school admin-istrator, generally does not have to exercise any conscious choice to operate in a racist/assimilationist manner. Individuals merely have to conform to the operating norms of the system, and *the institution [e.g the school] will do the discrimination for them.* Thus we can in our analysis move from 'evil motive discrimination' (actions *intended* to have a harm-ful effect on minority group members) to 'effects discrimination' (actions have a harmful effect whatever their motivation). Understanding this might save teachers from feeling angry, guilty and helpless (which many do when confronted with the genocide discourse).

But this is not enough for the needed thorough changes to be achieved. Here listening to and reading Jim can and often does make people real positive agents, optimistic and full of energy for starting to make necessary changes. I hope that the book you are about to read has this positive effect on you! THANK YOU, Jim!

Tove Skutnabb-Kangas

References

Cummins, J. (1976) The influence of bilingualism on cognitive growth: A synthesis of research findings and explanatory hypotheses. *Working Papers on Bilingualism*, No. 9.

Skutnabb-Kangas, T. and Toukomaa, P. (1976) *Teaching Migrant Children's Mother Tongue and Learning The Language of the Host Country in the Context of the Sociocultural Situation of the Migrant Family, Report Written for UNESCO.* Tampere: University of Tampere, Dept of Sociology and Social Psychology, Research Reports 15.

Preface

This book is intended to follow up the synthesis of theory, research, policy, and instructional practice related to the education of bilingual and multilingual students that I outlined in two previous books: *Language, Power and Pedagogy: Bilingual Children in the Crossfire* (Multilingual Matters, 2000), and *Negotiating Identities: Education for Empowerment in a Diverse Society* (2nd edn) (California Association for Bilingual Education, 2001).[1] Obviously, there have been major changes in this area during the past 20 years with respect to research findings, theoretical propositions, policy initiatives, and instructional practice in contexts around the globe. To illustrate, at this point virtually no serious researcher questions the legitimacy, in principle, of bilingual education for either 'majority' or 'minority' group students. Policymakers and media commentators who do question bilingual approaches for 'minority' group students are simply manifesting their ignorance of the research and their evidence-free ideological preconceptions (e.g. Haver, 2018). Theory has similarly shifted with the universal acceptance by researchers of dynamic models of bi/multilingualism and the elaboration of *translanguaging* as a key, albeit controversial, theoretical construct. Instructional practice is also evolving to acknowledge the feasibility and legitimacy of multilingual approaches that mobilise students' entire linguistic repertoire for learning even in highly diverse classroom contexts where teachers do not speak the multiple languages of their students.

Orientation towards Theory and Instructional Practice

Teachers have played a major role in the evolution of instructional practice from monolingual (dominant language only) to multilingual approaches. Some of the most significant initiatives have emerged from teachers taking the lead as *knowledge generators* (e.g. DeFazio, 1997), or teachers and university researchers working collaboratively to design, implement, and document multilingual instructional initiatives (e.g. Carbonara & Scibetta, 2020a, 2020b; Chow & Cummins, 2003; García & Kleyn, 2016; Little & Kirwin, 2019). The intersection of practice and theory in these accounts illustrates a major theme of this book: *theory and practice are infused within each other.* Practice generates theory which, in turn, acts as a catalyst for new directions in practice, which then inform theory, and so on.

This perspective is reflected in the analytic focus of the book. My interest starts and ends with what happens between teachers and students in classrooms. The focus of the book on theoretical concepts is, at the same time, intensely *practical*. The purpose of pursuing theoretical ideas is to contribute to changing instructional practices so that they become evidence-based and more effective in promoting equitable outcomes across social groups. In other words, although pursuit of theoretical ideas for their own sake is certainly legitimate, it is not the focus of this book; clarification and validation of theory is of interest to me only insofar as these ideas have relevance to classroom instruction and school organisation.

An implication of this analytic orientation is that the evaluation of any theoretical construct relevant to education should take into account the implications of that construct for educational policy and instructional practice. In order to elaborate more formally the relationships between theory and practice, I propose in Part 2 to extend the notion of *consequential validity* from its original formulation in the area of assessment (Messick, 1987, 1994) to the evaluation of theoretical constructs and propositions. In other words, I argue that we should examine the instructional consequences of implementing specific theoretical ideas or propositions; specifically, we should ask, as one evaluative criterion, to what extent a particular construct or claim is useful in promoting effective pedagogy.

The Centrality of Teacher Agency

Related to the notion of 'consequential validity' is the centrality assigned throughout the book to the role of teachers as agents of social and educational transformation. Teachers' instructional choices within the classroom play a significant role in determining the extent to which minoritised students will emerge from an identity cocoon defined by their assumed limitations (e.g. English language learner) to an interpersonal space defined by their talents and accomplishments, both linguistic and intellectual (Cummins, 2001a). I argue throughout the book, and especially in Chapter 11, that this process of pushing beyond normalised instructional boundaries positions teachers as knowledge generators and as co-creators of theory rather than as simply recipients of externally generated research-based instructional strategies, which they are expected to implement. Teacher agency, or what Ramanathan and Morgan (2007) call 'practitioner agency', is also at the heart of challenging the oppressive power structures that have subordinated minoritised students and communities over many generations.

This perspective has clear implications for the kinds of theoretical claims and discussions that I consider relevant to the issues discussed in this volume. A theoretical claim that has minimal short- or medium-term implications for the work of teachers may be intrinsically intriguing but is largely irrelevant to what this book is all about. Most of the theoretical constructs and claims discussed in these chapters derive predominantly from the work of teachers and are intended to act as a catalyst and resource for ongoing dialogue among educators, researchers, and policymakers.

Let me illustrate this point with reference to Makoni and Pennycook's (2005) claim that languages are 'invented' and cannot be viewed as discrete enumerable items. This claim is not controversial if it is taken to reference the fact that all languages are socially constructed and boundaries between them are fluid, porous, and changeable across time and space. However, Makoni and Pennycook go beyond this perspective. They argue that concepts that are premised on a notion of discrete languages, such as language rights, mother tongues, additive bilingualism, multilingualism, and codeswitching become just as problematic as the notion of discrete languages itself. They suggest that 'there is a disconcerting similarity between monolingualism and additive bilingualism in so far as both are founded on notions of language as "objects" … additive bilingualism and multilingualism are at best a pluralization of monolingualism' (2005: 148). Thus, they claim that the educational promotion of multilingualism and additive bilingualism leaves intact the monolingual assumptions about language that these constructs aim to critique. These constructs remain caught in the same paradigm that takes monolingualism as the norm. Rather than pursuing strategies of disinventing languages, the pluralisation strategy implied by notions of multilingualism and additive bilingualism reproduces existing oppressive structures. As discussed in Part 2 of this book, Makoni and Pennycook's position has been highly influential in shaping the *unitary translanguaging theory* proposed by Ofelia García and colleagues (e.g. García, 2009; Otheguy *et al.*, 2019).

The theoretical claims advanced by Makoni and Pennycook are both provocative and challenging and will undoubtedly be discussed for many years to come. However, do these claims have any short-term or medium-term relevance to the work of teachers, language planners, curriculum developers, or social justice activists? What do these claims imply for teacher agency? Makoni and Pennycook (2005: 141) suggest a 'situated' response to language planning and teaching issues: 'in some situations, the viable solution may lie in essentializing mother tongues, in other cases, in problematizing them'.

But isn't this what teacher agency is all about − making situated choices individually and collaboratively to challenge coercive relations of power and promote minoritised students' communicative and intellectual talents? How does the highly abstract notion of 'disinventing languages' contribute to teachers' instructional choices? Does it imply that teachers should *not* encourage minoritised students to develop literacy in both their languages (= additive bilingualism), teach for crosslinguistic transfer, or enable students to compare and contrast their languages? If teachers make the situated choice to 'essentialise' students' languages by pursuing these instructional strategies, isn't it a bit arrogant for university scholars to characterise them as still stuck in a monolingual paradigm?

By contrast, in the context of the present analysis, the educators whose inspirational multilingual practice is profiled in Chapter 11 *have* transformed the normalised monolingual paradigm within which they were socialised. Most would be offended to be told that their promotion of additive bilingualism or their commitment to develop their students' multilingualism is only marginally more enlightened than the monolingual orientation that continues to dominate most instructional practice.

In illustrating what a 'language disinvention' process might look like, Makoni and Pennycook ask, 'what would English look like if we were to analyse it using metadiscursive regimes from languages such [as] Hausa' (2005: 152-153). As documented in Chapter 11, many teachers across the globe are already enabling their students to compare and analyse their home languages in relation to the dominant school language. Theoretical constructs such as 'language disinvention' that deny the existence of languages and undermine the promotion of multilingualism, have *nothing* to contribute to teachers' efforts to promote their students' language abilities and awareness of similarities and differences between their languages. Theoretical constructs that are so far removed from classroom practice do not contribute to practitioner agency or act as a catalyst for further pedagogical innovation.

The point that I want to make here is that theoretical concepts that do not readily engage in two-way dialogue with instructional practice can safely be ignored by educators. Theoretical concepts that emerge from classroom practice and are jointly constructed by educators and university-based researchers are much more likely to fuel teacher agency and result in pedagogical transformation.[2]

Terminology

It is important to clarify some of the terminology in the book and the rationale for using a variety of terms or labels to refer to bilingual and multilingual students. First, I outline the meaning of the term *theory* and related terms as they are used in the present volume. *Theory* refers to a principle or set of principles proposed to explain or promote understanding of specific phenomena. To be considered valid, a theory must be capable of accounting for *all* the relevant phenomena that have been credibly established. A *theoretical proposition* or *claim* is a statement that purports to be evidence-based and valid. A *theoretical hypothesis* is a more tentative statement or prediction usually put forward so that its validity can be tested through research. A *theoretical construct* is an abstract explanatory variable or conceptual entity that is not directly observable, but which is used to account for observations, behaviour, or phenomena. Finally, a *theoretical framework* is a more elaborate grouping of interrelated theoretical propositions and constructs designed to account for phenomena, guide research, and/or legitimise particular instructional approaches.

It is important to note that theories are not true or false in any absolute sense. They are always partial, and subject to modification as new data emerge. Theories frame phenomena and enable interpretations of empirical data at a particular point in time and in a particular context. In other words, theoretical propositions and frameworks are in constant dialogue with empirical data. As noted previously, educational theories are also in constant dialogue with classroom realities. In short, the intersections between theories, empirical phenomena, and social realities are dynamic and constantly evolving.

The term *multilingual education*, as used in the present volume, refers to the use of two or more languages as mediums of instruction. It includes all forms of bilingual and L2 immersion programmes for both 'minority' and 'majority' background students in contexts around the world in which multiple languages are used to deliver academic content. The term *bilingual education* is used in a more specific sense as a subset of multilingual education to refer to formally established bilingual, dual language, content and language integrated learning (CLIL), and second language (L2) immersion programmes in which *two* languages are used for instructional purposes. I use the terms *multilingual learning, multilingual instruction, translanguaging pedagogy, crosslinguistic pedagogy, plurilingual pedagogy, bilingual instructional strategies* and *teaching through a multilingual lens* interchangeably to refer to classroom instruction that acknowledges, engages, and promotes the multilingual repertoires of students in linguistically diverse schools.

With respect to the terms employed to refer to students whose home language differs from the dominant language of the society, which is also typically the primary language of instruction in schools, I have chosen to follow the same approach elaborated in the book *Identity Texts: The Collaborative Creation of Power in Multilingual Schools* (Cummins & Early, 2011). In that book, we employed a variety of terms to refer to these students with the intention of highlighting the multiple identities that students adopt for themselves and the shifting identity positions that are projected upon them by societal institutions and educational practices and policies.

The generic term that I use to refer to these students is *multilingual students* or *multilingual learners*. The term *multilingual language learners* (MLLs) is currently used in some United States contexts (e.g. the state of Connecticut). I also use the term *plurilingual*, advocated by the Council of Europe, when I want to refer specifically to the dynamically integrated and intersecting nature of the linguistic repertoires of speakers of two or more languages. I use the term *bilingual students* when the context or research study focuses specifically on students with proficiency in two languages. At various places throughout the book, I use other terms to highlight the shifting perceptions and social realities of these students. For example, I use the term *minoritised* when it is appropriate to highlight the discriminatory power relations that operate in many societies to diminish the status and identities of students from diverse linguistic backgrounds. However, not all 'minority group' students are minoritised; for example, the English-speaking minority in Quebec is generally characterised as occupying a relatively privileged position economically and socially within the province. Similarly, French-speakers in Quebec, although a numerical minority within Canada, are not in any sense currently 'minoritised' within that province, although this was not always the case. Some scholars in the United States have objected to the term 'minority group students' because it appears to devalue the status of these students in comparison to 'majority group students'. Other scholars (e.g. Skutnabb-Kangas, 2000) have defended the use of the term 'minority' because of the important legal rights that certain minority groups have gained within educational and other social spheres.

Terms commonly used in official policies to refer to students such as 'English-as-a-second-language' (ESL), 'English-as-an-additional-language' (EAL), 'English-as-a-new-language' (ENL), 'English language learners' (ELL), and 'long-term English learners' (LTEL), are often seen as problematic because they define students only in terms of what they lack, namely adequate proficiency in English to achieve academically without additional instructional support. To counter this connotation, some scholars (e.g. García, 2009) have used terms such as 'emergent bilingual' to highlight the linguistic accomplishments of students rather than their presumed linguistic limitations. The terms 'bilingual' and 'multilingual' embody the same intention.

None of these terms is completely accurate in all contexts. For example, 'emergent bilingual' does not account for the fact that in many contexts students who arrive at school largely monolingual in their home language lose much of their fluency in that language over the course of schooling and often leave school with much less fluency in their home language than in the dominant school language. Similarly, the terms 'bilingual' and 'multilingual' do not capture the reality of many language learners in the very early stages of learning the school language when they may be largely monolingual in their home language. It is also important to note that many children growing up in multilingual social contexts around the world come to school essentially as simultaneous bi/multilinguals with knowledge of two or more languages differentiated by their domains of acquisition (e.g. home, neighborhood/playground, daycare/preschool, etc.). Thus, no one term captures the complex reality of the diverse array of acquisition contexts experienced by multilingual children and students.

Terms that focus on students' linguistic status intersect with terminology used to refer to students from social groups that have experienced long-term or more recent discrimination in the society. Terms such as 'minoritised', 'subordinated', 'oppressed', 'marginalised', 'racialised', 'dominated' have all been used to refer to the fact that students who experience academic underachievement frequently belong to social groups that have been subject to institutionalised racism or have been on the receiving end of coercive relations of power. Even within bilingual or dual language programmes designed to promote biliteracy, minoritised students sometimes experience discrimination because they speak nonstandard varieties of their home language, which the teacher views as 'incorrect' or inferior to the standard variety (García, 2020; McCollum, 1999).

In this volume, I use a variety of terms that reflect the shifting identity locations of students and their communities and the wide range of acquisition contexts that characterise the development of multilingualism. These terms carry different nuances of meaning and, like identities, these meanings are not static. The variety of terms reminds us that student identities shift in multiple ways according to the interactions they experience and the messages they receive in classrooms, schools, and other social contexts. As with the term *minority*, it is worth noting that not all multilingual students are marginalised or subordinated. Some have grown up and gone to school in highly privileged situations (e.g. those in private international schools).

Outline and Structure

The book is divided into three parts. Part 1 provides a personal account of how the theoretical ideas I have proposed since the 1970s were formulated and how they have evolved since that time into the early 2000s This process is described in broad detail in these chapters and the specifics can be pursued in considerably more depth in Cummins (2000) and Cummins (2001a).

Part 2 focuses on the evolution of research, theory, policy and instructional practice related to the education of multilingual learners over the past 20 years from the early 2000s to 2021. The initial chapter identifies three criteria for judging the legitimacy of any theoretical construct, claim or framework: (a) empirical adequacy, (b) logical coherence and (c) consequential validity. In subsequent chapters, these criteria are used to analyse:

- critiques of the construct of *academic language* and the distinction between conversational and academic language;
- the legitimacy of theoretical constructs that address the relationships between bilingual students' home and school languages (L1/L2) such as the interdependence hypothesis, the common underlying proficiency, and teaching for crosslinguistic transfer;
- controversies surrounding the construct of *translanguaging* (García, 2009; Williams, 1996) and theoretical propositions that have become associated with that construct such as the claim that the notion of 'a

language' is not legitimate; this claim implicates constructs such as additive bilingualism, the common underlying proficiency, and codeswitching as 'monoglossic' (and hence illegitimate) because they recognise 'language' as a credible sociolinguistic and psycholinguistic construct.
- the argument advanced by Flores and Rosa (2015) that additive approaches to minoritised students' bilingualism are permeated by discourses of appropriateness rooted in raciolinguistic ideologies.

The final chapter goes back to the classroom and draws on the work of inspirational educators to illustrate the kinds of classroom instruction that are implied by the research and theory considered in earlier chapters. As noted previously, theory and practice are infused within each other and much of the practice sketched in this chapter originated prior to the emergence of translanguaging as a theoretical construct. This practice has operated as a catalyst to generate theory. The chapter highlights the role of teachers as *knowledge generators* whose innovative practice, often in equal partnership with researchers, has opened up powerful directions to challenge coercive power structures and ideologies and to close opportunity gaps experienced by minoritised social groups.[3]

The Goal of the Book: Constructive and Critical Dialogue

A final point I want to make in framing the chapters that follow is that my overall goal in the book is to promote dialogue and respectful exchange in relation to issues that are central to the education of multilingual and minoritised students. The critique of theoretical claims and interpretations of research that are elaborated in Part 2 is intended to be constructive and in the spirit of critical dialogue. Much of the analysis in these chapters constitutes a response to critiques that have been made in relation to the theoretical constructs described in Part 1.

The alternative theoretical positions that are discussed in Part 2 can be seen as disputes within the family. All of the 'protagonists' are committed to social justice and antiracism in education; all have spent much of their academic lives to this point challenging societal and educational power structures that limit minoritised students' educational opportunities. Some (e.g. Ofelia García and colleagues) have created an extraordinary infrastructure for collaborative work with educators to transform school-based language policies and practices, with the goal of enabling minoritised students to expand their multilingual repertoires and develop the critical multiliteracies that our societies so badly need.

Thus, in joining this constructive and critical dialogue in pursuit of social and educational justice, I believe it is imperative to specify in as much detail as possible the instructional directions that are implied by various theoretical constructs. This involves extending the dialogue beyond the walls of universities and scholarly journals, crossing disciplinary borders and epistemological convictions, and rooting our discussions in the lives of educators, students and communities. The people we, as researchers, need to listen to and engage with, care nothing about whether we identify as sociolinguists, psycholinguists, sociologists, psychologists, or whether our inspiration comes from critical pedagogy, cultural studies, critical race theory, sociocultural theory, or any of the other myriad fractures that divide the academic world. They also don't care about whether our intellectual efforts are rooted in postmodernism, poststructuralism, positivism, or any other '-ism'.

Educators do care passionately, however, about their students and how to engage them in powerful learning. They are rightfully suspicious and often resistant to the 'theories' underlying the myriad instructional panaceas foisted on them every year by politicians and often ill-informed policymakers. Educators approach all theoretical ideas with the same overriding questions: *What does this idea have to do with my teaching? How can this idea contribute to my students' educational progress?* Thus, in order for theoretical ideas to take root and make an impact, they have to be validated *in situ* by teachers, school leaders, and administrators who are partners in the generation of knowledge. The family disputes debated in the pages of this, and many other academic books, won't be resolved in the pages of academic journals or in Twitter feeds or other forms of social media. But the credibility and usefulness of at least some of the theoretical ideas on all sides of these debates will slowly emerge from classroom practice and the insights of teachers and other educators who engage with and shape these ideas.

Notes

(1) Electronic copies of the *Negotiating Identities* book can be downloaded at no cost from https://www.gocabe.org/index.php/communications/cabe-store/
(2) I am grateful to Brian Morgan for insightful suggestions in relation to these issues.
(3) In Part 1 of this book, I have located myself in the narrative about how theoretical constructs I have proposed emerged and evolved. For readers who might want more background about how I position myself in relation to research and academic work, I have included a biographical statement at the end of the book. More detail can be found in two additional sources:
   • A paper entitled 'Echoes from the past: Stepping stones toward a personal critical literacy' (Cummins, 1997a). This paper was part of a collection of autobiographical essays edited by Christine Pearson Casanave and Sandra R. Schecter (1997) entitled *On Becoming a Language Educator: Personal Essays on Professional Development*.
   • The introductory chapter to a collection of my articles edited by Colin Baker and Nancy Hornberger (2001) entitled *An Introductory Reader to the Writings of Jim Cummins*.

Part 1

Evolution of a Theoretical Framework: A Personal Account

Introduction

My goal in this section of the book is to provide some background and insight into the origins of the theoretical constructs I have proposed over the past 45 years. In various publications (e.g. Cummins, 1981a, 2000, 2001), I described constructs such as the threshold hypothesis, the linguistic interdependence hypothesis, and the distinction between basic interpersonal communicative skills (BICS) and cognitive/academic language proficiency (CALP).[1] As these ideas evolved (e.g. Cummins, 1986, 1989, 1996), the psycholinguistic constructs were integrated into a broader sociological framework that explored ways in which identities are negotiated in teacher-student interactions and how this process of identity negotiation is rooted in patterns of historical and current societal power relations.

Thus, the framework represents an integration of different disciplinary perspectives including applied linguistics, psychology, sociology and pedagogy. This reflects the fact that all the interactions that take place between educators and students in schools can be viewed and analysed within the context of multiple frames of reference. None of these disciplinary perspectives is inherently superior to any of the others, but a more complete understanding of the dynamics and consequences of teacher-student interactions is likely to be obtained through a synthesis of different perspectives.

Chapter 1 provides an overview of the central theoretical claims of the framework. It outlines the relationships between psycholinguistic dimensions that focus on linguistic and cognitive characteristics of bilingual individuals and sociopolitical dimensions that highlight how power relations in the wider society, ranging from coercive to collaborative, influence the learning opportunities experienced by minoritised students within the context of schooling. In this chapter, I also attempt to position myself within the narrative of how these ideas evolved by connecting some of the broader themes to my own schooling experiences.

Chapter 2 discusses my initial attempt during the 1970s to resolve apparent contradictions in the way research on the cognitive consequences of bilingualism was being interpreted. Research studies conducted during the 1960s and early 1970s suggested that, under certain conditions, bilingualism might benefit aspects of students' cognitive and metalinguistic functioning. These findings were diametrically opposed to earlier claims, articulated since the 1920s, of negative cognitive consequences associated with bilingualism. Drawing on Vygotskian notions of linguistic mediation, I suggested that the consequences of bilingualism might depend on the extent to which students attained a threshold level of proficiency in their two languages as they progressed through schooling. Specifically, the levels of proficiency students acquired in their two languages might mediate their ability to understand instruction and attain an additive form of bilingualism that entailed cognitive, linguistic, and academic advantages (Cummins, 1976).

The developmental interdependence hypothesis, discussed in Chapter 3, was initially proposed in several papers in 1978 and 1979, with the goal of resolving an apparent contradiction in the outcomes of research on bilingual and second language immersion programmes. This contradiction was expressed as follows (Cummins, 1979a: 222): 'Why does a home-school language switch result in high levels of functional bilingualism and academic achievement in middle-class majority language children ... yet lead to inadequate command of both first (L1) and second (L2) languages and poor academic achievement in many minority language children?' Drawing on research conducted in Sweden (Skutnabb-Kangas & Toukomaa, 1976), as well as a variety of other findings suggesting consistently significant relationships between L1 and L2 literacy-related abilities among students in bilingual and second language immersion programmes, the interdependence hypothesis suggested that 'the level of L2 competence which a bilingual child attains is partially a function of the type of competence that child has developed in L1 at the time when intensive exposure to L2 begins' (1979a: 233).

The initial threshold and interdependence hypotheses focused specifically on the language competencies involved in schooling but did not elaborate in any formal way the theoretical construct of *language proficiency*. In the late 1970s and early 1980s (Cummins, 1979b, 1980a), I drew on empirical data regarding developmental trajectories of different components of language proficiency (both L1 and L2) and theoretical analyses of the construct of language proficiency to propose a distinction between cognitive/academic language proficiency (CALP) and basic interpersonal communicative skills (BICS). The empirical and theoretical rationale underlying this conceptual distinction is outlined in Chapter 4.

In Chapter 5, the relationship between minoritised students' academic achievement and societal power relations is discussed, drawing on both sociopolitical and psycholinguistic empirical and theoretical perspectives. Central to this analysis is the claim that patterns of teacher-student identity negotiation reflect the extent to which educators, individually and collectively, challenge the operation of coercive relations of power as they are manifested in educational structures, policies, practices and ideologies. The construct of *identity texts* is outlined as a core component of literacy instruction that affirms minoritised students' identities in opposition to coercive power relations in the wider society.

Finally, Chapter 6 addresses the question of which groups of students experience disproportionate academic difficulties and examines what evidence-based instructional responses can credibly be invoked to reverse these academic difficulties. These instructional responses include engaging students' multilingual repertoires, maximising literacy engagement, and implementing culturally empowering pedagogy that creates interactional spaces that affirm and expand student identities.

In discussing how these theoretical concepts were generated and how they evolved over time, I try to identify the specific issues or problems to which they were addressed, the empirical data from which they emerged and additional data that they helped explain, the logical connections that helped provide coherence to the ideas, and finally the implications of the research and theory for educational language policies and classroom instruction.

Note

(1) In discussing CALP, I initially used the term *cognitive/academic language proficiency* (Cummins, 1979b, 1984a) but later referred to the construct as *cognitive academic language proficiency*. I have reverted to the original term in this volume because it better reflects the fusion of cognitive and academic procedural and declarative knowledge (*knowing how* and *knowing that*) involved in school learning.

1 Core Ideas and Background Influences

The Framework in a Nutshell

The central proposition of the theoretical framework is that under-achievement among students from minoritised communities is caused by patterns of power relations operating both in schools and in the broader society. The corollary is that minoritised students will succeed education-ally to the extent that the patterns of teacher-student interaction in school challenge the coercive relations of power that prevail in society at large. This perspective was expressed as follows:

> Interactions between educators and culturally diverse students are never neutral with respect to societal power relations. In varying degrees, they either reinforce or challenge coercive relations of power in the wider soci-ety. Historically, subordinated group students have been disempowered educationally in the same way their communities have been disempow-ered in the wider society. (Cummins, 2000: 48–49)

This analysis explicitly highlighted the fact that power relations are not just abstract conceptual constructs – they are enacted by real people in specific institutional contexts. Teachers have agency and can act to challenge the operation of coercive power structures. They can also remain passive and become complicit, intentionally or unintentionally, with these power structures. Educators who enact coercive relations of power are often well-intentioned and totally unconscious that their actions and interactions are discriminatory. For example, in the past and unfortunately still today, some school psychologists who administer English-only cognitive ability tests to multilingual students may be unaware of how discriminatory these tests potentially are when adminis-tered to students who are still in the process of acquiring English and catching up to grade expectations in academic English (Cummins, 1984a). Their lack of awareness derives from the frequent absence of attention to issues related to bilingualism and language learning both in their profes-sional training and in more general educational policies.

The fact that racism and other forms of coercive power relations may be embedded in institutional and organisational structures does not alter the fact that educators who remain unconscious of or ignore these realities are complicit with the operation of these power structures. Effective teaching in linguistically, culturally, and racially diverse contexts *requires* educators to reflect on, and where necessary, challenge discriminatory structures, policies and instructional practices. Even in oppressive educational contexts, educators always have individual and collective choices – degrees of freedom to implement instructional practices designed to promote students' well-being and academic development:

> As educators we are faced with a choice; we either construct interpersonal spaces between ourselves and our students such that their options for identity formation are expanded or, alternatively, we constrict the interpersonal space such that students' voices are silenced and possibilities for self-expression are minimized. (Cummins, 1993: 30)

This analysis of societal power relations expanded and attempted to clarify psycholinguistic theoretical constructs I had advanced in the late 1970s and early 1980s. Specifically, I proposed a conceptual and empirical distinction between cognitive/academic language proficiency (CALP), reflected in the development of literacy and knowledge of academic subject matter, and basic interpersonal communicative skills (BICS) such as accent, oral fluency and sociolinguistic competence in both first and second languages (L1 and L2) (Cummins, 1979a, 1980a, 1981a). The BICS/CALP distinction emerged from an analysis of more than 400 psychological assessments administered to immigrant-background students in a western Canadian city (Cummins, 1980b, 1984a). It was reinforced by a reanalysis of data from the Toronto Board of Education showing that that at least five years' length of residence (LOR) was required for immigrant students from non-English speaking home backgrounds to catch up to grade expectations in L2 CALP, despite the fact that most students developed L2 conversational fluency much more rapidly (typically 1–2 years LOR) (Cummins, 1981c).

CALP, or what I later termed 'academic language proficiency,' represents a *fusion* of conceptual, linguistic, and academic knowledge. For example, a student's understanding of the word 'democracy' represents conceptual, linguistic, and academic knowledge associated with the subject matter of social studies. In the process of schooling, it is not possible to disaggregate these three dimensions, which are integrated in the student's understanding of the term. Empirical support for this conceptualisation of CALP includes the fact that on widely used measures of cognitive ability such as the various editions of Wechsler Intelligence Scale for Children (WISC), the vocabulary knowledge subtest represents the best index of overall cognitive ability, and also shows the highest correlation (0.74) of any of the WISC–V subtests with measures of overall academic achievement (Groth-Marnat, 2003; Kaufman *et al.*, 2016; Weiss *et al.*, 2016). This point is elaborated in Chapter 4.

The fusion of conceptual, linguistic, and academic knowledge is also evident in more extended examples of academic discourse (e.g. Uccelli *et al.*, 2015b). Consider, for example, the report of a science experiment written by a fluent speaker of the school language. We could certainly view such a report through the specific individual lens of conceptual knowledge, linguistic competence, and academic learning by identifying the ideas or conceptual units that are in the report, as well as the vocabulary, grammar, and discourse structures that are represented, together with the scientific content knowledge reflected in the student's writing. However, in the actual *performance* of writing the report, all of these dimensions are fused.[1]

In the late 1970s, I also argued that cognitive/academic proficiencies in both L1 and L2 are interdependent insofar as they are manifestations of a common underlying proficiency (Cummins, 1979b, 1981b). The 'common underlying proficiency' construct was used to explain why students in bilingual and second language immersion programmes experience no adverse effects in literacy and academic language development in the majority language despite spending much less instructional time through that language. In fact, students from minoritised communities tend to develop stronger majority language (L2) skills in bilingual programmes that divide the instructional time between L1 and L2 than in monolingual programmes that teach exclusively through L2. In other words, for students whose L1 is a minority language, the trend is towards an *inverse* relationship between achievement and instructional time through the majority language (e.g. Ferrón, 2012; Francis *et al.*, 2006; Lindholm-Leary & Borsato, 2006; National Academies of Sciences, Engineering, & Medicine, 2017; Valentino & Reardon, 2015). This seemingly counter-intuitive finding derives from the fact that the common underlying proficiency makes possible transfer of concepts, skills, and learning strategies across languages.

These psycholinguistic distinctions (e.g. BICS/CALP) and principles (e.g. crosslinguistic interdependence) are viewed as links in the causal chain that relate societal power relations to student outcomes:

> Both sets of constructs are essential components of the theoretical framework … The psycholinguistic constructs are focused more on *knowledge generation* (i.e. learning) while the sociopolitical constructs focus on *identity negotiation* and its rootedness in societal power relations. The point of the framework is that one dimension cannot be adequately considered without the other. They are two sides of the same coin. (Cummins, 2000: 50)

Unfortunately, the psycholinguistic dimensions of the framework have received far more attention from both proponents and critics than the fact that these constructs are nested within an analysis of the role of societal power relations in shaping student achievement. Specifically, little attention has been paid to the central proposition that minoritised students' opportunities to expand their language and literacy abilities are directly determined by the extent to which educators, individually and collectively, challenge patterns of coercive power relations that continue to permeate the organisational structures and interactional spaces of schooling.

This brief sketch of the core theoretical constructs and propositions that have evolved over the past 45 years raises a number of crucial questions that go beyond the merits or otherwise of these particular ideas. For example, how should we judge the legitimacy or credibility of any specific theoretical proposition, construct, or framework? To what extent should theoretical constructs or propositions be consistent with credible empirical evidence? This latter question assumes relevance in light of the fact that numerous critiques of the distinction between conversational fluency (BICS) and academic language proficiency (CALP), considered in Chapters 4 and 8, have ignored the empirical data that have been invoked in support of this distinction.

The issue of what criteria should be invoked to assess the legitimacy of any theoretical construct, proposition, or framework is discussed in Chapter 7. In the remaining chapters of Part 1, I describe the research and analysis that contributed to the evolution of the theoretical framework in order to provide a foundation for considering the extent to which these constructs and claims can be considered legitimate.

Early Influences

Many of the issues related to language learning and bilingual education considered in this book formed part of my personal learning experiences growing up in Ireland in the 1950s and 1960s. These issues include the acquisition of conversational and academic proficiency in a second language, the efficacy or otherwise of immersion and bilingual education, and the linguistic legacy of centuries of oppression at the hands of a more powerful nation. Social and educational policies enacted after the founding of the Irish Free State in 1922 were designed to revitalise the Irish language (Gaelic), which had declined rapidly during the 1800s. Policies such as the compulsory teaching of Irish throughout schooling, both as a subject and in some schools as a medium of instruction, were tolerated uneasily by much of the population. These issues were subjects of frequent media attention and at times acrimonious public discussion.

Although I was taught Irish as a subject at the equivalent of pre-kindergarten and kindergarten levels, my first intensive experience in learning the language came at the grade 1 level when I attended an 'all-Irish school' or Gaelscoil. Today in a North American context this would be labelled a dual language or two-way bilingual immersion programme insofar as some students spoke Irish as their home language, but the majority, including me, spoke only English at home. About 80% of the instruction was through the medium of Irish with only English language arts taught through English.

My parents' decision to send me to the Gaelscoil was not motivated by any special commitment to the revival of Irish. My older brother attended a nearby school, and it was convenient to send me to the closest school to his so that we could travel by bus together. There was no space available in my brother's school until the following year.

I recall no particular difficulty in picking up fairly fluent Irish during that school year. The process appeared largely automatic and I remember speaking it with friends later in the year going home in the bus in the afternoon. The following year, I left the Gaelscoil and went to the same school as my brother where I stayed for the next 11 years until graduation from secondary school. In this school as in most other Irish schools, Irish was taught as a subject for about 40 minutes a day. Despite the best efforts of teachers, the predominant focus was on the structure of the language itself; vocabulary and grammar were taught in isolation as autonomous structures; there was no authentic communicative context that would encourage spontaneous use of either oral or written language. As my peers and I grew older, we became increasingly conscious of the fact that there were very few communicative contexts anywhere in Ireland (or elsewhere in the world) where the language could be used in a functional way. The bulk of Irish cultural endeavor (music, literature, sports, etc.) was transacted in English, with the result that there were virtually no domains of language use unique to Irish. Students' motivation to learn the language was primarily extrinsic (to pass examinations) rather than intrinsic. Not surprisingly, I lost much of my oral fluency in Irish during those 11 years, despite more than a decade of formal study of the language. However, I did perform well in examinations. I had acquired relatively strong academic proficiency in the language but my ability to use the language in face-to-face interpersonal communication was less than it had been when I was eight years old.

Students who experienced sustained bilingual instruction in Irish-medium schools developed a very different pattern of Irish language skills than I did. For them, the language was functional, and fluency and literacy in Irish developed together through both use and study. Research studies conducted by O'Duibhir (2018: 171) reported that primary school students in Irish-medium schools 'attain very good communicative competence in Irish but lack grammatical accuracy'. This finding is consistent with the outcomes of second language immersion programmes in many other contexts where there is little exposure to the target language outside the school context.

My experience illustrates some principles that have been strongly supported in research conducted during the past 40 years:

- the centrality of communicative interaction in acquiring second languages;
- the limited utility of teaching languages only as school subjects when there is little opportunity for communicative interaction outside the school context;

- the efficacy of immersion in a second language environment for students from majority language backgrounds;
- the fact that bilingual education for students from either majority or minority language backgrounds results in no adverse effects on the development of academic proficiency in the majority language;
- and finally, the fact that conversational fluency and academic proficiency (in both first and second languages) can be distinguished and can develop in very different ways depending on the acquisition context.

Note

(1) The fusion of conceptual, linguistic, and academic knowledge in the performance of communicative tasks and in the learning process aligns with Swain's (2006) concept of *languaging*. Swain and Lapkin define this concept as follows

> Languaging is the use of language to mediate cognition and affect. When one languages, one uses language, among other purposes, to focus attention, solve problems and create affect. What is crucial to understand here is that language is not merely a means of communicating what is in one person's head to another person. Rather, language serves to construct the very idea that one is hoping to convey. (Swain & Lapkin, 2013: 105)

Based on Vygotsky's (2000) theoretical framework, Swain *et al.* (2011) identify two different forms of languaging – collaborative dialogue and private speech. Collaborative dialogue involves creating, negotiating, and solving problems with others while private speech involves communicating or 'talking' with ourselves for similar purposes, either out loud or internally.

2 Resolving Contradictions: Cognitive Consequences of Bilingualism

In the early 1970s, I went to Canada to pursue graduate studies in Educational Psychology at the University of Alberta. My engagement with issues of bilingualism and bilingual education came about as a result of receiving a graduate assistantship to work with Professor Metro Gulutsan who had started teaching graduate and undergraduate courses on this topic. Metro's interest in these issues derived not only from the fact that he was fluent in at least six languages but also from the recently enacted Canadian national policy of 'multiculturalism within a bilingual framework' that was proclaimed in 1971 as a result of deliberations in the late 1960s of the Royal Commission on Bilingualism and Biculturalism.

My dissertation research attempted to identify some of the cognitive effects of bilingualism in the context of a two-way French-English bilingual programme in Edmonton. The research built on the Peal and Lambert (1962) study that, in contrast to previous findings, had reported a general intellectual advantage in favour of bilinguals who had attained similar levels of fluency in both of their languages. Peal and Lambert suggested that the enriched linguistic environment experienced by bilinguals promoted greater cognitive flexibility, superiority in concept formation, and a more diversified set of mental abilities.

My research identified a similar pattern suggesting that 'some types of bilingualism facilitate verbal information processing' (Cummins, 1974: 74). A large number of studies conducted over the past 45 years have reported similar cognitive and metalinguistic advantages associated with bilingualism (see Adesope et al., 2010; Ardasheva et al., 2012; Bialystok, 2020a; Cummins, 2001a; Diaz, 1983; Mohanty, 2019; and Skutnabb-Kangas, 1975 for reviews). Barac and Bialystok (2011: 54) summarised their review of the research as follows: 'the experience of speaking two languages yields cognitive benefits in the areas of attentional control, working memory, abstract and symbolic representation skills, and metalinguistic awareness'. The most consistent findings are that bilinguals show more developed awareness of the structure and functions of language itself (metalinguistic abilities) and that they have advantages in learning additional languages (Adesope *et al.*, 2010; Grey *et al.*, 2018; Mohanty, 2019).

Initial Formulation of the Threshold Hypothesis

I returned to Ireland in 1974 and worked at the Educational Research Centre in St. Patrick's College, Dublin (the largest teacher education institution in the country). During my time there (1974–1976), I had the opportunity to further explore the issues that were the focus of my dissertation. My paper entitled 'The influence of bilingualism on cognitive growth: A synthesis of research findings and explanatory hypotheses' appeared in *Working Papers on Bilingualism* in 1976. The goal of this paper was to 'resolve inconsistencies between the results of recent studies which have reported that bilingualism is associated with positive cognitive consequences and earlier studies which suggested that bilingualism might adversely affect cognitive and scholastic progress' (1976: 1).

A starting point for the analysis derived from the very different sociolinguistic and sociopolitical contexts within which more recent and earlier studies were conducted. The recent studies reporting positive cognitive consequences associated with bilingualism were conducted in 'additive' contexts where bilinguals were adding a second language to their cognitive and linguistic repertoire. By contrast, earlier studies reporting lower cognitive and academic performance among bilinguals compared to monolinguals were carried out predominantly in 'subtractive' contexts where students' home languages were being actively suppressed within the school. The paper noted that 'negative stereotyping and discrimination against minority language groups ... are ... likely to play an important role in explaining the negative effects' (1976: 20). However, it also argued that 'there are intervening variables in the causal chain whose influence needs to be specified' (1976: 20). Specifically, drawing on the fact that language mediates much of our interaction with the world, and especially within the context of schooling, I suggested that the level of proficiency attained by bilingual students in their two languages might mediate the effects of bilingual learning experiences on cognitive and academic growth. In other words, there may be a threshold level of proficiency that bilingual students must attain both to avoid cognitive/academic difficulties and allow the potentially beneficial aspects of becoming bilingual to enhance cognitive/academic functioning.

In proposing the threshold hypothesis, I was aware that it was 'doubtless oversimplified' (1976: 28), but saw it as having heuristic value in stimulating further research on the developmental consequences of different forms of bilingualism acquired under varying sociolinguistic conditions. I raised the possibility that there might be not one but two thresholds; attainment of the lower threshold would be sufficient to avoid any negative cognitive/academic effects, but attainment of a second, higher, level of proficiency in both languages might be required to experience cognitive, linguistic, or academic advantages.

The threshold hypothesis was rooted explicitly in a Vygotskyian conception of the mediating role of language and speech both in cognitive functioning and in children's interactions with their environment. Vygotsky highlighted the possibility that bilingualism might be associated with positive or negative effects depending on a complex array of social and educational conditions:

> We must not ask whether being bilingual is always and everywhere favorable or inhibiting under all circumstances regardless of the concrete conditions in which the child is developing and of the patterns of that development which change at each age level. (Vygotsky, 1935/1997: 257)

The notion of a lower threshold essentially highlighted the consequences of inappropriate instruction. As expressed in Cummins (2000: 175): 'Simply put, students whose academic proficiency in the language of instruction is relatively weak will tend to fall further and further behind unless the instruction they receive enables them to comprehend the input (both written and oral) and participate academically in class'. When minoritised students are provided with minimal or no instructional support to learn the language of instruction, and when their home language is excluded from the school, they are unlikely to develop strong literacy skills in either language. This is precisely the rationale underlying the US Supreme Court's decision in the 1974 *Lau* v. *Nichols* case that mandated schools to provide effective instructional support to enable students to learn the language of instruction and to succeed academically.

Recent Research on Bilingual Cognitive Advantages and the Threshold Hypothesis

Bilingual cognitive advantages

An extensive body of research suggests that bilingualism might enhance what psychologists call *executive control* (e.g. Bialystok, 2020a; Kroll & Bialystok, 2013). Because bilingual children must develop cognitive mechanisms for controlling which of their languages gets used in particular contexts, they develop increased capacity for attending to external stimuli and this may result in better performance on other cognitive tasks. Kroll and Bialystok (2013: 497) summarised these findings as follows: 'In the realm of cognitive processing, studies of executive function have demonstrated a bilingual advantage, with bilinguals outperforming their monolingual counterparts on tasks that require ignoring irrelevant information, task switching, and resolving conflict'. Interpretation of these studies has been challenged by some researchers who claim that the evidence for bilingual advantages in cognitive control is weak or non-existent (e.g. Paap & Greenberg, 2013).[1]

The bilingual cognitive advantages suggested by numerous research studies may also protect bilinguals from cognitive decline associated with aging. Bialystok and Craik (2010) reported a comparison between 91 monolingual and 93 bilingual elderly patients who had been diagnosed with dementia. The age of dementia onset was four years later for the bilinguals than it was for the monolinguals. This finding has been replicated in subsequent large-scale studies (e.g. Alladi *et al.*, 2013).

Antoniou's (2019: 408) comprehensive review of the research evidence for and against bilingual advantages in executive functions, cognitive aging, and brain plasticity notes that some of the inconsistencies in the findings can be accounted for by the fact that '[b]ilingual advantages are unlikely to extend to all bilinguals under all circumstances', an observation similar to Vygotsky's (1935/1987) more than 80 years previously (see also Thordardottir, 2011). He pointed out that cognitively stimulating activities in general lead to cognitive benefits, brain changes, and improved cognitive aging outcomes. Thus, it is reasonable to expect lifetime use of two or more languages to promote similar benefits. According to Antoniou, this fact lends credibility to the following findings:

- The 'evidence is in favor of bilingualism delaying dementia incidence, with inconsistencies between studies arising due to study design or definitions of bilingualism' (Antoniou, 2019: 404).
- 'The emerging neuroscientific consensus is that bilingualism indeed alters the structure of the brain, as well as the networks that subserve numerous cognitive processes, including, but not restricted to, those involved in executive functions' (Antoniou, 2019: 407). Among the effects observed is the fact that bilinguals show greater brain matter density than monolinguals in several brain structures.

The threshold hypothesis

Within the broader context of research on the cognitive effects of bilingualism, research support for the notion of thresholds has continued to accumulate (e.g. Ardasheva *et al.*, 2012; Daller & Ongun, 2018; Lechner & Siemund, 2014; Ní Ríordáin & O'Donoghue, 2009) and useful insights about the effects of bilingualism on cognitive and linguistic functioning have been proposed on the basis of this research.

Daller and Ongun (2018) investigated the threshold hypothesis in the context of a study involving 100 Turkish–English successive bilingual children from middle-class backgrounds (mean age = 9 years, 4 months; range 7 years 1 month to 11 years, 9 months). Children's scores on receptive and productive vocabulary tests and a non-verbal cognitive ability test (Raven's Coloured Progressive Matrices) were compared to those of 25 Turkish monolingual children and 25 English monolingual children. Parents of the bilingual children completed questionnaires on their language dominance

(Turkish L1 versus English L2) and their language use at home. Daller and Ongun reported that although there was no overall difference between the bilingual and monolingual groups, there was a significant bilingual advantage in non-verbal cognitive ability for children whose parents used more L1 at home and had higher dominance scores for L1. These children performed significantly better in non-verbal cognitive ability than both of the monolingual control groups and bilingual children more exposed to English (L2) at home. The findings support Daller and Ongun's hypothesis that 'parental support for L1 will be beneficial as it improves exposure to the minority language, and this might in turn have positive consequences for the cognitive development of the children' (2018: 680). They draw the following conclusions in relation to the threshold hypothesis:

> Cummins' Threshold Hypothesis, which assumes a bilingual advantage for children with high proficiency in both languages, is also supported in our study but needs to be revised. High language proficiency, in our case, operationalised as vocabulary sizes in both languages, is related to general cognitive development, for example high nonverbal IQ scores. Parents who have a positive attitude towards L1 and use it' at home support the lexical and cognitive development of their children. (2018: 690)

They also note the implications of their findings for school language policies and pedagogy: 'Language policy that advocates the use of the dominant language in society (L2) at home may not be in the best interest of the bilingual children, and there is clear evidence that support for L1 is beneficial for the cognitive and linguistic development of the children' (2018: 690).

In a very different context, Ardasheva and colleagues (2012) tested aspects of the threshold hypothesis using large-scale data from a large Midwestern school district in the United States. They compared the academic performance of current English language learners (ELLs), former ELLs who had been redesignated as 'fluent English proficient' and native English-speaking (NES) students and summarised their findings as follows:

> Results of multilevel analyses indicated that after controlling for relevant student- and school-level characteristics, former ELLs significantly outperformed current ELL and NES students in reading (effect sizes: 1.07 and 0.52) and mathematics (effect sizes: 0.86 and 0.42) The results support Cummins's (1979, 2000) lower level threshold hypothesis predicting that upon reaching adequate proficiency in the language of schooling and testing, ELLs would no longer experience academic disadvantages. (2012: 769)

On the basis of their findings and the broader literature on cognitive benefits of bilingualism, Ardasheva and colleagues hypothesised that cognitive processing advantages associated with bilingual experiences may arise from children developing speaking proficiency in two languages through exposure to them on a regular basis (e.g. in the home). However, these cognitive processing benefits would translate into higher academic performance only when students developed proficiency in the language of schooling, particularly its literacy domains. They suggest:

> that the academic benefits associated with bilingualism may be available at both thresholds—in contrast to only at the higher threshold, as originally proposed by Cummins—by virtue of students gaining access to and being able to capitalize on aspects of bilingual advantages (i.e. cognitive processing benefits at the lower threshold and biliteracy advantage at the higher threshold). (2012: 798)

Bialystok's (2020a: 11) review of the research affirms the increased neuroplasticity of bilingual cognitive functioning observed in many studies. Her overall conclusion is consistent with the general notion of threshold effects:

> It is apparent that being more fluently bilingual or having been bilingual for a longer time confers larger benefits than do lesser bilingual experiences, but there is little understanding of the threshold for these effects. Similarly, suspending bilingualism and becoming more monolingual diminishes these effects...

In summary, more than 40 years after the threshold hypothesis was initially proposed, it continues to generate research, with much of it generally supportive of the claim that developing patterns of L1 and L2 proficiency mediate the cognitive, academic and metalinguistic consequences of bilingualism.

Implications for Language Policy and Classroom Instruction

In *Language, Power and Pedagogy* (Cummins, 2000), I analysed in some detail research evidence on the threshold hypothesis that had been published up to that point. I concluded that although the available evidence was consistent with the claim that threshold levels of L1 and L2 proficiency might act as intervening variables, the notion of linguistic thresholds was still speculative and not in any sense necessary to the overall theoretical framework I was proposing. I also made the point that, contrary to the views of both advocates and opponents of bilingual education, the threshold hypothesis, by itself, carried few policy implications.

Much more relevant to educational policy and classroom instruction is the, by now, overwhelming evidence that the continued development of literacy skills in two or more languages (additive bilingualism) results in positive educational, cognitive and metalinguistic consequences for bilingual students:

> For policy, this finding reinforces the legitimacy of strongly promoting bilingualism and biliteracy in school. Instructionally, the appropriate implication is that there should be an explicit focus on augmenting bilingual students' awareness of language in general and the roles that it plays

in their lives and in societal power relations. If we focus only on one of the bilingual's two languages, or keep them rigidly separate, then we miss a very significant opportunity to enhance bilingual students' linguistic and academic development. (Cummins, 2000: 198)

The evolution of theory and instructional practice over the past 20 years has brought about a major change in how educators and researchers view the school's role in promoting multilingual awareness and abilities among minoritised students. Prior to the turn of the millennium, scholarly and educational debate primarily argued the merits or otherwise of additive bilingual education versus subtractive monolingual education conducted exclusively in the school language. The latter option appeared to be the only possibility in contexts where students spoke multiple home languages. However, the focus has now shifted to exploring ways in which the diverse multilingual repertoires that students bring into the classroom can be harnessed as a resource to enrich the learning experiences of all students. The terms *translanguaging* (García, 2009), *crosslinguistic pedagogy* (Ballinger *et al.*, 2017) and *teaching through a multilingual lens* (Cummins & Early, 2015) have expressed the emerging understanding that even in highly multilingual classrooms, teachers can actively engage students' multilingual repertoires to enable them to use their languages as powerful tools to understand and act on their worlds. In other words, as a result of their collaboration in exploring innovative instructional approaches, educators and researchers today have a much greater understanding of how to ensure that all students gain access to the cognitive and linguistic benefits of bi/multilingualism.

Note

(1) An account of this controversy entitled *The Bitter Fight Over the Benefits of Bilingualism* was published in *The Atlantic* in February 2016 (Yong, 2016). See also Bialystok (2020b) for discussion regarding how to interpret null results in bilingualism research.

3 Linguistic Interdependence: Accounting for Patterns of Bilingual Academic Development

After returning to Canada in 1976, I eventually found a part-time research position in the Educational Psychology department at the University of Alberta. Although my research at that point primarily involved working with Professor J.P. Das on issues related to simultaneous and sequential cognitive processing (e.g. Cummins & Das, 1977), I was also able to pursue research and academic writing on issues related to the cognitive and academic development of bilingual students. In early 1977, my former dissertation supervisor, Professor Metro Gulutsan, invited me to browse through some reports and articles that had recently been sent to him. Among those reports was one prepared by Tove Skutnabb-Kangas and Pertti Toukomaa (1976) for the Finnish National Commission to UNESCO entitled *Teaching Migrant Children's Mother Tongue and Learning the Language of the Host Country in the Context of the Socio-Cultural Situation of the Migrant Family*. This report exerted a significant influence on the development of my thinking about bilingualism and educational attainment.

The Skutnabb-Kangas and Toukomaa UNESCO Report

I remember vividly my excitement as I read this synthesis of research documenting the performance of Finnish migrant children in Sweden on various verbal and nonverbal measures of cognitive and academic performance. I wrote to Professor Toukomaa on February 3, 1977, to express my appreciation for the report and to initiate contact and future collaboration (e.g. Skutnabb-Kangas & Cummins, 1988). Skutnabb-Kangas and Toukomaa (1976: 48) expressed the goal of their research as follows:

> The purpose of the study was to determine the linguistic level and development in both their mother tongue and Swedish of Finnish migrant children attending Swedish comprehensive school. Above all, attention was

paid to the interdependence between skills in the mother tongue and Swedish, i.e. the hypothesis was tested that those who have best preserved their mother tongue are also best in Swedish.

The findings of research carried out in two Swedish cities, as well as other studies involving the Finnish minority, showed that Finnish migrant students performed considerably below age norms and grade expectations on measures of both Finnish (L1) and Swedish (L2) verbal academic abilities. The measures in both Swedish and Finnish were standardised on monolingual populations in both contexts and included subtests typical of verbal ability test batteries (e.g. the Wechsler scales) such as vocabulary knowledge (antonyms and synonyms), verbal analogies, and sentence completion that are strongly related to the development of literacy skills in school. Other studies reviewed by Skutnabb-Kangas and Toukomaa (1976) showed that Grade 3 Finnish migrant students performed at the same level as Finnish students in Finland on a non-verbal abilities measure (Raven's Coloured Progressive Matrices) but several years below Finnish norms on the Finnish version of the Illinois Test of Psycholinguistic Abilities. Additional findings included:

- Parents, teachers, and the students themselves considered students' conversational fluency in both Swedish and Finnish to be well developed after several years' residence in Sweden despite the fact that their verbal academic proficiency in each language was considerably below grade expectations.
- Students who migrated around age 9–10 maintained a level of verbal academic Finnish close to Finnish students in Finland and attained Swedish verbal academic skills comparable to the level of Swedish students. By contrast, those who migrated at younger ages and started school in Sweden performed more poorly in both Finnish and Swedish.
- Significant relationships between Finnish and Swedish verbal academic performance were observed among students who immigrated to Sweden between ages 0-5 and those who immigrated between ages 9–11. For the younger immigrant group, the L1/L2 relationships 'showed that retaining the mother tongue has a clear relation to how well the Finnish children who were born in Sweden or moved before school age had learned Swedish' (1976: 60). For those who arrived in Sweden between ages 9 and 11, the findings showed that 'the better their verbal level in their mother tongue, the better they learn Swedish' (1976: 60).
- Students who moved to Sweden between ages 6 and 8 'do not demonstrate the interdependence between skills in the mother tongue and Swedish that was found for those who moved either earlier or later' (1976: 61).

On the basis of these findings, Skutnabb-Kangas and Toukomaa (1976) recommended predominantly Finnish-medium instruction both during the preschool years and throughout compulsory schooling (K-8) for Finnish L1 students, with formal teaching of Swedish to be introduced no sooner than age 9–10 (Grade 3). For groups that were not numerically large enough to make bilingual education feasible, they recommended that every effort should be made to promote literacy in their home languages in the early grades.

Problematic Characterisations of Language Proficiency and Literacy Development

In both the Cummins (1976) analysis of the cognitive effects of bilingualism and the Skutnabb-Kangas and Toukomaa (1976) report, students' language proficiency was posited as an intervening or mediating variable. As noted previously, this proposition is consistent with Vygotskian and sociocultural perspectives on language and cognitive development. It was also fundamental to the rationale underlying the *Lau* v. *Nichols* 1974 Supreme Court decision in the United States that was the precursor for the expansion of bilingual education in that context. The role of language proficiency as a mediating variable is very evident in contexts where students struggle to understand the language of instruction.

However, at the time, there was no theoretical or empirical consensus regarding what constituted 'language proficiency' (and this is still true today). The lack of specificity in the construct was acknowledged by both Cummins (1976) and Skutnabb-Kangas and Toukomaa (1976) who emphasised that their conception of 'language proficiency' referenced the kind of language that is used in schools and is closely related to the development of literacy and other dimensions of school achievement. Within schools, the linguistic and conceptual demands embedded in instruction increase significantly as students progress through the grades.

During the 1960s and 1970s, Swedish researchers and policymakers commonly used the unfortunate term 'semilingualism' to refer to the literacy and academic underachievement of migrant students in both Swedish and their home languages (see Paulston, 1975: 26-32 for a useful review of the Swedish research on this issue).[1] Skutnabb-Kangas and Toukomaa (1976) also employed the term, and their characterisation of the construct is paraphrased below:

- The research that supports the existence of semilingualism measured cognitive aspects of the language, understanding of the meanings of abstract concepts, synonyms, and vocabulary (1976: 21).
- We 'do not think semilingualism can be used or measured as a strictly linguistic concept at all' (1976: 22).
- There is obviously the danger that semilingualism will be treated as a characteristic of the student, i.e. a 'deficiency' invoked to explain the migrant student's poor school achievement. In fact, the term

highlights deficiencies in the educational system that miseducates migrant students. It is the educational system that needs to be changed, not the students (1976: 22).

• Semilingualism is a mediating variable and *not* the primary cause of the poor school achievement of migrant children, as teachers often claim; the basic factors behind both semilingualism and poor school achievement are societal (1976: 22).

In several articles I wrote in the late 1970s that drew on the Swedish research, I also used the term 'semilingualism' to highlight the consequences of school programmes that excluded minoritised students' home languages from the school and to refer to the lower threshold of language proficiency that I hypothesised minoritised students needed to acquire to avoid negative cognitive and academic consequences (Cummins, 1976, 1978a, 1979a). However, it soon became clear that the term was highly problematic and was being interpreted as pejorative regardless of how it was defined (Cummins, 1979b). In response to critiques of this and other theoretical constructs, I argued that there is little justification for continued use of the term insofar as it 'has no theoretical value and confuses rather than clarifies the issues' (Cummins, 1994a: 3814).[2]

I also pointed out, however, that there is considerable variation in the extent to which *all students* (both monolingual and bilingual) gain access to formal language skills associated with literacy, and educational discrimination against bilingual students continues to limit their opportunities to develop strong literacy skills in both of their languages. I cited Kalantzis *et al.* (1989: 31) who argued that all children should have the opportunity to develop mastery of formal language skills of speaking, reading and writing, which, in the modern world, are the means to certain sorts of futures and power. They note that academic researchers 'who have mastered the pinnacle of mainstream language' should not view as unproblematic the fact that a disproportionate number of minority students fail to realise the full range of options in their two languages (Cummins, 1994a).

In short, burying the construct of semilingualism 'does nothing, by itself, to resolve the issue of how should we conceptualize the nature of "language proficiency" and its relationship to academic achievement in monolingual and bilingual contexts' (Cummins, 2000: 105). Butler and Hakuta (2004: 131–132) address the same issue by stating that whatever term is used and whatever 'semilingualism' refers to, 'there are indeed individual differences in academic performance among L2 learners as well as monolingual students'. They point out that a key question seems to be to what extent such individual differences in academic performance among L2 learners can be attributed to their 'language proficiency' as opposed to their ability to master academic content knowledge. This question is discussed in Chapter 8.

Initial Theorising of Linguistic Interdependence

Several findings of the Skutnabb-Kangas and Toukomaa (1976) UNESCO report provided the seeds for the elaboration of the theoretical distinction between BICS and CALP and the formulation of the linguistic interdependence hypothesis. As noted previously, Skutnabb-Kangas and Toukomaa highlighted the fact that although parents, teachers, and the students themselves considered students' everyday use of Finnish and Swedish to be fluent, this 'surface fluency' was not matched by their school performance in literacy-related aspects of these languages nor on measures that required complex cognitive operations to be carried out through language (e.g. verbal analogies, mathematical problems, reading comprehension). The UNESCO report also highlighted the positive relationships between students' verbal academic performance in L1 and L2 and the fact that 'the children who knew Finnish best, also learned Swedish best' (1976: 17).

What I initially called the 'developmental interdependence' hypothesis emerged from connecting the Skutnabb-Kangas and Toukomaa (1976) findings with a broader set of data including consistently positive correlations between L1 and L2 literacy skills, and the achievement patterns of minority language students in bilingual programmes. The hypothesis proposed a relationship between the development of L1 and L2 proficiency in literacy-related aspects of language, such that students with a strong foundation in L1 were in a much better position to develop grade-appropriate language and literacy proficiency in L2 in comparison to those who had much less opportunity to develop a strong literacy-related foundation in L1. I argued that linguistic interdependence helped resolve the question of why a home-school language switch frequently leads to very different outcomes in majority and minority language learning situations. For students from majority language backgrounds in L2 immersion programmes, a home-school language switch followed by instruction through both languages after several years, resulted in relatively strong L2 development as well as grade-appropriate academic development in L1. The instructional conditions facilitate transfer of academic skills across languages. By contrast, many minority language students instructed exclusively through their L2 have no opportunity to develop L1 literacy skills and they also tend to perform considerably below grade expectations on measures of L2 literacy development. Under these circumstances, the lack of opportunity to develop L1 literacy skills results in a weak foundation upon which to build L2 literacy skills.

The hypothesis also helped explain the fact that in bilingual programmes for both minority and majority language students, less instructional time through the majority language resulted in no adverse consequences for students' academic development in that language. In both cases, transfer of knowledge across languages offset the reduced instructional time through the majority language. The major educational implication of the threshold and interdependence hypotheses was that 'if *optimal* development of a minority language child's cognitive and academic functioning is a goal, then the school programme must aim to promote an additive form of bilingualism involving literacy both in L1 and L2' (Cummins, 1979a: 247) (emphasis original).

In re-reading through these early attempts to formulate the interdependence and threshold hypotheses, I see several inaccuracies and inadequate formulations. Obviously, I was naive to use the toxic term 'semilingualism' to refer to underdeveloped literacy-related skills in each language. Despite the explicit rejection of a deficit position (Cummins, 1979a: 231), the deficit connotations of the term were seized upon by critics who generally ignored or dismissed the way the term was actually defined (see Cummins, 2000, for a detailed discussion of these issues). None of the critics have disputed the fact that historically many minoritised students have been denied opportunities to develop strong literacy skills in both their languages, which was the raciolinguistic reality the term 'semilingualism' attempted (very inadequately) to highlight.

The initial interdependence hypothesis was also problematically formulated in arguing that 'the inadequate development of L1 skills will limit the development of competence in L2' (Cummins, 1978a: 397) This implied that crosslinguistic transfer was one-way from L1 to L2, whereas later formulations of the interdependence hypothesis were explicit that transfer is potentially two-way, from L1 to L2 and from L2 to L1, depending on the sociolinguistic context and instructional conditions (e.g. Cummins, 1981a, 2001).

In addition, the initial formulation of the interdependence hypothesis implied an overly deterministic causality between L1 development and L2 literacy attainment. Clearly, there are many immigrant-background children born in the host country whose functional skills in the home language do not develop much beyond the context of everyday communication and who do not develop strong L1 literacy skills, but who nevertheless develop strong L2 literacy and academic proficiency (e.g. Volante *et al.*, 2017).

Finally, the suggestion that 'a low SES minority language child may have less knowledge of some aspects of language and may have developed different functional linguistic skills on entry to school than a middle class child' (Cummins, 1979a: 242) invited misinterpretation in the absence of more specificity regarding what 'less knowledge of some aspects of language' entailed. The specificity was elaborated in later publications that documented the fact that children growing up in low-income environments tend to have less access to print in their homes compared to more affluent children (because print, in the form of children's books, costs money), and this opportunity gap may result in less knowledge of school literacy conventions, and concepts about print on entry to school (e.g. Duke, 2000). Shirley Brice Heath's (1982) analysis of different communities' 'ways with words' highlighted some of the language and pre-literacy skills that middle-class children learn from growing up in a highly literate environment. Specifically, in talking about books:

> they repeatedly practice routines which parallel those of classroom interaction. By the time they enter school, they have had continuous experience as information givers; they have learned how to perform in those interactions which surround literate sources throughout school. They have had years of practice in interaction situations that are the heart of reading—both learning to read and reading to learn in school. ... They have developed ways of decontextualizing and surrounding with explanatory prose the knowledge gained from selective attention to objects. (1982: 56)

However, it is also important to highlight the fact, vividly illustrated by Ana Celia Zentella (2015: 75), that book reading is only one form of literacy engagement and that in many homes where there are few or no books, adults and older children foster literacy in a variety of other ways:

> Many Latino families pray every night, as I did, and children learn the words to those prayers and the songs they sing in church. ... When I was a child, I thought my Puerto Rican mother invented Scrabble because she cut paper bags into squares and wrote a letter of the alphabet on each; we sat on the floor and put words together. Mami also had me copy and memorize long poems in Spanish and English; I recited them to visitors and my father's Mexican society's *veladas* (cultural soirées), where I learned formal Spanish by imitating the guest speakers. My teachers never knew that I had those abilities...

The last sentence goes to the heart of the matter. Minoritised students are much more likely to experience academic difficulties when schools fail to recognise and build on the funds of knowledge (González *et al.*, 2005; Moll *et al.*, 1992) that students bring from their communities. Avineri and Johnson in their Introduction to the Invited Forum entitled *Bridging the 'Language Gap'*, to which Zentella (2015) contributed, note that it 'is undeniable that individuals who live in poverty face distinct challenges in academic contexts' (2015: 67). However, they highlight the consensus among Forum contributors that instead of focusing on modifying the language patterns of children who struggle academically, 'we propose rethinking the way schools and other educational programs engage students and families from linguistically diverse backgrounds such that what is highlighted is not deficits but strengths' (2015: 81).

Although in several respects inadequately expressed, my initial attempts to formulate the developmental interdependence hypothesis shared this perspective on the role of minoritised students' home language abilities as a powerful positive influence on their learning of the school language and their overall academic development.

Evolution of the Construct of Linguistic Interdependence

The interdependence hypothesis was elaborated in papers published in the late 1970s and early 1980s (e.g. Cummins, 1979b, 1980, 1981a; Cummins *et al.*, 1984). In a short paper published in *Working Papers in Bilingualism* entitled 'Cognitive/Academic Language Proficiency, Linguistic Interdependence, the Optimum Age Question, and Some Other Matters', I argued that 'both L1 and L2 CALP are manifestations of the one underlying dimension' (1979b: 199). In subsequent papers (e.g. Cummins, 1981a), I contrasted the Common Underlying Proficiency (CUP) model of bilingual proficiency with the Separate Underlying Proficiency (SUP) model. The assumptions underlying each of these models are visually represented in Figures 3.1 and 3.2.

The SUP model reflected the typical set of assumptions underlying opposition to bilingual education in the United States in the 1970s and 1980s, namely that minority students' proficiency in L1 is separate from their proficiency in English. Consequently, knowledge and skills learned through L1 will not transfer to English. This 'maximum exposure' or 'time-on-task' assumption (e.g. Porter, 1990) claimed that there is a direct relationship between exposure to a language (in home or school) and achievement in that language. Thus, if Spanish-speaking children come to school with minimal knowledge of English, then they need instruction in English (L2), not Spanish (L1). The commonsense appeal of this argument lies in the fact that it is clearly counter-intuitive to argue, as advocates of bilingual education do, that *less* instruction through English will result in *more* achievement in English. I pointed out, however, that 'despite its

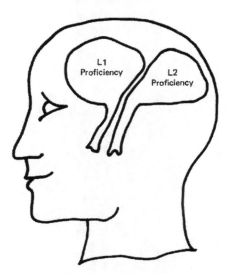

Figure 3.1 Separate Underlying Proficiency model

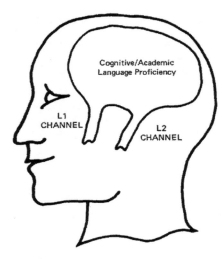

Figure 3.2 Common Underlying Proficiency model

intuitive appeal, there is not one shred of evidence to support the SUP model' (Cummins, 1981b: 23).

The research evidence from multiple sources can be explained only by positing a common underlying proficiency in which input in either language can promote development of the proficiency underlying both languages. Literacy-related aspects of the bilingual student's proficiency in L1 and L2 are seen as common or interdependent across languages, as illustrated in Figure 3.2. The 'dual iceberg' diagram (Figure 3.3) builds on the distinction between conversational and academic language proficiency (BICS/CALP) to illustrate the fact that common crosslinguistic conceptual

Figure 3.3 Dual Iceberg representation of bilingual proficiency

and academic proficiencies underlie the obviously different surface manifestations of each language.[3]

The following five major sources of research evidence consistent with
the CUP model were identified:

- Results of bilingual education and L2 immersion programmes showing that the amount of instructional time through the majority school
  language is either unrelated to, or inversely related to, achievement in
  that language (Cummins, 1981b).
- Studies showing that older immigrant students made faster progress
  in developing academic L2 skills than students who arrived at younger
  ages (e.g. Cummins, 1981c).
- Studies showing that use of a minority language in the home is not a
  handicap to students' academic progress in the majority school language (e.g. Bhatnager, 1980).
- Research showing consistently significant relationships between L1
  and L2 academic language proficiency (Cummins, 1979b).
- Experimental studies of bilingual information processing showing
  that bilinguals' lexical storage is neither completely undifferentiated
  with respect to language nor completely separated by language, but
  rather involves both common and discrete linguistic elements (e.g.
  Kolers, 1968; see also Buchweitz & Prat, 2013, for consistent neurolinguistic findings).

The implications of the CUP model for bilingual education programmes
were formally expressed by the interdependence hypothesis (Cummins,
1981b: 29):

> To the extent that instruction in Lx is effective in promoting proficiency
> in Lx, transfer of this proficiency to Ly will occur provided there is ade-
> quate exposure to Ly (either in school or environment) and adequate
> motivation to learn Ly.

In concrete terms, what this principle means is that in, for example, a
Spanish-English bilingual programme, Spanish instruction that develops
Spanish reading and writing skills (for either Spanish L1 or L2 speakers) is
not just developing *Spanish* skills, it is also developing a deeper conceptual
and linguistic proficiency that is strongly related to the development of
literacy in the majority language (English). In other words, although the
surface aspects (e.g. pronunciation, fluency, etc.) of different languages are
clearly separate, there is an underlying cognitive/academic proficiency that
is common across languages. This common underlying proficiency makes
possible the transfer of cognitive/academic or literacy-related proficiency
from one language to another. This is true even for languages that are dissimilar (e.g. American Sign Language and English, Spanish and Basque,
Dutch and Turkish, Chinese and English, etc.). The transfer of skills, strategies, and knowledge explains why spending instructional time through a

minority or non-dominant language entails no adverse consequences for the development of academic skills in the dominant language.

It is important to emphasise that the interdependence hypothesis envisages two-way transfer across languages (from Lx to Ly, and from Ly to Lx) provided the conditions articulated in the formal statement of the hypothesis are met. Thus, in a dual language programme that entails instruction through Spanish and English with the goal of developing literacy in both languages, one would expect two-way transfer across languages. However, in a monolingual English submersion programme, students' L1 conceptual and linguistic knowledge on entry to the programme will be applied to the learning of English language and literacy skills, but there is unlikely to be significant transfer from English to L1 language and literacy. This is because there is no exposure to L1 in the school and the exclusion of L1 from the school may communicate its lower status to students, thereby reducing their motivation to use and develop their L1.

Although the basic concept is essentially the same, different researchers have proposed alternative terms to refer to the notion of a common underlying proficiency. Baker (2011), for example, discussed the *common operating system,* Kecskés and Papp (2000) proposed a *common underlying conceptual base,* while Riches and Genesee (2006) labeled the phenomenon a *common underlying reservoir of literacy abilities.* I have also suggested (Cummins, 2000: 191) that the term *central processing system* represents a more dynamic way of expressing the reality referenced by the common underlying proficiency construct. All of these conceptions of linguistic interdependence incorporate both procedural and declarative knowledge – *knowing how* and *knowing that* – and have highlighted the importance of teaching for transfer across languages in both bilingual and monolingual programmes.

Recent Research on Linguistic Interdependence

There is extensive empirical research that supports the interdependence of literacy-related knowledge and skills across languages (e.g. Cobo-Lewis *et al.,* 2002a; Daller & Ongun, 2018; Edele & Stanat, 2016; Lindsey *et al.,* 2003; Prevoo *et al.,* 2015, 2016; Relyea & Amendum, 2020; Sparks *et al.,* 2008, 2009; see reviews by Baker, 2011; Dressler & Kamil, 2006; Cummins, 2001; Riches & Genesee, 2006; Geva, 2014). This evidence is considered in detail in Chapter 9 but is briefly previewed here in order to reinforce the legitimacy of the original theoretical claims regarding crosslinguistic interdependence.[4]

Research on crosslinguistic interdependence was clearly summarised by Dressler and Kamil (2006: 222) as part of the Report of the National Literacy Panel on Language-Minority Children and Youth (August & Shanahan, 2006). They concluded:

In summary, all these studies provide evidence for the cross-language transfer of reading comprehension ability in bilinguals. This relationship holds (a) across typologically different languages ...; (b) for children in elementary, middle, and high school; (c) for learners of English as a foreign language and English as a second language; (d) over time; (e) from both first to second language and second to first language.

These conclusions were reinforced in a synthesis of research regarding the education of English learners in the United States published by the National Academies of Sciences, Engineering, and Medicine (NASEM, 2017: 245):

> Conclusion 6-3: The languages of bilinguals do not develop in isolation from one another. Evidence indicates that certain aspects of dual language learning, processing, and usage are significantly and positively correlated and that the development of strong L1 skills supports the development of English-L2 skills. This interrelationship has been shown to be most evident in domains related to the acquisition of literacy skills and in languages that are typologically similar.

> Conclusion 6-4: Evidence reveals significant positive correlations between literacy skills in ELs' [English learners'] L1 and the development of literacy skills in English-L2. Educational programs that provide systematic support for the development of ELs' L1 often facilitate and enhance their development of skills in English, especially literacy.

Daller and Ungun (2018) report consistent findings in their well-designed study of 100 middle-class Turkish/English bilingual children in the UK. The children were in primary school with an age range from 7 to 11 years. They found strong crosslinguistic relationships for both receptive ($r = 0.61$) and productive vocabulary ($r = 0.73$) measures. They also found significant relationships ($p < .001$) between parents' preference for using Turkish (L1) in the home and vocabulary development in both Turkish *and* English. They summarise their findings as follows:

> Our findings clearly support Cummins' Interdependence Hypothesis. The vocabularies of our participants in L1 and L2 are related, and the development of the lexicon in L1 has a positive effect on the development of the lexicon in L2. The findings also support Cummins' CUP hypothesis for the vocabulary in both languages. ... Concepts that are developed in L1 are more easily available in L2 and this supports the development of L2 vocabulary. (Daller & Ungun, 2018: 689–690)

Although crosslinguistic relationships tend to be stronger between languages that are typologically similar, they are also evident in contexts involving dissimilar languages. For example, Chuang *et al.* (2012), using a sample of 30,000 Grade 9 Taiwanese students, reported correlations of 0.79 between Chinese and English reading ability. The fact that more than 60% of the variance in English reading could be accounted for by Chinese reading suggests that crosslinguistic interdependence operates even when there are few linguistic commonalities between the languages.

A similar conclusion can be drawn from research examining crosslinguistic relationships between oral/written languages and natural sign languages (e.g. American Sign Language [ASL]) (see Hoffmeister & Caldwell-Harris [2014] for a review). For example, Strong and Prinz (1997) investigated relationships between English literacy and ASL in a sample of 155 students between ages 8 and 15 attending a residential school for the deaf in California. Forty of the students had deaf mothers and 115 had hearing mothers. They reported that ASL skill was significantly correlated with English literacy and children with deaf mothers outperformed children with hearing mothers in both ASL and English reading and writing. They also reported evidence that the differences in English literacy between children of deaf mothers and children of hearing mothers could be accounted for by the differences in ASL proficiency between these two groups.

The research evidence suggests six major types of crosslinguistic transfer that will operate in varying ways depending on the sociolinguistic and educational situation:

- Transfer of conceptual elements (e.g. understanding the concept of *photosynthesis*).
- Transfer of specific linguistic elements (e.g. knowledge of the meaning of *photo* in photosynthesis).
- Transfer of more general morphological awareness (e.g. awareness of the function of *–tion* in *acceleration* [English] and *acceleration* [French]).
- Transfer of phonological awareness – the knowledge that words are composed of distinct sounds.
- Transfer of metacognitive and metalinguistic learning strategies (e.g. strategies of visualising, use of graphic organisers, mnemonic devices, vocabulary acquisition strategies, etc.).
- Transfer of pragmatic aspects of language use (e.g. willingness to take risks in communication through L2, ability to use paralinguistic features such as gestures to aid communication, etc.).

The question sometimes arises as to whether we are talking about crosslinguistic transfer or the existence of underlying attributes based on cognitive and personality characteristics of the individual. For example, is the relationship between L1 and L2 reading comprehension a result of transfer or the fact that reading comprehension in both languages is related to underlying cognitive attributes of the individual? The short answer to this question is *both*. The interdependence hypothesis incorporates both 'transfer' and 'underlying cognitive processes' as sources of the relationships between L1 and L2 literacy-related abilities. I pointed out (Cummins, 1991: 86) that 'consistent crosslingual relationships between aspects of L1 and L2 are reflective of underlying attributes of the individual in addition to characteristics of the input'. In other words, transfer and attributes are two sides of the same coin. The presence of the underlying attribute makes possible transfer across languages. Attributes (e.g. verbal cognitive abilities) and conceptual knowledge develop through experience; in other words, they are *learned*. Regardless of which language mediated their acquisition, when skills and knowledge exist within the individual's cognitive apparatus or central processing system, they are potentially available for two-way transfer across languages. In other words, transfer will occur from Lx to Ly or from Ly to Lx when the sociolinguistic and educational context is conducive to, or supports, such transfer. I summarised the sources of linguistic interdependence as follows:

> The positive relationship between L1 and L2 can thus be seen as deriving from three potential sources: (1) the application of the same cognitive and linguistic abilities and skills to literacy development in both languages; (2) transfer of general concepts and knowledge of the world across languages in the sense that the individual's prior knowledge (in L1) represents the foundation or schemata upon which L2 acquisition is built; and (3) to the extent that the languages are related, transfer of specific linguistic features and skills across languages. (Cummins, 2000: 191)

Implications for Language Policy and Classroom Instruction

The interdependence hypothesis and the notion of a common underlying proficiency provide an empirically supported and theoretically coherent foundation for both bilingual education and teaching for crosslinguistic transfer. Critiques of this hypothesis are discussed in Chapter 9, but for now it is sufficient to note some of the ways in which these ideas have influenced policy and instructional practice.

In the first place, the interdependence and CUP theoretical constructs provided an evidence-based antidote to the commonsense 'time-on-task' or 'maximum exposure' argument that English language learners will develop stronger English academic skills when they are taught exclusively through English. The interdependence hypothesis helped researchers and educators make sense of the extensive empirical evidence supporting bilingual education and provided a useful tool in North America and elsewhere to legitimise academic promotion of minoritised students' home languages.

Instructionally, interdependence/CUP highlighted the importance of teaching for crosslinguistic transfer both in monolingual programmes taught through the school language and in bilingual and L2 immersion programmes. The focus on teaching for transfer challenged the *two solitudes* orientation to students' languages that, for many years, dominated bilingual and L2 immersion programmes (Cummins, 2007a). It also highlighted the fact that in monolingual English-medium programmes (e.g. in Canada and the United States), the home language knowledge and abilities that children brought to school were relevant to their learning of English and should be built upon rather than ignored or suppressed.

The interdependence hypothesis also influenced assessment practices, particularly in the area of diagnostic assessment for students experiencing academic difficulties. It drew attention to the fact that academic or psychological assessment tests administered to bilingual and newly arrived immigrant students only in the school language could not be considered valid because these measures fail to assess the knowledge and cognitive abilities that are better developed in students' home language(s) (Cummins, 1984a). One concrete outcome of this increased awareness was the *Bilingual Verbal Abilities Tests* (BVAT) (Muñoz-Sandoval *et al.*, 1998), which was designed to assess bilingual students' combined verbal conceptual knowledge in L1 and L2.[5]

Finally, interdependence/CUP highlighted the fallacies involved in the (often well-intentioned) advice to parents and caregivers from teachers and other educational professionals that they should use the school language rather than their home language in interacting with their children. This advice undermines children's potential to develop strong conceptual and academic skills in their L1 and, in some cases, also compromises children's development of academic skills in the school language. As a result of the fact that teachers in many contexts are now more aware of the research relating to bilingual development, it is much more common today for educators to encourage parents and caregivers to use the home language consistently with their children in order to build up a strong conceptual foundation capable of sustaining academic development in both languages. Daller and Ungun's (2018) research provides direct empirical support for this policy direction.

Notes

(1) Paulston's (1975) review of the Swedish 'semilingualism' debate in the late 1960s and early 1970s presents a relatively balanced overview of the issues and findings. Her later report for the National Swedish Board of Education (Paulston, 1982: 54), however, is unequivocally dismissive of the construct: 'Semilingualism does not exist, or put in a way which is non-refutable, has never been empirically demonstrated'.

This conclusion ignores the very explicit way in which the construct was defined by Skutnabb-Kangas and Toukomaa (1976), which clearly referenced students' knowledge of the *academic* language of schooling. Empirical research carried out over many decades demonstrates that minoritised students subjected to racist discrimination, and in the case of many Indigenous students, active brutality, frequently leave school with low levels of literacy-related language skills in both of their languages (e.g. Truth and Reconciliation Commission of Canada, 2015).

In her 1975 article, Paulston (unintentionally) goes to the heart of the matter: 'I must admit that the first time I was exposed to the notion of semilingualism, I dismissed it out of hand as utter nonsense. Anyone trained in the tradition of structural linguistics knows very well that any language is perfectly adequate for the needs of its speakers' (1975: 27-28). This claim ignores the varied contexts in which we use spoken/signed and written language. Few would claim that a minoritised Spanish-speaking high school student whose monolingual miseducation in the United States has left him or her with English academic language and literacy competencies far below grade expectations has language skills 'perfectly adequate for his or her needs' within the context of schooling.

Related to this issue is the question of how we define 'language proficiency' and its relationship to literacy development. This issue has been addressed extensively in previous publications (Cummins, 1981a, 2000) and it is taken up again in Chapter 8.

(2)   Wickström (2015) documented the role that the construct of 'semilingualism' played in the Swedish home language reform legislation of 1976. He described it as 'a game-changing concept in the struggle to legitimise mother tongue teaching' (2015: 185). Despite the fact that it is currently 'discredited as a theoretical concept (Cummins, 2000: 104-105)', the gaps in both L1 and L2 academic language proficiency that it referenced 'legitimised the whole home language reform, from the stage of claims-making to that of implementation in the name of equality' (2015: 188).

(3)   As I noted in *Negotiating Identities* (Cummins, 2001: 188-189), the 'dual iceberg' visual metaphor built on sociolinguist Roger Shuy's depiction of 'language proficiency' as an iceberg: 'The metaphor of language proficiency as an iceberg was first proposed by Roger Shuy (1978) to distinguish between surface and deeper levels of language proficiency. Basic grammar, vocabulary, and phonology are "visible" above the surface but the less obvious semantic and functional proficiencies below the surface are much more significant for academic progress. The idea of representing bilingual proficiency (and the interdependence hypothesis) as a dual iceberg came to me in discussion with Roger Shuy and John Oller at a workshop organised by Margarita Calderón on a very hot February 1979 day in Riverside, California'.

(4)   The experiential reality of crosslinguistic transfer for multilingual students learning the language of instruction is clearly articulated by Aminah and Hira who were in their first year of learning English in Lisa Leoni's late elementary school English-as-a-second language class in the Greater Toronto Area. Lisa consistently encouraged her students to carry out creative writing and other assignments in their L1, and generally use their L1 as a stepping-stone to English.

> When I am allowed to use my first language in class it helps me with my writing and reading of english because if I translation in english to urdu then urdu give me help for english language. I also think better and write more in english when I use urdu because I can see in urdu what I want to say in english. (Aminah, original spelling retained).

> When I am allowed to use Urdu in class it helps me because when I write in Urdu and then I look at Urdu words and English comes in my mind. So, its help me a lot. When I write in English, Urdu comes in my mind. When I read in English I say it in Urdu in my mind. When I read in Urdu I feel very comfortable because I can understand it. (Hira, original spelling retained) (Leoni *et al.*, 2011: 55-56)

Hira's and Aminah's perception that Urdu and English are experientially *real* for them allows us to anticipate one of the major issues that will be considered in Part 2 of this book, namely, García and colleagues' argument that 'named languages' do not exist in the bilingual's linguistic system or 'mental grammar'. Otheguy *et al.* (2015: 281) expressed this claim as follows:

> The two named languages of the bilingual exist only in the outsider's view. From the insider's perspective of the speaker, there is only his or her full idiolect or repertoire, which belongs only to the speaker, not to any named language.

I suspect that Hira and Aminah, and many other people speaking, writing and learning languages might disagree.

(5)   The BVAT comprises three verbal tests derived from the Woodcock Johnson–Revised battery (Picture Vocabulary, Oral Vocabulary, and Verbal Analogies) together with translations of these tests into 15 additional languages. The test estimates the bilingual student's integrated verbal conceptual repertoire rather than measuring the student's knowledge of each language separately. Items that the student fails in English are subsequently assessed in the student's L1 in order to ascertain whether the student has that knowledge or ability developed in L1 despite the fact that it is not yet developed in English. The English score is combined with the increment from L1 testing of items missed in English and the total score (L2 + L1) is interpreted in relation to test norms (Cummins, 2001b). The notion of the bilingual student's integrated verbal conceptual repertoire is similar to the construct of total conceptual vocabulary (TCV) discussed by Daller and Ungun (2018) to refer to the vocabulary/concept knowledge that bilinguals have in both their languages combined, which is typically considerably larger than their vocabulary knowledge of either language in isolation.

Recent research in the United States among 62 Grades 2 and 4 Spanish-speaking English learners demonstrated that an expressive language 'conceptually scored vocabulary' measure administered in the fall and designed to assess overall or combined concept/vocabulary knowledge in Spanish and English, significantly predicted both English academic language proficiency and English reading comprehension administered in the spring of the same academic year. The authors express their findings as follows: 'a 1-point increase in fall conceptually scored expressive vocabulary was associated with a 0.56-point increase in academic English proficiency, controlling for grade level. ... a 1-point increase in conceptually scored vocabulary was associated with an average 0.26-point increase in English reading comprehension performance tested later in time, controlling for grade level and academic English proficiency' (Hwang *et al.*, 2020). Although not a direct test of the interdependence hypothesis, these findings are certainly consistent with the hypothesis. The fact that the significant predictive relationship remained even after English academic proficiency was partialled out suggests the influence of L1 vocabulary knowledge on the development of L2 reading proficiency. The authors provide no information on the specific instructional programme experienced by their elementary school participants, but it is likely that most, if not all, of the students were in English-only instructional contexts.

4 Language Proficiency and Academic Achievement

The distinction between basic interpersonal communicative skills (BICS) and cognitive/academic language proficiency (CALP) emerged from empirical findings and theoretical analysis. The initial catalyst for the distinction was an analysis of more than 400 teacher referral forms and psychological assessments of immigrant-background emergent bilingual students in western Canada. Many of the students referred for assessment were perceived by their teachers to have 'acquired English' but were still experiencing academic difficulties in classroom learning (Cummins, 1980b). This finding came into sharper focus as a result of a subsequent reanalysis I was able to carry out using research data from the Toronto Board of Education (Ramsey & Wright, 1974; Wright & Ramsey, 1970). The reanalysis showed that immigrant students born outside Canada who were learning English as an additional language required between 5 and 7 years, on average, to approach grade expectations in English academic proficiency. In other words, many students who were fluent in using English in everyday face-to-face interpersonal contexts required a considerable amount of additional time to catch up to their native English-speaking peers in academic aspects of the language.

The third piece of the puzzle emerged from my engagement in academic debates that were ongoing in the late 1970s and early 1980s about the nature of the construct of 'language proficiency' and how it should be measured. These debates had assumed some urgency as a result of the *Lau Remedies* issued in 1975 by the United States Department of Health, Education, and Welfare that required schools districts to implement bilingual instruction in any elementary school with 20 or more 'limited English proficient' students with the same primary language. Schools were required to evaluate the English language proficiency of students both in order to identify those who qualified for bilingual instruction and also to determine when these students had acquired sufficient proficiency in English to 'exit' from bilingual instruction back into mainstream classes. Attempts to specify and assess the extent to which students met these *Entry and Exit Criteria* highlighted the fact that there was no consensus

among researchers or educators about what constituted 'English proficiency' (Cummins, 1980c, 1980d).[1]

The range of theoretical perspectives was illustrated in the difference
between the model proposed by Hernandez-Chavez *et al.* (1978) that
specified 64 distinct proficiencies and Oller's (1978: 413) claim that 'there
exists a global language proficiency factor which accounts for the bulk of
the reliable variance in a wide variety of language proficiency measures'.
While acknowledging the legitimacy of positing a dimension of language
proficiency that is strongly related both to general cognitive abilities and
to academic achievement, I pointed out that 'with the exception of severely
retarded and autistic children, everybody acquires basic interpersonal
communicative skills (BICS) in a first language (L1) regardless of IQ or
academic aptitude' (1979b: 198). I distinguished BICS from cognitive/aca-
demic language proficiency which I defined as 'those aspects of language
proficiency which are closely related to the development of literacy in L1
and L2' (1980a: 177).

These roots of the BICS/CALP distinction are elaborated in the next
section. In discussing the evolution of these ideas, I use the terms *conversational fluency* and *academic language proficiency* interchangeably with
the acronyms BICS and CALP.[2]

Evolution of the Conversational/Academic Language Distinction

Teacher observations

In early 1978, I participated in a conference organised by the University
of Alberta for special educators and school psychologists working in the
two school districts in the city of Edmonton. My presentation focused on
the implications of bilingualism and language learning for special education assessment and instruction. After the presentation, I spoke informally
with a group of psychologists from one of the school districts who were
concerned about the extent to which the assessment instruments they were
using (mainly the Wechsler Intelligence Scale for Children – Revised
[WISC-R]) were valid for immigrant-background students who were in the
process of learning the school language. After this discussion, I realised
that the school systems were sitting on a wealth of data that could address
some of the concerns expressed by the psychologists. I subsequently submitted a proposal to the school district to analyse the teacher referral forms
and psychological assessments of New Canadian students who had been
assessed between 1975 and 1978, specifying the procedures that would be
put in place to assure the anonymity of all students, teachers and psychologists. The district responded favourably to this proposal and gave me access
to the relevant files for 428 students, which I copied and subsequently analysed using both qualitative and quantitative approaches.

Detailed analysis of the data was presented in various publications (e.g. Cummins, 1980b, 1981a, 1984a). The major finding of relevance in the present context is that throughout the teachers' referral forms and psychological assessment reports there were references to the fact that students' English communicative skills appeared considerably better developed than their academic language skills, as manifested both within the classroom and in the formal psychological assessment. The following examples illustrate this phenomenon:

> DM (105) arrived from Portugal at age 10 and was placed in a second-grade class; three years later in fifth grade, her teacher commented that 'her oral answering and comprehension is so much better than her written work that we feel a severe learning problem is involved, not just her non-English background'. (Verbal Ability score: <70, exact score not entered; Performance Ability score: 101)

> PS (094) was referred for reading and arithmetic difficulties in grade 2; her teacher commented that 'since PS attended Grade 1 in Italy, I think his main problem is language, although he understands and speaks English quite well.' (Verbal Ability score: 75; Performance Ability score: 84)

> GG (184) had been in Canada for less than a year when he was referred by his Grade 1 teacher who commented that 'he speaks Italian fluently and English as well. ... he is having a great deal of difficulty with the Grade 1 program'. She wondered if he had 'specific learning disabilities or if he is just a very long way behind children in his age group.' (Verbal Ability score: 65; Performance Ability score: 85)

The overall differences between Verbal and Non-Verbal (Performance) components of the WISC-R for the entire sample highlighted the fact that these emergent bilingual students were experiencing particular challenges in meeting the *linguistic* demands of the classroom learning environment. The mean Verbal and Performance Scale scores for the group were 77.9 and 89.1 respectively, 22 and 11 points below the norming sample mean of 100.

Similar differences between conversational and academic language proficiency were also identified in subsequent research among immigrant-background students. For example, Carolyn Vincent made the following observations based on her ethnographic study of a programme serving second generation Salvadorean students in Washington DC:

> All of the children in this study began school in an English-speaking environment and within their first two or three years attained conversational ability in English that teachers would regard as native-like. This is largely deceptive. The children seem to have much greater English proficiency than they actually do because their spoken English has no accent and they are able to converse on a few everyday, frequently discussed subjects. Academic language is frequently lacking. Teachers actually spend very little time talking with individual children and tend to interpret a small

sample of speech as evidence of full English proficiency. However, as the children themselves look back on their language development they see how the language used in the classroom was difficult for them, and how long it took them to acquire English. (Vincent, 1996: 195)

Academic language developmental trajectories

In 1978 I was offered a visiting scholar position in the Modern Language Centre of the Ontario Institute for Studies in Education in Toronto. Soon after taking up this position, I became familiar with the extensive research that was being carried out by the Toronto Board of Education on a variety of topics related to student achievement. One of the Board's research reports (Wright & Ramsey, 1970), was especially intriguing. In a survey of 25% of the Board's Grades 5, 7 and 9 classrooms that included 1210 immigrant students whose home language was other than English, Wright and Ramsey (also Ramsey & Wright, 1974) reported that students who arrived in Canada at ages 7 and younger attained grade norms on the seven measures of English language skills they administered, but students who arrived at older ages (8–15) performed considerably below grade norms. The data were interpreted as support for the existence of a critical or optimal age after which L2 acquisition becomes progressively more difficult. As I noted at the time (Cummins, 1979a), this finding appeared inconsistent with the findings regarding age on arrival reported by Skutnabb-Kangas and Toukomaa (1976). These authors found that Finnish background students who migrated to Sweden prior to the start of formal schooling or who started formal schooling in Sweden (age 7–8) performed more poorly in both Swedish and Finnish than those who migrated around the age of 9–10 after they had attained early literacy skills in Finnish.

The inconsistency in these reported findings troubled me for several months in 1979 until it occurred to me that Age-on-Arrival (AOA) and Length-of-Residence (LOR) were mirror images of each other. Although the Wright and Ramsey (1970) study gathered no specific information about students' LOR, it was possible to estimate LOR given the grade level of the student and his or her AOA. For example, if we assume that the average age of Grade 5 students is 11 years, then those who arrived in Canada at AOA 0-1 had been in Canada for approximately 11 years; those who arrived at AOA 2–3 had LOR of 9 years. Thus, the developmental trajectories that Ramsey and Wright (1974) attributed to AOA might equally result from differential opportunities to learn English deriving from how long students had been in Canada.

As described in Cummins (1981c), I was able to use the detailed information provided in the original Wright and Ramsey (1970) report to calculate students' LOR and analyse performance on the seven English proficiency tests as a function of LOR rather than AOA. I was also able to assess the influence of LOR and AOA on both standardised and raw scores. The standardised scores depicted students' linguistic performance in relation to how they compared to the total sample of students in their specific Grade level (5,386 students total across Grades 5, 7 and 9). The raw or absolute scores depicted the number of items students answered correctly on the test regardless of age or grade level. The difference between a students' absolute scores and their scores in relation to grade norms can be illustrated with reference to two (fictional) monolingual 6-year-old and 12-year-old students who both perform at grade level on a vocabulary test. Because the grade expectations in vocabulary for a 12-year-old are so much greater than for a 6-year-old, the 12-year-old will have learned much more vocabulary in absolute terms than the 6-year-old despite the fact that both are meeting the expectations for their respective grade levels.

The language tests administered in this study consisted of a group-administered Picture Vocabulary Test (PVT) derived from the Ammons Picture Vocabulary Test and a six-part test of English Competence (ECT) developed by the researchers, which was also group administered. The ECT included three measures of auditory perception that were prerecorded on tape and three measures designed to assess general vocabulary knowledge, knowledge of prepositional usage, and idioms. The auditory perception measures required students to mark the correct answers on a written answer sheet and thus may have assessed some degree of literacy skills in addition to the target language skills. Items in the six ECT measures all used high-frequency vocabulary and were designed such that native speakers should obtain a near-perfect score. The PVT, by contrast, was intended to distribute native speakers according to a normal curve (see Cummins, 1984a, for PVT standardised and raw scores distribution).

A consistent pattern of findings was obtained for the PVT and the three ECT measures that were designed to assess aspects of vocabulary knowledge and idioms. The performance of immigrant students on one of the ECT subtests designed to assess knowledge of prepositional usage (labelled by Wright and Ramsey, 1970, the *Functors* test) is depicted in Figure 4.1 (standardised scores) and Figure 4.2 (raw scores). On this 12-item subtest, as in other ECT subtests, there is relatively little variation among native speakers in performance (total sample means, grade 5: *9.8*; grade, 7: *11.1*; grade 9: *11.4*). Some examples from the test are presented below. Students were required to choose the preposition in column B that was appropriate to insert in each of the sentences in column A.

A	B
(1) I don't agree _____ you.	A: on
(4) She talks a lot _____ nonsense.	B: by
(5) _____ second thoughts, I stayed home.	C: with
(6) He led her _____ her arm.	D: of

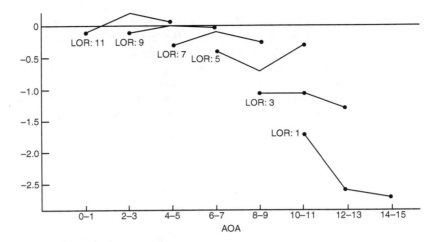

Figure 4.1 Prepositional usage test results. Vertical axis, standard deviation units, 0 = grade norm; horizontal axis, Age-on-Arrival (AOA); LOR = length of residence. From Cummins (1981c); Reproduced with permission.

Figure 4.1 presents students' scores in relation to how rapidly they catch up to Grades 5, 7, and 9 norms as determined by the total sample. The vertical axis shows scores in standard deviation units below the mean (grade norm). In other words, a score of minus 1 is the equivalent of 15 points on a standardised scale (such as an IQ test) where 100 is the mean and the standard deviation is 15). The horizontal axis displays students' age on arrival (AOA) in Canada. The joined lines show the scores for students who arrived at different ages but who have the same length of residence (LOR).

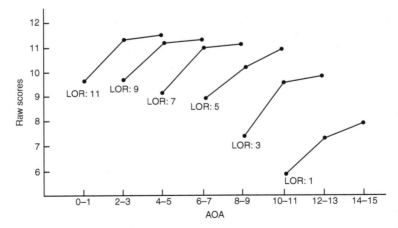

Figure 4.2 Prepositional test results. Raw scores (maximum = 12). From Cummins (1981c); Reproduced with permission.

The data presented in Figure 4.1 reveals the impact of LOR on students' performance during the initial 5–7 years they are learning English. Students who had been in Canada for one year performed between 1.5 and 2.5 standard deviation units below grade expectations. After three years LOR, they are about one standard deviation (15 standard score points) below the mean but it requires between 5 and 7 years for students to come close to grade expectations and even after this extended period of time learning English they are still about half a standard deviation below the norm. On two measures that attempted to assess aspects of English auditory processing, immigrant students came within a half standard deviation of grade expectations after three years LOR, although the fact that these measures entailed written responses suggests that they may also have been assessing aspects of English literacy.

These findings suggest that different acquisition trajectories characterise the attainment of conversational fluency as compared to academic language proficiency. As noted previously, teachers commonly observe that immigrant students acquire the societal language relatively rapidly (see also Snow & Hoefnagel-Höhle, 1979) and certainly a large majority of immigrant students are likely to acquire fluent conversational skills in the school language within three years of arrival. However, the reanalysis demonstrates that after three years of learning English there are still major gaps in performance with respect to literacy-related aspects of English. The data also show that for most of the comparisons, the effect of LOR on standardised test scores is largely independent of AOA. Only in the LOR 1 comparisons in Figure 4.1 is there a linear decrease in performance across the three AOA groups, with students who arrived at ages 10–11 performing better than those who arrived at later ages.

Figure 4.2 presents these same data in terms of students' absolute scores. It is clear that within each LOR level, there is a linear increase in absolute score with increasing AOA. This is most evident for students who arrive at ages 6–7 and later. In other words, when LOR is controlled, students who arrive at an older age learn more vocabulary in absolute terms than students who arrive at younger ages. This finding is exactly what would be predicted by the interdependence hypothesis and is consistent with numerous other research results relating to age and L2 learning (e.g. Snow & Hoefnagel-Höhle, 1979). Cummins (1980a: 184) interpreted the findings as 'showing that older L2 learners, whose L1 CALP is better developed, manifest L2 cognitive/academic proficiency more rapidly than younger learners because it already exists in the L1 and is therefore available for use in the new context'.

This was the first relatively large-scale study demonstrating that it took considerably longer for immigrant-background students to catch up academically than was required to attain conversational fluency in the school language. Subsequent research has reported very similar catch-up trajectories (e.g. Collier, 1987; Demie, 2013, 2018; Gándara, 1999;

Klesmer, 2004; Levin & Shohamy, 2008). This extended trajectory for immigrant-background learners to catch up in academic aspects of language is a result of both the challenges of learning academic language for all students and the fact that immigrant students are attempting to catch up to a moving target, namely, native speakers of the school language whose academic language and literacy skills are increasing significantly from one grade level to the next.

The depth of the empirical support for the differential trajectories in BICS and CALP among immigrant-background L2 learners can be illustrated with reference to Gándara's (1999: 5) summary of research in California. She identified a large discrepancy between the developmental patterns for oral L2 skills (measured by oral language tests) as compared to L2 reading and writing during the elementary school years:

> For example, while listening skills are at 80% of native proficiency by Level 3 (approximately 3rd grade), reading and writing skills remain below 50% of those expected for native speakers. It is not until after Level 5 (or approximately 5th grade) that the different sets of skills begin to merge. This suggests that while a student may be able to speak and understand English at fairly high levels of proficiency within the first three years of school, academic skills in English reading and writing take longer for students to develop.

Gándara (1999: 5) noted the significant implications of these findings for educational policy and classroom instruction: 'While some students are sufficiently fluent in English to participate in many classroom activities, it would be unreasonable to expect these students to perform academic tasks involving reading and writing in English at the same level as native English speakers until they have had sufficient time to develop these skills'.

Theoretical analysis of the 'language proficiency' construct

At a more theoretical level, the BICS/CALP distinction also served to qualify John Oller's (1978, 1980) claim that all individual differences in language proficiency could be largely accounted for by just one underlying global language proficiency dimension. Oller synthesised a considerable amount of data showing strong correlations between performance on cloze tests of reading, standardised reading tests, and measures of oral verbal ability (e.g. vocabulary measures). He concluded on the basis of this analysis that 'there is a language factor deeper than speech which pervades every kind of educational or psychological test that has been investigated so far (and this includes a surprisingly large and diverse array of tests)' (1980: 28).

I pointed out that Oller's theoretical position is consistent with a large body of research showing strong relationships between literacy skills and both verbal and, to a lesser extent, non-verbal intellectual abilities. For example, Strang (1945) reported correlations of between 0.80 - 0.84 between reading and verbal intellectual abilities and 0.41 -0.46 between reading and non-verbal intellectual abilities. Similarly, the strong relationship between vocabulary knowledge and reading comprehension has been demonstrated repeatedly. Grabe's (2004) review of research on teaching reading concluded that the 'relation between vocabulary knowledge and reading comprehension has been powerfully demonstrated in both L1 and L2 contexts' (2004: 49). As noted previously, vocabulary knowledge also represents the strongest predictor of overall cognitive ability on tests such as the Wechsler Scales (e.g. Kaufman *et al.*, 2016). In short, there is overwhelming empirical evidence for a theoretical construct that integrates verbal cognitive functioning, vocabulary knowledge, and reading comprehension.

However, Oller's claim that all variation in language proficiency could be reduced to a single global dimension ignored the fact that some of the major components of L1 functioning show minimal variation after the initial acquisition process (e.g. phonology, basic 'competence' in a Chomskian sense), while the variation in other components (e.g. oral fluency, accent, sociolinguistic competence) are largely unrelated to the development of cognitive and academic abilities during the course of schooling. I pointed out that 'the phonological, syntactical, and lexical skills necessary to function in everyday interpersonal contexts are universal across native speakers' (1980d: 84). In other words, after the acquisition of these competencies in the early years, there are no longer any meaningful individual differences among native speakers that are related to cognitive or academic performance. For example, if we take two monolingual English-speaking siblings, a 12-year-old child and a 6-year-old, there are enormous differences in these children's ability to read and write English and in the depth and breadth of their vocabulary knowledge, but minimal differences in their phonology, accent, or oral fluency. The six-year old can understand virtually everything that is likely to be said to her in everyday social contexts and she can use language effectively and appropriately in these contexts, just as the 12-year-old can. Thus, some aspects of children's L1 development (e.g. phonology) reach a plateau relatively early, whereas other aspects (e.g. vocabulary knowledge) continue to develop throughout our lifetimes.

In short, conversational fluency and academic language proficiency reflect distinguishable aspects of linguistic functioning that are characterised by the relative frequency they are manifested in the contexts of everyday face-to-face communication and performance of academic tasks in school. These differences invalidate Oller's (1980) theoretical claim that all variation in language performance reflects just one unitary proficiency dimension.[3]

Clarification and Elaboration of the BICS/CALP Distinction

In suggesting the term *Basic Interpersonal Communicative Skills* (BICS) to refer to the near-universal aspects of language proficiency that reach a plateau in the early years prior to the start of formal schooling, I emphasised that BICS was not proposed as a unitary dimension in any psychometric sense. Spolsky (1984: 42) pointed to the wide range of variation that can be identified among individuals in a range of conversational interactions: 'You might measure how well my pronunciation compares to a native speaker's, or how clear it is over a telephone; you might count the number of different words I use in a talk, or the speed of my syllable production; you might observe the structure of my sentences, or the effectiveness of my speech acts'. The point of distinguishing conversational fluency from academic language proficiency was not to deny either the complexity or major variation in conversational interactions but rather to point out that (a) all normally developing speakers (or signers) of any language develop the ability to use this language to attain their goals in everyday social contexts, and (b) the variation across individuals in various aspects of conversational fluency (e.g. accent, speed of syllable production, etc.) is not directly related to individual differences in the development of literacy-related aspects of language(s) in school (i.e. CALP).

As discussed in Chapter 8, the BICS/CALP distinction refers to the same reality as the distinction proposed by Hulstijn (2015: 21) between *basic language cognition* and *higher* or *extended language cognition*: 'Basic language cognition is the language cognition that all native speakers have in common; higher, extended language cognition is the domain where differences between native speakers can be observed'. The major distinguishing features of BICS and CALP are summarised in Table 4.1.

The linguistic differences between school language and conversational language outlined in Table 4.1 can be described in terms of differences of *register*. The term 'register' is used by linguists to refer to features of speech or writing characteristic of a particular type of linguistic activity (e.g. delivering a sermon, telling jokes, teaching a mathematics lesson in school, etc.). Gibbons (2007: 702) pointed out that the 'registers associated with academic learning traditionally code knowledge in ways that are linguistically unfamiliar to many students'. These registers include the specific technical language, grammatical patterns, and discourse structures specific to different subjects in the curriculum. For example, as students engage in scientific inquiry, they are frequently required to generate questions, make predictions, formulate hypotheses, recount the steps or procedures they followed in carrying out an experiment and generate explanations of their hypotheses and the phenomena they observed. According to Gibbons (2007: 702), these school-related registers 'usually involve more "written-like" discourse, which tends to be less personal, more abstract, more lexically dense, and more structured than the face-to-face everyday language with which students are familiar'.

Table 4.1 Differences between conversational fluency and academic language proficiency

Conversational fluency (BICS)	Academic language proficiency (CALP)
The ability to carry on a conversation in familiar face-to-face situations.	The extent to which an individual can comprehend and use the oral and written language that appears in the subject matter of academic disciplines and in classroom discussions about this subject matter.
Meaning is supported by facial expressions, gestures, eye contact, intonation, and the immediate context.	Meaning is made explicit through low-frequency vocabulary and discourse conventions that link concepts and ideas in precise ways; nominalisation (e.g. *acceleration*) and the passive voice are common features.
Developed by the vast majority of native speakers by the time they enter school at age 5 or 6; phonology and fluency, in particular, reach a plateau with minimal further development after age 5/6.	Develops together with BICS in the early years but becomes differentiated from BICS as a result of literate and academic activities in the home and school; continues to develop through the school years and beyond.
Involves utterances that are informationally transparent as a result of the immediate context and use of high-frequency words and expressions as well as relatively common grammatical constructions.	Involves informationally dense text and oral language where meaning is conveyed by less frequent vocabulary and more complex grammatical constructions, which are seldom used in face-to-face conversation.
In English, everyday conversational interactions draw predominantly from high-frequency Anglo-Saxon origin vocabulary.	As students progress through the grades, they increasingly encounter both in texts and classroom instruction low-frequency vocabulary that derives from Latin and Greek sources; CALP reflects the registers of language that children acquire in school and which they need to use effectively if they are to progress successfully through the grades.
Newcomer students who arrive in the early years of elementary school typically pick up L2 conversational fluency within 1–2 years when exposure in school and environment is sufficient; students who arrive at older ages may take longer to acquire L2 fluency and may retain traces of their L1 phonology in the new language.	Newcomer students typically require at least 5 years to catch up academically; this is because of the challenges that academic language and literacy pose for all students, and the fact that they are catching up to a moving target – native-speaking students continue to make gains in reading and writing skills and knowledge of low-frequency vocabulary every year.

This 'written-like' discourse is very different than the language of everyday communication, or *playground language* (Gibbons, 1991, 2015, 2017), which includes the language that 'enables children to make friends, join in games and take part in a variety of day-to-day activities that develop and maintain social contacts' (1991: 3). Gibbons pointed out that this language typically occurs in face-to-face situations and is highly dependent on the physical and visual context, and on gestures and body language. The cognitive and communicative demands of classroom language are very different, as illustrated by the requirement for students to understand sentences such as: *if we increase the angle by 5 degrees, we could cut the circumference into equal parts.* She noted that the language associated with cognitive functions such as hypothesising, evaluating, inferring, generalising, predicting, and classifying typically requires vocabulary, grammatical structures, and discourse conventions that seldom appear in everyday conversational interactions. These cognitive functions and associated language occur in all areas of the curriculum and are essential for school success, particularly as students progress through the grades.

Wong Fillmore (2009: 6–7) has also highlighted the strong empirical support for the distinction between everyday spoken language and the academic registers integral to learning and teaching in schools:

> Informational density is a hallmark of academic language, where a great deal of information is packed into individual sentences. The grammatical devices that enable this ... are only infrequently used in conversational language, according to linguists who have compared spoken and written languages of various types. (Biber *et al.*, 1998; Biber *et al.*, 1999)

One final point of clarification is important to emphasise. The BICS/CALP *distinction* was never conceived as representing a rigid *dichotomy* between social and academic language. Clearly, much of the interaction and instruction that goes on in schools involves everyday conversational structures and functions. Similarly, features that are characteristic of academic language are sometimes used in interpersonal interactions. Thus, as illustrated in Figure 4.3, it is more appropriate to conceive of the BICS/CALP distinction as a continuum along which patterns of language use will vary as a function of particular contexts. As students co-construct conceptual knowledge with their teachers, they expand their linguistic repertoire from everyday language to encompass the registers of schooling and the specific language features associated with different curriculum subjects (Gibbons, 2007).

In short, there is ample documentation (e.g. Bailey, 2007; Biber, 1986; Gibbons, 2007, 2017; Wong Fillmore & Fillmore, 2012) that the language

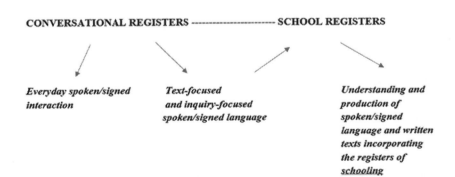

Figure 4.3 From everyday spoken/signed language to the language of schooling

typically used in educational contexts differs significantly from the language typically used in everyday social contexts. These differences lie in 'the *relative frequency* of complex grammatical structures, specialized vocabulary, and uncommon language functions' (August & Shanahan, 2010: 216) (emphasis original). These characteristics of academic language present learning challenges for *all* students – white middle-class students as well as minoritised students. The language demands of particular subject areas vary (e.g. Gottlieb & Castro, 2017) and students' ability to use academic registers of language continues to develop throughout their schooling.

Connecting BICS/CALP to degree of contextual support and cognitive demand

The BICS/CALP distinction quickly generated extensive discussion (and controversy) among applied linguists regarding its legitimacy and implications (e.g. Oller, 1980; Rivera, 1984). The distinction highlighted the absence of any coherent theoretical framework for relating 'language proficiency' to academic progress among both L1 and L2 learners, but it did so in a way that didn't fall neatly into categories derived from existing disciplinary perspectives in the broad field of applied linguistics (e.g. sociolinguistics, L1 and L2 language acquisition, L2 teaching, etc.). Not surprisingly, there were a significant number of critiques and (from my perspective) misinterpretations (outlined in the next section).

Some of these critiques pointed to the potential for acronyms to be misinterpreted (e.g. Spolsky, 1984). Because the acronyms seemed to be distracting at least some people from the reality of the distinction they referenced, I decided both to avoid using the labels BICS/CALP and to elaborate the distinction into two intersecting continua that highlighted the range of cognitive demands and contextual support involved in particular language tasks or activities (Cummins, 1981a) (Figure 4.4).[4]

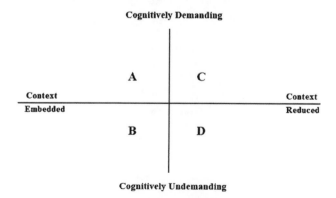

Figure 4.4 Range of contextual support and degree of cognitive involvement in communicative activities

In context-embedded communication the participants can actively negotiate meaning (e.g. by asking for clarification) and the language is supported by a wide range of meaningful interpersonal and situational cues. Context-reduced communication, on the other hand, relies primarily (or, at the extreme of the continuum, exclusively) on linguistic cues to meaning, and thus, successful interpretation of the message depends heavily on knowledge of the language itself. I used the term 'context-reduced' rather than 'decontextualised' in recognition of the fact that all language and literacy practices take place in particular social contexts. However, the range of supports to meaning in many academic contexts (e.g. textbook reading) is reduced in comparison to the contextual support available in face-to-face contexts. Internal and external dimensions of context were distinguished to reflect the fact that *context* is constituted both by what we bring to a task (e.g. our prior knowledge, interests and motivation – internal context) and the range of supports that may be incorporated in the task itself (e.g. visual supports such as graphic organisers – external context).

The lower parts of the vertical continuum consist of communicative tasks and activities in which the linguistic tools have become largely automatised and thus require little active cognitive involvement for appropriate performance. At the upper end of the continuum are tasks and activities in which the linguistic tools have not become automatised and thus require active cognitive processing. Persuading another individual in a face-to-face debate that your point of view is correct, and writing an essay, are examples of quadrant A and C skills respectively. Casual conversation is a typical quadrant B activity while quadrant D involves activities such as copying notes from the blackboard, filling in worksheets, or other forms of drill and practice activities. Numerous researchers have elaborated the kinds of tasks and activities that are characteristic of the four quadrants (e.g. Cline & Frederickson, 1996; Coelho, 2004).

This *Quadrants* framework stimulated discussion of the instructional environment required to enable immigrant-background students to catch up academically as quickly as possible. Specifically, I (and others) argued that effective instruction should focus primarily on context-embedded and cognitively demanding tasks (quadrant A). These tasks maintained high cognitive challenge while, at the same time, providing the internal and external contextual supports to enable learners to successfully meet these challenges. I pointed out that these task dimensions cannot be specified in absolute terms because what is 'context-embedded' or 'cognitively demanding' for one learner may not be so for another as a result of differences in internal attributes such as prior knowledge, interest, or motivation.

The BICS/CALP distinction was related to the theoretical distinctions of several other theorists including Bruner's (1975) *communicative and analytic competence*, Donaldson's (1978) *embedded and disembedded language* and Olson's (1977) *utterance and text* (Cummins, 1981b, 2000). The terms used by different investigators have varied but the essential distinction refers to the extent to which the meaning being communicated is strongly supported by concrete contextual and interpersonal cues (such as gestures, facial expressions and intonation present in face-to-face interaction) or supported by a smaller range of cues that are primarily linguistic in nature.

I also suggested (Cummins, 2001a) that conversational and academic language registers represent subsets of what Gee (1990) termed primary and secondary discourses. Primary discourses are acquired through face-to-face interactions in the home and represent the language of initial socialisation. Secondary discourses are acquired in social institutions beyond the family (e.g. school, business, religious and cultural contexts) and involve acquisition of specialised vocabulary and functions of language appropriate to those settings. Secondary discourses can be oral or written and are central to the social life of both non-literate and literate cultures. Examples of secondary discourse common in many non-literate cultures are the conventions of storytelling or the language of marriage or burial rituals that are passed down through oral tradition from one generation to the next. Oral forms of secondary discourse are in no way inferior to written forms, as illustrated in the fact that one of the greatest literary achievements of humanity, the Homeric epics of the Odyssey and the Iliad, existed for many centuries only in oral form prior to being written down (see Nurmela *et al.*, 2012, for discussion of 'oracy' and 'literacy' in the context of the implementation of mother-tongue based multilingual education in Nepal).

Within this conception, academic language proficiency reflects 'the extent to which an individual has access to and command of the oral and written academic registers of schooling' (Cummins, 2000: 67). These academic registers include the specialised vocabulary, grammatical and discourse structures, and functions of language that are characteristic of the social institution of schooling and which occur less frequently outside of the context of schooling. The secondary discourses of schooling are no different in principle and certainly not 'superior' in any sense to the secondary discourse of other spheres of human endeavor – for example, avid amateur gardeners and professional horticulturalists have acquired vocabulary related to plants and flowers far beyond the knowledge of those of us not involved in this sphere of activity. What makes acquisition of the secondary discourses associated with schooling so crucial, however, is that the life chances of individuals are directly determined by the degree of expertise they acquire in understanding and using these registers of language.

A more teacher-friendly version of the Quadrants framework was proposed by Mariani (1997) and elaborated by Gibbons (2009) and Wilson and Devereux (2014) (Figure 4.5). The quadrants in this case are also

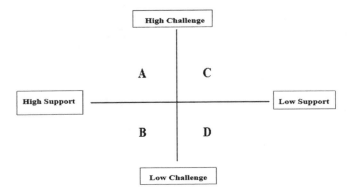

Figure 4.5 Challenge and support in learning tasks (based on Mariani, 1997)

expressed in terms of the underlying dimensions of instructional tasks and involve instructional continua ranging from High Challenge to Low Challenge (vertical) and High Support to Low Support (horizontal). The underlying dimensions are identical to those in Figure 4.4, but the 'Challenge Zone' framework (Gibbons, 2009) expresses more directly what teachers need to do to maximise learning – engage multilingual students in tasks that are cognitively challenging but incorporate the supports necessary to enable successful task completion.

Academic Language Proficiency: Theory and Practice in Dialogue

As noted previously, the BICS/CALP distinction emerged from observations by teachers and school psychologists who were concerned about classroom instruction and assessment realities experienced by immigrant-background students. As the distinction and the broader framework within which it is embedded (e.g. the interdependence hypothesis) became more widely known, researchers and educators began to explore the implications of these theoretical constructs for instructional practice in multilingual contexts. An example from the South African context (Starfield, 1994) illustrates the significant impact and the consequential validity (see Chapter 7) of these ideas for educators pursuing equity and social justice for minoritised students. Starfield's account also illustrates the synergy between the conception of CALP as a fusion of conceptual, linguistic and academic knowledge and abilities, and the constructs of the common underlying proficiency and linguistic interdependence.

The context for Starfield's discussion of the relevance of the construct of academic language proficiency and the quadrants framework was the Academic Support Programme (ASP) of the University Witwatersrand (WITS), Johannesburg, which was started in 1980 to enable black students who were English language learners to succeed in a predominantly white, English-medium university. These students had attended segregated schools operated by the apartheid-regime Department of Education and Training (DET). These schools provided L1 instruction up to and including the fourth grade after which students were transitioned to English-only instruction. Starfield noted that the DET K-12 schools were 'systematically structured to underequip black students for higher education' (Starfield, 1994: 176). Students frequently experienced difficulties in meeting the academic requirements of their university courses, with the result that many mainstream faculty members viewed students as having language problems while others appeared to believe that the students were cognitively unable to cope with university study. Mainstream faculty often wondered about the extent to which DET students' academic problems were rooted in linguistic or, alternatively, conceptual gaps.

In response to these issues, the ASP initially implemented a traditional English-for-academic-purposes (EAP) support programme focused on teaching academic language in isolation from academic content. Starfield (1994: 177) pointed out that this approach did not work very well and ironically simply reinforced perceptions of student deficits. The ASP changed direction on the basis of Cummins' (1984a, 1986) framework 'which helped ASP practitioners understand why the traditional EAP model could not work in the South African context and which provided the theoretical bases for the integrated approach to academic literacy now adopted'. The existing EAP programme did little to transform the context-reduced and cognitively demanding nature of typical academic literacy tasks such as writing an essay or reading a textbook. Of equal importance was the fact that students' previous education in segregated and structurally racist schools had provided minimal opportunity for students to develop a strong academic foundation in their L1:

> In the DET schools, however, academic literacy is barely acquired in the L1, for it ceases to be a medium of instruction after the fourth year, with insufficient time having been allowed for the acquisition of context-reduced, cognitively demanding skills. English then becomes the medium of instruction, requiring academic literacy acquisition via the L2. Content materials are, however, frequently too difficult for pupils to process given their limited English proficiency, so rote learning tends to predominate. (1994: 177)

Starfield located the 'problem' of students' academic difficulties at the university level squarely in the nature of the intervention designed to support them in upgrading their academic language skills. Certainly, students do need support in English language development, but they also require substantial assistance in content areas, which traditional EAP teachers are unable to provide. She responded to the question of whether DET students are experiencing linguistic or conceptual difficulties by arguing 'that these two dimensions are inextricably linked' (1994: 178).

Based on this insight, the ASP team reconceptualised the role of the ESL teacher and developed a content- and discipline-based model focused on enabling students to gain access to and take ownership of the specific conceptual networks and related linguistic functions and registers that underpin the knowledge structure of each discipline. The model dispensed with the separate language syllabus in favour of a content-driven syllabus in which the mainstream course determined the skills and processes taught and the conceptual focus of the instruction. Despite the fact that this model resulted in improved student performance, Starfield emphasised that its 'adjunct' nature was problematic insofar as it could be viewed as protecting the mainstream from change. Many educators and researchers have expressed similar concerns about 'satellite' ESL or heritage language programmes that have done little to bring about changes in mindset and instructional orientation in K-12 mainstream schools (e.g. Cummins & Cameron, 1994; Menken *et al.*, 2011; Wong Fillmore, 1982, 2014). This reality illustrates the need to integrate an analysis of psycholinguistic issues associated with language education with analysis of the ways in which societal power relations continue to perpetuate systemic racism and other forms of discrimination (see Chapters 5 and 6).

Initial Critiques of the BICS/CALP Distinction

The first batch of many critiques of the BICS/CALP distinction was voiced by several researchers at the Language Proficiency Assessment Symposium held March 14–18, 1981, at the Airlie House Conference Center in Warrenton, Virginia. The symposium was organised by Charlene Rivera with funding from the National Institute of Education, a federal agency based in Washington, DC. The main goals of the symposium were (a) to develop a working definition of communicative proficiency and (b) to 'make recommendations for the assessment of language minority students for the purpose of entry/exit into appropriate educational programs' (Rivera, 1984: xvi). Rivera edited four volumes based on presentations and discussions that took place at the symposium, one of which, entitled *Language Proficiency and Academic Achievement*, was focused almost entirely on critical analysis of the distinction between conversational fluency (BICS) and academic language proficiency (CALP). I outlined the rationale for the distinction in an initial chapter entitled 'Wanted: A theoretical framework for relating language proficiency to academic achievement among bilingual students' (Cummins, 1984b). This was followed by critiques of the proposed theoretical framework written by Fred Genesee (1984), Michael Canale (1984), Bernard Spolsky (1984), Rudolph Troike (1984) and Benji Wald (1984). In the final chapter, I responded to these critiques (Cummins, 1984c).

These critical analyses were, for the most part, constructive and useful, and served as a catalyst for clarification and elaboration of the theoretical constructs. One of the main themes running through these critiques was that the role of social factors in explaining differential school success was neglected in the framework in comparison to the importance assigned to cognitive and linguistic factors. I responded to this concern by noting that the causal primacy of sociolinguistic and sociopolitical factors was never in question, and cognitive/linguistic proficiencies were explicitly positioned as intervening variables rather than as independent causal variables.

Critics also pointed to lack of specificity in the ways that 'context' and 'contextual support' were conceived in the continuum between context-embedded and context-reduced meanings. In response, I suggested the distinction between internal and external context; as noted previously, the former refers to conceptual schemata that individuals have acquired as a result of their social interactions and prior experiences that facilitate understanding of content and language. External contextual factors refer to aspects of the language or instructional presentation that facilitate or (sometimes) complexify understanding of the context. For example, teachers and textbook writers frequently scaffold the presentation of academic content by adding graphic organisers, other visuals, and demonstrations.

Many subsequent critiques of the BICS/CALP distinction appeared over the following 20 years including Edelsky (1990), Edelsky et al. (1983), MacSwan (2000), Martin-Jones and Romaine (1986), Wiley (1996). I responded to these critiques in detail (Cummins, 2000, 2008a; Cummins & Swain, 1983) and will not revisit the issues in any depth in this chapter. The legitimacy of the distinction between conversational fluency and academic language proficiency is taken up again in Chapter 8 in the context of more recent critiques and debates about the construct of 'academic language'. I will comment at this point on just two of what I considered the most problematic features that characterised many of the early (1981–2000) critiques.

Dismissal/disinterest in empirical evidence

To my knowledge, none of the critiques (early or more recent) addressed the empirical evidence articulated as supporting the legitimacy of the BICS/CALP distinction. No critic commented on, or offered an alternative explanation for, the differential catch-up trajectories among immigrant-background students with respect to acquiring everyday conversational fluency in the school language as compared to catching up academically (e.g. Cummins, 1981c; Vincent, 1996). Critics also ignored the empirical evidence demonstrating that teachers and school psychologists frequently interpreted emergent bilingual students' conversational fluency in English as evidence that students had 'acquired English' with the result that verbal psychological tests (in English) were seen as 'valid' measures of cognitive functioning (Cummins, 1980b, 1984a). Similarly, the critiques ignored the role of the BICS/CALP distinction in highlighting the premature 'exit' from bilingual programmes of many bilingual students in the 1980s and 1990s in the United States. As documented in Cummins (1980c), emergent bilingual students were regularly being transferred from transitional bilingual programmes into English monolingual programmes on the basis of problematic tests that failed to assess the extent to which these students had developed sufficient knowledge of the academic registers of English to understand instruction. Finally, none of the critics of the BICS/CALP distinction commented on the research of Biber (1986) or Corson (1997) or many other researchers who documented major differences between the language registers of schooling and the language of everyday communication.

As I discuss in Chapter 7, in order to be considered credible, any critique of a theoretical construct or claim is *required* to address the empirical evidence advanced to support that claim. The evidence might be critiqued as problematic and thus not a credible source of support for the theoretical claim, or the evidence might be accepted as credible, but an argument made that this evidence can be more adequately accounted for by a different set of theoretical constructs. In Chapter 8, I present a detailed analysis of the legitimacy of the construct of 'academic language' and the more specific distinction between CALP and BICS in relation to the extent to which these constructs meet the criteria of empirical adequacy, logical coherence, and consequential validity.

Logically flawed distortions of the BICS/CALP distinction

When I first read the critique written by Edelsky *et al.* (1983), I was disturbed and extremely surprised that they characterised CALP as 'a language-related villain' (1983: 8). They also explicitly stated that I felt a 'need' to blame minoritised students for their failure to succeed at school. They characterised the BICS/CALP distinction as 'a spurious language proficiency dichotomy' (1983: 4) without ever addressing the empirical evidence that was advanced in support of the distinction or their rationale for characterising it as spurious.

Edelsky and colleagues (1983) further characterised CALP as a key component of a 'deficit theory' that 'blames' minoritised students for their academic underachievement. This argument is immediately suspect by virtue of the fact that Edelsky and colleagues offered no definition or explicit criteria for what constitutes a deficit theory (Cummins & Swain, 1983). A logically coherent critique would have:

- advanced empirical and logical arguments to justify the claim that the BICS/CALP distinction is 'spurious'; to be credible, these arguments would have to demonstrate that there are no systematic differences between the typical language registers used in everyday interpersonal communication and those used in academic contexts as students engage with increasingly complex academic content.

- articulated explicit criteria for what constitutes a 'deficit theory'; for example, as Merrill Swain and I commented in our response to Edelsky *et al*. (1983) 'does Wells' (1981) finding that low-SES children on entry to school have lower levels of literacy-related knowledge constitute a deficit position?' (Cummins & Swain, 1983: 24-25).

In short, the credibility of the critique by Edelsky and colleagues (1983) was undermined (in my eyes) by the fact that they chose not to acknowledge (or critique) the research evidence in support of the BICS/CALP distinction and they failed to articulate both what they meant by a 'deficit theory' and how the conceptual distinction between conversational fluency and academic language proficiency constituted such a deficit theory.[5]

Implications for Language Policy and Classroom Instruction

Since its initial articulation in the late 1970s, the distinction between BICS and CALP has influenced both policy and practice related to the instruction and assessment of second language learners. It has been invoked, for example, in policy discussions related to:

- The amount and duration of funding necessary to support students who are learning English as an additional language.
- The kinds of instructional support that English learners need at different stages of their acquisition of conversational and academic English.
- The inclusion of English learners in high-stakes testing mandated by state or national educational jurisdictions; for example, should immigrant-background students be exempt from taking high-stakes tests and, if so, for how long – 1, 2, 3, 4, or 5 years after arrival in the host country?
- The extent to which psychological testing through the school language of immigrant-background students for diagnostic purposes is valid and ethically defensible.

The distinction has been discussed positively in numerous books that aim to equip educators with the understanding and skills required to teach and assess linguistically diverse students (e.g. Cline & Frederickson, 1996, in the United Kingdom; Coelho, 2004, 2012, in Canada; Diaz-Rico & Weed, 2002, in the United States) and has been invoked to interpret data from a range of sociolinguistic and educational contexts (e.g. in the South African context, Broome, 2004; Starfield, 1994).

As noted previously, one of the initial (and ongoing) critiques of the BICS/CALP distinction is that it doesn't adequately account for sociopolitical and sociolinguistic determinants of minoritised students' academic achievement. This issue is discussed in Chapter 5.

Notes

(1) Forty years later, there is still no consensus among researchers, policymakers, or educators about what constitutes 'English proficiency'. Valdés (2020) cites a National Research Council (2011) report as identifying three different definitions employed across different states to identify the English language learner population:

> Importantly, the panel identified different conceptualisations of academic and social language measured by current tests as a significant aspect of the broader problems. It also emphasised that, given these different conceptualisations, state English Language Proficiency (ELP) tests: (1) have different number[s] of performance levels and (2) test different skills, which are described and measured differently. As a result, students classified at one level (e.g., intermediate) by one state might be classified at an entirely different level in another. (Valdés, 2020: 9)

I made a similar point 40 years previously, citing research showing that various measures of 'English language proficiency' had low correlations both among themselves and with standardised tests of literacy skills (Cummins, 1980c, 1980d).

(2) In temporarily avoiding use of the acronyms, I was responding both to concerns expressed about possible misinterpretations of their meaning and implications (Rivera, 1984) and multiple *actual* misrepresentations of the terms (see Cummins, 2000; Cummins & Swain, 1983). I emphasised, however, that 'the basic distinctions highlighted by these terms are unchanged' (Cummins, 1984a: 5). Despite the fact that from the early 1980s, I typically used the terms *conversational fluency* and *academic language proficiency* to refer to the distinction, educators concerned with teaching English learners predominantly continued to use the acronyms BICS and CALP. Thus, at this point, I use both sets of terms interchangeably. Lily Wong Fillmore (2009: 3) seems to have spoken for many educators when she noted that I had revised the initial terminology (BICS/CALP) 'but his first characterization is more memorable and apt than the subsequent description, which is why I continue using it'.

(3) It is worth highlighting the fact that Oller's (1978, 1980) general thesis regarding the existence of a global language proficiency factor as well as the narrower construct of CALP have been strongly supported by recent psychometric studies. Barr *et al.* (2019: 1007), for example, reviewed some of the relevant research as follows:

> Recent studies have consistently identified a general language factor as the strongest contributor to reading comprehension either in a bifactor model that includes decoding as the second factor (Foorman, Koon et al., 2015) or in bifactor models that include a general language factor in addition to specific factors for individual language components. (Kieffer *et al.*, 2016)

These psychometric studies (and Oller's research) obviously do not take account of dimensions of language proficiency that show minimal variation across individuals – what I have called *basic interpersonal communicative skills* and Hulstijn (2015, 2019) terms *basic language cognition* (see Chapter 8).

(4) In the original version of the Quadrants framework, the extremes of the 'cognitive' continuum were reversed from the current version, with 'cognitively undemanding' at the top of the vertical continuum and 'cognitively demanding' at the bottom. In Figure 4.4, I have put 'cognitively demanding' at the top of the continuum in order to bring the quadrants into alignment with the categories in the 'high challenge/high support', framework in Figure 4.5.

(5) This brief sampling of the controversy regarding the BICS/CALP distinction gives only a hint of the vehement rejection that the distinction evoked among some applied linguists. In contrast to the earlier academic critiques initially voiced at a conference in 1981 and later published in the Rivera (1984) volume, the Edelsky *et al.* (1983) critique was highly personalised as illustrated in claims such as: 'This unquestioning

acceptance of ... current school curricula is the flaw that we believe leads to all the rest of the errors. It accounts for Cummins' (1979) choice of data and for *his need to blame the learner for failure* by establishing a spurious language proficiency dichotomy' (1983: 4; emphasis added).

The issues surrounding the BICS/CALP distinction can be pursued in greater depth in Cummins (2000, 2013, 2017c) and in Chapter 8. The rejection of the distinction by some researchers contrasts with the almost universal acknowledgement of the practical implications of the distinction among educators directly engaged with supporting English learners in catching up academically (see, for example, https://www.colorin-colorado.org/faq/what-are-bics-and-calp).

5 Power Relations in School: Constructing or Constricting Identities?

Since the 1990s, there has been a large degree of consensus within the field of applied linguistics that the construct of *identity* is of central importance in understanding patterns of language learning and linguistic behaviour generally (e.g. Darvin & Norton, 2014; Gee, 2004; Norton, 2013; Norton Peirce, 1995; Toohey *et al.*, 2007). The centrality of both identity negotiation and societal power relations in understanding patterns of school achievement was clearly expressed by Ladson-Billings (1995: 485): 'The problem that African-American students face is the constant devaluation of their culture both in school and in the larger society'. The logical implication of this claim is that schools committed to reversing patterns of underachievement should implement instruction that actively challenges the devaluation of students and communities in the wider society.

Despite the current prominence of notions of identity negotiation and societal power relations in the academic literature relating to both language learning and achievement gaps between social groups, these notions have been largely ignored by 'mainstream' educational policymakers in many countries whose vision of school improvement is simply to increase the effectiveness with which standardised curricula are transmitted to students. This 'effectiveness paradigm' focuses on ensuring that students meet universal, one-size-fits-all standards, which are assessed by standardised or state-developed tests, all in the ultimate service of greater economic competitiveness. The mantra accompanying this mandate is that teachers must be held accountable for student attainment, which should be measured on a regular basis to ensure quality control (for analysis of this paradigm in recent United States educational policies, see Isola & Cummins, 2020; Ravitch, 2013).

In this chapter, I outline how the construct of *identity negotiation*, and its rootedness in patterns of societal power relations, emerged in my own attempts to understand underachievement among students from minoritised communities and to identify whole school approaches to reversing underachievement. As noted previously, the role of social determinants of underachievement among minoritised students was consistently acknowledged in all early formulations of the emerging theoretical framework. Sociocultural and sociopolitical influences such as poverty and historic patterns of racism directed at socially marginalised communities create 'opportunity gaps' (Boykin & Noguera, 2011) that have typically been exacerbated by educational malpractice (e.g. punishing students for speaking their L1 in school). Linguistic and cognitive factors were conceptualised as intervening variables that mediated students' interactions with their educational environment. The central role of societal variables was clearly reflected in the very different patterns of educational achievement observed across different minority groups (e.g. underachievement of Latinx students compared to the relatively strong achievement of many groups of Asian students in the United States) and within the same group across different societal contexts (e.g. underachievement of Finnish immigrant students in Sweden compared to strong achievement of Finnish immigrant students in Australia). Although educational policies in many countries focused on providing linguistic support to immigrant-background students (e.g. English-as-a-second-language teaching in the United States), these policies generally ignored the pernicious influence of broader societal factors related to power relations and identity devaluation.

My attempts to elaborate a coherent framework that specified the role of societal power relations in determining patterns of educational outcomes progressed through several stages during the 1980s, 1990s, and later. Initially, I highlighted the notion of *bicultural ambivalence* to reflect the fact that minority communities that experienced disproportionate school failure tended to be ambivalent in relation both to the dominant societal group and their own cultural group. (Cummins, 1981b). Subsequently, I integrated this construct with Ogbu's (1978) distinctions between autonomous, 'caste', and immigrant minorities (Cummins, 1982, 1986). According to Ogbu, so-called 'caste' or involuntary minorities frequently react to long-term oppression and exclusion from educational and economic opportunities by adopting an ambivalent or oppositional collective identity in relation to the dominant group.

The third elaboration focused directly on the way societal power relations determine both the structures of schooling and the ways in which educators define their roles in relation to minority students and communities (Cummins, 1986, 1989, 1990). The basic argument was that school failure among minoritised students will be reversed only when educators actively challenge historical and current patterns of disempowerment.

I subsequently expanded this theoretical claim by highlighting the ways in which teacher-student identity negotiation in schools reflected teachers' orientation to societal power relations ranging along a continuum from reinforcing coercive relations of power to promoting collaborative relations of power (Cummins, 1993, 1994b, 1996, 2001a). Within this theoretical framing, *empowerment* was defined as the collaborative creation of power.

An additional elaboration of this 'empowerment' framework involved theorising the construct of *identity texts* (Cummins, 2004a; Cummins & Early, 2011). This construct emerged from a cross-Canada project with my colleague, Margaret Early from the University of British Columbia, in which we worked collaboratively with educators to explore instructional innovations that harnessed students' multilingual and multimodal ways of learning and knowing. This *Multiliteracies Project* generated many examples of students' creative writing and artistic endeavors that expressed, extended and affirmed their academic and personal identities; hence the term 'identity texts'.

The final elaboration of the framework involved connecting the notion of 'empowerment', understood as the collaborative creation of power, with broader orientations to pedagogy that characterise contemporary educational discourse in different countries. Many proponents of critical pedagogy have contrasted teacher-centred transmission or 'traditional' instructional approaches – what Freire (1970) called 'banking education' – with critical or transformative approaches designed to promote equity and social justice. Located between these two pedagogical orientations is a pedagogical approach and philosophy that has been variously called 'progressive', 'sociocultural', or 'social constructivist'. This orientation aims to go beyond transmission of curriculum information by promoting student inquiry, but falls short of actively uncovering and challenging societal power imbalances associated with race, class, gender, sexual orientation, ability/disability, etc. Initially, like most other researchers and theorists who made similar distinctions, I characterised these orientations as separate from and opposed to each other (e.g. Cummins, 1996; Cummins & Sayers, 1995). However, in thinking more clearly about the fact that transmission of information, skills, and concepts is a major part of every teacher's job description, I came to see these pedagogical orientations not as opposed to each other or ordered according to a hierarchy of instructional virtue, but rather as *nested* within each other, with each orientation legitimate in principle but differentiated with respect to instructional focus and overall educational goals.

Bicultural Ambivalence

Although it was abundantly clear that societal power relations and identity negotiation between dominant and subordinated groups had characterised societies around the world since the beginnings of human history, in the 1970s and 1980s these relationships had not been extensively theorised with respect to *linguistic minorities* or the role of language of instruction in minority students' educational achievement. The initial rationale for bilingual education in the United States, for example, didn't move much beyond a superficial endorsement of the linguistic mismatch hypothesis that was patently inadequate to account for the empirical data (Cummins, 1979a). Constructs related to societal power relations or identity negotiation were largely absent from both academic publications and policy debates.

As I attempted to understand how societal factors interacted with students' linguistic and cognitive development and with educational provision, I initially identified a pattern of what I called *bicultural ambivalence* (Cummins, 1981b, 1982) that characterised the attitudes of many minoritised communities towards their own language and culture and that of the dominant group. I analysed data showing that factors such as socioeconomic status, acculturation as reflected in use of L2 at home, or language and cultural differences between home and school, were inadequate, by themselves, to account for the pattern of differential achievement by minority group students in different contexts. Thus, underachievement among minoritised group students was rooted in societal variables associated with relationships between minoritised and dominant group communities (Cummins, 1982).

The construct of 'bicultural ambivalence' was consistent with the observations of numerous researchers in a variety of international contexts. Skutnabb-Kangas and Toukomaa (1976: 29), for example, cited Heyman (1973) who highlighted this pattern among the Finnish community in Sweden:

> … many Finns in Sweden feel an aversion, and sometimes even hostility, towards the Swedish language and refuse to learn it or learn it under protest. There is repeated evidence of this, as there is, on the other hand, of Finnish people—children and adults—who are ashamed of their Finnish language and do not allow it to live and develop.

Similar patterns had been documented among minority Francophones in Canada (e.g. Mougeon & Canale, 1978–79; Wagner & Grenier, 1991) and among various minoritised communities internationally (e.g. Ogbu, 1978). The role of oppressive societal power relations in generating this bicultural ambivalence was illustrated in the judgment of the court in the case of the United States versus State of Texas (1981: 14):

> …the long history of prejudice and discrimination remains a significant obstacle to equal educational opportunity for these children. The deep sense of inferiority, cultural isolation, and acceptance of failure, instilled in a people by generations of subjugation, cannot be eradicated merely by integrating the schools and repealing the 'no Spanish' statutes.

The construct of 'bicultural ambivalence' reflected a similar reality to Freire's (1970/1981: 151) construct of *cultural invasion*, which he described as follows:

> In cultural invasion it is essential that those who are invaded come to see their reality with the outlook of the invaders rather than their own; for the more they mimic the invaders, the more stable the position of the latter becomes. For cultural invasion to succeed, it is essential that those invaded become convinced of their intrinsic inferiority.

In articulating a rationale for bilingual education as an alternative to the logically flawed and evidence-free linguistic mismatch hypothesis, I emphasised the sociocultural determinants of the academic difficulties experienced by many students from minoritised or subordinated backgrounds: 'A program that continues to promote students' L1 throughout elementary school is much more likely to reinforce children's cultural identity than one that aims to remove children as quickly as possible from any contact with, or use of, L1 in school' (1981b: 41). I invoked the notion of 'bicultural ambivalence' to argue that the success of bilingual education in promoting minoritised students' academic progress could be attributed, at least in part, to the fact that it validated the cultural and linguistic identity of students and their communities, thereby reducing their insecurity about their own language and culture and ambivalence towards the majority language and culture.

Although the theoretical construct of 'bicultural ambivalence' explicitly incorporated processes of societal power relations and identity negotiation, the operation and intersections of these processes were initially not elaborated in any detail. The construct was also limited insofar as it did not explain the variation in educational achievement across minority groups from similar socioeconomic status (SES) backgrounds and with similar educational experiences (e.g. home-school language switch). Some of these limitations were addressed by integrating the construct with the more extensive analysis of minority group achievement proposed by Ogbu (1978) whose minority group typology highlighted sociopolitical and sociocultural factors that could account for variation in students' educational outcomes.

Ogbu's Minority Group Typology

Ogbu (1978) initially distinguished between autonomous, 'caste', and immigrant minorities, and later reformulated these distinctions by contrasting voluntary and involuntary minorities (Ogbu, 1992). According to Ogbu (1978), autonomous minorities possess a distinct, racial, ethnic, religious, linguistic, or cultural identity and are generally not subordinated economically or politically by the dominant group. In the United States, Ogbu identified Jewish, Mormon and Amish communities as examples of autonomous minorities.

Involuntary minorities, on the other hand, were originally brought into the society against their will through slavery, conquest, colonisation, or forced labor. They have typically been viewed as inherently inferior by the dominant group, relegated to menial occupational positions, and denied assimilation into the mainstream economic, educational, and political life of the society. Involuntary minorities tend to experience long-term persistent underachievement as a result of the sustained discrimination and devaluation of identity to which they have been subjected in the wider society. Within the American context, Ogbu cites African Americans, Latinx communities (with the exception of Cubans), Native Americans and Hawaiian Americans as examples of involuntary minorities.

The third category identified by Ogbu was 'voluntary' minorities who emigrated to host countries with the intention of improving their lives and escaping difficult economic or political circumstances. They are typically positively oriented to the dominant group in their new society and want to integrate rapidly. At the same time, they are usually positively oriented to their home culture and have little ambivalence in regard to their sense of identity. Ogbu identified Chinese communities and Punjabi communities from India as examples of voluntary minorities in the United States. These groups may be subject to discrimination, and children may experience initial difficulties in school due to language and cultural differences, but over time they typically catch up and experience educational success.

Although both voluntary and involuntary minorities may experience discrimination and hardship, voluntary minorities, according to Ogbu (1992), have a comparative frame of reference that frequently positions their present circumstances as preferable to those they experienced in their country of origin. Their response to the challenges of immigration to a new society is often to work harder to succeed. Involuntary minorities, on the other hand, do not have access to a comparative frame of reference and are very much aware of the 'job ceiling' that limits how far they are likely to succeed in the society. In response to persistent devaluation of their identities and barriers to full participation in the society, they often develop either an ambivalent or oppositional collective identity in relation to the dominant group. They either partially internalise the devaluation of their identity or resist this process by taking on certain cultural behaviors that are opposed to dominant group norms in order to maintain their sense of security and self-worth. Adoption of an oppositional identity is one way of resisting the devaluation of their culture and language by the dominant group. This pattern is illustrated in Fordham's (1990) research showing that African American adolescents often regarded academic success as 'acting White'.

The situation of many refugee students around the world and of migrant workers in many European countries falls somewhere in-between Ogbu's voluntary/involuntary distinction. Migrant workers come willingly to the host country seeking better economic or political conditions but are often denied opportunities for assimilation into the host country (e.g. through segregated housing and schooling as well as restrictive citizenship policies). The second and subsequent generations then assume many of the characteristics of involuntary minorities.

As numerous critics have pointed out, the realities of minority group adaptation are considerably more complex in practice than revealed by Ogbu's typology (see Cummins, 1996, 1997b, 2001a). However, his distinctions do throw light on the general patterns of academic achievement among culturally diverse students and they help to explain variation in educational outcomes between minority group students exposed to similar educational conditions such as a home-school language mismatch. Furthermore, Ogbu's typology points to the centrality of issues related to societal power relations and identity negotiation in understanding school success and failure. I summarised my assessment of Ogbu's dichotomy between voluntary and involuntary minorities as follows:

> If conceived as a rigid dichotomy, the voluntary/involuntary distinction is not particularly helpful; however, it is extremely useful if conceived as a theoretical construct that highlights important patterns of how power relations operating in the broader society find their way into the structures and operation of schooling. The distinction must be conceived in dynamic rather than static terms and it must allow for the complementary explanatory role of other factors related to socioeconomic status (SES), 'race', culture, and language that may operate in specific situations. (Cummins, 1997b: 93)

An additional limitation of Ogbu's (1978, 1992) typology was that it largely ignored linguistic dimensions of these power relations and gave little concrete direction regarding pedagogical interventions that might reverse patterns of minority group underachievement. There was also little focus on the role of educator agency in challenging the operation of these power relations in schools.

I attempted to address these issues by focusing in concrete ways on how societal power relations operated in the organisation of schooling and in teacher-student interactions. Although I was very conscious of the ways in which the terms *empower* and *empowerment* had become superficial 'buzzwords' in 'corporate-speak' and in some educational contexts, I felt that it was important to reclaim these terms because they explicitly referenced power relations, unlike psychological terms such as 'self-esteem'. The core theoretical proposition in my attempts from 1986 onwards to theorise how societal power relations were infused in educational interactions was as follows: *Because educational underachievement among minoritised students is rooted in the societal power structure, educators individually and collectively who are committed to promoting students' academic success must challenge the ways in which this power structure operates in schools.*

Challenging the Disabling Structure of Societal Power Relations

In early April 1985, I was fortunate to have the opportunity to participate in a symposium entitled 'Minority Languages in Academic Research and Educational Policy' organised by Tove Skutnabb-Kangas and Robert Phillipson of Roskilde University in Denmark. The symposium was held at an inn (Sandbjerg Slot) located near the town of Sonderborg in southern Jutland. The remote location and the relatively small number of invited participants (approximately 20, primarily from European countries) resulted in intense discussions focused on minority language rights, anti-racist education, and bilingual education.

Upon returning to Canada, I tried to organise my notes and thoughts from the symposium and what resulted was the first draft of the paper that later appeared in the *Harvard Education Review*. The paper outlined a theoretical framework for analysing the school failure experienced by many minoritised students and the lack of success of multiple attempts at educational reform. The core of this framework focused on how schools positioned themselves in relation to societal power relations. I argued that educational reform initiatives had been largely unsuccessful because they did little to alter the relationships between educators and minoritised students, and between schools and minoritised communities. Despite multiple reform initiatives, the individual role definitions of teachers and the institutional role definitions of schools remained largely unchanged, thereby maintaining the power structures that continued to disable minoritised students. I argued that the individual and collective agency of educators, and how they positioned their identities in relation to societal power structures, were fundamental to any effective school improvement process. Specifically, the 'required changes involve *personal redefinitions* of the way classroom teachers interact with the children and communities they serve' (Cummins, 1986: 18) (emphasis original):

> It is in these interactions that students are disabled. In the absence of individual and collective educator role redefinitions, schools will continue to reproduce, in these interactions, the power relations that characterize the wider society and make minority students' academic failure inevitable. (Cummins, 1986: 33)

I described a number of concrete examples of 'empowering' educational initiatives that challenged disabling educational structures and relationships. To varying degrees, these initiatives incorporated students' languages and cultures into curriculum and instruction, they engaged minoritised communities as partners in their children's education, and they implemented pedagogy and assessment practices that connected to students' lives and enabled them to use the full range of their cognitive and linguistic talents to succeed academically.

Surprisingly (in retrospect), given the title of the paper, the concept of 'empowerment' was not elaborated in any detail. I simply noted that students who were empowered by their school experiences develop the ability, confidence, and motivation to succeed academically. These students participate competently in instruction as a result of having developed a confident cultural identity as well as appropriate school-based knowledge and interactional structures (1986: 23). In subsequent elaborations of this initial framework, the construct of 'empowerment' and its instructional implications were expanded in much more detail.[1]

After the 1986 Harvard Education Review (HER) article had been published, I was invited to prepare a monograph for a series of Teacher Training Monographs under development by the University of Florida. I prepared an expanded version of the HER article that included a more detailed description of 'empowerment pedagogy' and approaches to critical literacy. I also critically analysed the empirical credibility of claims advanced by academic critics of bilingual education.

The final chapter focused on parallels between the discourse published by media and academic critics of bilingual education and the debates that were ongoing at the time in regard to the United States' foreign policy and interventions in Latin America and elsewhere (e.g. the Iran/Contra controversy). I drew on Noam Chomsky's (1987) analysis of how the United States since the 1950s had systematically neutralised 'the threat of a good example' in the international arena by overthrowing democratically elected governments that were perceived as potentially threatening to American economic and political interests. I argued that the vehement arguments in the 1970s and 1980s against the 'internal threat' of bilingual education shared the same underlying structure as attempts to justify and rationalise the violent suppression of progressive social change in the international arena.

This last chapter was omitted in the version of the monograph disseminated by the University of Florida, presumably because it was perceived as likely to be controversial in that state. I subsequently submitted an updated version of the monograph to a mainstream publisher (with the encouragement of the publisher's education editor). The review process generated three very positive reviews (with some constructive suggestions which I subsequently incorporated) and one lengthy review (seven single-spaced pages) that was extremely negative.[2] Despite the education editor's strong objections, the manuscript was rejected by the publisher. In late 1988, I approached the California Association for Bilingual Education (CABE) to inquire whether they might be interested in publishing the monograph and they enthusiastically agreed to do so. The outcome was the book *Empowering Minority Students* (Cummins, 1989) that was widely disseminated in California and beyond.

A major theme of the book was that the debate about bilingual education essentially represented a 'surface structure' issue. The more fundamental issue was 'the extent to which educators, individually and collectively, are prepared to use their creative energies to devise and implement programs that challenge the racist attitudes and institutions that historically have disempowered minority communities and students' (1989: xi). In other words, a central argument was that educators *do* have the power to exercise agency in challenging disabling educational structures. However, in order to exercise that power, educators need to identify the *real* causes of underachievement among minoritised students. These causes go far beyond linguistic mismatch between home and school languages. The process of reversing underachievement requires a considerably broader set of instructional interventions and structural changes than simply providing some English-as-second-language or short-term L1 support.

As in the monograph prepared for the University of Florida, I argued that the ways in which 'power-over-others' (Galtung, 1980) was exercised was very similar in both domestic and international contexts. In both contexts, the dominant group seeks to reverse a sociopolitical change that they perceive as threatening their ability to control and exploit a traditionally dominated group: 'The structure of institutionalized racism that assaults minority students' cultural identity in schools and prevents empowerment is essentially the same structure in goals and functions as the structure that has attempted to maintain a "favorable climate" in third world countries for continued profitability for multinational companies' (Cummins, 1989: 127). I identified three discourse strategies that are used to manipulate information and create 'us' versus 'them' oppositions in both domestic and international arenas:

- *Limit the framework of discourse.* For example, in the bilingual education debate, limit the options that can be discussed to quick-exit transitional bilingual education versus English-medium structured immersion, omitting from consideration the much more effective additive bilingual programmes that promote biliteracy.[3]
- *Deny/distort empirical realities.* For example, refuse to acknowledge that *all* of the empirically demonstrated outcomes of bilingual education and second language immersion programmes refute the 'time-on-task' argument that students need maximum exposure to the dominant language if they are to succeed academically.
- *Ignore logical inconsistencies.* For example, eradicate minority students' home language in the early years of schooling by punishing them for using it in school and then attempt to teach these same 'foreign' languages at the high school level using traditional non-bilingual methods that have proven ineffective except for a small elite group of students.

The disabling social and educational structure propped up by these disinformation strategies (which appear tame compared to the disinformation strategies prevalent today) enables the dominant group to maintain, in Galtung's (1980) terms, 'power-over-others' 'while denying dominated groups (whether children in classrooms or migrant workers in fields) the opportunity to develop 'power-over-self'' (Cummins, 1989: 119).

Although the analysis in *Empowering Minority Students* addressed the role of societal power relations in disempowering minoritised students, it did not explicitly analyse issues related to how these power relations intersected with patterns of identity negotiation between teachers and minoritised students. These issues were subsequently explored in some articles (Cummins, 1993, 1994b) and elaborated in the book *Negotiating Identities: Education for Empowerment in a Diverse Society*, published by CABE in 1996, with an expanded second edition published in 2001.[4]

Human Relationships Are at the Heart of Schooling

This statement appeared on the first page of *Negotiating Identities* (Cummins, 1996). I pointed out that the interactions that take place between students and teachers and among students are more central to student success than any method for teaching literacy, or science or math: 'When powerful relationships are established between teachers and students, these relationships frequently can transcend the economic and social disadvantages that afflict communities and schools alike in inner city and rural areas' (Cummins, 1996: 1–2).

The framework proposed in *Negotiating Identities* (Figure 5.1) argues that relations of power in the wider society, ranging from coercive to collaborative in varying degrees, influence both the ways in which educators define their roles and the types of structures that are established in the

SOCIETAL POWER RELATIONS

influence
the ways in which educators define their roles (teacher identity)
and
the structures of schooling (curriculum, funding, assessment, etc.)
which, in turn, influence

the ways in which educators interact
with linguistically and culturally diverse students.

These interactions form
an
INTERPERSONAL SPACE
within which
learning happens
and
identities are negotiated.

These **IDENTITY NEGOTIATIONS**
either
Reinforce coercive relations of power
or
Promote collaborative relations of power

Figure 5.1 Societal power relations, identity negotiation, and academic achievement
(Adapted from Jim Cummins [2001a] *Negotiating Identities: Education for Empowerment in a Diverse Society*)

educational system. Coercive relations of power refer to the exercise of power by a dominant individual, group, or country to the detriment of a subordinated individual, group, or country. The assumption is that there is a fixed quantity of power that operates according to a zero-sum or sub-tractive logic; in other words, the more power one group has the less is left for other groups.

Collaborative relations of power, by contrast, reflect the sense of the term *power* that refers to *being enabled* or *empowered* to achieve more. Within collaborative relations of power, power is not a fixed quantity but is generated through interaction with others. The more empowered one individual or group becomes, the more is generated for others to share. The process is additive rather than subtractive. Within this context, empowerment can be defined as *the collaborative creation of power.* Schooling amplifies rather than silences minoritised students' power of *self*-expression regardless of their current level of proficiency in the domi-nant school language.

Educator role definitions refer to the mindset of expectations, assump-tions, and goals that educators, individually and collectively, bring to the task of educating linguistically and culturally diverse students. I pointed out that as educators, we are constantly sketching a triangular set of images reflecting our identity choices or role definitions:

- an image of our own identities as educators;
- an image of the identity options we highlight for our students;
- an image of the society we hope our students will help form.

The concept of *educator role definitions* highlights a similar reality to what García *et al.* (2016) later termed *stance* with specific reference to educators' philosophical orientation to translanguaging in the classroom. According to García and colleagues (2016: 50), the translanguaging stance 'is a necessary mindset or framework for educating bilingual students that informs everything from the way we view students and their dynamic bilingual performances and cultural practices to the way we plan instruc-tion and assessment'.

There is ample evidence that students who have been failed by schools predominantly come from communities whose languages, cultures and identities have been disparaged and devalued in the wider society. In the past, schools have reinforced patterns of disempowerment by punishing stu-dents for speaking their home language, or stigmatised varieties of those languages, in the school and ignoring or dismissing the knowledge and cul-tural values of minoritised communities. Schools typically viewed minori-tised students as inherently inferior, a judgment frequently legitimated by culturally biased IQ tests (Cummins, 1984a). Not surprisingly, students often disengaged themselves from school learning under these conditions.[5]

Educators' rejection of minoritised students' funds of knowledge (Moll *et al.*, 1992) is often unintentional and unconscious. For example, a large-scale study conducted by the U.S. Commission on Civil Rights (1973) in the American southwest reported that Euro-American students were praised or encouraged 36% more often than Mexican American students and their classroom contributions were used or built upon 40% more frequently than those of Mexican American students. I pointed out that 'under these conditions, many students might come to see themselves as not very bright academically' (Cummins, 2001: 2).

Numerous researchers also highlighted the fact that teachers can communicate ideologies of linguistic purism to students even in bilingual programmes ostensibly committed to promoting additive forms of bilingualism and biliteracy (e.g. Labov, 1972; Lippi-Green, 1997/2012; Valdés, 1997). Cummins (1981a: 32), for example, noted that '[d]espite the fact that Labov's analysis is universally accepted by linguists and sociolinguists, it is still disturbingly common to find administrators and teachers of language minority students in bilingual education programs disparaging the nonstandard version of the primary language (L1) which children bring to school and attempting to teach the standard version through explicit formal instruction'.

Educational structures refer to the organisation of schooling in a broad sense that includes policies, programmes, curriculum, and assessment. While these structures will generally reflect the values and priorities of dominant groups in society, they are not by any means fixed or static and can be contested by individuals and groups.

Educational structures, together with educator role definitions, determine the patterns of interactions between educators, students, and communities. These interactions form an interpersonal space within which the acquisition of knowledge and formation of identity is negotiated. Power is created and shared within this interpersonal space where minds and identities meet. The interactions between educators, students and communities are never neutral; in varying degrees, they either reinforce coercive relations of power or promote collaborative relations of power. As such, these teacher-student interactions constitute the most immediate determinant of student academic success or failure.

One of the most vivid accounts of how identities have frequently been negotiated in classrooms was provided by Virginia Vogel Zanger (1994) who documented the insights of a class of academically successful Latinx high school students into the social dynamics of their schooling experience. Focus groups of students were asked to discuss the reasons for the high drop-out rate of other Spanish-speaking students at the school and to recommend ways to make the school better for students from Spanish-speaking backgrounds. The student population at the school was about 40% Latinx, 40% African American and 20% White. Students' comments reflected the marginalisation they felt as well as lack of cultural respect and trust between teachers and students. Elsa, a student from the Dominican Republic, for example, noted 'You can't succeed in a place where no one respects you for what you are' (Zanger, 1994: 179), and she complained that 'teachers don't learn from us, they don't learn from anybody. They don't ask' (Zanger, 1994: 186). Another student described the alienation felt by many of her Spanish-speaking peers who had dropped out of school:

> They just feel left out, they feel like if no one loves them, no one cares, so why should they care? No one wants to hear what they have to say, so they don't say anything. (Zanger, 1994: 177)

I suggested that the insights of these successful students into the process of identity devaluation to which they were being subjected may have played an important role in helping them resist devaluation and refusing to live down to their teachers' expectations (Cummins, 1994b).

A central tenet of this framework is that effective education for students from minoritised communities *requires* educators to challenge coercive relations of power as they are manifested in the structures and processes of schooling. This obviously includes a challenge to ideologies rooted in systemic racism and/or linguistic imperialism (Phillipson, 1992; Skutnabb-Kangas, 2000). However, the framework also includes a range of discriminatory structures and ideologies that go beyond those rooted in racism. For example, deaf students have suffered major discrimination for generations as a result of educational policies that prohibit instructional use of natural sign languages (e.g. Snoddon & Weber, 2021).[6] Similarly, the well-documented and long-term underachievement of White working-class students in the United Kingdom (House of Commons Education Committee, 2014) clearly reflects discrimination based on social class, which is not readily captured within discourses of *racial* discrimination.

The framework assigns a central role to teacher agency in challenging the operation of coercive relationship of power. I highlighted the fact that individual educators are never powerless, although they frequently work in conditions that are oppressive both for them and their students. Despite the fact that educators rarely have complete freedom, they *do* have choices in the way they structure the interactions in the classroom:

> They ... determine for themselves the social and educational goals they want to achieve with their students. They are responsible for the role definitions they adopt in relation to culturally diverse students and communities. Even in the context of English-only instruction, educators have options in their orientation to students' language and culture, in the forms of parent and community participation they encourage, and in the way they implement pedagogy and assessment. ... In short, through their practice and their interactions with students, educators define their own identities. (Cummins, 2001a: 304)

I argued that minoritised students also go through a process of defining their identities in interaction with their teachers, peers and parents.

Although this process of negotiating identities is influenced by many societal and educational forces, it can never be fully controlled from the outside. Thus, within the interactional spaces where identities are negotiated, students and educators together can generate power that challenges structures and ideologies of injustice in significant ways (see Chapter 11 for concrete examples of educators and students collaboratively challenging coercive power structures).

Language Pedagogy and Empowerment

The role of teachers' orientation to language was explicitly highlighted in what I called the *Academic Expertise Framework* (Figure 5.2) which elaborated the construct of *interpersonal space* within the broader framework (Figure 5.1) (Cummins, 2001a). The Academic Expertise Framework proposed that academic development will be optimised when teacher-student interactions maximise both cognitive engagement and identity investment. Effective instruction will include a focus on meaning, a focus on language itself, and a focus on use.

The *focus on meaning* includes scaffolding strategies intended to make linguistic meanings comprehensible to students, but it goes beyond simply literal surface-level processing of language to include the development of critical literacy. Similarly, the *focus on language* involves promoting not just explicit knowledge of how the linguistic code operates (e.g. phonics, grammar, vocabulary) but also critical awareness of how language operates within society. If students are to participate effectively

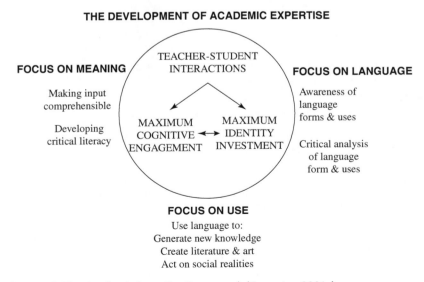

Figure 5.2 The Academic Expertise Framework (Cummins, 2001a)

within a democratic society, they should be able to 'read' how language is used to achieve social goals: to elucidate issues, to persuade, to communicate and share, to include, as well as socially problematic goals such as to deceive, to exclude, and to disempower (Janks, 2010, 2014). The *focus on use* component argues that optimal instruction will enable students to generate knowledge, create literature and art, and act on social realities.

The Academic Expertise Framework also makes clear that classroom instruction always positions students in particular ways that reflect the implicit (or sometimes explicit) image of the student in the teacher's mind. How students are positioned either expands or constricts their opportunities for identity investment and cognitive engagement. The integration of critical literacy throughout the Academic Expertise framework can be illustrated in the progression from comprehensible input to critical literacy in the Focus on Meaning component. The five phases outlined in Figure 5.3 are derived from a combination of Au's (1979) experience-text-relationship approach and Ada's (1988a, 1988b) creative reading framework. Each of the five phases progressively opens up possibilities for strengthening students' personal and academic identity. The phases

---

FOCUS ON MEANING:
FROM COMPREHENSIBLE INPUT TO CRITICAL LITERACY

Experiential Phase. Activate prior knowledge and build background knowledge; For example, in a science unit on photosynthesis, teachers and students brainstrom on "What makes plants grow?"

Literal Phase. Focus is on information contained in the text; Typical questions might be: When, where, how, did it happen? Who did it? Why?

Personal Phase. Students relate textual information to their own experiences and feelings; Teachers might ask: Have you ever seen (felt, experienced) something like this? Have you ever wanted something similar?

Critical Phase. Critical analysis of issues or problems arising from the text; involves drawing inferences and exploring generalizations. Teachers might ask: Is what this person said valid? Always? Under what conditions? Are there any alternatives to this situation?

Creative Phase. Translating the results of pervious phases into concrete action; How can the problem or issues be resolved? What role can *we* play in helping to resolve the problem. This phase might involve drama, role play, letters to editor, school principal, web site or newsletter publication of research/analysis/art, poetry, stories.

Figure 5.3 From Comprehensible Input to Critical Literacy (Cummins, 2001a)

illustrate how interpersonal spaces can be created between teachers and students that encourage students to share and amplify their experience and insights within a collaborative process of critical inquiry.

An additional elaboration of the empowerment framework articulated the construct of *identity texts* that brought together notions of identity investment and 'focus on use'.

Identity Texts: Affirmative Showcasing of Students' Identities

The theoretical construct of *identity texts* emerged in the context of my collaboration with Professor Eleni Skourtou and Vasilia Kourtis-Kazoullis of the University of the Aegean in Rhodes, Greece. In 1997, Eleni invited me to spend some time in Rhodes working with university faculty, educators, and parents who were engaged with various bilingual and multilingual issues both in families and schools. This was the first of many visits, and over the past 20+ years we have collaborated on a variety of projects in both Greece and Canada (e.g. Skourtou *et al.*, 2006).

During one of my visits to Rhodes in early 2004, Eleni and I were discussing the pedagogical significance of student-created dual language books written by emergent bilingual students in the context of the Canadian *Multiliteracies Project* led by Margaret Early and me (Cummins & Early, 2011; see also http://www.multiliteracies.ca/). Specifically, we focused on the fact that these student creations reflected not just cognitive, academic, and linguistic accomplishments but also expressed and shaped students' emerging identities. I suggested that the term *identity texts* could capture this intimate connection between literacy and identity. I subsequently described the concept and its relationship to the Academic Expertise Framework as follows:

> The Academic Expertise framework proposes that optimal academic development within the interpersonal space of the learning community occurs only when there is both maximum cognitive engagement and maximum identity investment on the part of students. The products of students' creative work or performances carried out within this pedagogical space are termed identity texts insofar as students invest their identities in these texts ... that then hold a mirror up to students in which their identities are reflected back in a positive light. (Cummins, 2004a: 72)

I pointed out that identity texts can be written, spoken, signed, visual, musical, dramatic, or combinations in multimodal form. When students share identity texts with multiple audiences (peers, teachers, parents, grandparents, sister classes, the media, etc.) they are likely to receive positive feedback and affirmation of self in interaction with these audiences. Although digital technologies are not essential to the creation of identity texts, they frequently act as an amplifier to enhance the process of production and dissemination.

The construct of 'identity texts' reinforced the argument that minoritised students will engage actively with literacy only to the extent that such engagement is identity-affirming. Creative writing and other forms of cultural production such as art, drama, computer animation, etc. represent an expression of identity, a projection of identity into new social spheres, and a re-creation of identity as a result of feedback from and dialogue with multiple audiences. This re-creation of identity through the production of identity texts assumes particular importance in the case of students from social groups whose languages, cultures, religions, and institutions have been devalued, often for generations, in the wider society. For these students, affirmation of identity constitutes a counter-discourse that enables them to repudiate the devaluation of identity that is embedded in the structures and relationships operating within many schools and other societal institutions.

Promoting Collaborative Relations of Power in the Context of Broader Pedagogical Orientations

The different orientations to pedagogy that have been discussed over the past century have frequently been presented as oppositional binaries (e.g. teacher-centred versus child-centred instruction, traditional versus progressivist pedagogy, phonics versus whole-language; 'banking' education versus liberatory education, etc). During the 1990s, I distinguished between traditional, progressive, and transformative orientations (e.g. Cummins, 1996; Cummins & Sayers, 1995). In the 2nd edition of the *Negotiating Identities* book (Cummins, 2001a), I used the term 'constructivist' in place of 'progressive', but the distinctions remained largely the same and were conceived as instructional alternatives that were in opposition to each other. However, I pointed out that the boundaries between the different orientations were not fixed, and although the three orientations were expressed as distinct categories, 'it is more appropriate to see them as points on a continuum that merge into one another. For example, a transformative orientation will usually include considerable explicit instruction and much classroom interaction will be constructivist in nature rather than focused directly on social realities' (2001a: 218).

In the course of one of the many discussions regarding pedagogy and equity issues that took place between Eleni Skourtou, Vasilia Kourtis Kazoullis and me during the time I spent in Rhodes in early 2004, it occurred to me that these distinctions were better conceived as *nested* within each other rather than as distinct oppositional categories. The next day, Vasilia suggested a variation of the visual representation of these relationships that is reproduced below (Figure 5.4). We used these nested pedagogical orientations to frame and interpret the outcomes of a partner class project involving collaborative inquiry between late elementary school students in Toronto, Canada and students in the Greek islands of Rhodes and Kassos (Skourtou *et al.*, 2006).

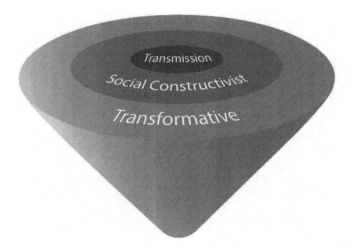

Figure 5.4 Nested pedagogical orientations. Design courtesy of Vasilia Kourtis-Kazoullis and Eleni Kazoulli; reprinted with permission.

Transmission-oriented pedagogy is represented in the inner circle with the narrowest focus. The goal is to transmit information and skills specified in curriculum directly to students. The importance of activating students' prior knowledge and developing learning strategies may be acknowledged within transmission or direct instruction approaches. However, in practice, activation of students' prior knowledge is often narrowly defined as revisiting content and skills that were taught in previous lessons.

Social constructivist pedagogy, occupying the middle pedagogical space, acknowledges the relevance of transmission of information and skills but broadens the focus to include the development among students of higher-order thinking abilities based on teachers and students co-constructing knowledge and understanding. The focus is on experiential learning, collaborative inquiry, and knowledge building. Theorists who endorse social constructivist or sociocultural approaches to pedagogy tend to build on Vygotsky's (2000) foundational work. The influential synthesis of the research on learning carried out by Bransford *et al.* (2000) is very much social constructivist in its emphasis on integrating factual knowledge with conceptual frameworks, activating students' pre-existing knowledge, and enabling students to take active control of the learning process through the development of metacognitive strategies.

Finally, transformative approaches to pedagogy broaden the focus still further by emphasising the relevance not only of transmitting the curriculum and constructing knowledge but also of enabling students to gain insight into how knowledge intersects with power. Transformative pedagogy uses collaborative critical inquiry to enable students to analyse and understand the social realities of their own lives and of their communities.

Students discuss, and frequently act on, ways in which these realities might be transformed through various forms of social action. The goal is to promote critical literacy among students with a focus on social realities relevant to issues of equity and social justice. In other words, transformative pedagogy enables students to scrutinise and actively challenge patterns of power relations in the broader society. Transformative approaches typically draw their inspiration from the work of Freire (1970) while also acknowledging the important influence of Vygotsky (2000).

The rationale for nesting these orientations within each other is to highlight the fact that features of transmission pedagogy are relevant to all kinds of learning. Transmission of information and skills becomes problematic only when it constitutes the predominant or exclusive focus of instruction. Thus, while it is important to reinforce students' awareness of how academic language works across the curriculum (e.g. Menken *et al.*, 2011), it would be highly problematic to focus primarily on teaching academic language in isolation from opportunities for students to use this language for powerful communicative purposes. Exclusive reliance on transmission pedagogy is likely to entail promotion of memorisation rather than learning for deep understanding, passive rather than active learning and minimal activation of students' prior knowledge. Similarly, a transformative orientation is not in any way opposed either to transmission of curriculum content or the co-construction of knowledge between teachers and students. Rather it builds on and expands transmission and social constructivist approaches in order to pursue a wider variety of pedagogical goals and a broader educational vision.

Project FRESA: Illustrating the Empowerment Framework

One of the most powerful examples of transformative pedagogy involving minoritised students that I am aware of is Project FRESA. This cross-age project, which took place over an entire school year in Mar Vista Elementary School in Oxnard, southern California, was initiated in 1999 by third-grade teacher Amanda Irma Pérez and fifth-grade teacher Michelle Singer. The school is surrounded by strawberry fields and a large majority of students in the two classes (45 out of 50) had family members who worked picking strawberries. The two classes met on a weekly basis to pursue the project. The following account is based on the work that students produced and interviews with the two teachers conducted by Kristin Brown (see Cummins *et al.*, 2007 for a detailed description).

Students initially brainstormed about what they knew and would like to know about strawberries. The students generated questions such as 'I wonder why the seeds are on the outside' and 'I wonder why the people who pick the strawberries wear scarves across their noses and mouths'. They reviewed the questions they had generated and decided what questions would be most appropriate to ask their parents. Students then analysed the questionnaire responses they received from their parents and looked for patterns that emerged across the responses. Cummins *et al.* summarised some of the students' findings as follows:

> They saw how long people had worked in the fields and how it had affected their health. 'My dad used to work in the fields, but he can't work now because of his back,' one child said. 'Really?' said another. 'That same thing happened to my grandfather.' Many of the most disturbing answers mentioned *fertilizantes*, the Spanish word the parents used for pesticides. 'Why do you have so many headaches?' the children had asked their parents. 'Por los fertilizantes' (because of the 'fertilizers,' one father said). Another child responded, 'No wonder my mom always has a headache. I didn't know that was why.' (Cummins *et al.*, 2007: 133)

As the project continued over the course of the school year, students engaged in inquiry that ranged right across the curriculum (science, social studies, math, language arts). They tracked the life span of strawberries from seeds to export markets. In addition to interviewing parents and other family members, students used the internet for additional research and invited community experts (from the Environmental Defense League and the California Rural Assistance League) to speak to their class. The teachers created a web site that contained students' poetry, artwork, graphs, and the results of their community investigations. Students also engaged in dialogue on local economics and profit analysis as part of their mathematics curriculum. They then carried their investigation beyond their community by connecting through email with students in a coffee-growing area of Puerto Rico, and in a strawberry-growing area of India. As the project grew, they also communicated by email with students in Paraguay who had worked picking strawberries and with strawberry growers in Chile who wanted to learn about working conditions in the United States.

The students also examined the websites of the major strawberry companies that operated in the Oxnard area. On the basis of their research, they wrote letters to several of these companies, asking questions such as 'How often do the workers receive breaks?' and 'Are there clean bathrooms on site?' They also decided to write letters to California's Governor, Gray Davis, to express their concerns about the use of pesticides and the working conditions their family members were experiencing in the fields. Throughout the project, each student wrote in their 'FRESA Journal' and the response received from the governor's office that encouraged them to continue 'to take an active role in public policy development' was photocopied for inclusion in each student's journal (although many students were skeptical about the sincerity of the governor's promise to investigate their concerns).

It is clear that the pedagogy implemented within Project FRESA incorporated all three of the pedagogical orientations discussed in the previous section. The teachers connected students' collaborative critical inquiry to the curriculum standards they were mandated to cover. Literacy engagement was pursued across the curriculum and the language forms and discourse conventions necessary for effective academic communication were taught in the context of students' use of language to effect social change. Students' identities as competent, engaged and intellectually powerful individuals were affirmed, as were their bilingual abilities which enabled them to discuss the issues with their family members and with other students in Latin American countries.

The instructional practice of Amanda Irma Pérez and Michelle Singer developed students' academic language as a tool that they could use for powerful social purposes, such as writing to the Governor or California and the CEOs of large companies. The way academic language was conceived and enacted in their classrooms was far removed from Nelson Flores' unqualified description of academic language as 'a raciolinguistic ideology that frames racialized students as linguistically deficient and in need of remediation' (2020: 22). Different conceptualisations of 'academic language' are discussed in detail in Chapter 8. For now, it is sufficient to note that enabling students to gain access to and use academic language registers, as well as other curriculum concepts and skills, will be greatly enhanced when explicit teaching is closely integrated with social constructivist and transformative orientations to pedagogy that challenge coercive relations of power.

Implications for Language Policy and Classroom Instruction

How can schools respond to the negative effects of societal power relations and colonial relationships that devalue the identities of students from marginalised social groups? Ladson-Billings expressed the essence of an effective instructional response: 'When students are treated as competent, they are likely to demonstrate competence' (1994: 123). In other words, educators, both individually and collectively, can challenge the devaluation of students' language, culture, and identity in the wider society by implementing instructional strategies that enable students to develop 'identities of competence' in the school context (Manyak, 2004). Students develop the belief that they have the ability to succeed academically, and as a result, they engage academically to a much greater extent than when their identities are implicitly or explicitly devalued.

A first step towards enabling students to develop identities of competence (and confidence) is for educators to examine implicit and explicit policies and instructional practices within their own schools. The following questions reflect the kinds of issues educators might discuss in developing coherent and evidence-based school policies that affirm students' identities:

- To what extent does the school view itself as a multilingual space in which students' languages are positioned as intellectual and educational resources?

- To what extent does instruction connect with students' multilingual and multicultural lives and extend their intellectual and personal horizons?
- To what extent is students' multilingual writing (e.g. dual language books) displayed prominently around the school?
- To what extent does instruction affirm the legitimacy of the language varieties that students bring to school and enable students to use these varieties as resources for learning?
- To what extent does instruction actively engage multilingual and newcomer students in higher-order thinking and creative inquiry into social issues?

The analysis of societal power relations and their impact on teacher-student identity negotiation presented in this chapter highlights the fact that, in the past, many schools (and the societies that funded them) actively created and reinforced opportunity gaps experienced by racialised and marginalised children and youth (e.g. Truth and Reconciliation Commission of Canada, 2015). Unfortunately, this process continues in more indirect and subtle forms today. When schools and teacher education programmes ignore the role of societal power relations, they risk devaluing minoritised students' identities, constricting their academic engagement, and limiting their opportunities for creative intellectual inquiry. This process can be reversed when educators, individually and collectively within schools, focus on shrinking opportunity gaps rather than inadvertently expanding them.

Certainly, additional challenges are faced by students whose home language differs from the language of the school, or who have grown up in families struggling with the effects of poverty, or who have faced multiple forms of discrimination. However, underachievement is not a direct result of these challenges. Instead, underachievement derives from the *school's failure* (a) to support students effectively in learning the school language, (b) to implement instructional strategies that respond to some of the most significant impacts of socioeconomic disadvantage and (c) to pursue antiracist and culturally sustaining pedagogies that affirm students' identities and promote collaborative relations of power. The intersections of these opportunity gaps and evidence-based instructional responses to them are discussed in the next chapter.

Notes

(1) The Cummins (1986) article was included in four subsequent compilations of articles published by the Harvard Education Review (HER) (Beauboeuf-Lafontant & Smith Augustine, 1996; Hidalgo *et al.*, 1990; Katzman *et al.*, 2005; Minami & Kennedy, 1991). It was also selected by the HER editors for their Classics Series, which consisted of 12 articles published in the HER between 1931 and 2000 that were judged to have made the most significant contributions to education during that period (Cummins, 2001c).

(2)   The tone and ideological orientation of this anonymous review written on April 16, 1988, can be gauged from the following extracts:

> The text reflects the Marxist ideology advocated by theorists such as Freire, Giroux, and Macedo. ... I would no more subject my credential candidates and education students to this vitriolic attack than I would ask them to drink battery acid. ... The influence of Freire is palpable here. ... I'm sorry but after almost two decades Freire seems dated, passé. The author should be blazing a new trail in a monograph, not following one as well worn (and as directionless) as this. ... I would not use this text under any circumstances. (Anonymous, 1988)

(3)   The term 'structured immersion' was proposed in the 1980s by opponents of bilingual education in the United States to refer to programmes for minority language students taught exclusively or predominantly through English (L2) (e.g. Baker & de Kanter, 1981). This use of the term 'immersion' is diametrically opposite to its original use in the context of Canadian French immersion programmes. The Canadian immersion programmes are bilingual programmes involving French and English as languages of instruction and are designed to promote active bilingual and biliteracy skills among students. By contrast, according to Baker (2001: 195), 'the language experience in a Structured Immersion program is "submersion" rather than "immersion". ... The first language is not developed but is replaced by the majority language. ... typically there is no native language support.' In order to highlight the subtractive nature of so-called 'structured immersion' programmes, most researchers refer to them as 'submersion' programmes (e.g. Cummins, 2000; Lambert, 1984; Skutnabb-Kangas, 2000).

(4)   Although the *Negotiating Identities* books (Cummins, 1996, 2001a) followed up and expanded many of the themes explored in *Empowering Minority Students*, the title was changed in two ways: first, to highlight the central role of teacher-student identity negotiation, and second, to avoid using the verb 'empower' in a transitive sense. As pointed out by several researchers (Clarke, 1990; Macedo, 1994; Ruiz, 1991), use of the verb in a transitive sense ('to empower someone'), suggests that educators are giving the gift of 'empowerment' to their students who are thereby consigned to the role of passive recipients rather than agents of their own empowerment. This was clearly not the intent of the original analysis, but to avoid misinterpretation, the *Negotiating Identities* books (1996, 2001) consistently highlight the opportunity for educators to create contexts of empowerment in their classrooms.

(5)   In a monograph entitled *Redesigning English-Medium Classrooms*, David Dolson and Lauri Burnham-Massey highlighted the relevance of societal power relations to the design of effective instruction:

> Throughout the history of public education, the school system has been unable or unwilling to systematically provide as effective programs for children from stigmatized minority groups, most notably Native Americans, African Americans, and Hispanics as it does for majority students. ... each of the mentioned groups has been historically subordinated through forms of violence (war, slavery, forced relocation, and/or genocide). ... Although this publication focuses on the specific needs of second-language learners, we acknowledge the outcome data that indicate that groups such as North American-born Hispanics, those believed to have already adapted to the U.S. culture and who are considered to be fluent in English, also suffer as a group from chronic underachievement in our schools. (Dolson & Burnham-Massey, 2011: 74)

(6)   The operation of coercive power relations can be illustrated in the evidence-free imposition of auditory/oral approaches to teaching deaf and hard-of-hearing children subsequent to the 1880 International Congress of Educators of the Deaf in Milan, Italy. Prior to that Congress, bilingual instructional approaches involving use of

natural sign languages to teaching deaf children had been common in many countries. The auditory/oral approach emphasises the development of any residual hearing with the assistance of hearing aids and the development of speech-reading skills and speech production. A major part of the rationale for an exclusive reliance on the auditory/ oral modality was the assumption that children will not make the effort to develop oral language if they are permitted to use the 'crutch' of sign language. Komesaroff provided a graphic description of the destruction of identity that oralism promoted in the Australian context:

> I was struck by the stories I heard, in particular, Deaf people's struggle with education. Those I met drew graphic images for me of their humiliation by oral educators. Moreover, they related that they had been forced to communicate through speech and lip-reading and had been denied access to Auslan [Australian sign language] throughout their school years. Deaf children from Deaf families arrived at school to find that their hearing teachers neither used nor tolerated their language. Forced to hide their hands beneath school desks, they found out-of-the-way places to use sign language in an attempt to avoid punishment. Those who were caught were forced to sit on their hands or had fingers jammed into desk drawers. The Deaf adults I met were still angry about their education. Because they believed their teachers' view that Auslan was the reason for their failure to become fully literate, they blamed their first language for their under-achievement. (Komesaroff, 2008: xi-xii)

6 Reversing Underachievement: An Integrated Framework

The preceding chapters have all focused directly or indirectly on hypothesised causes of underachievement among minoritised students and the instructional and organisational strategies schools can pursue to reverse underachievement. Educational policies in many countries explicitly reference equity issues as illustrated in federal policies enacted in the United States over the past 50 years with titles such as *Equality of Educational Opportunity, No Child Left Behind* and *Every Student Succeeds Act*. Few of these policies in any country have succeeded in their stated goals. This is illustrated in the 2019 National Assessment of Educational Progress (NAEP) in the United States. The periodical *Education Week* reported the dismal findings as follows:

> The latest scores from the National Assessment of Educational Progress, also known as the nation's report card, were just released—and things aren't looking good for the country's young readers. *Reading performance has dropped significantly* among both 4th and 8th graders since the last release two years ago. Just 35 percent of 4th graders are considered proficient by NAEP standards as of this year. That's down from 37 percent in 2017. And 34 percent of 8th graders scored at the proficient level or higher for this year, down from 36 percent in 2017. But that's only part of the story. In what should be very worrisome to literacy experts, teachers, and anyone concerned with inequity in education, *the lowest performers showed the biggest declines*. (Loewus, 2019) (emphasis added)

Similarly, in most European countries, large gaps in achievement have persisted between immigrant-background and non-immigrant-background students, reflecting the failure of countries around the world to close the achievement gap between students from marginalised and privileged backgrounds (e.g. OECD, 2010d).

In this chapter, I discuss the intersecting role of three broad sets of factors – language teaching/learning, socioeconomic status (SES), and societal power relations – in attempting to identify opportunity gaps that operate to sustain inequitable educational outcomes across social groups.

The preceding chapters have addressed issues related to language learning/teaching and societal power relations. The role of SES has not been addressed in any depth in previous chapters but its impact on student achievement has been repeatedly documented (e.g. Berliner, 2009; OECD, 2010d).

Clearly, the failure of many school systems to provide appropriate support to enable immigrant-background students to learn the language of instruction and catch up academically represents one broad set of causal factors. Underlying this failure are structural factors such as biased curriculum, teacher education programmes that ignore the linguistic and cultural diversity present in schools, no expectation on the part of policymakers that school leaders should know anything about how to support students in catching up academically, and tolerance within the educational system of misconceptions regarding issues such as how long it takes students to learn the language of instruction and the evidence-free belief that students' L1 will impede their acquisition of L2.

The failure of many school systems to provide effective support for students learning the school language obviously intersects with patterns of societal power relations, of which SES is one significant component as reflected in inequitable educational funding for socially privileged and disadvantaged communities (e.g. Kozol, 2005). The fact that it is not a priority in these societies to ensure that all teachers and school leaders are knowledgeable about instructional strategies that are effective in helping minoritised students catch up academically reflects coercive relations of power. Although there are exceptions, relatively few school systems can point to sustained policies and concrete initiatives that challenge the devaluation of minoritised students' identities. Until recently, curriculum documents and educational policies in most societies made no mention of issues related to identity negotiation and societal power relations. The inaccurate, patronising, and racist depiction of First Nations communities in Canadian curricula for most of the past century is just one of many examples that could be cited (Truth and Reconciliation Commission of Canada, 2015).

A central question for policymakers and researchers is 'How do these three sets of factors (language learning/teaching, SES, and marginalised status) that potentially exert a major impact on the achievement of minoritised students fit together'? 'How do they intersect in their impact'? and most importantly 'What evidence-based instructional responses are available to schools and educators to reverse the potentially negative impact of these factors'?

Surprisingly, the *integrated* nature of these questions and the instructional directions they imply have received relatively little attention from researchers. Researchers concerned with these three sources of potential educational disadvantage have worked largely in isolation from each other. Issues related to linguistically diverse students have been addressed primarily by applied linguists focused on issues related to language teaching/learning and bilingual/multilingual education. The role of social disadvantage has been addressed by researchers concerned with school improvement in general, but these researchers seldom discuss issues related to language learning and teaching, or issues related to the operation of societal power relations beyond SES. Issues related to racialised/marginalised students have been addressed by researchers focused on critical pedagogy and culturally responsive/relevant/sustaining instruction. Again, however, language issues associated with underachievement are rarely discussed, and social disadvantage is typically viewed as the consequence of racism and therefore subsumed within analyses of the educational effects of racism.

Thus, within the academic world, there has been little cross-disciplinary communication and few attempts at analytic integration among researchers concerned with the three distinct groups that tend to experience persistent underachievement: (a) immigrant-background students who are learning the language of instruction, (b) students experiencing the effects of poverty and other forms of social disadvantage and (c) students from socially marginalised communities who have experienced discrimination and racism, often over generations. These 'academic silos' are unfortunate and counter-productive because the reality is that although the three sources of potential disadvantage are conceptually distinct, a significant proportion of underachieving students fall into all three categories.

In this chapter, I summarise my own attempts over the past decade to integrate these three orientations to analysing underachievement, and the disciplinary perspectives they reflect, in order to identify evidence-based directions that schools could pursue to reverse underachievement. My analytic focus is on *instructional* initiatives, but these initiatives clearly imply broader organisational and policy changes, which I don't address in any detail (see Isola & Cummins, 2020, for discussion of these factors).

For ease of organisation, I have divided the chapter into three sections. The first section analyses relevant findings and interpretive claims of the Programme for International Student Assessment (PISA) implemented over the past 20 years by the Organisation for Economic Cooperation and Development (OECD). The PISA findings provide a vast reservoir of achievement data from more than 70 countries that includes assessment of the relationships between immigrant-background students' academic performance and factors such as SES and language spoken at home. The focus of the analysis of PISA findings in this chapter is on the impact of SES, language spoken at home, and reading engagement on students' reading achievement at age 15. In addition to reviewing PISA findings on these issues, I also include relevant findings from the broader research literature. Although PISA represents an invaluable resource for researchers and policymakers, the findings have not always been interpreted in a coherent and accurate manner either by PISA researchers themselves or by other researchers.

The second section examines a broader range of attempts by researchers to synthesise the research findings related to the achievement of multilingual students and also to assess the impact of various instructional programmes (e.g. bilingual education versus monolingual education in the school language). These research syntheses have been carried out primarily within the United States and reflect applied linguistics perspectives. The major problem with these reviews is that, in varying degrees, they focus primarily on linguistic variables and largely omit from consideration issues related to SES, societal power relations, and identity negotiation.

The third section presents an integrated framework that draws on the findings of both the PISA studies and the research synthesis reports in such a way that evidence-based instructional responses can be articulated. The foundation of the framework is that underachievement is observed predominantly among linguistically diverse students who are also experiencing the effects of social disadvantage and/or marginalised group status within the society. Thus, in addition to focusing on *language* issues, instruction must also address the opportunity gaps experienced by minoritised students and communities related to low-SES and societal discrimination. This will include maximising students' engagement with literacy (ideally in both L1 and L2) and enabling them to use language powerfully in ways that enhance their academic and personal identities.

Section 1. Analysis of the OECD PISA Findings

In the early 2000s, educational researchers and policymakers around the world gradually became aware of the OECD's PISA research. These studies were designed to assess the achievement of 15-year-old students in reading, science, mathematics and problem-solving and to identify some of the major social and educational factors that influence patterns of academic achievement among individual students and across different countries. The first set of studies was published in 2000 and involved about 315,000 students in 43 countries. Studies have been published at regular intervals since that time with an expanding range of students and countries involved.

PISA provides OECD member and participating non-member countries with a 'report card' on the effectiveness of their educational systems, including the relative success of students from socially disadvantaged and immigrant backgrounds. The economic implications of increasing diversity derive from the fact that immigrants represent human capital, and school failure among any segment of the population entails significant long-term economic costs in a knowledge-based economy.

Thus, it is not surprising that the relatively weak academic performance of the total sample of immigrant- and non-immigrant background

15-year-old students in some of the more affluent European countries gave rise to intense debate in these countries about how to improve students' literacy skills and overall educational success (e.g. Faas, 2014). These debates have become infused with sociopolitical and ideological discourses around diversity and immigration. For example, anti-immigrant sentiment in some European countries was fueled by claims that immigrant-background students' academic underachievement was undermining the effectiveness of the educational system and potentially contributing to long-term economic problems for the country. However, the PISA findings also challenge the credibility of this argument insofar as they demonstrate considerable variability across countries in the extent to which immigrant-background students succeed academically (Christensen & Segeritz, 2008; Christensen & Stanat, 2007; OECD, 2010a, 2010b, 2010c, 2010d, 2012, 2016; Stanat & Christensen, 2006). In other words, some countries are much more effective than others in enabling socially disadvantaged and immigrant-background students to succeed academically.

My personal engagement with the PISA findings was largely peripheral until I read the report written by Petra Stanat and Gayle Christensen (2006) entitled *Where Immigrant Students Succeed: A Comparative Review of Performance and Engagement in PISA 2003*. This report compiled PISA data on the academic performance of first- and second-generation immigrant-background students. First generation students (and their parents) were born outside the host country while second generation students are of immigrant background but were born in the host country. Using data from the PISA 2003 assessment involving 17 countries with significant immigrant student populations, the report examined how immigrant students performed primarily in mathematics and reading, but also in science and problem-solving skills.

Although legitimate issues have been raised in relation to the PISA project,[1] the research has identified significant inequities within educational systems and has contributed to useful discussions within and across countries about how schools can address underachievement in general, and among vulnerable populations in particular. For the first time, researchers and policymakers have had access to large-scale cross-national data on immigrant-background students that identified not only patterns of academic achievement over time in multiple countries but also relationships between achievement and variables such as SES, language spoken at home, and reading engagement. In this section, my focus is on the problematic ways the PISA data have been interpreted by a significant number of researchers and policymakers and, more generally, the failure of numerous researchers to analyse the data on minority group achievement in a logical and coherent way. As a result, educational policy and instructional practice in many countries remain largely evidence-free, despite the unprecedented volume of research from contexts around the world that is now available.

I first outline the early OECD findings regarding the achievement patterns of immigrant background students and then discuss some of the problematic ways in which these findings were interpreted by Stanat and Christensen (2006) and other OECD researchers. In the following section, I expand the analysis to four other research reviews of minority student achievement. In each case, the range of opportunity gaps associated with underachievement is inadequately identified and consequently the recommended instructional responses are incomplete.[2]

The 2003 and 2006 OECD Findings Regarding Immigrant Student Achievement

The PISA reading performance of 15-year-old first- and second-generation immigrant-background students from a selection of OECD countries is shown in Table 6.1. Students tend to perform better in countries such as Canada and Australia that have encouraged immigration during the past 50 years and that have a coherent infrastructure designed to integrate immigrants into the society (e.g. free adult language classes, language support services for students in schools, rapid qualification for full citizenship, etc.). Additionally, although systemic and individual racism persist in both countries, Canada and Australia have explicitly endorsed multicultural philosophies at the national level aimed at promoting respect across communities and expediting the integration of

Table 6.1 PISA Reading scores 2003 and 2006 (based on data presented in Christensen & Segeritz, 2008); Gen 1 = first generation students, Gen 2 = second generation students; negative scores indicate performance below country mean, positive scores indicate performance above country mean); 100 points represents one standard deviation.

	PISA 2003 Gen 1	PISA 2003 Gen 2	PISA 2006 Gen 1	PISA 2006 Gen 2
Australia	−12	−4	+1	+7
Austria	−77	−73	−48	−79
Belgium	−117	−84	−102	−81
Canada	−19	+10	−19	0
Denmark	−42	−57	−79	−64
France	−79	−48	−45	−36
Germany	−86	−96	−70	−83
Netherlands	−61	−50	−65	−61
Norway	−68	−59	−63	−42
Sweden	−89	−20	−68	−29
Switzerland	−93	−53	−85	−48
United Kingdom			−44	−7
United States	−50	−22		

newcomers into the broader society. In Canada (2003 assessment) and Australia (2006 assessment), second-generation immigrant-background students (born in the host country) performed slightly *better* academically than non-immigrant background native speakers of the school language. Some of the positive results for Australia and Canada can be attributed to selective immigration that favours immigrants with strong educational qualifications. In both countries, the educational attainments of adult immigrants are as high, on average, as those of the general population. This is also true of other countries (e.g. Ireland and New Zealand) where immigrant-background students perform relatively well.

By contrast, second generation students have tended to perform very poorly in countries that have been characterised by highly negative attitudes towards immigrants (e.g. Austria, Belgium, Germany). Christensen and Segeritz (2008: 18) highlight as particularly problematic the poor performance of second-generation students in many European countries: 'Of particular concern, especially for policymakers, should be the fact that second-generation immigrant students in many countries continue to lag significantly behind their native peers despite spending all of their schooling in the receiving country'. In some cases (Denmark and Germany in 2003; Austria and Germany in 2006) second generation students who received all their schooling in the host country performed more poorly than first generation students who arrived as newcomers and would likely have had less time and opportunity to learn the host country language. These data clearly suggest that factors other than simply opportunity to learn the host country language are operating to limit achievement among second-generation students in these countries.

Predictors of Reading Achievement in PISA and Related Research

Three major factors emerged across the PISA studies as strong predictors of reading achievement among immigrant-background 15-year-old students: SES, language spoken at home, and reading engagement. The OECD (2010d: 30) report expressed the overall pattern with respect to the SES and language spoken at home as follows:

> In most countries, immigrant students do not perform as well as native students on average. The performance gaps are more pronounced for immigrant students who speak another language at home other than the language of instruction, and for immigrants from low socio-economic backgrounds. (OECD, 2010d: 30)

Socioeconomic status

In general, the SES of individual students showed a strong negative relationship with reading achievement in the PISA studies: 'On average across OECD countries, 14% of the differences in student reading performance within each country is associated with differences in students' socio-economic background' (OECD, 2010a: 14). However, the report qualified this finding as follows:

> Regardless of their own socio-economic background, students attending schools with a socio-economically advantaged intake tend to perform better than those attending schools with more disadvantaged peers. In the majority of OECD countries, the effect of the school's economic, social and cultural status on students' performance far outweighs the effects of the individual student's socio-economic background. (OECD, 2010a: 14)

In other words, when students from low-SES backgrounds attend schools with a relatively advantaged socioeconomic intake, they tend to perform significantly better than when they attend schools with a socioeconomically disadvantaged intake.

Many other research studies have identified similar relationships between SES and student achievement. Snow *et al.* (1998), for example, noted a correlation of 0.68 between reading achievement and the collective poverty level of students in a school, a correlation that is considerably greater than the correlation of approximately 0.45 between reading achievement and early literacy indicators such as knowledge of the letters of the alphabet and phonological awareness. Gándara also highlighted the intersections between poverty and immigration status:

> Nearly two-thirds of immigrant children in the United States live near or below the poverty level. … Poverty has devastating effects on children's academic achievement, whether the students are English learners or native-born European Americans. … Poverty is a major predictor of absenteeism, poor grades and test scores, and high dropout rates. (Gándara, 2013: 160–161)

The difference between the SES of individual students and the collective SES of students within particular schools highlights the effects of housing and educational segregation on patterns of school achievement. The OECD (2012: 14) makes this point as follows: 'All things being equal, a more balanced social mix in schools would go a long way towards improving outcomes for both immigrant and non-immigrant students from disadvantaged backgrounds'.

Although the relationship between achievement and students' individual and collective SES is substantial, SES does not fully explain differences in immigrant-background students' reading performance either within or across countries:

> Socio-economic background is strongly associated with student performance; performance differences are substantially reduced after accounting for socio-economic factors such as the occupation and

education level of students' parents. However, it does not fully explain the observed performance disadvantage for immigrant students, and in most countries, substantial performance gaps for immigrant students remain even after accounting for socio-economic backgrounds. (OECD, 2010a: 37)

Language spoken at home – part of the problem or part of the solution?

Stanat and Christensen (2006) reported a negative relationship between 15-year-old immigrant-background students' use of their L1 at home and academic achievement in L2. Both first- and second-generation immigrant-background students who spoke their L1 at home were about a half-year behind their non-immigrant peers in mathematics and even further behind in reading. Similar discrepancies were reported in more recent PISA reports (e.g. Nusche, 2009; OECD, 2010, 2012). Christensen and Stanat (2007: 3) suggested the following interpretation of these findings: 'These large differences in performance suggest that students have insufficient opportunities to learn the language of instruction'. German sociologist, Hartmut Esser (2006: 64) similarly argued on the basis of PISA and other research data that 'the use of the native language in the family context has a (clearly) negative effect'. He further argued that retention of the home language by immigrant children will reduce both motivation and success in learning the host country language.

Several subsequent OECD reports have also attributed the performance gap associated with language use at home to the more limited exposure to the dominant school language resulting from L1 use in the home. For example, an OECD (2012) report entitled *Untapped Skills: Realising the Potential of Immigrant Students* summarised this interpretation of the data as follows:

PISA results suggest that students who mostly speak a different language at home from that which is used in school have significantly lower reading scores than those who tend to use the test language at home most of the time. This effect is very strong, accounting for a difference of about 30 points in reading scores, on average, between those who mostly speak the test language at home and those who do not... The language skills of parents, particularly of mothers, may not be sufficient to allow them to assist their children in their schoolwork. The objective needs to be more exposure to the host-country language, both in and out of school. (OECD, 2012: 12-14)

These interpretations of the PISA data can be summarised as follows: *Insufficient opportunity to learn the school language as a result of speaking a minority language at home leads to inadequate proficiency and academic underachievement in the school language.* Thus, in most, but not all OECD reports (see OECD, 2010c), students' L1 is positioned as part of the problem rather than as part of the solution. In these reports, linguistic mismatch and presumed lack of exposure to the dominant language are posited as independent causal variables despite the fact that we have known for more than 40 years that linguistic mismatch, by itself, cannot explain the empirical data (Cummins, 1979a, 1982, 1986).[3] The alternative interpretation of the data, which I elaborate later in this chapter, highlights the importance of engaging students' multilingual repertoires, maximising literacy engagement and promoting identity affirmation, as central components of effective literacy instruction for linguistically diverse students who are learning the language of instruction.

I critiqued the OECD interpretation of the relationship between home language use and achievement on multiple grounds including (a) the crudeness of the dichotomous home language index used in early PISA studies; (b) the claim that home use of L1 automatically translates into 'insufficient exposure' to the school language; (c) the fact that the relationship between achievement and L1 use at home is a relationship of association, not causation; (d) failure to consider alternative directions of possible causal relations, namely that success in learning the school language might lead to greater use of that language in the home rather than the opposite relationship; (e) failure to account for the findings of many other research studies that contradict the proposition that L1 use at home causes underachievement; (f) failure to acknowledge PISA findings that show no relationship between home L1 use and achievement in a majority of OECD countries when SES, length of residence in the host country, and other background variables were controlled; (g) the outcomes of bilingual education programmes, which refute the 'time-on-task' or 'maximum exposure' hypothesis underlying the 'insufficient exposure' claim (Cummins, 2008b, 2018).

Well-designed research studies carried out by Bhatnagar (1980) in Montreal, Canada and Dolson (1985) in Los Angeles, California, refute the proposition that use of L1 at home exerts an adverse impact on the learning of the school language and on academic achievement generally. In a study involving 273 Italian-L1 students who attended either English or French medium schools, Bhatnagar reported that students who used both Italian and either English or French (depending on the language of schooling) interchangeably in interactions with their parents performed significantly better academically and in their oral and written knowledge of the school language than their peers who predominantly used the school language in parental interactions. Age, cognitive ability and SES were controlled in these comparisons.

Dolson (1985) reported similar findings in a sample of 108 Grades 5 and 6 Spanish-speaking students who varied in the extent to which they continued to speak Spanish in interaction with their parents. Students in 'additive' home environments continued to use their L1 in interaction with their parents while those in 'subtractive' environments had switched to

English as their preferred home language. The groups were matched for initial home language, length of enrolment in school, and SES. Dolson summarised his findings as follows: 'Students from additive home bilingual environments performed significantly better than students from subtractive home bilingual environments on school measures of (a) mathematics skills, (b) Spanish reading vocabulary, (c) academic grade point average, (d) effort grade point average, and (e) retention' (1985: 148). The groups performed at a similar level on measures of English oral and reading skills.

Cobo-Lewis *et al.* (2002a) reported that initial differences in English language and literacy skills among Spanish-English bilingual children in the Miami area at kindergarten that were attributable to language spoken at home had largely disappeared by Grade 5, indicating no long-term negative consequences associated with L1 use at home. Prevoo *et al.* (2015) reported that students of Turkish language background who spoke more Turkish at home progressed as well in Dutch academic skills as similar-background students who spoke more Dutch at home. Furthermore, significant L1 to L2 relationships were observed for the initially Turkish-dominant group but not for the Dutch-dominant group, suggesting that crosslinguistic transfer of conceptual knowledge was occurring for the students with more L1 conceptual knowledge to transfer.

Agirdag and Vanlaar (2016) analysed more recent (2012) PISA data that included detailed questions on home language use rather than the dichotomous question on home language included in early PISA research. Their findings refute the claim that L1 use at home by immigrant-background students impedes L2 learning and school achievement. As in previous PISA studies, they identified an achievement gap between immigrant-background and native-speaking students in both reading and mathematics in a large majority of countries. The achievement gap narrowed but remained significant after students' background characteristics (e.g. SES) were taken into account. However, Agirdag and Vanlaar also reported that immigrant-background students who spoke their home language more often with their parents performed as well as those who spoke the dominant societal language with their parents. They found that in most countries involved in the OECD studies, home language use was unrelated to academic performance but in some countries, such as Canada, Finland and Singapore, speaking a minority language with parents was *positively* related to achievement in the dominant language.

In my review of the Stanat and Christensen (2006) report, I pointed to the fact that no relationship was found between home language use and achievement in the two countries where immigrant-background students were most successful (Australia and Canada) and the relationship disappeared for a large majority (10 out of 14) of OECD-member countries when socioeconomic status and other background variables were controlled (Stanat & Christensen, 2006, Table 3.5, pp. 200–202). The disappearance of the relationship in a large majority of countries suggests that language spoken at home does not exert any independent effect on achievement but is rather a proxy for variables such as socioeconomic status and length of residence in the host country (Cummins, 2008b: 495–496).

In short, differences between home and school languages are likely to be part of a broad causal matrix influencing immigrant students' academic performance, but it is a serious oversimplification to suggest a one-dimensional causal chain between linguistic mismatch and underachievement. Certainly, students need ample opportunities to learn the language of instruction and few researchers will argue about the importance of effective language support, but PISA provides no evidence that immigrant-background students have insufficient opportunities to learn the language of instruction as a result of L1 use at home, or that this is a cause of students' underachievement.[4]

Literacy engagement

The PISA data on the relationship between reading engagement and reading achievement among 15-year-old students focus on the general school population rather than specifically on immigrant background or low-SES students, although these groups are obviously included as part of the sample. The early PISA studies showed that 'the level of a student's reading engagement is a better predictor of literacy performance than his or her socioeconomic background, indicating that cultivating a student's interest in reading can help overcome home disadvantages' (OECD, 2004: 8). Cognitive psychologist, John Guthrie, reinforced this conclusion based on both National Assessment of Educational Progress (NAEP) and PISA data, noting that 9-year-old students in the 1998 NAEP study:

> whose family background was characterized by low income and low education, but who were highly engaged readers, substantially outscored students who came from backgrounds with higher education and higher income, but who themselves were less engaged readers. Based on a massive sample, this finding suggests the stunning conclusion that engaged reading can overcome traditional barriers to reading achievement, including gender, parental education, and income. (Guthrie, 2004: 5)

The OECD (2004: 8) authors were careful to point out that 'engagement in reading can be a consequence, as well as a cause, of higher reading skill, but the evidence suggests that these two factors are mutually reinforcing'.

More recent PISA findings (e.g. OECD, 2010a) confirm these trends. Engagement in reading was assessed through measures of time spent reading various materials, enjoyment of reading, and use of various learning strategies. Across OECD countries, reading engagement was significantly related to reading performance and approximately one-third of the relationship between reading performance and students' socioeconomic background was mediated by reading engagement. In other words, there was about a one-third overlap between the negative effects of low SES and the positive effects of reading engagement. The implication is that schools can potentially 'push back' about one-third of the negative effects of socioeconomic disadvantage by ensuring that students have access to a print-rich environment and become actively engaged with literacy. Brozo *et al.* (2007: 307–308) similarly articulated the implications of the PISA data for low-SES students as follows: 'Keeping students engaged in reading and learning might make it possible for them to overcome what might otherwise be insuperable barriers to academic success'.

The lower reading performance of students from socially disadvantaged backgrounds in comparison to their higher-SES peers can be attributed to the fact that many students from lower-income communities have significantly less access to print in their schools, homes, and neighborhoods than is the case for students from middle-income communities (Duke, 2000; Neuman & Celano, 2001). In comparison to more affluent families, parents living in poverty don't have the money to buy books or other cultural resources, such as iPads, smartphones and computers, for their children. The impact of this restricted access to books carries over into the summer months during which time, according to Allington and McGill-Franzen, SES-related reading gaps are exacerbated:

> Children from low-income families live in neighborhoods that offer fewer locations to buy or borrow books, attend schools where the numbers of books available are more limited, and live in homes where few books are found. … All this leads to some children spending summers with restricted access to books that could be read. This lack of access means that these children are less likely to read during the summer months. (Allington & McGill-Franzen, 2017: 175–176)

In short, there is an opportunity gap with respect to print access that has not been addressed by schools in most countries (see Allington & McGill-Franzen, 2017, 2018 for reviews of these data).

The OECD (2010a: 97) summarised the overall PISA findings on the effects of reading engagement as follows:

> Students who make reading an everyday part of their lives are able to build their reading proficiency through practice, which in turn can improve their confidence and encourage them to become more engaged in reading. In almost every country that took part in PISA 2009, the more students enjoy reading and the more engaged they become in reading for enjoyment – both off and on line – the higher their reading proficiency.[5] (OECD, 2010a: 97)

The OECD findings are reinforced by the extensive empirical research supporting the relationship between literacy engagement and attainment in both monolingual and multilingual educational contexts (e.g. Guthrie *et al.*, 2001; Krashen, 2004a; Lindsay, 2010, 2018). The National Academies of Sciences, Engineering, and Medicine (NASEM) (2017) 'Consensus Study' summarised the effects and implications of literacy engagement for English learners (ELs) in the United States as follows:

> Conclusion 8–4: Literacy engagement is critical during the middle school grades. During these grades, students are required to read and learn from advanced and complex grade level texts. For ELs, this problem is acute because instructional support for long-term English learners tends to emphasize skills instead of dealing with the barriers to their motivation to learn, engagement in the classroom, and literacy engagement. (2017: 326)

> Conclusion 8–9: Research on the literacy engagement of ELs and its relationship to educational outcomes is limited despite its potential importance. Current research indicates that literacy engagement may be an important factor for ELs in their learning to read, in their academic language learning from school texts, and in their literacy and academic achievement. Literacy engagement may be even more important for ELs than for students whose first language is English because (1) learning to read in a language one is still learning is difficult, and literacy engagement can support ELs' efforts to learn despite those difficulties; and (2) literacy is necessary to learning academic language. If ELs do not read well and are not motivated to read, they will find it difficult to learn the academic language required for reclassification. (NASEM, 2017: 327)

In summary, there is persuasive evidence from multiple sources that engaging students actively in literacy activities, both in school and in out-of-school contexts, promotes literacy attainment. This evidence includes both L1 and L2 contexts. This research strongly suggests that a sustained focus on maximising literacy engagement is an essential component in reversing underachievement among socially disadvantaged students.

Although most of the research has focused on reading, it seems appropriate to broaden the focus from simply *reading engagement* to *literacy engagement* in light of the fact that there is considerable research documenting the role of extensive writing not only in developing writing expertise but also in improving reading comprehension (Graham & Herbert, 2010). A sampling of the extensive research on print access and literacy engagement is summarised in Appendix 6.1.

In the next section, I examine several reviews of the research literature carried out by credible and respected researchers concerning the academic achievement of minority group students. These reviews attempted to identify evidence-based causes of underachievement and to make recommendations regarding effective educational interventions to address these causal factors. However, while these reviews make important contributions, they suffer from limitations in their interpretation of the research evidence. These misinterpretations have major implications for how we understand the nature of academic underachievement experienced by minoritised students and the educational interventions that might be effective in reversing underachievement.

Section 2. Research Reviews Focused on Reversing Underachievement

During the past 15 years, in addition to the OECD reports reviewed in the previous section, four major syntheses of research evidence have been published regarding the academic achievement of linguistically diverse students whose L1 is different from the dominant language of instruction at school. These research syntheses have focused primarily on research and policy issues in the United States. Two comprehensive reviews were published in 2006: the report of the National Literacy Panel on Language-Minority Children and Youth entitled *Developing Literacy in Second-Language Learners* (August & Shanahan, 2006, 2008a) and a volume edited by Genesee *et al.* (2006) entitled *Educating English Language Learners: A Synthesis of Research Evidence.* Four years later, the California Department of Education (2010) published a volume of six chapters (plus an Introductory chapter) written by 12 prominent research-ers, including several involved in the earlier research syntheses, entitled *Improving Education for English Learners: Research-Based Approaches.* This volume highlighted the instructional implications and applications of the research evidence.

An adjunct monograph (Dolson & Burnham-Massey, 2011) entitled *Redesigning English-Medium Classrooms: Using Research to Enhance English Learner Achievement,* was originally intended as a final chapter of the California Department of Education volume. However, the chapter highlighted some major inconsistencies between the research evidence and California State law and policy, such as the fact that state (and federal) law at the time proclaimed that English learners should acquire English profi-ciency within one year of instruction whereas the research shows clearly that much more than one year is required for English learners to catch up academically (e.g. Cummins, 1981c; Parrish *et al.*, 2006). The authors were not willing to omit reference to these inconsistencies and thus the chapter was not included in the California Department of Education (2010) volume but was instead published as a separate monograph by the California Association for Bilingual Education. For purposes of this chapter, I am including the Dolson and Burnham-Massey monograph as a component of the overall California Department of Education (2010) project.

The fourth research synthesis was published by the National Academies of Sciences, Engineering, and Medicine (NASEM, 2017) enti-tled *Promoting the Educational Success of Children and Youth Learning English: Promising Futures.* This report was compiled by a committee of 19 prominent American researchers in the area of second language learn-ing and minority group achievement and was peer reviewed by multiple additional researchers in these areas.

These four syntheses of the empirical research make important con-tributions in compiling and critically analysing the research findings. For example, all of the research syntheses carried out by United States researchers acknowledged the legitimacy both of students' L1 as a cognitive resource and bilingual education as a policy option. However, only the NASEM (2017) report acknowledged the significant role played by literacy engagement in the development of students' reading comprehension skills, and only the Dolson and Burnham-Massey (2011) report highlighted the role of societal power relations and teacher-student identity negotiation in determining minoritised student outcomes.

Thus, most of the reports exhibit some limitations in the ways in which the research has been interpreted and linked to educational policy and classroom instruction. Underlying these limitations is the fact that these reports focus primarily on *language* differences between home and school, and students' consequent need to learn the school language, in isolation from the social context within which these language differences are embedded. As a result, their instructional prescriptions highlight more effective ways to develop students' academic language proficiency without systematically integrating these instructional responses with those that are implied by the research on SES and marginalised group status. Thus, the reports fail to identify instructional interventions that are of central importance for students' academic achievement. In the next section, I review the four research syntheses in relation to (a) areas of consensus and (b) limitations in the reports.

Areas of Consensus in the Research Syntheses

All of the reports agree on the need for schools to modify instruction in order to support students in learning the school language. Goldenberg (2008: 14), for example, in discussing common themes emerging from August and Shanahan's (2006) National Literacy Panel (NLP) report and the Genesee *et al.* (2006) report, notes three key conclusions that are common to both reports:

- Teaching students to read in their first language promotes higher levels of reading achievement *in English*;
- What we know about good instruction and curriculum in general holds true for English learners as well; but
- When instructing English learners in English, teachers must modify instruction to take into account students' language limitations. (emphasis original)

The first conclusion reinforces the findings of many other reviews of the literature on bilingual education (e.g. Cheung & Slavin, 2012; Cummins, 2001a; McField & McField, 2014; Rolstad *et al.*, 2005; Slavin & Cheung, 2005) and establishes bilingual education as a legitimate policy option for teaching linguistically diverse students. The McField and McField analysis is particularly interesting insofar as it is a meta-analysis of the various meta-analyses that were carried out over the previous 30+ years. They reported that both sustained and transitional bilingual programmes showed greater effectiveness than English-only programmes in teaching English literacy skills. Sustained or 'strong' bilingual programmes continued L1 instruction through the elementary school grades with the goal of promoting additive bilingualism involving literacy in L1 and L2. Transitional or 'weak' programmes typically exited students into all-English programmes after only 1–2 years of bilingual instruction. Sustained/additive programmes demonstrated a highly significant effect (effect size: $d = 0.41$) in comparison to English-only models. The positive effect for early-exit transitional programmes was considerably less ($d = 0.19$). McField and McField concluded: 'There is no doubt that, when it comes to English acquisition, native-language instruction is part of the solution, not part of the problem' (2014: 289).

Goldenberg's (2008) second conclusion is essentially saying that the findings of the National Reading Panel (NRP) (2000) with respect to effective reading instruction also apply to literacy instruction for linguistically diverse students. As expressed by Goldenberg (2008: 17): 'The NLP found that ELLs learning to read in English, just like English speakers learning to read in English, benefit from explicit teaching of the components of literacy, such as phonemic awareness, phonics, vocabulary, comprehension, and writing'. This seemingly innocuous interpretation of the research is problematic on two grounds. First, the NRP reported that after Grade 1, normally achieving and low achieving students experienced no benefits with respect to reading comprehension from systematic phonics instruction (Ehri *et al.*, 2001). Thus, some significant qualifications are required in the blanket statement that explicit teaching of the components of literacy 'benefit' students' reading development (for more elaboration, see critiques of the NRP by Cummins, 2007b; Garan, 2001; Krashen, 2004b; Pressley *et al.*, 2004, among many others). Second, neither the NRP nor the NLP, while emphasising the centrality of systematic phonics instruction, adequately reviewed the research showing that reading engagement was strongly related to reading comprehension (see Appendix 6.1). As a consequence, neither research synthesis recommends that educators attempt to maximise students' reading engagement. The other research syntheses (California Department of Education, 2010; Genesee *et al.*, 2006) likewise ignore the research on reading engagement. Thus, while it is certainly appropriate and necessary to focus on developing students' language awareness and to teach many aspects of language explicitly, the impact of this explicit instruction will be considerably less in the absence of literacy engagement.

The third conclusion identified by Goldenberg (2008) to emerge from the NLP and the Genesee *et al.* (2006) reports is not particularly informative. No researcher currently advocates a return to 'submersion' or sink-or-swim instructional policies where no modifications are made to support linguistically diverse students in comprehending curriculum content and acquiring the language of instruction. Unfortunately, neither the NLP nor Genesee *et al.* reports were able to specify in any detail, on the basis of the research, how instruction should be modified. August and Shanahan (2008b: 9) explain one of the reasons why they found so few research studies that could inform instruction: 'Unfortunately, because there have been too few experimental studies, research has not yet provided a complete answer to what constitutes high-quality literacy instruction for language-minority students'. Goldenberg pointed out that the NRP (2000) report synthesised findings from more than 400 experimental or quasi-experimental studies of instruction in phonological awareness, phonics, vocabulary, reading fluency, and reading comprehension but the NLP could identify only 17 such studies involving linguistically diverse students. The limitations of focusing almost exclusively on experimental or quasi-experimental research have been pointed out by numerous critics of both the NRP and NLP reports (e.g. Cummins, 2007b; Pressley *et al.*, 2004).

Fortunately, however, many of the same authors adopted a more open orientation to the instructional implications of the research in their contributions to the California Department of Education (2010) research synthesis. Detailed and useful elaborations of evidence-based instructional practices for linguistically diverse learners are included in this volume. These are summarised below in terms of four overlapping instructional mandates:

- Scaffold instruction to support students' language comprehension and production.
- Activate students' existing background knowledge and build new background knowledge as needed.
- Teach academic language explicitly.
- Enable students to use their L1 as a cognitive resource either through bilingual education programmes or within English-medium programmes.

Scaffold instruction

The term *scaffolding* refers to the provision of instructional supports that enable learners to carry out tasks and perform academically at a higher level than they would be capable of without these supports. Dolson and Burnham-Massey (2011: 41) describe scaffolding (or 'sheltered') instructional strategies as follows: 'In sheltered settings, teachers make content comprehensible through a variety of techniques that include the use of visual aids, modeling, demonstrations, graphic organizers, vocabulary previews, predictions, adapted texts, cooperative learning, peer tutoring, multicultural content, and native language support'. The best known and most widely used comprehensive instructional system developed for linguistically diverse students is the Sheltered Instruction Observation Protocol (SIOP) model, which is described by Echevarria and Short (2010) in the California Department of Education volume.

Activate and build background knowledge

There is virtually universal agreement among reading and learning theorists that effective instruction for all students activates their background knowledge and builds on it as needed (e.g. Bransford *et al.*, 2000). Snow *et al.* (1998: 219) expressed the centrality of background knowledge as follows: 'Every opportunity should be taken to extend and enrich children's background knowledge and understanding in every way possible, for the ultimate significance and memorability of any word or text depends on whether children possess the background knowledge and conceptual sophistication to understand its meaning'. Consistent with this perspective, SIOP emphasises the importance of linking new concepts explicitly to students' background experiences and past learning. Both Lindholm-Leary and Genesee (2010) and Dolson and Burnham-Massey (2011) interpret background knowledge in relation to the construct of *funds of knowledge* (González *et al.*, 2005), which implies a much broader connection to students' lives and cultural realities than narrower conceptions of background knowledge which might focus only on content learned in previous lessons. Clearly, connecting instruction to minoritised students' lives validates the legitimacy of their experience, culture and language, thereby affirming students' identities.

Teach academic language explicitly

All of the research syntheses endorse the necessity of teaching academic language explicitly and consistently across the curriculum. Echevarria and Short (2010), for example, highlight the importance of articulating clearly defined content and language objectives in all subject areas. Dutro and Kinsella (2010) provide detailed strategies for expanding secondary English Learners' (EL) vocabulary knowledge throughout the school day. The OECD (2010b) has also argued for an explicit and consistent focus on developing students' awareness of how academic language works in the different content areas in order to help struggling learners catch up academically.

Use students' L1 as a scaffold and cognitive resource

The research syntheses carried out in the United States consistently endorse both bilingual education as a legitimate programme option for emergent bilingual students and, in linguistically diverse classrooms, the inclusion of students' L1 within the predominantly English-medium class-room. Snow and Katz, for example, cite the Lucas and Katz (1994) study which found that, in exemplary programmes, a wide variety of L1/primary language uses were observed:

> [S]tudents are encouraged to use their primary language to assist one another, tutor other students, interact socially, ask/answer questions, write in the primary language, and use bilingual dictionaries. In the larger school context, exemplary schools provide instruction in the students' native culture and history, libraries maintain collections of native language books, teachers encourage parents to read to their children in the native language at home and to be actively involved in school activities, and schools communicate with parents in the first language. (Snow & Katz, 2010: 87)

August and Shanahan (2010: 235) also highlight the fact that 'effective literacy instruction for English learners is respectful of the home language'. As examples of successfully implemented practices, they list (a) providing books in students' L1 during school reading time, (b) previewing and reviewing storybook reading in students' L1, (c) allowing students to converse and write in L1 as well as L2, (d) allowing some use of L1 in instructional conversations, (e) providing L1 vocabulary support through targeted translation of passages and individual vocabulary items, including building awareness of cognate connections.[6]

It is clear from these syntheses of research (and from the classroom examples discussed in Chapter 11) that opening up the instructional space to include students' home languages as resources for learning can (a) scaffold comprehension and production of L2, (b) more effectively activate students' background knowledge, much of which is likely to be encoded in L1 and (c) develop awareness of L1/L2 crosslinguistic connections and how academic language operates more generally. Showing respect for students' L1 in these ways also clearly communicates a positive message to students and their families with respect to the value of bilingualism in their lives and its legitimacy as a cognitive and personal resource. These forms of identity affirmation also represent an instructional challenge to historical and current societal power relations that devalue marginalised students' cultures and languages. Numerous crosslinguistic or 'translanguaging' instructional initiatives implemented by inspirational educators over the past 30 years are described in Chapter 11.

The promising instructional strategies outlined above are also emphasised in the NASEM (2017) report, as illustrated in the following conclusions:

> Conclusion 8-1: The following instructional practices are effective in developing elementary school-aged ELs' knowledge of academic subject matter: providing explicit instruction focused on developing key aspects of literacy; developing academic language during content area instruction;

providing support to make core content comprehensible; encouraging peer-assisted learning opportunities; capitalizing on students' home language, knowledge, and cultural assets; (NASEM, 2017: 325)

Conclusion 8-8: There is less research on effective instructional practices for high school ELs than for the other grade spans. However, some promising practices include a focus on academic language development that embraces all facets of academic language and includes both oral and written language across content areas; structured reading and writing instruction using a cognitive strategies approach and explicit instruction in reading comprehension strategies; opportunities for extended discussion of text and its meaning between teachers and students and in peer groups that may foster motivation and engagement in literacy learning; (NASEM, 2017: 327)

Limitations in the Research Syntheses

As noted previously, there are two major limitations in the way the research findings have been interpreted in the four US syntheses. Specifically, research supporting the roles of print access/literacy engagement was ignored or dismissed in three of the four reviews, and the role of societal power relations and identity affirmation was minimally addressed in most of the contributions to these reviews. Dolson and Burnham-Massey's (2011) monograph is an exception insofar as it explicitly endorses culturally sustaining pedagogies that focus on identity and social justice in their discussion of effective practices for linguistically diverse learners (e.g. the autobiographical writing strategies documented in Ada & Campoy's, 2003, *Authors in the Classroom* and the *Bridging Multiple Worlds* programme developed by Bhattacharya *et al.* 2007).

In contrast to most of the US research syntheses, the OECD PISA studies highlight the central role that reading engagement plays in predicting reading achievement among 15-year-old students in countries around the world. However, this finding is not emphasised in PISA reports that discuss policy and instructional implications of their research (e.g. OECD, 2015). PISA likewise says very little about identity issues, presumably because constructs such as 'identity' were not amenable to quantitative measurement. The following sections briefly outline some of the problematic ways in which research relating to literacy engagement and identity affirmation was interpreted in the NLP report (August & Shanahan, 2006).

Print access/literacy engagement

The OECD's (2010a) documentation of the role of reading engagement in literacy development contrasts with the virtual dismissal of this research in the NLP volume. For example, Shanahan and Beck's (2006) review of studies that encouraged reading and writing, or involved adults reading to children, could identify only nine such studies that they deemed worthy of inclusion. By contrast, Lindsay's (2010, 2018) meta-analysis of 108 studies of 'print access' identified 44 'rigorous' studies that employed experimental or quasi-experimental designs (see Appendix 6.1). Shanahan and Beck reviewed only one of the nine research studies compiled by Elley (1991, 2001). They focused on the Fiji 'book flood' experiment (Elley & Mangubhai, 1983; Mangubhai, 2001) which Elley (1991) summarised. They largely dismiss the findings because of what they claim are reporting flaws in the study. For example, they claim that it was not possible to tell whether the pretest was in the students' native language or English and the author (Elley) did not document what was done to account for attrition over the two years of the study (Grades 4 and 5).

These claims suggest that Shanahan and Beck (2006) may not have consulted the original study (Elley & Mangubhai, 1983), which they did not reference, or Mangubhai's (2001) later account of it, relying instead on Elley's (1991) summary. It is clear from Elley and Mangubhai (1983) that all testing was carried out in English, including the pretest measures. Mangubhai (2001: 149) is also explicit on this point: 'In February, 1980, pupils in Grades 4 and 5 in 15 rural schools were tested using a specially prepared ESL reading test and 12 schools were selected and matched to produce three equivalent groups'. Attrition was also not an issue because the study was not longitudinal. Grades 4 and 5 classes in 1980 and Grades 5 and 6 classes in 1981 were tested as independent units, and results reported by grade level, with the result that any attrition of students between the 1980 and 1981 assessments would have been irrelevant to the results. In fact, the Elley and Mangubhai study is one of the most robustly designed of all of those considered in the NLP research synthesis. It involved random assignment of schools to treatments, relatively large sample sizes within each treatment, statistical controls for Grade 4 pretest differences that were not resolved through random assignment, and replication of the original Grades 4 and 5 results through a second year of Grades 5 and 6 testing.

Identity affirmation

The NLP panel concluded that 'there is surprisingly little evidence for the impact of sociocultural variables on literacy learning' (August & Shanahan, 2008b: 8). They acknowledged that a significant number of ethnographic and case studies provide examples of teachers giving legitimacy to students' personal, communal, or cultural backgrounds in the classroom, but they did not find rigorous evidence that sociocultural validation in the school benefited students' literacy outcomes. This conclusion appears to reflect the excessively narrow criteria the NLP adopted with respect to adequacy of research design and the need to isolate variables so that their separate impact could be assessed. This is rarely possible in field research where multiple variables overlap and interact.

Certainly, many sociologists and anthropologists would take issue with the claim that their disciplines have contributed no credible evidence regarding the sociocultural and educational conditions that influence students' achievement. They might also point to the fact that the NLP omitted several *quantitative* studies that point to the influence of sociocultural factors. For example, Portes and Rumbaut concluded on the basis of their large-scale study of second-generation immigrant students that maintaining links to the home culture and language is associated with higher educational achievement:

> The findings from our longitudinal study consistently point to the benefits of selective acculturation. This path is closely intertwined with preservation of fluent bilingualism and linked, in turn, with higher self-esteem, higher educational and occupational expectations, and higher academic achievement. (Portes & Rumbaut, 2001: 274)

Bankston and Zhou (1995: 14) similarly point out that 'identification with Vietnamese ethnicity, Vietnamese reading and writing abilities, attitudes toward future education, and current study habits all have significant [positive] effects on current educational outcome'. In addition, the many experimental studies that have documented the deterioration of task performance when negative stereotypes are communicated to the individual (termed *stereotype threat* by psychologist Claude Steele, 1997) have highlighted mechanisms through which societal power relations, reflected in teacher expectations, can influence task performance.

It is noteworthy that the conclusions of the NLP in relation to sociocultural factors (Goldenberg *et al.*, 2006) are not even accepted by the policymakers who coordinated the California Department of Education (2010) volume to which two of the authors contributed. In her Introduction to that volume, Aguila (2010: 12) pointed to the 'substantial and compelling research to support the notion that powerful sociocultural factors strongly influence the outcomes of programmes for English learners and other minority students and students of low socioeconomic class'. She goes on to endorse culturally responsive pedagogy (Gay, 2000) aimed at countering 'the racism, prejudice, and discrimination [these students] experience in schools and society' (2010: 13). However, as noted above, with the exception of the fact that they endorse the educational legitimacy of students' bilingualism, other chapters in the California Department of Education volume make little attempt to integrate their prescriptions for academic language instruction with culturally responsive or sustaining pedagogy.

In summary, although there are gaps in all the research reviews, the following instructional strategies emerge prominently as evidence-based and effective:

- Scaffold comprehension and production of language (e.g. Gibbons, 2015).
- Reinforce academic language across the curriculum (e.g. Zwiers, 2008).
- Engage students' multilingual repertoires (e.g. Little & Kirwin, 2019).
- Maximise literacy engagement (e.g. Guthrie, 2004).
- Connect with students' lives and the knowledge, culture and languages of their communities (e.g. Moll *et al.*, 1992).
- Affirm students' identities by enabling them to use their language and literacy skills to carry out powerful intellectual and creative academic work (e.g. Cummins & Early, 2011).

Obviously, each of these broad instructional strategies can be specified in considerably more detail. For example, in the theoretical framework outlined in the next section, I include two additional interventions as integral to evidence-based instructional responses designed to counter the devaluation of identity experienced by marginalised students and communities. These responses – *Decolonise curriculum and instruction through culturally sustaining pedagogy* and *Valorize L1/L2 language varieties* – are clearly implied by broader orientations such as affirming students' identities, connecting to students' lives, and engaging students multilingual repertoires, but have been specified explicitly to make connections to broader themes in the scholarly literature (e.g. Battiste, 2013; Delpit, 1995; García, 2020; Hammine, 2019; López-Gopar, 2016; Macedo, 2019; Motha, 2006; Prax-Dubois & Hélot, 2020; Salaün, 2013; Taylor, 2011).

Section 3. An Integrated Framework: Evidence-Based Instruction That Responds to Opportunity Gaps

The integrated framework that I present in this section is based on three questions: (a) Which groups or 'categories' of students experience disproportionate school failure? (b) What potential causal factors or 'opportunity gaps' can be identified as sources of educational disadvantage? (c) What instructional responses designed to respond to these opportunity gaps are implied by the research evidence? Each of these questions is discussed in the sections that follow.

Which Students Experience Disproportionate Underachievement?

The international literature on patterns of academic achievement (e.g. OECD, 2010d; Van Avermaet *et al.*, 2018) identifies three groups (excluding students with special educational needs) that are commonly seen as potentially educationally disadvantaged: (a) students whose L1 is different from the language of school instruction, (b) students from low-SES backgrounds and (c) students from communities that have been marginalised or excluded from educational and social opportunities as a result of discrimination in the wider society.

Table 6.2 specifies some of the societal conduits through which these potential opportunity gaps operate to create educational disadvantage. It also identifies evidence-based educational interventions that respond to these potential disadvantages. Some communities in different countries are characterised by all three risk factors (e.g. many Spanish-speaking students in the United States, many Turkish-speaking students in different European countries). In other cases, only one risk factor may be operating (e.g. middle-class African American students in the United States, middle-class white Romanian students in Italy). Although these three sets of social conditions constitute risk factors for students' academic success, they become realised as actual educational disadvantage only when the school fails to respond appropriately or reinforces the negative impact of the broader social factors.

As noted previously, researchers concerned with each of these three sources of potential educational disadvantage have worked largely in isolation from each other. Issues related to linguistically diverse students have been addressed primarily by applied linguists concerned with second language learning and bilingual education issues. For the most part, these researchers have not focused directly on the ways in which social disadvantage or societal power relations affect patterns of student achievement. The analyses presented in August and Shanahan (2006, 2008a), Genesee *et al.* (2006), and the California Department of Education (2010) volumes reflect this orientation.

Analyses of the ways in which low-SES undermines student achievement have been published by researchers concerned with school improvement and educational reform in general. Researchers such as David Berliner (2009), Linda Darling-Hammond (2010), Jonathan Kozol (2005), Pedro Noguera (2003), Robert Rothstein (2004) among others have highlighted opportunity gaps faced by socially disadvantaged and racialised students and have also identified specific ways in which schools can address these opportunity gaps (e.g. Carter & Welner, 2013). Some of these researchers have focused on pedagogical issues (e.g. Boykin & Noguera, 2011) but, for the most part, they have not directly addressed problematic issues related to literacy instruction or the relative merits of bilingual education compared to English-medium programmes.

Issues related to racialised/marginalised students have been addressed by researchers focused on critical pedagogy which is designed to challenge the ways in which societal power structures undermine the educational opportunities afforded to students from marginalised communities (e.g. Wink, 2010). Prominent anti-oppressive critical approaches been variously labelled culturally relevant (Ladson-Billings, 1995), culturally responsive (Gay, 2010) and culturally sustaining (Paris, 2012). These researchers focus primarily on the ways in which power differentials and systemic racism affect the academic development of students from racialised communities. Researchers concerned with multicultural education in the United States (e.g. Banks, 2016; Nieto & Bode, 2018) have also addressed these issues and have highlighted the need for schools to adopt a critical antiracist orientation to issues of systemic racism. Researchers whose focus has been on the effects of racism and other forms of educational discrimination have addressed how to implement antiracist education (e.g. Dei, 1996; Lee, 1985), but have tended to focus less on issues related to bilingual education, second language learning, and approaches to literacy instruction.

Obviously, important contributions to understanding the roots of underachievement and ways of reversing underachievement have been made by researchers representing all three of these broad orientations. Several researchers have drawn from more than one of the three orientations and so the boundaries sketched above are by no means rigid. For example, the prolific scholarly writing of Ofelia García (e.g. 2009, 2017), although rooted in applied linguistics, has highlighted the need to inject critical antiracist perspectives into the education of linguistically minoritised students both in bilingual and English-medium programmes.

One of the first initiatives to bring bilingual education into dialogue with critical pedagogy and literacy education was the volume published by the California Association for Bilingual Education entitled *Reclaiming Our Voices: Bilingual Education, Critical Pedagogy & Praxis* (Frederickson, 1995). The essence of the construct of *empowerment*, understood as the collaborative creation of power, was expressed by Adriana Jasso and Rosalba Jasso, two high school students who had immigrated from Mexico several years previously. In their teacher Bill Terrazas' class, they found their voice:

> The most exciting thing we can remember is going into the classroom and having one of those deep and powerful dialogues [in which] we shared and examined our own lives. ... Our classroom was full of human knowledge; all of us knew something different and we were confident enough to share it with each other. We had a teacher who believed in us; he didn't hide out power; he advertised it. (Jasso & Jasso, 1995: 252)

Despite these attempts to bridge the gap between different interpretive lens, for the most part researchers whose focus is on social disadvantage and/or critical pedagogy have not addressed issues related to language and literacy in any detail. By the same token, applied linguists focused on language issues and cognitive psychologists concerned with reading and literacy issues have largely ignored the impact of power relations and identity negotiation. The framework presented in this section attempts to integrate these various perspectives with the goal of identifying coherent instructional responses that can be pursued individually and collectively by educators within schools.

Opportunity gaps associated with underachievement

As noted previously, none of the risk factors outlined in Table 6.2 operates as a causal agent in isolation. They become associated with underachievement primarily when combined with other risk factors (e.g. home-school language switch, low-SES, marginalised status) and/or in the absence of effective evidence-based instruction that addresses the risk factor. For example, a home–school language switch becomes an educational disadvantage only when the school fails to provide appropriate instructional supports required to enable students to learn the school language and catch up academically. Similarly, the effects of racism in the wider society can be significantly ameliorated when the school implements instruction that affirms students' identities and actively challenges the devaluation of students and communities in the wider society.

Table 6.2 Evidence-based instructional responses to sources of potential underachievement.

Student background	Linguistically Diverse	Low-SES	Marginalized Status
Sources of potential disadvantage	Failure to understand instruction due to home-school language differences	Inadequate healthcare and/or nutrition	Societal discrimination
		Housing segregation	Low teacher expectations
		Lack of cultural and material resources in the home due to poverty	Stereotype threat
		Limited access to print in home and school	Stigmatization of Ll/L2 language varieties
			Identity devaluation
Evidence-based instructional response	Scaffold comprehension and production of language across the curriculum	Maximize print access and literacy engagement	Connect instruction to students' lives
	Engage students' multilingual repertoires		Decolonize curriculum and instruction through linguistically and culturally sustaining pedagogy
	Reinforce academic language across the curriculum	Reinforce academic language across the curriculum	Valorize and build on L1/L2 language varieties
			Affirm student identities in association with academic engagement

With respect to *linguistically diverse students*, the risk factor is fairly obvious: if newcomer multilingual students do not understand the language of instruction, and if minimal support is provided to enable them to access curriculum content and learn the school language, they are very likely to fall behind their native-speaking peers in academic progress. This is particularly problematic for newcomer students at the secondary level who have limited time to catch up academically and gain the educational qualifications that will determine their futures.

Many of the sources of potential underachievement associated with *social disadvantage* are beyond the capacity of individual schools to address (e.g. housing segregation) but the potential negative effects of other factors can be ameliorated by school policies and instructional practices. In this regard, a major source of potential disadvantage is the limited access to print that many low-SES students experience in their homes, neighborhoods, and schools (Duke, 2000; Neuman & Celano, 2001). Additionally, the increased pressure that teachers in schools serving low-SES students experience to ensure that these students meet academic expectations often results in more limited curriculum options and pedagogy that is less stimulating and inquiry-based (Cummins, 2007b; Isola & Cummins, 2020). The logical inference that derives from these differences is that schools serving low-SES students should (a) immerse them in a print-rich environment in order to promote literacy engagement across the curriculum and (b) focus in a sustained way on how academic language works and enable students to take ownership of academic language by using it for powerful (i.e. identity-affirming) purposes.

It is important to note that the construct of literacy engagement involves a socialisation process that goes beyond simply solitary reading. As reading theorist Frank Smith (1988) pointed out more than 30 years ago, all learning is social, and developing strong literacy skills involves *joining the literacy club* where learners engage in reading and writing (or various kinds of media production) together with other members of the club: 'The classroom should be a place full of meaningful and useful reading and writing activities, where participation is possible without evaluation and collaboration is always available' (1988: 12). Uccelli and Phillips Galloway (2018: 69) make a similar point in emphasising the importance of complementing extensive exposure to engaging texts with 'plenty of opportunities for meaningful text-based discussions and writing'. They advocate a multipronged approach 'that exposes students to language through speech and print, and that scaffolds understanding and language skills through text-based discussion'.[7]

With respect to students from *marginalised communities*, the central risk factor is devaluation of identity expressed through the interrelated impact of various forms of direct and institutionalised racism, stereotype threat, and low teacher expectations. The effects of constant devaluation of culture are manifested in the well-documented phenomenon of *stereotype threat* (Steele, 1997). Stereotype threat refers to the deterioration of individuals' task performance in contexts where negative stereotypes about their social group are communicated to them. This impact of negative stereotypes clearly reflects the intersection of societal power relations, identity negotiation, and task performance.

Among linguistically diverse students, devaluation of identity is frequently enacted in the process of excluding, either explicitly or implicitly, students' home languages from the life of the school. Despite increasing evidence of the benefits of bilingualism for students' cognitive and academic growth, schools in many contexts continue to prohibit students from using their L1 within the school, thereby communicating to students the inferior status of their home languages and devaluing the identities of speakers of these languages (e.g. Agirdag, 2010; Agirdag & Vanlaar, 2016).

It is important to note that some bilingual programmes may also contribute to devaluation of minoritised students' identities if they fail to affirm the legitimacy of the varieties of students' home languages that they bring to the classroom (Alfaro & Bartolomé, 2017; McCollum, 1999). As Escamilla *et al.* (2014) point out, the majority of Latinx students currently in US classrooms are simultaneous bilinguals who frequently speak varieties of Spanish that are influenced by contact with English. Teachers need to validate and extend these language varieties, ideally in a programme that focuses on developing literacy in Spanish and English simultaneously and fosters both language awareness and two-way transfer across languages. The *Literacy Squared* programme developed and evaluated by Escamilla and colleagues over the past 15 years illustrates powerfully the benefits of this approach (e.g. Soltero-González *et al.*, 2016).

Power relations associated with devaluation of identity are typical of colonial contexts where the coloniser adopts a self-image of inherent superiority in relation to the colonised and works to ensure that the colonised internalise a sense of their own inherent inferiority (Fanon, 1967). Similar processes of 'cultural invasion' (Freire, 1970) have been inflicted on Indigenous groups in many parts of the world. In these contexts, students' home languages are typically suppressed, their community funds of knowledge dismissed as irrelevant to 'education', and the curriculum and instruction they experience are infused with racist assumptions that reinforce low teacher expectations (Battiste, 2013; Delpit, 1995; López-Gopar, 2016; Macedo, 2019; Salaün, 2013; Skutnabb-Kangas, 2000).

Canadian First Nations educator and scholar Marie Battiste (2013: 175) expressed this reality very clearly: 'Every school is either a site of reproduction or site of change. In other words, education can be liberating, or it can domesticate and maintain domination. It can sustain colonization in neo-colonial ways or it can decolonize'. Battiste's assessment highlights not only the historical and current reality of identity destruction among

Indigenous youth in schools across Canada and internationally, but also the opportunity for schools to repudiate neocolonial structures of disempowerment. The empowerment framework (Figure 5.1) similarly identifies teacher agency or choice as a central pivot in challenging the ways that coercive relations of power manifest themselves within schools and educational systems more generally.

Evidence-based instructional responses

As noted previously in this chapter, international research on the education of multilingual students has highlighted a variety of instructional strategies that respond directly to the potential causes of educational disadvantage among linguistically diverse, socially disadvantaged, and marginalised students. These strategies are incorporated into the framework (Table 6.2). All of the strategies are relevant to the three 'categories' of underachieving students, but some strategies respond more specifically to the potential sources of disadvantage affecting one group more than others. For example, scaffolding comprehension and production of language is particularly relevant for students who are learning the language of instruction whereas decolonising instruction and affirming students' identities respond directly to the experience of students from marginalised groups whose identities have been devalued in the wider society.

These instructional strategies overlap and intersect as they respond to the opportunity gaps that contribute to multilingual students' underachievement. For example, as described in Chapter 11, projects carried out in Canada and elsewhere have encouraged newcomer students to write in their home language about topics that connect with their lives and then translate this writing to English (e.g. Cummins & Early, 2011). These projects not only engage students' multilingual repertoires and affirm students' identities as creative writers with multilingual talents, but also scaffold students' learning of the school language as they collaborate with other students and adults to translate their writing from their L1 to the school language. This translation process was supported by various human and technological resources depending on what was available in different contexts (e.g. teachers or educational assistants who speak community languages, parents with some fluency in the school language, other multilingual students, community volunteers, and even technological resources such as Google Translate).

The intersections of dual language writing, identity, and learning are poignantly described by Hira, a Grade 5 student learning English in teacher Lisa Leoni's ESL classroom in the Toronto area. As described in Chapter 11, Lisa encouraged her students to write in their home languages as well as in English so that they could use their full cognitive and multilingual resources in learning:

When I am allowed to write stories in Urdu, I feel very comfortable because when I write English its difficult for me. If I write in Urdu I feel very comfortable because in Pakistan People speak in Urdu and we also write in Urdu. Teacher give me a little work to do but I want to be smart and I want to do a lot of work. Teacher gives the little work because I can't speak in English. I want to be smart to tell teacher I know English very much. (original punctuation and spelling retained)

With respect to instructional strategies that respond to social disadvantage, the relevance of promoting literacy engagement has been demonstrated in multiple studies that have reported a strong relationship between reading engagement and reading achievement. Teachers, individually and collectively within schools, can't do much to reverse the effects of social realities such as housing segregation or food insecurity, but they have considerable influence on how they develop students' literacy skills. The research data show very clearly that immersing low-SES students in a print-rich school environment can contribute significantly to reversing underachievement (see Appendix 6.1).

How can schools counteract the negative effects of societal power relations that devalue minority group identities? If devaluation of identity alienates students from active engagement in learning, then it is clear that educators, both individually and collectively, must challenge this devaluation by implementing instructional strategies that enable students to develop 'identities of competence' (Manyak, 2004) in the school context. These instructional strategies will communicate high expectations to students regarding their ability to succeed academically and support them in meeting academic demands by affirming their identities and connecting curriculum to their lives. This process of creating contexts of empowerment by connecting instruction to students' lives was vividly illustrated by Lisa Delpit:

> To deny students their own expert knowledge is to disempower them. Amanda Branscombe, when she was working with Black high school students classified as 'slow learners', had the students analyze RAP songs to discover their underlying patterns. The students became the experts in explaining to the teacher the rules for creating a new RAP song. The teacher then used the patterns the students identified as a base to begin an explanation of the structure of grammar, and then of Shakespeare's plays. Both student and teacher are expert at what they know best. (Delpit, 1988: 288)

In multilingual contexts, connecting to students' lives automatically implies engaging their multilingual resources. For example, research carried out over the past 20 years in postcolonial and Indigenous education contexts, has highlighted the benefits of *L1-based multilingual education programmes* that use students' home languages as mediums of instruction at least through to the end of primary school and ideally into secondary school (e.g. Benson & Kosonen, 2021; Heugh *et al.*, 2012; Mohanty, 2019). Benson (2019: 121) expressed this point as follows: 'Recent research suggests that access, equity and empowerment of non-dominant groups requires a systematic approach to maintaining and developing non-dominant languages in order to create the strongest foundation possible for literacy and learning'. Analysis of multilingual contexts where formal research on these issues has not been carried out (e.g. Iran) reaches similar conclusions (e.g. Kalan, 2016).

Conclusion

Underachievement is observed predominantly among linguistically diverse students who are also experiencing the effects of social disadvantage and/or discrimination and devaluation of identity both in schools and in the wider society. Thus, instruction must also address the sources of potential disadvantage experienced by low-SES and marginalised group students. Appropriate instructional responses will include maximising students' engagement with literacy (ideally in both L1 and L2) and enabling them to use language powerfully in ways that enhance their academic and personal self-concept. In a social context where the identities of marginalised group communities have been devalued, effective identity-affirming instruction requires that educators, individually and collectively, challenge the societal power structures that position students as socially inferior and less capable academically. For multilingual students, this challenge to societal power structures will include recognising students' home languages as intellectual accomplishments and mobilising these languages as resources for learning within the classroom.

This analysis of educational underachievement among multilingual immigrant-background students differs from most previous analyses in the following ways:

- It asserts that underachievement is not directly related to the switch between the language of the home and the language of the school. Instead, underachievement is rooted in the failure of schools to respond in an evidence-based way to the challenges minoritised students face as a result of (a) poverty, (b) racism and other forms of discrimination and (c) the need to learn the school language, often with minimal support from the school.
- It asserts that educators within schools, working individually and collectively, *can* challenge the operation of societal power structures by implementing evidence-based instructional strategies that (a) support students in learning the language of instruction, (b) promote literacy engagement across the curriculum and (c) affirm student identities in association with powerful uses of L1 and L2.

Notes

(1) As one example of the widespread concerns about PISA, 83 prominent educators and academics from around the world wrote an open letter entitled *OECD and Pisa tests are damaging education worldwide* to Dr Andreas Schleicher, director of the PISA project. The letter was published in *The Guardian* newspaper (May 6, 2014). The major damage to education was identified as follows:

> Finally, and most importantly: the new Pisa regime, with its continuous cycle of global testing, harms our children and impoverishes our classrooms, as it inevitably involves more and longer batteries of multiple-choice testing, more scripted 'vendor'-made lessons, and less autonomy for teachers. In this way Pisa has further increased the already high stress level in schools, which endangers the wellbeing of students and teachers. (*The Guardian*, May 6, 2014)

Certainly, the widespread use of high-stakes standardised tests, scripted 'teacher-proof' lessons, and suppression of teacher autonomy have all exerted highly negative effects on the effectiveness of education in general and on the life experiences of teachers and students in particular (see, for example, Cummins, 2007b; Isola & Cummins, 2020). However, all these trends were well-established in both the United States and United Kingdom (and many other countries) long before the PISA data began to exert an impact on educational policy making. It is worth noting that the OECD (2010b: 50) itself reported no educational benefit to the systematic use of standardised tests and deplored the 'punitive' accountability system operating in the United States subsequent to the implementation of the No Child Left Behind legislation in 2002 (OECD, 2010b: 75). In short, it is important to view the PISA data critically and cautiously, but it is also important to acknowledge the impact of PISA findings on discussions regarding equity in education. For example, PISA has consistently reported that the most effective educational systems are also the most equitable insofar as they have lower achievement gaps between different SES groups (e.g. OECD, 2010d). In an ideal world where scientific data outweighed entrenched ideologies, this kind of finding might have exerted more of an impact on educational policy than it has to this point.

(2) The concept of *opportunity gaps* has been discussed by numerous researchers in recent years to highlight potential sources of minoritised students' underachievement (e.g. Blankstein & Noguera, 2016; Boykin & Noguera, 2011; Carter & Welner, 2013; see also http://schottfoundation.org/). Isola and Cummins described the concept as follows:

> These opportunity gaps include social conditions, such as segregated and unsafe housing, inadequate access to health care and nutrition, and poverty, which reduces parents' ability to provide access to books and other cultural resources. Opportunity gaps also derive from educational conditions, such as lack of access to early childhood education, attendance at under-resourced schools staffed by inexperienced teachers, and instructional approaches focused on preparing students to take high-stakes standardized tests rather than engaging them in intellectual inquiry and critical thinking. (Isola & Cummins, 2020: vi)

As noted in Table 6.2, fewer opportunities to gain access to print and engage actively with literacy represents a major opportunity gap for low-income students. Guthrie *et al.* (2001: 159) reported a significant impact of opportunity to read on students' reading performance on the National Assessment of Educational Progress (NAEP): 'The effect of opportunity to read on achievement was mediated by engaged reading, meaning that engagement was the link between the instructional practice of providing reading opportunity and measured achievement in reading'.

(3) The attribution of underachievement to insufficient exposure to the dominant language by OECD researchers clearly echoes assumptions underlying the discredited Separate Underlying Proficiency model and the associated maximum exposure hypothesis discussed in Chapter 3. Nevertheless, arguments such as these, based on the PISA data, have played a major role in contexts such as Germany where the merits of bilingual education programmes as compared to monolingual German-only programmes have been vigorously debated among both researchers and policymakers (e.g. Esser, 2006; Gögolin, 2005).

(4) In addition to their problematic interpretation of a causal relationship between underachievement and speaking a minority language at home, Stanat and Christensen (2006) and Christensen and Stanat (2007) interpreted the research on bilingual education and the interdependence hypothesis in inaccurate ways (see Cummins, 2008c for a detailed analysis). This is illustrated by their characterisation of the interdependence hypothesis:

> Traditionally, the 'interdependence hypothesis' dominated research on the effectiveness of language support. This hypothesis suggests that students will only be able to become proficient in a second language if they already have a good command of their first language. Although few people today maintain the strict version of this hypothesis, the assumption that first-language proficiency is a crucial prerequisite for second-language acquisition is still widespread. Moreover, the empirical support for this assumption is weak. (Christensen & Stanat, 2007: 3-4)

As should be clear from Chapter 3, this description seriously misinterprets the interdependence hypothesis. The Cummins (1979a) article, which they cited, explicitly rejected simplistic linguistic explanations of minority students' academic difficulties such as the UNESCO (1953: 11) statement that 'it is axiomatic that the best medium for teaching a child is his mother tongue'. Furthermore, Christensen and Stanat's assessment that the empirical support for the interdependence hypothesis is 'weak' is contradicted by the findings of numerous comprehensive reviews of the research literature (e.g. Dressler & Kamil, 2006; Lindholm-Leary & Borsato, 2006). Their skepticism in regard to the efficacy of bilingual education ignores extensive research showing 'that language-minority students instructed primarily in their native language (primarily Spanish) as well as English perform, on average, better on English reading measures than language-minority students instructed only in their second language (English in this case). This is the case at both elementary and secondary levels' (Snow, 2006: 639). These findings are clearly interpretable within the context of the interdependence hypothesis (see Chapters 3 and 9 for detailed analysis).

(5) These broad trends can be illustrated by the Swedish PISA 2009 data. Garbe *et al.* (2016) note that there was a difference of 115 points (equivalent to almost three years of schooling) in reading performance among Swedish 15-year-old students who reported being highly engaged in reading (top quarter) and those who reported being much less engaged in reading (bottom quarter). This difference was significantly higher than the average in other European countries (99 points difference). Large differences in reading performance were also observed between students who were aware of efficient reading strategies and those who were much less aware of these strategies (understanding, remembering, and summarising strategies).

(6) As noted earlier in this chapter, some OECD authors have inappropriately interpreted correlational data as causal and argued that immigrant-background students' use of L1 at home contributes to underachievement. However, at least one OECD publication has advocated more affirmative (and evidence-based) school policies in relation to the bilingual realities of immigrant-background students:

> Valuing the mother tongue of immigrant students is an essential part of developing a positive and appreciative approach to diversity and identity. It means seeing

students' language capacities as part of their personal, social and cultural identity and welcoming it as a tool for learning and understanding. (OECD, 2010c: 49)

(7) Smith's (1988) notion of 'joining the literacy club' draws on the same considerations as Gee's (2001) construct of *affinity group* in which individuals who are 'members' of the group share an identity as a 'certain kind of person'. People in the group share *'allegiance to, access to, and participation in specific practices* that provide each of the group's members the requisite experiences' (2001: 105) (emphasis original). According to Gee, engagement with the shared practices that define the affinity group generates the power of belonging for its members.

The significance of linking literacy with students' emerging identities was brought home to me when I visited an elementary school in southern Ontario with a group of visiting Italian educators and policymakers on June 22, 2010. Outside one of the classrooms, students had displayed a series of printouts that began with the sentence starter *Reading makes me powerful because*... Obviously, the teacher had been discussing with students what the purpose of reading is, and they then wrote about why and how reading made them powerful. Among the insights shared by students were the following:

• Reading makes me powerful because I get smarter and I learn more facts. I learn new words and I will never forget.
• Reading makes me powerful because I learn new words and I love reading!
• Reading makes me powerful because when I grow up I can find a better job than people who can't read. Somebody can also trick you to do something that will get you in trouble [if you can't read well]. Reading gives you new words to learn. It gives my brain new ideas. It helps your vocabulary so when you need to write something you can use longer and harder words. In school you can get a better mark using more words.

The last observation reflects an exuberance about reading that unfortunately is denied to many students in our schools today.

Appendix 6.1 Empirical Support for the Construct of 'Opportunity to Read'

In introducing the construct of *opportunity to read*, Hiebert and Martin (2010) point out that in any sphere of human endeavour – medical diagnosis, flying an aircraft, or programming computers – people become proficient by participating extensively in the activity. However, when it comes to teaching students to read in schools, policymakers, researchers, and many educators have paid little attention to the amount of reading that students actually do. Hiebert and Martin describe 'opportunity to read' as a critical but neglected construct in reading instruction.

In light of the fact that the role of print access and literacy engagement in promoting literacy expertise has been largely ignored by policymakers and many researchers (e.g. August & Shanahan, 2006), I have decided to supplement the summary of this research in Chapter 6 with a more detailed review in this Appendix. I can only speculate as to why some researchers are resistant to acknowledging this research. For some cognitive psychologists associated with scripted programmes such as 'direct instruction' (Carnine *et al.*, 2003), the roots of this resistance appear to lie in an antipathy to the notion of 'balanced literacy', which they interpret as a return to 'whole language' approaches that they perceive as neglecting explicit and systematic teaching of phonological awareness and phonics (see Cummins, 2007b, for analysis of these issues).

This ideological orientation was evident in the funding criteria adopted by the 'Reading First' evaluation panel established under the Bush administration to distribute funds to school districts with the goal of supporting low-income students to develop strong reading skills. This 'Reading First' programme, with a price tag of $6 billion, was implemented with admirable intentions but disastrously flawed logical and empirical assumptions. The evaluation panel withheld funding from states and school districts that proposed to use instructional approaches or programmes deemed to be 'balanced' or tainted by whole-language assumptions. As a result, its massive investment of funding failed to show any benefits for reading comprehension or reading engagement (Gamse *et al.*, 2008). A scathing review of the Reading First programme written by the United States Office of the Inspector General quoted an email exchange between the Reading First Director and a staff member regarding one of these instructional programmes in which the Director stated:

> 'Beat the [expletive deleted] out of them in a way that will stand up to any level of legal and [whole language] apologist scrutiny. Hit them over and over with definitive evidence that they are not SBRR [scientifically based reading research], never have been and never will be. They are trying to crash our party and we need to beat the [expletive deleted] out of them in front of all the other would-be party crashers who are standing on the front lawn waiting to see how we welcome these dirtbags. (Office of the Inspector General, 2006: 24)

Unfortunately, similar attitudes towards 'balanced literacy' are evident in the 'Science of Reading' movement that has emerged in the United States in recent years. Championed by journalist Emily Hanford (2018), this approach revisits the so-called 'reading wars' by once again setting up a false opposition between phonics and balanced literacy instruction. New York Times reporter, Dana Goldstein (2020) endorsed this false opposition as follows: 'The 'science of reading' stands in contrast to the 'balanced literacy' theory that many teachers are exposed to in schools of education. That theory holds that students can learn to read through exposure to a wide range of books that appeal to them, without too much emphasis on technically complex texts or sounding out words'.

This caricature of 'balanced literacy' is far from my understanding of the concept. I have always understood that a balanced literacy instructional approach focuses *equally* on ensuring that all students develop strong decoding skills and that they continue to expand their language development throughout the preschool and school years. Ironically, despite the fact that proponents of the 'Science of Reading' approach constantly invoke the National Reading Panel's (NPR) (2000) emphasis on systematic phonics instruction, they consistently fail to note that the NPR reported that systematic phonics instruction showed *no impact* on reading comprehension beyond Grade 1 for normally achieving and low achieving readers. They also fail to note that the NRP strongly advocated balanced approaches to reading and rejected any opposition between systematic phonics instruction and engagement with authentic texts (Cummins, 2007b). For example, the NRP emphasised that 'systematic phonics instruction should be integrated with other reading instruction to create a balanced reading programme' (2000: 2–136). The NRP also advocated the use of high-quality literature and cautioned that phonics 'should not become the dominant component in a reading programme, neither in the amount of time devoted to it nor in the significance attached' (2000: 2–136). The NRP expressed concern about 'the commonly heard call for "intensive, systematic" phonics instruction' (2000: 2–135) and drew attention to the possible effects of scripted programmes on teachers' orientation to instruction: 'Although scripts may standardize instruction, they may reduce teachers' interest in the teaching process or their motivation to teach phonics' (2000: 2–135).

In light of these ongoing unproductive debates about reading instruction, it may be timely to remind policymakers and media pundits that any invocation of the 'science of reading' should consider the actual empirical research, some of which is summarised below.

Studies Focused on the General School Population

Print access improves reading performance (Lindsay, 2010, 2018)

Print access and literacy engagement are obviously two sides of the same coin. Without ample access to print, literacy engagement is unlikely. The most comprehensive analysis of the relationship between print access and educational outcomes was carried out by Jim Lindsay (2010, 2018) who identified 11,616 potentially relevant reports on this topic. These reports were reduced to 108 research studies that were suitable for meta-analysis. Lindsay's meta-analysis of these studies concluded that print access plays a causal role in the development of reading skills.

Lindsay examined several categories of research studies. First, correlational studies showed highly significant effect sizes for the impact of print access on all outcome variables: attitudes towards reading, motivation to read, reading behaviour, basic language abilities, emergent literacy skills, reading performance, writing performance, and general achievement. Subsequent analyses focusing on 'rigorous' experimental and quasi-experimental research studies, found that 'interventions that lend print materials (e.g., books and magazines) to children or give print materials to children *cause* improved attitudes towards reading, increased reading behavior, improved emergent literacy skills, and improved reading performance' (2018: 50; emphasis original). When books are given to children (as opposed to just being lent) effects are also found for children's motivation to read. The effects of these print-access interventions were found to be considerably greater, on average, than those found for most other types of educational intervention. Lindsay summarised the overall outcomes of the meta-analysis as follows:

> The results confirm the intuitive belief held by many educators: Providing books and magazines to children—either by lending the materials to them or giving the materials to keep—improves their attitudes towards reading, the amount of reading that they do, their acquisition of basic literacy skills, and their reading performance. (Lindsay, 2010: 34)

The positive impact of print exposure increases over time (Mol & Bus, 2011)

This meta-analysis of the effects of print exposure and extensive reading covered the range of preschool to university. The authors reported moderate to strong relationships between print exposure and students' reading performance. They summarised their findings as follows:

> For all measures in the outcome domains of reading comprehension and technical reading and spelling, moderate to strong correlations with print exposure were found. The outcomes support an upward spiral of causality: Children who are more proficient in comprehension and technical reading and spelling skills read more; because of more print exposure, their comprehension and technical reading and spelling skills improved more with each year of education. For example, in preschool and kindergarten print exposure explained 12% of the variance in oral language skills, in primary school 13%, in middle school 19%, in high school 30%, and in college and university 34%. Moderate associations of print exposure with academic achievement indicate that frequent readers are more successful students. (Mol & Bus, 2011: 267)

Preschool print exposure accelerates literacy development (Neuman, 1999)

Neuman investigated the effects on children's language and literacy development of 'flooding' more than 330 child-care centers in the United States with high-quality children's books at a ratio of five books per child. The study sampled 400 3- and 4-year-old children randomly selected from 50 centers across 10 regions and 100 control children from comparable centers not involved in the project. Findings indicated that 'children's concepts of print, writing, letter name knowledge, and concepts of narrative improved substantially over the year's intervention compared to those of the control group (1999: 308). A follow-up study of a subsample in kindergarten produced what Neuman termed 'striking' results: 'Even after

6 months had elapsed, results indicated that the gains made by children in the Books Aloud program were still very much evident' (1999: 305).

Preschool 'literacy saturation' significantly predicts later reading comprehension in the adolescent years (Wylie & Thompson, 2003; Wylie *et al.*, 2006)

Wylie and colleagues' longitudinal research carried out in Aotearoa/ New Zealand from preschool through age 16 identified five components of early childhood environments that contribute significantly to students' academic and social progress through adolescence (age 16). These include (a) staff responsiveness to children, (b) staff actively guiding children in activities, (c) staff asking children open-ended questions, (d) staff joining children in their play and (e) providing a print-saturated environment. The first four components of what constitutes 'high-quality preschool environments' are not surprising in light of the importance of child-adult interaction in promoting children's development. However, the importance of a 'print-saturated' environment is seldom acknowledged in the US literature on preschool programmes. Most children from higher-SES backgrounds experience a 'print-saturated' environment in their homes during the preschool years but, unfortunately, this is rarely the case among children from lower-SES backgrounds.

Early childhood centers that achieved the highest rating for provision of a print-saturated environment encouraged print awareness in children's activities, they had a lot of printed material visible around the center at children's eye-level or just above, and they offered children a range of readily accessible books. By contrast, centers that were rated in the lowest category had no books, posters, or other forms of writing on display.

The longitudinal findings showed that at age 10, for children from low-income homes, there was a difference of 18 percentage points in reading comprehension between those who attended the least and most print-saturated early childhood centers. At age 14, students who had attended non-print-focused early childhood centers scored 12–15 percentage points lower than the three other quartile groups who had experienced greater print saturation in their early childhood centers.

The findings reported by Wylie and colleagues resonate with the conclusions of McGill-Franzen *et al.* (2002) who compared the orientation to literacy within five preschools serving students from varying SES backgrounds. The authors reported that preschools serving students from low-income predominantly African American backgrounds provided far fewer opportunities for children to become socialised into literacy than those serving a religious (Jewish) community and a university-affiliated community:

Children had less access to print, fewer opportunities to participate in literacy, and little experience listening to or discussing culturally relevant literature ... poor children and children of color are socialized to practice a different literacy, one that offers limited experiences with books and is less connected to personal and community identity. (McGill-Franzen *et al.*, 2002: 443)

Reading engagement exerts a causal impact on school achievement (Sulllivan & Brown, 2013)

In an ongoing British longitudinal study involving a nationally representative sample of several thousand students, Sullivan and Brown (2013) reported that children who were read to regularly by their parents at age 5 demonstrated significantly stronger performance on vocabulary, spelling and math tests administered at age 16 than those who did not experience this early exposure to books. Furthermore, the amount of pleasure reading students reported at age 10 significantly predicted later scores at age 16. The authors were able to demonstrate a causal relationship between reading engagement and reading achievement that was not dependent either on the socioeconomic background of the parents or on cognitive or academic ability: 'Once we controlled for the child's test scores at age five and ten, the influence of the child's own reading [at age 16] remained highly significant, suggesting that the positive link between leisure reading and cognitive outcomes is not purely due to more able children being more likely to read a lot, but that reading is actually linked to increased cognitive progress over time' (2013: 37).

Several other studies demonstrate the same pattern of significant relationships between print access/literacy engagement and reading achievement (e.g. Allington & McGill-Franzen, 2017, 2018; Cunningham & Stanovich, 1997; Sparks *et al.*, 2014). In short, multiple research studies provide highly credible evidence that literacy engagement plays a central role in literacy attainment. Research carried out specifically with L2 learners is consistent with the overall pattern of strong relationships between literacy engagement and academic language learning.

Studies Focused on L2 Learners

Extensive reading in L2 promotes L2 reading comprehension (Nakanishi, 2015)

This meta-analysis of 34 studies involving mainly university and secondary school students in Japan (total sample size = 3,942 participants) reported a moderately strong effect size (d = 0.46) for contrasts between groups that engaged in extensive reading in their L2 and those that did not engage in extensive L2 reading. Nakanishi concludes that 'the available research to date suggests that extensive reading improves students' reading proficiency and should be a part of language learning curricula' (2015: 6).

L2 reading is more effective than L2 teaching in promoting L2 learning (Elley, 1991, 2001; Elley & Mangubhai, 1983; Mangubhai, 2001)

In a tightly controlled experimental study, Elley and Mangubhai (1983) examined the effects of a 'book flood' programme in which grades 4/5 (1980) and grades 5/6 (1981) students learning English (L2) in Fiji simply read books either alone or with the guidance of their teacher during their 30-minute daily English lessons. The students who experienced the 'book flood' performed significantly better over a two-year period than students taught through more traditional methods. Elley (1991, 2001) similarly documented the superiority of book-based English language teaching programmes among elementary school students in a variety of other Asian contexts.

Numerous other research studies with multilingual students demonstrate the same pattern of results. These include Tizard *et al.* (1982), Hafiz and Tudor (1989), Collins (2005) and Roberts (2008).

One additional study (Chen *et al.*, 2018) involving a randomised book-reading intervention implemented in Uyghur-Mandarin bilingual preschools in Xinjiang Province in China is worth mentioning. The intervention took place over the course of one school year and involved not only the reading by teachers or bilingual classroom assistants of specially created Uyghur-Mandarin bilingual picture books to 4- and 5-year-old children, but also 20 minutes daily of language learning activities based on the themes and content of the picture books. There were 256 children participating in the experiment with 134 in classes randomly assigned to the intervention group and the remainder in classes assigned to the control group that did not experience the bilingual book reading intervention. Chen *et al.* (2018) reported that the intervention resulted in more rapid development of Chinese receptive vocabulary (effect size = 0.68) and Uyghur expressive vocabulary (effect size = 0.38). The authors conclude that 'well-designed book-reading programmes can benefit language minority children by supporting the development of both home and school languages simultaneously' (2018: 206).

This conclusion seems legitimate, but it is difficult to disaggregate the effects of more time spent by the teachers in reading picture books to children from the effects of additional focused vocabulary instruction associated with the book reading. The teachers in the intervention classrooms also received professional development on how to implement the book reading and language instruction intervention that the control teachers did not receive until the following year. Despite these cautions, the findings are obviously consistent with those of Neuman (1999) and Wylie *et al.* (2006) that 'literacy saturation' or 'book flooding' can significantly benefit preschool children's language and literacy development. Furthermore, in a bilingual pre-school context, the benefits extend to both languages. Unfortunately, enlightened preschool programmes that promote children's proficiency in both Uyghur (L1) and Chinese (L2) are no longer in operation in Xinjiang Province.

Part 2

Critical Analysis of Competing Theoretical Claims

Introduction

The chapters in Part 2 shift perspective from a narrative account of the evolution of theoretical constructs and frameworks to a more analytic focus on the underlying issues and the legitimacy of particular ways of framing phenomena related to the education of minoritised students. Although most of the interpretations of research findings and theoretical claims and conclusions presented in Part 1 have been broadly accepted by a majority of researchers in the field, controversy has persisted over the course of many years in relation to certain theoretical claims and constructs. Specifically, a number of researchers reject the legitimacy of the construct of 'academic language'. Criticism has also been directed at claims of linguistic interdependence and the construct of the 'common underlying proficiency' on the grounds that these constructs are rooted in static 'monoglossic' conceptions of bi/multilingualism rather than reflecting the dynamic 'heteroglossic' organisation of multilingual cognitive and linguistic functioning. Some variations of this perspective also reject the construct of specific languages as discrete conceptual entities, insisting that only the verb forms 'languaging' and 'translanguaging' are legitimate. Finally, the constructs of 'additive bilingualism' and 'additive approaches to bilingualism' have been rejected on the grounds that these constructs are permeated by discourses of appropriateness and raciolinguistic ideologies that stigmatise the nonstandard varieties of L1 and L2 spoken by minoritised students.

In order to evaluate the legitimacy of these critiques, together with the validity of the theoretical claims and constructs proposed in preceding chapters, it is essential to articulate explicit criteria for assessing the credibility of theoretical claims and the legitimacy of theoretical constructs in the broad area of language education (and the social sciences more generally). In Chapter 7, I identify three criteria for judging the legitimacy of any theoretical construct, claim or framework: (a) empirical adequacy, (b) logical coherence and (c) consequential validity. In subsequent chapters, these criteria are used to analyse opposing theoretical claims regarding academic language, linguistic interdependence, translanguaging and additive approaches to minoritised students' bilingualism.

In order to set the stage for analysis of alternative theoretical perspectives, it is important to be clear about the empirical foundation upon which theoretical arguments and claims are constructed. The research findings reviewed in Part 1 represent the structure that supports theoretical claims relating to the difference between academic and conversational language (CALP/BICS), crosslinguistic interdependence, and the impact of teacher-student identity negotiation as reflections of societal power relations. Any critique of these theoretical claims should identify to extent to which the theoretical claim is rejected because (a) it is not supported by the empirical data, (b) it is logically incoherent, or (c) it has resulted in problematic policies or instructional practices that undermine the educational opportunities experienced by minoritised students (consequential validity). The following propositions reflect the research findings outlined in Part 1:

- The language required for academic success in school differs in significant ways from the language we typically use in everyday conversational interactions.
- Immigrant-background students who are learning the school language as L2 typically require at least 5 years to catch up academically to native speakers; by contrast, relatively fluent everyday conversational fluency is usually acquired within 1–2 years.
- Consistently significant crosslinguistic relationships between L1 and L2 academic and literacy skills are observed when students have sustained opportunities in school to develop these skills.
- Sustained growth in reading and writing skills is strongly related to the extent to which students become actively engaged with literacy.
- Students from lower-income backgrounds frequently have significantly less access to print in their homes, neighborhoods, and schools than is the case with students from higher-income backgrounds.
- Multilingual students' home languages are *not* a cause of underachievement. Students' home languages represent important tools for thinking, communication within the family, and future economic and personal opportunities.
- In bilingual education programmes implemented for both 'minority' and 'majority' language students in countries around the world, students make relatively strong progress in the minority language at no cost to their academic development in the majority language. Minoritised students in bilingual programmes that sustain L1 literacy instruction through the course of elementary school and beyond typically develop stronger L2 literacy skills than comparison groups in L2-medium programmes.
- Even in countries committed to equality and quality schooling for all, societal power relations strongly influence the structure of schooling (curriculum, assessment, teacher education, home language support, etc.) and the interactions between teachers and students (negotiation of identity).

- Identity matters. Devaluation of minoritised students' academic and personal identities within schools is the fastest way to encourage them to disengage academically. By the same token, affirming students' personal, cultural, intellectual, and academic identities by means of linguistically and culturally sustaining instruction promotes academic engagement and achievement.

The four chapters in this section argue that the theoretical constructs of academic language, linguistic interdependence, and additive bilingualism are all consistent with the empirical data. Critiques of these constructs, as well as of the Council of Europe (2001, 2020) construct of *plurilingualism*, are characterised by a problematic pattern of logical *non-sequiturs*. Specifically, critics have attributed a variety of discriminatory instructional practices to these theoretical constructs without ever demonstrating a causal connection between the constructs and problematic instruction. For example, critics have argued that the constructs of 'academic language' and 'additive bilingualism' stigmatise minoritised students' fluid 'non-standard' language practices (e.g. Flores, 2019; García, 2020; Valdés, 2017). They have also argued that the construct of linguistic interdependence and teaching for crosslinguistic transfer reflect monoglossic ideologies that promote rigid separation of languages for instructional purposes. The construct of plurilingualism has also been implicated in promoting a neoliberal corporate agenda (e.g. Flores, 2013; García, 2018, 2020). The 'evidence' invoked to support these claims consists of examples of problematic instructional practices or of misguided broader policy initiatives. However, no logical or empirical connection has ever been established between the theoretical constructs and the problematic instructional policies and practices.

In other words, the theoretical constructs have been made the *scapegoat* for problematic instructional practices, despite the fact that there is no intrinsic, logical, or empirical connection between the two. To illustrate, the construct of academic language reflects clear differences between the language we typically use in everyday interpersonal contexts and the language and literacy demands of school subjects that increase as students progress through the grades (see Chapter 3). This distinction applies to the language demands faced by middle-class white students just as much as the demands faced by emergent bilingual and minoritised students. In other words, it is logically independent of particular instructional practices and says *nothing* in itself about how minoritised students should be educated. The fact that minoritised students continue to be miseducated in many countries around the world is not in any way intrinsically connected to the question of whether there are differences in the relative frequency with which certain discourse structures, grammatical constructions and specialised vocabulary are employed in everyday face-to-face contexts as compared to academic contexts.

An analogy can be made with the concept of democracy. The concept of democracy is systematically perverted by autocratic regimes around the world and is also undermined in some countries that ostensibly proclaim their commitment to universal suffrage (e.g. through widespread and ongoing attempts to suppress the voting rights of racialised minorities, as in the 2020 US presidential election, and virtually all federal elections in the United States over the past 200+ years). However, the operation of these power relations that undermine the democratic process does not invalidate the concept of democracy itself. It is logically invalid to scapegoat or blame *democracy itself* for these perversions of democracy in practice.

7 How Do We Assess the Legitimacy of Theoretical Constructs and Claims?

Virtually all of the issues discussed in this book revolve around the relationships between educational research, theory and instructional practice. Academic debates, media controversies and policy decisions regarding the education of minoritised students have all invoked varying interpretations of the empirical research on bilingual education. Competing theoretical claims, propelled as much by 'commonsense' and political ideologies as by research findings, have also vied for ascendency both in the media and in the pages of academic journals. For example, as noted previously, efforts to provide bilingual education for minority groups in the United States have been strenuously opposed by many media commentators and policymakers who characterised bilingual education as counter-intuitive on the grounds that less instruction through English must surely mean less opportunity to acquire English. President Ronald Reagan was one of those who expressed this perspective in a speech on March 2, 1981, arguing that 'it is absolutely wrong and against American concepts to have a bilingual education program that is now openly, admittedly dedicated to preserving their native language and never getting them adequate in English so they can go out into the job market' (Clines, 1981).

Concerns, rooted in ideology, have also been expressed that education partly through Spanish might promote separatist tendencies and fracture national unity. Even commentators widely viewed as 'liberal' expressed concern that bilingual education would fragment the United States. For example, eminent historian Arthur Schlesinger Jr., in his 1991 book *The Disuniting of America*, declared:

> In recent years the combination of the ethnicity cult with a flood of immigration from Spanish-speaking countries has given bilingualism new impetus. ... Alas, bilingualism has not worked out as planned: rather the contrary. Testimony is mixed, but indications are that bilingual education retards rather than expedites the movement of Hispanic children into the English-speaking world and that it promotes segregation rather than it does integration. Bilingualism shuts doors. It nourishes self-ghettoization, and ghettoization nourishes racial antagonism. (Schlesinger, 1991: 108–109)

Schlesinger goes on to assert that monolingual English-only education is required to give minoritised students the opportunity to learn English and succeed in the society: 'Using some language other than English dooms people to second-class citizenship in American society. ... Monolingual education opens doors to the larger world' (1991: 109).

The arguments that 'bilingualism shuts doors' and 'monolingual education opens doors to the larger world' are clearly absurd. But what is interesting in the present context is that assertions such as these can be made by serious scholars with no sense of obligation to provide supporting empirical evidence or to assess the extent to which their claims embody contradictory logic. Clearly, explicit criteria are required to evaluate the credibility of alternative theoretical claims that address issues of social and educational policy.

The need for explicit criteria can be further illustrated by examining the superficially more credible claim that 'time on task' is the major variable determining attainment in any school subject. Based on this theoretical claim, it has been argued in several contexts that maximum exposure to the school language is essential for minority group students to learn the language rapidly and effectively. In the United States context, for example, Rosalie Pedalino Porter in her book *Forked Tongue: The Politics of Bilingual Education* made the case for time on task as follows:

> Effective time on task—the amount of time spent learning—is, as educators know, the single greatest predictor of educational achievement; this is at least as true, if not more so, for low-socioeconomic-level, limited-English students. Children learn what they are taught, and if they are taught mainly in Spanish for several years, their Spanish-language skills will be far better than their English-language ones. (Porter, 1990: 63–64)

Similar arguments were made by Rossell and Baker (1996) and Rossell and Kuder (2005). The research reviews conducted by these authors claimed to demonstrate that 'structured immersion' programmes (i.e. monolingual English-medium programmes) are superior in their outcomes to bilingual programmes that use students' L1 as a medium of instruction in addition to English. These literature reviews have been strongly criticised on multiple grounds (e.g. Cummins, 1999), but, again, they raise the issue of what criteria should be invoked to assess the credibility of varying interpretations of both the research findings and theoretical claims made on the basis of these research findings. For example, what criteria should be used to judge theoretical constructs and claims I have made in the preceding chapters such as the distinction between conversational and academic language proficiency, the interdependence/common underlying proficiency hypothesis, and the claims regarding the role of literacy engagement and identity texts in promoting minoritised students' academic engagement and attainment?

In the next section, I summarise arguments I have advanced since the early 1980s regarding the relationship between research, theory, and instructional practice. I then elaborate the three criteria, mentioned previously, for evaluating the legitimacy or credibility of any theoretical construct, claim, or framework: (a) empirical adequacy, (b) logical coherence and (c) consequential validity. I illustrate the application of these criteria with reference to empirical and theoretical claims made by researchers concerned with the academic achievement of minoritised students.

Research, Theory, Policy and Instructional Practice

Research findings become interpretable for policy and practice only through theory

During the 1980s and 1990s, the only thing that academic opponents and advocates of bilingual education seemed to agree on with respect to research on the effectiveness of bilingual programmes was that it was of almost universally poor quality (August & Hakuta, 1997; Baker & de Kanter, 1981; Greene, 1998; Rossell & Baker, 1996). Greene, for example, could find only 11 'methodologically acceptable' studies out of the hundreds of potentially relevant studies in the research literature. The credibility of even these studies was questioned by other researchers (see Cummins, 1999). The reality is that it has proven extremely difficult to carry out experimental or quasi-experimental research in complex educational contexts where the treatment variable of interest (e.g. bilingual instruction) is intertwined and interacting with many other variables that affect programme outcomes.

In opposition to the perspective reflected in the dominant controlled experimentation research paradigm, I argued that there is an enormous amount of relevant and interpretable research, both internationally and within the United States, that speaks directly to the bilingual education policy issues (e.g. Cummins, 1983, 1999). I suggested that the policy issues have remained confused and contested at least partly because the bulk of the relevant research has been largely ignored, both by advocates and opponents of bilingual education. The relevance of this research is not apparent within the dominant paradigm because many of the studies fail to meet stringent criteria of acceptability within this paradigm. However, when we examine the research from the perspective of an alternative theoretically oriented scientific paradigm, its relevance is immediately apparent.

The alternative paradigm claims that the relevance of research for policy is mediated through theory. In complex educational contexts, research findings become relevant for policy purposes only in the context of coherent theoretical models or frameworks. It is the *theory* rather than the individual research findings that permits the generation of predictions about programme outcomes under different conditions. Research findings themselves cannot be directly applied across contexts. For example, the fact that students in a Spanish-English bilingual programme in New York City performed well academically in relation to grade norms (Beykont, 1994) tells us very little, by itself, about whether a similar programme might work with Turkish-speaking immigrant-background students in Hamburg, Germany.

However, when certain patterns are replicated across a wide range of sociolinguistic and sociopolitical contexts, the accumulation of consistent findings suggests that some stable underlying principle is at work. This principle can then be stated as a theoretical proposition or hypothesis from which predictions can be derived and tested through the accumulation of additional data.

This process is in the mainstream of scientific inquiry. In most scientific disciplines, knowledge is generated not by evaluating the effects of particular treatments under strictly controlled conditions but by observing phenomena, forming hypotheses to account for the observed phenomena, testing these hypotheses against additional data, and gradually refining the hypotheses into more comprehensive theories or models that have broader explanatory and predictive power.

This process can be illustrated through the prediction of weather patterns. Scientists generate knowledge in this discipline by observing phenomena (e.g. the conditions under which hurricanes appear) and build up theoretical models that attempt to predict these phenomena. With further observations they test and refine their predictive models. There is no control group, for obvious reasons, yet theory-based predictions are constantly being tested and refined. In the same way, I argued that a much wider body of research data is both theoretically and policy relevant than typical reviews in the area of bilingual education suggested. For example, case studies of particular programmes, or evaluations that assess student progress in relation to grade norms, are potentially theoretically relevant. They become relevant for theory and policy when their outcomes are assessed in relation to the predictions derived from particular hypotheses or theoretical frameworks.

In the context of educating multilingual learners, the process of knowledge generation can be illustrated by the articulation and ongoing testing of the interdependence hypothesis. As outlined in Chapter 3, the hypothesis was initially advanced to account for a variety of research findings that were available in the 1970s. It was stated formally in Cummins (1980c, 1981b), specifying explicitly the conditions under which positive L1/L2 relationships could be anticipated. Since the time of its initial articulation, a large number of additional studies have been carried out that have produced findings consistent with the hypothesis under a wide variety of sociolinguistic and sociopolitical conditions (see Chapter 9). These emerging findings have also served to refine the developmental aspects of the hypothesis, the dimensions of academic language proficiency that are involved in crosslinguistic transfer, and the extent to which linguistic similarity between the bilingual's two languages influences the degree of L1/L2 relationship. The process of theory generation and refinement parallels the process of predicting weather patterns and other scientific phenomena.

In contrast to research findings, theories are, by definition, applicable across contexts. The validity of any theoretical principle is assessed precisely by how well it can account for the research findings in a variety of contexts. If a theory cannot account for a particular set of research findings, then it is an inadequate or incomplete theory. Although no individual research finding can 'prove' a theory or definitively confirm a hypothesis, any research finding can disconfirm or refute a theory or hypothesis. Thus, the criterion of validity for any hypothesis is extremely stringent – it must be consistent with *all* the research data or at least be able to account in a credible way for inconsistencies (e.g. inadequate implementation of a programme).

Viewed through this lens, the two hypotheses that dominated debate surrounding bilingual education in the United States during the 1970s and 1980s, namely the *linguistic mismatch* and *maximum exposure* hypotheses, are both patently inadequate. The linguistic mismatch hypothesis predicts that in every situation where there is a switch between home language and school language, students will encounter academic difficulties. The maximum exposure hypothesis, as articulated with reference to bilingual education in the United States, predicts that any form of bilingual education that reduces the amount of instructional time through the medium of English will result in academic difficulties in English. As noted previously, both of these predictions are refuted by a massive amount of research evidence.

Qualitative research contributes to knowledge generation just as significantly as quantitative research

Educational policymaking in many countries has been dominated by the perspective that only quantitative research is relevant to policy and only experimental and quasi-experimental studies can generate causal inferences about the effect of a 'treatment' or instructional programme. These studies attempt to assess the impact of the experimental intervention in comparison to a control or comparison group that has not experienced the treatment or intervention. Thus, the National Reading Panel (NRP) (2000) regarded as 'scientific' only experimental or quasi-experimental studies of reading, omitting a vast amount of equally relevant non-experimental and qualitative research (Cummins, 2007b). The National Literacy Panel on Language-Minority Children and Youth (August & Shanahan, 2006, 2008a) assigned a supportive but limited role to qualitative research, as illustrated in the following quotation: 'Ultimately, [qualitative] studies can generate only hypotheses about the influence instruction may have on learning (because they make no systematic manipulation of the instruction, they have no control group)' (August *et al.*, 2008: 133). As a result of this narrow perspective on what constitutes legitimate research, August and Shanahan could identify very few research studies that addressed the impact of sociocultural variables on minority students' literacy development. The research of Ladson-Billings (1995), Bankston and Zhou (1995) and many others was ignored.

In contrast to this perspective, I argued (e.g. Cummins, 2009a, 2009b) that ethnographic and case study research contribute to theory and knowledge generation in two ways. First, this research establishes phenomena that require explanation, thereby helping to build and test theoretical models. The second way in which qualitative data contribute to knowledge generation derives from the fact that any phenomenon established credibly by observation (qualitative or quantitative) can refute theoretical propositions or policy-related claims. As noted above, any theoretical claim or proposition must be consistent with *all* the empirical data; if not, the proposition requires modification or qualification to account for the data.

These two processes can be illustrated in Reyes' (2001) multi-year classroom observation study of biliteracy acquisition by English-dominant and Spanish-dominant primary grades students in a dual language programme. Students received initial literacy instruction only in their dominant language (L1) but were found to spontaneously transfer their reading and writing knowledge across languages, despite the fact that they received no formal phonics or decoding instruction in their second language. Reyes attributed this transfer to the fact that the programme strongly promoted writing for authentic purposes in each language, and also attempted to affirm the status and legitimacy of Spanish (as well as English) in the classroom.

Reyes' study contributes to scientific knowledge by establishing the phenomenon (which is also supported by many other studies) that, under appropriate conditions, students can spontaneously develop reading and writing skills in their second language without overt literacy instruction in that language. This phenomenon is consistent with claims of crosslinguistic transfer of academic skills, and it also refutes the theoretical claim that systematic phonics instruction is always *necessary* to develop literacy skills in a language.

In short, contrary to the perspective expressed by August and Shanahan (2006, 2008a), ethnographic and case study research are in the *mainstream* of scientific inquiry, capable not just of generating hypotheses but also of testing and refuting hypotheses.

Educators and researchers collaborate in the generation of knowledge

The relationship between theory and practice is two-way and ongoing: practice generates theory, which, in turn, acts as a catalyst for new directions in practice, which then inform theory, and so on. The process is dialogical. To illustrate, as outlined in Chapter 4, the initial impetus for making the distinction between basic interpersonal communicative skills (BICS) and cognitive/academic language proficiency (CALP) came from discussions with school psychologists who were concerned about the potential for bias in their own cognitive assessment practices with bilingual children. Classroom teachers and school psychologists had generated a significant amount of observational data in the form of teacher referral forms and psychological assessment. The analysis of these teacher referral forms and psychological assessments revealed the consequences of conflating conversational fluency in English (L2) with proficiency in academic registers of English. The BICS/CALP theoretical distinction, in turn, focused attention on and generated changes in policies and practices related both to instruction and assessment.

Theoretical claims or frameworks that integrate these claims are not valid or invalid, true or false. Theories frame phenomena and provide interpretations of empirical data within particular contexts and for particular purposes. They represent ways of viewing phenomena that may be relevant and useful in varying degrees depending on their purpose, how well they communicate with their intended audience, and the consequences for practice of following through on their implications.

Ideally, educators contribute to the knowledge generation process in two ways: they generate knowledge through their innovative instruction and they also critically assess the legitimacy of theoretical constructs by considering their implications for classroom practice. This perspective on the symbiotic relationship between research observations, theory generation and instructional practice is very different from traditional conceptions of research. Implicit assumptions about the relationships between research and instructional practice often position researchers as the generators of knowledge who then 'mobilise' it to improve educational effectiveness. Teachers are positioned within this discourse as passive recipients of knowledge, which they are charged with infusing into their instructional practice. This conception of the relationship between research and practice certainly describes the traditional process and it represents a legitimate strategy for improving education. However, it is by no means the only legitimate strategy nor the most powerful direction for change.

An alternative strategy, illustrated by the rapid increase during the past 20 years of creative instructional initiatives in multilingual classrooms (see Chapter 11), is to encourage teachers (and school administrators) to pursue instructional innovation and, together with researchers, document the effects of these innovations on students' academic engagement and learning. Within this conception, instructional innovations *create knowledge*, and teachers who pursue and document these innovations become *knowledge generators*. Teachers are positioned as agents of school-based language policies rather than simply being tasked with implementing top-down policies or 'best practices' generated beyond the classroom by policymakers or researchers. Within this collaborative orientation to knowledge generation, researchers typically observe teachers' instructional initiatives, document them, analyse the principles or claims underlying the observed practice, and synthesise these principles across diverse contexts in order to assess the extent to which they can account for the observed data. In this way, the theoretical intuitions, hypotheses, and potential insights that emerge from this process can be brought into direct dialogue with instructional practice, resulting in practice and theory serving as reciprocal catalysts for each other.

A similar orientation to research collaboration between researchers and educators was advanced by Jeffrey Duncan-Andrade and Ernest Morrell (2008) in their book *The Art of Critical Pedagogy: Possibilities for Moving from Theory to Practice in Urban Schools*. They point out that more informative and useful data can result from research agendas committed to collaboration with participants as colleagues rather than subjects: 'With the insertion of multiple voices into the conversation, the process of identifying problems and researching solutions becomes more democratic' (2008: 141). This collaborative and 'additive' approach recognises the complexity of each situation and encourages educator agency in pursuing instructional innovations and solutions to local problems. The orientation in the present volume, and in many of the projects discussed in Chapter 11, expands the scope of the collaborative approach advocated by Duncan-Andrade and Morrell by highlighting not only the possibilities of moving from theory to practice but, equally significant, the possibilities of moving from practice to theory. Educators are positioned as knowledge generators who work collaboratively with researchers in pushing the boundaries of innovation, thereby creating insights that contribute to the process of theory generation.

Prasad and Lory have similarly highlighted the vital role that teachers and students play in theory building 'as they collaboratively take risks and critically push the boundaries of what is possible in classroom spaces'. In the research-practice partnership Gail Prasad pursued with educators in a linguistically diverse elementary school in a midwestern school district in the United States (see Appendix 11.1); the reciprocal nature of practice and theory was foregrounded:

> Theory/ies offer explanatory frameworks for understanding practice, and practice drives theory building because theory/ies must be able to account for what has happened in the past, describe what is happening in the present, and predict what will happen in the future. When theory/ies are unable to meet any of these conditions, theoretical frameworks must be interrogated, revised, and/or reconceptualized. (Prasad & Lory, 2020: 810)

Criteria for Assessing the Legitimacy of Theoretical Constructs and Claims

The literature on scientific inquiry emphasises the importance of ensuring that claims and supporting arguments are consistent with the entirety of the relevant empirical evidence and are internally coherent and non-contradictory. Britt *et al.* (2014), for example, point out that in evaluating any scientific claim or argument, it is necessary to assess whether the evidence is sufficient to support the claim. This involves 'weighing the extent to which the totality of the support can overcome counterevidence or competing claims ... and considering the degree to which counter arguments and opposing evidence is rebutted, explained, or dismissed' (Britt *et al.*, 2014: 116). Britt and colleagues point out that although completely unqualified assertions often tend to be more persuasive to readers, '[q]ualifiers of scope (e.g. generally, always) and certainty (e.g. probably, suggests) are especially significant in academic and scientific writing' (Britt *et al.*, 2014: 116).

This analytic process is often neglected in popular discussions of scientific concepts (e.g. climate change). von der Mühlen *et al.* (2016), for example, compared the performance of college students and scientists in accurately judging the plausibility of arguments and recognising common argumentation fallacies. They reported that the superior performance of scientists was mediated by their strategy of evaluating in an analytic manner the internal consistency and empirical foundation of the arguments. By contrast, students often relied on intuitive assertion-based judgements reflecting the extent to which the claim, and supporting evidence or argumentation, was consistent with their prior attitudes, beliefs and knowledge. In the chapters that follow, I return to this distinction between assertion-based claims that are frequently 'evidence-free' and more rigorous analysis-based claims that seriously address the relevant empirical evidence.

In evaluating the legitimacy of theoretical constructs and claims that have been advanced in relation to the education of minoritised students, I propose three criteria:

- *Empirical adequacy* – to what extent is the claim consistent with all the relevant empirical evidence?
- *Logical coherence* – to what extent is the claim internally consistent and non-contradictory?
- *Consequential validity* – to what extent is the claim useful in promoting effective pedagogy and policies?

These criteria operationally define what is meant by *legitimate* or *credible* in the current context. The first two criteria reflect the generally accepted analytic processes common to all scientific inquiry. The third criterion was initially articulated in the area of educational testing by Messick (1987, 1994) who argued that discussions of the validity of any assessment procedure or test should take into account the consequences, intended or unintended, of applying or implementing this procedure. For example, research (reviewed by Ravitch, 2013) has documented that extensive use of high-stakes standardised testing during the era of the No Child Left Behind legislation in the United States (2002–2015) resulted in a narrowing of the curriculum to focus only on content that would be assessed in the test. This, in turn, exacerbated the existing 'pedagogical divide' whereby low-income students who were at risk of failing the tests experienced a significant increase in drill-and-practice test-preparation instruction in comparison to more affluent students who were less likely to be considered at risk of failure (Cummins, 2007b). In a similar way, the criterion of consequential validity requires that theoretical claims and constructs in the area of language education (and education more generally) should be assessed in relation to their implications for both classroom instruction and educational language policies. In other words, such claims should be subjected to a classroom 'reality check' to assess the credibility or usefulness of their instructional implications.

Empirical adequacy

The process of evaluating the extent to which a theoretical claim is consistent with the empirical data can be illustrated with reference to a well-designed study of almost 1,200 Russian- and Turkish-speaking 9th grade students (aged approximately 15 years) in Germany (Edele & Stanat, 2016). The study focused primarily on investigating the relationship between L1 listening comprehension and German (L2) reading comprehension skills. Significant relationships were found for both groups between L1 listening comprehension and L2 reading comprehension that were independent of background variables such as SES, non-verbal cognitive ability, and type of school. These findings are discussed in Chapter 9. Of primary interest in the present context is the finding that 'frequent use of L1 in the family is negatively associated with students' L2 reading comprehension' (2016: 174). The authors interpret this finding as evidence for a competing relationship between the time available for learning L1 and L2, as suggested by the time-on-task argument: 'According to this argument, the frequent use of L1 in the family has negative effects on the proficiency level that a student will reach in L2 because it limits the learning time available for the acquisition of L2'.

An initial challenge to this theoretical claim involves reconciling it with research showing superior academic performance in the school language among emergent bilingual students who continued to use their L1 at home (e.g. Bankston & Zhou, 1995; Bhatnager, 1980; Dolson, 1985). Other studies have shown no long-term negative effects on development of the school language as a result of using L1 at home (e.g. Mancilla-Martinez & Lesaux, 2011; Cobo-Lewis *et al.*, 2002a). In order for the unqualified claim that L1 use in the home negatively impacts the development of literacy in the school language to be credible, the authors would need to account for discrepant empirical findings that refute this theoretical proposition.

The empirical adequacy of Edele and Stanat's (2016) theoretical claim of causality between L1 use at home and lower L2 literacy attainment is also called into question by virtue of the fact that no data were available for length of residence in Germany among those born outside the country. In the Russian-speaking sample, 54% of the students were born outside of Germany whereas only 11% of the Turkish-speaking sample were born outside of Germany. Length of residence for those born outside of Germany is relevant because in comparison to immigrant-background students born in Germany or those who arrived at an early age, recently arrived students who are still in the process of acquiring German are more likely to use L1 at home, and also to perform more poorly on measures of German proficiency. Consider, for example, the situation of an immigrant student who arrives in Germany at age 13; this student is likely to perform poorly in relation to grade expectations on measures of German proficiency at age 15. Because her L1 fluency is likely to be better developed at this stage than her German fluency, she is also likely to continue using L1 at home with her parents who may know very little German. By contrast, students who arrive at an early age are likely to have much greater opportunity to acquire German academic skills in school and, as a result, switch from L1 to German in the home. Their parents will have also lived in Germany for a considerable period of time, and many are thus likely to have developed at least everyday receptive skills in German. Thus, the potential impact of L1 use at home is confounded with the impact of length of residence in the host country, with the result that no causal inferences can be drawn.

Logical coherence

The importance of ensuring logical coherence in theoretical claims and frameworks can be illustrated by examining the logical *incoherence* that characterises the rationale for early-exit transitional bilingual programmes in the United States and internationally. This model was the most widely adopted programme model in the United States context following the *Lau* v. *Nichols* Supreme Court decision in 1974. Today, early- or quick-exit programmes have been largely discredited in the United States in favour of various forms of *dual language* programme that maintain instruction in both English and Spanish (or other languages) at least throughout elementary school (Grade 6, approximately age 12). Many of these dual language programmes are 'two-way' insofar as they admit students from both English-dominant and Spanish-dominant backgrounds.

The rationale for quick-exit transitional programmes derives from the discredited linguistic mismatch hypothesis that assumes students will fail academically if they do not receive initial literacy instruction through their L1. However, the rationale also endorses the equally discredited maximum exposure hypothesis by ensuring that minority students spend as little time as possible in the bilingual programme before being 'exited' to all-English instruction. I expressed the confused internal logic of this rationale as follows:

> On the one hand, transitional programs assume that bilingual instruction in the early grades will be *more* effective in raising the level of *English* proficiency of [emergent bilingual] students than instruction only through the medium of English. In other words, *less* time through the medium of English will result in *greater* development of the English language skills underlying literacy. ... [Thus], in the initial grades the SUP [separate underlying proficiency] model is rejected in favor of the CUP [common underlying proficiency] model. However, despite the implicit endorsement of a CUP model in the early grades, transitional programs revert to a SUP model by assuming (without any evidence) that children's English skills will not develop adequately unless they are mainstreamed to an English-only program. ... The extent of the logical contradiction involved in the mainstreaming process can be seen in the fact that minority students in the early grades of transitional programs are expected to make so much progress in the cognitive/academic skills underlying English literacy that after two or three years they should be at a level where they can compete on an equal footing with their unilingual English-speaking peers who have had all their instruction in English. (Cummins, 1980c: 52–52) (emphasis original)

I pointed out that the *less equals more* rationale of the CUP model is consistent with the research evidence, but the time frame is unrealistic. The data (even in 1980!) showed that the impact of bilingual instruction was cumulative insofar as emergent bilingual students tended to catch up to grade expectations in English literacy only in the later grades of elementary school (for more recent data see Lindholm-Leary & Borsato, 2006).

This analysis of the problematic rationale underlying quick-exit transitional bilingual programmes is still highly relevant in the international arena. Submersion (L2-only) and quick-exit transitional programmes are still the norm in low-income postcolonial contexts despite the fact that, according to Heugh (2011a, 2011b), these programmes provide minimal return on investment and are essentially designed to fail. She pointed out in relation to the sub-Saharan African context: 'The evidence is clear: only well-resourced programmes that use the first language as medium of instruction for a minimum of six years will allow students an equal chance of becoming sufficiently proficient in the international language of wider communication and their other academic studies' (2011b: 257).

Benson (2019) similarly highlighted the limitations of early-exit transitional models of multilingual education (MLE) in which learners' L1 is used for only 1–3 years before 'exit' to a programme that uses the dominant language exclusively. According to Benson, early-exit models represent a very weak version of MLE because they typically fail to develop a strong foundation for literacy and cognition in students' L1, with the result that students are ill-prepared to transition to exclusive use of the dominant instructional language.

Benson (2019) pointed out that while short-term use of L1 is preferable to ignoring it, much greater gains in learner achievement are observed in more additive, pedagogically sound approaches that aim to maintain and develop students' L1 at least through the 5–7 years of primary schooling: 'use of learners' best languages (known as L1s) for literacy and learning across the curriculum provides a solid foundation for basic and continuing education and for transfer of skills and knowledge to additional languages' (2019: 29). This has been established not only through research in Europe and North America but also in low-income settings such as Eritrea and Ethiopia that implemented instruction through learners' home languages during the eight years of primary school (e.g. Heugh et al., 2012).[1] Additionally, L1 instructional use has been linked to increased parent involvement and greater participation of girls and women in education.

In short, the 'entry and exit fallacies' documented in the implementation of early-exit transitional bilingual programmes in the United States context are equally relevant to current debates on educational language policies in low-income postcolonial contexts. The rationale for these programmes is logically incoherent, which is a major reason why they also lack convincing empirical support in comparison to strong additive programmes that maintain L1 instruction (in addition to the dominant language) throughout the elementary school years (e.g. Heugh et al., 2012; Ramirez, 1992).

Consequential validity

The relevance of the criterion of consequential validity to evaluating the legitimacy of theoretical constructs can be illustrated by the claim (Makoni & Pennycook, 2005, 2007a; García & Lin, 2017) that human languages are 'invented' and don't exist as discrete 'countable' entities. García and Lin (2017: 127) expressed this claim as follows in describing what they label the 'strong' version of translanguaging: 'a theory that poses that bilingual people do not speak languages but rather, use their repertoire of linguistic features selectively'. Rather than referring to languages as though they actually exist as countable entities or legitimate constructs, García and colleagues in multiple publications (e.g. García & Kleifgen, 2019; García & Li Wei, 2014) use the verb forms *languaging* and *translanguaging* in order to position language as a social practice in which learners engage rather than a set of structures and functions that they learn. In other words, they adopt a mutually exclusive (either-or) position with respect to language (noun form) and languaging (verb form). A heteroglossic theoretical orientation, according to this perspective, requires adoption of the verb form (*trans/languaging*) as legitimate, and the noun form (*language*) as monoglossic and hence illegitimate. It is not possible to view both verb forms and noun forms as legitimate constructs.

The claim that discrete languages don't exist except as ephemeral social constructions has been disputed on multiple grounds (see Chapter 10). Here, my concern is with the consequential validity of this claim – what does it imply for language policies and educational practice? Makoni and Pennycook (2007a) were very clear about the logical consequences of this theoretical position. They acknowledged that, according to this analysis, constructs such as language rights, mother tongues, multilingualism and code-switching are also illegitimate. Grin highlighted the implications of this claim:

> Very practically, language is a key category in much of human rights law; denying the existence of languages blocks the access of minoritised groups to it. But more fundamentally, if languages in general do not *really* exist, if they are misleading constructs, this is true of small languages as well. Why, then, fight for them? It would be absurd. ... This is why the advocates of the notion of 'languaging', particularly when they go one step further and deny the existence of languages, are not just making scientifically spurious claims. They are also, willingly or not, the objective allies of linguistic imperialism and linguistic injustice. (Grin, 2018: 260) (emphasis original)

MacSwan (2020: 1) elaborated on this critique by arguing that to deny the existence of 'language' as a legitimate construct is 'inconsistent with a civil rights orientation on language education policy'. Lau and Van Viegen (2020a: 11) similarly point to the consequences of erasing discrete languages for speakers of marginalised languages: 'recognizing the existence of an internally differentiated system corresponds with overt support of children's often ignored multilingual language resources, particularly for children from minoritized communities'.

The problematic consequences of the argument that discrete languages don't exist in the individual's cognitive apparatus are also evident at the level of everyday discourse and educational practice. For example, carried to its logical conclusion, this claim implies that it would be illegitimate for a child to express an utterance such as 'I speak Spanish at home but English in school'. It would also be illegitimate for web sites such as *Ethnologue* (www.ethnologue.com) to refer to and provide information about the 7,106 languages and dialects that humanity has generated. One could also not talk about Spanish-English (and other) bilingual programmes since these languages do not exist. To claim that languages exist as social constructions or 'inventions' but have no objective cognitive reality raises the issue of what is 'reality' and what is a 'social construction'.

Otheguy *et al.* (2015: 293) distance their position from that of Makoni and Pennycook (2007) by asserting that because of the social importance of distinguishing between bilinguals and monolinguals 'we are not simply abandoning the distinction or scuttling the concepts of language and bilingualism' and for the same reason 'we continue to talk in some settings about languages and even about a particular language'. They recognise that these notions continue to have real consequences in the lives of minoritised people. However, they emphasise that in accepting terms like 'language', 'a language', 'monolingual', and 'bilingual' 'we are using categories that have nothing to do with individuals when seen from their own linguistic perspective ... these concepts are not appropriate for discourse dealing with mental grammar'.

This claim immediately runs into the problem that individuals, who presumably have more access to their own linguistic perspective than external theorists, perceive themselves as using specific languages in particular sociolinguistic contexts. Teachers in bilingual programmes also see themselves and their students as using language constructions and utterances that are associated with particular languages. Experientially, neither teachers nor students in their language use and performance distinguish between sociolinguistic behaviours and their mental grammar. Thus, from the perspective of pedagogical translanguaging or crosslinguistic pedagogy, and language education policy, the distinction between 'mental grammar' and educational reality proposed by Otheguy *et al.* (2015) is largely irrelevant.

The lack of educational relevance is also evident in the fact that García and colleagues in multiple publications refer to discrete languages as though they actually *do* exist as part of the individual's linguistic and mental repertoire. For example, García and Kleifgen (2019: 9–10) in discussing a research study by Espinosa and Herrera (2016) talk about how the researchers told students to use their entire linguistic repertoire to state the main idea from their reading. Students drew from all their language resources: 'Some used English, others Spanish, and yet others used both Spanish and English'. There is a clear logical incongruity in using labels such as *Spanish* and *English* as though they actually referred to real conceptual entities within the individual's cognitive apparatus while at the same time claiming that these conceptual entities don't exist. How does the claim that 'bilingual people do not speak languages' (García & Lin, 2017: 126) fit with the acknowledgement that some bilingual students 'used English, others Spanish, and yet others used both Spanish and English'?

The inconsistency between García and colleagues' theoretical proposition that languages do not exist within the bilingual's linguistic system and their frequent reference to students who actually do speak languages is all the more incongruous in light of Otheguy *et al.*'s (2019: 630) critique of MacSwan (2017) for doing essentially the same thing:

> MacSwan consistently uses the names of the two languages as firm guides for assigning utterances, parts of utterances, and elements of the underlying system to what for him is either one psychologically real language or the other. MacSwan (2017, page 181 among others) speaks of English words and Spanish words, English sentences and Spanish sentences and, more important, of English rules and Spanish rules ... (Otheguy *et al.*, 2019: 630)

In short, there is nothing to be gained theoretically or pedagogically from the assertion that 'bilingual people do not speak languages'. This claim is likely only to sow confusion among educators and policymakers and to distract from the shared goal of promoting multilingual abilities among minoritised students. There is no dispute about the fact that languages are socially constructed with porous boundaries, but languages are also experientially, instructionally, and socially *real* for students, teachers, policymakers, curriculum designers, politicians, and most researchers. Students and teachers across the globe use languages, they study and learn languages, they compare languages, and in effective classrooms they have fun with languages. Students invest significant cognitive effort in learning languages because they want to speak languages. They would likely be dismayed to learn that nobody speaks languages.

There is no conceptual difficulty in reconciling the construct of translanguaging, understood as the integrated process through which multilingual individuals use and learn languages, with the experiential and social reality of different languages, understood as historical, cultural, and ideological constructs that have material consequences and determine social action (e.g. language planning, bilingual programmes, etc.) (Cummins, 2017a). Expressed differently, there is no compelling reason to adopt a binary *either-or* dichotomy between the verb form *trans/languaging* and the noun form *language* rather than a *both-and* position that acknowledges both the legitimacy of the construct of *translanguaging* and the experiential and social legitimacy of languages.

Skutnabb-Kangas (2009, 2015) has also argued that individuals and groups have the right to claim a language as their own and there is no contradiction between treating languages as both processes and, at the same time, as concrete entities. Skutnabb-Kangas and Heugh (2012: xvii) in introducing their edited volume on mother-tongue based multilingual education, similarly acknowledge the philosophical debate about whether languages are 'invented', but point out that 'we work with practical notions of what languages are and how they function inside educational institutions and how they may be used to facilitate the best possible access to quality education'. In other words, philosophical debates about whether languages *really* exist have very little practical or theoretical relevance to language policies or language instruction in educational institutions around the world. Kubota (2020: 318) has lucidly expressed a similar point: 'Furthermore, when so many incidents of raciolinguistic hatred are happening in our community, isn't it more important to recognise all languages as valid, legitimate and essential for human rights and humanity, rather than trying to make linguistic boundaries blurred and fuzzy'?

In summary, the criterion of consequential validity highlights the fact that theoretical constructs, propositions and frameworks are always *situated*. They don't emerge in a scientific or social vacuum. Theories are always located within particular discursive contexts; they propose interpretations of specific observations or phenomena that are of concern to various stakeholders (e.g. researchers, educators, policymakers). The extent to which any particular theoretical framing communicates effectively with these stakeholders and enables appropriate social action is intrinsic to the situated validity of the theory. Danièle Moore has made a similar point in noting that theoretical concepts travel and change as a result of their evolving relationships to the social phenomena they address. She notes that we need to consider the historical, geographical and social circumstances that give rise to certain concepts and how these concepts take on different shapes as a result of these social, political, and historical forces that are reflected in institutional structures and individual perspectives (Moore *et al.*, 2020).

Thus, the validity of the proposition that languages don't exist as legitimate conceptual or discrete entities must be assessed not only in terms of its empirical and logical credibility, but also in relation to the extent to which the benefits of any social and educational action to which this proposition might give rise outweigh the problematic consequences that it might generate. As discussed above, it is difficult to discern any social or educational benefits associated with this proposition, but the problematic consequences are very evident.

Concluding Thoughts

In this chapter, I have argued that creation of theoretical hypotheses, propositions, and models is an intrinsic and essential component in the generation of knowledge. Isolated research findings become relevant for social policy and educational practice only when they are integrated into coherent theoretical frameworks. There are typically many different ways of organising or interpreting observed phenomena, each of which may be consistent with the empirical data. For example, different disciplines (e.g. neurology versus cognitive science) may describe and explain the same phenomenon quite differently but in equally valid ways. Also, within a

particular discipline, the observed phenomena may be synthesised legitimately into very different theoretical frameworks depending on the purpose of the framework, the audience envisaged, and the outcomes desired.
This process is analogous to observing any object (e.g. a house that we are
considering buying); when we move and shift our perspective, we see a
different image although the object of our observation has not changed in
any way. Thus, theoretical frameworks provide alternative perspectives on
particular phenomena in specific contexts and for particular purposes.

In light of the centrality of theory, it is essential to articulate criteria
for evaluating the credibility of theoretical constructs and claims. The
criteria of empirical adequacy, logical coherence, and consequential validity provide a framework for assessing the legitimacy of theoretical propositions. For example, these criteria enable us to distinguish between
evidence-free ideological claims and evidence-based, logically coherent,
and pedagogically useful claims. Thus, unqualified assertions such as
Schlesinger's (1991) 'bilingualism shuts doors' can immediately be dismissed as evidence-free, logically incoherent, and immensely counter-
productive with respect to its social and educational consequences.

The empirical adequacy, logical coherence and consequential validity
of any theoretical claim or framework are never absolutes. A more detailed
and complex theoretical framework may be more adequate in capturing
specific details of particular phenomena and their social or educational
impact. However, gains in specificity and/or complexity may be made at
the expense of usefulness (consequential validity). Too much detail may
lead educators and policymakers to lose sight of the 'big picture' while
excessive theoretical complexity or language that is alien to educators and
policymakers will reduce the likelihood of implementation.

For example, the 'empowerment' framework outlined in Part 1 of this
book is clearly far less theoretically sophisticated than a framework based
on French philosopher Michel Foucault's theories (e.g. Foucault, 1984).
However, it is arguably considerably more useful than a Foucauldian
account in communicating insights to educators about how patterns of
teacher-student identity negotiation in schools are inseparable from societal power relations. It also speaks directly and specifically to the ways in
which educators can exercise agency through their own instructional
practice to challenge the operation of coercive power relations. None of
this is surprising – the empowerment framework was formulated with the
intention both of elucidating the deep structure of educational practice in
relation to minoritised students and contributing to educators' attempts
to transform this practice. Foucault's framework was not focused specifically on educational contexts, educators were not its primary audience,
and while it certainly intended to elucidate, immediate transformation of
oppressive educational structures was not a primary aim.

The point here is that theoretical constructs, claims, and frameworks
are situated in time, place and context. While the criteria of empirical

adequacy and logical coherence apply to all theoretical propositions, the criterion of consequential validity is context specific. Theory is always dialogical in the sense that it expresses an ongoing search for understanding among collaborating partners (e.g. researchers, educators, policymakers) with shared goals in particular social and educational contexts. Just as oral and written language is meaningless outside of a human communicative and interpretive context, so too theory assumes meaning only within specific dialogical contexts.

Note

(1) Several authors have expressed concern about the encroachment of English into teacher education programmes in Ethiopia (e.g. Benson *et al.*, 2012; Heugh *et al.*, 2012; Liddicoat & Heugh, 2015). Liddicoat and Heugh, for example, note that starting in 2005, the Ethiopian government diverted 44% of the teacher education budget to invest additional resources in English, thereby reducing the use of mother tongues in teacher education. Despite these pressures, however, the Ethiopian 8-year mother tongue-medium (MTM) policy from 1994 is still being fully implemented in multiple languages (personal communication, Carol Benson). Evaluation data (Heugh *et al.*, 2012: 254) provide strong support for the superiority of extended mother-tongue instruction: 'Students who receive eight years of MTM education, and whose teachers are correspondingly trained in the MT [mother-tongue], achieve the highest scores across the curriculum, except where significant socio-economic deprivation applies'. Additional perspectives on MTM education in Ethiopia are provided by Benson (2021) and James (2021).

8 Is 'Academic Language' a Legitimate Theoretical Construct?

In this chapter, I consider two different variations of the question that forms the title: (1) To what extent is the construct of 'academic language' empirically adequate, logically coherent, and consistent with instructional practice endorsed by educators focused on equity and social justice? (2) To what extent does the specific distinction between 'academic language proficiency' (CALP) and conversational fluency (BICS) meet these same criteria of legitimacy? These questions obviously overlap but they are not identical. The general question about the legitimacy of 'academic language' is independent of the particular conception of 'academic language' incorporated in the CALP/BICS distinction, and it applies to all educational contexts, with no particular focus on multilingual or second language contexts. By contrast, the CALP/BICS distinction represents one prominent but controversial account of the construct of 'academic language' that emerged from research on L2 academic development among immigrant-background students. While its origins were in multilingual education contexts, it also references a distinction that applies to students in both monolingual and multilingual contexts.

Some researchers who endorse the general construct of 'academic language' or acknowledge the specific linguistic demands of schooling, have critiqued the CALP/BICS distinction on the grounds that it oversimplifies both conversational interactions and academic language, or devalues the cognitive complexity and instructional centrality of interpersonal communication (e.g. Bailey, 2007; Bunch, 2013; Scarcella, 2003). Others reject both the general construct of 'academic language' and the specific distinction between academic language proficiency and conversational fluency (e.g. Flores & Rosa, 2015; García, 2020; García & Solorza, 2020; MacSwan, 2000; MacSwan & Rolstad, 2003; Petrovic & Olmstead, 2001; Rolstad, 2014, 2017; Valdés, 2004, 2017; Wiley & Rolstad, 2014).

In contrast to critics of the academic language construct, numerous researchers accept the legitimacy of the construct. These researchers have proposed instructional strategies and/or theoretical frameworks designed to support teachers in enabling minoritised students to catch up academically to fluent speakers of the school language and develop strong literacy skills in both the school language and L1 (e.g. Anstrom *et al.*, 2010; Bailey, 2007; Bunch *et al.*, 2014; DiCerbo *et al.*, 2014; Schleppegrell, 2004; Wong Fillmore, 2009, 2014; Wong Fillmore & Fillmore, 2012; Wong Fillmore & Snow, 2018; Uccelli & Phillips Galloway, 2018; Uccelli *et al.*, 2015a, 2015b). Others accept the legitimacy of the construct but argue that it should be conceptualised as one important component of the broad repertoire of semiotic tools required for *academic communication* (Haneda, 2014).

In the sections that follow, I review three major themes that have emerged in critiques of the general construct of 'academic language' and then examine the rationale proposed by those who endorse the legitimacy of the construct. I then discuss the more specific issues that arise in relation to the legitimacy of the CALP/BICS distinction, focusing primarily on more recent critiques.

Section 1. Critiques of the Construct of 'Academic Language'

Three broad themes have emerged in critiques of the legitimacy of the academic language construct:

- The constructs of 'academic language' and 'academic language proficiency' are illegitimate because language development is essentially complete by the time the child enters school around age 5. Thus, 'language proficiency', *by definition*, has no relationship to academic learning, literacy development, or the cognitive functioning involved in schooling.
- Academic language is synonymous with 'standard language'. Thus, teaching 'academic language' to minoritised students inevitably and invariably entails replacing their 'inferior' home linguistic varieties with the standard language. In other words, the construct of 'academic language' is aligned with a deficit view of minoritised students' L1 and L2 language varieties.
- The construct of 'academic language' as elaborated in the US Common Core State Standards (CCSS) reflects an 'autonomous' orientation to language and literacy that ignores the social, economic and political contexts in which language and literacy practices are embedded. This privileging of 'autonomous' over 'ideological' perspectives inevitably gives rise to deficit orientations to the spoken language of minoritised students and to the language of communities who have not developed print literacy.

A common characteristic of these claims is that they are typically made without qualifications of scope or certainty and without evaluating counterevidence or claims, thereby violating basic principles of scientific analysis (Britt *et al.*, 2014).

Claim 1. Language Proficiency is Independent of Literacy and Academic Knowledge

This position (MacSwan, 1999, 2000; MacSwan & Rolstad, 2003; Petrovic & Olmstead, 2001; Rolstad, 2017) is derived from a Chomskian perspective that children's acquisition of 'core grammar' in their home language is essentially complete by about age 5. Rolstad expressed the view that language is an inherent human ability unrelated to literacy, cognitive abilities, and academic achievement as follows:

> Indeed, by the time they arrive at school, children have already learned most of the rules of their home language, and possess an essentially adult-like grammar. … Children's biological endowment for language underlies these special linguistic achievements, and suggests that all children should be linguistically successful, regardless of their social status. (Rolstad, 2017: 498)

Based on the same set of assumptions, MacSwan (1999: 268) argued, without qualifications, that language is independent of literacy and content area knowledge. He suggested that it is reasonable to include literacy as part of the definition of *second-language* proficiency but in the case of schoolchildren's first-language development, literacy-related knowledge, conceptual knowledge, and content-area knowledge must be excluded from any conception of language proficiency or competence. MacSwan and Rolstad (2003: 333) expressed their position very clearly: 'schooling plays little role in developing language proficiency in the context of native language ability'.

As part of their rationale for this position, MacSwan (1999) and MacSwan and Rolstad (2003) suggested that to include literacy as an aspect of 'language proficiency' implies that members of nonliterate cultures and societies, as well as pre-literate emergent bilingual children, have relatively low 'language proficiency'. In other words, any linkage of 'literacy', 'conceptual knowledge', or school-based content knowledge to 'language proficiency' automatically constitutes a deficit orientation to minority students' and pre-literate peoples' language and culture. Rolstad elaborated on the connection (or lack thereof) between education and language as follows:

> School is one social/situational context of many possible ones in which language is used and shaped, but the language we use in that context is itself no more complex than any other variety. … Instead, many within education and psychology have posited dichotomies of language proficiency – representing linguistic differences as linguistically different ability levels – to explain school failure among children in disadvantaged communities, cutting across both monolingual and bilingual communities. (Rolstad, 2017: 499)

In critiquing MacSwan's position, I pointed to the counterevidence and instructional consequences of defining 'literacy' as independent of 'language'. For example, it implies that any literacy-related knowledge such as range and depth of vocabulary, ability to understand and use formal discourse patterns, as well as reading and writing expertise have minimal or no relationship to language proficiency as defined within the social context of schooling (Cummins, 2000).

The radical nature of the positions advanced by MacSwan (1999), MacSwan and Rolstad (2003) and Rolstad (2017) can be seen in relation to a concrete example used by Lily Wong Fillmore (2009: 4) to illustrate the challenges for all students in understanding typical academic texts. The example is taken from a Grade 5 language arts anthology: *'In the typical western town, the buildings were often skirted with a sidewalk of wooden planks, along with hitching posts and water troughs for horses'*. It is highly likely that most educators would find it at least bizarre to claim that this sentence does not involve language (because language development is complete at age 5, and thus vocabulary that is not part of the typical 5-year-old's linguistic repertoire cannot qualify as 'language'). Additionally, any individual differences among Grade 5 students in their ability to understand this sentence are unrelated to differences in their knowledge of language (because after age 5, there are *no* academically meaningful individual differences in language knowledge or proficiency).

Furthermore, the curriculum content area of 'Language Arts' becomes meaningless, as do instructional strategies that are frequently seen as central to effective pedagogy for all students such as teaching language across the curriculum, engaging in instructional conversations about textual meanings, and developing critical language awareness. It would also be meaningless to talk about developing students' ability to use language for various cognitive functions such as hypothesising, predicting, identifying cause-effect relationships etc.

The idiosyncratic nature of this position can be appreciated by contrasting it with the perspective expressed by Christian Faltis and Sarah Hudelson, both of whom have been critical of the conceptual distinction between CALP and BICS:

> Language and literacy cannot be separated. Put another way, both spoken language and written language are language. They are different sides of the same coin. Central to both is the creation and construction of meaning. Both are socially constructed. Both are developed in and through use, as learners generate, test, and refine hypotheses. (Faltis & Hudelson, 1998: 101–102)

This perspective regarding the fusion of language, learning, and literacy is shared by the vast majority of educators and educational linguists. Palmer and Martínez (2013: 270–271), for example, point to one of the problems with the terms 'English language learner' and 'English learner' in the United States context: 'Are we not all learners of the English language throughout our lives, given that language accompanies us as we learn about new ideas and engage with new people?' In the same volume, Bunch (2013: 299) notes: 'Language has long been understood to play a central role – perhaps *the* central role – in teaching and learning'. Barr *et al.* in their description of 'core academic language skills' (CALS) similarly point out:

> We view language development as inseparable from context and affected by learners' accumulated opportunities to participate in literacy practices inside and outside of school. Contrary to widespread belief, language development continues after the early years, with learners expanding not only their vocabulary but also their grammatical and discourse proficiencies throughout adolescence and potentially throughout life as they navigate an increasing number of social contexts. (Barr *et al.*, 2019: 982)

Gottlieb and Castro make the same point throughout their immensely useful book *Language Power*, as illustrated in their statement of the overall goal of the book: 'It is our intent to ensure that every teacher has an understanding of the importance of academic language use in their craft, no matter who their students are and what their discipline is' (2017: xvi).

The same perspective is made explicit in a recent report from the European Union Commission entitled *Education Begins with Language* in which the authors highlight key lessons regarding the language of schooling:

- **The language of schooling is a highly complex and foundational skill for learning:** it has a variety of complex formal registers and grammatical structures which structure thought and expression, which are crucial for learning in formal educational settings. ...
- **Every teacher is a language teacher:** given the complexity of the language of schooling and its importance for pupils to succeed at school, *all* teachers have a role to play in supporting their pupils to master the language of schooling. It is important to continue raising awareness among subject teachers of their role in developing the language of schooling through linguistically sensitive teaching. (Staring & Broughton, 2020: 13) (emphasis original).

I pointed out that if language development is largely complete by age five, it implies that Nobel Literature Prize laureate Toni Morrison had no more language proficiency than a 5-year-old child (Cummins, 2000). Because language development, literacy learning, and academic achievement are conceptualised *a priori* as unrelated, this dismissal of the construct of 'academic language' has nothing to say to educators about how they can expand students' expertise in using academic registers of language and enable them to become powerful users of language.

Petrovic and Olmstead (2001) dissented from this argument by claiming that it is 'linguistically true' that Toni Morrison had no more linguistic expertise than a 5-year-old child: 'To the extent that this can be read as blaming the 5-year-old for not having the literary repertoire that schooling has yet to give her, one could indeed interpret it as a deficit model' (2001: 408). I am at a loss to describe this as anything other than absurd. Petrovic and Olmstead appear to be claiming that all teachers who teach 'Language Arts' in school and believe (for some reason) that their goal is to expand their students' agility and expertise in using oral and written language (e.g. in debating issues such as systemic racism) are complicit with discourses of linguistic deficit and view all kindergarten students as linguistically deficient. No teacher who tries to expand students' language and literary repertoire beyond the preschool years believes that this endeavor constitutes *blaming* preschool children, or characterising them as 'linguistically deficient', because they don't yet have the language and literacy expertise of students in grades 1–12.

Rolstad proposed the construct of *second language instructional competence* (SLIC) which acknowledges linguistic progression during the school years among *L2 learners* but 'is not relevant to children's native language, which flourishes naturally within its community of use' (2017: 502). The weirdness of this position can be illustrated with reference to The English Language Development Standards developed by the World Class Instructional Design and Assessment (WIDA) consortium (WIDA Consortium, 2012). WIDA standards, and instructional strategies that are aligned with these standards, are used in more than 40 US states to support and assess ELLs' academic language development. The standards and instructional strategies specify academic language progressions aligned with cognitive functions associated with each of the major content areas. The WIDA academic language performance criteria that are assessed within and across grade levels include Linguistic Complexity, Language Forms and Conventions, and Vocabulary Usage.

According to the logic of MacSwan and Rolstad's (2003) theoretical claims about language development, it would be acceptable in principle to use the WIDA framework to support *second* language development among ELLs. However, it would not be legitimate for teachers of fluent English speakers to focus on linguistic complexity, language forms and conventions, and vocabulary usage across the curriculum because these aspects of their native language 'have already flourished naturally within their communities of use'. Personally, I am much more persuaded by Bunch's (2013: 299) position that language has long been understood to play a central role – perhaps *the* central role – in teaching and learning.

The alternative theoretical positions outlined above are presented diagrammatically in Figures 8.1 and 8.2.

My reading of the research related to language and school achievement suggests that the general relationships depicted in Figure 8.2 are consistent with the theoretical understanding of the vast majority of researchers (although obviously not all would endorse the constructs of CALP and CALS). By contrast, the relationships depicted in Figure 8.1 represent an extreme outlier position based on a highly restricted understanding of the nature of language and language development.

The theoretical claims advanced by MacSwan, Rolstad, and others, and by implication their rejection of the construct of 'academic language',

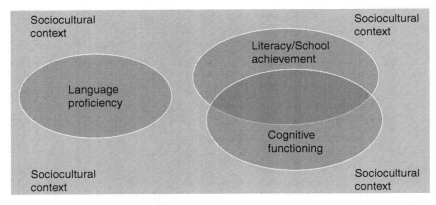

Figure 8.1 Theoretical understanding of 'language development' as independent of cognitive functioning and literacy/school achievement

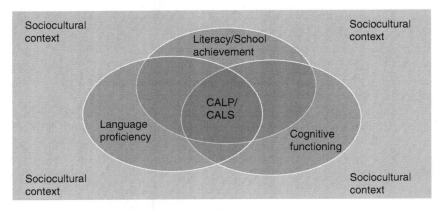

Figure 8.2 Theoretical understanding of 'language development' as intersecting with cognitive functioning and literacy/school achievement in the context of schooling; CALP = cognitive/academic language proficiency, CALS = core academic language skills (Uccelli *et al.*, 2015a)

do not fare well when assessed in relation to the criteria for evaluating theoretical constructs and claims discussed in Chapter 7. With respect to *empirical adequacy*, their claims are refuted by the extensive research literature (discussed previously) showing highly significant relationships, after the early grades of schooling, among various measures of academic language proficiency such as vocabulary knowledge, reading comprehension and verbal cognitive functioning (e.g. Grabe, 2004). These data are much more consistent with the claim, expressed previously, that students' academic *performance* in school reflects a *fusion* of linguistic, academic and cognitive knowledge and functioning involving both declarative and procedural knowledge.

With respect to logical coherence, the claim that language development is complete at age five essentially denies that there is any involvement of *language* in the expansion of vocabulary, grammatical knowledge, and the development of students' insight about how language functions in various forms of discourse over 12 years of schooling. In order to consider the consequential validity of this position, I invite the reader to engage in a mind game where, in a professional development workshop, Language Arts teachers are informed that they are not teaching language (and it might even reflect a deficit orientation to believe they are). Teaching how language works in different disciplines, according to this position, is also a futile exercise because language is unrelated, and essentially irrelevant to, literacy and academic content knowledge.

In short, (for obvious reasons, in my view) this challenge to the theoretical legitimacy of the constructs of 'academic language' and 'academic language proficiency' has not gained much traction in educational policy or instructional practice.

Claim 2. Because the Construct of 'Academic Language' is Inseparable from the Construct of 'Standard Language', Educational Policies and Instructional Practice that Position Academic/Standard Language as Superior to Nonstandard Varieties of Language Stigmatise Minoritised Students' Spoken Varieties of L1 and L2

This claim is rooted in the fact that in both monolingual English classrooms in the United States and in some bilingual classrooms, the 'nonstandard' varieties spoken by minoritised students are often devalued either intentionally or inadvertently by teachers who view the more formal 'standard' variety of L1 and L2 as superior and more appropriate. The critiques advanced by Guadalupe Valdés (2004, 2017) and Ofelia García (2009, 2020; García & Solorza, 2020) overlap considerably and I examine these critiques separately from the critique advanced by Nelson Flores and Jonathan Rosa (2015).

To what extent does the construct of 'academic language' operate to stigmatise the language practices of minoritised students as argued by Valdés and García?

In discussing the ways in which varieties of nonstandard English in the United States such as African American Vernacular English (AAVE), Native American English and Chicano English have been stigmatised in both school and out-of-school contexts, Valdés noted that:

> Concern about the limitations and negative impact of the varieties of English spoken, especially by African American students, has a lengthy history in the field of education, and even though extensive research has been carried out by a number of researchers on the impact on students of negative attitudes toward their home varieties of language ... views and beliefs about AAVE endure. ... Moreover, instrumentalist language ideologies that argue for the direct and/or explicit 'teaching' of the Standard inadvertently embrace deficit theories of minority students' language. (Valdés, 2017: 333)

Valdés goes on to argue that the construct of 'academic language' operates in a similar way to 'standard language' to construct a symbolic/ideological border dividing those who 'have' academic language from those who do not. She notes that in many educational discussions academic language is often blended or conflated with 'standardness'. She summarised her concerns as follows:

> In sum, the scholarly and professional discourse that has positioned the imprecise notion of academic language as fundamental to student achievement suggests that the use of language as a boundary object is moving rapidly toward the establishment of a new and enhanced symbolic border between two different categories of students: users of academic language and users of non-academic language in American schools ... [thereby] depriving historically disadvantaged students of their original social and linguistic capital. (Valdés, 2017: 338–339)

Two examples illustrate the ways in which this devaluation of cultural and linguistic capital has been enacted in schools over many years, long before the construct of 'academic language' entered mainstream educational discourse. In the first case, Ramphal (1983) carried out a micro-ethnographic study of 14 reading lessons give to West Indian Creole speakers of English in a Toronto-area school. The study demonstrates vividly how the stigmatisation of minoritised students' variety of English effectively excluded them from participation in learning. Ramphal reported that teachers consistently corrected students' miscues at the word level, thereby denying students the opportunity to self-correct. One student was interrupted so often in his oral reading in one of the lessons that he was able to read only one sentence, consisting of three words, uninterrupted. I summarised Ramphal's conclusions as follows: 'Ramphal suggests that teachers' constant focus on surface features of the text and of students' dialect prevented students from focusing on the meaning of what they were reading and also fostered dependent behaviour in that students knew that whenever they paused at a word the teacher would automatically pronounce it for them' (Cummins, 1984a: 238).

The second example highlights similar instructional malpractice, albeit well-intentioned, in a middle school dual language programme ostensibly designed to promote biliteracy among native Spanish-speaking and native English-speaking students. McCollum (1999) documented how Spanish-speaking students in this programme came to prefer English over their home variety of Spanish as a result of the ways in which the teacher, who was from their own community, constantly corrected their speech and made negative comments about their nonstandard Spanish or use of 'vernacular' constructions. According to Alfaro and Bartolomé:

> Equally incomprehensible to these native Spanish speakers was why their fluent communication in their vernacular was criticized, yet their native English-speaking peers were lauded when they produced incomplete Spanish phrases. Not only was their Spanish vernacular devalued, their teacher also [devalued] the English they spoke. In effect, the Spanish-speaking students were being muzzled because they did not speak Standard versions of either Spanish or English. (Alfaro & Bartolomé, 2017: 23)

Similar concerns have been expressed by García (2020) and García and Solorza (2020) in arguing that 'standard language' and 'academic language' operate in similar hierarchical ways to devalue the varieties of Spanish and English spoken by Latinx students in the United States. García (2020) identified two predominant mainstream misunderstandings of Latinx bilinguals: (a) they have language deficiencies, especially in English and (b) their language deficiencies extend to Spanish because what they lack is academic language. She claims, correctly, that the concept of a standard language has been constructed by nation-states and their institutions in order to control those whose language and knowledge systems are rendered invalid. In this process, the 'language of bilingual communities has been made deficient by imposing the knowledge-system of white monolingual middle-class people' (2020: 2). She describes the role of 'academic language' in this process of linguistic and cultural subordination as follows:

> In the last few years, schools have imposed another language construct that restricts our view of Latinx bilingual students as knowledgeable about language. This construct is what has been called *academic language*. It is now said that Latinx bilingual students fail not just because they do not 'have' English or Spanish, but because they also do not have academic language. ... Thus, the concept of academic language adds to the burden and the failure of Latinx bilingual students and renders their knowledge of language and bilingualism as non-academic, popular, intuitive, incomprehensible, or simply wrong. (García, 2020: 2–3) (emphasis original)

It is clear from the observations of García, Valdés, McCollum, Ramphal and others that devaluation of minoritised students' identities can occur in both monolingual and bilingual programmes as a result of misconceptions on the part of teachers about the appropriateness and 'correctness' of the varieties of L1 and L2 that students bring to school. As McCollum's research demonstrates, it is not only 'white monolingual middle-class people' that participate in this process of devaluation but also, in some situations, bilingual teachers from minoritised communities who unintentionally stigmatise students' language and cultural knowledge. It is also clear, that when teachers conflate 'academic language' with 'standard language' and stigmatise students' language, culture, and identities in the course of trying to teach literacy and academic language proficiency, they are inadvertently reinforcing stereotypes and coercive relations of power (see Figure 5.1 and Table 6.2). Rather than connecting to students' lives and affirming students' identities, they are invalidating students' experiences, talents, and identities.

Clearly these examples of instructional malpractice are indefensible and implicate not only the lack of awareness of some individual educators but also the systemic structures (e.g. teacher education programmes, professional development priorities, etc.) that perpetuate these practices. But to what extent do these unfortunate examples of misguided practice invalidate the legitimacy of the construct of 'academic language'? Apart from designating the construct of academic language as 'imprecise', neither García nor Valdés address the empirical data that have been invoked to support the legitimacy of the construct. They do not engage with the issue of whether the linguistic registers typically involved in 'everyday' linguistic interactions outside of school are identical to or distinct in certain ways from the linguistic registers operating across the curriculum and in classroom interactions that attempt to socialise students into fluid use and understanding of these registers (Gibbons, 2015).

To illustrate, García and Solorza (2020: 5) note that many scholars 'describe academic language as having long and complex sentences and using subordinating conjunctions, including frequently long noun phrases with embedded clauses; using nominalization, that is, using verbs or adjectives as nouns or noun phrases; and employing complex and unfamiliar vocabulary (Bailey 2007; Di Cerbo *et al.* 2014; Scarcella 2003; Schleppegrell 2004, 2012; Snow and Uccelli 2009, among others)'. They acknowledge that 'formulations such as these often describe the language of written academic texts' (2020: 5) but note that this language is not characteristic of typical teacher-student classroom interactions. This argument ignores the fact that success in school for *all* students depends on the extent to which they develop competence in reading increasingly complex *written* texts and learning how to *write* coherently for a variety of audiences across the curriculum. Thus, the characteristics of 'academic language' that García and Solorza summarise (and do not dispute) create significant learning challenges for white middle-class students as well as for minoritised students.

My reading of their work suggests that Valdés and García are more concerned with the ways in which the construct of 'academic language' has been inappropriately coopted to legitimise problematic instructional practices than with the extent to which this construct legitimately reflects language registers that are prominent within the context of schooling. This interpretation is based on the fact that (a) neither researcher has challenged or addressed in any depth the nature of the language registers used in schools (e.g. Wong Fillmore & Fillmore, 2012) and (b) both have affirmed the importance of teaching minoritised students the standardised academic language that permeates academic texts and school subjects across the curriculum.

Valdés (2004: 123), for example, noted that she is 'also not arguing that students should not be taught the conventions of academic language'. She cited approvingly the TESOL (1997) ESL Standards that, among other descriptors, specified that students will use English

> to obtain, process, construct and provide subject matter information in written form. They will retell information, compare and contrast information, persuade, argue, and justify, analyse, synthesise and infer from information. They will also hypothesise and predict, understand and produce technical vocabulary and text features according to the content area. (Valdés, 2004: 121)

In other words, she endorsed the legitimacy of teaching the academic registers associated with subject matter content, and also the cognitive functions that students use to acquire, interpret, and act on information. She elaborated the pedagogical focus of her concerns as follows:

> What I am questioning is whether academic language can, in fact, be taught or learned effectively in the self-contained, hermetic universes of ELL classrooms. ... Students must be encouraged to see themselves as having something to say, as taking part in a dialogue with teachers, with students in their classroom, with students in their school, with members of their communities, and with other writers who have written about issues and questions that intrigue them. (Valdés, 2004: 123)

Valdés' concern with segregated ELL classrooms is well-founded. Callahan *et al.*, for example, reported that 'students placed in ESL coursework exit high school with significantly less academic content, even when accounting for English proficiency, prior achievement, generational status, ethnicity, parental education, years in U.S. schools, and school level factors' (2010: 26). The alternative pedagogical strategies proposed by Valdés are entirely consistent with the emphasis in the present volume on connecting instruction to minoritised students' lives, validating their spoken varieties of L1 and L2, affirming their identities, and generally promoting pedagogies of powerful communication (Walker, 2014).

García similarly acknowledges the importance of engaging students in studying aspects of standard and academic language such as syntax, vocabulary, and discourse structure in ways that do not devalue the nonstandard varieties of L1 and L2 that minoritised students bring to the classroom: 'A translanguaging literacies approach also includes strategies such as translation and cross-linguistic study of syntax, vocabulary, word choice, cognates, and discourse structure to advance students' metalinguistic awareness of their own bilingual practices, thus heightening their engagement with texts' (García & Kleifgen, 2019: 13). García has also acknowledged the reality of academic and standard language and the need to teach these registers explicitly:

> Because literacy relies on the standard, the standard language itself is taught explicitly in school, and it *certainly needs to be taught*. ... We are not questioning the teaching of a standard language in school; without its acquisition, language minority children will continue to fail and will not have equal access to resources and opportunities. But we have to recognize that an *exclusive* focus on the standard variety keeps out other languaging practices that are children's authentic linguistic identity expression. (García, 2009: 36) (emphasis original)

What researcher or theorist over the past 60 years has argued that instruction should focus *exclusively* on the standard variety and prohibit minoritised students from using their authentic spoken varieties of L1 and L2? Ever since Labov (1969, 1972) established 'the logic of nonstandard English', there has been consensus among researchers and applied linguists that schools should build on the linguistic resources that students bring to school as part of a process of affirming the 'funds of knowledge' that exist in minoritised communities (Moll *et al.*, 1992). I assume that what García intends to communicate here is that the teaching of biliteracy, together with L1 and L2 academic and standard language skills, should also include affirmation of minoritised students' authentic languaging practices, a sentiment that virtually every contemporary applied linguist endorses.[2]

This interpretation is reinforced by García's (2013) apparent endorsement of the Common Core State Standards (CCSS) with their explicit emphasis on teaching academic language. In an introductory article to the pioneering CUNY-NYSIEB Guide for Educators (Celic & Seltzer, 2013) entitled *Theorizing Translanguaging for Educators*, García directly discussed the question of how translanguaging fits with the CCSS. She noted that a translanguaging pedagogical approach enables emergent bilingual students to meet the CCSS even when their English language is not fully developed. She pointed out that every instructional strategy in the Translanguaging Guide indexes in the sidebar of the page the relevant common core standard. She elaborated on the compatibility of translanguaging with the CCSS as follows:

> In addition, the theory of translanguaging fits well with the theory of language as action that is contained in the Common Core State Standards. Translanguaging offers bilingual students the possibility of being able to

gather, comprehend, evaluate, synthesize and report on information and ideas using text-based evidence; engage with complex texts, not only literary but informational; and write to persuade, explain and convey real or imaginary experience, even as their English is developing. (Celic & Seltzer, 2013: 3–4)

This perspective is very far removed from Wiley and Rolstad's claim, reviewed later in this chapter, that 'the CCSS reflect ... an autonomous, deficit orientation' (2014: 38). But it also seems very far removed from García's (2020) claim that the construct of 'academic language' subordinates the linguistic knowledge and expertise of minoritised students. Clearly, enabling minoritised students to understand and use academic registers (ideally in L1 and L2) by means of the powerful instructional strategies elaborated in the Translanguaging Guide (Celic & Seltzer, 2013) does not in any way position their language knowledge and expertise as deficient, or devalue their linguistic, cultural, and intellectual identities. In short, García's (2020) problem with 'academic language' seems to be with the problematic ways in which it has too often been taught rather than with the construct itself.

To what extent is there any substance to García and Solorza's (2020: 8) claim that the major problem with respect to the construct of 'academic language' is that the 'emphasis on academic language has driven instruction away from what scholars have called an asset-based approach to education'. This claim is weakened by their admission in the following sentence that 'the linguistic and cultural practices of Latinx bilingual students have always been devalued'. Thus, their case against the construct of academic language rests on two questionable propositions:

(1) raciolinguistic discrimination directed against the language practices of Latinx students has become more prevalent over the past decade, during which there has been an intensified focus on teaching academic language (as illustrated for example in the CCSS) than was the case in the 1980s, 1990s and 2000s;

(2) This purported intensification of raciolinguistic discrimination can be attributed to the construct of 'academic language'.

No evidence is presented to support either of these propositions. The miseducation of Latinx students obviously continues in many US schools but, to my knowledge, no researcher has presented any evidence that the situation is currently worse than it has been in the past, prior to the emphasis on 'academic language'. By the same token, there is no intrinsic relationship between the construct of 'academic language' and asset-based approaches to education. The inspirational research and school/university collaborations pursued by García and colleagues (and many other educators – see Chapter 11) have demonstrated how asset-based approaches (such as those outlined in Table 6.2) can develop minoritised students' knowledge of academic language and enable them to use it powerfully in a variety of communicative contexts.

In short, despite their concerns with the way the construct of 'academic language' has been interpreted instructionally in some US educational policies and classroom practices, neither Valdés nor García have unequivocally disputed the legitimacy of the construct. Valdés acknowledges that conventions of academic language should be taught 'in classrooms that are open to multiple texts and multiple voices' (2004: 123), and García affirms rather than refutes the legitimacy of academic/standard language by arguing that it 'certainly needs to be taught' (2009: 36).

The positions articulated by both Valdés and García appear similar to that advanced by Lisa Delpit (1988, 1995) more than 30 years ago. Delpit argued that teachers must recognise the potential conflict between minoritised students' home discourses and the discourse of the school. The appropriate instructional approach, according to Delpit, involves a *both/ and* rather than *either/or* orientation. A decontextualised focus on standard academic language risks devaluing the varieties of language(s) and the registers that students and communities use in everyday social interactions. However, attempts to affirm students' language varieties without explicitly teaching them the 'codes of power' infused in academic language risk excluding them from educational achievement and economic participation. According to Delpit (1988: 285) the Black community wants 'to ensure that the school provides their children with discourse patterns, interactional styles, and spoken and written language codes that will allow them success in the larger society'. She quoted a parent who demanded 'My kids know how to be Black – you all teach them how to be successful in the White man's world'. The appropriate way for teachers to do this, according to Delpit (1995: 164) is to transform the school discourse so that Black students can see themselves within it: 'To do so, they must saturate the dominant discourse with new meanings, must wrest from it a place for the glorification of their students and their forbears'. The poem entitled 'The Hill We Climb' written by Amanda Gorman, and recited by her at the January 2021 inauguration of President Joe Biden (and Kamala Harris as Vice President), illustrates powerfully how minoritised young people are more than capable of saturating the dominant discourse with new and emancipatory meanings.

To what extent is 'academic language' permeated by discourses of appropriateness and raciolinguistic ideologies (Flores & Rosa, 2015)?

Theoretical claims

In an influential article entitled 'Undoing appropriateness: Raciolinguistic ideologies and language diversity in education', Flores and Rosa (2015) argued that additive approaches to the education of bilingual students, heritage language learners, and Standard English learners are inherently problematic because 'discourses of appropriateness' lie at their core. They suggested that these discourses of appropriateness 'involve the conceptualization of standardized linguistic practices as objective sets of linguistic forms that are understood to be appropriate for academic settings' (2015: 150). Furthermore, these standardised linguistic practices are anchored in raciolinguistic ideologies 'that conflate certain racialized bodies with linguistic deficiency unrelated to any objective linguistic practices' (2015: 150). As a result of this process, 'long-term English learners, heritage language learners, and Standard English learners can be understood to inhabit a shared position as raciolinguistic Others vis-à-vis the white listening subject' (2015: 151).

Common to Flores and Rosa's (2015) concern with the ways in which discourses of appropriateness impact the educational experiences of these three groups or categories of students is the construction, in educational policy and practice, of their nonstandard linguistic varieties as inferior to the formal standardised 'academic' language taught in school. They reject what they view as 'rigid' distinctions between 'academic' and 'social' language use on the grounds that so-called 'academic' language is effectively used outside of formal school contexts and 'social' language is effectively used in conventional classroom settings. They claim that as a result of what they label the 'crude dichotomy' (2015: 159) between academic and nonacademic linguistic practices, the language dexterity of fluent speakers of a language such as Spanish, which students have learned in the home, is often stigmatised in formal academic contexts, thereby illustrating the operation of raciolinguistic ideologies and discourses of appropriateness.

With respect to long-term English learners, Flores and Rosa critique Olsen's (2010) description of these students as having high functioning social language, weak academic language and significant gaps in reading and writing skills. They argue that Olsen depicts long-term English learners as 'deficient in the academic language that is appropriate for a school context and necessary for academic success' (2015: 157). Also seen as problematic are Olsen's (2010: 33) pedagogical recommendations that instruction for these students should focus on 'powerful oral language, explicit literacy development, instruction in the academic uses of English, high quality writing, extensive reading of relevant texts, and emphasis on academic language and complex vocabulary'. Finally, they dispute Olsen's recommendation that long-term English learners should receive additive instruction that develops their home language literacy skills. Flores and Rosa summarise their critique by claiming that Olsen's recommendations for supporting long-term English learners' academic development are 'squarely focused on molding them into white speaking subjects who have mastered the empirical linguistic practices deemed appropriate for a school context' (2015: 157).

With respect to heritage language learners, Flores and Rosa endorse Valdés' (2001) rejection of 'prestige' varieties of linguistic practice as inherently more sophisticated than 'nonprestige' varieties. But they critique her 'embrace' of an additive approach to heritage language education in which heritage language learners must build from their proficiencies developed outside of the classroom in order to master the language that is appropriate in an academic setting. This approach, they argue, implicitly accepts the distinction between social and academic uses of language and is insufficient to address the raciolinguistic ideologies produced by the white speaking subject.

The third focus of the Flores/Rosa critique is Delpit's (1988, 2006) approach to educating African American standard English learners. Delpit advocated explicit teaching of the linguistic 'codes of power' where 'the point must not be to eliminate students' home languages, but rather to add other voices and discourses to their repertoires' (2006: 163). This orientation appears entirely consistent with that proposed by Valdés (2004). Flores and Rosa note that Delpit endorses a critical additive approach where students learn the codes of power while they are also 'helped to learn about the arbitrariness of those codes and about the power relationships they represent' (Delpit, 2006: 45). However, they also claim that it is 'clear that Delpit views the codes of power as a discrete set of practices [and as] objective linguistic practices rather than ideological phenomena' (2015: 165).

In order to 'undo' appropriateness in language education, Flores and Rosa (2015) suggest that we need to shift the focus of scrutiny to the white listening subject. They advocate a critical heteroglossic perspective that both 'legitimizes the dynamic linguistic practices of language-minoritized students while simultaneously raising awareness about issues of language and power' (2015: 167). A pedagogical focus on critical language awareness combined with a heteroglossic rather than a monoglossic perspective has the potential to open up space for unmasking the racism inherent in dominant approaches to language education.

Critique of the Flores/Rosa theoretical claims

The legitimacy of Flores and Rosa's (2015) theoretical claims with respect to 'academic language' can be analysed with reference to the criteria of empirical adequacy, logical coherence and consequential validity. Their claims fall far short of credibility in relation to all three criteria. A major problem throughout their analysis is that they repeatedly rely on blanket assertions with no qualifications regarding the social and educational conditions under which these assertions might be credible.

Empirical adequacy

Flores and Rosa conflate 'standard language' with 'academic language', claiming that both are embedded in discourses of appropriateness that reflect 'racialized ideological perceptions rather than objective linguistic categories' (2015: 152). As noted previously, they also question the distinction between linguistic practices that are appropriate for academic and social uses.

In equating standard language with academic language and implying that there is no empirically credible distinction between the language registers people typically use in everyday social interactions and the language registers students encounter in academic contexts, Flores and Rosa ignore a significant amount of research pointing to characteristics of written/academic language found in textbooks, novels, newspapers and schools, that differ significantly from the language we typically use in interpersonal face-to-face social interactions (e.g. Biber, 1986; Corson, 1995, 1997; Massaro, 2015; Wong Fillmore, 1982, 2009, 2014; Wong Fillmore & Fillmore, 2012). Bailey (2007: 9), for example, noted that differences between social and academic language lie in 'the relative frequency of complex grammatical structures, specialized vocabulary, and uncommon language functions'. Recent reviews of this issue that reinforce Bailey's conclusions include Cummins (2017c), DiCerbo et al. (2014), Heppt et al. (2016), Uccelli et al. (2015a, 2015b), Volodina et al. (2020).

Flores and Rosa's (2015) claims that there is no legitimate distinction between social and academic registers of language and that academic registers are permeated with discourses of appropriateness and raciolinguistic ideologies are simply asserted with no attempt to even consider empirical evidence that might be at variance with these claims. As pointed out by von der Mühlen et al. (2016), evidence-free assertion-based claims cannot be considered empirically credible. Thus, any attempt to dismiss the legitimacy of the construct of academic language that fails to even consider the empirical evidence is unconvincing.

Logical coherence

Flores and Rosa's (2015) claims regarding academic language also fail to meet the criterion of logical coherence. To illustrate, they note that Delpit (1988, 2006) advocates a critical instructional approach that attempts to demystify the arbitrary nature of codes of power and help students understand the power relationships these linguistic forms represent. Yet in the next paragraph, they claim that Delpit views the codes of power as a discrete set of objective linguistic practices rather than as ideological phenomena.

I have no idea how Flores and Rosa reached this conclusion. Delpit's statement that the codes of power are arbitrary seems very far from Flores and Rosa's claim that she views them as 'objective linguistic practices'. Their claim that she doesn't view the codes of power as ideological phenomena is hard to reconcile with her statement that the codes of power are embedded in societal power relations.[3]

An additional example of logical inconsistency involves Flores and Rosa's (2015: 167) denial that they are suggesting that 'people from racialized or language-minoritized communities should not seek to engage in linguistic practices deemed appropriate by mainstream society'. But it appears that they *are* suggesting that teachers who attempt to extend students' access to these linguistic practices are (inadvertent) agents of raciolinguistic ideologies and discourses of appropriateness.

Flores and Rosa might object that their analytic focus is on abstract theoretical constructs such as raciolinguistic ideologies, discourses of appropriateness, and objective linguistic forms rather than the actual instructional work of teachers. They note, for example, that their analysis focuses on racial hierarchies rather than individual practices. *However, racial hierarchies find expression only through the instructional practices of individual teachers.* For example, few researchers would dispute a claim that teachers who encourage minoritised students to replace their L1 with English are complicit with, and agents of, raciolinguistic ideologies, albeit inadvertently in many cases. By the same token, if the construct of 'academic language' is rooted in raciolingustic ideologies, then teachers who teach students how academic language works in any explicit way are clearly complicit in perpetuating raciolinguistic ideologies.

The other side of this coin is that if the pernicious effects of racial hierarchies are to be resisted or undone, it will surely be through the agency of teachers, students, and community members. Menken *et al.* (2011: 103) express this point as follows: 'promoting multilingualism in classroom settings relies on teachers, who are at the epicenter of language policy implementation in schools'. Thus, the claim that 'abstract theoretical constructs' are unrelated to the work of teachers is highly problematic and raises the question: 'Why write about these abstract theoretical constructs if they are not relevant to what teachers do in their classrooms'?

A final logical issue involves the criteria for deciding which (academic) language registers are permeated with discourses of appropriateness and raciolinguistic ideologies. The absence of any qualifications of scope or certainty (Britt *et al.*, 2014) in Flores and Rosa's analysis suggests that they view all forms of standard and academic language as constituting 'racialized ideological perceptions'. Does this theoretical claim imply that the writings of Gloria Anzaldúa, Te-Nehisi Coates, Frederick Douglass and Toni Morrison, among many others, are infused with raciolinguistic ideologies? If the academic registers used by these authors are not characterised by raciolinguistic ideologies, then which academic registers, if any, are infused with raciolingistic ideologies? What are the criteria for deciding whether a textbook, novel, or article is innocent or guilty in this regard? Are educators of colour who promote their students' acquisition of academic registers also afflicted with the 'white gaze' and raciolinguistic ideologies?

In summary, Flores and Rosa's unqualified assertion that the construct of 'academic language' and approaches to teaching academic language are permeated by discourses of appropriateness and raciolinguistic ideologies invokes the following flawed logic:

Because

some educators who teach language arts to minoritised students in both bilingual and English-medium programmes disparage, implicitly or explicitly, students' fluid non-standard language varieties and practices by failing to affirm and build on these language varieties and practices as they teach standard academic language skills,

therefore

all educators who teach literacy and academic language skills to minoritised students are complicit in the marginalisation of students' fluid language varieties and practices.

It is important to emphasise that this analysis in no way disputes the reality either of discourses of appropriateness or raciolinguistic ideologies (e.g. McCollum, 1999; Labov, 1969, 1972; Lippi-Green, 1997/2012; Ramphal, 1983). Clearly, the teaching of language arts (in L1 and/or L2) in many school systems may be prescriptive in orientation (as pointed out by García, 2020 and Valdés, 2017), and standards documents such as the Common Core State Standards in the United States may reinforce prescriptive orientations in some school contexts. However, there is no unique or inherent linkage between the theoretical construct of 'academic language' and misguided instructional approaches that attempt to teach academic language in highly problematic ways. Both Valdés (2017) and García (2009; García & Kleifgen, 2019), and many other researchers (e.g. Cummins, 2001a; Wong Fillmore, 1982, 2009, 2014) have pointed to ways of developing minoritised students' expertise in using academic registers of language that affirm rather than devalue students' linguistic and cultural capital.

Consequential validity

Flores and Rosa's (2015) analysis also falls short with respect to the criterion of consequential validity. As one example, noted previously, they critique Olsen's (2010: 33) argument that instruction for long-term English learners should promote their home language literacy skills together with powerful oral language, explicit literacy development, instruction in the academic uses of English, high quality writing, extensive reading of relevant texts, and emphasis on academic language and complex vocabulary. Flores and Rosa claim that these instructional approaches are designed to mold minoritised students into 'white speaking subjects,' but they tell us very little about what teachers should do to avoid this outcome apart from a vague instructional focus on critical language awareness that valorizes the home language practices of minoritised students.

Certainly, few if any progressive educators would argue against a pedagogical focus on critical language awareness or instruction that valorizes the home language practices of minoritised students (see, for example, Table 6.2 and Cummins, 2001a). But how is this focus in any way inconsistent with Olsen's recommendations that instruction should support students' home language literacies and expand their abilities to use oral and written language in powerful ways? Are Flores and Rosa (2015) suggesting that teachers should *not* encourage the development of powerful oral language, high quality writing, and extensive reading of relevant texts? If it is problematic for teachers to focus on powerful oral language, what should they focus on instead? If extensive reading of relevant texts is a problematic instructional goal, how should teachers expand their students' literacy skills? Are teachers who provide conceptual and linguistic feedback on minoritised students' academic writing complicit with discourses of appropriateness?[4]

In short, Flores and Rosa's critique of the construct of 'academic language' and teachers' attempts to expand minoritised students' access to academic language registers has no empirical basis, is logically flawed, and devoid of clear pedagogical directions for teachers. Blanket generalisations simply asserted without qualifications risk undermining the overall credibility of potentially useful theoretical constructs such as discourses of appropriateness and raciolinguistic ideologies.

Claim 3. The Construct of 'Academic Language' Reflects an 'Autonomous' Orientation to Language and Literacy that Ignores the Social, Economic and Political Contexts in which Language and Literacy Practices are Embedded

This claim primarily reflects the critique of the BICS/CALP distinction written by Terrence Wiley (1996) to which I responded in detail (Cummins, 2000). More recently, Wiley and Rolstad (2014), in an article entitled 'The Common Core State Standards and the Great Divide', have reprised this critique with a more general focus on what they view as the uncritical emphasis on 'academic language' in the Common Core State Standards (CCSS). In this section, I focus on the Wiley and Rolstad critique and, in particular, the overly simplistic and rigid way they interpret the distinction between autonomous and ideological orientations to literacy proposed initially by the late eminent British 'New Literacies' theorist Brian Street (1984).[5]

I argue that when viewed as a conceptual distinction to highlight the kinds of evidence and theoretical assumptions that underlie different approaches to literacy research and instructional practice, the contrast between autonomous and ideological orientations represents a useful heuristic tool. However, when adopted as a rigid *either-or* dichotomy that involves rejecting *a priori* the legitimacy of alternative orientations to literacy research, the autonomous/ideological distinction loses all credibility. In place of a scientifically unproductive dichotomy, I propose a *both-and* perspective that acknowledges (a) that autonomous and ideological orientations are each capable of generating legitimate research questions and usefully investigating language and literacy issues according to the modes of inquiry appropriate to their respective disciplines, (b) that each research orientation has contributed significantly to our understanding of language and literacy development among minoritised students and (c) that it makes far more sense to combine the insights from both orientations in designing effective literacy instruction for minoritised students rather than disparaging and dismissing the 'opposing' research tradition. The framework presented in Table 6.2 reflects this 'both-and' orientation to literacy research and theory.

Autonomous and ideological orientations to literacy and academic language: Oppositional or complementary?

An oppositional perspective

Wiley and Rolstad (2014: 39) describe the autonomous orientation as concentrating 'on formal mental properties of decoding and encoding text, and comprehending vocabulary, without consideration of how these processes are embedded within socio-cultural contexts'. Within this orientation, literacy development is studied from the perspective of individual psychological development. By contrast, the ideological orientation emphasises literacy practices as being embedded in, and shaped by, social, economic and political institutions and the power relations operating within these contexts.

Wiley and Rolstad point out that social practices scholars are not uninterested in individual cognitive development but these scholars argue that 'language and literacy skills or proficiencies are best understood and analyzed in social context, rather than as independent, autonomous skills, and that language and literacy emerge from social practice' (2014: 39). They state explicitly, and without qualification, that 'the CCSS reflect ... an autonomous, deficit orientation' (2014: 38). Their basic thesis is elaborated in their conclusions:

> The Common Core State Standards (CCSS) initiative places a strong emphasis on the development of 'academic English,' though little effort has been made to define the construct. One sees the persistence of the idea that language itself is the gateway to greater cognitive development, and that the language of the literate somehow contributes special qualities which permit access and insight into academic disciplines which other forms of language do not allow. ... It is simply not the case that literacy and academic language involve higher order cognition, while other domains in which we use specialized language do not. (Wiley & Rolstad, 2014: 51)

Their argument here is that just as in the 'Great Divide' debate, where some scholars argued that 'literate' people have cognitive advantages in comparison to so-called 'nonliterate' people, claims that were debunked by Scribner and Cole (1978), the CCSS emphasis on 'academic English' implies that this form of language confers special educational and cognitive advantages on people. In opposition to the CCSS emphasis on 'academic language', Wiley and Rolstad claim that expertise in understanding and using literate or academic language confers no more advantage than other forms of language on students attempting to access science, math and social studies content.

This claim immediately raises the question of what is meant by 'other forms of language' are we talking about the language of horticulture, the language of Facebook interactions, or the language of casual, everyday interaction between friends, or all registers of language used in out-of-school contexts? It seems at least highly counter-intuitive, not to mention contrary to considerable research evidence (e.g. Barr *et al.*, 2019; Phillips Galloway & Uccelli, 2018), to claim that students who have developed familiarity with and expertise in using general academic registers have no more advantage in accessing subject matter disciplinary content within the sociocultural context of schooling than students whose knowledge of general academic registers is much less strongly developed.

With respect to Wiley and Rolstad's claim that higher order cognition is involved in human endeavours outside of academic and print literacy-related contexts, what educator or applied linguist has ever argued that this is not the case?[6] I know of no serious educational scholar concerned with the education of minoritised students who endorses any form of deficit orientation to students' cognitive or academic development. Thus, Wiley and Rolstad's (2014) invocation of the 'Great Divide' debate relating to the cognitive abilities of 'literate' versus 'nonliterate' peoples seems little more than a dubious rhetorical device intended to smear by analogy theorists who believe that the construct of 'academic language' has empirical and logical substance.

Wiley and Rolstad do not reference any empirical support for their assertion that knowledge of academic language is essentially independent of the development of students' ability to access and gain insight into academic disciplines. Nor do they acknowledge any of the research that contradicts their position showing strong relationships between academic language skills and school performance in content-area disciplines (e.g. Grabe, 2004; Kaufman *et al.*, 2016). For example, the dimensions of 'core academic language skills' (CALS), identified by Uccelli and colleagues by means of extensive empirical research, demonstrate that academic language skills are strongly related to academic performance across the curriculum (e.g. Uccelli *et al.*, 2015a, 2015b; Barr *et al.*, 2019). These relationships are clearly referenced in at least three of the seven domains of CALS identified empirically by these authors: *Domain 1: Unpacking Dense Information at the Word and Sentence Level*; *Domain 5: Understanding Metalinguistic Vocabulary*; and *Domain 7: Recognizing Academic Language*. Domain 1 is described as follows: 'Skill in comprehending (a) complex words and (b) complex sentences helps readers to unpack dense information in academic texts' (Barr *et al.*, 2019: 987). Other scholars have similarly identified skills such as *focusing on informational density in content-area texts* as central components of the development of academic expertise (e.g. Bunch, 2013; Wong Fillmore, 2009, 2014). In short, contrary to Wiley and Rolstad's claims, there is overwhelming empirical evidence showing strong relationships between academic language skills and school performance across the curriculum.

I suspect that Wiley and Rolstad would dismiss any empirical research that casts doubt on their assertion that 'academic language' is unrelated to disciplinary knowledge as emanating from an autonomous orientation and consequently not credible. This dismissal of all research deriving from an autonomous orientation logically also applies to the research conducted by a large majority of applied linguists, cognitive psychologists, and second language educators who have explored the nature of academic language and ways of enabling students to read and produce complex academic text. For example, the bulk of empirical evidence referenced by theorists such as Bunch (2013), Bunch *et al.* (2014), Gibbons (2015), Hiebert and Mesmer (2013), Uccelli *et al.* (2015a, 2015b) and Wong Fillmore and Fillmore (2012) draws predominantly on psychological and applied linguistics research that owes little to ideological perspectives. Are all of these, and many other theorists, complicit with deficit orientations to minoritised students' academic development? Should all of the research and theory related to the role of scaffolding academic content in order to make it comprehensible for learners (e.g. Gibbons, 2015) be rejected simply because it is alleged to reflect an autonomous perspective? If the CCSS focus on academic language reflects a deficit orientation to minoritised students' language and cognition, then why should the researchers cited above (among many others) who have discussed how to implement the CCSS not also be rebuked for promoting a deficit agenda?

The most useful (and truly inspirational) resource that provides guidance for teachers of multilingual students to implement the CCSS is the CUNY-NYSIEB Translanguaging Guide (Celic & Seltzer, 2013; García, 2013), which aligns translanguaging strategies with relevant Common Core standards. Wiley and Rolstad's (2014) unqualified claim that the CCSS reflect an autonomous, deficit orientation logically implies that the Translanguaging Guide and its authors are complicit with a deficit orientation to minoritised students' language and literacy skills. The absurdity of this position reflects the superficiality of the assertion-based theoretical claims that constitute the Wiley and Rolstad (2014) analysis.

Clearly, as pointed out previously, any credible analysis of why deficit orientations allegedly permeate the CCSS, but (perhaps) not the work of scholars who have discussed how the CCSS instructional goals might be implemented, requires *criteria* for what constitutes a deficit orientation and what does not. It is not sufficient simply to cite Valencia's (1997) definition of a deficit theory as holding 'that the student who fails in school does so because of internal deficits or deficiencies…' (Rolstad, 2017: 501) without explaining why the CCSS conception of 'academic language' constitutes a deficit theory whereas the work of most other cognitive psychologists and applied linguists who discuss how students can be supported in accessing and using complex text is innocent of these charges. Claims regarding deficit theories that fail to conduct this kind of analysis do not meet the criterion of logical coherence.

A final point concerns Wiley and Rolstad's implication that educators and/or researchers who give credence to the construct of 'academic language' believe that ELLs cannot engage in intellectually challenging work until they have fully developed academic language and literacy. They express this perspective as follows:

> The alleged Great Divide, whether expressed as cognitive deficits or as a never ending 'achievement gap,' does not aid in our understanding, nor does the expectation that children cannot engage in intellectually stimulating work until after they have developed academic language and literacy. Instead, we support the efforts of educators who seek to engage students in interesting, challenging work which can then lead to the expansion of students' linguistic repertoires and their development of literacy, rather than the other way around. (Wiley & Rolstad, 2014: 51)

Once again, no citations are offered to indicate which researchers have ever argued that children should be excluded from intellectually stimulating work until after they have developed grade-appropriate academic language and literacy. The fact that these practices do occur in far too many school contexts (e.g. Callahan et al., 2010) does not automatically imply that any *researchers* endorse these forms of instructional malpractice. I can think of no current researcher who has argued that ELLs who receive appropriate teacher support are *not* capable of engaging in higher order thinking and reading of challenging texts long before they have caught up academically to grade expectations in academic English. Certainly, none of the scholarly articles or support documents aimed at interpreting the implications of the CCSS for teacher education or ELL instruction (e.g. Bunch, 2013; Council of Great City Schools, 2014; García, 2013; Hiebert & Mesmer, 2013; Wong Fillmore, 2014) have argued that the ability to use academic English is a prerequisite for understanding academic content or engaging in intellectually stimulating academic work. To illustrate, the *Framework for Raising Expectations and Instructional Rigor for English Language Learners* published by the Council of Great City Schools to support teachers in helping ELLs meet the academic challenges of the CCSS, expressed its 'theory of action' in the following way:

> ... English Language Learners are capable of engaging in complex thinking, reading and comprehension of complex texts, and writing about complex material. If teachers are given time to analyze the CCSS and plan effective lessons based on the standards and using grade-level appropriate, complex texts, ELLs *will* acquire the reasoning, language skills, and academic registers they need to be successful across the curriculum and throughout the school day. (Council of Great City Schools, 2014: 3)

In short, Wiley and Rolstad's claim that 'the CCSS reflect ... an autonomous, deficit orientation' (2014: 38) amounts to little more than an evidence-free and logically incoherent assertion. The fact that the CCSS and the Council of Great City Schools (2014), together with numerous researchers (e.g. Uccelli *et al.*, 2015a, 2015b; Wong Fillmore & Fillmore, 2012), give credence both to the reality of 'academic language' and research supporting the construct does not automatically transform these researchers into deficit theorists.

A complementary perspective

In discussing the impact of literacy policies on school curricula, I examined the claims to knowledge of two opposing orientations to literacy research (Cummins, 2015). Rather than using the loaded terms 'autonomous' and 'ideological', I used the minimally value-laden terms *individualistic orientations to literacy research* and *social orientations to literacy research*. I pointed out that recent educational policies in both the United Kingdom (UK) and United States (US) have drawn heavily on the claims of researchers whose orientation is individualistic and have largely ignored the research and theory of those whose work is rooted in social orientations to literacy. I suggested that literacy policies in both contexts have failed to achieve their goals of reducing achievement gaps because (a) research deriving from social orientations was ignored and (b) research deriving from individualistic orientations was interpreted by both researchers and policymakers in highly problematic ways (Cummins, 2007b, 2015).

The individualistic orientation views reading as a cognitive process that takes place within the heads of individuals whereas the social orientation views reading and other aspects of literacy as social practices intimately dependent on context. The former orientation is predominantly rooted in the discipline of cognitive psychology and relies on quantitative research methods, ideally experimental and quasi-experimental studies, to test hypotheses and generate knowledge (e.g. Ehri *et al.*, 2001; National Reading Panel, 2000). By contrast, researchers who view literacy as a set of social practices argue that it cannot be reduced to a single linear quantifiable dimension. The term *multiliteracies* (New London Group, 1996) was introduced to highlight the multimodal and multilingual dimensions of literacy practices (see also Haneda, 2014, in relation to the connection between academic language and the broader toolkit of mediational means used to achieve goals of personal importance). The work of these researchers and theorists is often referred to as *The New Literacy Studies* (e.g. Pahl & Rowsell, 2005). This work draws on a more varied set of disciplinary orientations, including anthropology and sociology, and relies predominantly on qualitative research methods such as critical ethnographies to articulate claims and generate knowledge.

The oppositional orientation that characterises individualistic and social orientations to literacy research is illustrated in the dismissal by both sides of research reflecting the opposing orientation. Wiley and Rolstad's (2014) rejection of individualistic/autonomous orientations was analysed in the previous section. The dismissal of social orientations to research by scholars representing an individualistic orientation rooted in cognitive psychology was illustrated in Chapter 7 by August *et al*.'s (2008) claim that qualitative research can only generate hypotheses about the influence of instruction on learning because it makes no systematic comparisons between treatment and control groups. As a result of its individualistic orientation to research, the National Literacy Panel (NLP) could draw virtually no conclusions regarding the impact of sociocultural variables on linguistically diverse students' academic achievement.[7]

I argued that this oppositional perspective between individualistic and social orientations to research is scientifically unnecessary and unproductive (Cummins, 2008a, 2015). A complementary perspective that recognises the specific contributions to knowledge of both orientations is likely to yield more useful information and insights to guide instruction and policy (Pearson, 2004). Issues related to schooling, equity and literacy are clearly rooted in societal ideologies and power structures (see Chapters 5 and 6). However, this does not mean that a social practices perspective that highlights social and contextually specific dimensions of cognition and literacy is the best or only way to address all questions of literacy development. It is equally legitimate to ask questions regarding issues such as the following:

- What cognitive processes are operating within the heads of individuals as they perform cognitive or linguistic tasks (e.g. Bialystok, 2020a)?
- How long does it typically take linguistically diverse students to catch up to grade expectations in school-related language and literacy skills (e.g. Cummins, 1981c)?
- What are the effects of reinforcing students' knowledge of how academic language works across the curriculum as opposed to teaching the school language only in Language Arts or language support contexts (e.g. Callahan *et al*., 2010)?
- What are the effects of literacy engagement on reading comprehension (e.g. Guthrie, 2004)?

None of these questions reflect an 'ideological' or social orientation to language and literacy teaching and development, but research focused on these questions has contributed in substantial ways to promoting equity in schooling for bilingual students.

An unfortunate consequence of the oppositional orientation to the distinction between individualistic and social orientations to literacy instruction and research (or 'autonomous' versus 'ideological' orientations) is that each side tends to generate caricatures of the other. For example, in describing differences in instructional practices between autonomous and ideological orientations, Skutnabb-Kangas and McCarty (2008) point out that an autonomous perspective emphasises discrete language skills, often taught through direct instruction and scripted phonics programmes. It is certainly accurate to claim that this type of instructional approach is rooted in an autonomous perspective that largely ignores social realities associated with literacy (see Cummins, 2007b, for a critique). However, it is not accurate to claim that all researchers who give credence to cognitively and individually oriented research advocate this kind of restrictive (and largely evidence-free) instructional approach to teaching reading and writing. For example, as someone who gives credence, in principle, to both individualistic and social research orientations, I am in full agreement with the legitimacy and importance of Skutnabb-Kangas and McCarty's (2008: 4) description of literacy pedagogy rooted in ideological perspectives: 'An *ideological* view binds reading and writing to oracy, emphasizing the development of different literacies (and multiliteracies) for different purposes through meaningful social interaction and critical examination of authentic texts' (emphasis original).

In short, it is no more defensible for researchers who endorse a social or ideological orientation to language and literacy to dismiss, in principle, research emanating from an autonomous or individualistic orientation than it is for individualistic-oriented researchers to dismiss the legitimacy of social-oriented or 'New Literacies' research. The claims to knowledge of each orientation should be examined on their merits rather than on the particular research ideology they reflect. In this regard, I have argued that many of the claims regarding reading development, rooted in an individualistic orientation to research, proposed by the National Reading Panel (NRP) (2000) and the National Literacy Panel (August & Shanahan, 2006, 2008a) are empirically unsupported (Cummins, 2007b, 2015). Similarly, many claims that profess an ideological or social practices orientation are logically flawed and without empirical support (e.g. Flores & Rosa, 2015; Wiley & Rolstad, 2014).

Thus, the construct of 'academic language' is not automatically invalidated simply because much of its empirical support derives from psycholinguistic and classroom-based research. By the same token, any credible account of how literacy and academic language (in L1 and L2) should be developed in schools must go beyond a psycholinguistic focus and take account of how societal power relations create opportunity gaps that can be addressed only through equity-oriented and culturally sustaining instruction (Boykin & Noguera, 2011).

Section 2. Legitimacy of the Construct of 'Academic Language': Empirical, Theoretical and Instructional Perspectives

As noted in Chapter 4, over the past 40 years in numerous publications, I have highlighted the empirical basis for the distinction between 'academic language proficiency' and 'conversational fluency' (e.g. Cummins, 1981b, 1984a, 2000, 2008a). Briefly stated, in monolingual contexts the distinction reflects the obvious differences between the fluent interpersonal communicative skills that (most) children bring to school at age 5 or 6, and the expanded range of language registers they acquire through literacy and during 12 years of schooling. It also reflects the difference in time periods typically required for immigrant-background students to acquire a reasonable degree of fluency in face-to-face situations compared to the length of time required to catch up academically to grade expectations in literacy and subject matter content. I also argued (Cummins, 2000) that the legitimacy of the difference between 'academic' and everyday language is supported by (a) Biber's (1986) analysis of a corpus of authentic discourse gathered from a wide range of communicative situations, both written and oral; (b) Corson's (1995, 1997) documentation of the lexical differences between English everyday conversational language and textual language, the former deriving predominantly from Anglo-Saxon sources and the latter from Graeco-Latin sources; and (c) Snow and Hoefnagel-Höhle's (1979) longitudinal analysis of L1 and L2 development among English speakers learning Dutch in a naturalistic setting.

To my knowledge, none of the critics of the construct of 'academic language' has questioned the credibility of the empirical evidence supporting the construct. In recent years, this empirical evidence has been powerfully elaborated by the research programme of Paola Uccelli of Harvard University and colleagues who have conceptualised and investigated what they term *Core Academic Language Skills* (CALS). I review this research in the next section.

With respect to theoretical contributions that support the construct of 'academic language', I review the work of Jan H. Hulstijn of the University of Amsterdam. Hulstijn does not focus directly on 'academic language' but his distinction between *basic language cognition* and *extended language cognition* provides important perspectives on the nature of the 'language cognition' that schools attempt to promote.

Finally, I review the insights about 'academic language' that derive from instructional perspectives and particularly the collaborative work with teachers carried out over many years by Lily Wong Fillmore of the University of California, Berkeley. This work highlights the importance of understanding the challenges posed by academic language for *all* students, first language learners as well as students learning the school language, if we are to teach it effectively.

Uccelli and Colleagues' Core Academic Language Skills (CALS)

The starting points for the research agenda that Paola Uccelli and colleagues have pursued over the past decade are discussed in the paper 'The Challenge of Academic Language' (Snow & Uccelli, 2009). The authors pointed to the fact that although there is widespread agreement that the development of academic language skills poses challenges for both L1 and L2 learners, there is still no precise or validated consensus regarding the linguistic characteristics of academic language. They noted that language can be more or less academic depending on the prevalence in particular texts or utterances of traits that are typical of academic language (e.g. nominalisation and lexical density). Thus, there is no basis for designating 'academic language' as a separate category that has passed some threshold qualifying it as 'academic'. They also noted that although academic communication poses particular kinds of challenges compared to other forms of language (e.g. explaining the theory of evolution as compared to negotiating the purchase of onions), it is not necessarily more complex than colloquial language in any absolute sense. It is, however, more relevant to success in school than most forms of colloquial language. Informal colloquial language does vary among native speakers but, in most contexts, not in ways that are particularly consequential for educational success.

Snow and Uccelli (2009) articulated a research agenda for exploring the nature of academic language, which Uccelli and colleagues have pursued in impressive ways. Uccelli *et al.* (2015b) proposed the construct of *Core Academic Language Skills* (CALS), which they defined as: 'a constellation of the high-utility language skills that correspond to linguistic features that are prevalent in academic discourse across school content areas and infrequent in colloquial conversations' (2015b: 338). Phillips Galloway *et al.* elaborated the CALS construct as follows:

> CALS refer to knowledge of the lexical, syntactic, and discourse resources used for completing common communicative functions in classroom learning communities. CALS encompass knowledge of abstract vocabulary, intricate sentence structures, connective words, and phrases (e.g., *therefore, as a result*), and stance markers (e.g., *probably, it might be true* …) that are of high utility for their prevalent use in written academic discourse to precisely and concisely express information, to logically organize thinking, and to express perspectives reflectively. (Phillips Galloway *et al.*, 2020: 4)

Uccelli and colleagues also developed the Core Academic Language Skills Instrument (CALS-I), which they defined as 'a theoretically grounded and psychometrically robust innovative tool' (2015b: 337) to assess and explore the CALS. They reported that CALS independently predicted reading comprehension, even after controlling for academic vocabulary knowledge, word reading fluency, and sociodemographic factors (e.g. SES).

Uccelli *et al.* (2015a) locate their research within a sociocultural pragmatics-based view of language development in which language is conceptualised as inseparable from social context, and language learning is viewed as context-dependent and usage-based. Thus, language proficiencies emerge as the result of individuals' socialisation and enculturation histories. It is worth noting that the authors see no contradiction between this social practices theoretical orientation and their use of the kind of assessment instruments that Edelsky *et al.* (1983: 9) described as 'out-of-context, irrelevant nonsense'.

Uccelli *et al.* (2015b) point to the gap that may exist, for all learners, between the colloquial language of the home and community and the academic language of schooling. Young learners are successfully enculturated into the language of face-to-face communication within their communities; however, these colloquial conversations and interactions through social media are not always aligned with language and literacy practices characteristic of school such as the language of argumentation and written informational discourse:

> As a consequence, many colloquially fluent students may not have been granted sufficient opportunities to be socialized into academic-language and literacy practices either at home or at school. ... The available ethnographic and quantitative research findings point to students from minoritized linguistic communities and from high-needs environments as particularly likely to experience a larger distance between the ways language is used outside of school and the ways it is used in school texts. (Uccelli *et al.*, 2015b: 339)

Barr *et al.* (2019) are careful to point out that academic language development is just one of many dimensions of language proficiency that develop through adolescence. It is part of the much larger process of achieving what they term 'rhetorical flexibility', understood as the ability to use 'an increasing repertoire of lexico-grammatical and discourse resources appropriately and flexibly in an expanding variety of social contexts, for instance, mastering the language skills of youth conversation, sportscasts, or religious communities' (2019: 986). However, core academic language skills reflect the discourse patterns and challenges of language and literacy use within the social context of schooling to a greater extent than other registers of language development.

The seven domains of CALS were identified either on the basis of existing empirical evidence related to their role in text comprehension or on the basis of persuasive arguments in the scholarly literature related to their relevance to text comprehension. These domains, as operationalised in the Core Academic Language Skills–Inventory (CALS-I), are summarised below (Barr *et al.*, 2019):

Domain 1: Unpacking dense information at the word and sentence level. This domain includes the ability to use morphological and syntactic skills to comprehend complex words and sentences.

Domain 2: Connecting ideas logically. This domain tests understanding of connectives such as *consequently, as a result, although*, etc.) that indicate how ideas are related to each other.

Domain 3: Tracking participants and themes. This domain assesses students' ability to track expressions that refer to the same participants or themes throughout an academic text (e.g. *Water evaporates at 100 degrees Celsius. This process …*).

Domain 4: Organising analytic texts. This domain reflects students' skill in recognising organisational structures characteristic of academic discourse such as argumentative texts (e.g. *thesis, argument, counter-argument, conclusion*) and paragraph-level structures (e.g. *compare/* contrast; *problem/solution*).

Domain 5: Understanding metalinguistic vocabulary. Although the relationship between reading comprehension and this subset of general academic vocabulary has not been specifically investigated, skill in understanding words that refer to thinking or discourse processes (e.g. *hypothesis, generalisation, argument*) has been hypothesised to play an important role in comprehension and school learning (Astington & Olson, 1990).

Domain 6: Understanding a writer's viewpoint. This domain assesses the student's understanding of linguistic markers that express the writer's stance in relation to the content of a proposition (e.g. *It is quite obvious from the research data that climate change is happening*).

Domain 7: Recognising academic language. This domain reflects the student's ability to distinguish between academic and colloquial language features in a text.

In a large-scale study of more than 7,000 Grades 4–8 students in the United States, Barr *et al.* (2019) reported the following three major findings:

- CALS, as measured by the CALS-I instrument, represents a unidimensional set of skills best represented by a higher-order factor composed of distinguishable but interrelated lower-order task-specific factors: 'cross-disciplinary academic language proficiency, as operationalized in this study, is best represented as a unitary construct made up of a constellation of distinguishable skills that co-develop, most likely as students engage with all these skillsets concurrently when participating in academic discussions and reading and learning at school' (2019: 1006).
- CALS showed strong criterion validity when compared to a standardised assessment of reading comprehension.
- CALS captured variability across Grades 4 to 8, with older students performing better but with considerable individual differences within grades.

Phillips Galloway and Uccelli (2019a) also demonstrated a strong relationship between CALS and the quality of science writing among Grades 4–7 students. The researchers controlled for students' reading comprehension of the source text, the impact of student characteristics such as grade,

English proficiency status, SES, and special education status, and the features of students' summaries (misspelling ratio, topic, length, ratio of copied text). They reported that 'both academic language skills and comprehension of the source text make unique contributions to science summary writing quality for students in grades four to seven' (2018: 750).

An additional study (Phillips Galloway & Uccelli, 2019b) examined the development of academic language skills and reading comprehension in a sample of Grades 6–7 emergent bilinguals and their English proficient peers ($n = 573$). Findings indicated that growth rates in CALS over the two years of the study were positively associated with growth rates in reading comprehension, and initial levels of CALS predicted rates of growth in reading comprehension. The authors argue for the potential for CALS-focused instruction to promote adolescent learners' reading comprehension development.

With respect to the question posed in the title of this chapter, the CALS research presents a strong case that 'academic language' *is* a legitimate theoretical construct. Uccelli and colleagues have clearly addressed the concern expressed by García (2020) and Valdés (2004, 2017) that the notion of 'academic language' is 'imprecise'. Not only have Uccelli and colleagues specified precisely the dimensions they view as 'core' to the construct of 'academic language', they have also operationalised these dimensions in the CALS-I instrument and demonstrated the unidimensional coherence of the construct, as well as criterion validity with measures of reading comprehension (Barr *et al.*, 2019; Phillips Galloway, 2019b) and science summary writing (Phillips Galloway & Uccelli, 2019a). Thus, the claims of these researchers regarding the legitimacy of the construct of 'academic language' go a considerable way to meeting the criterion of empirical adequacy.

The researchers are cautious, however, to acknowledge that further research is required to demonstrate the construct validity of CALS. Barr *et al.* also note that the 'larger construct of academic language proficiency includes both cross-disciplinary and discipline-specific skills, and in no way does this study suggest that the overarching academic language proficiency construct is unidimensional' (2019: 1011). In other words, although their research provides evidence for unidimensionality of *cross-disciplinary* language skills, there may be specific skills involved in the language of math, science, history, and other disciplines that are distinguishable empirically from CALS. They also highlight the fact that language usage and development, as well as reading comprehension, are *situated* and vary by contexts of use. Thus, their findings are not necessarily generalisable to language skills in general or to contexts of language use that differ significantly from the educational contexts experienced by their samples of students.

With respect to logical/theoretical coherence, García and Solorza (2020) have critiqued the work of Uccelli and colleagues (2015a) on a number of counts. They argued that the construct of CALS reifies the concept of language as a named autonomous entity without addressing how it has been constructed by processes of colonisation and nation-building. They also argue that CALS presents language learning as a simple linear developmental skill focused on acquiring characteristics of what is assumed to be a single valid white middle-class linguistic and cultural norm.

This critique of the CALS construct is not persuasive to me. In the first place, as discussed in a previous section, it is more productive to view so-called autonomous and ideological orientations to language as complementary rather than as oppositional to each other. Secondly, it is logically inconsistent to dismiss standard academic language as the property of white middle-class students when García (2009: 36) herself, together with other colleagues (e.g. Celic & Seltzer, 2013: 17), has clearly articulated the need to teach standard academic language to minoritised students. As Uccelli *et al.* (2020) have argued, all students have the right to have their voices heard and the right to develop the academic language skills that will enable them to project their voices powerfully into multiple social spheres. They specifically address how the CALS framework can be applied to the education of Latinx students by documenting how CALS can be used to affirm and amplify students' voices as they engage in critical reflection and discussion of social issues: 'Integrating insights from our teacher-researcher collaborations, we call for practices and dispositions that *amplify* language resources and awareness and *affirm* students' voices by engaging teachers and students in reflecting about language, context, and power while scaffolding CALS across content areas and grades' (2020: 75) (emphasis original). These goals seem to be completely aligned with those of the CUNY-NYSIEB Translanguaging Guide (Celic & Seltzer, 2013; García, 2013), further undermining García and Solorza's (2020) critique of the CALS project.

As far as consequential validity is concerned, Uccelli *et al.* (2015) highlight some of the pedagogical applications of the CALS in the context of the emphasis in the CCSS to expose students to more complex texts: 'Thus, a potential pedagogical application of the CALS-I might be to help make the crucial role of students' academic language skills visible to educators and researchers and to support them in identifying language features in the complex texts that students must read at school and in designing lessons that incorporate the expansion of students' academic language skills as an important pedagogical goal' (2015: 1101). García and Solorza (2020: 7) adopt a very different perspective with respect to the consequential validity of CALS: 'The danger of how CALS is being taken up by policy makers and educators is that the construct is being used to further enregister Latinx bilinguals who language differently, as not only lacking "academic language", but also cognitive skills'. This argument echoes the critiques of BICS/CALP by researchers such as Edelsky *et al.* (1983), MacSwan and Rolstad (2003) and others. García and Solorza present no evidence or examples of how CALS is being used to stigmatise Latinx students as lacking linguistic and cognitive skills.

My perspective on this issue is that it is counter-productive for researchers to make the construct of 'academic language' a scapegoat for the miseducation of minoritised students. It makes far more pedagogical sense (1) to acknowledge that the development of academic and literacy skills presents challenges for *all* students that go beyond the challenges of acquiring everyday interpersonal language skills and (2) to work collaboratively with educators and teacher educators to implement asset-based instructional approaches that have demonstrated their effectiveness in enabling minoritised and non-minoritised students to overcome these challenges and to use language in powerful and identity-affirming ways (e.g. CUNY-New York State Initiative on Emergent Bilinguals, 2021; Isola & Cummins, 2020; Little & Kirwin, 2019; Nieto & Bode, 2018). Gottlieb and Castro (2017: 7) express a similar perspective: 'an intentional focus on language provides more equitable opportunities for students to interact with academic discourse and assures that all students have the tools to participate meaningfully in activities designed to mediate learning'.[8]

In short, the CALS construct has demonstrated its utility as a conceptual framework to promote what Uccelli *et al.* (2019) term 'critical rhetorical flexibility' among both Latinx students and the general school population. This initial credibility with respect to consequential validity will undoubtedly be refined and elaborated as more educators become aware of the CALS framework and begin to apply it in their classrooms. The CALS research also highlights the *lack of credibility* of claims that the construct of 'academic language' reflects a deficit orientation to minoritised students' language and cognition (MacSwan, 2000; MacSwan & Rolstad, 2003; Rolstad, 2017; Wiley & Rolstad, 2014) or that educators' attempts to promote academic language skills are permeated by discourses of appropriateness and raciolinguistic ideologies (Flores & Rosa, 2015).

Hulstijn's Theory of Basic and Extended Language Cognition

Dutch linguist Jan Hulstijn (2011, 2015, 2019) proposed what he termed *Basic Language Cognition* (BLC) theory to address a variety of issues related to variability in bilingualism and L1 and L2 acquisition. He used the term 'language cognition' as synonymous with language proficiency and language ability to refer both to 'knowledge of language and the ability to access, retrieve and use that knowledge in listening, speaking, reading or writing' (2015: 20-21). The theory proposed a distinction between basic and extended or 'higher' language cognition, which he described in the following way:[9]

BLC refers to the language cognition in the oral domains (comprehension and production of speech) that is acquired and thus shared by all adult native speakers. ... Extended language cognition is the domain of oral and written language use where differences between native speakers can be observed, that is, language cognition not acquired or shared by all native speakers. (Hulstijn, 2019: 160-161)

Hulstijn (2015) noted that the distinction between basic and extended language cognition (ELC) represents a dichotomy rather than a continuum. This dichotomy is unified within the construct of 'language proficiency' or 'language cognition'. He argued that the preference for a dichotomy rather than a continuum 'is based on the fact that, in the domains of lexis, morpho-syntax and pragmatics, there is a minority of elements (words, constructions, expressions) that occur extremely frequently, while there is a large majority of elements that occur infrequently' (2015: 22).

BLC involves lexical items and grammatical structures that occur frequently in speech in any communicative situation and is shared by all adult first-language speakers, regardless of age, literacy, or educational level. Within the BLC construct, the individual's knowledge of phonetics, prosody, phonology, morphology and syntax is largely implicit and unconscious whereas lexical-pragmatic knowledge is largely explicit and conscious. In both cases, this knowledge is processed with a high degree of automaticity.

ELC, on the other hand, involves low-frequency lexical items and uncommon morphosyntactic structures that can occur in both written text and spoken utterances. These utterances are frequently more complex lexically and grammatically and they are often longer than those reflecting BLC. According to Hulstijn (2011: 231), ELC discourse 'pertains to topics other than simple everyday matters, that is, topics addressed in school and colleges, on the work floor, and in leisure-time activities'. Any differences in language proficiency/cognition that result from experiences with literacy will affect only ELC because, by definition, BLC is invariant across individual native speakers in adult native speaker populations.

The relevance of the BLC/ELC distinction in the present context is that the constructs of 'academic language' and 'academic language proficiency' represent one domain of language use, involving both general academic and specific disciplinary registers, within the broader construct of extended or nonshared language cognition. Thus, unlike MacSwan (1999) and Rolstad (2017), Hulstijn does not regard the construct of 'language proficiency' as pertaining only to the nonvariant species-universal shared language development that occurs in the early years. The construct of 'language proficiency' extends beyond 'basic', 'universal', or 'shared' language development into the realm of individual differences among 'native' or L1-speakers in their access to a wide variety of language registers, some of which are associated with literacy and schooling. This understanding of 'language development' is similar to that of many other educators, researchers and theorists (e.g. Cummins, 2000; Uccelli & Snow, 2009; Wong Fillmore, 2014).

Hulstijn (2011, 2015) recognised the similarity between his constructs of BLC and ELC and the BICS/CALP distinction but pointed out that there are important differences in specificity and theoretical context. According to Hulstijn, BICS is defined only in a general way whereas BLC 'explicitly refers to the distinction between language reception and production, to the distinction between representation and online processing of linguistic information, and to particular linguistic domains (phonetics, prosody, phonology, morphology, syntax, and the lexicon)' (2011: 233). Furthermore, there is a significant difference in the motivation or purpose underlying the two distinctions. Hulstijn notes that whereas the BICS/CALP distinction was 'proposed to help solve a practical issue, my notions of BLC and HLC [higher language cognition] and the accompanying hypotheses aim to help explain a more fundamental problem of understanding individual differences in language ability' (2011: 233).

These are valid observations. The BICS/CALP or conversational/academic language distinction was focused primarily on identifying and addressing multiple examples of educational malpractice associated both with assessment of intellectual and academic performance of minoritised students and inappropriate placement of these students in particular programmes. It was also intended simply as a conceptual distinction relevant only to educational contexts rather than as a more general theoretical framework for conceptualising the construct of 'language proficiency'. Hulstijn's distinction is much more detailed in its linguistic specification and its purpose goes far beyond the specific realm of schooling. He also describes the BLC/ELC distinction as a 'dichotomy', whereas BICS/CALP was elaborated in terms of intersecting continua (see Chapter 4).

However, despite these differences, the two sets of distinctions clearly point to the same underlying reality. Some aspects of language proficiency develop in the early years and are largely invariant among adult L1 speakers whereas other aspects extend this early development into specific domains or contexts of language use and vary significantly among L1 speakers after the early years. Literacy and schooling experiences are major drivers of these individual differences among native speakers within the specific context of education.

In short, Hulstijn's theoretical framework adds specificity and breadth to the constructs of 'academic language' and 'academic language proficiency' even though he does not use or discuss these constructs in any specific way.

Wong Fillmore's Instructional Exploration of Academic Language

How can instructional innovation contribute to our theoretical understanding of academic development among monolingual and bilingual students? As noted in Chapter 7, the documentation of innovative instruction creates *phenomena* that require explanation and can call into question existing theoretical assumptions. In discussing future directions for clarifying the linguistic demands of schooling, I suggested that instructional interventions involving collaboration between researchers and educators represented a fruitful direction to advance our understanding:

> The most productive direction to orient further research on this topic, and one that can be supported by all scholars, is to focus on creating instructional and learning environments that maximize the language and literacy development of socially marginalized students. ... Deeper understanding of the nature of academic language and its relationship both to conversational fluency and other forms of literacy will emerge from teachers, students, and researchers working together in instructional contexts collaboratively pushing (and documenting) the boundaries of language and literacy exploration. (Cummins, 2008a: 81)

Lily Wong Fillmore has long been concerned with the specific language skills English language learners need to participate fully in classroom instruction (e.g. Wong Fillmore, 1982). She has explored this issue by means of classroom-based research involving observations of students engaging with academic learning and through collaborations with teachers to enable students to analyse complex academic text. She described characteristics of the academic register students need to acquire as follows:

Informationally dense discourse and complex noun phrases made so by clauses and phrases that elaborate and modify head nouns are just two of the key features of academic English. Other notable features include:

- specificity of reference, in which full noun phrases are preferred over pronouns, except in references that refer to something that has just been mentioned.
- frequent use of nouns that derive from verbs and adjectives; for example, *information* from *inform*, *conversation* from *converse*, *moderation* from *moderate*, and so on.
- use of the passive voice; for example, the buildings 'were often skirted' with a sidewalk of wooden planks, a bank 'made of solid brick,' and so on. (Twenty-five percent of all finite verbs in academic writing are in the passive voice.)
- grammatically complex sentence structure, made so by subordination, coordination and adjunct phrases and clauses. (Wong Fillmore, 2009: 7)

In working collaboratively with educators in New York City and other contexts, Wong Fillmore (2009, 2014; Wong Fillmore & Fillmore, 2012) explored the question of how anyone learns this kind of language. In order to understand complex sentences, readers need to unpack the information contained in these sentences and use structural cues to interpret the intended relationships between the parts. She highlighted the central importance of two sets of experiences for native speakers and second language learners to acquire expertise in accessing and using academic registers: (a) active engagement with the language of texts and (b) instructional conversations focused on language in the materials students are using in school:

> We knew this: No one can be a fully proficient reader or writer without a command of such language, and we also recognized that those of us who have it learned it by doing massive amounts of reading and writing. The fact is that academic language can be learned only from texts in which it used, and only by interacting with those texts in nonsuperficial ways: it calls for the reader to read not only for meaning and understanding, but also with attention to how things are said. Discussions of such texts are an important aspect of the learning process, as are efforts to write about the materials in the text. (Wong Fillmore, 2014: 628-629)

With respect to literacy engagement, Wong Fillmore (2009) argued that students need opportunities to get acquainted with books, the world of print, and the language of literacy. She cited the 1985 report of the Commission on Reading, *Becoming a Nation of Readers*, which concluded that reading aloud to children is the single most important activity for building the knowledge required for eventual success in reading. Thus, in preschool, adults should read stories aloud to students, and students should experience conversations about those stories with adults and schoolmates as well as dramatic plays with props that are centered on the stories. Students should also be enabled to engage in artistic and musical activities that encourage them to play with the concepts, themes, and language from those stories (Wong Fillmore, 2009). As discussed in Chapter 6, longitudinal research carried out in Aotearoa/New Zealand from preschool through age 16 has shown that this type of 'literacy saturation' in the early years significantly predicts later reading comprehension in the adolescent years (Wylie & Thompson, 2003; Wylie *et al.*, 2006).

In order to enable learners to 'see' how things are said in complex texts, teachers need to draw their attention to the structures found in sentences and help them notice how meaning is packed into phrases, clauses, and sentences. Wong Fillmore developed a series of strategies with MaryAnn Cucchiara (2019) and New York educators from kindergarten through high school that involved teachers spending about 15 minutes each day discussing one or two 'juicy' sentences drawn from texts the class was working on in subjects such as science, history, or literature. The teachers led students in a conversation about the various parts of the sentence (displayed on a chart or whiteboard) figuring out what information was packed into each phrase and clause and what made the sentence complex. After reading the sentence aloud a few times, teachers asked questions such as, 'So what is this sentence about?' 'Take a look at this part.

Who can tell me something about it? Talk to the person next to you and compare your ideas about what it means'.

Wong Fillmore (2009, 2014) argued that this focus on systematically reinforcing students' awareness and knowledge of how academic language works across the curriculum is particularly important for English language learners who are frequently deprived of (a) access to complex grade-appropriate texts, (b) the instructional support required to help them gain access to the meaning of such texts and (c) guidance in understanding how such texts are constructed linguistically.

> What we find when we look at the school programs for ELLs is a compendium of practices and conditions that add up to a formula for disastrous outcomes. ELLs are often in classrooms and schools filled with nothing but ELLs, learning English from, and practicing it with, one another. They are provided instruction on English grammatical structures and vocabulary divorced from content that might make the linguistic materials meaningful or reveal how they might be deployed communicatively. They are taught to read with instruction focused on building decoding skills, and scant attention is given to reading for understanding or for learning. (Wong Fillmore, 2014: 625)

Although no formal evaluation has been carried out on the effectiveness of the instructional strategies implemented by Wong Fillmore and educators in seven cities across the United States, she noted that 'there are indications that it has given many ELLs the boost into English and literacy they have needed' (2014: 630). According to Wong Fillmore, teachers remain supportive of the approach because they see how it enables their students to make sense of texts that once seemed impossibly difficult for them.

Maryann Cucchiara (2019), former director of research and development for English learners in New York City Public Schools, worked with Wong Fillmore to develop the instructional strategies intended to demystify the academic language of complex texts. She described the broader changes in professional development and whole-school instructional approaches that resulted from the focus on academic language implemented in the initial 'laboratory' schools:

> The approach that grew out of the lab sites … includes seminars for district and instructional leaders, teacher training, and laboratories of practice in which to observe, create, replicate, and assess these instructional practices. … we worked with the Council of the Great City Schools to develop a series of five online courses … that build on one another to transform teaching practices with practical tools, examples, and practice. (Cucchiara, 2019: 36)

She noted that more districts are providing models of professional learning based on the conviction that all students, including ELLs, have the capacity to benefit from rich and robust instruction. Whole-school structural changes have resulted from the initial project such as co-teaching between classroom and specialist ESL teachers to enable ELLs to learn in mainstream classrooms with their peers who are fluent in English. In addition, rather than being pulled out of mainstream classrooms for isolated skill instruction with simplified texts, ELLs 'are more often sitting side by side with their native speaker classmates, joining in on compelling and complex social studies, science, math, and English language arts lessons and seizing opportunities to learn and grow in promising ways' (Cucchiara, 2019: 36).

These observations provide powerful and credible evidence that the instructional focus on 'academic language' developed by Wong Fillmore and Cucchiara has the potential to 'engage students in interesting, challenging work which can then lead to the expansion of students' linguistic repertoires and their development of literacy, rather than the other way around' (Wiley & Rolstad, 2014: 51). The fact that the instructional innovations implemented by Cucchiara (2019), Wong Fillmore (2009, 2014) and the Council of Great City Schools (2014) are aligned with the Common Core State Standards (CCSS) yet result in virtually identical pedagogical approaches to those endorsed by Wiley and Rolstad (2014), highlights the lack of credibility of their claim that the CCSS reflect an autonomous deficit orientation to minoritised students' language and literacy development.

In the present context, Wong Fillmore's work illustrates how the construct of 'academic language' can be instructionally deployed within classrooms to demystify for emergent bilinguals (and all students) how this register of language is structured and how learners can use it productively in talking and writing about academic content. Wong Fillmore, together with many other researchers and educators (see, for example, Cucchiara, 2019; DiCerbo et al., 2014), clearly identified the specific challenges inherent in complex academic text that make it more difficult for many students to process in comparison to everyday conversational language. The instructional strategies she and colleagues devised are logically coherent insofar as they respond directly to the gap between colloquial and academic language. The consequential validity of these strategies is reflected in the fact that they were developed and widely implemented in collaboration with both ESL specialists and classroom/subject matter teachers.[10]

When we view this instructional focus on academic language through the lens of the various critiques of the construct considered previously in this chapter, it is evident that language proficiency does not cease to develop after the early years, as claimed by MacSwan (2000), Rolstad (2017) and others, but rather is intimately related to the disciplinary language of academic subject matter and depends on sustained engagement with complex academic text across the curriculum for its continued development through the school years. This engagement with academic text takes place primarily through talk and dialogue with teachers and peers.

With respect to Valdés' (2017) and García's (2020) concern that the construct of academic language creates a symbolic/ideological border dividing those who 'have' academic language from those who do not, it seems clear that the culprit here is not 'academic language' as such, but rather the *educational malpractice* that *prevents* many emergent bilingual students from gaining access to and engaging with the language of complex texts. As emphasised by Uccelli and colleagues, Wong Fillmore, and other researchers (e.g. Bunch *et al.*, 2014), instructional conversations aimed at explicitly demystifying how academic language works are *required* to erase symbolic or ideological borders related to academic language that have been erected as a result of misguided instruction. These instructional conversations, however, will only be effective when they take place in a school context that builds on minoritised students' cognitive expertise and linguistic varieties of L1 and L2.

To what extent does the critique of the construct of 'academic language' made by Flores and Rosa (2015) apply also to the instructional strategies pioneered by Wong Fillmore and educator colleagues? Recall that Flores and Rosa (2015) claimed that the instructional approaches proposed by Laurie Olson (2010) to support long-term ELLs in catching up academically as well as Lisa Delpit's (1988) insistence that African American students be supported in gaining access to the linguistic 'codes of power' were permeated by discourses of appropriateness and raciolinguistic ideologies. To what extent are the instructional strategies designed to demystify how academic language works, elaborated by Cucchiara (2019) and Wong Fillmore (2009, 2014), likely to mold minoritised students into 'white-speaking subjects'? Is Wong Fillmore's focus on 'juicy sentences' permeated by discourses of appropriateness and raciolinguistic ideologies?

I believe that Flores and Rosa's claim that the construct of 'academic language', and by implication, all instructional approaches designed to reinforce students' knowledge of academic language, are permeated by raciolinguistic ideologies would be ridiculed by the vast majority of educators committed to social justice and educational equity. Not only are such claims logically incoherent and devoid of empirical evidence (as documented previously), they are also highly offensive to educators whose instructional efforts to promote minoritised students' literacy skills in L1 and L2 are being implicitly dismissed, without exception or qualification, as raciolinguistic (i.e. 'racist').

Section 3. To What Extent are Recent Critiques of the CALP/BICS Distinction Valid?

Critiques of the CALP/BICS distinction overlap with more general critiques of the construct of academic language and most of these issues have been considered in previous sections of this chapter. I will examine the specific critiques of BICS/CALP primarily in the context of the ways they are addressed in two recent sources: (a) a special issue of the *International Multilingual Research Journal* (2014: 8/1) focused on 'Rethinking Language at School', much of which was devoted to critique of the BICS/CALP distinction and (b) the Baker and Wright (2017) textbook *Foundations of Bilingual Education and Bilingualism* (6th edn). Previous editions of this highly regarded textbook were single authored by Colin Baker of the University of Bangor in Wales, one of the most respected international authorities on issues related to bilingualism and bilingual education. The updated 6th edition was co-authored with Wayne Wright of Purdue University in the US state of Indiana, an authority on issues related to bilingual education in the United States.

Bunch (2014) succinctly outlined both the contributions of the BICS/CALP distinction and the range of criticisms that have been leveled at the distinction:

> It has been helpful to uncover the limitations and misuse of language proficiency tests, articulate language demands that language minority students are likely to face in mainstream classrooms, and highlight the responsibility of educators to help students meet those demands. It has also been criticized for privileging certain class-based varieties of language, confusing oral language and written literacy, conflating language proficiency and academic achievement, and ignoring the sociolinguistic context of language use. (Bunch, 2014: 71)

Faltis (2014) explains his concerns with the CALP/BICS distinction in a particularly clear and useful way. He notes that although he had initially uncritically incorporated the dimensions of BICS and CALP into his teaching and writing, he became convinced by critiques of these dimensions that what Cummins really meant by CALP was that it was cognitively more complex and consequently more cognitively enriching than BICS. Specifically, 'this assertion both confounds language ability with academic achievement and privileges the language of the educated classes, espousing the belief that the language of CALP is inherently superior to other varieties of language' (2014: 63). He quotes MacSwan and Rolstad:

> Rather than identifying cultural and linguistic *differences* which privilege some children, Cummins describes CALP as having specific context-independent properties from which advantages related to academic achievement are derived, and sees school as the agency by which basic conversational skills are transformed into the linguistically complex language of the educated classes. (MacSwan & Rolstad, 2003: 331) (emphasis original)

In other words, according to Faltis (and MacSwan & Rolstad, 2003), the BICS/CALP distinction portrays linguistic differences as differences in language ability, which relate to variation in social and educational class membership.

However, Faltis declared himself much more comfortable with Cummins' later definition of CALP as 'registers of language that children acquire in school and which they need to use effectively if they are to progress successfully through the grades' (2000: 66). He notes that registers involve specialised language use, usually but not exclusively lexical, for particular knowledge systems:

> Referring to academic language as a register avoids the implication that school language is inherently more complex or enriching than BICS. It simply says that academic language is one of many different registers that learners may acquire in order to belong to certain socio-cultural groups, in this case, those affinity groups that recognize and use academic language and literacy to carry out their primary practices. ... In this manner, learners who do not acquire the academic language register are not cognitively deficient; rather, they chose to acquire other registers that afford them access to and recognition in different, non-academic affinity groups. (Faltis, 2014: 63)

Let us examine some of the issues raised by Bunch (2014), Faltis (2014) and MacSwan and Rolstad (2003). More detailed discussion of these issues can be found in Cummins (2000, Chapters 3 and 4) and Cummins (2008a, 2013, 2017c).

Is There a Fundamental Difference between Defining CALP in Terms of 'Proficiency' as Compared to Defining it in Terms of 'Register'?

Clearly Faltis (2014), Wiley and Rolstad (2014) and others (e.g. Petrovic & Olmstead, 2001) believe that there is a major difference between these formulations because 'proficiency' is seen to reflect an autonomous orientation to language whereas 'register' reflects a social practices or ideological orientation. As noted previously, I see these two orientations, which I have termed 'individualistic' and 'social', not as oppositional but as complementary to each other. If we acknowledge that there is variation *within* social groups in the extent to which students have gained access to linguistic registers associated with schooling, then it is also legitimate to talk in terms of the extent to which students have developed expertise or proficiency in understanding and using different academic registers. As one notable example, the construct of 'proficiency' is intrinsic to the Council of Europe's (2020) conceptual framework for language teaching, learning, use and assessment. In short, use of the terms 'proficiency' or 'skills' (Uccelli *et al.*, 2015a) to refer to the extent to which students gain access to linguistic ad academic registers does not in any sense imply a deficit orientation to children's cognitive or linguistic abilities.

Does the Construct of CALP Imply that School Language is Inherently More Complex or Enriching, or Superior to BICS, and are Learners Who Develop Less Expertise in Using Academic Language Registers Cognitively Deficient?

The claim that CALP or 'academic language' reflects a 'superior' or 'improved' form of language in comparison to the language of everyday conversation represents a core element of virtually all arguments that CALP incorporates a deficit orientation to minoritised students' language and cognition (e.g. Edelsky *et al.*, 1983; MacSwan & Rolstad, 2003). The 'logic' is that if CALP is superior to BICS, then minoritised or low-SES students who may have 'less CALP' are, by definition, inferior, or linguistically/cognitively deficient.

The only problem with this 'logic' is that I have *never* argued that school language is inherently more complex or enriching or superior to the language of everyday social interactions. Why would I make such an argument? *It is totally irrelevant to the issues to which the CALP/BICS distinction was directed.* Furthermore, anybody who has engaged in conversational analysis will testify to the inherent complexity of social interactions. The CALP/BICS distinction simply drew attention to the fact that the language demands students encounter *within the social context of schooling* are different from and go beyond the language demands of *everyday* social interactions in the ways described by many linguists and educators (e.g. Cucchiara, 2019; Wong Fillmore & Fillmore, 2012).

As discussed previously, some theorists (MacSwan, 1999; MacSwan & Rolstad, 2003; Rolstad, 2017), deny that there are any language demands within schooling because language development has essentially ceased by the time children arrive in school around age 5 or 6. Furthermore, these theorists argue that for native speakers of a language, schooling has minimal impact on expanding 'language proficiency' beyond what 5-6-year-old children bring to school (MacSwan & Rolstad, 2003). MacSwan and Rolstad's entire critique of the BICS/CALP distinction, which has been uncritically accepted by numerous researchers (e.g. Baker & Wright, 2017; Bunch, 2014; Faltis, 2014; Wiley & Rolstad, 2014), hinges on this *a priori* and profoundly counter-intuitive theoretical assertion. The fact that, for some of these researchers, the radical claim that schools play virtually no role in developing students' knowledge of language directly contradicts much of their own scholarly writing (e.g. Faltis & Hudelson, 1998; Bunch, 2013), suggests that they may not have fully processed the theoretical basis and implications of the MacSwan/Rolstad critique of BICS/CALP, which were discussed earlier in this chapter.

Does CALP Privilege Certain Class-Based Varieties of Language, Specifically the Language of 'Educated Classes'?

The simple answer to this question is 'absolutely not'. As in the case of core academic language skills (CALS) (Uccelli *et al.*, 2015a, 2015b), the construct of 'CALP' refers simply to the academic registers that all students will encounter within the social context of schooling. It says *nothing* about possible differences between social groups in any aspect of language development or academic language skills. The characteristics of these academic registers of schooling have been repeatedly documented, as described previously in this chapter and in Chapter 4. The cautions articulated by Phillips Galloway *et al.* (2020: 5) in relation to how the CALS construct should be interpreted apply equally to the construct of CALP:

> In privileging these skillsets for assessment, we do not imply that CALS is categorically distinct from language resources learned in other contexts. CALS comprise knowledge of Spanish and English language resources *more likely* to co-occur with school learning tasks (Snow & Uccelli, 2009), but which may also be used for communication in homes and communities (just as the language used in home settings is *also* used for learning at school). In addition, in focusing on ALs [academic languages] we are not suggesting that this language development is more consequential than that which results from adolescents' participation in other discourse communities (sports teams, religious groups, with peers online).

With respect to Phillips Galloway and colleagues' (2020) first point, it is worth noting that critics of the BICS/CALP distinction have frequently mischaracterised it as a 'dichotomy' (e.g. Edelsky *et al.*, 1983; Rolstad, 2017) or as 'polar opposites' (Jensen & Thompson, 2020), implying a rigid universal categorical difference rather than a conceptual distinction directed at a particular set of issues in the specific context of schooling. When critics characterise it as a rigid dichotomy rather than a conceptual distinction, they often consider that they have refuted the legitimacy of the distinction on the grounds that components of 'academic language' are used in everyday conversational interactions and everyday colloquial language is used in academic interactions and learning in school (e.g. Flores, 2020; Flores & Rosa, 2015; Jensen & Thompson, 2020). As noted previously, this characterisation of the BICS/CALP distinction is inaccurate, sets up a 'straw person', and totally misses the point. The point is that there are differences in the relative frequency with which certain features of language occur in everyday interactions outside of school contexts as compared to the language demands faced by *all* students in disciplinary learning and literacy development within the context of schooling.

To my knowledge, not one of the critics of the BICS/CALP distinction has disputed this proposition, which is the central tenet of the theoretical distinction.

An additional point, as Phillips Galloway *et al.* (2020) point out, is that CALS (and CALP) is not universally more consequential than the language registers that adolescents use in various other discourse communities. For example, CALS/CALP is probably not particularly functional within the adolescent discourse community of video games, which for many adolescents is far more salient than the discourse community of schooling. However, by definition, and as these researchers have repeatedly demonstrated empirically, CALS/CALP *is* more consequential within the specific discourse community of the school.

The fact that schools in many contexts have discriminated against the languages and language varieties that minoritised and socioeconomically excluded students have brought to school is unrelated to the terminology used to characterise the extent to which students gain access to the academic registers of schooling (e.g. CALP, CALS). To argue otherwise is essentially to claim that the educational difficulties experienced by some minoritised students are caused by the *inherent nature of the academic registers of schooling* rather than by the misguided instructional practices implemented in far too many schools in the United States and internationally.

Does CALP Conflate Language Proficiency, Academic Achievement and Cognitive Functioning?

In contrast to the *a priori* dismissal of any relationship between language proficiency and academic achievement proposed by MacSwan (1999), MacSwan and Rolstad (2003) and Rolstad (2017), the construct of CALP or academic language proficiency posits a strong and consistent relationship, after the primary grades, between academic language skills and achievement in academic subject matter across the curriculum. Extensive empirical evidence of these relationships has been reported by Grabe (2004), Uccelli and colleagues (e.g. Uccelli & Galloway, 2018), and many other researchers.

The fact that there is a consistent relationship between academic language skills and academic achievement does not imply that language proficiency and academic achievement are identical. Academic subject matter knowledge is not reducible to linguistic concepts. Similarly, the cognitive functions involved in academic tasks (e.g. hypothesising, analysing cause/effect relationships, etc.) are closely related to, but not identical with, the academic language we use to carry out these cognitive functions. The operation of these cognitive functions is not confined only to academic contexts but is also clearly evident in out-of-school contexts that do not involve print literacy.

However, as discussed in previous chapters, although the cognitive, academic, and linguistic dimensions of CALP are conceptually distinct, these dimensions are frequently *fused* both in the process of acquiring academic knowledge and in carrying out academic tasks (see, for example,

Starfield, 1994). The instructional implications of the fusion of cognitive, academic, and linguistic dimensions within the construct of CALP was expressed as follows:

> *Cognitive*—instruction should be cognitively challenging and require students to use higher-order thinking abilities rather than the low-level memorisation and application skills that are tapped by typical worksheets or drill-and-practice computer programs.
>
> *Academic*—academic content (e.g. science, math, social studies, art) should be integrated with language instruction so that students acquire the specific language or registers of these academic subjects.
>
> *Language*—the development of critical language awareness should be fostered throughout the program by encouraging students to compare and contrast their languages (e.g. phonics conventions, grammar, cognates, etc.) and by providing students with extensive opportunities to carry out projects investigating their own and their community's language use, practices, and assumptions (e.g. in relation to the status of different varieties and power relations associated with language policies and practices). (Cummins, 2000: 98)

To What Extent does the Construct of CALP Ignore or Unintentionally Obscure the Fact that Task-Oriented Talk is a Crucial Component of Academic Engagement?

Bunch (2014: 71) expressed concern that the contrast between 'academic' and 'social' language can unintentionally mask the productive ways in which students use a wide variety of linguistic resources to engage with academic tasks: 'In engaging in academic tasks, students' language may include features of interpersonal communication, as well as nondominant regional and social dialects, ... "errors" to be expected in the speech and writing of second language learners, and normal dysfluencies associated with spontaneous talk of even the most competent English speakers'.

The importance of interactive talk for learning and language/literacy development was explicitly acknowledged by Cummins (2000: 79) in emphasising that academic language proficiency develops in a matrix of social interaction and students need ample opportunities to talk with each other and to the teacher about academic tasks in order to expand their command of academic language: 'Talking about the text in a collaborative context ensures that higher order thinking processes (e.g. analysis, evaluation, synthesis) engage with academic language in deepening students' comprehension of the text'. The obvious fact that we use our entire conceptual and linguistic repertoire to discuss and engage with academic tasks, and socially manage collaborative conversations and group work, is not in any way inconsistent with the well-documented differences between the language demands of school as compared to everyday social interaction.

To What Extent is CALP 'Context-Independent' and a 'Prerequisite' for Participating Successfully in Academic Tasks?

Baker and Wright (2017) misrepresent the BICS/CALP distinction in concluding that 'early theories made a distinction between everyday context-embedded conversational language and decontextualised academic language and argued that cognitive academic language proficiency is a prerequisite for academic success in school' (Baker & Wright, 2017: 168). Although I occasionally used the term 'decontextualised' in initial formulations of the BICS/CALP distinction, I quickly switched to the term 'context-reduced' in recognition of the fact that all language and literacy practices are contextualised (e.g. Cummins, 1981b). This does not mean, however, that the degree and range of contextual supports for meaning are equivalent in typical academic contexts, such as textbook reading, in comparison to the contextual supports available in face-to-face contexts (e.g. intonation, eye-contact, gestures, reference to the immediate situation, etc.). Thus, as discussed previously, the CALP/BICS distinction was conceptualised in terms of two intersecting continua related to degree of contextual support and cognitive demand rather than as dichotomous 'context-independent' (MacSwan & Rolstad, 2003) or 'decontextualised' constructs.

The assertion that CALP or knowledge of academic language is a 'prerequisite' for academic participation (Aukerman, 2007; Baker & Wright, 2017; Bunch, 2014) is similarly misleading and inaccurate. Aukerman, for example, misinterpreted the CALP/BICS distinction when she argued in the context of initial literacy instruction that 'I believe it is ultimately destructive to view proficiency in decontextualised language as a prerequisite for successful participation in school' (2007: 632). I agree completely with her argument – it would be absurd for anyone to make such a claim. If CALP were a prerequisite for academic learning, how would any student develop CALP? Together with theorists such as Wong Fillmore (2009, 2014), I have argued that CALP is developed through face-to-face interaction in home and school and in the process of actively engaging with literacy, discussing ideas with peers and adults, and becoming aware of how the registers of academic language work across different disciplines. Opportunities for collaborative learning and talk about text are crucial constituents of academic language learning (e.g. Cummins, 2000). Thus, there is no inconsistency or incompatibility between the construct of CALP and the fact that all students, including emergent bilingual students, use everyday conversational language to grapple with ideas as well as to display their academic work for various audiences (what Bunch [2014] calls the 'language of ideas' and the 'language of display').

Concluding Thoughts

The case articulated previously for the legitimacy of the construct of 'academic language' applies equally to the distinction between academic language proficiency and conversational fluency (CALP/BICS). The distinction is supported by substantial empirical evidence pointing to (a) differences between everyday colloquial language and the language demands of schooling, (b) strong relationships between academic language proficiency and the learning of subject matter content and (c) strong relationships between academic language proficiency and both reading comprehension and academic writing performance (e.g. Barr *et al.*, 2019; Uccelli *et al.*, 2015a, 2015b; Uccelli & Galloway, 2017). The logic underlying the distinction is transparent, and evident in the fact that conversational fluency in everyday social contexts reaches a plateau roughly around the age of about 6 whereas our academic language skills continue to expand through 12 years of schooling and beyond.

Clearly, cognitive skills are involved in virtually all forms of social interaction, and spoken communicative interactions are integral to much of the academic work that students undertake in schools. But in everyday social interactions, much of our spoken language use and comprehension is largely effortless, automatised, and involves minimal cognitive load (Sweller *et al.*, 2019). By contrast, academic learning in school (and learning new skills and knowledge in out-of-school contexts) is frequently cognitively demanding and dependent on various forms of instructional scaffolding to reduce the cognitive and linguistic load to manageable levels (e.g. Bunch *et al.*, 2014). When the BICS/CALP distinction was initially introduced, educators very quickly grasped the logic underlying the distinction because it fit directly with their experience and their instructional goals in the classroom. The distinction explained how many emergent bilingual students could quickly attain conversational fluency in English and yet continue to experience difficulties in catching up to grade expectations in English literacy and other academic content.

With respect to consequential validity, the BICS/CALP distinction drew attention to the potential for discriminatory assessment of emergent bilingual students when their L2 conversational fluency was taken as an index of academic L2 acquisition. It highlighted the need for *all* teachers to reinforce academic language across the curriculum to support students in catching up academically. And, finally, the fact that academic language is found predominantly in written text rather than in everyday spoken conversation reinforced the importance of maximising print access and literacy engagement from an early age.

How did such a simple straightforward idea become so controversial? I don't have a satisfactory answer to this question. But a partial answer resides in the fact that the various critiques were accepted uncritically and without analysis by many scholars. For example, in contrast to previous editions of the *Foundations of Bilingual Education and Bilingualism*, the 6th edition of this classic textbook characterised the BICS/CALP distinction as an early (i.e. outdated), oversimplified, problematic and misleading account of language proficiency in both bilingual and monolingual populations (Baker & Wright, 2017: 164–168). The various criticisms of the BICS/CALP construct were reported uncritically and, unlike previous editions which largely reserved judgment, were explicitly identified as valid. For example, Baker and Wright (2017) approvingly cite Wiley and Rolstad's (2014: 51) claim that it is 'simply not the case that literacy and academic language involve higher order cognition, while other domains in which we use specialised language do not'. They accept uncritically Wiley and Rolstad's evidence-free assertion that the construct of CALP implies that people who use specialised registers of language in domains outside of the school (e.g. horticulturalists, auctioneers, stand-up comedians, etc.) do not use higher order cognition. This is a gross distortion by both Wiley and Rolstad (2014) and Baker and Wright (2017) of everything I have written about the BICS/CALP distinction.

None of the many critiques of BICS/CALP, to my knowledge, has even addressed, let alone disputed in any systematic way, the empirical evidence supporting the distinction between the linguistic demands of everyday face-to-face communication and the linguistic demands of schooling. The closest they have come is to dismiss any and all assessment data as 'out-of-context irrelevant nonsense' that measures only 'test-wiseness' (e.g. Edelsky *et al.*, 1983: 9), or as illegitimate because it emanates from an autonomous orientation to language and literacy (Wiley, 1996; Wiley & Rolstad, 2014). As discussed in Chapter 7, critiques that fail to address the empirical adequacy of a theoretical claim or construct have a credibility problem.

An additional example of inadequate analysis comes from Bunch's (2014) listing of some of the critiques of the BICS/CALP distinction in which he notes that critics have claimed that CALP conflates language proficiency with academic achievement. As discussed previously, he fails to take account of the fact that this criticism is based solely on MacSwan and Rolstad's (2003) theoretical claim that language proficiency is *a priori* totally independent of literacy development and academic achievement. Clearly, Bunch does not share this conception of language proficiency and language development as totally independent of everything that happens instructionally in schools (e.g. Bunch *et al.*, 2014). Yet, his uncritical articulation of this radically counter-intuitive criticism lends credibility to a position he would clearly oppose.

In summary, just as the construct of 'academic language' satisfies the criteria of empirical adequacy, logical coherence, and consequential validity, so too does the BICS/CALP distinction. As a conceptual distinction applying to both L1 and L2 contexts, with clear implications for instruction and assessment of minoritised students, it makes no claim to be a comprehensive theory of language proficiency. Thus, claims that the distinction is 'oversimplified' miss the point (Cummins, 2000, 2008a). It is not in any sense opposed to or incompatible with a distinction such as Bunch's (2014) language of ideas and language of display – the two sets of distinctions are addressed to very different questions.

I have sympathy with Bunch's (2013) concern that teacher education programmes in the United States tend to focus on the BICS/CALP distinction, despite multiple critiques, without pursuing issues of language instruction and assessment in more depth. Obviously, teachers' pedagogical knowledge should include much more than the fact that there are significant differences between informal everyday conversational interactions and the academic language demands of schooling. However, I would contend that the BICS/CALP distinction is not a bad place to start in developing this pedagogical knowledge. Its implications for instruction and assessment are immediately relevant:

- It explains why emergent bilingual students who have gained considerable fluency in the school language (L2) may still exhibit large gaps in L2 literacy skills for several additional years.
- It highlights the reasons why *all* teachers should be prepared to reinforce academic language in a sustained way across the curriculum for both L1 and L2 learners.
- It explains one very significant reason why 'quick-exit' transitional bilingual programmes don't tend to work particularly well for emergent bilingual students.
- It refutes the rationale for highly problematic assessment and accountability policies incorporated into federal legislation such as the No Child Left Behind (2001) Act that mandated that English language learners be assessed by high-stakes standardised tests after just one year of learning English (this was extended to three years in the 2015 Every Student Succeeds Act [ESSA]).
- And, going full circle to the origins of the distinction, it highlights the need for change in the ways in which exceptional students are identified (both at the 'gifted' and 'handicapped' ends of the continuum); specifically, it provides a strong impetus to explore multilingual assessment procedures at least during the initial five years of learning the school language (e.g. Schissel *et al.*, 2019).

These immediate applications to instructional practice and educational policy explain why many teacher educators have continued to incorporate the BICS/CALP distinction into their programmes over the past 40 years.[11]

Notes

(1) Thomas and Collier's (1997) *Prism model* incorporates the same elements as Figure 8.2, namely sociocultural, linguistic, academic and cognitive processes, although these components are arranged somewhat differently, with social and cultural processes located in the center of the prism that is bounded on three sides by L1 + L2 academic, cognitive and language development. All components are seen as interdependent in complex ways. The Prism model was developed to account for the findings of Thomas and Collier's research involving more than 700,000 ELLs. One of their major conclusions was that 'the most powerful predictor of academic success in L2 is

formal schooling in L1. This is true whether L1 schooling is received only in home country or in both home country and the U.S.' (1997: 39). They express their perspective on the interdependence of language, cognition, and academic development as follows: 'Language and cognitive development go hand in hand. Language is the vehicle for communicating cognitively. In school, we develop students' cognitive growth through academic work across the curriculum in science, social studies, mathematics, language arts, and the fine arts' (1997: 40).

(2) Although it is beyond the scope of this chapter to address in any detail, it is worth acknowledging Richardson's (2014) critique of Labov's focus on AAVE as part of the problem with respect to reading and academic success. In opposition to Labov's analysis, she argues that the problem lies in the fact that 'poor Black people are trapped in a cycle of structural racism, and it will take more than changing our syntax, phonology, and vocabulary to fix that' (2014: 191–192).

(3) Flores and Rosa's (2015) critique of Delpit's argument regarding the need to teach explicitly how the linguistic codes of power operate also appears inconsistent with the strong endorsement of Delpit's position in the CUNY-NYSIEB Translanguaging Guide (Celic & Seltzer, 2013), which was produced as part of a project directed by Nelson Flores. Celic and Seltzer note that it is critical for bilingual and emergent bilingual students to learn the codes and rules discussed by Delpit (1995), 'which are often those that refer to white, middle- class cultural norms' (2013: 17). They note that explicitly teaching minoritised students how to recognise and play by these rules equips them with the dominant cultural knowledge that they will need in their future lives where they are likely to be judged on the extent to which they have gained the linguistic agility to use these codes of power together with a variety of other registers of language. Once students have gained access to these arbitrary standardised norms, they 'can then *question* and *challenge* the culture of power, thinking about who created these codes and rules and why' (2013: 17). (emphasis original).

(4) The problematic nature of Flores and Rosa's (2015) claims regarding Olsen's (2010) pedagogical recommendations is reinforced when Olsen's recommendations are compared to those of other researchers. Table 8.1 compares Olsen's pedagogical priorities with those of Bunch *et al.* (2014) and Cummins (this volume, Chapter 6). In all three cases, the focus is on supporting academic development among ELLs. Olsen's specific concern is with 'long-term English learners' while Bunch and colleagues' review of research-based instructional strategies is oriented towards the curriculum standards articulated in the Common Core State Standards (CCSS). In all three cases, the listing of instructional options is not in any order of priority.

Clearly, there is considerable overlap in the three sets of instructional priorities. For example, an explicit focus on the language of academic text is common to all three sets of instructional strategies. Why do Olsen's pedagogical recommendations merit the accusation that they are designed to mold ELLs into 'white speaking subjects' (Flores & Rosa, 2015: 157) but (perhaps) the other pedagogical priorities are innocent of this charge? If the Bunch *et al.* instructional priorities are equally complicit with raciolinguistic ideologies, then explicit criteria for making this claim should be articulated. Furthermore, the detailed empirical evidence cited by Bunch *et al.* in support of their choice of pedagogical strategies should either be refuted or accounted for in some way (see Chapter 7).

Flores and Rosa (2015) imply that any focus on developing students' awareness of linguistic features of text (Bunch *et al.*, 2014) or reinforcing academic language across the curriculum (Cummins, 2001), or teaching the codes of power (Delpit, 1988) automatically renders this instructional focus uncritical and implicated in raciolinguistic discourses of appropriateness. This implication is refuted by the fact that Delpit (1988, 1995) and Cummins (2001a; this volume) and many other authors (e.g. Janks, 2014) have strongly advocated that teachers promote critical inquiry into language forms and uses in ways that challenge coercive relations of power.

Table 8.1 Pedagogical strategies for supporting emergent bilingual students

Olsen (2010)	Bunch et al. (2014]	Cummins (this volume)
Promote:		
Home language literacy and language development	Use of students' home language	Engage students' multilingual repertoires
Emphasis on academic language and complex vocabulary	Focusing students on linguistic features of text	Reinforce academic language across the curriculum
Instruction in the academic uses of English	Attention to text structure Integrated pedagogical scaffolding	Scaffold comprehension and production of language across the curriculum
Powerful oral language	Stimulating reading engagement	Maximise literacy engagement
Extensive reading of relevant texts	Comprehension strategy instruction	Connect instruction to students' lives
Explicit literacy development		Decolonise curriculum and instruction through culturally sustaining pedagogy
High quality writing	Building and activating background knowledge	
	Promoting disciplinary literacy	Valorize and build on L1/L2 language varieties
		Affirm identities in association with academic engagement

(5) Although the title of the Wiley and Rolstad (2014) article references the CCSS and the 'Great Divide', the bulk of the article is devoted to a repudiation of the BICS/CALP distinction. Since they include virtually no analysis of the CCSS itself, my interpretation of their position is that the construct of 'academic language' automatically implies a deficit position in relation to the language and culture of minoritised students.

(6) It is universally accepted that our experiences growing up in particular social and environmental contexts determine the kinds of cognitive skills we develop. Thus, Inuit young people growing up in the 1940s Canadian Arctic without access to formal schooling were unlikely to have developed formal print literacy, science, or mathematics skills, but they would have developed a wide range of higher order cognitive skills related to surviving on the land through navigating, hunting, and trapping as well as a deep knowledge of their community's culture and history. Their cognitive skills would have developed in a different direction from those of students who experienced formal schooling in southern Canada, but it would be absurd to claim that their cognitive skills are in any way inferior or less well developed than those of young people who had experienced schooling.

Similarly, as Nurmela et al. (2012) point out, the oral culture and traditions of so-called 'nonliterate' communities reflect highly accomplished forms of reasoning, memory, decision-making, and dispute-resolution. A concern for language planners involved in extending schooling and literacy to these communities is that the concept of 'literacy' can render the cultures of Indigenous communities invisible, marked and negative: 'it "minoritises" them, and hides and rationalises power relations instead of exposing and questioning them' (Nurmela et al., 2012: 162). These authors argue that children who currently grow up in oral environments should not be subjected to education that is predominantly focused on reading and writing. Communities should be given the opportunity to maintain the benefits of oral traditions at the same time as they become literate to a high level in their own and wider societal languages. By the same token, any form of schooling that aspires to connect to students' lives and engage community funds of knowledge, must prioritise the oral language and cultural traditions that students bring to school. This perspective is entirely consistent with the theoretical frameworks discussed in Part 1 of the present volume.

(7)   A fascinating example of the clash between individualistic and social orientations to language and literacy research that is still highly relevant today can be seen in the debate between James Paul Gee and Catherine Snow in the *Journal of Literacy Research* (1999-2001). This debate was occasioned by a critical review written by Gee (1999) of the Snow *et al.* (1998) National Research Council report on prevention of reading difficulties. Gee argued that the social dimensions of reading were largely ignored in the report and, in particular, the role of poverty as a contributor to reading difficulties was minimally addressed. He pointed out that broader indices of language development that reflected the impact of SES were just as strongly related to reading achievement as phonological awareness, which the report focused on as a critical variable. Underlying the problems with the report, he argued, was a conception of reading as an autonomous process divorced from the social realities of children's lives. Gee also highlighted the role of societal power relations and identity negotiation between teachers and students as contributors to students' underachievement:

> The fact that children will not identify with, or even will disidentify with, teachers and schools that they perceive as hostile, alien, or oppressive to their home-based identities and cultures is as much a cognitive as a political point. ... To ignore these wider issues, while stressing such things as phonemic awareness built on controlled texts, is to ignore, not merely what we know about politics, but also what we know about learning and literacy as well. (Gee, 1999: 360)

In her response, Snow (2000) denied that social realities were ignored in the National Research Council report. She noted that Snow *et al.* (1998) pointed to the correlation of 0.68 between reading achievement and the collective poverty level of students in a school and acknowledged that this correlation is considerably greater than the correlation of approximately 0.45 between reading achievement and early literacy indicators such as knowledge of the letters of the alphabet or phonological awareness. However, Snow *et al.* then largely ignored these data, preferring to focus on individual cognitive variables. Snow defended the emphasis in the report on the cognitive subskills involved with literacy development on the grounds that instruction could address these effectively whereas schools were relatively impotent to change the social conditions of learners. She also challenged the claims of New Literacy Studies, arguing that 'If Gee really wishes to promote the impact of the New Literacies approach, he would do well to invest his time in conducting the sort of empirical research that proponents of phonological awareness have produced, rather than simply arguing for his position as the politically and morally correct one' (Snow, 2000: 116).

Gee (2000) responded by pointing out that New Literacies theorists view skills not simply as internal cognitive states but as the means whereby individuals participate in culturally, historically, and institutionally situated social practices. In this sense, skills are not fixed but rather change according to the social context and students' modes of participation in these contexts. He suggested that if this social perspective had been given greater weight, a very different report would have emerged with dramatically different policy implications.

(8)   Uccelli and Galloway (2017) dismiss any notion that academic language is 'superior' to the colloquial language used in out-of-school contexts. They note that students whom they interviewed often characterised the colloquial language they used in everyday contexts as 'incorrect' or 'inferior' reflecting the fact that they had 'internalized the hierarchical societal values associated with different ways of using language' (2017: 402). Uccelli and Galloway instead argue for promoting students'

ability to communicate successfully across boundaries and to move flexibly across cultures, communities, and ways of speaking, goals also promoted by culturally sustaining and critical pedagogies (Duncan-Andrade & Morrell, 2008; Paris & Alim, 2017):

> In our view, mastering CALS does not entail using formulaic structures according to prescriptive rules but, instead, using language resources flexibly in the service of effective communication and learning. A successful language user is one that has at her or his disposal the resources and awareness to participate flexibly and effectively in a variety of academic and nonacademic contexts. ... Certainly, among the many ways of using language, school needs to focus on expanding students' academic language resources to support their academic achievement. Yet, our research suggests that this learning will be more effective if students' voices and their own ways of making meaning are heard and incorporated into the discussion. (Uccelli & Galloway, 2017: 403)

This perspective is clearly consistent with the views expressed by Valdés (2004, 2017) and García (2009, 2020). However, in contrast to the concerns expressed by these and other researchers (e.g. Flores & Rosa, 2015) in regard to the construct of 'academic language', Uccelli and Galloway see no conflict between expanding students' academic language resources on the one hand, and incorporating their voices and ways of making meaning into classroom instruction on the other.

(9) Hulstijn has employed different terms to refer to the distinction between basic and extended language cognition. In his 2011 article, the two constructs were named basic language cognition (BLC) and higher language cognition (HLC). In his 2015 book, he used the label 'extended' rather than 'higher' language cognition and in 2019, the terms 'shared' and 'nonshared' are used alternatively with 'basic' and 'extended'.

(10) The 'juicy sentences' approach pioneered by Wong Fillmore and colleagues (e.g. Wong Fillmore & Blum Martinez, 2015) has recently been integrated into the EL Education grades K-5 and 6–8 Language Arts Curricula. Videos illustrating the 'Deep Dive' into language approach can be viewed at: https://eleducation.org/resources/implementing-language-dives and https://eleducation.org/resources/small-group-language-dive-long-version. This approach is described as follows on the latter website:

> A Language Dive empowers students to analyze, understand, and use the language of academic sentences by slowing down to have a conversation about the meaning, purpose, and structure of a compelling sentence from a complex text or tool. Following the engaging deconstruct-reconstruct-practice routine of the Language Dive, students play with the smallest 'chunks' of the sentence, paying close attention to how language works, acquiring the necessary facility with academic English, and fostering overall language ability.

It is important to clarify here that 'smallest chunks' refer to phrases and clauses, not individual vocabulary items (personal communication, Lily Wong Fillmore, March 15, 2021).

EL Education is a non-profit organisation that develops open-source curriculum materials that are freely accessible on its website. According to EdReports, the EL Education's Language Arts curricula are rated extremely highly (https://www.edreports.org/reports?s=ela). EL Education is strongly committed to equity and antiracism (https://eleducation.org/who-we-are/our-commitment-to-equity-and-antiracism), illustrating the fact that explicitly reinforcing academic language across the curriculum is fully consistent with an antiracist instructional approach and does not in any sense reflect a raciolinguistic ideology.

(11) Seltzer (2019) also expressed concern that the BICS/CALP distinction continues to be taught uncritically in TESOL and bilingual teacher preparation programmes. She suggested that '[r]esearch has highlighted the deficit perspectives inherent to conceptual frameworks that distinguish between home and school language' (2019: 988). Here she seems to conflate two different referents for home and school language: (1) home language referencing a language such as Spanish in the US context, with English being the school language and (2) home language referencing the languaging practices in which students engage outside of school contexts as compared to the 'academic' language of schooling. My interpretation of her argument is that she regards both of these distinctions as problematic and implicated in deficit perspectives.

A challenge for theorists operating within this orientation to translanguaging theory, which in Chapter 10 I label *unitary translanguaging theory* (UTT), is to address the internal contradictions that crop up repeatedly. For example, as noted previously, García (2009: 36) argued that teachers *must* teach the standard academic language in order not to disadvantage minoritised students. This position clearly acknowledges specific characteristics of the 'school language' that pose challenges for students beyond their out-of-school languaging. It seems unlikely that Seltzer (2019) would characterise García's argument as a deficit position, particularly since Celic and Seltzer (2013: 17) also endorse the need for minoritised students to learn the codes of power 'which are often those that refer to white, middle-class cultural norms'.

If Seltzer's argument is more focused on deficit perspectives inherent in distinguishing between, for example, Spanish as the home language and English as the school language, then it would be useful to address apparent inconsistencies in the way these terms are utilised by researchers operating within the same broad project (the CUNY-New York State Initiative on Emergent Bilinguals – https://www.cuny-nysieb.org/). For example, Menken and Sánchez (2019), in an important article documenting the outcomes of school-based professional development focused on translanguaging pedagogy, utilise the terms 'home language' and 'home language practices' a combined total of 36 times, as illustrated in the following quotations:

> Teachers also made the linguistic landscape of their classrooms multilingual, whereby students' *home languages* were visually displayed. ... For example, teachers in participating schools created word walls, cognate walls, and false cognate walls in English and students' home languages. (2019: 750–751) (emphasis added)

> Although scholars of TESOL and bilingual education have for years recommended that educators incorporate students' *home languages* in instruction ... the schools in our sample—like most across the United States—failed to do so prior to their involvement in CUNY-NYSIEB. By systematically bringing students' languages into their classrooms, teachers in the project normalized the fact that students live in bilingual households and that their bilingualism is a resource for them. (2019: 753) (emphasis added)

9 Are 'Linguistic Interdependence' and the 'Common Underlying Proficiency' Legitimate Theoretical Constructs?

The linguistic interdependence hypothesis has generated far less controversy than either the threshold hypothesis or the distinction between BICS and CALP. As noted in Chapter 3, the validity of the hypothesis has been supported in virtually all major reviews of L1/L2 relationships (e.g. Dressler & Kamil, 2006; Geva, 2014; National Academies of Sciences, Engineering, and Medicine [NASEM], 2017; Riches & Genesee, 2006).

Despite the extensive empirical support for the construct, a number of investigators have rejected 'interdependence' and 'crosslinguistic transfer' either on theoretical grounds (e.g. García & Li Wei, 2014) or on the basis of research that generated findings seemingly inconsistent with predictions derived from the hypothesis (e.g. Berthele & Lambelet, 2018; Berthele & Vanhove, 2020). Other researchers have suggested some qualifications to the hypothesis while accepting its general legitimacy (e.g. Genesee et al., 2006; Geva, 2014; Prevoo et al., 2015; Proctor et al., 2010; Sierens et al., 2019, 2020). A number of these investigators have sought to account for the fact that crosslinguistic relationships are less consistently observed in aspects of 'oral language proficiency' (e.g. listening comprehension, vocabulary knowledge) as compared to indices of literacy development (e.g. decoding skills, reading comprehension). These investigators have tried to establish a theoretical basis for hypothesising the extent to which different language literacy skills are interdependent (e.g. Proctor et al., 2010).

Clearly, the criterion of 'empirical adequacy' requires that findings that appear inconsistent with the interdependence hypothesis be accounted for and inconsistencies resolved. These apparently contrary findings are reviewed later in this chapter. I argue that the apparent inconsistencies reflect (a) the nature of 'oral language' tests used in many studies involving preschool and primary school students and (b) the fact that students in these studies often have not had sufficient time and/or opportunities to develop academic skills in both languages. Under subtractive instructional conditions, minimal interdependence and crosslinguistic transfer are likely to be observed.

Prior to reviewing critiques and suggested qualifications to the interdependence hypothesis, I summarise some of the recent research that strongly supports crosslinguistic interdependence.

Section 1. Recent Research Supporting Crosslinguistic Interdependence

Spanish and English Core Academic Language Skills are Interdependent Among Students in Dual Language Programmes

Phillips Galloway *et al.* (2020) investigated the crosslinguistic relationships between Spanish and English core academic language skills (CALS) as well as their unique and shared contributions to English reading comprehension among 165 Grades 4 and 5 students in Spanish-English dual language programmes. They chose to carry out the research with students in dual language programmes (most of whom spoke Spanish at home) on the grounds that these students were in the process of being simultaneously socialised into Spanish- and English-speaking discourse communities. Because students were developing literacy in both languages, 'the language skills we assess are not subjected to the subtractive impacts of English-only instruction in which U.S. bilingual learners learn distinct sets of language skills at home and at school' (2020: 6).

Phillips Galloway and colleagues (2020) note that previous studies of crosslinguistic relationships involving L1 and L2 vocabulary knowledge produced mixed results. They attribute this pattern to a variety of factors. First, Spanish-English bilinguals in the United States experience considerable diversity of L1/L2 learning opportunities related to language use patterns in home and school. For example, there is often little overlap between the Spanish vocabulary acquired in the context of the home and the English vocabulary acquired primarily in the context of English-medium schooling. This variability in acquisition contexts according to language can diminish the relationship between L1 and L2 vocabulary knowledge. Similarly, the two languages also frequently serve different communicative functions in home and school contexts.

Variability in the context of schooling will also affect the degree of crosslinguistic relationship for vocabulary and other academic language measures. For example, in contrast to English-only programmes, there is likely to be much greater overlap between Spanish and English vocabulary and communicative functions in dual language programmes that develop language and literacy in both Spanish and English. Thus, stronger cross-linguistic relationships would be predicted in these contexts than in monolingual programmes.

A final consideration is the fact that measures of vocabulary knowledge used in many previous studies (e.g. Picture Vocabulary tests) assess children's general vocabulary knowledge, involving home, school, and other contexts, rather than the specific vocabulary knowledge that has high utility within the context of the school. For example, these tests frequently ask students to name items that are pictured, thereby limiting the range of vocabulary that is assessed. Many school-related abstract concepts (e.g. *analyse*, *predict*, etc.) do not lend themselves easily to visual presentation. Even the more difficult low-frequency vocabulary in these tests frequently involve items that are not of high utility in academic settings (e.g. *transom*, *chevron*, etc.). Thus, according to Phillips Galloway and colleagues, the global nature of vocabulary, syntax and discourse assessments used in previous studies is likely to contribute to the varied patterns of relationships in studies that investigated L1/L2 crosslinguistic relationships involving these variables.

Because their research focused on the specific context of the school, Phillips Galloway and colleagues (2020) employed Spanish and English versions of the CALS-I assessment battery described in the previous chapter. These measures were intentionally designed to test school-relevant language skills, specifically high-utility lexical, syntactic and discourse features prevalent in school texts across the curriculum.

Phillips Galloway and colleagues investigated two hypotheses: (1) bilingual learners' academic language proficiencies 'constitute a relevant subset of language proficiencies that support their literacy achievement' (2020: 2); (2) bilinguals' well-developed skills in one language (Lx) positively influence their language and literacy achievement in a second language (Ly) (the Linguistic Interdependence Hypothesis). The first hypothesis relates to the extent to which CALS (or CALP) is significantly related to reading comprehension skills in English. The second hypothesis examines the extent to which students' Spanish (L1) CALS/CALP is related to English reading comprehension and how the strength of this crosslinguistic relationship compares to the within-language relationship between English CALS/CALP and English reading comprehension. Phillips Galloway and colleagues point out that these two hypotheses have been extensively linked and discussed theoretically but have seldom been investigated empirically within the same research study.[1]

With respect to the first research question, Phillips Galloway and colleagues reported that English CALS-I scores were positively and significantly correlated with both English word reading fluency and with English reading comprehension. Relationships between English CALS-I and English reading comprehension were significantly greater than those between English CALS-I and English word reading fluency. Spanish

CALS-I scores were positively and significantly correlated with Spanish word reading fluency. The findings strongly support the authors' first hypothesis.

With respect to the linguistic interdependence hypothesis, Phillips Galloway and colleagues reported the following crosslinguistic relationships:

> Spanish CALS-I and English CALS-I performances were strongly and positively correlated, as would be expected for learners exposed and instructed in academic Spanish and English at school (Grade 4, $r = 0.71$, $p < .001$; Grade 5, $r = 0.67$, $p < .001$). Additionally, ... we observed that the relation between Spanish CALS-I scores and English reading comprehension was also positive and strong (Grade 4, $r = 0.51$, $p < .001$; Grade 5, $r = 0.63$, $p < .001$); and that word reading fluency in Spanish and English were moderately and positively correlated (Grade 4, $r = 0.38$, $p < .001$; Grade 5, $r = 0.53$, $p < .001$). (Phillips Galloway et al., 2020: 8)

Path analysis confirmed that Spanish CALS predicted English reading comprehension almost as strongly as was the case for English CALS. The standardised coefficient for Grade 4 Spanish CALS predicting English reading comprehension was 0.29 and for Grade 4 English CALS predicting English reading comprehension the coefficient was 0.31. The Grade 5 figures were 0.33 for Spanish CALS and 0.35 for English CALS.

In summary, Phillips Galloway and colleagues (2020) provide strong evidence that Spanish and English academic language skills are interdependent and reflective of a common underlying crosslinguistic dimension that includes English reading comprehension.[2]

Inuktitut Proficiency at Grade 3 Predicts Grades 4–6 Growth in French and English Proficiency

A comprehensive longitudinal study carried out over a 12-year period in a remote Inuit community in Nunavik, Québec (Usborne et al., 2009) provided compelling evidence of positive crosslinguistic relationships. Students, all of whom spoke Inuktitut as their home language, received instruction exclusively in Inuktitut from Kindergarten through grade 3 after which parents could choose either English-medium or French-medium instruction for their children from grades 4 through to the end of secondary school. Using a battery of specially constructed culturally appropriate parallel tests in the three languages, the researchers examined the relationships between students' baseline grade 3 proficiency in Inuktitut and their growth in English or French proficiency between grades 4 and 6. The sample included 110 students, 49 in the French stream and 61 in the English stream. The language tests assessed vocabulary knowledge (colours, numbers, letters and body parts) and sentence reading and comprehension (sentence completion task) and were individually administered. Hierarchical linear modelling was used to analyse the data. Usborne *et al.* summarised the findings as follows:

> These results indicate that for every one point increase in baseline Inuktitut, second language scores across subsequent years increased by 0.45 points when all other predictors were held constant. ... Furthermore, for every one point increase in baseline second language scores, second language scores across subsequent years increased by 0.23 points, when all other predictors were held constant. (2009: 677)

In other words, the crosslinguistic effect was about double the within-language effect in predicting growth in English and French language skills.

Baseline grade 3 Inuktitut scores also predicted Grades 4-6 Inuktitut proficiency. However, minimal overall growth was observed in Inuktitut proficiency between grades 3 and 6, which the authors attribute both to possible ceiling effects in the Inuktitut proficiency measures and the fact that instruction in Grades 4-6 was exclusively in English or French. The authors conclude that the findings support the interdependence hypothesis: 'having a strong basis in Inuktitut is predictive of later strength rather than weakness in a second language' (2009: 680).

The authors raise concerns about the extent to which a transitional programme of the type implemented in this community is adequate to ensure survival of the Indigenous language. Despite the fact that the programme was not intended to be assimilationist, Inuktitut scores reached a plateau after Grade 3 and no significant improvement in proficiency beyond Grade 3 levels was observed over the 12 years of the study. Usborne and colleagues recommended further efforts to include Inuktitut as a meaningful component of the curriculum throughout all the years of schooling. The major reasons this direction had not been pursued by the school system was due to the challenges of generating Inuktitut curriculum materials beyond Grade 3 and the difficulty of finding certified Inuit teachers to teach in higher grade levels.[3]

L1 Listening Comprehension Predicts L2 Reading Comprehension Among Russian- and Turkish-Speaking Students in Germany

As noted in Chapter 7, Edele and Stanat (2016) investigated the relationships between L2 reading comprehension and L1 listening comprehension among 502 Russian-speaking and 662 Turkish-speaking Grade 9 (15-year-old) students in Germany. The study used data collected as part of the National Educational Panel Study (NEPS), a nationwide longitudinal study of education in Germany. Edele and Stanat were able to examine the crosslinguistic relationships between L1 listening comprehension and various measures of German proficiency including reading comprehension, listening comprehension, receptive vocabulary, and reading fluency while controlling for the effects of non-verbal reasoning, family characteristics (e.g. SES, number of books in the home, cultural possessions), and type of school students attended (ranging from more 'academic' to more 'vocational' in orientation).

The Edele and Stanat study is exceptional in the number of variables they were able to examine that might moderate the relationships between L1 and L2. They were also able to compare the patterns of interdependence across two dissimilar languages. They point out that Russian is considerably more similar to German (both are Indo-European languages) than is the case for Turkish (which is not Indo-European) and this enabled them to examine the extent to which linguistic similarity and distance affected interdependence.

Edele and Stanat reported highly significant relationships between L1 listening comprehension and German reading comprehension for both groups of students. These relationships persisted when controls for L2 listening comprehension, L2 reading fluency, family characteristics and cognitive ability were introduced into the regression equations. They concluded that 'the linear regression models confirmed our first hypothesis that students with advanced listening comprehension in L1 are also likely to attain high levels of reading comprehension in L2' (2016: 173).

The fact that the crosslinguistic effect was similar for Turkish and Russian indicated that the relationships were not due to specific linguistic similarities between languages. Rather, according to Edele and Stanat, transfer between linguistically distant languages may reflect the operation of higher-level language skills, such as the use of metacognitive strategies or higher-order semantic knowledge.

The authors also examined the extent to which L1/L2 interdependence is greater at higher levels of L1 listening comprehension than at lower levels. In other words, to what extent is there support for a L1 threshold effect mediating L1/L2 transfer or interdependence? They found evidence for such an effect in the Turkish sample, but not in the Russian sample where the L1/L2 relationship was linear. They concluded:

> Our findings thus suggest that in languages with a low degree of similarity, transfer of L1 listening comprehension to L2 reading comprehension is restricted to higher levels of L1 listening comprehension, as suggested by the threshold assumption. ... In languages with a higher degree of similarity, by contrast, transfer also seems to occur at lower levels of L1 listening comprehension. (Edele & Stanat, 2016: 175)

Although the Edele and Stanat (2016) investigation of linguistic interdependence is more comprehensive than most previous studies with respect to sample size and variety (two different linguistic groups), and inclusion of cognitive, linguistic, and family moderator variables, two limitations should be noted. First, for students born outside of Germany, length of residence in Germany was not included in the analyses. As noted in Chapter 7, this variable is directly related to students' opportunity to learn German and can affect language use at home (more recent arrivals with less opportunity/time to learn German are more likely to use L1 at home) as well as the strength of L1/L2 relationships. It was for this reason that Cummins *et al.* (1984) partialled out the effects of length of residence in calculating L1/L2 relationships in their sample of Japanese- and Vietnamese-background students in the Canadian context.

A second limitation concerns vagueness in the construct definition of 'listening comprehension'. Edele and Stanat (2020: 176) note that 'vocabulary knowledge explains large proportions of variability in listening comprehension' and thus the limitations of typical oral vocabulary measures articulated by Phillips Galloway and colleagues (see previous section) may also apply to the listening comprehension measure used in this study.

This vagueness in the conceptualisation of 'listening comprehension' reflects the more general lack of coherence in the notion of 'oral language proficiency' that is evident in the scholarly writing of many researchers in this area (e.g. August & Shanahan, 2006; Melby-Lervåg & Lervåg, 2011; Saunders & O'Brien, 2006). For example, the empirical data reviewed by Saunders and O'Brien reveal very clearly that the notion of 'oral language' is meaningless as a theoretical construct. Some manifestations of 'oral language' are strongly related to academic language measures while other aspects are unrelated. Measures of 'oral language' do not consistently relate to each other, casting doubt on the legitimacy of the construct of 'oral language proficiency'.[4]

The relevance of the distinction between conversational and academic language skills (BICS/CALP) discussed in the previous chapter can be seen in the problematic way Edele and Stanat interpret their data. They make the inaccurate claim that the interdependence hypothesis up to this point has not included transfer of 'oral language comprehension skills':

> The finding of a transfer of L1 listening comprehension is also important from a theoretical perspective. Cummins's (2000) influential notion of language interdependence posits that academic language skills in particular should transfer across languages. Although current definitions of academic language include features of oral and written language (see Nagy & Townsend, 2012; Snow, 2010), the transfer hypothesis assumes the transfer of L1 literacy skills but not of oral language comprehension skills (see, e.g., Cummins, 2000, p. 173). Our findings, however, suggest that theoretical notions of linguistic transfer should also include the oral domain. (Edele & Stanat, 2016: 176)

The interdependence hypothesis and the notion of crosslinguistic transfer have *always* explicitly included the oral domain. As outlined in the previous chapter and in Chapter 4, definitions of 'academic language proficiency' and 'literacy-related' language reference both oral and written language. For example, in critiquing the way the construct of 'oral language proficiency' was used in the August and Shanahan (2006, 2008a) reports, I noted that 'it is unclear to what extent oral vocabulary knowledge can be separated either logically or empirically from written vocabulary knowledge; for example, is there any fundamental difference in comprehension requirements between listening to a lecture on photosynthesis and reading the same lecture on photosynthesis?' (Cummins, 2009b: 383). I made the point in many publications that aspects of conversational language (BICS) (e.g. phonology) are unlikely to transfer across languages but the construct of CALP or 'literacy-related' language includes all of the oral language knowledge (e.g. vocabulary, metalinguistic awareness, etc.) that is strongly related to literacy development.

These two limitations are relatively minor and do not detract from the overall relevance and impact of one of the most significant and carefully implemented research studies in this area.

In Trilingual Contexts, Interdependence of Academic Language Proficiency Occurs Across the Three Languages in Multidirectional Ways

A series of studies carried out in Basque-Spanish bilingual programmes in the Basque Country demonstrated not only that Basque and Spanish language and literacy skills are significantly related but also that degree of bilingualism exerts a positive effect on English (L3) acquisition (e.g. Cenoz, 2013b; Cenoz & Gorter, 2011). Studies carried out in Israel have also demonstrated significant crosslinguistic relationships of literacy-related skills across multiple languages such as Arabic, Hebrew, English and Circassian (Abu-Rabia, 2005) and Arabic, Hebrew and English (Abu-Rabia & Siegel, 2003). Haim (2015) summarised the research on interdependence of academic proficiency (AP) in multilingual contexts as follows:

(a) bilinguals may indeed have certain advantages with respect to the development of L3 proficiency and metalinguistic awareness, (b) literacy in two or three languages fosters a higher level of metalinguistic awareness, (c) crosslinguistic transfer occurs in different dimensions of AP, such as grammar, syntax, reading, and writing, (d) transfer of dimensions of AP can occur in various directions, that is, from L1 to L2/L3 but also from L3 to L2/L1 and also from L2 to L3 and vice versa, (e) cross-linguistic transfer can occur across languages that are typologically distant, and (f) cross-linguistic transfer of AP may be related to other factors, such as the level of proficiency in each one of the languages used by the language learner, the language program, or typological distance. (Haim, 2015: 700)

Haim's (2015) own investigation of these issues in a sample of 274 Russian-speaking 11th graders studying through Hebrew (L2) and learning English (L3) produced consistent findings. She reported that students' Russian (L1) academic proficiency assessed by writing measures, studying Russian at school, and self-report through a 'can do' questionnaire, significantly predicted academic proficiency in both Hebrew and English independently of any interaction with arrival age, gender, or socioeconomic status. Reading comprehension and writing in Hebrew significantly predicted performance on parallel measures of these literacy skills in English.

Haim interpreted her findings as supportive of both holistic models of flexible multilingualism (e.g. Cook, 1992; Herdina & Jessner, 2002; Jessner, 2008) and the interdependence of language knowledge within the common underlying proficiency or common underlying conceptual base (Kecskés & Papp, 2000). She also pointed to the significant contribution of L1 to academic performance in L2 and L3: 'Denying access to immigrants' home language in the school context during primary school years may curtail their development of AP not only in their L1 but also in their subsequent languages' (2015: 710). She suggested using a translanguaging pedagogical approach to develop metacognitive and metalinguistic awareness and enhance crosslinguistic transfer.

Kindergarten Students' L1 Proficiency Predicts Later L2 Academic Development

Two relatively large-scale longitudinal studies carried out in the United States (Relyea & Amendum, 2020; Thompson, 2015) provide compelling evidence that students' L1 literacy-related knowledge at the kindergarten level is strongly related to their academic trajectories in English during the course of elementary school and beyond. Relyea and Amendum reported that 'initially well-developed Spanish reading competence plays a greater role in English reading development than English oral proficiency' (2019: 1150). Thompson (2015) similarly reported that emergent bilinguals' kindergarten performance on academic language tests in both L1 and L2 were about equally related to later English academic growth through the elementary school years and beyond.

The Relyea and Amendum (2020) study

Relyea and Amendum investigated the extent to which Spanish-speaking bilingual students' development of (pre)reading skills in Spanish, assessed at the kindergarten level, was related to developmental change in English reading between kindergarten and Grade 4. The sample consisted of 312 students drawn from a nationally representative sample of US school children who participated in the Early Childhood Longitudinal Study, Kindergarten Class of 2010–2011 (ECLS-K: 2011). The students were 99.7% Hispanic and came from 124 schools across the United States. Students were assessed at six points between the fall of kindergarten and the spring of Grade 4 with a battery of tests measuring Spanish reading, English reading, and English oral language abilities. The English oral language measures assessed listening comprehension (following directions) and receptive vocabulary (identifying pictures).

Relyea and Amendum reported two major findings of relevance in the present context:

- Bilingual Spanish-speaking kindergarten students who demonstrated stronger Spanish reading performance outperformed those with weaker Spanish reading performance in kindergarten English reading, and exhibited higher rates of English reading growth through the end of fourth grade. Initial concurrent correlations in the fall of kindergarten between Spanish and English reading competence were moderate to strong (0.68 - 0.69), but the fact that early Spanish reading predicted the rates of English reading *growth* suggests that the effects of cross-linguistic transfer are not temporary but rather increase over time. Relyea and Amendum (2020: 1160) concluded: 'The transfer effect of initial Spanish reading on the long-term developmental changes in English reading is evident'.
- A second major finding was that students' English oral proficiency moderated the contribution of initial Spanish reading ability to English reading development. Specifically, similar levels of initial English reading performance were found for bilingual students with weaker English oral proficiency but stronger Spanish reading ability, and bilingual students with stronger English oral proficiency but weaker Spanish reading ability. However, the group with stronger Spanish reading ability made greater gains at a faster rate relative to those with stronger English oral proficiency but weaker Spanish reading ability. Relyea and Amendum (2020: 1161) concluded: 'Despite initially weaker English oral proficiency, bilingual students with strong Spanish reading performance demonstrated greater English reading growth than their counterparts with stronger English oral abilities'.

Relyea and Amendum (2020: 1162) addressed the practical implications of their findings by highlighting the importance of promoting sustained development of both Spanish and English language and literacy: 'Because findings demonstrate an advantage for students with stronger Spanish literacy performance, maintaining Spanish proficiency and developing Spanish academic vocabulary may be important to support English language and literacy achievement and growth'.

The Thompson (2015) study

In a large-scale longitudinal study of 202,931 students who entered the Los Angeles Unified School District (LAUSD) between 2001 and 2010 as English language learners in kindergarten, Thompson (2015) investigated how long it took students to develop sufficient English academic proficiency to be reclassified as no longer needing English language support services. The sample consisted predominantly of native-Spanish speakers (94%) and students from low-income backgrounds (95%).

During the period the study was conducted, the LAUSD assessed all students in both their primary language and English on entry to kindergarten. Thompson refers to assessments at kindergarten entry as 'measures of students' initial academic language proficiency because these assessments focus on the types of language valued and used in school contexts and do not capture students' full range of language use in other contexts or their knowledge of non-dominant language varieties' (2015: 340–342). The L1 assessments were categorised on a 4-point scale with a score of 1 representing the lowest proficiency level. English assessments were categorised on a 5-point scale. Thompson points out that the highest score students can attain on the English measure and still be considered an English learner (EL) is Level 3 (Intermediate). Thus, for purposes of the study, students who scored Level 3 at kindergarten entry were classified as having high levels of academic English proficiency relative to their peers. Thompson summarised her findings as follows:

> Results corroborate prior research suggesting that English proficiency, when defined to encompass text-based literacy practices, does not develop quickly. Although a majority of students attain speaking and listening proficiency in English after only 2 years in the district, attaining proficiency on measures of reading and writing in English takes considerably longer. Specifically, the time necessary for at least 60% of students who enter LAUSD as ELs [English learners] in kindergarten to score proficient on literacy-based measures ranges from 4 to 7 years. ... Boys, native Spanish speakers, and students whose parents have lower levels of education are all less likely to be reclassified than their peers, after controlling for other factors. In addition, students' likelihood of reclassification varies dramatically based on their initial academic language proficiencies both in English and their primary language. (Thompson, 2015: 331)

The last point speaks directly to the interdependence hypothesis. Thompson reported that students who entered kindergarten with high levels of L1 academic language proficiency (i.e. Level 4) were 12% more likely to be reclassified as English proficient than students who entered with low levels of L1 academic language proficiency (i.e. Level 1). Those who entered kindergarten with high levels of English academic proficiency (Level 3) were 13% more likely to be reclassified than those with low levels of initial English proficiency (Level 1). Students who entered kindergarten with high levels of proficiency in both their languages (English and L1) were 24% more likely to be reclassified after nine years than students who entered with low levels of academic L1 proficiency and low levels of academic English proficiency.

In summary, Thompson concluded that 'a student's academic language and literacy skills in her home language play an important role in her acquisition of a second language' (2015: 358). The impact of initial L1 proficiency on rate of L2 academic language acquisition was almost the same as the impact of initial L2 (English) proficiency (12% versus 13%).

This pattern of findings is obviously consistent with predictions derived from the interdependence hypothesis.

Deaf Children's Development of Proficiency in a Natural Sign Language Predicts the Development of Reading and Writing Skills in the Dominant School Language

During the past 25 years, numerous empirical studies have been carried out to investigate the relationship between students' proficiency in a natural sign language (such as American Sign Language [ASL]) and the development of their literacy skills in the dominant school language (e.g. English in the United States). The initial study focusing on this issue was carried out by Prinz and Strong (1998) (see also Strong & Prinz, 1997) and the findings of this study were briefly summarised in Chapter 3. Subsequent research has shown similar patterns of findings consistent with predictions derived from the linguistic interdependence hypothesis. All of these studies suggest that the common underlying proficiency operates in similar ways regardless of whether the languages in question use different modalities (manual/spoken/written) or the same modality (spoken/spoken; written/written).

In their study involving 155 students between ages 8 and 15 attending a residential school for the deaf in California, Prinz and Strong also reported evidence that the differences in English literacy between children of deaf mothers and children of hearing mothers could be attributed to the differences in ASL proficiency between these two groups. When ASL level was held constant, differences in English literacy performance disappeared for the high and medium ASL groups, while differences remained among the low ASL group. Prinz and Strong explained these findings as follows:

> The implication here is that the scores in English literacy of students with deaf mothers are not superior to those of students with hearing mothers at the medium and high levels of ASL ability. This finding suggests that ASL skills may explain the different academic performance between the two groups—a notion that is consistent with Cummins' theory of cognitive and linguistic interdependence. At low levels of ASL skills, children may benefit from having a deaf parent possibly related to factors such as parental acceptance of the child, good parent-child communication, and emotional stability. (Prinz & Strong, 1998: 53)

Strong and Prinz (1997: 37) summarised the implications of their findings as follows: 'The implication of this research is straightforward and powerful: Deaf children's learning of English appears to benefit from the acquisition of even a moderate fluency in ASL'.

Niederberger (2008; also, Niederberger & Prinz, 2005) reported a study carried out in Switzerland with 39 deaf students aged between 8 and 17 which showed that the linguistic competencies necessary to support the learning of written language *can* be developed through a natural sign language, either as an alternative or as a complement to language skills developed orally. Significant correlations were found between students' French sign language proficiency and their morpho-syntactic and narrative skills in written and spoken French indicating that there are crosslinguistic and crossmodal interactions between natural French sign language and oral/written French. This again shows that linguistic interdependence operates between sign and written language in a similar manner to the relationship that exists between two oral/written languages.

The positive relationship between ASL and English literacy abilities is supported by several other studies. Hoffmeister *et al.* (1998), for example, reported significant positive correlations between ASL and reading comprehension among 50 deaf students aged 8–16 years. Similar findings were reported by Fish *et al.* (2005) who tested all students above the age of 7 who had no identified disabilities at two bilingual/bicultural schools for the deaf in the northeastern United States (N = 190, ages 7–20 years old). Forty of the students had deaf parents and 150 had hearing parents. The authors reported highly significant correlations between students' ASL proficiency and an English vocabulary measure from the Stanford Achievement Test. These correlations held for both the entire sample and within each of the deaf groups. In addition, deaf students with deaf parents performed better on both the ASL and English vocabulary measures than deaf students with hearing parents.

Padden and Ramsey (1998) also found significant correlations between ASL proficiency and English reading among 31 students ranging from grades 4–8. They suggested that the relationship between ASL and English reading must be cultivated by certain forms of instruction that draw students' attention to correspondences between the languages (i.e. teaching for crosslinguistic transfer):

> What emerges is an interrelationship between a set of language skills, specifically fingerspelling, initialized signs, reading, and competence in remembering ASL sentences as well as knowledge of ASL morphology and syntax. Students who perform best on tests of ASL and fingerspelling also perform well on a measure of reading comprehension. (Padden & Ramsey, 1998: 44)

> It is argued that deaf readers must *learn* to exploit fingerspelling and initialised signs as tools for reading, and must have guided practice doing so. They learn to do this ... from teachers and from other signing deaf readers in homes and in instructional contexts where the set of skills needed to become a signing deaf reader is implicitly acknowledged. (Padden & Ramsey, 1998: 39)

Singleton *et al.* (1998) reported a relationship between ASL and English writing ability among children of hearing parents for older (age 9+) but not for younger children (age 6–9). The authors summarise their findings as follows:

> Our preliminary results indicate that after age 9, high ASL-fluent deaf children of hearing parents were outperforming their less ASL-fluent peers on several English writing tasks. At this point, we have found no such correlation between ASL proficiency and English skills for the younger children in our sample (ages 6–9). However, it is important to note that at this young age, the children are producing very little English text in their classroom activities and in the writing samples we collected. It is possible that our present method for writing sample analysis fails to capture important differences in these shorter samples. It is also possible that the association between high ASL proficiency and improved English writing skills only emerges after the preliteracy stage. (Singleton *et al.*, 1998: 25)

Another research study carried out by Singleton and her colleagues with 72 deaf elementary school students reported a significant relationship between students' ASL proficiency and their writing skills in English. Specifically, they found that:

> Low-ASL-proficient students demonstrated a highly formulaic writing style, drawing mostly on high-frequency words and repetitive use of a limited range of function words. The moderate- and high-ASL-proficient deaf students' writing was not formulaic and incorporated novel, low-frequency vocabulary to communicate their thoughts. (Singleton *et al.*, 2004: 86)

The authors concluded their article by emphasising the importance of writing instruction that encourages deaf students to write for substantive and authentic purposes:

> In closing, we wish to emphasize the importance of writing stories that have something to say. Deaf students who generate repetitive and formulaic sentences are not demonstrating that they are true writers. While the ASL-proficient students lacked important grammatical elements in their stories, their writing demonstrated original and creative expression. These children are indeed thinking and creating. Therefore, as educators, the onus is upon us to harness those novel thoughts that might be expressed so fluently in ASL and develop instructional techniques that can connect this creativity to their developing literacy skills in English. (Singleton *et al.*, 2004: 100)

Further evidence for the applicability of the interdependence hypothesis to the cross-modal relationships between ASL and English reading comes from a study by Chamberlain and Mayberry (2008). They investigated ASL-English reading relationships among 40 adults who were profoundly deaf from birth and whose main language was ASL. The adults were classified as good or poor readers using a Grade 8 reading level cutoff. The good readers showed high levels of ASL syntactic and narrative comprehension skills whereas the poor readers had low levels of ASL skill. ASL syntactic and narrative comprehension skills also predicted reading comprehension skills on both the Stanford and Gates-McGinitie reading tests. They also found that the good readers experienced earlier access to ASL (average age 4 years old) than the poor readers (average age 7 years old), highlighting the importance of early exposure to meaningful linguistic interaction. The authors concluded that sign language *can* serve as the linguistic basis for reading despite the differences in modality that exist between ASL and English. They suggested that deaf students follow a unique path in comparison to hearing children in developing reading proficiency; they discover this path alone while engaged in reading books or other material.

Linguistic interdependence between sign language and written language was also reported in a study involving 15 deaf students aged 13–17 by Menéndez (2010) in Catalonia, Spain. Students were attending a bilingual school in which Catalan Sign Language was used to support the acquisition of written skills in Catalan, Spanish and English. Menéndez' study used contrastive analysis to identify areas of possible lexical, morphological and syntactic contact between Catalan Sign Language (SL) and written English. His analysis provided evidence of extensive positive transfer across languages and he expressed his conclusions as follows:

> Empirical data provided in this study show evidence of linguistic transfer from SL to written at the lexical, morphological and syntactic levels. Other data presented in the literature review show linguistic transfer at a pragmatic level (story grammar, narrative and cohesion). ... Therefore, Cummins' Linguistic Interdependence Theory is here supported as being correctly applied to sign bilingual education. (Menéndez, 2010: 218)

Hermans *et al*. (2010) reviewed several studies carried out in the Netherlands that drew similar conclusions. For example, Hermans *et al*. (2008) found a significant correlation between vocabulary knowledge in Sign Language of the Netherlands (SLN) and reading vocabulary among 87 deaf students in bilingual programmes aged 8–12 years when age, short-term memory, and nonverbal intelligence were controlled. Similarly, Ormel (2008) found a significant relationship between deaf students' receptive vocabulary in spoken Dutch and Sign Language of the Netherlands among 62 Deaf children in bilingual programmes aged 8-12 years after age was partialled out. Hermans *et al*. (2010) replicated these findings in showing significant correlations for expressive vocabulary and morpho-syntactic skills in spoken Dutch and SLN for a group of older children (aged 5.7 to 8.10 years) but not for younger children (aged 4.1 to 5.4 years). They interpret the lack of correlation at the younger age as reflecting the fact that students' SLN skills may not yet have been developed to a level where transfer can take place.

In summary, the research evidence shows consistent significant relationships between students' proficiency in natural sign languages and their development of reading and writing skills in the dominant school language. Transfer between sign language and written/spoken language has been reported at lexical, morphological, syntactic and pragmatic levels (e.g. Menéndez, 2010; Padden & Ramsey, 1998). Thus, the positive relationships can be attributed to transfer of conceptual elements (knowledge of the world) across languages, transfer of metacognitive and metalinguistic elements, and transfer of some specific linguistic elements (e.g. fingerspelling, initialised signs).

Migrant Students' L1 Literacy Skills Predict School Literacy Skills in Switzerland

This project (Berthele & Lambelet, 2018; Berthele & Vanhove, 2020; Vanhove & Berthele, 2018) described the development of literacy skills among Portuguese L1 speakers in both French- and German-speaking regions of Switzerland from the beginning of Grade 3 to the end of Grade 4 in both of their languages. It also aimed to test the interdependence hypothesis by examining the relationships between students' Portuguese and French/German literacy skills at three different times over the course of two school years. The sample consisted of 114 students who attended French-language schools and 119 who attended German-language schools. Three language/literacy tasks were administered to assess reading comprehension, narrative writing, and argumentative writing. These tests were administered at the beginning of third grade (average age 8 years and 8 months), at the end of third grade (average age 9 years and 3 months) and at the end of fourth grade (average age 10 years and 3 months). Of the Portuguese participants, 73% in French-speaking Switzerland and 97% in German-speaking Switzerland attended Portuguese language classes for about two hours per week with a focus on literacy development.

Berthele and Vanhove (2020) articulated three predictions which they claimed were derived from the interdependence hypothesis:

(1) An individual's score at time T predicts his or her score in the same skill in the other language at time T + 1.
(2) Crosslinguistic effects from the school language to the heritage language are stronger than the other way around.
(3) Crosslinguistic effects between French and Portuguese are stronger than those between German and Portuguese.

The first prediction is the only one that directly tests the interdependence hypothesis. As Berthele and Vanhove acknowledge, their second prediction 'is nowhere explicitly stated in the interdependence literature' (2020: 555). The interdependence hypothesis has always envisaged transfer across languages as potentially two-way, depending on the sociolinguistic and instructional conditions. There is no compelling rationale for proposing that crosslinguistic effects will be stronger from L2 (the major language of instruction) to L1, particularly in contexts where L1 literacy is not being strongly promoted within the school.

The third prediction is also not a test of the interdependence hypothesis. As noted in Chapter 3, similarity of specific linguistic elements (e.g. cognates) is only one of many components of academic language proficiency that might potentially transfer across languages. The extensive literature on this topic (e.g. Edele & Stanat, 2016; Usbourne *et al.*, 2019, previously reviewed in this chapter) shows that positive crosslinguistic relationships occur almost as frequently between languages that are dissimilar (e.g. American Sign Language/English, Basque/Spanish, German/ Turkish, Inuktitut/French and English etc.) compared to those that are similar (e.g. French/Portuguese). Swain *et al.* (1991), for example, reported that among grade 8 multilingual students in a French/English bilingual programme, heritage language literacy was a more potent predictor of French language and literacy skills than was linguistic similarity between the heritage language and French.

Thus, my examination of these predictions will focus primarily on the first prediction regarding longitudinal relationships across languages. The cross-language and within-language correlations reported by Berthele and Lambelet (2018) and Berthele and Vanhove (2020) are presented in Tables 9.1 and 9.2.

Table 9.1 Correlations of Portuguese, French, and German reading comprehension scores with Portuguese reading comprehension scores from the previous year

Testing point	French region		German region	
	P/F	P/P	P/G	P/P
T1-T2	.43	.70	.44	.63
T2-T3	.58	.69	.59	.69

Source: Based on data presented in Berthele and Vanhove, 2020, and Vanhove and Berthele (2018).
Note: T1, T2, T3 = Time 1, 2 and 3; P/F = correlation between Portuguese Time 1 and French Time 2, and Portuguese Time 2 and French Time 3; the same pattern holds for P/P, and P/G. The N for these correlations ranges from N = 80 to N = 96.

Table 9.2 Correlations of the school language (French or German) reading comprehension scores with Portuguese reading comprehension scores from the previous year

Testing point	French region		German region	
	F/P	F/F	G/P	G/G
T1-T2	.49	.65	.23	.54
T2-T3	.50	.68	.61	.60

Source: Based on data presented in Berthele and Vanhove, 2020, and Vanhove and Berthele (2018).
Note: T1, T2, T3 = Time 1, 2 and 3; F/P = correlation between French Time 1 and Portuguese Time 2, and French Time 2 and Portuguese Time 3; the same pattern holds for F/F, G/P, and G/G. The N for these correlations ranges from N = 77 to N = 100.

Vanhove and Berthele (2018) summarised the data in Table 9.1 by noting that relatively good readers in Portuguese tend to be relatively good readers in Portuguese one year later, and relatively good readers in Portuguese also tend to be relatively good readers in French or German one year later. As would be expected, the within-language correlations are stronger than those between languages, although all relationships are highly significant.

The same general pattern of crosslinguistic relationships holds for the data presented in Table 9.2 which depicts the relationships between reading comprehension in the school language at Time 1 and Time 2 and Portuguese reading comprehension at Time 2 and Time 3. One difference is the relatively low initial correlation ($r = 0.23$) between German and Portuguese at Times 1 and 2, which then 'bounces back' to a strong correlation ($r = 0.61$) between Time 2 and Time 3. This crosslinguistic relationship is equivalent in strength to the within-language relationship between German reading comprehension scores at Time 2 and Time 3 ($r = 0.60$).

Vanhove and Berthele carried out regression analyses for reading comprehension, narrative writing, and argumentative writing to assess whether a model with the participants' previous scores in both languages yields more accurate estimates than one with the participants' previous scores in the same language only. For all three dimensions of literacy, they found that 'there is indeed an added value in modelling the participants' previous scores in both languages when estimating their scores in a particular language a year later' (2018: 105). As expected, the within-language effect was stronger than the cross-language effect for reading comprehension and argumentative writing, but the cross-language effect was equivalent to the within-language effect in the case of narrative writing.

This research study is well designed, and the findings are clearly consistent with the construct of linguistic interdependence. The fact that the observed crosslinguistic relationships are longitudinal rather than cross-sectional and are replicated across two sets of languages and two different time periods adds to the confidence with which the findings can be interpreted as reflecting the operation of a common underlying proficiency.

Other aspects of the correlations depicted in Tables 9.1 and 9.2 can readily be interpreted in the context of the interdependence hypothesis. For example, the correlations from Portuguese to the school language are 15 points higher at T2-T3 as compared to the earlier T1-T2 (French: 0.43 T1/T2 versus 0.58 T2/T3; German: 0.44 T1/T2 versus 0.59 T2/T3). This pattern is noteworthy in light of considerable data (reviewed in Cummins, 2001) showing that as students gain more opportunity to develop literacy in both their languages, crosslinguistic relationships tend to increase in strength. Hakuta (1985: 66), for example, reported data from a Spanish-English bilingual programme to the effect that 'when the students first entered the bilingual program [at kindergarten], their abilities in Spanish and English were unrelated. However, by the end of three years, there were correlations as strong as $r = .70$ between the languages'. Hakuta interpreted this pattern of findings as indicating that development of either language can be used as a foundation for the other: 'children who came in with a strong base in their native language, Spanish, ended up with the strongest abilities in English, a finding that supports Cummins's contention of the interdependence of the languages of the bilingual' (1985: 66).

The relatively low initial correlation (Table 9.2) between German and Portuguese ($r = 0.23$) compared to French and Portuguese ($r = 0.49$) can also plausibly be interpreted on a *post hoc* basis. The greater linguistic similarity (e.g. cognate relationships) between French and Portuguese as compared to German and Portuguese might 'kick-start' the transfer process at an earlier stage for Portuguese students being educated through French as compared to German. However, this effect 'washes out' in the subsequent set of relationships (T2-T3: $r = 0.50$), as a result of the fact that as literacy and knowledge of the world increase, so too does conceptual transfer between the languages. This interpretation is consistent with the increase from 0.23 (T1-T2) to 0.61 (T2-T3) for the German results. The static pattern for French/Portuguese correlations between T1/T2 (0.49) and T2/T3 (0.50) suggests that linguistic similarity facilitates both linguistic and conceptual transfer at a relatively early stage of literacy development but then reaches a point of diminishing returns. This interpretation is consistent with the way in which Edele and Stanat (2016) interpreted their findings, considered previously in this chapter, regarding the different patterns of L1/L2 transfer in languages with a high degree of similarity as compared to languages with a low degree of similarity.

Surprisingly, the authors of this well-designed research project reject the interdependence hypothesis as an explanation for their findings. They adopt this position on the basis of several considerations. First, their second and third predictions regarding the interdependence hypothesis were not supported by the data. Transfer from the school language to students' L1 was no greater than transfer from students' L1 to the school language (Prediction 2) and the overall crosslinguistic relationship between French and Portuguese was no greater than between German and Portuguese (Prediction 3). As noted previously, neither of these predictions is intrinsic to the interdependence hypothesis.

Berthele and Vanhove's critique of the interdependence hypothesis

In addition to rejecting the interdependence hypothesis as a result of the lack of support in their data for Hypotheses 2 and 3, Berthele and Vanhove also raise the following two objections:

Cross-sectional correlations of measures across two or more languages within subjects may well be explained in terms of underlying linguistic proficiency, but they may just as well be due to the correlation of measurement errors or due to general, non-linguistic cognitive skills (working memory, general intelligence, world knowledge, and test-wiseness, to name but a few), whereas longitudinal correlations can at least be accounted for as the by-product of imperfectly measured variables. (Berthele & Vanhove, 2020: 562)

The authors' attribution of their findings to measurement errors is entirely unconvincing. Not only are their own findings consistent across language differences and different times of measurement, but the broader research literature has consistently demonstrated crosslinguistic relationships in reading comprehension performance for more than 40 years. The fact that hundreds of studies carried out in vastly different linguistic, sociolinguistic, and sociopolitical contexts show consistent evidence for moderate to strong crosslinguistic relationships is remarkable. Measurement errors would typically operate in a random fashion. These relationships, by contrast, are systematic rather than random. They obviously do not operate in isolation from highly varied contextual conditions, but the consistency of the findings, despite major contextual variation, suggests that this is a real and educationally significant relationship.

The authors' second attempt to explain away their own data is equally problematic. It assumes a rigid distinction between 'linguistic' and 'non-linguistic' cognitive skills and implies that working memory, 'general intelligence', and world knowledge are independent of the construct of 'language proficiency'. Once again, we come back to the question, discussed in previous chapters, of what is meant by 'language proficiency'. To illustrate this issue with a concrete example, we can refer to a study carried out by Cain *et al.* (2004) which reported that 'working memory sentence span' correlated at highly significant levels ($p < .001$) with variables such as reading comprehension, verbal ability (IQ), and vocabulary knowledge. This raises the question of whether 'working memory sentence span' is a linguistic or a cognitive variable? Is vocabulary knowledge a linguistic or a cognitive variable? Is 'verbal ability' a linguistic or a cognitive variable?

Berthele and Verhove (2020) acknowledge that there is crosslinguistic transfer of concepts such as 'photosynthesis' that reflect conceptual knowledge. They claim that this type of 'transfer' is uncontroversial and does not call for empirical investigation (2020: 551). The authors do not regard this type of transfer as reflecting *linguistic* skills, which in their study they operationalised by means of reading and writing skills. The logic here is untenable. The authors' position involves arguing that their reading comprehension test does not reflect cognitive skills or measure students' conceptual knowledge or knowledge of the world. The fact that they operationalise linguistic skills by using reading and writing measures also suggests that they see no difference between the constructs of 'literacy' and 'language proficiency'. Although some aspects of 'language proficiency' become strongly related to literacy during the school years, few researchers, with the possible exception of Oller (1980), would claim that the constructs are identical.

Berthele and Verhove's position can be expressed as follows:

(reading comprehension = language proficiency) ≠ conceptual knowledge

Thus, if a student were reading a passage on 'photosynthesis', their previous knowledge of this concept (or lack thereof) would have no influence on their understanding of the passage. Or, if students were reading about the second world war, their background conceptual knowledge of the events and issues in this conflict would exert no influence on their comprehension of the text. Almost a century of research evidence relating to the role of background knowledge refutes this perspective (e.g. Bartlett, 1932). As I have argued in previous chapters, reading comprehension, academic language proficiency, and conceptual knowledge are fused in the performance of typical academic tasks. Thus, understanding the concept of 'photosynthesis' reflects academic language proficiency as much as it does conceptual knowledge.

In summary, this small sample of recent studies reinforces the conclusions of numerous research reviews that affirm the legitimacy of the construct of linguistic interdependence (e.g. NASEM, 2017). A persistent question underlying debates about this and other issues (e.g. assessment of eligibility for language support services) relates to the construct of 'language proficiency' itself. I have tried to be clear that the component of 'language proficiency' that I have labelled 'academic language proficiency' or 'CALP' reflects a *fusion* of linguistic, cognitive and academic knowledge and skills (see Figure 8.2). Uccelli and colleagues' (2015a, 2015b) construct of CALS similarly incorporates linguistic, cognitive and subject matter dimensions. By contrast, in many publications and research articles, the notion of 'language proficiency' is either left undefined or discussed in terms of internally incoherent notions of 'oral language proficiency' that confound rather than clarify the issues (e.g. August & Shanahan, 2006, 2008a; Melby-Lervåg & Lervåg, 2011) (see Appendix 9.1 for further discussion of this point).

The next section reviews the theoretical critique of the interdependence hypothesis proposed by Ofelia García and colleagues (e.g. García, 2009; García & Li Wei, 2014). I then examine the perspectives of other researchers who have proposed qualifications or modifications to the interdependence hypothesis, while at the same time supporting its general legitimacy.

Section 2. Theoretical Critique: Does Linguistic Interdependence Imply a Monoglossic Orientation to Multilingualism?

García and colleagues (e.g. García, 2009; García & Li Wei, 2014) have argued that the notion of a common underlying proficiency and teaching for crosslinguistic transfer imply a *monoglossic* conception of bi/

multilingualism that is at variance with dynamic models of multilingualism. Dynamic models of multilingualism incorporate a *heteroglossic* orientation that reflects the fluid and permeable boundaries of language use in bilingual communities. According to García and colleagues, monoglossic language ideologies conceptualise monolingualism as the norm whereas heteroglossic ideologies position bi/multilingualism as the norm. Heteroglossic perspectives also view the individual's linguistic resources as rooted in an integrated non-differentiated cognitive organisation.

On the basis of this dichotomy, García and Li Wei (2014: 62) critique scholars 'who still speak about L1, L2 and code-switching'. They also argue that we can now 'shed the concept of *transfer*... [in favor of] a conceptualization of *integration* of language practices in *the person of the learner*' (emphasis original) (2014: 80). They question the notion of a common underlying proficiency because, in their eyes, it still delineates a conception of bilingualism as 'double monolingualism' involving separate L1 and L2, and separate linguistic features: 'Instead, translanguaging validates the fact that bilingual students' language practices are not separated into an L1 and an L2, or into home language and school language, instead transcending both' (2014: 69).

The argument by García and colleagues that the construct of a common underlying proficiency and teaching for crosslinguistic transfer reflect a monoglossic orientation to bi/multilingualism follows directly and logically from their theoretical claim that the construct of 'a language' is illegitimate. As noted in Chapter 7, García and Lin (2017: 127) expressed this point as follows: 'bilingual people do not speak languages'. If there is only one linguistic system with features that are totally integrated rather than being associated with any particular 'language', then, clearly, it is meaningless to talk about transfer from one language to another.

I argue in this section that García and colleagues simply assert this proposition with no supportive analysis. They also fail to engage with the claim (Cummins, 2007a) that the notion of a common underlying proficiency is not in any way inconsistent with dynamic models of multilingualism. Underlying the logically flawed assertion that 'we can shed the concept of transfer' are three intersecting problematic theoretical claims: (1) 'languages' don't exist as legitimate conceptual entities; (2) any theoretical construct that endorses the legitimacy of the construct of 'languages' is, by definition, monoglossic; and (3) the monoglossic/heteroglossic distinction represents a binary dichotomy rather than a continuum – if a construct is not heteroglossic according to the way García and colleagues characterise the term, then it must be monoglossic.

To what extent is there legitimacy to the claims (García, 2009; García & Li Wei, 2014) that the construct of a common underlying proficiency and the pedagogical practice of teaching for crosslinguistic transfer are monoglossic in ideology and inconsistent with dynamic models of bilingualism? In the sections that follow, I examine these claims with respect to empirical adequacy, logical coherence, and consequential validity. First, however, I sketch the evolution of dynamic conceptions of bilingualism over the past 30 years.

Most Dynamic Models of Multilingualism Do Not Reject the Construct of 'Languages'

García's (2009) rejection of monoglossic orientations to multilingualism builds on similar perspectives articulated by numerous scholars during the past 30+ years (e.g. Cook, 1992, 2007, 2016; Grosjean, 1982, 1989; Herdina & Jessner, 2002; Jessner, 2006). Common to these positions is the conceptualisation of multilingualism as a dynamically integrated system rather than a static accumulation of separate language skills. Grosjean (1989) initially highlighted the fact that the bilingual is not two monolinguals in one person and this insight was subsequently elaborated in Cook's (1992, 2007, 2016) concept of *multi-competence*, which emphasised that multi-competence is not comparable to monolingual competence in each language. Herdina and Jessner (2002) and de Bot *et al.* (2007) elaborated this perspective by proposing a dynamic systems theory, which argued that knowledge of additional languages influences the development not only of the second language but also the development of the overall multilingual system, including the first language. Dynamic systems theory highlights the fact that the entire psycholinguistic system of the bi- and multilingual is transformed in comparison to the relatively less complex psycholinguistic system of the monolingual. As expressed by Jessner (2006: 35), there is 'a complete metamorphosis of the system involved and not merely an overlap between two subsystems'.

These theoretical propositions are not in any way controversial. Virtually all theorists and researchers currently endorse some form of dynamic systems theory that highlights the transformation of the cognitive and linguistic system brought about by the acquisition of multiple languages. As one example, the concept of *plurilingualism* that undergirds many of the language teaching and language policy initiatives promoted by the Council of Europe and the European Centre of Modern Languages over the past 20 years is firmly grounded in a dynamic conception of language functioning (e.g. Beacco *et al.*, 2016; Coste *et al.*, 2009; Council of Europe, 2001, 2020; Lau & Van Viegen, 2020a; Moore *et al.*, 2020; Piccardo, 2013, 2016). There is also widespread support in the academic literature for the propositions that (a) multilingual/plurilingual individuals draw on the totality of their linguistic resources in communicative interactions and (b) classroom instruction should encourage students to use their full linguistic repertoire in flexible and strategic ways as a tool for cognitive functioning and academic learning (e.g. Cummins, 2007a). Educators were implementing these instructional strategies long before the construct of translanguaging entered mainstream academic discourse (e.g. Chow & Cummins, 2003; Cummins *et al.*, 2005; DeFazio, 1997; Kirwin, 2014, 2020; Little & Kirwin, 2018, 2019).

None of these 'early' models of dynamic bilingualism have seen it necessary to reject the construct of 'languages' in order to highlight the complex crosslinguistic interactions that take place in the cognitive systems of multilinguals. Thus, the rejection of 'languages' (noun form) in favour of 'translanguaging' (verb form) is not an intrinsic or necessary component of a dynamic conception of multilingualism.

Obviously, as Jessner (2006) points out, dynamic models of bilingualism go far beyond the linguistic interdependence hypothesis or common underlying proficiency in specifying how languages are organised and interact cognitively. The common underlying proficiency construct was addressed to a very different set of issues, as outlined in Chapter 3, and made no attempt to chart the complexities either of multilingual communication or neurolinguistic and cognitive organisation of languages in our brains. But this does not mean that there is any incompatibility or inconsistency between these constructs and dynamic systems theory. I made this point in elaborating the theoretical basis for teaching for crosslinguistic transfer and arguing against 'two solitudes' models of bilingualism and bilingual education:

> The theoretical constructs elaborated by Cook (1995) and Jessner (2006) are not in any way inconsistent with the notion of a common underlying proficiency (CUP). ... What all these constructs share is a recognition that the languages of bi- and multilinguals interact in complex ways that can enhance aspects of overall language and literacy development. They all also call into question the pedagogical basis of monolingual instructional approaches that appear dedicated to minimizing and inhibiting the possibility of two-way transfer across languages. (Cummins, 2007a: 234)

Empirical Adequacy: There is Strong Empirical Support for the Common Underlying Proficiency Construct and Teaching for Crosslinguistic Transfer

The corollary of this observation is that there is minimal empirical support for rejection of the common underlying proficiency construct or for 'shedding' the concept of transfer as proposed by García and colleagues (García, 2009; García & Li Wei, 2014). The empirical data in relation to this issue has been reviewed in Chapter 3, and also previously in this chapter. The constructs of common underlying proficiency and teaching for crosslinguistic transfer are also consistent with a growing body of neurolinguistic research, summarised by NASEM (2017: 243):

> A growing body of research dating back to the 1960s reveals that the two languages of bilinguals do not exist in isolation and to the contrary, are highly interactive. ... *The two languages of bilinguals share a cognitive/*

conceptual foundation that can facilitate the acquisition and use of more than one language for communication, thinking, and problem solving. It is the sophisticated and complex management of two linguistic systems that is thought to engender the development of superior cognitive skills in bilinguals relative to monolinguals. Research on the acquisition, comprehension, and production of two languages during second language learning and bilingual performance has revealed that *both linguistic systems are differentially accessible and activated at virtually all times* (e.g., Gullifer et al., 2013; Kroll et al., 2014). Even when using only one language, bilinguals access the meaning of words in both languages, although accessibility and salience of meaning in the active language are stronger. (NASEM, 2017: 243) (emphasis added)

Research studies that investigated the effects of teaching for crosslinguistic transfer (e.g. Hopewell, 2011; Tamati, 2016) report positive outcomes. Tamati (2011, 2016) elaborated what she called the *transacquisition approach* in the context of *kura kaupapa Māori* programmes in Aotearoa/New Zealand, which were developed and implemented in the 1980s with the goal of revitalising the Māori language. The transacquisition approach consisted of several instructional interventions, implemented over an 8-week period with 24 Year (Grade) 7 and 8 students, designed to enable them to use both their languages simultaneously to promote biliteracy development and acquire academic knowledge. The goal was to teach explicitly for two-way transfer across languages. Tamati reported the following major finding from the quantitative analyses:

> The quantitative findings from the intervention study showed that the kura students' academic language, academic understanding, and reading comprehension in English improved significantly as a result of the eight-week intervention programme. The magnitude of the improvement was large and the rate of improvement very fast, well beyond what would be expected among similarly-abled English-medium students. (Tamati, 2016: iv)

Hopewell's (2011) intervention study involving 49 Grade 4 students enrolled in two biliteracy classes compared the difference in English reading comprehension when students were invited to use both Spanish and English to write written responses to English texts as compared to when they were confined to English only. She reported evidence of better performance when students were enabled to draw on their entire linguistic repertoire. The effect of expanding the learning space to include Spanish was particularly strong when students read and discussed an English text that was congruent with their experience of family life as compared to a text that reflected content that was more school-based.

The positive outcomes associated with the Literacy Squared programme that explicitly pursues crosslinguistic pedagogy in the context of simultaneous literacy instruction in both languages can also be viewed as supportive of the legitimacy of both the common underlying proficiency construct and teaching for crosslinguistic transfer (Escamilla *et al.*, 2014; Soltero-González *et al.*, 2016; Sparrow *et al.*, 2014).

Finally, it is important to highlight the useful visual metaphor by means of which Tamati (2016) illustrated what she called the Interrelational Translingual Network (ITN) that reflects the common underlying proficiency or common operating system of the bilingual individual. The distinctive growth pattern of the kahikatea tree, native to Aotearoa/New Zealand (depicted on the cover of this volume), is characterised by a network of entangled roots that bind multiple trees together, thereby enhancing the strength of each individual tree (Figure 9.1). According to Tamati (2016: 9) 'each tree entwines its buttressed roots with its neighbours to form a thick, matted footing that supports all the trees in waterlogged swampy soils'. Applied to language learning and multilingualism, the metaphor suggests that individual languages are rooted in a dynamic network of connections but can still be distinguished as legitimate conceptual entities. This visual metaphor contrasts with García's (2009: 8) metaphor of banyan trees 'which grow up, out, down, horizontally, or vertically through the air until they come upon something solid'. Sometimes it is impossible to distinguish individual trees because the branches and roots of multiple trees are so intertwined. García suggests that the banyan tree is an apt metaphor for languages which, she claims, cannot be distinguished as discrete cognitive or linguistic entities. In Tamati's formulation, by contrast, the roots are intertwined but each individual tree is clearly distinguishable. There is no rationale for denying the individual and collective existence of trees (languages) just because they are sustained by an underlying network of interconnections.

Figure 9.1 Intertwined roots of kahikatea trees
(https://www.gettyimages.ca/detail/photo/kahikatea-tree-at-yarndleys-bush-royalty-free-image/1149526308)

Logical Coherence: The Binary Dichotomies of Monoglossic/ Heteroglossic and Language/Translanguaging Oversimplify and Distort Dynamic Crosslinguistic Relationships

What is the rationale for adopting 'either/or' dichotomies on an *a priori* basis to represent bilingual cognitive organisation and pedagogical orientations rather than grounding these categorisations in empirical data, or a more fluid set of hypotheses regarding patterns of L1/L2 cognitive organisation? For example, rather than an impermeable dichotomy between 'monoglossic' and 'heteroglossic' orientations, why not explore the possibility of a theoretical continuum with a range of potential L1/L2 relationships depending on the sociolinguistic and pedagogical context?

I have already (Chapter 7) pointed to the arbitrary nature of the 'either-or' dichotomy between the verb form *trans/languaging* and the noun form *language*. There is no logical or empirical reason to erect a false opposition between these constructs, and then to dismiss the noun form 'language' as illegitimate under all discoursal and rhetorical conditions associated with individuals. A large majority of applied linguists (together with educators and policymakers) acknowledge the legitimacy of both 'languaging' and 'languages' within appropriate communicative and discoursal contexts. Even strong proponents of translanguaging who are sympathetic to the notion of a unitary linguistic system acknowledge the legitimacy of a both/and rather than either/or perspective. For example, Angel Lin and Jay Lemke, in a broad ranging discussion about current issues and controversies related to translanguaging, address concerns from minoritised groups about the possible erasure of their languages and identities implied by the notion of a unitary undifferentiated linguistic system. Lemke makes the following point:

> Not to say 'It's either translanguaging or it's named language systems'. It can be both, for different purposes. Yes, indeed, if you want to codify your heritage language, that's fine. Right? It serves a purpose for you. (Lin *et al.*, 2020: 65)

Unfortunately, however, this more flexible perspective is at variance with the assertion of a rigid monoglossic/heteroglossic dichotomy advanced by García and colleagues. These authors (e.g. Otheguy *et al.*, 2015, 2019) have presented no logical rationale or empirical evidence to support the *dichotomous* nature of hetroglossic versus monoglossic orientations rather than other possibilities such as a continuum between these two end points.

This can be illustrated by MacSwan's (2017) rebuttal of their claims regarding the monoglossic nature of the theoretical construct of codeswitching. MacSwan (2017: 179) pointed out that the characterisation of codeswitching research as monoglossic in orientation is 'merely asserted and not tied to an actual analysis of theoretical proposals in the literature, nor are any actual relevant citations provided'. His detailed analysis of research in the areas of codeswitching and bilingual language development supports what he calls an integrated multilingual model that posits both shared and discrete grammatical and lexical resources rather than the unitary undifferentiated model advocated by García and colleagues. This integrated model of multilingual competence is consistent with the common underlying proficiency construct proposed by Cummins (1981b). In short, MacSwan (2017) makes a credible case that there are additional options other than a binary oppositional contrast between 'monoglossic' and 'heteroglossic' ideological and theoretical orientations.

In the same way, García and colleagues' characterisation of the common underlying proficiency and teaching for transfer as 'monoglossic' in orientation fails the test of logical coherence. Prior to García's (2009) elaboration of the construct of translanguaging, I challenged monolingual instructional assumptions in both L2-only and bilingual/immersion programmes that were based on what I called the 'two solitudes' model of bilingual instruction (Cummins, 2007a). This rejection of monolingual instructional assumptions was rooted theoretically in both the linguistic interdependence hypothesis and dynamic conceptions of bilingualism. García and colleagues have acknowledged this rejection of monolingual instructional assumptions but have not engaged analytically with the argument that the constructs of linguistic interdependence, teaching for crosslinguistic transfer, and additive bilingualism are entirely consistent with heteroglossic conceptions of bi/multilingualism. In multiple publications, there has simply been a ritual repetition of *a priori* claims that the linguistic interdependence hypothesis and the construct of a common underlying proficiency represent monoglossic ideologies (e.g. García, 2009; García & Li Wei, 2014). In some cases, the implication has been that because of their alleged monoglossic orientation, these constructs reflect deficit conceptions in regard to minoritised students' bilingualism (e.g. Flores & Rosa, 2015).

My point here is that theoretical disagreement and dialogue represent an integral process in how knowledge gets generated (Cummins, 2000). However, *avoidance* of theoretical dialogue is antithetical to the process of knowledge generation. In asserting that the notion of a common underlying proficiency and the proposal to teach for crosslinguistic transfer are 'monoglossic' in orientation, García and colleagues fail to consider or rebut the opposing claims (a) that teaching for crosslinguistic transfer challenges the 'two solitudes' (i.e. monoglossic) orientation to teaching minoritised students and (b) that the construct of a common underlying proficiency arose in opposition to the subtractive notion of a 'time-on-task' or 'maximum exposure' (separate underlying proficiency) conception of bilingualism and bilingual education. By classifying, without any qualification, both the common underlying proficiency construct and the separate underlying proficiency construct as equivalently 'monoglossic' and essentially no different from each other, they undermine the sustained efforts of countless educators, policymakers, and researchers to implement equitable and antiracist bilingual education for minoritised students. As Britt and colleagues (2014) point out, completely unqualified assertions often tend to be persuasive to readers, but they seldom hold up to scientific scrutiny.

Consequential Validity: 'Shedding' the Concept of Crosslinguistic Transfer Yields no Pedagogical Gains

The problematic consequences for language pedagogy and policy that arise as a result of the claim that languages have no cognitive reality and don't exist as 'countable' entities have been discussed in Chapter 7. Cummins (2017: 414) pointed to similar issues that arise when the concept of crosslinguistic transfer and the instructional strategy of teaching for transfer are invalidated: 'If not teaching for transfer, how should teachers in a Spanish/English bilingual program conceptualize what they are doing when they draw students' attention to similarities between *encontrar* and *encounter*, or when they remind students about the similarities between Spanish and English in conventions for paragraph formation?'

The consequences of dismissing concepts such as 'home language', 'school language', and crosslinguistic transfer become obvious in the fact that these concepts are regularly invoked by translanguaging researchers who have ostensibly rejected the legitimacy of these concepts. For example, Flores and Schissel (2014: 473), in the context of an insightful discussion of the New York State Bilingual Common Core Initiative (2013), make the point that 'students can use translanguaging to build on the skills that they already have in their home language as they master content that will eventually transfer to English'. In this one sentence, Flores and Schissel appear to confirm the legitimacy of the concepts 'home language', 'school language' (English) and crosslinguistic transfer, despite the fact that these concepts have been designated as monoglossic and illegitimate within the translanguaging framework they endorse.

A similar set of contradictions is evident in García and Kleifgen's (2019: 13) argument, cited previously, that a translanguaging approach to literacies instruction would include strategies such as translation, crosslinguistic study of syntax, vocabulary, cognates and discourse structure. In relation to this very reasonable statement, educators might well ask questions such as the following: If languages have no cognitive or linguistic reality, what are we translating between? What does *crosslinguistic* mean if languages don't really exist within the individual's linguistic system and if there is no transfer between languages? If languages are *real* only in a social sense but not a linguistic sense, how should we interpret cognates?

In summary, neither linguistic interdependence nor the common underlying proficiency construct implies a monoglossic orientation to multilingualism. These constructs are fully consistent with dynamic models of multilingualism insofar as they highlight the fact that the languages of bilingual individuals do not constitute 'two solitudes' but rather intersect and interact in complex ways. Thus, García and colleagues' claim that the common underlying proficiency construct and teaching for transfer reflect monoglossic ideologies fails to satisfy the criteria of empirical adequacy, logical coherence, and consequential validity.

Section 3. Suggested Modifications and Qualifications to the Linguistic Interdependence Hypothesis

A number of researchers have suggested modifications to the linguistic interdependence hypothesis based on their research findings. These suggestions are clearly useful and have contributed to our understanding of the conditions under which two-way crosslinguistic transfer is likely to occur. However, several of the studies have not fully taken into account the conditions for transfer that have already been specified within the interdependence hypothesis. Many of the studies also employ the problematic construct of 'oral language proficiency' in their examination of L1/L2 relationships. As noted previously, I have argued (Cummins, 2009b) that this construct is incoherent because, in theory, it can encompass dimensions of language/literacy proficiency that have nothing in common apart from the fact that they do not directly involve print-based written language.

In the sections below, I review several of the studies and reviews that have proposed qualifications to the interdependence hypothesis and then focus on the legitimacy of the construct of 'oral language proficiency' because it has been pervasive in psychologically oriented research on both reading development and L1/L2 relationships.

Prevoo and Colleagues (2015)

This study was entitled 'A Context-Dependent View on the Linguistic Interdependence Hypothesis' and its initial premise appears to have been that the hypothesis was proposed without any consideration of the way the sociolinguistic, sociopolitical and educational contexts might moderate the extent and nature of L1/L2 relationships. The only citation for the interdependence hypothesis was Cummins (1979a), with the result that the more formal statement of the hypothesis (Cummins, 1980c, 1981b, and numerous subsequent publications) was not considered. As noted in Chapter 3, the formal statement specified that crosslinguistic transfer from Lx to Ly (and, by implication, from Ly to Lx) would occur provided there is adequate exposure to each language (either in school or environment) and adequate motivation to learn each language. Cummins (1980a: 179) also noted that 'these relationships do not exist in an affective or experiential vacuum'. The degree of transfer depends on the measures utilised (the hypothesis focused only on CALP) and on the context, specifically opportunities to develop both languages within the school and motivation to do so. Thus, it is inaccurate to claim (Prevoo *et al.*, 2015) that the interdependence hypothesis lacks attention to contextual variables that moderate the degree of L1/L2 relationships.

Obviously, investigations that probe the conditions under which interdependence occurs such as those carried out by Prevoo *et al.* (2015) and numerous other researchers (e.g. Cobo-Lewis *et al.*, 2002a, 2002b; Cummins *et al.*, 1984) are important in refining the interdependence hypothesis. For example, Prevoo and colleagues' (2015) study of L1/L2 vocabulary relationships (measured by oral picture vocabulary tests) in a sample of 104 5- and 6-year-old Turkish-speaking children in the Netherlands reported that positive transfer from Turkish to Dutch vocabulary was found among children whose mothers reported that they spoke more Turkish than Dutch at home but not in the group of children who were reported to speak more Dutch than Turkish. Socioeconomic status exerted no impact on these patterns of relationships. These findings are fully interpretable within the context of the interdependence hypothesis as formally stated (Cummins, 1981b). Turkish-background students who spoke more Dutch than Turkish at home are likely experiencing a subtractive process whereby their L1 is being partially replaced by their L2. Under these circumstances, minimal crosslinguistic transfer would be expected. By contrast, 5/6-year-old children who speak Turkish predominantly at home are continuing to develop their knowledge of that language while they are acquiring Dutch at school. Under these circumstances, transfer effects are more likely to occur.[5]

Genesee and Colleagues (2006) and Geva (2014)

A review of crosslinguistic relationships authored by Fred Genesee, Esther Geva, Cheryl Dressler and Michael Kamil (2006) was written as part of the report of the National Literacy Panel on Language-Minority Children and Youth (August & Shanahan, 2006). Genesee and colleagues acknowledged the influence and usefulness of the interdependence hypothesis for explaining procedural knowledge that underlies language use in academic or cognitively demanding tasks, but they suggest that, by itself, the hypothesis is not sufficient to identify what specific skills or abilities are transferred. Both Genesee *et al.* (2006) and Geva (2014) suggested that crosslinguistic relationships can be interpreted within two main frameworks – linguistic interdependence and contrastive analysis. They note that linguistic interdependence theory posits a common underlying proficiency that makes possible positive crosslinguistic transfer (from L1 to L2 and from L2 to L1) whereas the contrastive analysis framework focuses on structural similarities and differences between L1 and L2 (e.g. phonology, syntax, semantics) that will affect the extent of positive or negative transfer across languages.

Geva's (2014) brief but useful review of the interdependence hypothesis was written as the Introduction to a special journal issue focused on cross-language transfer. Drawing on the findings of Geva and Ryan (1993), she suggested that much of the crosslinguistic 'transfer' can be accounted for by common underlying cognitive processes that underlie performance in L1 and L2. Geva (2014) concluded that the process of crosslinguistic transfer is highly complex, involving not just specific aspects of L1/L2 such as vocabulary, morphological awareness, and syntax, but also specific components of literacy and cognition together with social, affective, contextual and instructional factors.

Clearly, as Genesee *et al.* (2006) point out, it is informative to identify the specific skills and knowledge that transfer from one language to another, and considerable progress has been made in this regard (e.g. Geva, 2006; Koda, 2008; Phillips Galloway *et al.*, 2020). It is also important to learn more about the specific sociolinguistic, sociopolitical and educational contexts that promote L1/L2 transfer. However, the way both Genesee *et al.* (2006) and Geva (2014) interpret the interdependence construct is somewhat at variance with the way it has been described in numerous publications (e.g. Cummins, 1980c, 1981b, 1991, 2000, 2001). Almost from its inception (Cummins, 1979b), the interdependence hypothesis was integrated with the CALP/BICS distinction, and it specified that oral and written CALP (literacy-related) skills would show positive crosslinguistic relationships under conditions where both languages continued to develop during the elementary school years. Thus, specific skills and abilities would show crosslinguistic relationships to the extent that they were integral to the overall construct of CALP within languages. For example, those aspects of L1 development that are facilitative for L1 reading comprehension should also facilitate L2 reading comprehension in contexts where both languages are promoted in school. Cummins (1984a: 144) expressed this perspective as follows:

> What are some of the literacy-related skills involved in the common underlying proficiency? Conceptual knowledge is perhaps the most obvious example. An immigrant child who arrives in North America at, for example, age 15, understanding the concept of 'honesty' in his or her L1 only has to acquire a new *label* in L2 for an already-existing concept. ... By the same token, subject matter knowledge, higher-order thinking skills, reading strategies, writing composition skills etc. developed through the medium of L1 transfer or become available to L2 given sufficient exposure and motivation. (Cummins, 1984a: 144) (emphasis original)

Genesee *et al.*'s (2006a: 157) interpretation of the common underlying proficiency differs significantly from the description quoted above:

> In particular, it is not entirely clear what Cummins means by his construct of *common underlying proficiency*. We take it to refer to procedural knowledge that underlies language use for academic or higher order

cognitive processes and entails, for example, the skills involved in defining words or elaborating ideas verbally as is often required when language is used for academic purposes. We differentiate Cummins' notion of common underlying proficiency from underlying cognitive abilities... We also assume it does not refer to structural features of the type that figure in the contrastive analysis framework. (Genesee *et al.*, 2006a: 157)

Similarly, Geva (2014: 5–6), following Geva and Ryan (1993), proposed that 'L1 and L2 higher level skills (e.g. the activation of prior knowledge in the L1 and L2) may be better understood by considering individual differences in underlying cognitive processes such as working memory, phonological awareness, and rapid automatized naming that are thought to be part of one's general, cognitive make-up'.

As noted previously, the interdependence hypothesis incorporates both 'transfer' and 'underlying cognitive processes' as sources of the relationships between L1 and L2 literacy-related abilities. Individual differences in these cognitive processes constitute 'attributes' of the individual, and L1/L2 relationships reflect the fact that these attributes manifest themselves in cognitive and academic tasks in both languages. Thus, there is no opposition between notions of 'transfer' and 'underlying cognitive processes' as sources for L1/L2 relationships.

My conception of linguistic interdependence and the common underlying proficiency construct is also very much at variance with Genesee *et al.*'s (2006) interpretation that the common underlying proficiency construct does not include either underlying cognitive abilities or structural similarities between languages. The six major types of crosslinguistic transfer identified in Chapter 3 include conceptual knowledge, common linguistic elements, and metacognitive and metalinguistic processes. Furthermore, in contrast to Genesee *et al.*'s interpretation, the construct includes declarative as well as procedural knowledge. I see minimal difference between the common underlying proficiency construct and the *common underlying reservoir of literacy abilities* construct (Riches & Genesee, 2006), which Genesee *et al.* described as follows:

> English-language learners are best conceptualized as having a reservoir of knowledge, skills and abilities that serve second-language learning and use. Some of these will be the same skills and knowledge possessed by monolinguals, and others will be unique to bilinguals and encompass discrete language skills, related to, for example, phonology and grammar, as well as knowledge and experience acquired through the medium of the first language and first-language learning. (Genesee *et al.*, 2006a: 172)

It is perhaps not surprising that the construct of the common underlying proficiency remains unclear to some researchers in view of the fact that the nature of the construct of *language proficiency* (and particularly *oral language proficiency*) remains confused and contested, as discussed in a later section.

In summary, despite the concerns expressed by Genesee *et al.* (2006a) and Geva (2014) regarding the conceptualisation of linguistic interdependence, the research findings they review overwhelmingly support the basic tenets of the interdependence hypothesis, namely, that positive crosslinguistic relationships will be observed when educators (and/or parents/caregivers) support the continued development of both languages over the course of literacy acquisition in school. The fact that various components of cognition (e.g. working memory, executive function, etc.), metalinguistic awareness, as well as academic knowledge may be involved in these relationships does not in any way undermine the validity of the hypothesis. As noted previously, L1/L2 relationships predominantly involve CALP, which is conceived as a fusion of linguistic, cognitive/conceptual, and academic knowledge and processes.

Proctor and Colleagues (2010, 2017)

Based on their research involving 91 Grade 4 Spanish-English bilinguals, all of whom had received literacy instruction in Spanish as well as English, Proctor and colleagues (2010) proposed an *interdependence continuum* in which the strength of crosslinguistic relationships varies according to the similarities of specific linguistic skills between the two languages. In the context of this model, lower-level text skills related to decoding are likely to show strong crosslinguistic relationships, reading comprehension moderate relationships, and oral language skills considerable variability depending on the specific oral language measures used.

Proctor *et al.* (2010) reported that Spanish and English alphabetic knowledge (decoding skills) were moderately related and loaded on the same factor in their analysis. Oral language skills, measured by listening comprehension and picture vocabulary measures, were strongly related to reading comprehension within languages but were unrelated to similar oral language skills across languages. Structural equation modeling showed patterns of crosslinguistic relationships that were consistent with the interdependence continuum. The composite Spanish–English alphabetic knowledge variable predicted both Spanish and English reading comprehension, albeit to a much lesser degree than the within-language relationships between oral language proficiency in Spanish and English and reading comprehension in each language. There was also a small but significant positive relationship between Spanish and English reading comprehension.

In short, the findings of the Proctor *et al.* (2010) study are consistent with the notion of an interdependence continuum. The educational implications highlighted by the authors align with the bilingual instructional strategies identified by numerous other researchers (e.g. Cummins, 2001, 2007a, 2017a; García & Kleifgen, 2019; García & Kleyn, 2016):

The instructional conclusion to be drawn from this research is that English literacy attainment may in fact be aided by native language and literacy development. However, it is not sufficient to simply provide access to L1 language development (e.g., teacher and student use of the L1 in instructional settings). Rather, to reap the potential benefits of interdependence, instruction must focus on language and literacy development in both languages, and indeed focus directly on explicitly teaching for transfer. (Proctor *et al.*, 2010: 18)

A subsequent study carried out by Proctor *et al.* (2017) provided further support for the interdependence hypothesis. The authors investigated the relationships between Spanish oral language skills (vocabulary and syntax, measured at the grade 2 level) and the subsequent development of English reading comprehension and oral language skills (vocabulary, morphology, semantics, syntax) among 156 bilingual Latinx students in second through fifth grade whose first language was Spanish and whose second language was English. All students had been educated in English-medium programmes with no formal support for Spanish language literacy development. The findings indicated that early levels of Spanish syntax knowledge (but not vocabulary) predicted students' fifth-grade English oral language skills and reading comprehension as well as students' growth in these skills between grades 2 and 5. Spanish syntax was also positively related to growth in English semantic knowledge assessed by a measure of students' awareness of conceptual relations between words (e.g. fence, *window*, *glass*, rug).

The research studies carried out by Proctor and colleagues (e.g. 2010, 2017) are well-designed and add significantly to our knowledge of the conditions under which crosslinguistic transfer occurs. However, the reality of crosslinguistic transfer is likely to be considerably more complex than what can be expressed on a simple linear continuum based primarily on linguistic similarities/differences between languages. For example, the continuum hypothesis might have problems explaining the documented interdependence between languages that have relatively few common elements (e.g. the positive relationships observed between proficiency in a natural sign language and reading comprehension in the dominant language). It is also worth noting that the interdependence continuum hypothesis was not supported in a study by Sierens *et al.* (2020) that attempted to test the hypothesis directly. The wide variation in sociolinguistic, sociopolitical, and educational conditions under which bilingual students develop proficiency in their languages will also mediate the extent to which crosslinguistic interdependence is observed. Proctor and colleagues acknowledge some of these issues as follows:

Finally, we acknowledge that Spanish language gains and loss are possible given the sociolinguistic realities of bilingualism in the United States. For some children, growth is possible because of support at home, and loss is possible due to lack of such support. Both factors may serve to predict English outcomes for Spanish-English bilingual Latino children. (Proctor *et al.*, 2017: 388)

Meta-Analytic Studies of Linguistic Interdependence

Two meta-analytic syntheses of research have attempted to throw light on patterns of linguistic interdependence. Norwegian researchers Melby-Lervåg and Lervåg (2011) analysed the results of 47 studies that investigated crosslinguistic transfer of oral language, decoding and phonological awareness. They also intended to examine crosslinguistic dimensions of reading comprehension but were unable to do so because their sample of research studies contained too few analyses of L1/L2 reading comprehension relationships to support a meta-analysis. Dutch researchers Prevoo and colleagues (2016) carried out a more extensive meta-analysis involving 86 studies that investigated relationships between L1 oral language proficiency and various indices of school achievement, including literacy attainment.

Both meta-analyses found evidence of crosslinguistic interdependence. In the case of Melby-Lervåg and Lervåg, L1/L2 phonological awareness and decoding skills showed moderate to strong crosslinguistic relationships, with smaller, but still statistically significant, relationships between L1 and L2 oral language variables. Prevoo *et al.* (2016) reported weak, but significant, positive relations between L1 oral proficiency and L2 early literacy and reading variables, and between L2 oral proficiency and L1 early literacy.

The outcomes of any meta-analysis depend to a considerable extent on the selection criteria that determine which studies will be included in the analysis and the range of moderator variables (e.g. socioeconomic status [SES]) that are available to help interpret the findings. In this regard, the selection criteria adopted by Melby-Lervåg and Lervåg are quite problematic, and only a limited number of moderator variables were included, whereas both the selection criteria and moderator variables included in the Prevoo *et al.* (2016) meta-analysis appear more adequate.

The Melby-Lervåg and Lervåg meta-analysis

Melby-Lervåg and Lervåg (2011) base their meta-analysis of crosslinguistic transfer on the fact that existing research findings regarding crosslinguistic transfer of oral language skills and phonology show large variations in results between studies. They suggest that a meta-analysis 'is needed both to examine the overall strength of the relationships and to examine moderator variables that may explain variation in the relationships between studies' (2011: 115).

Their inability to conduct an analysis of relationships between L1 and L2 reading comprehension reflects the study selection criteria adopted by

Melby-Lervåg and Lervåg rather than an actual paucity of studies reporting correlations between L1 and L2 reading comprehension. Narrative reviews of crosslinguistic relationships between L1 and L2 reading comprehension (e.g. Cummins, 1991; Dressler & Kamil, 2006; Fitzgerald, 1995; Lindholm-Leary & Borsato, 2006) reveal a large number of such studies. The selection criteria that reduced the 795 full-text articles addressing crosslinguistic relationships to the 47 studies examined in the 2011 meta-analysis included the provisions 'Did not report sufficient data for effect size calculation' and 'Less than 4 hours a day L2 instruction' (2011: 118). The fact that certain studies did not report sufficient data for effect size calculation obviously excludes them from the meta-analysis. However, this does not mean that these are inadequate studies or any less relevant to the issues under investigation than studies that did include these data. Thus, this criterion potentially entails a significant loss of relevant data.

Melby-Lervåg and Lervåg (2011) provide no rationale as to why studies with less than 4 hours a day of L2 instruction were excluded. This criterion eliminates studies with more than one hour a day of L1 instruction and consequently excludes most studies involving bilingual programmes for both majority- and minority-group students. As noted previously, opportunity to continue to develop L1 and L2 language and literacy skills throughout elementary school is highly predictive of L1/L2 crosslinguistic relationships.[5]

Although Melby-Lervåg and Lervåg (2011) include moderator variables such as SES, age, and instructional language in their meta-analysis, the complexity and variability of the social and educational contexts within which bilingual students develop are not adequately captured by binary categories such as L2 instruction versus both L2 and L1 instruction. The instructional environments potentially captured by 'both L2 and L1 instruction' range from quick-exit transitional programmes to fully bilingual/biliterate programmes involving at least 50% L1 instruction K-6.

Melby-Lervåg and Lervåg reported a relatively small but statistically significant meta-correlation between L1 and L2 oral language (assessed by listening comprehension and vocabulary measures) ($r = 0.16$, p < .01) and a moderate to large correlation between L1 and L2 phonological awareness and decoding. They interpreted these differences in terms of the greater complexity of oral language compared with phonological awareness and decoding. A general cognitive procedure can be applied to the limited number of L1 and L2 letter-sound combinations whereas no such general procedure is applicable to vocabulary acquisition. Melby-Lervåg and Lervåg (2011) also reported large variation across studies in L1/L2 correlations for all domains of language. In the case of decoding skills, this variation was moderated by writing system and instructional language. Specifically, stronger relationships were observed in samples where both L1 and L2 were alphabetic than in samples where L2 was alphabetic and L1 was ideographic, and in samples where students were instructed in both L1 and L2 compared with L2 only.

It was possible to examine the relationships between L2 reading comprehension on the one hand, and L1 decoding and L1 oral language on the other, in only a small number (6-8) of studies. A small to moderate significant relationship with L2 reading comprehension was found for L1 decoding and a minimal and non-significant relationship was found for L1 oral language.

Melby-Lervåg and Lervåg's (2011) results are informative but limited. A majority of the studies they analysed tested bilingual students who were in subtractive educational contexts where instruction was through L2, and L1 skills were not being promoted in school. It is likely that even in contexts where bilingual instruction was being implemented, the programme was transitional in orientation with no real commitment to promote sustained literacy development in L1. This likelihood is reinforced by the exclusion of any studies involving more than one hour daily of L1 instruction. Thus, the relatively weak crosslinguistic relationship for oral language is likely to reflect the fact that most of the students sampled had only limited opportunities to develop L1 literacy skills while they were acquiring L2 language and literacy skills.

A second issue concerns the nature of the oral language measures used in many of the studies. For younger students in lower grades of elementary school, assessment of vocabulary has typically involved administration of picture vocabulary tests which, as noted previously, are inadequate to assess school-related low-frequency vocabulary because many of these words are abstract and difficult to represent visually (e.g. words such as *integrity, intrinsic, persist*, from Coxhead's, 2000, Academic Word List) (Phillips Galloway *et al.*, 2020). Furthermore, for emergent bilinguals, vocabulary is often contextually specific. L1 vocabulary is primarily associated with home and L2 vocabulary associated with school, thereby diminishing the likelihood of crosslinguistic relationships.

The roles of contextual variables and opportunity to acquire L1 and L2, in mediating L1/L2 oral language relationships are illustrated in more detail in Appendix 9.1 where I review several of the studies in the Melby-Lervåg and Lervåg (2011) meta-analysis that showed negative or minimal crosslinguistic relationships.

The Prevoo and colleagues' (2016) meta-analysis

Prevoo and colleagues carried out a comprehensive meta-analysis of 86 studies involving 23,049 students in order to identify the relationships between L1 and L2 oral language variables and various indices of school attainment including dimensions of early literacy, reading comprehension, spelling, mathematics, and overall academic achievement. They were able to assess the effects of multiple moderators in their analyses including variables such as age/grade level, specific oral language measure, specific reading measure, and participation in L1 classes or bilingual education programmes. The major findings in relation to crosslinguistic relationships are outlined below:

- Significant positive crosslinguistic relationships were found between L1 oral language measures and both early literacy and reading comprehension L2 measures, but not with indices of spelling, mathematics, or general academic achievement.
- These crosslinguistic relationships were less than the within-language relationships, which were positive and significant for all school outcomes.
- Crosslinguistic relationships were bidirectional: L1 oral proficiency → L2 early literacy and L2 reading comprehension; L2 oral proficiency → L1 early literacy.

The following moderator effects were found:

- Within- and cross-language associations of L1 oral proficiency with early literacy in L1 and L2 were stronger when vocabulary was the language proficiency measure compared to studies that used a general or composite oral language proficiency measure.
- Within-language relations between oral language proficiency and reading were moderated by the grade level or age of the children, with stronger relationships observed for older as compared to younger children.
- The relationship between oral L2 proficiency and L2 reading was stronger for reading comprehension than for (pseudo)word reading (decoding).
- The crosslinguistic relationship between L1 oral proficiency and L2 reading was stronger for samples in which the majority of students participated in L1 language classes either outside of the regular school programme ($r = 0.22$, p < .01) or in a bilingual programme (full bilingual or transitional) ($r = 0.21$, p < .01) compared to samples in which the majority of students were in L2-only programmes ($r = 0.07$).

Prevoo *et al.* (2016) note that they found no negative crosslinguistic relationships, indicating that the subtractive bilingualism hypothesis that L2 develops at the expense of L1 was not supported. They proposed a task-dependent bidirectional transfer hypothesis, stating that in addition to within-language effects of oral language proficiency on school outcomes, cross-language transfer from L1 to L2, and from L2 to L1, can occur. The extent of this transfer depends on the type of oral language proficiency task and the type of school outcome that is being measured. The authors conclude that their findings support the interdependence hypothesis:

The positive cross-language associations between L1 oral proficiency and L2 early literacy and reading found in our meta-analyses are in line with the *interdependence hypothesis* (Cummins, 1979), which states that competence in L2 is partly based on competence in L1. This would converge with findings from neuroimaging studies that the same brain regions are active in L1 and L2 processing (Abutalebi, 2008; Buchweitz & Prat, 2013). (Prevoo *et al.*, 2016: 262) (emphasis original)[6]

Concluding Thoughts

More than 40 years of research, including several comprehensive meta-analyses of this research, has supported the interdependence hypothesis and the related construct of a common underlying proficiency. Specific contextual, developmental, exposure and measurement conditions are prerequisites for the observation of positive crosslinguistic L1/L2 relationships (see Appendix 9.1). Analysis of apparent counterevidence in studies that reported negative L1/L2 relationships for some dimensions of proficiency showed that bilingual students in these studies typically did not experience sufficient opportunity to develop their L1 language and literacy skills as they were acquiring L2. Thus, the hypothesis satisfies the criterion of empirical adequacy.

With respect to logical coherence, the interdependence hypothesis has been challenged (e.g. García & Li Wei, 2014) only on the grounds that 'languages' have no cognitive reality and don't exist as linguistic or conceptual entities; consequently, it is illegitimate to talk about crosslinguistic transfer. As discussed previously in this chapter and in Chapter 7, this argument is unconvincing and problematic on multiple grounds (e.g. Grin, 2018).

With respect to consequential validity, the major instructional implication of this hypothesis is that minoritised students' educational outcomes will benefit when schools support L1 language and literacy development in addition to L2. Virtually all applied linguists concur with this instructional goal, despite the fact that the educational experience of the majority of emergent bilinguals remains subtractive in most educational contexts.[7]

Despite the widespread acceptance of the interdependence hypothesis and its educational implications, there are still major challenges in postcolonial low-resource, and minoritised educational contexts in implementing bilingual programmes that reflect the empirical evidence (e.g. Bahry & Zholdoshalieva, 2012; Benson, 2019; Heugh, 2011a, 2011b; Skutnabb-Kangas & Heugh, 2012; Taylor, 2014). Similarly, in North American and European contexts, the educational experience of emergent bilingual students seldom includes promotion of L1 literacy in addition to L2 literacy. Positive changes have occurred in the United States in recent years as a result of 'two-way' or dual language bilingual programmes that promote biliteracy for Spanish-dominant and English-dominant students within the same instructional model (e.g. Escamilla *et al.*, 2014). However, bilingual programmes are feasible only in contexts where there is a concentration of students from a particular language background. As a response to the diversity of languages and cultures in typical classrooms in contexts such as Europe, North America and Australia, educators have begun to explore the instructional potential of *translanguaging* or *crosslinguistic pedagogy*, which involves positioning students' multilingualism as a cognitive, linguistic, and educational resource within the classroom. The theoretical underpinnings of this strategy are discussed in the next chapter.

Notes

(1) Following Prevoo *et al.* (2015), Phillips Galloway and colleagues (2020) interpret the linguistic interdependence hypothesis as positing only a one-way rather than a two-way relationship between Lx and Ly. That erroneous impression may have been derived from initial articles on the hypothesis (e.g. Cummins, 1979a), which were focused on the role of minority students' L1 in supporting L2 development, but the crosslinguistic relationships were always seen as two-way and reciprocal. The formal statement of the interdependence hypothesis (Cummins, 1981b: 29) envisages the possibility of two-way influence from Lx to Ly and from Ly to Lx. Cummins (2001a: 175) explicitly affirmed the reciprocal relationships as follows:

> In general, transfer is more likely to occur from the minority to the majority language because of the typically greater exposure to literacy in the majority language outside of school and the strong social pressure to learn it. However, when the sociolinguistic conditions are right, two-way transfer across languages *does* occur. This has been demonstrated in both minority contexts (Verhoeven, 1991a, 1991b) and majority contexts (Cashion & Eagan, 1990) (emphasis original)

(2) Another notable study of Spanish and English literacy development among students in a dual language programme was reported by Sparrow *et al.* (2014). The programme followed the 'Literacy Squared' pedagogical model developed by Escamilla *et al.* (2014) that focuses on simultaneous development of literacy in Spanish and English and explicit teaching for transfer across languages. The dataset for the study consisted of Spanish and English reading and writing performance scores involving 872 K–3 participants in 2009-2010, 1,199 K–4 participants in 2010-2011, and 1,411 K–5 participants in 2011-2012. All crosslinguistic correlations were highly significant ranging from 0.54 to 0.75 for Spanish/English reading and from 0.53 to 0.75 for Spanish/English writing. These crosslinguistic correlations were consistently higher than the within-language correlations between reading and writing scores (Spanish reading/writing correlations ranged from 0.40 to 0.68 and English reading/writing correlations ranged from 0.37 to 0.62). Similar to the Phillips Galloway *et al.* (2020) study, Sparrow and colleagues' findings constitute strong support for the interdependence hypothesis and highlight the potential benefits for literacy development of systematically teaching for transfer across languages.

(3) Insightful perspectives on the current status of bilingual education in Nunavut and Nunavik can be found in Skutnabb-Kangas *et al.* (2019) and Walton and O'Leary (2015).

(4) The problematic nature of Saunders and O'Brien's (2006: 14) conceptualisation of 'oral language proficiency' can be gauged from the fact that they include contrasting

language behaviours such as 'exchanging greetings' and 'delivering or composing lectures' within the same theoretical construct. This issue is discussed in more detail in Appendix 9.1.

(5) It should be noted that transfer effects among emergent bilingual children are often not observed in the initial years of elementary school because of widely divergent exposure to both languages in any typical sample. Consider, for example, a sample of students in kindergarten and grade 1 who have had varying amounts of exposure to the school language (L2) in their homes and environment. One would expect a minimal or even negative relationship between measures of L1 and L2 language proficiency at this stage because students who have had the most exposure to L1 at home are likely to have had the least exposure to L2 before they start school. They are thus likely to perform better on measures of L1 proficiency and less well on measures of L2 language proficiency than their peers who have had more exposure to L2 in their homes. By the same token, those who have had more exposure to L2 are likely to have had less exposure to L1 and will consequently perform less well on measures of L1 proficiency. Thus, a minimal or possibly negative relationship between the two languages would be expected under these conditions.

However, crosslinguistic interdependence of literacy-related skills typically emerges strongly at older ages in school contexts where literacy in both languages is promoted (e.g. Hakuta, 1985, 1987; Oller & Eilers, 2002). As noted previously, picture vocabulary tests of receptive vocabulary (as used in most studies involving younger elementary school students) are not particularly good measures of the specific vocabulary knowledge that has high utility within the context of the school (Philipps Galloway *et al.*, 2020).

(6) One additional meta-analysis (Jeon & Yamashita, 2014) reported findings relevant to the interdependence hypothesis. The meta-analysis of L1/L2 reading comprehension involved 22 independent correlations from 17 studies involving 2,257 participants ranging from kindergarten to college levels. Consistent with the interdependence hypothesis, a highly significant correlation of 0.50 was found between L1 and L2 reading comprehension. Not surprisingly, this was less than the correlation between L2 reading comprehension and both L2 grammar ($r = 0.85$) and L2 vocabulary knowledge ($r = 0.79$), but the findings nevertheless suggest an important role for L1 literacy-related knowledge in the acquisition of literacy skills in L2.

Another relevant study involving 10,331 16-year-old Norwegian students using data from two national reading tests was reported by Brevik *et al.* (2016). The authors reported that L1 reading was the strongest predictor of students' English (L2) reading proficiency. Norwegian reading comprehension and academic language knowledge (vocabulary and grammar) together accounted for 41% of the variance in English reading proficiency.

(7) McQuillan and Tse (1996) reported that 85% of academic articles published in the United States from 1984-1994 were in favour of bilingual education compared to only 45% of media articles. More recently, Lewis and Davies (2018) reported that 95% of academic articles published between 2006 and 2016 were in favour of bilingual education compared to 45% of media articles. I am grateful to Dr Steve Krashen for bringing these articles to my attention.

Appendix 9.1 The Centrality of 'Opportunity to Learn' in Assessing L1/L2 Interdependence

Across the range of studies focused on 'oral language proficiency' considered in the meta-analyses conducted by Melby-Lervåg and Lervåg (2011) and Prevoo *et al.* (2016), considerable variation was found in the strength of relationships between L1 and L2 oral language variables and between L1 oral language and L2 reading comprehension and decoding skills. At first sight, some of these relationships would appear to constitute negative evidence in relation to the interdependence hypothesis. For example, in the Proctor *et al.* (2006) study, grade 4 students' Spanish (L1) and English (L2) picture vocabulary scores were negatively correlated (−0.32, p < .001) as were Spanish and English listening comprehension (−0.25, p < .01). To what extent does this pattern of correlations constitute counterevidence to the interdependence hypothesis?

I argue here that these findings are not inconsistent with the hypothesis of linguistic interdependence. As outlined in Chapter 3, the interdependence hypothesis specified that positive Lx/Ly bidirectional relationships in literacy-related aspects of academic language proficiency would be observed under conditions where students had adequate exposure to both languages and adequate motivation to learn these languages. I am using the term 'opportunity to learn' to include both of these conditions. In the following sections, I examine some of the research studies that reported negative or minimal crosslinguistic relationships.

To What Extent is There Counterevidence to the Interdependence Hypothesis?

Proctor and colleagues (2006) and related studies

The Proctor *et al.* study reported the strongest *negative* correlations between L1 and L2 oral language proficiency among the 37 sets of correlations entered in the Melby-Lervåg and Lervåg (2011) meta-analysis. The negative correlations noted above involved fourth grade students, most of whom had been in school since kindergarten or pre-kindergarten. After five or six years of schooling and three to four years of literacy instruction, one might expect that bilingual students would have had sufficient time and opportunity to learn both languages and transfer knowledge and skills across languages as predicted by the interdependence hypothesis. However, when the context is examined in more detail, the apparent inconsistency with the interdependence hypothesis can easily be resolved.

The sample in the Proctor *et al.* (2006) study consisted of 135 Spanish–English bilingual fourth graders from three large, urban elementary schools in Boston, Chicago and El Paso, Texas. The authors point out that the schools were largely segregated institutions with significant populations of Latinx students from low socioeconomic status backgrounds. Thus, students would likely have had minimal exposure to English outside of the school. All schools used the highly structured Success for All curriculum (Slavin *et al.*, 1996), available in both English and Spanish. However, this curriculum does not allow for simultaneous L1 and L2 literacy instruction, with the result that students learning to read in Spanish received no literacy instruction in English until they exited from the Spanish programme. Similarly, students receiving literacy instruction in English received no literacy instruction in Spanish. The authors point out that most students who received Spanish language instruction spent between two and three years learning to read in Spanish. In other words, for many students in the programme, English literacy instruction would likely have started only in Grade 3 and they would have received only about one year of English literacy instruction prior to the administration of the tests (average age of the sample was 10 years and 1 month, which suggests that tests were administered early in the Grade 4 year). For some students, English literacy instruction may have started even later than Grade 3. Duursma *et al.* (2007), who used a sample from the same schools, reported that there was variation in the timing of transition to English-medium instruction among students who received initial literacy instruction in Spanish, with some children transitioning at the end of second grade and others at the end of third or fourth grade.

The effects of opportunity to learn in the Proctor *et al.* (2006) study can be seen in the L1/L2 correlations where differences in the language of initial literacy instruction was controlled. This variable explained 19% of the variance in English reading comprehension. With language of initial literacy instruction controlled, the negative correlations between Spanish (L1) and English (L2) picture vocabulary and listening comprehension were reduced to −0.05 and −0.04 respectively. With more time and ongoing opportunities to expand literacy skills in L1 and L2, the interdependence hypothesis would predict that these essentially zero correlations would become positive, reflecting cross-linguistic transfer. This prediction is supported by the positive correlation (0.25, p < .05) between Spanish and English reading comprehension when language of instruction was controlled. Additionally, in the model that provided the best fit to the data, Spanish picture vocabulary made a small but statistically significant contribution to English reading comprehension.

Similar considerations related to opportunity to learn L1 and L2 apply to the Duursma *et al.* (2007) study that involved the same pool of participants. The non-significant negative correlation of -0.19 between Spanish and English Picture Vocabulary measures at the fifth grade is easily attributable to the fact that students have had minimal opportunity to transfer vocabulary knowledge across languages because of the structure of both the bilingual and monolingual programmes.

Lack of opportunity to learn can also explain the negative L1/L2 picture vocabulary correlation (−0.20, N = 68 third grade students) reported by Swanson *et al.* (2008). Students attended all-English instructional programmes in which no support was provided for Spanish (L1) literacy development.

A fourth study that reported negative L1/L2 relationships (Ordonez *et al.*, 2002) involved a sample of fourth and fifth grade students from two different school districts (Boston and Santa Barbara) who had received either bilingual instruction or English-only instruction. The authors described the context of their study as 'subtractive' where students were losing their knowledge of Spanish as they acquired English. The study reported a significant a negative correlation (−0.23, p < .05) between English and Spanish picture vocabulary measures but also a much stronger positive correlation (0.43, p < 0.01) between English and Spanish with respect to students' ability to provide word definitions that reflected their knowledge of semantic hierarchies (e.g. car is a type of vehicle). Although this word definition task clearly reflects 'oral language', it was not included in Melby-Lervåg and Lervåg's (2011) meta-analysis, presumably because it was not a standardised test.

Cobo-Lewis and colleagues (2002a, 2002b) and related studies

Several US studies show convergence of English (L2) and Spanish (L1) oral language knowledge over time, which reflects the *developmental* aspects of L1/L2 interdependence. For example, Cobo-Lewis *et al.* (2002a) reported large differences on multiple English language proficiency measures at kindergarten between Miami-area students who spoke both English and Spanish at home as compared to those who spoke only Spanish at home, but these differences were significantly reduced by Grade 2 and largely eliminated by Grade 5. Similarly, differences in English oral language performance between students in largely English-medium (90% English, 10% Spanish) and those in the dual language programme (60% English, 40% Spanish) were large at kindergarten, but beyond kindergarten the two programmes 'appeared to produce largely comparable results' (2002a: 96).

Convergence of English and Spanish oral language knowledge over time is also evident in a longitudinal study conducted among 392 Puerto Rican background students in the New Haven Spanish-English bilingual programme (Hakuta, 1987). For the initial cohort of students, a non-significant correlation (0.11) between English and Spanish Picture Vocabulary tests was found at the kindergarten level but by Grade 2, the correlation had risen to 0.56 (p < .001). Similar progressions were reported for the subsequent cohort. Hakuta (1987: 1383) concluded: 'Thus, in the early grades, the two languages are uncorrelated, but the relative abilities in the two languages become similar over time'.

The pattern of L1/L2 relationships reported by Cobo-Lewis *et al.* (2002b) appears at first sight to cast doubt on the extent of interdependence for oral language measures. Analysis of crosslinguistic relationships involving Grades 2 and 5 students in bilingual and largely monolingual programmes showed that literacy measures in English and Spanish were strongly related and loaded on the same factor but oral language measures (two picture vocabulary tests, one oral vocabulary test, and one verbal analogies test) loaded on separate English and Spanish factors. The authors concluded that the interdependence hypothesis was strongly supported for L1 and L2 reading and writing skills but not for oral language skills.

As pointed out by Cummins (2004b), this conclusion is problematic in light of the correlations among the Grades 2 and 5 English and Spanish oral language variables, which were less than for the literacy variables but nevertheless highly significant. The English/Spanish correlations ($N = 704$) for the residualised standard scores (which controlled for group membership) on the literacy measures ranged from 0.44 (Passage Comprehension) to 0.68 (Letter-Word Knowledge). The correlations for the oral language measures ranged from 0.10 ($p = .01$) (Woodcock Picture Vocabulary test) to 0.45 ($p < .0001$) (Woodcock Verbal Analogies test). The correlations for English and Spanish Oral Vocabulary (synonyms/antonyms) and Peabody Picture Vocabulary Test were 0.31 ($p < .0001$) and .33 ($p < .0001$) respectively. Thus, the authors' conclusion that 'oral language skills were largely unrelated at the level of individual subjects' (Cobo-Lewis *et al.*, 2002b: 132) is not consistent with the data. Clearly, the relationships among the L1/L2 literacy measures are greater than those for the oral language measures, but the data also provide evidence for interdependence among the oral L1/L2 measures. It is also worth noting that the crosslinguistic correlation for the oral Verbal Analogies test was just as strong as for the written Passage Comprehension test, suggesting again that no clear distinction can be drawn between oral and written measures. The data are consistent with an interpretation that both oral Verbal Analogies and written Passage Comprehension reflect the fusion of language and cognitive abilities signified by the construct of CALP.

Sierens and colleagues (2019, 2020)

Sierens and colleagues reported two research studies that examined linguistic interdependence among Turkish-background preschool and Grade 1 school children in the Dutch-speaking region of Belgium (Flanders). Sierens *et al.* (2019) found significant L1/L2 relationships in their sample of 154 children of Turkish background (aged 4 to 6), attending Flemish preschool: 'Regression analyses revealed that Turkish L1 vocabulary size significantly predicted Dutch L2 vocabulary size, which is in line with interdependence theories' (2019: 1269). They elaborated this interpretation as follows:

> The results indicate that in emergent bilingual children who were learning academic L2 in an immersion-like context, there was a modest positive yet significant relationship between receptive vocabulary knowledge in L1 and L2. This finding appears to support the linguistic interdependence hypothesis regarding oral vocabulary. (Sierens *et al.*, 2019: 1290–1291)

Despite the clear support in their findings for linguistic interdependence, the authors suggest that individual differences in underlying cognitive processes rather than linguistic interdependence may account for the L1/L2 relationships they observed. They provide minimal logical or empirical support for this interpretation and it appears to rest of the assumption that it is possible to separate the impact of cognitive and linguistic factors in the development of vocabulary knowledge. By contrast, in this book I have articulated the position that there is a fusion of cognitive, linguistic, and academic knowledge in the performance of conceptual/linguistic tasks.

It is also important to bear in mind that despite the support for linguistic interdependence in the Sierens *et al.* (2019) study, any L1/L2 receptive vocabulary relationships observed at the preschool stage are likely to be unstable as a result of the nature of picture vocabulary measures (Phillips Galloway *et al.*, 2020) and the differences in relative amounts of L1/L2 exposure in the homes of minoritised students.

The linguistic interdependence hypothesis was also supported in a second longitudinal study involving 75 Turkish–Dutch bilingual children attending Dutch-medium schools. Sierens *et al.*, 2020) assessed children's listening comprehension in Dutch and Turkish using a sentence comprehension test when they were in preschool and a test of their ability to understand more extended discourse in Grade 1. Correlational, multiple regression, and path analyses revealed significant positive crosslinguistic relationships between Dutch and Turkish sentence comprehension proficiency within Time 1 and Time 2. For the preschool sentence comprehension measure the crosslinguistic correlation was 0.46 (p < .001) and for the Grade 1 discourse comprehension measure the crosslinguistic correlation was 0.59 (p < .001).

Interpretation of the cross-time relationships is more complicated. Sierens *et al.* (2020) report positive crosslinguistic correlations between Time 1 sentence comprehension scores and Time 2 discourse comprehension scores. Turkish preschool sentence comprehension correlated 0.50 (p < .001) with Dutch Grade 1 discourse comprehension, and Dutch preschool sentence comprehension correlated 0.35 (p = .002) with Turkish Grade 1 discourse comprehension. These relationships are clearly consistent with the interdependence hypothesis. The regression analyses conducted by Sierens *et al.* are difficult to interpret due to the entry of a large number of 'control' variables including vocabulary, phonological awareness, and print concepts in Step 1 of the analyses, resulting in a nonsignificant unique effect of Turkish preschool sentence comprehension on Dutch grade 1 discourse comprehension. The path analysis results for Time 1 Turkish (sentence comprehension) on Time 2 Dutch (discourse comprehension) showed a small and nonsignificant direct effect (0.14) and a medium indirect effect (0.37), resulting in an aggregated significant medium-sized standardised path coefficient (0.51).

Sierens *et al.* (2020) interpret these findings as indicating a lack of L1/L2 relationships over time but it is not at all clear that this interpretation is supported by their data. The over-time correlations are significant with a stronger Turkish to Dutch (0.50) than Dutch to Turkish (0.35) relationship. The aggregated direct and indirect effects in the path analysis also show a significant relationship. Based on the L1/L2 concurrent relationships observed, Sierens *et al.* suggest that the findings support the interdependence hypothesis for both sentence comprehension and discourse comprehension variables.

Goodrich and colleagues (2013, 2016)

In two studies involving Spanish-speaking preschoolers in the United States, Goodrich and colleagues investigated L1/L2 transfer effects for language and emergent literacy skills. Goodrich *et al.* (2013) carried out an experimental study in which 94 children were randomly assigned to one of three instructional conditions. The control condition was the regular English-medium preschool programme in the Head Start center the children attended. The two experimental conditions involved 21 weeks of small-group pull-out instruction focused on oral language, phonological awareness and print knowledge either in an English-only context or a transitional Spanish/English context where instruction was provided in Spanish for the first 9 weeks and thereafter in English for the remaining 12 weeks. The intervention sessions took place 4 times per week and each session lasted about 20 minutes. The researchers examined whether children's initial pretest skills in one language moderated the impact of the intervention on those same skills in the other language at post-test.

The authors reported significant crosslinguistic relationships ($p < .01$) for the Print Knowledge measure and two phonological awareness measures (Elision and Blending) across all 12 concurrent and pretest/post-test correlations. By contrast, only two out of eight correlations involving Receptive and Definitional vocabulary were significant ($p < .05$), a finding that is consistent with other investigations of vocabulary knowledge at this early stage of schooling. The authors interpret the crosslinguistic phonological awareness relationships as reflecting 'language-independent' influences because 'sounds are the same across languages' (2013: 422). By contrast, the minimal relationships for the vocabulary measures reflected the language-specific nature of vocabulary knowledge.

However, the experimental design enabled the authors to examine the extent of actual *transfer* of knowledge and skills across languages rather than simply the co-occurrence of skills across languages provided by correlations: 'By experimentally manipulating instruction in this study, we were able to examine the degree to which ability level in L1 influenced learning in L2' (2013: 422). Goodrich *et al.* summarised their findings as follows:

> Results for vocabulary outcomes indicated that Spanish-speaking LM [language minority] children transferred specific linguistic information

about vocabulary across languages. Children with higher initial vocabulary knowledge in one language benefited more from the intervention on vocabulary outcomes in the other language than did children with lower initial vocabulary knowledge. These children were exposed to adequate amounts of instruction in English and Spanish to allow their prior Spanish and English vocabulary knowledge to facilitate the acquisition of new vocabulary knowledge in the language of instruction. (Goodrich *et al.*, 2013: 422–423)

Similar findings were found for elision skills leading the authors to interpret their results in terms of the 'Matthew Effect' (the rich get richer). They claim that their study is unique in reporting that this effect occurs across languages rather than just within languages.

Goodrich *et al.* (2016) reported similar findings in a subsequent study involving two independent samples of Latinx preschool children in Los Angeles (N = 96) and Miami (N = 116). Children were administered measures of receptive, expressive, and definitional vocabulary in Spanish and English at two time points approximately 9–12 months apart. The authors predicted that children who initially knew a word in Lx but not Ly would be significantly more likely to acquire that word in Ly at a later time. This prediction was supported in both samples for receptive and expressive vocabulary knowledge, but not for definitional vocabulary. The authors interpret their findings as follows:

This finding provided support for the narrow notion of transfer, in which specific information can be transferred from L1 to L2 and vice versa. For example, children who knew the word *perro* in Spanish were more likely to acquire the word *dog* in English than were children who did not know *perro* in Spanish. (Goodrich *et al.*, 2016: 987)

The authors suggest that the lack of similar findings for definitional vocabulary may be due to the fact that this component of vocabulary knowledge may develop later than receptive or expressive vocabulary, with the result that preschool children do not have adequate definitional representations of words in L1 to utilise when learning L2.

Goodrich *et al.* (2016: 989) also concluded that 'knowing a word in both languages acted as a protective factor for the memory of the word, reducing the likelihood that it would be forgotten'. They suggest that 'if knowing a word in both languages increases the likelihood that knowledge of the word is retained over time, bilingual vocabulary instruction (rather than English-only instruction) would increase language minority children's memory for words' (2016: 989).

The Goodrich *et al.* (2013, 2016) studies are well-designed and provide useful information regarding patterns of L1/L2 relationships and transfer. For example, their research demonstrates empirically that knowing a word in one language can act as a sort of magnet for acquisition of the meaning of that word in a second language, given appropriate conditions of exposure. However, cautious interpretation of some aspects of their findings is warranted in light of the volatility observed across multiple studies with respect to crosslinguistic vocabulary knowledge among children in preschool and in the early grades of primary school. In these early years, variables such as language spoken at home, instructional language(s), and the nature of the specific vocabulary measures can dramatically affect the pattern and strength of crosslinguistic relationships. As noted previously, as students progress through the middle grades of elementary school and beyond, crosslinguistic vocabulary relationships tend to become stable and highly significant.

An additional consideration is that the distinction these authors make between general language-independent and language-dependent or specific transfer is not always easy to determine, as they themselves recognise for aspects of phonological awareness and print concepts (Goodrich *et al.*, 2013). For example, vocabulary knowledge is regarded as a language-specific trait but as discussed previously, vocabulary knowledge becomes increasingly fused with knowledge of concepts and with subject-specific knowledge as students move beyond the early grades of elementary school. Thus, vocabulary knowledge cannot be easily separated in practice from conceptual knowledge and underlying cognitive processes, which Goodrich *et al.* regard as language-independent.

What conclusions can we draw from this more detailed analysis of studies in which some findings or interpretations of findings appear at first sight to be inconsistent with the interdependence hypothesis? Four conclusions appear warranted: (1) context matters, (2) grade level and L1/L2 developmental trajectories matter, (3) for immigrant students, length of residence (LOR) matters and (4) the extent to which 'oral proficiency' measures assess *academic* language proficiency matters. These issues are elaborated in the following sections.

Degree of Interdependence Reflects Context, Time, Exposure and Measurement

Instructional and sociolinguistic context

The degree of L1/L2 interdependence depends on the extent to which the sociolinguistic and instructional context are conducive to the development of additive as opposed to subtractive bilingualism. As noted previously, interdependence of academic language proficiency is much more likely to be fostered in contexts where minoritised students have opportunities to develop literacy in both languages than in contexts where their home language is ignored or actively excluded from the school. While L1 knowledge at the kindergarten level may predict later L2 literacy attainment (e.g. Relyea & Amendum, 2020; Thompson, 2015), it may not be significantly related to L2 knowledge at the kindergarten level because of the varied opportunities to acquire each language that are typical of any emergent bilingual sample.

The sociolinguistic and instructional context are also relevant to the question of whether schools should always attempt to teach for transfer and promote L1/L2 interdependence. Australian researcher Stephen Harris (1990) made a persuasive argument for caution in teaching for transfer in his seminal book *Two Way Aboriginal Schooling: Education and Cultural Survival*. Harris suggested that the gap in world views between Aboriginal and western cultures is so great that bilingual education programmes should clearly separate western and Aboriginal cultural domains, with English used exclusively for the former and Aboriginal languages for the latter. He suggested that using the Aboriginal language as a means of teaching the concepts of western schooling risks undermining the Aboriginal culture and contributing to language and cultural shift. Harris is not questioning the importance or legitimacy of bilingual education for Indigenous communities but rather the most effective ways of allocating instructional resources to ensure cultural and linguistic survival as well as strong academic development in conventional school subjects.

These considerations are relevant to Indigenous communities around the world who should be encouraged and enabled to make instructional decisions informed by the local sociolinguistic and sociopolitical context. Unfortunately, as Australian educator Beth Graham points out in her moving and poignant memoir, Indigenous communities in Australia (and elsewhere) are still excluded from meaningful participation in schools and the broader society and this coercive process of exclusion diminishes members of the dominant group as much as it does the minoritised group: 'If we would only listen to their stories, songs and wisdom, we may find a new way of belonging to this ancient land' (Graham, 2020: 267).

L1/L2 developmental trajectories

For early literacy-related skills (e.g. phonological awareness, alphabetic knowledge, etc.), the strong L1/L2 positive relationships observed in the meta-analyses can be attributed to the fact that a general cognitive procedure (e.g. learning that words can be divided into smaller units, which can then be used to decode text) can be applied in a similar fashion in both languages. By contrast, no specific procedural knowledge can be applied to the acquisition of vocabulary, which is dependent on the quality and quantity of exposure to each language. In particular, print access and literacy engagement are crucial for the expansion of school-related vocabulary/concept knowledge. Because development of vocabulary is a process that is ongoing throughout schooling and beyond, time and opportunity to develop both L1 and L2 vocabulary are prerequisites for crosslinguistic transfer. Students' knowledge of school-related vocabulary increases as they progress through the grades and this growth in school-related vocabulary will be reflected in greater interdependence in contexts where the school is promoting both L1 and L2 literacy (e.g. Phillips Galloway *et al.*, 2020).

Length of residence (LOR)

As noted in Chapter 4, LOR is typically strongly related to the development of L2 language and literacy skills among immigrant students, but often negatively related to the maintenance/development of L1 language and literacy skills. The rationale for controlling LOR was expressed by Cummins *et al.* (1984: 71) in a study of Japanese-speaking and Vietnamese-speaking students in the Canadian context: 'It is necessary to partial out LOR because it is positively related to the development of English Academic Proficiency, but negatively related to Japanese Academic Proficiency, thereby masking the relationships between Japanese and English Academic Proficiency'. Thus, research studies that do not partial out LOR risk underestimating the relationships between L1 and L2 proficiency (e.g. Nieminen & Ullakonoja, 2017).

Measuring 'oral language proficiency'

The incoherence of the construct of 'oral language proficiency' can be gauged by considering the definition of the term in the August and Shanahan (2008b: 1) report of the National Literacy Panel: 'For purposes of this review, *oral language proficiency* denotes knowledge or use of specific aspects of oral language, including phonology, vocabulary, morphology, grammar, and discourse domains. It encompasses skills in both comprehension and expression' (emphasis original). Inconsistencies quickly emerge in the way the construct is discussed. For example, despite the fact that the definition of oral language proficiency includes knowledge and use of phonology, later chapters frequently treat oral language proficiency and phonology as separate constructs. This is illustrated in the claim that 'phonological processing skills are better than oral language proficiency as predictors of word reading skills' (August & Shanahan, 2008a: 50). More fundamentally, vocabulary knowledge and phonological processing clearly follow different developmental trajectories after the initial grades, which raises the question of why they should be considered components of a construct called *oral language proficiency.*

Furthermore, it is unclear to what extent oral vocabulary knowledge can be separated either logically or empirically from written vocabulary knowledge. For example, is there any fundamental difference in comprehension requirements between listening to a lecture on 'Threats to Democracy' and reading a printed copy of the same lecture?

The problematic nature of the 'oral language proficiency' construct can be further illustrated in the definition provided by Saunders and O'Brien:

Developing proficiency in oral English involves acquiring vocabulary, gaining control over grammar, and developing an understanding of the subtle semantics of English ... [as well as] learning how to use the language to interact successfully with other speakers of the language. Oral interactions can vary considerably from exchanging greetings to initiating and sustaining conversations to negotiating collaborative tasks to giving and/or receiving directions to telling or listening to stories to delivering or comprehending lectures. (Saunders & O'Brien, 2006: 14)

Obviously, these dimensions of language proficiency or communicative competence are all legitimate functions. On the basis of this description, one might be tempted to define 'oral language proficiency' as the ability to use language effectively in contexts that do not directly involve reading or writing. However, to what extent can one credibly view 'delivering lectures' as part of the same construct as 'exchanging greetings'? Is 'delivering a lecture' ('oral proficiency') very much different than 'composing a lecture' ('written proficiency')? Most of us would intuitively regard 'composing a lecture' (in our head or on paper) as reflecting advanced literacy skills. We would also regard 'delivering a lecture' as reflecting advanced literacy skills unless we reduce the notion to simply reading a lecture composed by someone else. If 'delivering a lecture' reflects advanced literacy skills, then why would we define this language function as a component of 'oral language' rather than literacy abilities?

The relevance of this issue in the present context is that it is not at all clear whether 'vocabulary' as measured by Picture Vocabulary tests in the early grades of elementary school reflects the same construct as 'vocabulary' measured by vocabulary subtests associated with reading comprehension test batteries (Phillips Galloway et al., 2020). Thus, Picture Vocabulary tests only partially assess 'literacy-related knowledge' whereas oral or written vocabulary tests administered after the primary grades that are not limited to vocabulary that can be 'pictured' are clearly assessing academic language proficiency (CALP) and would be expected to show similar patterns of L1/L2 relationships as is the case for reading comprehension.

In support of this proposition, consider Grabe's literature review, which noted the abundance of data showing strong relationships between vocabulary and reading:

In an early large-scale study, Thorndike (1973) surveyed research in 15 countries ... and reported median correlations across countries and age groups of r = .66 and r = .75 for reading and vocabulary. Stanovich (2000) reported on research that supports this relationship, noting strong correlations between vocabulary and reading for third through seventh-grade L1 students (r = .64 to .76). (Grabe, 2004: 49)

The fourth-grade correlations between reading comprehension and both oral vocabulary knowledge and listening comprehension reported by Proctor et al. (2006) are consistent with these data. English reading comprehension correlated strongly with both English vocabulary knowledge ($r = 0.73$) and English listening comprehension ($r = 0.76$) while Spanish reading comprehension correlated 0.70 and 0.77 with the equivalent Spanish variables.

Carver (2000) argued that the relationships between vocabulary and reading comprehension were so strong that the variables were indistinguishable. A similar position was advanced by Pike (1979) in a study of vocabulary and reading subtests of the Test of English as a Foreign Language (TOEFL). Correlations ranged between 0.88 and 0.94, suggesting that vocabulary and reading subtests were assessing the same construct. Other studies in very different contexts demonstrating strong relationships between vocabulary knowledge and reading comprehension include Schoonen et al. (1998) and Qian (2002).

In summary, vocabulary knowledge and reading comprehension are distinguishable in the early grades of school but they increasingly merge into a unitary construct by late elementary school. An obvious reason for this pattern is that access to low-frequency vocabulary comes primarily through written texts as the language demands of schooling increase after the initial primary grades. As Stanovich (2000) points out, the research evidence suggests a reciprocal causal relationship between vocabulary and reading such that vocabulary knowledge increases reading comprehension and more extensive reading results in vocabulary growth.

What does this analysis imply for L1 and L2 crosslinguistic relationships? Essentially, it suggests that after the primary grades of elementary school, we should expect to find the same kind of positive crosslinguistic relationships for vocabulary knowledge (assessed in oral or written modes) as have been demonstrated for reading comprehension. This prediction depends on students having sufficient opportunities to develop literacy and other academic skills in both L1 and L2.

Conclusion

The original formal statement of the interdependence hypothesis (Cummins, 1980c, 1981b) specified adequate exposure to L1 and L2 and adequate motivation to learn L1 and L2 as conditions for crosslinguistic interdependence. The elaboration of these conditions in this chapter has identified specific contextual, developmental, exposure, and measurement conditions that are prerequisites for the observation of positive crosslinguistic L1/L2 relationships. These conditions incorporate the considerations proposed by Prevoo et al. (2015, 2016) that include the role of context (e.g. bilingual programme versus L2-only programme) and measurement of constructs (reading comprehension tests versus discrete reading skills tests). However, they also highlight the lack of theoretical coherence in much of the cognitive psychology literature regarding the construct of 'oral language proficiency' and the need to prioritise the construct of 'opportunity to learn L1 and L2' in meta-analyses of L1 and L2 relationships.

10 Unitary Translanguaging Theory and Crosslinguistic Translanguaging Theory: A Comparative Analysis

In previous chapters, I critiqued certain components of the theoretical orientation to translanguaging proposed by García and colleagues (e.g. García, 2009; García & Li Wei, 2014; García & Kleifgen, 2019).[1] Specifically, in Chapter 7, I highlighted problematic aspects of aligning translanguaging theory with the proposition that languages don't exist as countable linguistic entities. In Chapter 9, I disputed the characterisation of constructs such as the linguistic interdependence hypothesis, the 'common underlying proficiency', and teaching for crosslinguistic transfer as 'monoglossic', and hence not only theoretically illegitimate but also implicated in oppressive and racist educational structures and ideologies.

In this chapter, I analyse translanguaging theory in more depth, focusing on the distinction articulated by García and Lin between what they termed 'strong' and 'weak' versions of translanguaging theory:

> On the one hand, there is the strong version of translanguaging, a theory that poses that bilingual people do not speak languages but rather, use their repertoire of linguistic features selectively. On the other hand, there is a weak version of translanguaging, the one that supports national and state language boundaries and yet calls for softening these boundaries. (García & Lin, 2017: 126)

García and Lin cite the work of Cummins (2007a, 2017a) in relation to crosslinguistic interdependence and the importance of teaching for transfer across languages as representative of the so-called weak version of translanguaging. In contrast to the 'weak' version of translanguaging theory, they support the so-called strong version of translanguaging, understood as a linguistic theory, but they also suggest that bilingual education programmes should combine the weak and strong versions of translanguaging theory:

> On the one hand, educators must continue to allocate separate spaces for the named languages although softening the boundaries between them. On the other hand, they must provide an instructional space where translanguaging is nurtured and used critically and creatively without speakers having to select and suppress different linguistic features of their own repertoire. (García & Lin, 2017: 127)

The distinction between alternative versions of translanguaging theory proposed by García and Lin is useful in drawing attention to and facilitating analysis of key points of contrast between different theoretical propositions associated with the construct of translanguaging. Rather than adopt the semantically loaded terms *strong* and *weak*, I use the terms *Unitary Translanguaging Theory* (UTT) and *Crosslinguistic Translanguaging Theory* (CTT) to highlight distinguishing features of the alternative theoretical orientations identified by García and Lin. The term 'unitary' characterises one of the central features of García and colleagues' translanguaging theory: 'Rather than possessing two or multiple autonomous language systems, speakers viewed as bilingual/multilingual select and deploy particular features to make meaning and to negotiate particular communicative contexts from a *unitary linguistic repertoire*' (García, 2017: 163) (emphasis original). Otheguy *et al.* (2019) similarly espouse what they call a unitary view arguing that bilingualism and multilingualism, despite their sociocultural reality, occupy a single, undifferentiated cognitive terrain that has no correspondence in a dual or multiple linguistic system.

In contrast to this position, the CTT claims that bilinguals actually *do* speak languages, involving multiple registers and porous boundaries, and effective teaching promotes conceptual and linguistic transfer across languages. The term 'crosslinguistic' references the fact that although 'languages' can be viewed as conceptually distinct experiential entities, they *do* intersect and interact in dynamic ways in the cognitive and linguistic functioning of the individual.[2]

The different orientations of UTT and CTT to the legitimacy of the construct of *language* should not obscure the fact that both theoretical perspectives view languages as socially constructed, they reject rigid instructional separation of languages, and they condemn the frequent devaluation of the linguistic practices that many minoritised students bring to school. Both orientations to translanguaging theory also endorse dynamic conceptions of multilingual cognitive functioning. And, finally, UTT and CTT both view translanguaging pedagogy that connects with students' lives and draws on their entire linguistic repertoire as a central component in the struggle for social justice and equity in education.

In the next section, I outline the evolution of the term 'translanguaging' from its origins in the Welsh-English bilingual education system to its current usage in academic and educational contexts. I then systematically compare UTT and CTT orientations and critique the UTT claim that additive orientations to minoritised students' bilingualism reflect monoglossic and raciolinguistic ideologies that contribute to social marginalisation and educational exclusion of these students (e.g. Flores, 2019; Flores & Rosa, 2015; García, 2017, 2019). Finally, I examine the orientation to translanguaging theory incorporated in several related models of multilingualism and bilingual education, specifically the extent to which their claims are more aligned with the CTT as compared to the UTT framework.

Section 1. Evolution of Translanguaging Theory

Origins in the Welsh Context

The construct of *translanguaging*, or in Welsh *trawsieithu*, was introduced in the 1980s by Cen Williams (1994, 1996, 2000) in the context of Welsh-English bilingual programmes that were focused on revitalising the Welsh language. The term drew attention to the systematic and intentional alternation of input and output languages in bilingual instruction. Colin Baker (2001) originally brought the construct to wider international attention in the 3rd edition of his comprehensive textbook *Foundations of Bilingual Education and Bilingualism*. He described 'translanguaging' as follows:

> This term describes the hearing or reading of a lesson, a passage in a book or a section of work in one language and the development of the work (i.e. by discussion, writing a passage, completing a work sheet, conducting an experiment) in the other language. That is, the input and output are deliberately in a different language, and this is systematically varied. (Baker, 2001: 281)

Gwyn Lewis, Bryn Jones and Colin Baker (2012b: 667) elaborated this description by noting that translanguaging represents 'a distinct pedagogic theory and practice that seeks to consciously vary the language of input and output but with dual-language processing ... because deeper learning may occur when both languages are activated'. These authors proposed a tripartite distinction between (a) classroom translanguaging (both planned and serendipitous), (b) universal translanguaging involving linguistically fluid interactions in a variety of interpersonal contexts and (c) neurolinguistic translanguaging involving research into brain activity modulations when both languages are activated (Lewis *et al.*, 2012a). Lewis and colleagues highlight the ways in which the conceptualisation of translanguaging shifts perceptions of minority group bi/

multilingualism from separate and diglossic to integrated and heteroglossic and 'from ideology that accented the subtractive and negative nature of bilingualism to one that expresses the advantages of additive bilingualism where languages in the brain, classroom, and street act simultaneously and not sequentially, with efficient integration and not separation' (2012b: 668). They also argue, citing the interdependence hypothesis, that translanguaging is an effective and efficient way of enabling crosslinguistic transfer (Lewis *et al.*, 2012a: 645). Williams (2000: 139) likewise argued that translanguaging instructional strategies provide students with opportunities to develop additive bilingualism.

In short, these authors see no conflict between their conception of 'translanguaging' and notions of 'additive bilingualism', teaching for crosslinguistic transfer, the personal and social existence of 'languages', and the reality of 'languages' being processed cognitively in our brains.

Elaboration of the Construct by García and Colleagues

During the past decade, the term *translanguaging* has come to dominate academic discussions regarding pedagogy in bilingual and L2 immersion programmes as well as pedagogy for multilingual and immigrant-background students in mainstream programmes taught through the dominant school language (e.g. Carbonara & Scibetta, 2020a, 2020b; Hornberger & Link, 2012; Leung & Valdés, 2019; Little & Kirwin, 2018; Makalela, 2018; Mary & Young, 2017; Mertin, 2018; Panagiotopoulou *et al.*, 2020; Paulsrud *et al.*, 2017; Slembrouck & Rosiers, 2018; Spiro & Crisfield, 2018; Tsokalidou & Skourtou, 2020). This unprecedented expansion of research and theoretical discussion was sparked by Ofelia García's (2009) book *Bilingual Education in the 21st Century: A Global Perspective* and sustained by the prolific publications of García and colleagues since that time. García (2009) extended the original Welsh construct of translanguaging to highlight the dynamic heteroglossic integrated linguistic practices of multilingual individuals and to endorse the legitimacy of instruction that integrates rather than separates the languages of emergent bilingual students. In many subsequent publications, García and colleagues elaborated the theoretical dimensions of translanguaging, and also explored with educators how translanguaging pedagogies could be implemented in classroom contexts. The City University of New York (CUNY) New York State Initiative on Emergent Bilinguals (CUNY-NYSIEB) (https://www.cuny-nysieb.org/) has developed an impressive and inspirational set of resources, guides, and instructional examples to support educators in pursuing translanguaging instructional initiatives both in bilingual and English-medium programmes (CUNY-New York State Initiative on Emergent Bilinguals, 2021).

Although some scholars (e.g. Edwards, 2012; Grin, 2018) dispute the usefulness and legitimacy of the term *translanguaging*, there is widespread support in the academic literature for the propositions that multilingual individuals draw on the totality of their linguistic resources in communicative interactions and that classroom instruction should encourage students to use their full linguistic repertoire in flexible and strategic ways as a tool for cognitive and academic learning. For example, as noted previously, virtually all theorists and researchers currently endorse some form of *dynamic systems theory* that highlights the transformation of the cognitive and linguistic system brought about by the acquisition of multiple languages (e.g. de Bot *et al.*, 2007; Herdina & Jessner, 2002).

Contradictory Origins of Unitary Translanguaging Theory

When we examine the evolution of translanguaging theory in the work of García and colleagues, we are immediately faced with a glaring contradiction. García and colleagues in multiple publications (e.g. García, 2009; García & Li Wei, 2014) highlight two significant influences on the development of their theoretical framework: (a) the work of Cen Williams in Wales who initially coined the term and (b) the theoretical claims of Makoni and Pennycook (2005) that languages are invented and don't exist as countable entities.

García and colleagues distanced themselves somewhat from the Makoni and Pennycook position by acknowledging that languages do exist in the sphere of social discourse, but they extended Makoni and Pennycook's claims by denying the reality of 'languages' within our linguistic and cognitive system – hence the legitimacy of the construct of 'languaging' but not the construct of 'languages'. In her Foreword to Makoni and Pennycook's (2007b) book, García highlighted the profound impact of their theoretical insights on her own thinking:

> This book has engaged me in a key question that must surround the ways in which we think about bilingual education in the future: What would language education look like if we no longer posited the existence of separate languages? How would we teach bilingually in ways that reflect people's use of language and not simply people as language users? (García, 2007: xiii)

The positions adopted by García and colleagues with respect to 'academic language' (Chapter 8), the common underlying proficiency, teaching for crosslinguistic transfer (Chapter 9), and additive bilingualism (this chapter) can all be traced directly to the theoretical claims advanced by Makoni and Pennycook (2005, 2007a). As noted in the Preface, Makoni and Pennycook suggested that 'there is a disconcerting similarity between monolingualism and additive bilingualism in so far as both are founded on notions of language as "objects" ... additive bilingualism and multilingualism are at best a pluralization of monolingualism' (2005: 148). Thus, they claim that the educational promotion of multilingualism and additive bilingualism leaves intact the monolingual assumptions about language that these constructs aim to critique. These constructs remain caught in the same paradigm that takes monolingualism as the norm. Thus, rather than pursuing strategies of disinventing languages, the pluralisation strategy implied by notions of multilingualism and additive bilingualism reproduces existing oppressive structures. All of these claims are recycled in the rigid dichotomy that García and colleagues erect between heteroglossic (dynamic) and monoglossic (static) orientations to bi/multilingualism and their consignment of 'weak' or crosslinguistic versions of translanguaging theory to the monoglossic orientation (see Figure 10.1).

The immediate problem that arises for UTT theorists with this dichotomy is that the adoption of the Makoni/Pennycook theoretical framework logically entails a *rejection* of the original Welsh concept of translanguaging. The pedagogical translanguaging framework advanced by Williams and other Welsh researchers (Lewis *et al.*, 2012a, 2012b) endorses the constructs of additive bilingualism and teaching for productive contact between languages. Welsh and English are clearly distinguished within the emergent bilingual's cognitive and linguistic system. According to the logic advanced by UTT theorists, the Welsh concept of translanguaging is monoglossic in orientation and falls squarely within the category of 'weak' or crosslinguistic translanguaging theory.

Table 10.1 illustrates the very different conceptions of translanguaging theory that constitute the twin pillars of UTT. It is clear that the position articulated by Welsh researchers is diametrically opposed to the unitary and undifferentiated conception of translanguaging that owes its inspiration to the theoretical framework advanced by Makoni and Pennycook (2005, 2007a). Emphasis has been added in all of the quotations in Table 10.1.

The Welsh researchers clearly do not see additive bilingualism or teaching for crosslinguistic transfer as problematic. They endorse the cognitive and linguistic reality of languages in talking about crosslanguage semantic remapping. By contrast, although they have never acknowledged the contradiction, UTT theorists adopt the Makoni/Pennycook position

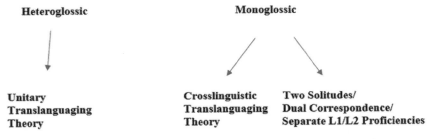

Figure 10.1 UTT conception of heteroglossic/monoglossic dichotomy with CTT consigned to the monoglossic category

Table 10.1 Contrast between the endorsement of additive bilingualism and the cognitive reality of languages in the Welsh conceptualisation of translanguaging and the rejection of these constructs as oppressive within UTT

Translanguaging in the Welsh Context	Status of 'Languages' in the Makoni/ Pennycook and UTT Framework
'It could be argued that the constant switching from one language to the other, and the fact that *sections of the notes were read in English and then explained in Welsh*, provided students with opportunities to develop their individual bilingual capabilities; that it was a means of translanguaging and another form of *creating an opportunity for additive bilingualism*'. (Williams, 2000: 139) Translanguaging shifts perceptions of minority group bi/multilingualism 'from ideology that accented the subtractive and negative nature of bilingualism to one that expresses *the advantages of additive bilingualism*' (Lewis et al., 2012b: 668).	'By talking of monolingualism, we are referring to a single entity, while *in additive bilingualism and multilingualism the number of 'language things' has increased*. Yet the underlying concept remains unchanged' (Makoni & Pennycook, 2005: 148) '[S]tandard language and additive bilingualism have been used as instruments to minoritize the language practices of some bilinguals and rendering them as deficient' (García, 2020: 16)
Pedagogical translanguaging 'allows more effective learning due to *crosslanguage* semantic remapping that occurs when the encoded information in *one language* is retrieved to enable production in the *other language*' (Lewis et al., 2012a: 650).	'In our view, the myriad lexical and structural features mastered by bilinguals occupy a cognitive terrain that is not fenced off into anything like the two areas suggested by the two socially named languages. ... *[The] position that, while allowing for some overlap, the competence of bilinguals involves language specific internal differentiation ... which we have called the dual correspondence theory ... has had pernicious effects in educational practices*' (Otheguy et al., 2019: 625).

that notions of additive bilingualism (and codeswitching, crosslinguistic transfer etc.) are still locked into a monoglossic paradigm and hence reflect pernicious social and educational forces that represent a retarding obstacle to minoritised students' academic opportunities.

Dissenting Voices

Despite the general consensus about the legitimacy of the core principles underlying the construct of translanguaging and the pedagogical directions it implies, a number of theorists have expressed concern about the multitude of claims advanced by García and colleagues. For example, Jaspers (2018: 2) described translanguaging as 'a terminological house with many rooms' and pointed to the problematic nature of stretching the construct of translanguaging to encompass a wide range of disparate theoretical claims:

In sum, translanguaging can apply to an innate instinct that includes monolinguals; to the performance of fluid language use that mostly pertains to bilinguals; to a bilingual pedagogy; to a theory or approach of language; and to a process of personal and social transformation. By any standard this is a lot for one term. (Jaspers, 2018: 3)

He noted that some of the claims regarding the transformative power of translanguaging are inconsistent with research showing more modest outcomes (e.g. Sierens & Van Avermaet, 2014). He also questioned the 'lack of qualifications and caveats' (2018: 4) regarding many of the transformative claims in the translanguaging literature. While agreeing with much of the political agenda behind translanguaging and the need for 'a linguistic makeover' in present-day education, Jaspers expressed doubt that the current promotion of translanguaging is capable of delivering this linguistic makeover, let alone transformation of inequalities in the wider society. He pointed to the dilemma for educators and scholars who promote linguistic equality and diversity deriving from the fact that 'at the end of the road, pupils will be evaluated for their skills in a monolingual, academic type of language' (2018: 9).

Ballinger *et al.* (2017) have also pointed to the vagueness associated with the multiple uses of the term 'translanguaging', which, they claim, encompasses a theory of cognitive processing, societal use of multiple languages in communicative interactions, classroom language use behaviours among emergent bilingual students, and teaching practices that attempt to harness students' multilingual repertoires to enhance learning. They propose the umbrella term *crosslinguistic pedagogy* as preferable to translanguaging to refer to pedagogical practices that support and encourage learners to draw on their full linguistic repertoire in the classroom.

Researchers involved with Canadian French immersion programmes (e.g. Ballinger *et al.*, 2017, 2020; Lyster, 2019) have cautioned against the use of translanguaging on the grounds that it risks undermining students' motivation and opportunity to use the minority language (i.e. French). Lyster (2019: 349) expressed the point as follows: 'translanguaging pedagogies have the potential to jeopardize the use of the minority language in certain contexts of bilingual education. This is because, when there is competition in schools between majority and minority languages, the majority language always prevails'. These authors are not opposed, in principle, to crosslinguistic pedagogy that brings the two languages into productive contact and encourages two-way transfer across languages. Rather, they advocate instructional strategies that support crosslinguistic connections within the bilingual or L2 immersion programme, while at the same time maintaining largely separate instructional spaces for each language. An example of how they have pursued this goal is described in Chapter 11 (see also Cummins, 2014a).

In short, while most researchers reject linguistic hierarchies and support the pedagogical goals associated with the construct of translanguaging, there is also a sense of unease among researchers, outside of core

UTT advocates, about the empirical adequacy, logical coherence and instructional consequences of some propositions that have been advanced in relation to translanguaging theory.

Section 2. Unitary and Crosslinguistic Theoretical Orientations

I have argued that as the concept of translanguaging evolved into its 'strong' or 'unitary' versions over the past decade, it acquired a considerable amount of *extraneous conceptual baggage* that risks undermining its overall credibility (Cummins, 2017a, 2017b). This extraneous conceptual baggage includes the following interrelated propositions that have been loosely woven together into the theoretical framework elaborated by UTT advocates:

- Languages are 'invented' and don't exist as discrete 'countable' entities (e.g. Makoni & Pennycook, 2007).
- The multilingual's linguistic system is internally undifferentiated and unitary, reflecting the fact that 'languages' have no linguistic or cognitive reality (e.g. García, 2009).
- Codeswitching is an illegitimate monoglossic construct because it assumes the existence of two separate linguistic systems (e.g. Otheguy *et al.*, 2015, 2019).
- Additive bilingualism is an illegitimate monoglossic construct because it similarly assumes the existence of two separate languages that are added together in bilingual individuals (e.g. García, 2009).
- For similar reasons, the notion of a *common underlying proficiency* and teaching for crosslinguistic transfer imply a monoglossic conception of bilingualism (e.g. García & Li Wei, 2014).
- 'Academic language' is an illegitimate construct, as is the distinction between the language typically used in social and academic contexts (e.g. Flores & Rosa, 2015; García & Solorza, 2020).
- Additive approaches to minoritised students' bilingualism are rooted in raciolinguistic ideologies (e.g. Flores & Rosa, 2015).
- Teaching biliteracy involves teaching standardised language norms in a prescriptive way that stigmatises and suppresses students' authentic varieties of L1 and/or L2 (e.g. Flores & Rosa, 2015).[3]

I have argued that all of these propositions are problematic (Cummins, 2021). In varying degrees, they are unsupported by empirical research, they are logically inconsistent, and they undermine important potential contributions of the construct of translanguaging to effective and equitable pedagogy. Some of these issues have been discussed in previous chapters. Specifically, I have disputed claims that the construct of 'languages' is illegitimate, that crosslinguistic interdependence and teaching for transfer reflect monoglossic ideologies, and that the construct of 'academic language' is spurious and implicated in discourses of appropriateness and raciolinguistic ideologies. MacSwan (2017) has similarly asserted the legitimacy of the construct of 'codeswitching' in opposition to the claim by García and colleagues that it is monoglossic in orientation.

In this chapter, my focus is on the following two central claims of UTT:

- The multilingual's linguistic system is internally undifferentiated and unitary, reflecting the fact that 'languages' have no linguistic or cognitive reality; because additive bilingualism implies the existence of 'languages', it is an illegitimate monoglossic construct.
- Additive bilingualism involves 'the enforcement of named languages as wholes to be used separately [which] stigmatizes even further [minoritized speakers'] more dynamic and fluid multilingual practices' (García, 2019: 157). Furthermore, discourses of appropriateness rooted in raciolinguistic ideologies lie at the core of additive approaches to language education (Flores & Rosa, 2015).

In contrast to the theoretical claims advanced by advocates of UTT, the CTT framework affirms the legitimacy and pedagogical importance for teachers to (a) adopt additive approaches to minoritised students' bilingualism and biliteracy, (b) actively and explicitly build students' awareness regarding how language and languages work in academic contexts and (c) teach for transfer of concepts, skills, and learning strategies across languages.

To What Extent are Interpersonal and Pedagogical Translanguaging Legitimate Constructs?

In comparing UTT and CTT, it is important to establish initially the extent to which the core constituents of translanguaging theory, endorsed by both UTT and CTT advocates, are legitimate according to the criteria of empirical adequacy, logical coherence, and consequential validity. Although codeswitching/translanguaging and use of nonstandard varieties of English and/or L1 are still stigmatised in many schools and university contexts, as well as in the job market (Delpit & Dowdy, 2002; Flores & Rosa, 2015; Lippi-Green, 1997/2012; Weber, 2015), I know of no researcher in recent years who has disputed the legitimacy of these interpersonal language practices. There is consensus among applied linguists and other researchers that schools should build on the linguistic resources that students bring to school as part of a process of affirming the 'funds of knowledge' that exist in minoritised communities (González et al., 2005; Moll et al., 1992). In short, although division exists regarding the extent to which codeswitching is a legitimate construct that can be conceptualised as one manifestation of translanguaging (e.g. MacSwan, 2017; Otheguy et al., 2015, 2019), there is no academic debate about the legitimacy of interpersonal translanguaging, understood as the fluid communicative use of the individual's entire linguistic repertoire (what Lewis *et al.*, 2012a, labelled 'universal translanguaging').

With respect to pedagogical translanguaging, there are numerous documented examples of educators mobilising minoritised students' multilingual resources long before the construct of translanguaging had entered North American educational discourse (Auerbach, 1993, 2016; Chow & Cummins, 2003; Cummins *et al.*, 2005; DeFazio, 1997; García & Sylvan, 2011; Lucas & Katz, 1994). Many of the insights about multilingual instructional strategies we have gained over the past 30 years have been generated by educators who have often worked in collaboration with university researchers to document their initiatives. Documentation of these early instructional initiatives, together with more recent examples (e.g. Carbonara & Scibetta, 2020a, 2020b; Chumak-Horbatsch, 2019; Chumak-Horbatsch *et al.*, 2020; Cummins & Persad, 2014; García & Kleyn, 2016; Little & Kirwin, 2019; Menken & Sánchez, 2019; Prasad, 2016; Prasad & Lory, 2020) has demonstrated that multilingual instructional strategies (i.e. pedagogical translanguaging) can scaffold higher levels of academic performance, build critical language awareness, engage students actively with literacy in both their home and school languages, and affirm students' identities. Ballinger *et al.* (2020: 269) reach similar conclusions on the basis of the research, noting that when instruction reflects and supports learners' full range of language and literacy skills, learners become more engaged with literacy in general and critical biliteracy in particular, make more effective use of reading and writing strategies, develop greater morphological awareness and report more positive identity development.

In summary, the legitimacy of pedagogical translanguaging is supported by extensive research demonstrating that mobilising students' multilingual and multimodal repertoires can connect curriculum to students' lives, scaffold learning, affirm their identities, and reinforce their knowledge of how language works as an oral and written communicative system. With respect to consequential validity, the recent theoretical focus on translanguaging, together with earlier multilingual instructional initiatives, has resulted in a significant increase in educators' interest in exploring ways of incorporating minoritised students' home languages into instruction. Thus, the construct of translanguaging (broadly defined) can be viewed as legitimate from the perspectives of empirical adequacy, logical coherence and consequential validity.

To What Extent does UTT Meet the Criteria of Empirical Adequacy, Logical Coherence and Consequential Validity?

Empirical adequacy

Several researchers have called into question the empirical adequacy of the claim that 'named languages' are social constructions that have sociopolitical reality but are not distinguishable within the mental system of individuals (García, 2009; Otheguy *et al.*, 2015, 2019). As noted previously, MacSwan (2017) argued that the unitary undifferentiated model advocated by García and colleagues is inconsistent with a multitude of linguistic data and analysis. He pointed out that for François Grosjean (1982) who initially made the case that the bilingual is not just the sum of two monolinguals, 'bilingualism is not just social and political; it is also psychologically real' (2017: 190). MacSwan argued that it is mistaken and counter-productive to claim on the basis of the colonial history of language differentiation that individual bilingual grammars are internally unitary and undifferentiated. On the contrary, linguistic analysis supports an integrative multilingual model that posits both shared and discrete grammatical and lexical resources rather than the unitary undifferentiated model advocated by García and colleagues. MacSwan also repudiated the UTT claim that codeswitching research adopts a dual competence monoglossic perspective on bilingual mental grammar that privileges the monolingual speaker.

Grin (2018: 256) has likewise disputed the empirical basis for a unitary undifferentiated model noting that neurolinguistic research shows that 'the very fact of using different languages mobilises different areas of the brain and reflects the need, for bilingual language users switching between languages, to *inhibit* one language in order to speak the other' (emphasis original). Information processing research going back to the 1960s likewise supports a conception of bilingual language processing that entails both shared and discrete components. Kolers (1968: 82), for example, summarised his research as follows: 'Our work showed that some information can be stored in such a way that it is readily accessible in either of two languages. Other information is, in terms of its accessibility, closely bound to the language by which it was stored in the mind'.

Bhatt and Bolonyai (2019) have also disputed the empirical and logical basis for claims of differences between translanguaging and codeswitching, and the characterisation of codeswitching as monoglossic, and translanguaging as heteroglossic. Their analysis of evidence for these claims advanced by advocates of UTT suggests that even a cursory look at the empirical data 'reveals that there isn't *any* discernible difference between translanguaging and code-switching' (2019: 15) (emphasis original). They also review compelling data from studies of aphasia demonstrating that the different languages of bilinguals have specific patterns of neural representation and organisation. For example, they cite the case of JZ, a Basque-Spanish bilingual individual with aphasia, whose linguistic functioning in each language was affected in markedly different ways by his aphasia:

> JZ's aphasia impacted his languages to different degrees: his first language, Basque, was more impaired than his second language, Spanish. In

particular, the Bilingual Aphasia Test revealed deficits in first language production, but intact production in his second language. Such differential language loss does not find an account in translanguaging theory: a unitary linguistic system cannot explain why one language is impacted (more) than another in differential bilingual aphasia. (Bhatt & Bolonyai, 2019: 18)

I would add the qualification that although the findings of case studies such as this cannot be accounted for by UTT, they are totally consistent with the claims of CTT.

Otheguy *et al.* (2019) responded to MacSwan's (2017) critique by characterising it as a *dual correspondence theory*, which posits that bilinguals possess two separate linguistic systems whose boundaries coincide with those of the two named languages. They dismiss MacSwan's rejection of dual competence models and his characterisation of his position as an *integrated multilingual model* that includes both shared and discrete grammatical and lexical resources in the linguistic system of the multilingual: 'Recognizing that some areas of grammar and vocabulary are shared does not distinguish MacSwan's proposal from the claims traditionally made by proponents of the dual correspondence theory' (Otheguy *et al.*, 2019: 631).

I believe it is a major mischaracterisation of MacSwan's (2017) position (and that of CTT more generally) to conflate it with a 'dual correspondence' or 'two solitudes' notion of bilingualism. I return to this point later in the chapter (see Figure 10.2). It is sufficient to note at this point that serious questions have been raised about the empirical adequacy of the unitary undifferentiated model of bilingual language processing advanced by UTT advocates.

Logical coherence

Although the perspectives of García and colleagues (e.g. García, 2019; Otheguy *et al.*, 2015, 2019) and Flores and Rosa (2015) regarding additive bilingualism overlap in multiple ways, I will discuss the logical coherence of their claims separately. Both sets of researchers characterise additive bilingualism as monoglossic and inextricably linked to the imposition of standardised language that marginalises the fluid linguistic practices of minoritised students. Their respective emphases differ somewhat in the fact that García and colleagues base part of their critique on the proposition that the bilingual's linguistic system is unitary and undifferentiated while Flores and Rosa argue that additive *approaches* to bilingualism are permeated by raciolinguistic ideologies. Because of the absence of any qualifications in their condemnation of additive approaches, it is unclear to what extent Flores and Rosa would characterise the educators profiled in Bartlett and García's (2011) inspirational volume *Additive Schooling in Subtractive Times* as inadvertently complicit with raciolinguistic ideologies.

Logical coherence in García and colleagues' claims. 1. The unitary nature of mental grammar

Although Otheguy *et al.* (2019) dispute the empirical basis of MacSwan's (2017) critique of unitary translanguaging, their initial claims for the unitary nature of the bilingual's linguistic system were based on logical and theoretical arguments rather than empirical arguments. Otheguy *et al.* expressed their position as follows:

> The point that needs repeating is that a named language *cannot* be defined linguistically, cannot be defined, that is, in grammatical (lexical or structural) terms. And because a named language cannot be defined linguistically, it is not, strictly speaking, a linguistic object; it is not something that a person speaks. (Otheguy *et al.*, 2015: 286) (emphasis original)

In other words, because grammarians cannot come up with a coherent set of linguistic criteria to distinguish so-called 'languages' from each other and from related dialects, languages must be viewed solely as social constructs rather than as linguistically 'real' objects or entities. MacSwan's (2017: 186) detailed analysis of this position concluded that Otheguy *et al.*'s 'ideas about mental architecture are not sufficiently detailed to permit empirical investigation'.

From the perspective of the present volume that is concerned primarily with language education issues, the more significant point is that questions concerning the extent to which 'languages' are represented in the individual's mental grammar are largely *irrelevant* to the provision of equitable, engaging, and culturally sustaining instruction for minoritised students. Educators who are committed to challenging disempowering structures and processes in school and society tend not to be overly concerned about whether their Spanish/English bilingual students are *actually* speaking 'languages'. They know that the languages they and their students speak are socially, linguistically, cognitively, instructionally and experientially real. Like the educators profiled in Bartlett and García's (2011) book *Additive Schooling in Subtractive Times*, they are aware of the subtractive forces in both school and society, and the instructional and social challenges faced by their students in developing Spanish language and literacy skills in addition to English language and literacy skills. I would be surprised if any of them gave much consideration to the status of 'languages' in their students' mental grammar.

In the same way, a child who says 'I speak English to my Mom but French to my Dad' is not sharing any revelation about her mental grammar. She is simply stating the experiential and social reality of her communication practices. Yet, UTT advocates have put themselves in the strange position of having to declare this type of statement illegitimate because 'a named language ... is not something that a person speaks' (Otheguy *et al.*, 2015: 256). In short, UTT advocates frequently and consistently confound the social/experiential with the cognitive/linguistic. They would presumably assent to the legitimacy of the child's comment about her use of French and English on the grounds that this comment is referencing the social reality of languages, but at the same time they appear to be claiming that the child is incorrect in saying that she speaks these specific languages.[4]

The doubtful proposition that people don't speak languages (García & Lin, 2017; Otheguy *et al.*, 2015, 2019) generates numerous additional logical conundrums for advocates of UTT. For example, in contrasting 'strong' (UTT) and 'weak' (CTT) versions of translanguaging theory, García and Lin (2017: 126) characterise the 'weak' version as 'one that supports national and state language boundaries, and yet calls for softening these boundaries'. It is not at all clear what is meant by 'supporting national and state language boundaries'. Does this refer to political beliefs, educational policies, language usage, cognitive/linguistic processing or all of the above? How does 'supporting national and state language boundaries' differ from García and colleagues' acknowledgement that (a) languages have social reality, (b) '[m]inoritized languages must be protected and developed if that is the wish of people' (García & Lin, 2017: 127) and (c) 'bilingual education must develop bilingual students' ability to use language according to the rules and regulations that have been socially constructed for that particular named language'? (García & Lin, 2017: 126). García and Lin's argument that minoritised languages should be promoted together with the dominant language sounds a lot like promotion of additive bilingualism; likewise, their claim that the teaching of emergent bilinguals' languages must adhere to the 'rules and regulations' associated with each language suggests that students' fluid linguistic practices should be expanded to encompass literate and standard forms of the language.

It seems that García and Lin are essentially acknowledging that there are no differences in the instructional practices that are implied by so-called strong and weak versions of translanguaging (e.g. Cummins, 2007). *If this is the case, then the claims of UTT that languages have no cognitive reality and the bilingual's mental grammar is unitary are essentially of no relevance to educators or educational policymakers.*

Logical coherence in García and colleagues' claims. 2. The multiple conflations of additive bilingualism.

Despite the fact that García and Lin (2017) can logically point to no instructional differences between UTT and CTT, García and colleagues elsewhere claim that CTT and UTT imply very different approaches to instruction, largely as a result of contrasting conceptions of 'additive bilingualism'. As noted previously, CTT does not view the construct of 'additive bilingualism' as in any way problematic, let alone monoglossic. The term simply references an instructional orientation designed to build on and develop minoritised students' multilingual repertories. As noted by Cummins (2017a, 2017b), the term emerged in opposition to the construct of subtractive bilingualism at a time when schools typically encouraged emergent bilingual students to replace their home languages with the dominant language of schooling. Within this discursive context, the promotion of additive bilingualism challenged coercive relations of power by promoting instructional practices and policies that enabled students to develop their home languages rather than replace them with the dominant school language.

By contrast, the construct of 'additive bilingualism' takes on sinister and coercive overtones within UTT as an instructional approach and educational philosophy that *enforces* named languages as discrete wholes to be used separately, thereby marginalising the dynamic and fluid linguistic practices of emergent bilingual students (García, 2019: 157). Two recent examples of UTT advocates inappropriately conflating additive bilingualism with 'two solitudes' or 'dual correspondence' conceptions of bilingualism are cited below. García expressed this perspective as follows:

> The construction of languages as autonomous entities, and bilingualism as simply additive has worked against the language practices of minoritized bilingual communities. The bilingualism of Latinx bilingual students is not simply additive; it is dynamic (García 2009). Thus, merely acknowledging or even using what is seen as the students' first language in education does not in any way uncover the ways in which standard language and additive bilingualism have been used as instruments to minoritize the language practices of some bilinguals and rendering them as deficient. (García, 2020: 16)

Otheguy *et al.* (2019) similarly argued that additive bilingualism, as it has been used in the research literature up to this point, represents 'the addition of an autonomous and separate named second language' (2019: 648). They argue that a 'much healthier educational climate is created by teachers who adopt the unitary view sponsored by translanguaging' (2019: 625). They suggest that the concept of additive bilingualism might be redeemed if it were 'seen as the addition of lexical and structural features to the bilingual's expanding unitary language system' (2019: 648) as opposed to the addition of a separate named language. Specifically, the 'former is the true driver of bilingual proficiency; the latter has often been its retarding obstacle' (2019: 648).

This characterisation of 'additive bilingualism' by García (2020) and Otheguy *et al.* (2019) is at variance with the way virtually every other theorist has used the term over the past 40 years. To illustrate, British researcher, Ruth Swanwick (2017a) in an article entitled 'Translanguaging, learning and teaching in deaf education' noted that the ideological roots of the term 'translanguaging' are located in an additive view of bilingualism and bilingual language use in education. She elaborated this perspective as follows:

> The addition to one's language repertoire is considered to be an enrichment of the linguistic and cultural experience of the individual that enhances but does not compromise the existing repertoire. Additive bilingual education strives to develop learners' proficiency in both, or all, of their languages and to respect, value and celebrate the linguistic and cultural heritage that individuals bring to the classroom. (Swanwick, 2017a: 236)

She highlighted the fact that the emphasis on the language repertoire of individuals represents an important additive feature of translanguaging. The language experiences and repertoires of deaf children vary enormously, and sophisticated hearing technologies and global digital technologies have opened up multiple additional avenues for communication, with the result that, on a daily basis, deaf children are exposed to and use sign, spoken, and written language(s) with varying degrees of fluency. In short, Swanwick (2017a) clearly sees no opposition between an additive view of bilingualism, and translanguaging conceived as both an individual communicative strategy and pedagogical approach. She certainly does not drive a binary wedge between additive bilingualism and translanguaging, characterising the former as monoglossic and the latter as heteroglossic.

Claims regarding the pernicious effects of the construct of additive bilingualism on educational practices rest on its conflation with 'two solitudes' or dual correspondence theory. A more persuasive argument would have attempted to actually *document*, rather than simply assert, the equivalence of 'two solitudes' perspectives with CTT constructs such as additive bilingualism, interdependence/common underlying proficiency, and teaching for crosslinguistic transfer. One might also have expected UTT advocates to showcase *at least one example* of how promoting additive bilingualism or teaching for crosslinguistic transfer has been a 'retarding obstacle' to the development of bilingual proficiency among minoritised students.

Certainly, as I have argued for more than 40 years, separate underlying proficiency or 'two solitudes' orientations to bilingual education and the development of bilingual proficiency are highly problematic (e.g. Cummins, 1981b). But any coherent argument that 'additive bilingualism' and teaching for crosslinguistic transfer are indistinguishable from 'two solitudes' assumptions in their pernicious effects on education necessitates at least two components: (1) it would have to address the fact that these constructs were proposed as a *repudiation* of dual correspondence or separate underlying proficiency claims; (2) it would have to actually document, rather than simply assert *ex cathedra*, the pernicious effects on educational practice brought about over the past 40 years by these constructs.

In short, the dismissal by García and colleagues of constructs associated with CTT such as additive bilingualism, linguistic/interdependence/ common underlying proficiency, and the importance of teaching for crosslinguistic transfer, is premised on a logically flawed and scientifically problematic identification of these constructs with dual correspondence theory.

In the four points below, I elaborate on the multiple conflations and logical *non-sequiturs* evident in the claims by UTT advocates regarding additive bilingualism and related constructs.

1. Additive bilingualism and dynamic bilingualism occupy different discursive contexts

The construct of 'additive bilingualism' was employed long before the theoretical landscape shifted to highlight the dynamic nature of bilingual cognitive processes. The term referenced language education issues, not issues related to bilingual linguistic processes or mental architecture. Thus, García's contrast between 'additive bilingualism' and 'dynamic bilingualism' represents a false opposition – these are incommensurable concepts that cannot logically be compared or contrasted. García's (2020) claim that 'additive bilingualism' references mental architecture is not reflected in the way *any researcher* has used this term over the past 40+ years (e.g. Canagarajah, 2006; Lewis *et al.*, 2012b; Molyneux *et al.*, 2016; May, 2011; Nieto & Bode, 2018; Plüddemann, 2015; Williams, 2000).

2. Additive bilingualism acknowledges the social and existential reality of 'languages'

The appearance of conflict between notions of additive bilingualism and dynamic models of bilingualism is based on the fact that researchers who invoke the former construct also typically ascribe legitimate meaning to terms such as home language and school language, whereas the legitimacy of these referents is dismissed by UTT advocates. If the ascription of social and experiential legitimacy to terms such as 'Spanish', 'English', home language' and 'school language' automatically consigns a theoretical construct to monoglossic infamy, then certainly 'additive bilingualism' would belong there. However, as discussed previously, there are multiple logical problems with this perspective, not least being the fact that use of these terms implies nothing about the individual's mental grammar.

3. The everyday connotations of the term 'additive' are confounded with the discursive meaning of 'additive bilingualism'

As Cummins (2017b) pointed out, it is not difficult to see how the L1 + L2 connotation of the term 'additive' could be interpreted as implying compartmentalisation of the bilingual's two languages. However, even a superficial examination of the discursive context in which the term 'additive bilingualism' has been used shows that compartmentalisation and separation are not in any way implied. As noted previously, the term has been used exclusively in the discursive context of challenging subtractive orientations to minoritised students' bilingualism and outside of this context it is semantically empty. Consider the semantic equivalence of the following two sentences that a teacher of bilingual students might utter: 'My instructional goal is to promote bilingualism and biliteracy among my students' and 'My instructional goal is to promote additive bilingualism and biliteracy among my students'. The word *additive* adds virtually nothing to the basic meaning of the statement. If anything, it entails the connotation that the teacher sees herself as building on, or adding to, the language repertoires that students bring to school. Yet, within UTT, the first sentence would (presumably) be regarded as legitimate whereas the second sentence would be dismissed as illegitimate because of its putative monoglossic character resulting from the intrusion of the term 'additive'. In short, there is nothing remotely contradictory in promoting additive bilingualism (i.e. expanding students' multilingual repertoire) through translanguaging or crosslinguistic pedagogy.

4. The term 'additive bilingualism' does not imply language separation or inert compartmentalisation

The superficiality of the claim that 'additive bilingualism' is a monoglossic concept can also be seen in the fact that if we were to substitute the term 'active bilingualism' in all of the discursive contexts where 'additive bilingualism' has been used over the past 40+ years, the case for its monoglossic character would simply fall apart. I expressed this point as follows:

> Nothing is lost semantically by this proposed change. Active bilingualism fits easily into current dynamic heteroglossic frameworks, and it retains its power to challenge the undermining of minoritised students' bilingual and biliteracy development. The argument that additive bilingualism reflects a monoglossic ideology simply disappears with the elimination of the term. (Cummins, 2017b: 242)

A related point, as any baker knows, is that the addition of two or more substances does not mean that they remain inert and separate from each other. Thus, as Cenoz and Gorter (2013) emphasise, a Basque/Spanish bilingual student who adds English to her repertoire of skills will benefit from the dynamic interdependence, intersections, and cross-fertilisation among the three languages, particularly if teachers teach for crosslinguistic transfer. This again highlights the point that 'additive' in no way implies static, inert, separate, autonomous, or independent. The process of crosslinguistic intersection and interaction within the common underlying proficiency is a core theoretical proposition within CTT.

In short, García and colleagues' (2009, 2020) conflation of 'additive bilingualism' with separate (non-dynamic) bilingualism and with standardised language has no logical or empirical basis. This is reflected in the fact that these equivalencies are simply asserted without logical argumentation or empirical justification.[5]

The logical challenges for UTT in characterising the bilingual's linguistic system as unitary and totally undifferentiated can also be illustrated with reference to the cognitive processing of bimodal bilingual deaf children. In applying translanguaging theory to the bimodal bilingual context, Swanwick (2017b: 97) highlighted the ways in which sign, spoken, and written languages interact in multiple, complex, and fluid ways. She noted that bimodal bilingual deaf children 'translanguage "internally" as they use their own knowledge of one language to mediate learning in the other'. Within UTT, this description of children's linguistic processing is illegitimate because the bilingual's (deaf or hearing) linguistic system is undifferentiated, and therefore there are no distinguishable languages that can mediate learning in other languages. By contrast, Swanwick's account is obviously consistent with CTT in highlighting the dynamic interactions between languages in the bilingual's linguistic system.

In short, UTT theorists conflate 'additive bilingualism' with monoglossic, dual competence, or separate underlying proficiency conceptions of bilingualism despite the fact that the construct of 'additive bilingualism' has been invoked for more than 40 years to argue *against* separate underlying proficiency (Cummins, 1981a, 1981b) or *two solitudes* (Cummins, 2007) conceptions of bilingualism. These theorists offer no explanation as to why they interpret additive bilingualism exclusively as referencing patterns of internal cognitive *linguistic* processing rather than as part of the *social* and *instructional* landscape experienced by students and teachers at school. They acknowledge that 'named languages' are real and legitimate social constructs but it appears that the 'named languages' implied within the construct of 'additive bilingualism' can only be conceived as monoglossic constructs within the bilingual's internal cognitive/linguistic system and have no reality as social constructs.

The fact is that the construct of 'additive bilingualism' *implies nothing with respect to how bilinguals process languages*. No researcher who has invoked the construct of 'additive bilingualism' has claimed that additive bilingualism refers to the mental architecture underlying bilinguals' processing of language.

Thus, the conflation of additive bilingualism with monoglossic ideologies is arbitrary and unsubstantiated. It lacks credibility because it is simply asserted with no empirical evidence, analytic discussion, or qualifications. No research is cited by UTT advocates to support any connection between the construct of additive bilingualism and patterns of bilingual language processing *for the simple reason that there is none*. Within the oversimplified dichotomy of heteroglossic/monoglossic, a convincing case could have been made for the heteroglossic qualities of additive bilingualism, and teaching for crosslinguistic transfer, because of the intersection and interdependence of languages incorporated into these theoretical constructs.

In my reading, the basic (and legitimate) point that UTT advocates wish to convey is that the fluid language practices and varieties of all students (bilingual and monolingual) should be affirmed and built upon by schools in all programme types. Students' language repertoires should be actively acknowledged as crucial cognitive tools and intrinsic dimensions of their evolving identities. It is also valid to point out that some so-called bilingual programmes have failed to connect instruction to students' lives and affirm their linguistic talents. But it is logically problematic to make blanket assertions, with no qualifications, that *all* additive bilingual programmes, and *all* largely monolingual programmes that adopt an additive approach, marginalise students and stigmatise their fluid language practices.

Logical coherence in Flores and Rosa's claims

Flores and Rosa (2015) have made the blanket assertion that additive approaches to language education designed to promote biliteracy skills are inherently problematic because they are permeated by discourses of appropriateness fueled by raciolinguistic ideologies. This position implies that all researchers and educators who endorse additive approaches to students' language and culture are inadvertently complicit with these discourses of appropriateness and raciolinguistic ideologies. The fact that this is an extremely idiosyncratic perspective can be illustrated by comparing it to the description of additive bilingualism offered by critical theorists Sonia Nieto and Patty Bode in their influential book *Affirming Diversity: The Sociopolitical Context of Multicultural Education*:

> *Additive bilingualism* refers to a framework for understanding language acquisition and development that *adds* a new language, rather than *subtracts* an existing one. This perspective is radically different from the traditional expectation in our society that immigrants shed their native language as they learn their new language, English. ... Additive bilingualism supports the notion that two is better than one—that English *plus* other languages can make us stronger individually and as a society. (Nieto & Bode, 2018: 194) (emphasis original)

Before analysing Flores and Rosa's assertion regarding the racist nature of additive approaches to bilingualism, it is important to acknowledge the validity and relevance of some aspects of their analysis. For example, it is clear that raciolinguistic ideologies *do* exist and that they exert pernicious effects on minoritised students' academic engagement and achievement (e.g. Labov, 1972; Lippi-Green, 1997/2012; Motha, 2006). It has also been long recognised that ideologies of linguistic purism communicated by teachers to students can undermine bilingual students' confidence and competence in both their home and school languages. At this point, despite ongoing discriminatory instructional policies and practices within schools, there is no dispute among educational researchers and applied linguists that 'educators must recognise, validate, and build on the diverse and rich repertoire of language practices that multilingual learners bring with them to school' (Martin *et al.*, 2019: 26). Inspirational educators have been showing for many years how this can be implemented in linguistically diverse classrooms (e.g. Bartlett & García, 2011; Chow & Cummins, 2003; DeFazio, 1997; García & Sylvan, 2011).

Thus, Flores and Rosa's (2015) analysis is a useful reminder of the ongoing reality of both raciolinguistic ideologies and discourses of appropriateness. However, their claim that raciolinguistic ideologies and discourses of appropriateness are *intrinsically and inevitably* implicated in additive approaches to bilingualism and biliteracy is asserted without reference to any empirical evidence that would support this claim.

With respect to logical coherence, Cummins (2017b) pointed to numerous contradictions and inconsistences in the theoretical claims advanced by Flores and Rosa (2015). One inconsistency involves their claim that discourses of appropriateness permeate additive approaches to language education and their simultaneous claim that they are 'not suggesting that advocates of additive approaches to language education should abandon all of their efforts to legitimize the linguistic practices of their language-minoritized students' (2015: 167).

The first claim entails a blanket condemnation, without qualification or nuance, of all forms of additive approaches to language education on the grounds that these pedagogical directions are permeated by raciolinguistic discourses of appropriateness. The second claim suggests that under certain unspecified circumstances, additive approaches *can* be mobilised to legitimise the linguistic practices of minoritised students. However, this second claim, which contradicts the initial claim, cries out for clarification and elaboration. Does this second claim mean that teachers should abandon only *some* of their efforts to promote additive bilingualism? If so, which instructional components are problematic, and which are acceptable? Is it acceptable for teachers to promote reading, writing, and other academic skills together with additive forms of bilingualism so long as they also 'shift the focus to scrutiny of the white listening subject' (Flores & Rosa, 2015: 167)? If this is in fact the position that Flores and Rosa are advocating, it is unclear why they argue against additive approaches to bilingualism – their argument is against *uncritical* instructional approaches generally that fail to challenge coercive relations of power.

The argument that additive approaches to bilingualism are permeated by discourses of appropriateness and raciolinguistic ideologies invokes the following flawed logic:

Because
some educators who adopt additive approaches to minoritised students' bilingualism in both bilingual and English-medium programmes fail to affirm and build on students' language varieties and practices, thereby disparaging implicitly or explicitly, these language varieties and practices,

therefore
all educators who adopt additive approaches to bilingualism involving the sustained teaching of academic skills in two languages are complicit in the marginalisation of students' fluid language varieties and practices.

An additional issue with respect to logical coherence derives from the fact that more recent claims articulated by Flores (2019) regarding the construct of additive bilingualism appear to contradict his earlier analysis. Specifically, despite his earlier claim that discourses of appropriateness, fueled by raciolinguistic ideologies, permeate additive approaches to language education, he has more recently suggested that additive bilingualism is not necessarily infused with raciolinguistic ideologies. The limitation to additive bilingualism resides in the fact that it attributes the educational underachievement of Latinx students to linguistic difficulties rather than to racism:

> In short, from a raciolinguistic perspective, the limitation to additive bilingualism is not that it is 'infused with raciolinguistic ideologies' (Cummins, 2017, p. 415) but rather that it offers a purely linguistic analysis of a phenomenon that is highly racialized. Despite nods to structural inequality, at the core of additive bilingualism is a similar theory of change as the one that lies at the core of subtractive bilingualism – that the root of the problems confronted by Latina/o students is linguistic in nature. (Flores, 2019: 56)

Flores (2019) provides no rationale or explanation for reversing his assertion that additive approaches to bilingualism are permeated by raciolinguistic ideologies. But leaving aside that apparent reversal, one can ask about the validity of his claim that additive bilingualism offers a purely linguistic analysis of a highly racialised phenomenon. Obviously, the abstract concept of additive bilingualism is not making any theoretical claims and so the question becomes: To what extent do proponents of additive bilingualism offer a purely linguistic analysis of underachievement among Latinx students rather than identifying the racialised power structures that undermine students' academic engagement and achievement?

Clearly, some advocates of additive bilingualism focus largely on the linguistic and educational benefits of promoting biliteracy, but this is certainly not the case generally. For example, May (2014: 9) pointed out that despite the critique of additive bilingualism as monoglossic, the concept of additive bilingualism goes far beyond the monolingual orientation of much second language acquisition (SLA) theorising: 'the notion of additive bilingualism ... still presents a strikingly different basis for analyzing language learning than the monolingual norms, and related dismissal and/or subtractive views of bilingualism, found within mainstream SLA'. Similarly, the analysis of societal power relations and their impact on student/teacher identity negotiation discussed in Chapters 5 and 6 and in Cummins (1986, 2001a) integrates conceptions of additive bilingualism with a detailed analysis of how societal power relations are actualised through patterns of teacher-student identity negotiation in schools. Furthermore, as noted previously, I have long argued that linguistic factors, and specifically the flawed and evidence-free linguistic mismatch hypothesis, are entirely inadequate to account for the underachievement of Latinx and other minoritised students (e.g. Cummins, 1979a).

Consequential validity

With respect to consequential validity, the stigmatisation of additive bilingualism as monoglossic and implicated in 'watchful adherence' to standardised language norms raises the question of how this perspective should be communicated to educators who, for many years, have promoted additive bilingualism as a challenge to subtractive ideologies in schools. Attempts to convey this message are likely to result in pedagogical confusion on the part of educators, not least because it is simply inaccurate to claim, as UTT advocates do, that the construct of additive bilingualism necessarily and inevitably entails separate and non-interacting language systems. To the extent that 'additive bilingualism' has been integrated with the construct of the 'common underlying proficiency' or related constructs such as Baker's (2011) 'common operating system', it references bilingual language functioning as intersecting and interdependent systems within a shared conceptual space.

In their response to MacSwan (2017), Otheguy et al. (2019: 646–649) do address issues of consequential validity by discussing the 'pernicious' educational implications of adhering to the dual correspondence theory. They appear to categorise every researcher and theorist who does not explicitly endorse the unitary translanguaging theory as supporting the dual correspondence theory. The only problem with this rhetorical strategy is that, to my knowledge, *there are no researchers or theorists who support dual correspondence models of bilinguals' linguistic functioning.* In discussing these issues, the only researchers they mention as supporting dual correspondence are MacSwan (2017) and Cummins (2017b), both of whom have argued strenuously *against* dual correspondence models, which MacSwan labels 'dual competence' models and I have variously termed 'separate underlying proficiency' or 'two solitudes' models.

An additional issue concerning consequential validity faced by UTT advocates relates to the assessment of bilingual students' literacy attainment in L1 and L2 in bilingual programme evaluations and research. As noted previously, Otheguy et al. (2015: 293) claim that it is legitimate to make reference to 'named languages' in discussions of social identity and sociolinguistic behavior but not in discourse dealing with mental grammar. Because performance on a reading comprehension test or on academic language tasks such as the CALS-I scales (Phillips Galloway et al., 2020) would not normally be regarded as falling within the discourse domains of social identity or sociolinguistic behaviour, it is unclear whether it is even possible to make reference to this kind of language-specific literacy performance within the boundaries of UTT. If people do not speak languages, they presumably do not read or write languages, and thus to talk about Spanish reading comprehension or English writing abilities becomes meaningless.

An obvious consequence of this is that within the scope of UTT it would be illegitimate to discuss the vast majority of Spanish/English programme evaluations and research studies such as those reviewed in Chapter 9. Spanish-speaking parents who wonder about the wisdom of enrolling their child in a Spanish/English bilingual programme, such as the Literacy Squared programmes evaluated by Escamilla and colleagues (e.g. Escamilla *et al.*, 2014; Soltero-González *et al.*, 2016; Sparrow *et al.*, 2014) would be out of luck seeking advice from UTT theorists because there is nothing they can logically say about separate Spanish and English language and literacy abilities.

UTT advocates might argue that although assessment of separate Spanish and English literacy skills is illegitimate and invalid, for practical purposes we have to act as if these separate constructs meant something. This might explain why, despite their rejection of distinguishable languages operating in the bilingual's linguistic system, García and colleagues *do* assign credibility to bilingual education evaluation research that measures the two languages of instruction separately. For example, García and Woodley (2015: 139) review the major research and meta-analytic studies of bilingual education showing that 'students in bilingual programs outperform those in English-only programs on tests of academic achievement'. Academic achievement in these research studies typically refers only to achievement in *English*, which, within UTT, is a meaningless linguistic category.

The problem here is that after a while the pretense runs thin. We pretend for practical purposes that people speak languages even though we believe they don't. We praise our child for doing well on a Spanish test even though we know that there is no such thing as competence in the named language 'Spanish'. Spanish/English bilingual programmes would not exist in the United States if researchers had not been able to tell parents, policymakers, and the general public that there is unequivocal research evidence that children experience no adverse effects on their English language and literacy development despite spending 50% or more of their instructional time through Spanish. The constructs of linguistic interdependence and the common underlying proficiency came into being largely to explain these phenomena (see Chapter 3). As hypothesised by the interdependence hypothesis, minoritised students in bilingual programmes experience no adverse effects on development of language and literacy skills in the dominant language because they transfer conceptual and linguistic knowledge and skills across languages. It is not at all clear that the strictures of UTT would permit any discussion, let alone explanation, of crosslinguistic transfer because, as noted by García and Li Wei (2014), the construct specifies transfer across conceptually distinct languages.[6]

The most unfortunate aspect of the claims made by UTT theorists regarding the unitary/undifferentiated nature of the bilingual's mental grammar and the monoglossic nature of 'additive bilingualism', and its supposedly 'pernicious' and 'retarding' impact on minoritised students' linguistic and academic identity, is that the confusion these claims are likely to evoke among educators and policymakers is *completely unnecessary*. There is nothing to be gained theoretically or pedagogically from the assertion that 'bilingual people do not speak languages'. Similarly, the counter-intuitive and empirically unsupported claim that additive instructional approaches that promote biliteracy among minoritised students are essentially racist amounts to little more than an unqualified overgeneralisation that risks undermining the overall credibility of a critical translanguaging approach to teaching minoritised students. The rhetorical contortions required to justify these counter-intuitive and evidence-free positions rapidly reach a point of diminishing returns.

In short, the critique by UTT theorists of additive approaches to biliteracy, which reflect teachers' attempts to expand minoritised students' access to academic registers in both L1 and L2, has no empirical basis, is logically flawed, and devoid of clear pedagogical directions for educators. In the final section of this chapter, I briefly review a number of recently proposed theoretical frameworks that incorporate the construct of translanguaging. My goal is to assess the extent to which these frameworks are consistent with the theoretical propositions derived from UTT as compared to CTT.

Section 3. The Role of Translanguaging in Recent Multilingual Education Frameworks

A number of other theoretical approaches to multilingual education have been proposed during the past decade under the influence of García's (2009) elaboration of the construct of translanguaging. These include Creese and Blackledge's (2010) concept of *flexible bilingualism*, Cenoz and Gorter's (2014) *focus on multilingualism*, Slembrouck and colleagues' (2018) *functional multilingual learning*, Weber's (2014, 2015) *flexible multilingual education*, and the *holistic model for multilingualism in education* proposed by Duarte and Günther-van der Meij (2018). I briefly review the ways in which these authors integrate the construct of translanguaging into their frameworks. I also examine how translanguaging connects with earlier frameworks such as the *plurilingualism* framework developed by researchers associated with the Council of Europe (e.g. Beacco *et al.*, 2016; Council of Europe, 2020; Moore *et al.*, 2020; Piccardo, 2016) and Hornberger's (1989, 2003; Hornberger & Link, 2012) *Continua of Biliteracy*, which addresses in a comprehensive way the complexities of multiple forms of literacies in linguistically diverse contexts. All of these approaches view the boundaries between languages as permeable and share the goal of 'turning multilingualism into a powerful didactic tool' (Slembrouck *et al.*, 2018: 18). However, unlike UTT, these theoretical proposals do not propose an absolute *either-or* dichotomy between *language* and *languaging* or claim that the notion of *a language* is an illegitimate psycholinguistic construct.

Flexible/Functional Conceptions of Multilingualism in Education

Creese and Blackledge (2010)

Drawing on their ethnographic case studies of community-run complementary schools in the UK that taught Gujarati, Turkish, Bengali and Chinese to students from those language communities, Creese and Blackledge (2010) documented how teachers and students engaged in flexible bilingual interactions involving frequent translanguaging between the community language and English. They suggest that as participants engage in *flexible bilingualism*, the boundaries between languages become permeable. They note in relation to the transcript of a Gujerati- and English-speaking student, that she uses her languages to make meaning, transmit information, and perform identities drawing on her entire linguistic repertoire to connect with her audience.[7]

Although the instructional ideologies expressed by teachers were just as likely to endorse separation of languages as flexible bilingualism, the pedagogy observed by the researchers predominantly reflected the overlapping of languages rather than strict language separation. They conclude that 'flexible bilingualism is used by teachers as an instructional strategy to make links for classroom participants between the social, cultural, community, and linguistic domains of their lives' (2010: 112).

Slembrouck and colleagues (2018)

The *Functional Multilingual Learning* approach advocated by researchers from the University of Ghent in Belgium (e.g. Slembrouck *et al.*, 2018; Slembrouck & Rosiers, 2018) aims to move beyond the binary debate between L2-submersion provision for immigrant-background students and bilingual education programmes, which are often not feasible in linguistically diverse school contexts that might have up to 20 languages represented in individual schools. It proposes to bring a translanguaging focus into the classroom on the grounds that minoritised children's lifeworlds involve many forms of translanguaging, which are characteristic of multilingual spaces outside the context of the school. A major pedagogical aim for the school should be to unlock the learning potential of the translanguaging practices that multilingual students bring to the school. Slembrouck and Rosiers (2018: 183) characterise Functional Bilingual Learning as being 'primarily about the adoption of a positive orientation to the linguistic repertoires which children bring to school and a commitment to the productive exploitation of these repertoires as didactic capital, for example, as a scaffold for learning the language of schooling or, more generally for acquiring knowledge'.

Slembrouck and colleagues discuss their attempt to implement a functional multilingual approach in four primary schools in the Ghent area (see also Sierens & Van Avermaet, 2014). In two of the schools, the intervention included the teaching of Turkish literacy to students from Turkish home backgrounds. The outcomes of this 'Home Language in Education' (HLiE) project were mixed. No impact on Dutch reading comprehension was found among Turkish students as a result of the intervention but some other 'softer' benefits were noted:

> In the case of the HLiE project, the quantitative findings showed a growth in self-confidence among the learners. The qualitative findings point to enhanced well-being, and increase in commitment and the development of more interactive learning environments. (Slembrouck, 2018: 34)

The authors also reported that the intervention significantly changed teachers' perceptions of multilingual learners and the challenges they experienced in the school environment. In discussing the lack of impact on Dutch reading comprehension, Slembrouck *et al.* (2018) note that their quantitative research focused on capturing language-specific proficiency rather than multilingual competence, thereby reflecting the 'two solitudes' assumption that multilingual proficiency can be captured adequately by conducting tests in two languages, on separate occasions, and with separate instruments for each language. They conclude that they (and, I would add, applied linguists generally) are still quite a few steps removed from adequately conceptualising assessment of multilingual proficiency.

One additional framework (Weber, 2014, 2015) incorporates the notion of 'flexible bilingualism' as a central pedagogical concept.

Weber (2014, 2015)

Weber argued that what he calls *flexible multilingual education* programmes enable schools to fully acknowledge the hybrid and transnational linguistic repertoires that young people actually use in highly diverse societies. He points out that from a pedagogical point of view, monolingual instruction through the dominant language is the worst possible programme for fostering emergent bilingual and minoritised children's language development. Instead, teachers need to build on students' home language resources in order to further their acquisition of the dominant school language. The essence of flexible multilingual education, according to Weber (2015: 80) is that 'the good language teacher encourages the children to draw upon all the linguistic resources already at their disposal, thus enabling them to transfer knowledge from their first language(s) to the target language, and in this way improving and speeding up the process of language development'.[8]

Weber (2014, 2015) includes all the varieties of particular languages that learners speak as an integral part of their multilingual repertoire. He argues that the concept of translanguaging includes switching between standard and local varieties of a particular language. There is no such thing as a 'pure' language and certainly 'standard' forms of any particular language are not in any way superior linguistically or cognitively to non-standard or so-called dialectal varieties of a language. Thus, he argues that linguistic varieties exist on continua and are involved in a continuous process of contact and change. They constantly 'leak into each other' (2015: 31) because they are not clearly bounded entities.

Weber (2015), similarly to Otheguy *et al.* (2015), points out that the distinction between a 'language' and a 'dialect' is a matter of politics, as illustrated in the fact that somebody who speaks only Bavarian and Standard German would typically be considered monolingual, because 'Bavarian' is considered a dialect of German, whereas somebody who speaks Luxembourgish and German would be considered bilingual despite the fact that Luxembourgish and Bavarian are similarly distant from standard German. However, unlike Otheguy *et al.* who argue on this basis that 'languages' have no linguistic reality and consequently our mental grammar is unitary and undifferentiated rather than being populated by 'countable' linguistic entities, Weber suggests an alternative approach to mapping our linguistic resources, namely that we need to count *all* the languages and dialects in our linguistic repertoires:

> If the distinction between language and dialect is a matter of politics, then we cannot rely upon it for a definition of multilingualism. We will just have to include all the varieties that a person speaks, whether they are perceived as languages or dialects. (Weber, 2015: 29)

Holistic Conceptions of Multilingualism in Education

Cenoz and Gorter (2014)

In multiple publications Jasone Cenoz and Durk Gorter have proposed a holistic approach to multilingualism in education (e.g. Cenoz, 2013a; Cenoz & Gorter, 2011, 2014; Cenoz & Santos, 2020). A central concept is what they call *Focus on Multilingualism* which they relate to constructs such as 'flexible bilingualism' (Creese & Blackledge, 2010), 'translanguaging' (García, 2009), and continua of biliteracy (Hornberger, 1989). They distinguish three dimensions of this approach: (1) the multilingual speaker; (2) the whole linguistic repertoire and (3) the social context.

As noted by Grosjean (1982, 1989) and Cook (1992, 2007, 2016), *multilingual speakers* differ qualitatively from monolinguals in the ways they learn and use languages. They use their languages in dynamic and flexible ways for different purposes depending on the context and interlocutors. The focus on the multilingual individual's *whole linguistic repertoire* contrasts with what Cenoz (2013a) terms 'atomistic views of multilingualism' that analyse languages separately as independent entities. In fact, the boundaries between the languages of multilingual speakers are soft, and in communicating or carrying out academic tasks multilingual speakers draw on their entire linguistic repertoire using their languages as a resource. Finally, language practices always take place within particular *social contexts*, frequently involving multiple modalities in which the boundaries between languages and between different semiotic tools are often blurred.

The 'Focus on Multilingualism' framework involves a pedagogical emphasis on integrating the discrete languages of the school curriculum with the fluid discursive practices of multilingual students. Cenoz and Gorter (2014: 242) suggest that 'languages can be distinct entities because they are treated as such by social actors in the school context', but pedagogically, the erection of solid boundaries between languages is not helpful. They argue for a pedagogical translanguaging approach involving flexible crosslinguistic boundaries that actively promotes synergies between the different languages. Teaching for crosslinguistic transfer enables multilingual students to tap into their entire linguistic repertoire in ways that enhance their metalinguistic awareness and development of competence in all their languages.

Duarte and Günther-van der Meij (2018, 2020)

These authors have proposed an ambitious holistic model of multilingualism in education that was developed in collaboration with teachers in a design-based project in the Netherlands. The model incorporates translanguaging as a core instructional lens or approach. There are three major dimensions to the model proposed by Duarte and Günther-van der Meij (2018, 2020):

- The model focuses on effective approaches for both national minority groups and migrant students and can thus be applied to a wide variety of schools. Although not explicitly specified by Duarte and Günther-van der Meij, some aspects of the model (e.g. a focus on 'language awareness') could presumably also be applied to 'mainstream' instructional settings that are not characterised by significant linguistic diversity.
- The model addresses the multilingual attitudes, knowledge and skills of both teachers and students, and teachers are encouraged to

innovate in how they implement and combine different instructional strategies.

- The model distinguishes between five different approaches to multilingual education that range across a continuum between acknowledgement of different languages and their actual use in instruction. The five approaches are specified as language awareness, language comparison, receptive multilingualism, Content and Language Integrated Learning (CLIL), and 'Immersion'. The latter two categories involve use of officially recognised languages as mediums of instruction, whereas the other categories involve teachers engaging with languages they do not necessarily share with their students. Language awareness activities involve exploration of languages and dialects that students speak or that are present in the social environment (see Hélot *et al.*, 2018). Language comparison involves comparison by students of typologically related and unrelated languages. Receptive multilingualism involves fostering receptive skills among typologically similar languages as well as positive attitudes among students to language learning in general. CLIL involves teaching one or two content areas (e.g. Geography) through a target language with the goal of developing both content knowledge and language proficiency. Finally, 'immersion' appears to refer to an organised bilingual programme where a considerable amount of instruction is delivered through a language that is not the students' home language (such as French immersion programmes in Canada).

Duarte and Günther-van der Meij (2020) identify three different functions of translanguaging practices in school that can be implemented across the five different instructional contexts they identify:

- *Symbolic* functions aim to recognise and valorize migrant languages within mainstream education. Acknowledging students' languages in this way doesn't require the teacher to understand or speak students' languages.
- *Scaffolding* functions provide temporary but systematic bridges to support students in linking their existing multilingual repertoire to other school languages (e.g. the dominant language of schooling). The teacher is not required to know students' languages in order to encourage them to use their languages to learn or clarify content.
- The *epistemological* function of translanguaging involves the teacher using different languages for instructional purposes to enhance academic content and language knowledge.

Duarte and Günther-van der Meij (2018, 2020) have carried out several studies that investigate how teachers implement translanguaging strategies within the context of their holistic model. Over the course of a two-year project, teachers' attitudes towards migrant students' languages changed considerably such that by the end of the project all teachers were incorporating migrant students' languages into their lessons. Teaching for crosslinguistic transfer from the home language to Dutch emerged as a major focus of teachers' instruction. Duarte and Günther-van der Meij (2018: 34) quote a school principal involved in the project who highlighted the fact that migrant students' languages reinforce the learning of Dutch and Frisian rather than constituting a threat to these languages:

> Actually, we see that because the pupils are already familiar with certain concepts in their mother tongue, they can more easily link a second concept onto that and that enables us to compare languages in the middle and upper grades.

The framework proposed by Duarte and Günther-van der Meij (2018, 2020) has the advantage of being more detailed and comprehensive than many of the other approaches discussed above. The fact that it encompasses both students and teachers within its scope contributes to its usefulness. The explicit focus on forming researcher/educator partnerships in the development of both pedagogical activities and the theoretical framework itself reflects a perspective of 'teachers as knowledge generators' (Cummins, in press), which is likely to have contributed to the positive change in orientation towards multilingual students and their languages that the researchers documented.

However, in other contexts, the continuum from language acknowledgement to instructional use of multiple languages might look very different. For example, the category of 'receptive multilingualism' has not featured prominently in most other accounts of translanguaging pedagogy. There is also a certain disjunction between the initial three categories that are explicitly, but not exclusively, focused on the languages of migrant students and the language use categories of CLIL and 'immersion' that, in many contexts, tend to include primarily dominant group students and may, in fact, pay very little attention either to students' home languages or making connections between languages. Thus, it is not clear that the five categories actually form a continuum.

It is also unclear where larger-scale projects such as the creation of dual language books (e.g. Chow & Cummins, 2003; DeFazio, 1997; García & Sylvan, 2011) would fit on this continuum. These projects clearly go beyond 'language awareness' but do not fit easily into other categories on the continuum. Finally, it would be useful for Duarte and Günther-van der Meij to clarify what they mean by 'immersion'. The term is used in a variety of ways, sometimes as a problematic euphemism for 'submersion' (as is the case with 'structured immersion' in the United States context that refers to a monolingual programme with minimal if any instructional supports for minoritised students), sometimes to refer to L2 bilingual programmes intended primarily for dominant group students (e.g. Canadian French immersion programmes), and sometimes to refer to language revitalisation programmes that may include native speakers of both dominant and minority languages.

These minor concerns should not obscure the valuable contribution that Duarte and Günther-van der Meij's holistic model represents. But their framework illustrates the fact that models are likely to be context-specific and may need to be adjusted and/or re-invented to incorporate the sociopolitical and sociolinguistic realities of different educational situations. However, the collaboration between researchers and educators in the construction and mutual infusion of theory and innovative practice represents a knowledge-building process that can profitably be emulated elsewhere.

In the next section, two influential frameworks that predate the emergence of translanguaging as a central analytic construct are considered.

The Council of Europe's Construct of Plurilingualism

Around the same time as dynamic systems theories of bilingualism were being articulated (e.g. Herdina & Jessner, 2002), researchers associated with the Council of Europe elaborated the construct of *plurilingualism* to refer to the dynamically integrated and intersecting nature of the linguistic repertoires of bilingual and plurilingual individuals. These repertoires include unevenly developed, fluid, and constantly shifting competencies in a variety of languages, dialects and registers (Coste *et al.*, 1997/2009; Galante, 2020; Piccardo, 2013, 2016; Piccardo & North, 2020; Taylor & Snoddon, 2013). Because language users draw on the totality of their linguistic resources in both interpersonal and academic contexts, it follows that classroom instruction should encourage and promote this dynamic and integrated use of multiple registers and skills. Piccardo (2016: 7) expressed this point as follows: 'A plurilingual classroom is one in which teachers and students pursue an educational strategy of embracing and exploiting the linguistic diversity present in order to maximize communication and hence both subject learning and plurilingual/pluricultural awareness'.

The construct of plurilingualism provided a theoretical foundation for related Council of Europe initiatives such as the *Common European Framework of Reference for Languages* (CEFR: Council of Europe, 2001, 2020) and the *European Language Portfolio* (Little, 2005). These developments have injected new life into discussions of language teaching and bilingual education, particularly in the European context. Piccardo (2016: 16) documented many initiatives in curriculum development and instruction generated by discussion around the construct of plurilingualism that are 'potentially very inspiring for pedagogical innovation'. The plurilingualism framework also undergirds many of the impressive pedagogical innovations documented by researchers based in North America such as Galante (2020), Prasad (2016) and in the volume edited by Lau and Van Viegen (2020b).

The construct of plurilingualism is clearly compatible with translanguaging pedagogies insofar as both constructs embrace dynamic conceptions of bilingualism and porous boundaries across and within languages (e.g. 'monolingual' individuals' ability to shift from one register or social variety to another depending on context, interlocutors, and communicative demands). However, beyond these obvious compatibilities, some differences emerge.

Plurilingualism theorists associated with the Council of Europe have proposed a clear distinction between plurilingualism and multilingualism. The former is seen as expressing the mutual influence, interconnections, and dynamic relations among languages, registers, and dialects *within the individual* while the latter refers to the presence of languages *in the society*. However, many researchers (e.g. Conteh & Meier, 2014; May, 2014; MacSwan, 2017) do not accept the usefulness or legitimacy of this distinction and continue to use the term 'multilingualism' to refer both to societal multilingualism and to knowledge of multiple languages by individuals. These researchers all endorse dynamic conceptions of multilingualism (rather than 'multiple monolingualisms') and the pedagogical approaches they advocate are largely indistinguishable from those promoted by researchers who prefer the term 'plurilingualism'.

Some scholars (e.g. Flores, 2013; García, 2018, 2019) have critiqued the construct of plurilingualism, as conceived by the Council of Europe, on the grounds that it promotes a neoliberal corporate agenda. For example, García (2018: 883) argued that the construct ignores power imbalances between speakers of different languages and 'in today's globalized neoliberal economy, plurilingualism is exalted as a tool for profit making and personal gain'. In a similar way to critiques of 'academic language' and 'additive bilingualism', this claim confounds the *construct of plurilingualism*, as articulated in the scholarly literature (e.g. Piccardo & North, 2020), with the reality of ongoing social and educational policies and instructional practices that continue to marginalise minoritised students, communities, and their languages.

It is important to highlight the fact that within the Council of Europe's advocacy of plurilingualism the languages of immigrant-background and marginalised groups have been explicitly included (e.g. Beacco *et al.*, 2017; Little, 2010). For example, a commitment to legitimise migrants' linguistic repertoires is explicitly acknowledged in the Introduction to a volume that reported the proceedings of a symposium organised by the Council of Europe focused on the linguistic integration of adult migrants in Europe:

> Secondly, in the course of the symposium the role played by adult migrants' linguistic repertoires and language biographies was often stressed. There is in principle no contradiction between welcoming new languages and supporting plurilingualism on the one hand and helping migrants to acquire the language of their host country on the other. On the contrary, as a number of contributions show, the one supports the

other when teachers devise activities that give legitimacy to migrants' linguistic repertoires and exploit them in their classes. (Beacco *et al.*, 2017: 2)

The European Union has also funded a variety of research and development projects focused on topics such as *linguistically sensitive teaching* that explicitly explore how schools in multiple European countries can implement inclusive approaches to students' languages with particular emphasis on the diverse languages that migrant-background and minority group students bring to the school. For example, the *Linguistically Sensitive Teaching in All Classrooms* (http://listiac.org) project aims to help current and future teachers become more linguistically sensitive in their beliefs, attitudes, and actions.

In addition to the inaccuracy of claiming that academic writing and social policies deriving from the construct of plurilingualism ignore power imbalances, there are logical incongruities in implicating plurilingualism with a neoliberal corporate agenda. According to this logic, any set of skills or abilities (e.g. educational qualifications) that could qualify as economic cultural capital would be subject to the same problematic claims of neoliberal complicity. For example, because gaining a university degree is consistent with corporate priorities and contributes to a nation's economic development in a neoliberal society, should we then shut down universities? By the same token, because expanding our plurilingual abilities potentially contributes to social mobility and economic development, should we then stop teaching languages in schools and universities? The conflation of plurilingualism with a corporate neoliberal agenda is simply asserted, without empirical evidence, in these critiques and appears to me to be entirely unconvincing. Promotion of plurilingualism/multilingualism for *all* community groups, and especially among those who have been marginalised as a result of xenophobia and racism, clearly challenges the operation of coercive power relations in the broader society and is consistent with the way the construct has been employed in the academic literature (e.g. Galante, 2020; Lau & Van Viegen, 2020b; Moore *et al.*, 2020; Piccardo, 2016; Prasad & Lory, 2020).

García and Otheguy (2020) moderate their critique of plurilingualism somewhat in an article entitled 'Plurilingualism and translanguaging: Commonalities and divergences'. Rather than a blanket condemnation of the construct of plurilingualism as embedded in a neoliberal corporate agenda, García and Otheguy acknowledge the emphasis on linguistic rights promoted by the Council of Europe and the focus on extending the benefits of plurilingualism to refugees and black and brown immigrants. They claim that plurilingualism in language education has been a valuable construct and a big step forward: 'Plurilingualism insists on giving all students recognition of, and access to, their language practices and identities, even if, for those who are minoritized, these are only temporary benefits' (2020:

24). They claim that the focus is still on supporting minoritised students in gaining proficiency in the named national language: 'The emphasis is on changing refugee students' national and linguistic identities, rather than affirming theirs, even when those are leveraged temporarily at the beginning of the educational career' (2020: 23).

By contrast, according to García and Otheguy (2020: 32), the theoretical formulation of translanguaging has a transformative potential to affirm students' dynamic multilingual realities by disrupting the concept of named languages and the power hierarchies in which languages are positioned in ways that 'the concept of plurilingualism may not always do'. Despite this distinction between the two concepts, García and Otheguy acknowledge that plurilingual and translanguaging pedagogical practices sometimes look the same, and sometimes they even have the same practical goals:

> For example, educators who say they use plurilingual pedagogical practices might insist on developing bilingual identities, and not solely use plurilingualism as a scaffold. And educators who claim to use translanguaging pedagogical practices sometimes use them only as a scaffold to the dominant language, not grasping its potential. (García & Otheguy, 2020: 31)

In García and Otheguy's (2020) reformulation of Garcia's (2018, 2019) critique of plurilingualism, the differences between translanguaging and plurilingualism become truly nebulous. They acknowledge that it is essentially impossible to differentiate plurilingual from translanguaging pedagogical practices. They also acknowledge implicitly that both constructs can be aligned, or fail to be aligned, with transformative educational goals. The only difference, it appears, is that García and colleagues' conception of translanguaging dismisses the construct of 'languages' whereas this construct is not repudiated within plurilingual theory. As discussed previously, a credible case can be made that this theoretical claim undermines rather than strengthens the potential impact of the construct of translanguaging on educational policy and pedagogical practice.[9]

In contrast to researchers who condemn the construct of plurilingualism as inherently 'neoliberal' or as less pedagogically transformative than translanguaging, Kubota (2020: 317) has presented a more nuanced perspective that applies to both translanguaging and plurilingualism: 'To contribute to actual social change, translanguaging and plurilingualism need to find a closer synergy with critical multiculturalism, by exploring deeper questions of linguistic and cultural inequalities in relation to colonialism, imperialism, capitalism, and associated language ideologies'. Thus, rather than dismissing the *construct of plurilingualism* as irretrievably neoliberal, Kubota points to the theoretical embeddings and connections that are required for this construct, and the construct of 'translanguaging', to contribute to transformative social and educational change.

Other researchers who have adopted a plurilingual framework likewise see no theoretical or logical barriers to aligning it with a critical or transformative orientation to societal power relations. Englander and Corcoran (2019: 61), for example, argue that a 'critical, plurilingual approach challenges rather than reinforces particular inequitable and asymmetrical relations of power within the existing neoliberal world order'.

In one of the most insightful discussions of the origins of plurilingualism and its relationship to translanguaging, Danièle Moore, in conversation with Sunny Man Chu Lau and Saskia Van Viegen (Moore *et al.*, 2020), makes the point that there are minimal differences between translanguaging and plurilingualism either in theoretical orientation or pedagogical implications. Moore notes that plurilingual and intercultural education (PIE) focuses on the intertwined and interwoven conceptions of language usage and competence, thereby marking a clear break from educational visions of separate and isolated identifiable languages:

> Languages are viewed as, rather than separate entities in the brain, connected in multiple ways and having mutual and dynamic influence on one another. Rather than attempting to maintain learners' languages in isolation, and ignore various cultural ways of learning, teachers need to help learners to become aware of and draw on their existing knowledge and previous experience, in and out of school, and be encouraged to transfer them to new learning contexts. (Moore *et al.*, 2020: 39–40)

Moore notes that 'PIE promotes the interdependence between languages, disciplinary knowledge and semiotic means' (Moore *et al.*, 2020: 40) and she explicitly acknowledges its consistency both with Grosjean's (1989) wholistic view of bilingualism and Cummins' Common Underlying Proficiency model 'which points to the common underlying cognitive knowledge and abilities that bi/plurilingual individuals draw on for meaning making and language performance' (2020: 33). Both of these theoretical orientations theorise bilingualism as a combined repertoire of linguistic resources and they reject conceptions of bilingual competence as the simple sum of two monolingual, discrete competencies.

Hornberger's Continua of Bi/Multiliteracy

Nancy Hornberger's (1989) *Continua of Biliteracy* framework is undoubtedly the most comprehensive model of biliteracy and multiliteracies that has been proposed to date. Since its appearance more than 30 years ago, it has expanded and refined itself to accommodate new findings and perspectives, as any useful framework should. As part of this process, Hornberger and Link (2012) integrated the construct of translanguaging into the Continua framework and, in the process, expanded the scope and utility of both theoretical perspectives.

The essence of the Continua model is succinctly expressed by Hornberger and Link (2012: 268): 'The continua model posits that *what* (content) biliterate learners and users read and write is as important as *how* (development), *where and when* (context), or *by what means* (media) they do so' (emphasis original). The dimensions of content, development, context, and media are nested within each other and each is characterised by reciprocally intersecting continua. For *development*, language skills develop along L1/L2, receptive/productive, and oral/written continua. For *context*, the continua range from micro to macro, oral to literate, and bi(multi)lingual to monolingual. For *content*, the range extends from minority to majority perspectives and experiences, from vernacular to literary styles and genres, and from contextualised to decontextualised language texts. Finally, multiliteracies can be mapped along continua characterised by simultaneous to successive exposure, dissimilar to similar linguistic structures, and divergent to convergent scripts. Any literacy event or practice can be located within the multidimensional space provided by these intersecting continua and analysed from a variety of disciplinary perspectives.

Societal power relations are infused within the Continua such that the initial descriptors, outlined above, within the development, context, content, and media continua reflect traditionally less powerful literacy practices while the second descriptors, at the opposite end of the continuum, reflect traditionally more powerful practices. The mapping of the matrices generates opportunities for social and educational actors to open up implementational and ideological spaces within which inequities of access to powerful forms of language and literacies can be contested.

Hornberger and Link (2012: 268) note that translanguaging practices in the classroom 'have the potential to explicitly valorize all points along the continua of biliterate context, media, content, and development'. They analyse a variety of translanguaging scenarios to illustrate how translanguaging can be seamlessly integrated with the Continua framework. In a Foreword to Hornberger's (2003) edited volume, I summarised the potential of the framework as an analytic tool as follows:

> It has become a dynamic tool for mapping the literacy landscape and for highlighting the extremely limited conceptions of literacy embedded in many educational policies. Furthermore, it enables us to analyze with precision and detail the social injustices perpetuated by policies that intentionally eradicate the multilingual literacies that children bring to school. (Cummins, 2003: xi)

Summary: Recent Multilingual/Plurilingual Frameworks are Consistent with CTT

Very similar pedagogical assumptions underlie all of the frameworks and instructional approaches briefly reviewed in this section. These approaches incorporate translanguaging as a useful conceptual construct to highlight multiple ways in which the classroom learning environment can be expanded from a closed monolingual to an open multilingual space. Common to all of these perspectives is a commitment to connect instruction to the lives of minoritised students and to valorize the varieties of language they bring to the classroom. The frameworks also affirm the porous and constantly changing nature of languages and their dynamic and intersecting use by multilingual learners.

However, none of the frameworks suggest that 'languages' are devoid of linguistic reality or that teaching for crosslinguistic transfer is an illegitimate instructional exercise. Teaching for crosslinguistic transfer is explicitly highlighted in some accounts (e.g. Duarte & Günther-van der Meij, 2018). In others (e.g. Hornberger & Link, 2012; Slembrouck *et al.*, 2018), there is no hesitation in using terms such as 'home language' (L1) and 'school language' (L2). Hornberger's Continua framework explicitly distinguishes between vernacular and literary styles and genres, a distinction similar to the distinction made in the present volume between conversational and academic registers of language. Thus, these theoretical formulations can be seen as more consistent with CTT than with UTT.

Concluding Thoughts

This chapter has critically analysed two central claims of UTT: (a) the linguistic system (or 'mental grammar') of multilingual people is unitary and undifferentiated, reflecting the proposition that 'languages' have no linguistic or cognitive reality; (b) additive bilingualism represents an illegitimate monoglossic construct that is permeated by discourses of appropriateness fueled by raciolinguistic ideologies. As such, additive bilingualism is viewed as stigmatising the fluid multilingual practices of minoritised students and enforcing the imposition of standard languages and pedagogies of linguistic separation in bilingual programmes.

I argued that these claims are devoid of empirical support, are logically flawed, and detract from the implementation of powerful and effective multilingual pedagogies for minoritised students.

In contrast to UTT, CTT proposes that the construct of 'languages' *is* legitimate, and that people *do* speak languages, which to teachers and students are socially, linguistically, cognitively, instructionally and experientially real. UTT seriously misrepresents the claims of CTT when it characterises constructs such as 'additive bilingualism' and teaching for crosslinguistic transfer as 'monoglossic', and when it suggests that promotion of additive bilingualism entails the imposition of standard languages and pedagogies of linguistic separation. 'Additive bilingualism' is a sociolinguistic and sociopolitical construct that says *nothing* about the bilingual's mental grammar, linguistic processing, or cognitive architecture. It has been used almost exclusively over the past 40 years in the discursive context of challenging monolingual submersion programmes that promote subtractive bilingualism among minoritised students.

The 'additive bilingualism' construct also has no logical or intrinsic connection to the teaching of standard forms of L1 and L2. UTT advocates who have demonised the construct have not identified even one researcher who has claimed that additive bilingual programmes should teach only standard forms of L1 and L2 and exclude students' nonstandard varieties from the classroom. Obviously, this type of inappropriate instructional practice does occur in some monolingual and bilingual programmes (e.g. McCollum, 1999), but there is nothing in the construct of 'additive bilingualism' that endorses, supports, or implies such practices.

Likewise, the unqualified claim that additive approaches to minoritised students' bilingualism are permeated by raciolinguistic ideologies (Flores & Rosa, 2015) is simply asserted with no supportive analysis. It ignores the fact that additive approaches to minoritised students' culture and language explicitly challenge coercive power relations by asserting students' right to develop strong biliteracy skills and to have their home languages reinforced rather than undermined by the school system.

The problematic nature of many of the claims embodied in UTT can be traced to the binary dichotomy between monoglossic and heterglossic orientations to multilingualism that is at the core of the theory. Why should the theoretical constructs in CTT be categorised as 'monoglossic' rather than 'heteroglossic'? What is monoglossic about positing a shared conceptual, linguistic, and cognitive space where languages interact in dynamic ways and where two-way crosslinguistic transfer occurs? What is monoglossic about repudiating 'two solitudes' orientations to bilingual pedagogy in favour of bilingual instructional strategies and 'teaching through a multilingual lens' (Cummins, 2007; Cummins & Persad, 2014)?

These constructs are consigned to the monoglossic category because they maintain that languages have cognitive and linguistic reality in addition to social reality. In the eyes of UTT advocates, following Makoni and Pennycook (2005, 2007a), this disqualifies them from being categorised as heteroglossic. Once constructs such as additive bilingualism are identified as monoglossic, it follows that they are implicated in all of the oppressive practices and ideologies that are intrinsic to this designation.

But what if we regarded the heteroglossic/monoglossic distinction as a continuum rather than a dichotomy? In a similar way to the multiple continua discussed by Hornberger (1989), we could map different constructs and frameworks along the continuum without having to locate them in one of two binary categories. As depicted in Figure 10.2, CTT would be clearly identifiable as 'heteroglossic' insofar as it endorses both dynamic conceptions of bilingualism and translanguaging pedagogies focused on teaching for productive contact and active transfer across languages. These characteristics explicitly locate CTT in a different category from 'two solitudes' or 'dual correspondence' (Otheguy et al., 2019) models of bilingualism, especially since the 'common underlying proficiency' construct was proposed 40 years ago in direct opposition to

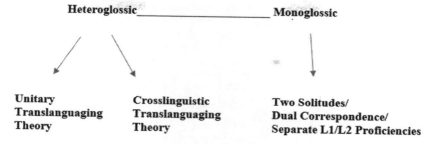

Figure 10.2 CTT conception of heteroglossic/monoglossic continuum with CTT located at the heteroglossic end of the continuum

'separate underlying proficiency' notions of bilingualism (e.g. Cummins, 1980c, 1981b). MacSwan's (2017) Integrated Model of Individual Bilingualism might occupy a similar location as a variant of heteroglossic conceptions of bilingualism that avoids the empirical and logical pitfalls of UTT. Both CTT and MacSwan's model posit shared and discrete linguistic resources rather than the unitary and undifferentiated model proposed by UTT advocates.

Within this conception, UTT and CTT could be seen as variations of a heteroglossic orientation to multilingualism with no need to consign CTT to a monoglossic category with all of the negative attributions that follow from that designation. Areas of difference between CTT and UTT such as the positing of fluid boundaries between languages (CTT) as compared to no boundaries and no languages (UTT) could be assessed on their merits with respect to empirical adequacy, logical coherence, and consequential validity, as this chapter has attempted to do.

The final chapter moves from analysis of theoretical concepts to description and analysis of instructional practice. As noted in previous chapters, theory and practice are infused within each other. Translanguaging theory has evolved from instructional practice, and has, in turn, guided instructional practice. The final chapter explores the inspirational work of teachers and school administrators with the goal of continuing the dialogue between practice and theory in which knowledge and insight are generated.

Notes

(1) For ease of expression, I am using the citation 'García and colleagues' to refer to the following publications that represent a sample of the extensive scholarly output produced by Ofelia García and colleagues over the past decade: Bartlett & García, 2011; Flores, 2019; Flores & Rosa, 2015; García, 2009, 2014, 2017, 2018, 2019, 2020; García & Woodley, 2015; García & Kleifgen, 2019; García & Kleyn, 2016; García & Lin, 2017; García & Li Wei, 2014; García & Otheguy, 2014; García & Sylvan, 2011; Kleyn, 2019; Martin *et al.*, 2019; Otheguy *et al.*, 2015, 2019.

(2) The distinction between UTT and CTT is not always clear even to those who appear to be generally supportive of García and colleagues' position. Bartlett and Koyama (2014: 246), for example, describe García's position as follows: 'Based on the belief

that bilinguals have two or more dynamically interdependent language systems whose interactions create new structures that are not found in monolingual systems, García (2014) has proposed a model of dynamic bilingualism'. This description is much more aligned with CTT propositions than with the unitary model espoused by García and colleagues. UTT proposes that there is just *one* dynamic undifferentiated language system and dismisses crosslinguistic positions that posit two or more dynamically interdependent and interacting language systems as 'monoglossic'.

(3) Many of the problematic claims in relation to additive approaches to bilingualism and raciolinguistic ideologies discussed in this chapter relate specifically to the prolific publications of Nelson Flores. I focus primarily on the Flores and Rosa (2015) article as representative of this work. I also locate this work within the general theoretical framework elaborated by García and colleagues on the grounds that these authors cite Flores' work extensively and have co-published with him. However, it is not clear that García would endorse all of the theoretical claims made by Flores. For example, Flores and Rosa's claim that additive approaches are embedded in discourses of appropriateness would also seem to apply to the book written by Bartlett and García (2011) entitled *Additive Schooling in Subtractive Times: Bilingual Education and Dominican Immigrant Youth in the Heights.*

(4) As noted previously, Skutnabb-Kangas (2009) made a similar point in the context of mother-tongue based multilingual education. She argued that Indigenous and minoritised peoples have the right to decide for themselves whether they have a named mother tongue(s) rather than these decisions being made by researchers or government administrators. She questioned the extent to which the voices of marginalised peoples are 'heard and respected by researchers and government representatives, or are they silenced, marginalised, ridiculed, stigmatised'? (2009: 57).

(5) Another example of inaccurate and empirically unfounded assertions about 'additive bilingualism' can be found in Flores and Schiessel's (2014) characterisation of the construct. They identify two monoglossic ideologies operating in educational policies and practices related to emergent bilingual students. The first approach is that of 'subtractive bilingualism' that argues for replacement of students' home language with the national or school language. Equally monoglossic is 'additive bilingualism' which they describe as follows: 'The second perspective is additive bilingualism, which explicitly rejects monolingualism but continues to reproduce monoglossic language ideologies by advocating the development of balanced bilingualism—equal competencies in two languages' (2014: 457). I have searched the research literature published over the past 40 years and have found no instance of the many researchers who invoke the construct of 'additive bilingualism' linking it with the development of 'balanced bilingualism'. As discussed previously, researchers who have invoked the construct of 'additive bilingualism' advocated for continued development of emergent bilinguals' home language while they were acquiring the school language, but they did not conflate 'balanced bilingualism' with 'additive bilingualism'. From the early 1980s, the notion of 'balanced bilingualism' was increasingly recognised as a problematic and not particularly useful construct (e.g. Baker, 2001). Thus, contrary to what Flores and Schiessel assert, 'additive bilingualism' does not imply 'balanced bilingualism', and there is no logical or empirical connection between the two constructs.

(6) In many contexts of assessment, tests administered in separate languages underestimate emergent bilinguals' competence in both languages, particularly if the scores are interpreted in relation to monolingual norms (e.g. Cummins, 1984a). In recent years, within the fields of applied linguistics and educational psychology, researchers have explored the feasibility of both formative and summative multilingual assessment in order to address this issue (e.g. Flores & Schissel, 2014; Monsrud *et al.*, 2019; Muñoz-Sandoval *et al.*, 1998; Schissel *et al.*, 2018, 2019; Shohamy, 2006, 2011). Although

attention to this issue is important, we are likely still a long way from any feasible implementation of widespread multilingual assessment. In the meantime, separate assessment of bilingual students' language and literacy skills is likely to remain the norm in most educational contexts. Furthermore, in programme evaluation research, policymakers, educators, and parents typically and legitimately want to know how well students' proficiency and literacy in each language has developed since most bilingual programmes aspire to develop students' abilities to function academically at a high level in each language.

(7) Creese and Blackledge (2010) note that at the time of this interaction, this Gujerati- and English-speaking student may not have been explicitly aware of Gujerati and English as distinct languages. Similarly, for many of the Spanish-speaking communities in New York City studied by García and colleagues, there may be minimal consciousness on the part of speakers regarding which languages or combinations of languages they are using on any particular occasion. In these situations, this is typical of the fluid translanguaging practices that constitute what Lewis *et al.* (2012a) labelled 'universal translanguaging'. However, it is problematic to generalise from these situations to *all* contexts of spoken and written language use. For example, students and individuals who are learning an additional language are typically very conscious of the cognitive effort they are making to internalise its features and they are also sometimes painfully aware of what they can and cannot do with the language in comparison to what they can do in their home or stronger language (see Aminah's and Hira's reflections about English and Urdu in Chapter 3, Footnote 4).

Similarly, in discussing critical plurilingual pedagogies related to academic publishing in English by speakers of other languages, Englander and Corcoran (2019) make it clear that scholars are very conscious of which language they use for which purposes, and they also see clearly the power imbalances and burdens placed on those who use English as an additional language: 'When writing in English for scholarly publication, adherence to the gatekeepers' notion of Standard English in the text may be the most advantageous. However, conducting research, thinking about data, planning papers and writing them may be performed with any and all the language resources available' (2019: 61).

(8) Weber's use of the term 'multilingual education' differs from its use in the present volume where it refers to the use of two or more languages as mediums of instruction with the purpose of developing literacy and academic knowledge in multiple languages. His construct of flexible multilingual education refers not to a formal bilingual or multilingual education programme, but to what in this volume has been variously termed 'translanguaging pedagogy', 'multilingual learning', 'crosslinguistic pedagogy' or 'bilingual instructional strategies'. These pedagogical approaches promote classroom instruction that acknowledges, engages, and promotes the multilingual repertoires of students in linguistically diverse schools.

Weber also sets up a problematic opposition between 'flexible multilingual education' and 'mother-tongue education programmes' which he interprets as focusing on maintaining or revitalising particular minority languages rather than prioritising the educational success of the individual student. This is certainly not the understanding of 'mother-tongue based multilingual programmes' reflected in the writings of those who have written extensively on the topic (e.g. Benson, 2019; Benson *et al.*, 2012; Heugh, 2011a; Heugh *et al.*, 2012; Skutnabb-Kangas, 2000, 2009, 2015). The programmes discussed and evaluated by these researchers have been focused directly on promoting equitable educational opportunities and academic success for minoritised students in low-resource and postcolonial contexts.

(9) In discussing the sociopolitical motivations and impact of different forms of bilingual and second language programmes, García and Otheguy (2020) make some inaccurate

claims regarding the history and global impact of Canadian French immersion programmes:

> In Québec in 1974, the Francophone numerical majority gained political control with the rise to power of the Québecois party. As a result, some powerful Anglophone parents demanded that the school system develop the bilingualism of their children. Immersion bilingual programs were organized, in which Anglophone children were first taught only in French. ...
>
> It is this Canadian immersion model that has spread today to the so-called English-medium instruction (EMI) programs that have proliferated all over the world, especially in Asia. These programs are fueled by the desire to teach English so as to facilitate access to the symbolic goods that English supposedly represents. (García & Otheguy, 2020: 19)

The first French immersion programme in the St. Lambert suburb of Montreal started in 1965 long before the Parti Québecois came to power. The activist parents whose efforts *during the early 1960s* resulted in the initial programme were not motivated by any immediate political issues. Rather, they were 'frustrated by the limited opportunities that existed for their English-speaking children to learn fluent French' (Jezer-Morton, 2020).

The claim that Canadian French immersion programmes provided the model for the global spread of English-medium 'immersion' programmes is also inaccurate. Monolingual English-medium (L2) programmes, whether implemented as submersion programmes in postcolonial contexts in Africa or South Asia, or in international schools serving an affluent clientele, are entirely different from the French immersion model which strongly promotes students' (English) home language after the initial 'immersion' in French in kindergarten and Grade 1. Typically, L1 English-medium instruction is introduced in Grade 2, and by Grade 4 the instructional time allocation has become 50% English and 50% French. In other words, French immersion programmes are bilingual programmes, taught by bilingual teachers, whose goal is bilingualism and biliteracy. They are quite distinct in theory and implementation from the problematic monolingual English-medium programmes cited by García and Otheguy (2020).

García and Otheguy also attribute the problematic instructional philosophy of language separation that characterized the initial French immersion programmes (and is still dominant in these programmes) to the influence of additive bilingualism. They point out that the 'process was completely reliant on the philosophy of additive bilingualism' (2020: 19). The fallacious logic in this claim is immediately evident in the fact that the term additive bilingualism was not coined until a decade after the French immersion programmes were initiated. Thus, the instructional separation of languages in French immersion programs could not have been reliant on the philosophy of additive bilingualism because the construct did not exist at the time these programmes were started. In their evaluation of the initial St. Lambert immersion programme, Lambert and Tucker (1972) made no reference to the notion of additive bilingualism.

Furthermore, Lambert (1974, 1975) articulated the distinction between additive and subtractive bilingualism with specific reference to the subtractive experiences of minority groups who were forced to replace their languages with the dominant language. He argued that the 'important educational task of the future, it seems to me, is to transform the pressures on ethnic groups so that they can profit from an *additive* form of bilingualism' (1975: 68) (emphasis original). Thus, as argued throughout this volume, the construct of additive bilingualism is rooted, from its origins, in a sociopolitical challenge to the subtractive societal and educational forces, operating over generations, that robbed minoritised students of their culture and languages.

Part 3

Instructional Practice in Dialogue with Theoretical Concepts

Introduction

This final section, comprising just one lengthy chapter, focuses on instructional practice, and engages with the following questions: (1) What are the implications for instructional practice of the theoretical concepts and analysis discussed in preceding chapters? and (2) How does practice inform theory? As discussed in Chapter 7, this book is written from the perspective that theory and instructional practice are infused within each other. The theoretical issues discussed in the preceding chapters have been informed by instructional practice, and in turn, the theoretical constructs and frameworks that have emerged from observations of practice are designed both to account for the observed reality and also to guide educational policies and instructional practices.

The instructional examples of transformative pedagogy, including translanguaging/crosslinguistic pedagogy, described in this section illustrate the dialogical relationship between practice and theory. All the initiatives were implemented with the broad goal of engaging multilingual and/or minoritised students actively in the learning process as a means of promoting academic success. They can readily be described in relation to the eight instructional strategies outlined in Table 6.2 and Table 8.1. Some initiatives incorporate most of these instructional strategies while others reflect just a single strategy. Several initiatives described in this chapter were conceived and implemented primarily by teachers prior to the emergence of translanguaging as a potent theoretical concept. Others were directly influenced by the theoretical elaboration of the translanguaging concept by García and colleagues. The projects that preceded the emergence of translanguaging reflected teachers' general understanding of the relevance of students' home languages for their educational success, but they broke new ground in showing how students' knowledge of multiple languages could be harnessed productively in the classroom even when teachers did not speak most of these languages.

Two broad themes run through the projects described in Chapter 11. I have labelled these themes (1) *Actuality implies possibility* and (2) *Teachers as knowledge generators*. In the sections below, I describe these themes with specific reference to the Canadian context, but I believe that they are equally applicable to crosslinguistic and culturally sustaining instructional initiatives that have been implemented internationally (see, for example, Mary *et al.*, 2021).

Actuality Implies Possibility

Educators' orientation to linguistic diversity in Canadian schools has gone through several stages over the past 50 years. In the case of multilingual students from immigrant backgrounds, monolingual assumptions dominated instructional practice until the 1980s. It was common for teachers to encourage multilingual students to use only English (or French in Quebec) in school and teachers sometimes reprimanded or even punished students for non-compliance. Teachers and other school personnel (e.g. psychologists, school leaders) frequently advised parents to switch to the school language in their interactions with children at home.

As research emerged highlighting both the benefits of bi/multilingualism for children's academic and cognitive development and the destructive influence of language loss for children's communication with parents and grandparents in the home (e.g. Wong Fillmore, 1991, 2000), these discriminatory practices gradually faded and teachers became more tolerant of students' occasional use of their home language in school. Most teachers no longer suggested to parents that they should switch to English or French in the home. However, teaching in school remained monolingual. English or French were used exclusively in mainstream instruction partly because there seemed to be no way that students' home languages could be integrated into the classroom since teachers did not speak these languages. Ironically, the fact that provincially funded heritage language programmes operated in several provinces outside of regular school hours communicated to mainstream classroom teachers that they did not need to concern themselves with students' home languages (Cummins & Danesi, 1990).

Gradually, this orientation, which I have labelled 'benign neglect' (Cummins, 2019), began to change in the late 1990s when educators and university-based researchers, working in collaboration, started to explore the possibilities of bringing students' home languages and the dominant school language into productive contact. Twenty years later, a wide range of projects carried out across Canada (and elsewhere) have documented the feasibility and effectiveness of crosslinguistic pedagogy in multilingual classroom contexts where teachers do not speak the languages of most of their students (see Appendix 11.1).

With respect to knowledge mobilisation – the translation of research into instructional practice – the logic underlying the impact of these projects on educational policy and instructional practice can be expressed as *actuality implies possibility*. Educational initiatives that have been successfully implemented or 'actualised' in one context can, in principle, be implemented elsewhere. Successful implementation in a particular context demonstrates proof of concept. Context is clearly important in the sense that initiatives implemented in one context are likely to require modification in other contexts. But the projects summarised in this section demonstrate that it is no longer possible to claim that multilingual students' home languages cannot be integrated productively into classroom instruction.

Teachers as Knowledge Generators

As noted in Chapter 7, the role of teachers as knowledge generators is explicitly incorporated into the criterion of consequential validity which assesses the usefulness of a theoretical construct or claim for pedagogical practice. In the context of educating multilingual students, teachers have contributed to knowledge and theory generation by demonstrating the feasibility and impact of connecting instruction to students' lives (e.g. Denos *et al.*, 2009; Norton & Tembe, 2020) and by implementing translanguaging/crosslinguistic instructional approaches (e.g. CUNY-New York State Initiative on Emergent Bilinguals, 2021; García & Kleyn, 2016.) Teachers also have a clear role to play in assessing the credibility of theoretical claims advanced by researchers. Some of these claims immediately lose credibility when subjected to classroom reality checks. This is illustrated by claims discussed in previous chapters such as the claim that promotion of additive bilingualism is permeated by raciolinguistic ideologies, or that teaching for crosslinguistic transfer reflects a monoglossic orientation to language, which renders it an illegitimate instructional practice.

Researchers are likely to take the initiative in pursuing the other two criteria for evaluating theoretical constructs and claims discussed in Chapter 7. They have the expertise and opportunity to carry out empirical research (or review existing research) with the goal of assessing the extent to which theoretical claims are supported by empirical data. Because their job descriptions typically involve scholarly publication, they may also have more opportunity than teachers to analyse the logical coherence of theoretical propositions. However, in the context of educational research, the criteria of empirical adequacy and logical coherence are incomplete by themselves. Our knowledge of effective practice in teaching plurilingual/multilingual learners, as well as in other spheres of instruction, will advance only when these criteria are aligned with the criterion of consequential validity in a dialogue between theory, research, policy, and practice.

The recent experience of multilingual instructional projects described in this section illustrates the powerful impact generated by collaboration between educators and researchers. By the same token, failure to engage in this two-way collaborative dialogue, and subject theoretical propositions to classroom reality checks (consequential validity), risks undermining the credibility of theoretically important constructs such as translanguaging and raciolinguistic ideologies.

At this point, the number of published projects involving crosslinguistic pedagogy, broadly defined, is far too extensive to describe in any detail. I have chosen to describe several projects in some detail and to summarise others briefly in Appendix 11.1. I have organised the projects that I describe in more depth according to those that were implemented prior to the explosion of attention to the concept of 'translanguaging' and those that were strongly influenced by the emergence of that construct subsequent to García's (2009) book. A large majority of both earlier and more recent projects involve collaboration between educators and university-based researchers, but the earlier projects show clearly the primary role of teachers as knowledge generators whose instructional initiatives have contributed to theory, whereas in the later projects the theoretical elaboration of 'translanguaging' has typically acted as a catalyst or at least a significant influence on the instructional initiatives pursued by educators.

11 Teachers as Knowledge Generators: Learning from Inspirational Pedagogy

During the past 25 years, a large number of books and articles have been published documenting innovative approaches to teaching multilingual and minoritised students. The projects that have given rise to this documentation fall into two broad overlapping categories. Some projects have focused on translanguaging and/or crosslinguistic pedagogy with the goal of engaging students' multilingual resources. These projects can, in principle, take place both in bilingual/L2 immersion programmes and in programmes involving students from multiple language backgrounds taught primarily or exclusively through the dominant school language. Most of the documented projects, with some exceptions (e.g. Lyster *et al.*, 2009), fall into the latter category partly because 'two solitudes' assumptions have been the norm in many bilingual and L2 immersion programmes.

The second category of projects have focused on what we have called *identity texts* (e.g. Cummins, 2004; Cummins & Early, 2011), which were described in Chapter 6. These projects extend the classroom instructional space to enable students to engage in creative writing and artistic endeavours that express and affirm their emerging academic and personal identities. These projects frequently involve multiple languages, but the concept of 'identity texts' is equally applicable to monolingual as well as multilingual contexts.

An additional difference between the two categories of project that are considered in this chapter is that translanguaging initiatives can include relatively 'small steps' that focus on developing language awareness and curiosity (e.g. Duarte & Günther-van der Meij, 2018; Majima & Sakurai, 2021) whereas identity text projects are usually more sustained with a focus on individual and collective creative products or artifacts that hold a mirror up to students in which their identities are reflected back in a positive light. Despite these differences, many of the projects and instructional initiatives considered in this chapter fall into both categories.

The first section lays out a broad map of the translanguaging/identity texts landscape with instructional initiatives discussed in relation to four categories that vary in complexity from simple activities to sustained projects. I then examine in more depth several of the early projects implemented prior to the emergence of the theoretical construct of 'translanguaging'. Some of these projects were written up and published after translanguaging emerged as a descriptive and interpretive lens but the instructional innovations were initiated by educators motivated to engage multilingual students in learning and affirm their identities. More recent translanguaging and identity text projects are then examined. The initiative for these projects often came from university researchers influenced by the theoretical conceptualisation of translanguaging articulated by García and colleagues. The final section changes the lens to examine various translanguaging and identity text initiatives in relation to the evidence-based instructional responses articulated in the framework for reversing underachievement discussed in Chapter 6.

Section 1. Teaching Through a Multilingual Lens: Four Categories of Instructional Initiative

Four categories of teaching through a multilingual lens can be distinguished (Cummins, 2014b). These range from the very simple to the more elaborate and can be implemented in both primary and secondary schools across the grade levels. These categories could be used as an initial, somewhat crude, tool for educators who are committed to pursuing *Language Friendly* initiatives in their schools to think about what the notion of a *language friendly school* implies in actuality (Le Pichon *et al.*, 2020: see http://languagefriendlyschool.org):

- Simple everyday practices to make students' languages visible and audible within the school.
- Encouraging students to use their home languages for typical school activities such as reading, research, note-taking.
- Using technology in creative ways to build awareness of language, geography, and intercultural realities.
- Dual language project work.

Simple Everyday Practices to Make Students' Languages Visible and Audible Within the School

Although the activities listed below can easily be implemented in any school context, their symbolic value for students and communities should not be underestimated. They illustrate how teachers can build powerful relationships with their students by implementing policies and practices that explicitly acknowledge students' languages and cultures within the school.

(1) Each day, one or more students brings a word or phrase from their languages into the classroom and explains why they chose that word/phrase and what it means. All students and the teacher learn the word or phrase and its equivalent in the school language. The multilingual words and translations into the school language that the class has learned can be displayed in a 'multilingual corner' in the classroom. The words can also be included in a computer file that can be printed out or displayed on a smartboard on a regular basis for review by students and teachers.

(2) All students including the teacher learn simple greetings (e.g. hello, thank you) in the languages of the classroom. Students who speak these languages are the 'teachers'. The 'teachers' can also show their peers and teacher how to write a few simple expressions in different scripts (e.g. Arabic, Chinese, Greek, etc.).

(3) During the morning announcements or school assemblies, students and/or teachers give greetings and say a few words in different languages (with follow-up translation in the school language).

(4) Examples of students' work in both school and home languages are prominently displayed in classrooms, in school corridors and at the entrance to the school in order to reinforce the message to parents, grandparents, caregivers, community members, and students that students' linguistic talents are seen as educational and personal assets within the school.

(5) School signs (e.g. for the main office) are displayed not only in the school language but also in languages of the community (see Figure 11.1). Students could also be invited to construct and display multilingual versions of other signs in the school (e.g. Exit signs).

These simple activities have the potential to sensitise students to the sounds and writing systems of different languages and counteract the ambivalence and even shame that many students develop in relation to their languages. The acceptance of students' languages within the classroom can also be linked to other curricular content. For example, if a Syrian student has brought an Arabic word to share with the teacher and her classmates, the activity could be extended to showing where Syria is on a map of the world and explaining some salient aspects of its culture and history. These kinds of activities contribute not only to building students' (and teachers') awareness of language but also to their knowledge of geography and other cultures.

The celebration of students' languages within the classroom is illustrated in the wall display depicted in Figure 11.2 from Perminder Sandhu's grade 4 classroom. In Perminder's classroom, students wrote about their languages, discussed the importance of continuing to speak their languages, and worked in pairs to create dual language and multilingual books, often with the help of their parents (see Giampapa, 2010; Giampapa & Sandhu, 2011; and http://www.multiliteracies.ca/index.php/folio/view-Document/38/11470). She clearly articulated the ways in which active

Figure 11.1 Multilingual sign for the school office in Crescent Town Public School, Toronto District School Board. The School Board supplies these signs in up to 10 languages for any school that requests them. Photo credit, Jim Cummins.

promotion of students' linguistic and cultural capital represents a process of negotiating identities:

> It informs my practice through and through. It runs in the bloodstream of my classroom. It's all about relationships, how we validate students' identities, how they accept their own identities. That ethos is fundamentally important—it is not an add-on. (Cummins *et al.*, 2005:42)

Figure 11.2 Celebration of students' languages in Perminder Sandhu's Grade 4 class in Coppard Glen Public School. Photo credit, Jim Cummins.

Students Use Their Home Languages for Reading, Research, Note-Taking and Other Academic Work

(6) Teachers can encourage newcomer and bilingual students to use the internet to access home language resources relevant to their schoolwork. This might involve activating and expanding their background knowledge of content (e.g. researching cell structure and function in the human body). Building up students' L1 knowledge in this way will make content and texts in the school language more comprehensible and promote two-way transfer across languages. Online curricular resources in multiple languages are available through programmes such as Binogi (www.binogi.com).

(7) Teachers can invite newcomer and bilingual students to use their home languages for group planning of projects that will be presented to the wider class in the school language. In these cases, students' limited knowledge of the school language does not prevent them from using their full cognitive capacities in carrying out the project. Figure 11.3 illustrates this process in the context of a project where students explored similarities and differences between their home languages and English.

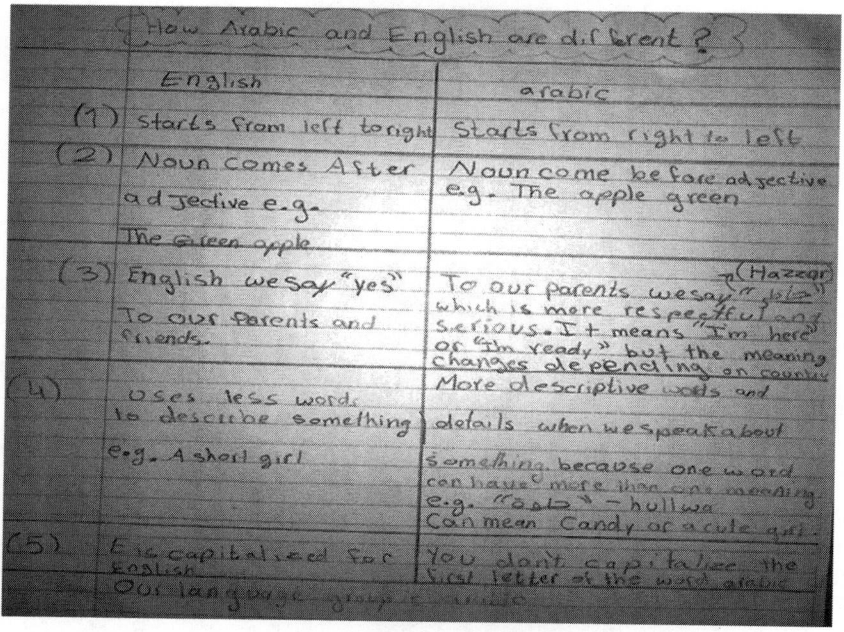
How Arabic and English are diffrent ?

	English	arabic
(1)	Starts from left to right	Starts from right to left
(2)	Noun comes After adjective e.g. The green apple	Noun come before adjective e.g. The apple green
(3)	English we say "yes" To our parents and friends.	To our parents we say "[illegible]" (Hazeer) which is more respectful and serious. It means "I'm here" or "I'm ready" but the meaning changes depending on country
(4)	uses less words to describe something e.g. A short girl	More descriptive words and details when we speak about something because one word can have more than one meaning e.g. "[illegible]" – hullwa Can mean Candy or a cute girl.
(5)	E is capitalized for English	You don't capitalize the first letter of the word arabic

Our language group is arabic

Figure 11.3 Grade 4 Arabic-speaking English learners in Robin Persad's class at Thornwood Public School, Peel District Board of Education, compared features of English and Arabic. Reprinted with permission of Robin Persad.

(8)   Teachers can encourage parents or caregivers of newcomer students to read and/or tell stories in the home language to their children. Children can also be encouraged by parents and teachers to engage in shared storytelling and/or reading in the home both with parents and siblings. These activities expand home language knowledge into literate spheres and also expand children's knowledge of the world.

(9)   It is important to ensure that the school library has a good collection of home language and dual language books for students to check out and read. Figure 11.4 shows part of the home language book collection in Crescent Town school in Toronto. The school used some of the additional funds it received as an inner-city school to keep the school library open after normal school hours between 4pm and 7pm several days per week in order to encourage parents to use the library with their children after they picked them up from school (see Cummins *et al.*, 2015 and Markus *et al.*, 2021, for additional initiatives from Crescent Town and other schools in the Toronto District School Board).

Dual language books written by students in the school can also be included in the school or classroom library (see Chow & Cummins, 2003). The school could also work with parents to set up a home language book exchange in the school library where parents could donate home language books that their children have finished reading or have grown out of. Other parents could then borrow these books to read at home with their children. The advantage of this kind of initiative goes beyond just providing children with reading materials in their home language; it also promotes genuine collaboration between parents and the school, communicates to parents the importance of reading with children and actively developing their children's home language abilities.

Figure 11.4 Library books in multiple languages, Crescent Town Public School, Toronto District School Board. Photo credit, Jim Cummins.

(10) Teachers can invite community members to come to class to read and/or share their stories in the school language or community languages (e.g. about coming to a new country) (Naqvi *et al.*, 2015). If the visitor uses a community language, translation can be provided by the community member himself or herself or by other multilingual individuals who speak that language (e.g. a home language teacher or bilingual parents). Naqvi and colleagues (2013) have reported that this kind of classroom exposure to literacy in multiple languages results in stronger linguistic growth.

(11) In social studies at upper primary or high school levels, teachers can encourage students to research curriculum content, social issues and current affairs using internet sources in their home languages. For example, TED talks are available through subtitles and transcripts in more than 100 languages. Arabic subtitles are available for more than 8,000 TED talks. Parents can be encouraged to get involved in this process by watching videos or TED talks and discussing them with their children. Students then bring this information back to class and differences in perspectives across different languages, cultures, and ideologies can be discussed.

(12) In science, multilingual students can be encouraged to use their home languages in project work. For example, if students were working in groups to create posters of the various bodily systems (e.g. respiratory system, digestive system, etc.), students could label the various organs and parts of the body in their home languages as well as in the school language. Students could then use these posters to teach a lesson on the human body for younger students in the same school.

(13) Initiatives pursued by Rania Mirza, at the time a teacher in the York Region District Board of Education, included having volunteer students teach their languages to other students during the lunch break, and encouraging students to keep a travel journal, written in whatever language they choose, when they visit their countries of origin during school holidays. Rania also encouraged newcomer students to use L1 diaries to reflect on their learning and to become aware of differences and similarities between their L1 and English (Cummins *et al.*, 2012). American teacher, Lori Langer de Ramirez (2012) has also described the operation of student-run language classes in Herricks Public Schools in Long Island, New York.

Teachers and Students Use Technology in Creative Ways to Build Awareness of Language, Geography and Intercultural Realities

(14) Encourage students to use Google Translate (www.translate.google. com) or other free translation web sites for a wide variety of purposes. For example, newcomer students could write a story or text in their home language and then use Google translate to generate a

rough version in the school language. This rough version is usually sufficient to enable the teacher and other students to understand what the student is trying to express. The teacher and/or other students can then help the newcomer student edit this rough version into coherent text in the school language.

(15) Google Earth can be used to 'zoom into' the towns and regions of students' countries of origin. Students can compare aspects of their countries of origin to the social, geographical, and climate realities of their new country. For example, in the study of history, students from particular language groups could work together to create a timeline showing what was happening in their countries of origin at particular stages of history. In science, students could investigate what the effects of climate change are likely to be in their countries of origin in comparison to their new country.

(16) Students' languages can be integrated in creative ways into a variety of content instruction. For example, grade 5 teacher Tobin Zikmanis at Thornwood Public School taught a Data Management mathematics unit using data from a language survey of the entire school's student population carried out by his students. Students generated three questions for the survey and collected the data working in small groups. After compiling the data, they then used spreadsheet software to generate a variety of graphs (e.g. pie charts, bar graphs) to display and disseminate their findings (see Figure 11.5). Zikmanis (personal communication) reported that students were so engaged in analysing their data that many of them did not want to go out for recess. A variety of mathematics activities could be carried out using this kind of data (e.g. probability of students in a class speaking particular languages).

Dual Language Project Work

(17) Students can write and web-publish dual language books or web-publish curriculum-related project work using programmes such as PowerPoint. Students can also create videos using iPads or similar technologies. For example, in Floradale Public School near Toronto, teacher-librarian Padma Sastri worked with students to create short dual language books (http://multiliteracies.ca/index.php/folio/view-Project/5). See also Cohen, 2011; Cohen and Leoni, 2012; Giampapa, 2010; Giampapa and Sandhu, 2011.

(18) Students can express their ideas and insights through poetry (or other genres of writing) in both the home and school language. Poetry allows the author to express profound meanings in relatively few words. Students could write initially either in the school language or home language, depending on their comfort level in each language. Then they could translate from one language to another, possibly working with other students from the same language

Grade 5 - Languages spoken

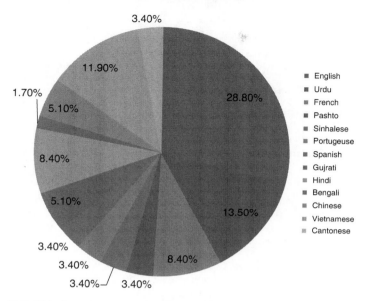

Figure 11.5 Slide from PowerPoint presentation by grade 5 teacher Tobin Zikmanis documenting language survey project in Thornwood Public School, Peel District Board of Education. Reprinted with permission of Tobin Zikmanis.

background. In a qualitative study involving Spanish/English bilingual adolescents, Jiménez *et al.* (2015) demonstrated the power of crosslinguistic translation to provide opportunities for students to deepen their awareness of language and understanding of texts at the lexical, syntactic, and semantic levels.

Examples of multiple themes for stimulating student (and parent and teacher) writing can be found at http://authorsintheclassroom. com/examples-of-books-index/. These themes include: *I am books, Where I'm from books, I can books*, as well as themes focusing on *A person in my life, My name, Understanding the past, creating the future* (Ada & Campoy, 2003).[1]

(19) Students can collaborate with partner classes in distant locations (across the world or across the city) to carry out a variety of projects involving dual or multiple languages. These projects could focus on social justice issues in different countries (e.g. environmental policies, climate change, income disparities), language awareness, or other substantive curriculum-relevant content (see Cummins *et al.*, 2007 and Skourtou *et al.*, 2006, for examples).

This listing of the kinds of crosslinguistic and identity text projects that have been (and can be) carried out in multilingual classrooms illustrates the fact that imaginative innovation is neither costly, complex, or radical. For example, it is hardly a radical proposal to suggest that educators should encourage students to use the full range of their intellectual and linguistic talents in carrying out projects or learning tasks.

Section 2. Crosslinguistic Pedagogy Prior to the Emergence of Translanguaging

Initial Challenges to Linguistic Separation

As noted previously, bilingual and L2 immersion programmes continue to be dominated by 'two solitudes' or language separation assumptions. These assumptions were built in *a priori* to French immersion programmes in Canada, which were initiated in the mid-1960s (Lambert & Tucker, 1972), and have continued to influence bilingual programmes for both 'majority' and 'minority' group students in many countries since that time. Lambert expressed this assumption clearly in the context of Canadian French immersion programmes:

> No bilingual skills are required of the teacher, who plays the role of a monolingual in the target language ... and who never switches languages, reviews materials in the other language, or otherwise uses the child's native language in teacher-pupil interactions. In immersion programs, therefore, bilingualism is developed through two separate monolingual instructional routes. (Lambert, 1984: 13)

Although no empirical evidence had ever been presented to support this monolingual principle (Cummins, 2007a), early attempts to challenge the dogmatic separation of languages in bilingual instruction unfortunately did not gain much traction. Faltis (1989), for example, wrote a robust defense of Jacobsen's (1981) *new concurrent model* that advocated systematic intersentential codeswitching as a means of teaching content to students raised in bilingual communities where this type of codeswitching is common. The sociolinguistic context and instructional rationale are very similar to those that stimulated García and colleagues' advocacy of translanguaging pedagogy, but at the time the impact on policy and instructional practice was minimal.

In a very different context, Angel Lin's (1996) study of classroom Cantonese-English codeswitching in Hong Kong schools provided empirical evidence that strict language separation was not instructionally sustainable for many teachers. The classrooms she observed were ostensibly 'English-medium' but operated in a Cantonese-English oral mode and English written mode. Rather than characterising this instructional codeswitching as inherently problematic and a failure to faithfully implement an English immersion model, Lin highlighted the sociocultural, linguistic, and educational functions it served. According to Lin, these practices represented teachers' and students' pragmatic and expedient response to cope with the symbolic domination of English in the Hong Kong context. However, because official policies discouraged bilingual classroom practices, teachers were largely unwilling to acknowledge codeswitching and bilingual language use in the classroom. As a consequence, there was no discussion at either policy or school level of the most appropriate approaches to bilingual language use for instructional purposes.

Lin's study was (to my knowledge) the first empirical research to cast doubt on the legitimacy of linguistic segregation in bilingual and L2 immersion contexts. Like the work of Jacobson (1981) and Faltis (1989), it was largely ignored at the time by researchers, educators and policymakers involved in bilingual and L2 immersion programmes. One reason for this is that most researchers involved with bilingual education and L2 immersion were coming from cognitive psychology and applied linguistics research orientations that (at the time) tended to pay little attention to sociopolitical considerations such as the symbolic domination of English in colonial and postcolonial contexts.

Lin (1996, 1997) highlighted the negative consequences associated with the failure of policymakers to critically assess alternative approaches to developing bilingualism among Hong Kong students. She pointed out that the local, pragmatic, and expedient crosslinguistic practices in the classrooms she observed were not effective for promoting either Chinese or English academic literacy skills. These practices did not affirm the value or support the development of Chinese academic literacy, thereby perpetuating the ideological domination of English academic monolingualism. With respect to the development of English skills, students had to 'resort to rote memorization and copying to cope with the English written work and examinations in these schools' (1997: 287). Lin called for the development of 'viable bi/tri/multi-lingual education approaches that will enable the majority of students to bridge the multiple linguistic gaps between their home world and their school world: the gaps between their mother tongue (Cantonese) and Chinese literacy, between Cantonese and spoken English, and between Chinese literacy and English literacy' (1997: 288).

During the 1990s, a small number of educators in the United States began to systematically explore possibilities for incorporating minoritised students' home languages into English-language instruction.

Early Examples of Crosslinguistic Instruction in the United States

Three examples from the United States illustrate the emergence of crosslinguistic approaches to teaching learners of English in the late 1980s and 1990s. These examples focus on classroom contexts involving diverse groups of learners and make no assumption that teachers understand or speak any of the languages represented in the classroom. Elsa Auerbach's

(1993, 2016) influential paper, focused primarily on adult learners of English, highlighted the fact that English-only instructional approaches were devoid of empirical support and were essentially ideological biases masquerading as established research. Tamara Lucas and Anne Katz (1994) documented the many ways in which teachers of emergent bilingual students in exemplary schools enabled students to draw on their multilingual resources to complete classroom tasks and to engage academically. Their purpose was to 'reframe the debate' from the entrenched oppositions of *bilingual education* versus *English-only* to the broader issues of how and why teachers should engage students' multilingual repertoires as a normal component of classroom instruction. Finally, Anthony DeFazio's (1997) documentation of crosslinguistic instructional practice at the International High School at LaGuardia Community College in New York City illustrated both the feasibility and academic affordances of transforming classroom spaces from English-only to multilingual instructional zones. García and Sylvan (2011) provided an updated account of the pedagogical approach pioneered in this school and in other schools in the 'Internationals' network sharing the same philosophical approach. Each of these contributions is briefly described in the following sections.

'The issue isn't whether to leverage students' primary linguistic resources, but how' (Auerbach, 2016: 937)

This quote comes from Auerbach's reflection on her original article that appeared in *TESOL Quarterly* in 1993. She summarised the main points in that article as follows:

> My goal in 'Reexamining' was to problematize the then widely accepted axiom that English is the only acceptable medium of communication in ESL classes. I argued that this taken-for-granted insistence on using only English was rooted in regimes of ideology rather than in evidence-based findings regarding its effectiveness for English acquisition. ... My argument was not that teachers should indiscriminately enable use of learners' first language, but that they should be selective, mindful, and respectful in their approach to this issue. (Auerbach, 2016: 936–937)

In her original article, Auerbach (1993: 9) reviewed evidence showing that 'L1 and/or bilingual options are not only effective but necessary for adult ESL students with limited L1 literacy or schooling and that the use of students' linguistic resources can be beneficial at all levels of ESL'.

'[T]he use of the native language is so compelling that it emerges even when policies and programs mitigate against it' (Lucas & Katz, 1994: 558)

Lucas and Katz (1994) described nine exemplary K–12 programmes in which English was the primary language of instruction but in which students' L1 was used in multiple ways for instructionally useful purposes. The following examples illustrate the range of bilingual instructional activities that were observed:

- At one site the teacher devised a group writing assignment in which students used their L1. At another site, students read or told stories to each other using their L1 and then translated them into English to share with other students.
- Students from the same language backgrounds were paired together so that students who were more fluent in English could help those less fluent.
- Students were encouraged to use bilingual dictionaries as a resource to understand difficult text.
- Students were encouraged to discuss school work, and get help at home in their native languages from family members.
- Books in students' L1s were provided and students were encouraged to read them.
- Awards were given for excellence in languages that are not commonly studied (e.g. a high school senior award in Khmer language ability).

The authors cite Auerbach's (1993) arguments for mobilising students' L1 resources in concluding that 'monolingual English speakers or teachers who do not speak the languages of all of their students can incorporate students' native languages into instruction in many ways to serve a variety of educationally desirable functions' (1993: 558).

The Lucas and Katz (1994) research builds on an earlier study by Lucas *et al.* (1990) that examined characteristics of six high schools that had been recognised for their success in educating Latinx minoritised students. The authors identified eight features of these high schools that promoted educational success for these students. The first characteristic listed by Lucas and colleagues was: *Value is placed on students' languages and cultures.* The entire school staff 'gave language minority students the message that their languages and cultures were valued and respected, thus promoting the self-esteem necessary for student achievement' (Lucas *et al.*, 1990: 322). Other pedagogical features of these schools included high expectations for all students, strong support for parental involvement, and an entire school commitment to create contexts of empowerment for language minority students. All of these features are clearly consistent with those emphasised in Chapter 6 and throughout this volume.

'Students use both English and their native language for all phases of learning and assessment' (DeFazio, 1997: 103)

The International High School (IHS) in La Guardia Community College, New York City, was founded in 1985 and offers learners of English a four-year comprehensive programme where they can satisfy state mandated subject matter requirements while they are learning English

(DeFazio, 1997; DevTech Systems, 1996). The school web site outlines the current philosophy and programme at IHS as follows:

> IHS offers a rigorous college preparatory program for students who are learning the English language in a multicultural educational environment. IHS accepts students who are English language learners and who have been in the United States fewer than four years at the time of application. Once admitted, the students remain with the school for their entire high school career. They receive a substantive high school/college curriculum taught with a content-based English-as-a-new-language approach. At the same time, students maintain and further develop their native language skills by engaging in peer-mediated instructional activities using materials and resources in English as well as their native languages. (http://www.ihsnyc.org/)

Since its inception, the IHS has pursued numerous instructional innovations including portfolio rather than standardised test assessment, interdisciplinary curriculum, career education across the curriculum, collaborative peer-supported learning, close contacts and collaboration with the wider community, and a focus on language awareness and engaging students' multilingual repertoires across curricular tasks and projects (DeFazio, 1997). Students' first languages are integrated into all phases of learning and assessment. For example, in developing their portfolios in the various interdisciplinary programmes, students write in both their first language and English, according to their choice. Other students or members of the wider community assist in translating material that has been written in a language the teachers do not know. Among the other instructional initiatives noted by De Fazio are the following:

- Students write an autobiography or a biography of another student using their choice of English, L1 or both languages.
- Students work in groups to carry out comparisons of English and their L1s including topics such as the sounds in different languages (using the International Phonetic Alphabet) and crosslinguistic differences in syntax and other aspects of the languages.
- Students write multilingual children's books on some aspect of language or linguistics (e.g. 'How the Chinese Got Language' or 'The Monster that Ate Polish Words').
- Students interview community members about social dimensions of language such as dialect, language prejudice, bilingual education, etc.

The success of the initial IHS has given rise to a network of almost 30 international schools in New York City and elsewhere in the United States that serve only English language learners. García and Sylvan (2011: 393–394) described the ongoing commitment to plurilingual pedagogy in these schools as follows:

The IHS classrooms are noisy, active, and interactive places. Students are generally sitting in groups of three to four ... talking, arguing, trying to make their points, and collaborating on a project together. In so doing, they are using different language practices, including those they bring from home. In a multilingual-plurilingual model classroom, an observer will hear several languages at once and may see materials in many languages. ... In short, teachers in IHS classrooms use dynamic plurilingual pedagogy and build on translanguaging in the classroom. By allowing individual students to use their home language practices to make sense of the learning moment, these IHSs go beyond traditional second-language programs ...or traditional bilingual education programs.

The academic outcomes of the instructional programme at IHS are impressive. According to DeFazio (1997), entering students score in the lowest quartile on tests of English proficiency, yet more than 90% of them graduate within four years and move on to post-secondary education. DevTech Systems (1996) reported that the drop-out rate among limited English proficient students at IHS was only 3.9% compared to almost 30% in New York City as a whole.

Early Examples of Crosslinguistic Instruction in the European Context

'[C]hildren respond far beyond expectations to an environment that encourages them to demonstrate who they are and what they can do' (Kirwin, 2020: 52)

Scoil Bhríde (Cailíní) (St. Bridget's School for Girls) is a primary school located in the western suburbs of Dublin, Ireland. In the school year 2014-15, it had more than 300 pupils, almost 80% of whom spoke a language other than English at home. In total, 51 home languages were spoken by the pupils. Over a period of 20 years (1994-2014), the school principal, Déirdre Kirwin worked with school staff and in collaboration with Trinity College Dublin professor David Little to implement plurilingual pedagogies that would connect with pupils' lives and affirm their plurilingual identities. The school's pedagogical orientation was shaped by the following five principles:

- *An inclusive ethos:* 'effective schooling depends on being open to the experience and knowledge pupils bring with them' (Little & Kirwin, 2018: 317).
- *An open language policy and integrated approach to language education:* English is the major language of instruction throughout primary school, but Irish is taught as a subject and used informally by teachers in interaction with pupils from the two years of preschool (Junior and Senior Infants) through the six years of primary school. French is introduced in years 5 and 6. Teachers encourage pupils to become conscious of connections between their home languages and these three languages. No restrictions are placed on pupils' use of their

home languages inside or outside the classroom. According to Little and Kirwin (2018: 321), 'Pupils are engaged with language, its uses and varieties throughout the school. They welcome new pupils because they bring new languages with them'.

- *A strong emphasis on the development of literacy skills:* Literacy development is encouraged in pupils' home languages as well as English, Irish, and French. 'Not only are [home languages] visible throughout the school, from Junior Infants to Sixth Class, in classroom and corridor displays; they are also used to support the development of pupils' English language skills' (Little & Kirwin, 2018: 323).
- *Teaching methods that strive to be as explicit as possible:* Teachers promote a reflective approach to learning that encourages self-awareness and self-assessment among pupils.
- *Respect for teachers' professional autonomy:* Teachers are expected to comply with the school's inclusive ethos and its open language policy, and to emphasise literacy engagement and explicit teaching methods. However, they have wide latitude in how they implement these policies, and their professional judgment and autonomy are respected within the school community.

Little and Kirwin (2018, 2019) and Kirwin (2020) have documented multiple examples of how these pedagogical principles were put into practice at Scoil Bhríde. They also document the enthusiasm of both teachers and pupils for the multilingual pedagogical approach implemented in the school. Despite the large immigrant-background school population coming from primarily lower socioeconomic backgrounds, the school's standardised test scores in English and mathematics (administered every year between First and Sixth Class) have consistently been at or above the national average. This contrasts with the significant underachievement in most European countries of first- and second-generation immigrant-background learners, particularly when they are clustered in schools with large concentrations (more than 25 percent) of learners from similar immigrant backgrounds (OECD, 2010d, 2015).

Little and Kirwin (2019) conclude that encouraging immigrant-background learners to use their home languages inside and outside the school promotes crosslinguistic comparisons and the development of language awareness, both of which contribute to pupils' educational success. This approach stimulates pupils to transfer skills and knowledge from school languages to home languages (and vice-versa) and supports parents in developing their children's home language literacy skills.

'Class discussion that focuses on migrant languages and cultures leads to co-construction of knowledge and skills' (Auger, 2014: 229)

The *Comparons Nos Langues* project initiated in the early 2000s by Nathalie Auger of Université Paul Valéry in Montpellier focused on how teachers encouraged recently arrived immigrant students to compare their languages with French. Numerous language awareness activities were developed and implemented in schools serving newcomer migrant students in southern France. A 23-minute DVD was also produced to illustrate the various activities (available on YouTube at: https://www.youtube.com/watch?v=_ZlBiAoMTBo). A guide to support teachers in encouraging multilingualism and activating crosslinguistic transfer is also available (Auger, 2004, 2008). Auger (2014: 231) argues that these language awareness activities generate empowerment for migrant pupils and challenge the predominant negative representations of migrant languages in the French educational system: 'The notion of empowerment is very important for the pupils as well as their teachers because ... the traditional culture of learning and teaching does not really allow empowerment to take place. Thanks to these activities, teachers' and pupils' negative representations of first languages are transformed'.

A recent year-long ethnographic study carried out by Naraina de Melo Martins Kuyumjian (2020), a doctoral student working under the direction of Professor Auger, documented the impact of language awareness and intercultural activities implemented in a highly diverse kindergarten classroom in southern France. Building on 17 previous projects implemented in Europe and North America (e.g. Armand & Maraillet, 2013; Candelier et al., 2007; Prasad, 2016), Kuyumjian developed a portfolio of activities involving 80 hours of intervention over the course of the school year. The impact of these activities was compared to a comparison kindergarten class that experienced the usual kindergarten curriculum. Findings demonstrated the potential of an instructional focus on language awareness and intercultural sensitivity to promote children's knowledge of the school language and to position them in positive ways with respect to their identity and self-confidence. The instructional activities also promoted a greater degree of collaboration among students in comparison to the teacher-centred and individualistic orientation of the comparison classroom.

'The language awareness model ... can be a first step in making our schools multilingual' (Hélot & Young, 2006: 87)

Christine Hélot and Andrea Young, based at the University of Strasbourg in the Alsace region of France documented the impact of a 3-year project focused on language awareness and parental involvement in the Alsatian town of Didenheim, not far from the German and Swiss borders. The project was initiated by elementary school teachers in the year 2000 as a way of legitimising regional and immigrant languages, and also to sensitise students to the wide variety of languages and cultures spoken by students and their teachers in the school. The teachers invited parents to present aspects of their language and culture to three classes of children aged six to nine during Saturday morning sessions. More than a dozen parents volunteered and over the course of the project, the children encountered 18 different languages and their related cultures through pedagogical activities prepared by parents in collaboration with teachers.

In discussing the outcomes of the project, Hélot and Young noted that the children 'loved the activities and looked forward to their Saturday morning sessions with great curiosity' (2006: 79-80). The children's questions 'showed their thirst for knowledge about language and languages once the programme had started, as well as about the people who speak these languages' (2006: 81). They highlighted the range of activities that a language awareness curriculum for young children can include: 'from singing to cooking, to learning different rules of politeness, to human geography, history of migration, reading and writing, learning to listen to new sounds to differentiate them, finding clues to understand a language close to French, and, last but not least, feeling respect for languages spoken by one's peers' (Hélot & Young, 2006: 81).

The potential impact of this kind of project to challenge societal power relations and affirm the identities of minoritised students and communities is illustrated by the experience of Turkish-background children and their families. In the words of one teacher: 'Now they exist in the class, before they did not really exist' (2006: 80). Hélot and Young interpreted this comment as follows:

> What she meant was that the children made their presence felt, that they had their hands up and participated much more in class activities. In other words that they found their voice in French once their home language had been acknowledged in their school. The project was also much talked about in the Turkish community, who welcomed it because such collaboration is still very rare in French primary schools. (Hélot & Young, 2006: 80–81)

This project illustrates well the theme of teachers as knowledge generators. Hélot and Young emphasise that the project was started by the teachers themselves, and the teachers and parents ran the project according to their own agenda. The researchers participated by engaging in participant observation, taking notes, and capturing some of the interactions on video.

Early Examples of Crosslinguistic Instruction in Canada

Numerous crosslinguistic pedagogy projects were implemented across Canada during the late 1990s and early 2000s. In this section, I summarise just three of these projects chosen on the basis of the unique contribution they made at the time of their implementation. The *Dual Language Showcase* was conceived and implemented by Grade 1 teacher Patricia Chow at Thornwood Public School near Toronto in the context of a collaborative project initiated by Sandra Schecter of York University (Schecter & Cummins, 2003). This was the first Canadian project to document the fact that teachers could mobilise students' languages for instructional purposes even when they themselves didn't speak these languages. The project also sowed the seeds of what we later called *identity texts* (see Chapter 5) by demonstrating the impact on student identity of writing and classroom publishing dual language stories, and then later showcasing these stories on the recently invented World Wide Web (Chow & Cummins, 2003).

The second example, entitled *Linking languages through a bilingual read-aloud project* (Lyster *et al.*, 2009), is included because it is one of the very few attempts to implement crosslinguistic pedagogy in the context of French immersion programmes. As noted previously, separation of languages remains a foundational principle within these programmes, but Montreal-area researchers Roy Lyster, Susan Collins and Cynthia Ballinger explored an intriguing way to bring French and English into productive contact while maintaining instructional separation of languages.

The third example is a quasi-experimental investigation of a bilingual reading intervention carried out by University of Calgary researchers Rahat Naqvi and colleagues (2013). This project is significant because it is a well-designed quantitative study that demonstrates that listening to books read in a student's home language can exert a significant positive impact on reading skills in the dominant school language.

Students' 'knowledge of additional languages was a resource to be shared rather than an impediment to be overcome' (Chow & Cummins, 2003: 52)

The *Dual Language Showcase* emerged from a broader collaborative project (Schecter & Cummins, 2003) initiated in 1998 in which university researchers (Schecter and Cummins) worked collaboratively with educators in two highly diverse elementary schools (Thornwood and Floradale) in the Peel Board of Education near Toronto. The goal was to explore effective pedagogical practices in multilingual and multicultural contexts. In both these schools at the time of the project, between 70% and 80% of students came from home backgrounds other than English. Grade 1 teacher, Patricia Chow, initiated the Dual Language Showcase project as a way of engaging students actively in literacy activities that involved their home languages as well as English. An additional component of the project was the active involvement of parents in helping their children craft stories in the L1 and, in some cases, to translate between L1 and English.

Over the course of 15 years, Thornwood students in Grades K through 5 created dual language texts in multiple languages that were posted on the school's website. In some cases, newcomer students or those who had developed L1 literacy skills wrote initially in the home language but more frequently students drafted their stories in English and then worked with parents (and sometimes teachers who spoke their L1) to create their L1 version. More recent multilingual teaching initiatives at Thornwood can be viewed at: https://spark.adobe.com/page/fQLZZPiY8LORx/.

The Dual Language Showcase exerted a significant impact on both Ontario Ministry of Education and school district policymakers and educators in demonstrating that teachers *could* expand the instructional space beyond simply an English-only zone to include students' and parents' multilingual and multimodal repertoires even when they themselves didn't speak the multiple languages represented in their classrooms. It opened up pedagogical possibilities for many of the subsequent multilingual pedagogy projects that are listed in Appendix 11.1. Cummins and Early (2011: v) in their book on *Identity Texts* acknowledged the impact of this project: 'Many of the case studies in the book owe their inspiration to the Dual Language Showcase'. Students in these projects (and their parents) took enormous pride in their creative dual language writing and illustrations, which were frequently shared on school or university websites or in the school library as hard-copy books displayed on the same shelves as the 'real' authors whose books students were reading in their classrooms.

The Dual Language Showcase was just one of the ways in which Patricia Chow validated students' languages and cultures. She described her approach as follows:

> Being of Chinese descent, and having grown up in French-speaking Quebec, I am in a position to share my knowledge of both Chinese and French with my students. I attempt to increase students' knowledge of other languages and cultures in a variety of low-key and unobtrusive ways, especially in the first term of school. For example, I say hello or good morning in other languages when taking attendance, sing songs in French, and ask students to share their bilingual skills when counting. In addition, I put posters with a variety of languages represented on the class bulletin boards. The students love to see their languages displayed in this way and understand that their languages are acknowledged and valued in the classroom. They are therefore not inhibited in displaying their knowledge of additional languages and take pride in their linguistic expertise. (Chow & Cummins, 2003: 46–47)

Patricia attempted to integrate a multilingual dimension in teaching subjects across the curriculum. As one example, as part of her Chinese New Year activities she included an addition activity sheet requiring students to do simple computation using Chinese numerals. This activity stimulated some of the students to create math activity sheets in their own languages: 'I was surprised and delighted when my students spontaneously started creating their own arithmetic sheets using numbers written in Arabic, Gujarati, and Tamil' (Chow & Cummins, 2003: 47).

Sandra Schecter and I were extremely impressed by the multilingual instructional initiatives undertaken by Patricia and by other teachers in the school (see Chow & Cummins, 2003) and I promised to put in writing my perception of the significance of these initiatives. In an email sent to Patricia on January 19, 2000, I made the following points with specific reference to the multilingual math activities:

- These activities communicate to students that what they know and their prior experience are important. Their knowledge of additional languages is an accomplishment that should be acknowledged, respected, and celebrated. It raises their status in the eyes of other children, which is important because as learners of English, they may have felt inadequate about their English proficiency at some points.

- These activities communicate to children that you, as their teacher, are interested in what they bring to the classroom and that you regard their language and culture with respect as important resources.
- The same message is communicated to parents who presumably helped some of the children carry out the project.
- The math activity integrates math with language development and awareness and motivates children to engage with math.
- You could follow up the activity and build multicultural awareness and geography knowledge by identifying children's countries of origin on the map and have children or their parents bring in cultural arti-facts, photos, or just talk about whatever aspects of their countries they want to communicate to you and their classmates. (paraphrased from Chow & Cummins, 2003: 49–50).

This exchange, and the inspirational pedagogy implemented by educa-tors in Thornwood and Floradale schools over many years (Cohen, 2011; Cummins *et al.*, 2005; Sastri *et al.*, 2010), illustrates the dialogue between practice and theory and the ways in which they become fused within each other. Also illustrated is the role of teachers as knowledge generators and the supportive role that university-based researchers can play in these projects. Finally, the Dual Language Showcase and its aftermath reflects the theme of *Actuality Implies Possibility* – the pioneering instructional innovations pursued by Patricia Chow and her colleagues inspired educa-tors in subsequent projects to explore additional crosslinguistic pedagogi-cal approaches (see Cummins & Early, 2011; Stille & Prasad, 2015).

Easy-to-implement bilingual read-aloud projects can foster productive language contact, language awareness, and literacy engagement in bilingual and L2 immersion programmes

Lyster *et al.* (2009) documented the outcomes of a biliteracy interven-tion in an urban school district in the Montreal area in which the French and English teachers of three different classes read aloud to their students (ages 6 to 8) from the same storybooks (the *Magic Tree House* series) over four months. The teachers alternated the reading of one chapter during French-medium instruction and another during English-medium instruc-tion; for example, on Monday, Chapter 1 might be read in French, and then on Tuesday Chapter 2 would be read in English, followed by Chapter 3 in French on the following day. In the school district, 38% of elementary school students were French L1 speakers, 53% were English L1 and 9% spoke another language at home. French was the major language of instruction with English taught by a different teacher for between 3 and 5 hours per week, depending on the particular school.

The researchers set out to explore how the presence of both English- and French-dominant students in the same classroom – and the linguistic resources that they represent – could be acknowledged and used as an instructional resource for teaching. They were also interested in the extent to which the reading-aloud project might foster collaboration between English and French teachers working with the same group of students. Up to that point, collaboration and even contact between the English and French teachers had been minimal.

The intervention generated strong enthusiasm among both teachers and students. Lyster *et al.* (2009: 378) summarised the findings as follows:

> One of the most interesting results of this exploratory study was the high level of motivation that it generated among students, as observed in their interest in being read the stories aloud in both languages as well as volunteering to retell previous happenings and predict upcoming events. Moreover, their interest in continuing to read similar stories on their own was striking.

The project was successful in *initiating* cross-linguistic collaboration between the teachers in the sense that they discussed individual students and their reaction to the stories. However, there was 'no collaboration on common activities, exploiting the various curricular themes that emerged from stories; nor was there any collaboration driven specifically by language learning objectives' (2009: 378). Lyster *et al.* suggested that more intervention and guidance would be needed to support teachers in extending the crosslinguistic collaboration, particularly in a context where a culture of collaboration might not exist due to the fact that no time is built into the school day to encourage such collaboration.

They illustrated the kind of crosslinguistic collaboration that might be pursued with reference to a follow-up writing project implemented by one of the French teachers. This teacher asked students to invent their own Magic Tree House adventure for the two protagonists, using the familiar structure and vocabulary of the books. Lyster *et al.* (2009: 379) suggested that this would be 'an ideal activity for collaboration among students with different language dominances, in which sections of the story could alternate back and forth between languages'.

This project illustrates the fact that even in a bilingual programme that is committed to maintaining separate spaces for each language, creative collaboration between teachers is possible to bring the two languages into productive contact. The impact of this kind of initiative on students' literacy engagement (in both languages) is reflected in the fact that students were highly motivated to check out Magic School House books from the school library after listening to them in both languages.

Listening to dual language books significantly benefited kindergarten children's pre-reading skills in the dominant school language

Rahat Naqvi and colleagues at the University of Calgary set out to explore the extent to which listening to stories read in both English and other languages might affect kindergarten students' acquisition of early reading abilities, specifically alphabet knowledge, knowledge of print conventions, and the meaning of printed words, as measured by the Test of Early Reading Abilities (TERA) (Reid *et al.*, 2001). The sample consisted of 105 children (45 comparison, 60 treatment) with diverse language backgrounds (35% English, 31% Punjabi, 16% Urdu, 18% other languages) from eight kindergarten classes in four schools. Within each school, school administrators randomly assigned one kindergarten class to the treatment group and the other to the comparison group.

Both treatment and comparison groups received the 15–25-minute reading intervention three times per week over an 11-week period. For each reading, children in the comparison group were read to in English only, whereas children in the treatment group were read to in English and another language (i.e. either French, Punjabi, or Urdu). The classroom teacher read the story in English (and sometimes French) while trained community members from immigrant backgrounds read the Punjabi, Urdu, and sometimes French stories. In both groups, children were encouraged to ask questions, make predictions, summarise and share their thoughts and feelings related to the story content. Pre- and post-intervention testing with the three subtests of the TERA were administered, using different forms of the test.

The findings indicated that children who were read to using dual language books demonstrated significantly greater gains in their recognition of printed letters and words than children who were read to in English only. Children who spoke the targeted languages (Punjabi and Urdu) at home accounted for the significant differences, but children who did not speak the targeted languages were not negatively affected by listening to dual language stories. The authors interpret the results as follows:

> We propose that exposing the UP group (i.e. native Urdu and Punjabi speakers) to different languages and scripts alongside their home language supported the development of these children's concepts of words, letters, and graphophonic representation. This conceptual development, we argue, is under-girded by metalinguistic awareness (i.e. knowledge of the form of language as distinct from its content), which has been shown to be important for early reading development, particularly for students who may be learning to read in a language they do not speak at home. (Naqvi *et al.*, 2013: 10)

In summary, this well-controlled study suggests that even a relatively short-term exposure to home language literacy engagement within the school can positively affect students' emerging literacy skills in the school language.

Section 3. Translanguaging Theory as a Catalyst for the Expansion of Crosslinguistic Pedagogy

It is hard to overstate the dramatic impact of Ofelia García's (2009) book and the subsequent collaboration between university-based researchers at the City University of New York (CUNY) and educators in the New York City metropolitan area. The CUNY-New York State Initiative on Emergent Bilinguals project (CUNY-NYSIEB) has produced a wealth of instructional resources for teachers (e.g. https://www.cuny-nysieb.org/translanguaging-resources/translanguaging-guides/) together with a continuous stream of influential scholarly articles and books produced by García together with colleagues working in her research team. Numerous edited books focusing on translanguaging/heteroglossia initiatives and theory have been published in contexts around the world (e.g. Alisaari *et al.*, 2020; Creese & Blackledge, 2014; CUNY-New York State Initiative on Emergent Bilinguals, 2021; García & Kleyn, 2016; Juvonen & Källkvist, 2021; Lau & Van Viegen, 2020b; Panagiotopoulou *et al.*, 2020; Paulsrud *et al.*, 2017; Wedin, 2017). Special issues of academic journals have also focused on translanguaging issues (e.g. *EAL Journal*, Issue number 8, Spring 2019; Prada & Nikula, 2018). In addition, translanguaging theory has been used as a lens to describe and interpret pedagogical initiatives that pre-dated the emergence of the construct itself (e.g. Little & Kirwin, 2018).

In this section, I describe three notable contributions to the translanguaging literature that are less well known than the prolific work of García and colleagues. The work of my Toronto colleague, Roma Chumak-Horbatsch (2012, 2019) on *Linguistically Appropriate Practice* is focused on equity and social justice for young immigrant-background children. According to Chumak-Horbatsch, social justice is routinely denied to these children when their first languages are ignored or actively excluded from educational contexts – this constitutes linguistically *inappropriate* practice.

The research carried out by Valentina Carbonara and Andrea Scibetta (2020a, 2020b) in northern Italy constitutes a second important contribution to our understanding of translanguaging. These researchers from the Università per Stranieri di Siena worked collaboratively with teachers in highly diverse schools to explore the potential of translanguaging pedagogy to affirm and mobilise students' individual and collective multilingual repertoires.

Finally, Latisha Mary and Andrea Young's (2017, 2021) documentation of translanguaging initiatives undertaken by one preschool teacher in the Alsace region of France illustrates the power of teacher agency in transforming the educational experience of minoritised students and their families.

Linguistically Appropriate Practice (LAP)

Roma Chumak-Horbatsch (2012) of Ryerson University in Toronto identified and implemented a range of multilingual instructional practices at the preschool and primary grades level. Drawing on the dynamic bilingualism framework proposed by García (2009), Chumak-Horbatsch described LAP as follows:

> LAP is a new classroom practice that extends current inclusive practices and reflects the principles of dynamic bilingualism. ... LAP views immigrant children as emergent bilinguals, acknowledges their unique language and literacy needs, focuses on the social and communicative aspects of language, encourages translanguaging, promotes bilingualism, and builds partnerships with families. (Chumak-Horbatsch, 2012: 57)

Examples of each of the following five themes, into which LAP activities are organised, are provided below. All the activities were field-tested by Chumak-Horbatsch working with teachers in linguistically and culturally diverse school contexts.

- Charting home languages.
- Using home languages in the classroom.
- Linking the home and classroom.
- Bringing the outside world into the classroom.
- Sharing books and newspapers with children.

Create home language graphs

First, teachers and children together make a colour-coded home language chart, listing on a large sheet of construction paper the different languages spoken by children in the classroom. The languages should be listed in alphabetical order. Update the chart as new children arrive in the classroom throughout the year. Children could also add their drawings of the flags of their families' countries of origin, corresponding to the languages they speak, using the information contained in the world flag database (www.flags.net/mainindex.htm). Finally, the teacher could work with the children to create visual representations using bar graphs, pie charts, etc. of the number of children in the classroom who speak each language.

What do you see?

Using picture books with brightly coloured illustrations (e.g., of food, body parts, furniture, etc.), the teacher, parent, or child points to each object and asks the children 'What do you see'? This can be done not only as a way of building vocabulary in the classroom language but also to promote transfer of knowledge across languages. After asking 'What do you see'? in the classroom language, the teacher can ask children to name the object in their home languages. The teacher and the other children try to repeat and learn the names of objects in different languages. Parents can also take part in this game in the classroom and the teacher can encourage them to play the game at home with their children in their home languages.

Parents and grandparents in the classroom

Parents and/or grandparents together with the teacher can read aloud dual language books together, with the parent/grandparent reading a page in his/her home language followed by the teacher reading the same page in the classroom language. Another activity involves the children with the help of parents and grandparents creating a chart that lists the ages of the children and their grandparents. Other information can also be added to the list, such as the languages spoken by children, parents, and grandparents.

Bringing the outside world into the classroom

Children can be encouraged to notice signs in multiple languages in their neighbourhoods and in the neighbourhood of the preschool centre. While they are out walking with their child, parents (or grandparents) could take digital photographs of home language signs in their neighbourhoods and either bring the digital copies or electronically send these signs to the preschool teacher for discussion in the classroom. The child (with the help of the parent) could explain to the teacher and other children what the sign says. The teacher could then compile a collage of the signs in multiple languages that defines the children's landscape

Sharing books and newspapers with children

Among the activities suggested in *Linguistically Appropriate Practice* for socialising children into the world of books and literacy are the following:

- *Talk to children about books and newspapers.* Describe features of books such as author(s), illustrator(s), publisher, front and back cover, table of contents, text, font, and page numbers. Similarly, describe newspaper components such as name, size, black and coloured print, advertisements, etc.
- *Story time.* As the teacher reads books to the children, s/he can invite children to provide home language translations for words or phrases. In a classroom context where children's languages are actively welcomed, children will respond enthusiastically to this

invitation to showcase their expertise and linguistic knowledge. Family members can also be invited to participate in story time and to use similar crosslinguistic strategies in reading books in L1 at home to their children (e.g. asking for the meaning of words or phrases in the school language).

- *Visiting the public library.* These visits alert children and their parents/grandparents to the presence of public libraries and the fact that many libraries have books and other materials in a variety of languages. The teacher can encourage children and other family members to join the public library and borrow books in the languages of both the home and classroom.
- *Create multilingual newspapers and dual language or multilingual books.* Children and their parents can be encouraged to create individual or group dual language books such as those created in the Early Authors Project (Bernhard *et al.*, 2006). These dual language books can be modelled after similar books read to the children in the classroom. Similarly, children and their parents can participate in creating a multilingual newspaper modelled after the newspapers that teachers have read to children in class.

A follow-up book expanded the scope of LAP to the full range of K-12 multilingual classrooms. Chumak-Horbatsch (2019) collaborated with educators from around the world to bring their multilingual instructional practices into public view. The activities and resources described in this book were created and implemented by teachers and synthesised in a highly readable way by Chumak-Horbatsch. The tone and scope of the book can be gauged in Chumak-Horbatsch's closing comments as she reflects on her five-year fact-finding LAP journey:

> During my many interactions with children, teachers and families, I saw LAP in all its excitement and richness. I witnessed creative teaching and busy, vibrant learning. I saw understanding and pride as newcomers, bilinguals and monolingual children worked together and shared their learning. In classrooms, auditoriums and libraries, I saw families opening up the world to children by sharing their knowledge, their languages and their literacies.
>
> I visited schools where home languages were seen, heard, used and included in the curriculum. ... I saw children reach out to newcomers, help each other and learn from each other. I observed them using their home languages and listening to stories and narratives read in languages they did not understand. What they did understand, however, is that these are the languages of their classmates and friends—and that they matter. (Chumak-Horbatsch, 2019: 146)

Chumak-Horbatsch's (2019) volume represents an important complement to the compilation of translanguaging/LAP instructional activities and resources published by researchers and educators working with the CUNY/NYSIEB project (e.g. Celic & Seltzer, 2013; CUNY-NewYork State

Initiative on Emergent Bilinguals, 2021). The latter is focused primarily on the experience in the United States whereas *Using Linguistically Appropriate Practice* reflects a more international orientation. Chumak-Horbatsch recently collaborated with two Ontario French language teachers, Shelina Adatia and Serena Quintal, to document ways in which a multilingual/plurilingual focus could be injected into the teaching of French in both core French (taught as a subject) and French immersion (Chumak-Horbatsch *et al.*, 2020). The linguistic and personal enrichment generated by this multilingual focus is also vividly illustrated in Adatia's (2019) award-winning short video *La richesse de la diversité – The richness of diversity*.

L'AltRoparlante project

In what is perhaps the most comprehensive empirical investigation of translanguaging to date, Valentina Carbonara and Andrea Scibetta (2020a, 2020b) carried out a Transformative Action-Research project in Italy that involved analysis of classroom interaction and students' work in five highly diverse schools, three of which extended into middle school grade levels. In addition to observation of teachers' instruction, data were derived from parent questionnaires and multiple interviews and focus groups with 18 teachers and 122 students. According to Carbonara and Scibetta (2020b), the name of the project derives from a pun that combines the Italian words *altro* (other) and *altoparlante* (loudspeaker). Thus, *L'AltRoparlante* 'is a sort of magical instrument, allowing all children to raise their own voice and express themselves "in another way", for example in other languages or in other modes' (2020b: 4). The project started in 2016 and was recognised with the 'European Language Label' in 2018 (see Figure 11.7).

Initially, the project team worked with participating teachers to communicate research findings and instructional strategies associated with translanguaging. Monthly meetings were conducted to plan activities, share feedback on teaching initiatives, and discuss relevant readings regarding translanguaging. The researchers then guided teachers in the collection of information about the linguistic repertoires of students and their families as a way of increasing teachers' awareness of how students used their languages in different contexts, students' attitudes towards their multilingual repertoires, and potential assumptions or perceptions students or family members might have regarding the legitimacy of different languages in the context of the school, which the researchers labelled 'language regimes'.

After initial guided implementation, teachers became more autonomous and creative in exploring translanguaging instructional possibilities with their students in the realms of oracy, literacy and other subject-matter content. Many activities were inspired by the CUNY-NYSIEB project, such as the designing of lesson plans around a multilingual culminating

Figure 11.6 Andrea Scibetta, Valentina Carbonara, Professor Carla Bagna and Jim Cummins, Siena, February 2020. Photo credit, Jim Cummins.

Figure 11.7 'European Language Label' designation awarded to L'AltRoparlante project. Photo credit, Jim Cummins.

product (Celic & Seltzer, 2013). With older students, teachers were able to focus explicitly on issues such as language rights and social inequalities, guiding students towards critical or transformative reflection on how power relations operate in society.

The authors highlight a variety of positive outcomes on students' metalinguistic awareness, academic engagement, and attitudes towards multilingualism in general and their home languages/dialects in particular. As students expanded their awareness of language and experienced the legitimacy of their multilingual/multicultural repertoires, native Italian-speaking students also began to reclaim their regional dialects as part of their identity.

An analysis of student focus groups, each composed of 3–4 students, in two of the participating schools documented the impact of the project on the students. All students were interviewed twice: initially in January 2017, at the beginning of the project (36 focus groups), and then in June 2017, at an advanced phase of implementation of translanguaging pedagogy in their classrooms (35 focus groups). These 71 focus groups were video-recorded, yielding a corpus of almost 600 minutes that was analysed by means of the N-Vivo software programme for themes and progression of perceptions and attitudes from Time 1 to Time 2. Carbonara and Scibetta summarised the major findings as follows:

> Our results show how activities that spur students' perception of class linguistic repertoires lead to empowerment dynamics, to the fading of language regimes, and to the affirmation of an idea of global citizenship. From a linguistic perspective, L'AltRoparlante fostered metalinguistic awareness and fluid multilingual communicative practices, as well as a more positive attitude towards language diversity in class. Immigrant minority languages, usually confined to a minoritized position, began to be conceived by students as educational resources for learning and meaning-making. (Carbonara & Scibetta, 2020b: 17)

In summary, the extremely rich data collected by Carbonara and Scibetta (2020a, 2020b) illustrate the ways in which students' diverse languages provide a gateway through which teachers can affirm the cultures and languages of minoritised students and communities, thereby challenging the societal power relations that stigmatise community talents and identities. We see in the accounts of both students and teachers involved in the project that translanguaging pedagogy, when implemented effectively, is much more than just an instructional strategy. It enables teachers and students – both monolingual dominant language speakers and multilingual speakers – to re-imagine their roles and identities. Teachers in this and other projects, whether labelled translanguaging, crosslinguistic, or LAP, quickly learn to appreciate that the best way to teach the dominant language and promote students' academic engagement is to start where students are and accept everything they bring from their homes, including their languages, dialects, and cultural knowledge.

Resisting Dominant Discourses in a French Preschool

To make headway, you have to go against the flow. These words express the pedagogical and social philosophy of Sylvie, a preschool teacher working with highly diverse children and families in a low socio-economic area in the northeast of France. They also form part of the title of a chapter written by University of Strasbourg researchers and teacher educators, Latisha Mary and Andrea Young (2021) that describes and analyses Sylvie's pedagogical practice and orientation to language education. At the time of their detailed ethnographic study of Sylvie's classroom during the period September 2014 to July 2015, Sylvie was head teacher of her school and had been teaching for 35 years, 31 of which were in multilingual contexts and 18 in pre-primary classrooms (*école maternelle*).

The data collected by Mary and Young (2017, 2021) consisted of video-recordings of interactions and activities involving Sylvie, her teaching assistant, pupils and their families. Every two weeks observational field-notes were collected, and recorded interviews were conducted with members of the classroom learning community, including parents. Four in-depth interviews were conducted with Sylvie over the course of the academic year and Sylvie also contributed personal written reflections on her classroom practices.

Over the course of her teaching career, Sylvie had come to reject the assimilationist instructional practices that were the norm within the French educational system. She learned words and phrases of the various languages of her pupils as a result of interacting with them in the classroom and talking with their parents. She used the limited knowledge she had of these languages regularly in the classroom to facilitate children's learning. Unlike many of her colleagues over the years, Sylvie welcomed children's languages into the classroom and encouraged her pupils to use their languages in discussing books that they had listened to or browsed through. She also invited parents to spend time in her classroom and to read books in their languages to the children. In one of her interviews with the researchers, Sylvie noted that some other teachers and the school inspector considered her classroom to be chaotic: these teachers 'had said that it was chaos in my classroom, parents in the playground, parents in the corridors, in the classrooms, headscarves in the school, well, everything you can imagine' (Mary & Young, 2021).

Mary and Young (2017) identified four overlapping purposes of translanguaging in Sylvie's classroom:

- *To meet children's basic needs.* For example, on one occasion when a Turkish-speaking child was distressed, Sylvie used the little Turkish she had learned to comfort the child and she asked her assistant to bring in an older Turkish child to translate for him.
- *To make connections between home and school.* For example, Sylvie made links to children's home culture by initiating an activity using plasticine about the making of *lahmacuns* (Turkish pizzas popular with Turkish families).

- *To build on children's prior knowledge and scaffold their learning of French.* For example, in an activity where Sylvie read a story book to the children in French and a parent read the Turkish version in parallel, Sylvie repeated what children said in Turkish and also used simple Turkish phrases inserted into her French reading and dialogue with the children. According to Mary and Young, Sylvie 'makes use of translanguaging to scaffold the children's understanding of the story and to maintain their attention and engagement in the activity' (2017: 121).
- *To foster engagement with literacy.* The previous example also illustrates the way Sylvie used translanguaging in both spontaneous and teacher-initiated situations to foster literacy engagement. Mary and Young point out that encouraging children to interact with print resources in the language of their choice resulted in extensive engagement with books: 'Literacy played an important part in the life of this classroom and children were frequently observed attentively poring over picture books which they were either looking at by themselves or huddled together and discussing animatedly with their peers' (2017: 121–122).

One theme that resonates throughout Mary and Young's (2021) account of Sylvie's instructional practice is what I have called *educator role definitions* (see Chapter 5) and what García *et al.* (2016) have called a *translanguaging stance* (see also Menken & Sánchez, 2019). Mary and Young (2021) highlight Sylvie's beliefs and ideologies about language, including her commitment to social justice, her positive image of the children, her critical awareness of the role language played in people's lives, and her willingness to challenge prevailing monolingual discourses and practices. According to Mary and Young, Sylvie's exercise of agency or 'articulation of choices' involved questioning the normalised assumptions about curriculum, assessment, and instruction that constrict identity options and academic engagement among emergent bilingual students.

In short, once again, Sylvie's instructional practice illustrates the role of teachers as knowledge generators. The research study conducted by Mary and Young (2017, 2021) documented pedagogical initiatives that had evolved over many years as a result of *choices* that Sylvie had made regarding what it meant to educate the minoritised emerging bilingual children in her preschool classes. Many of the evidence-based instructional responses outlined in Table 6.2 are readily identifiable in Sylvie's interaction with children and parents. She regularly engaged children's multilingual repertoires as a way of both scaffolding instruction and affirming children's cultural and linguistic identities. She consistently attempted to connect instruction with children's lives. And she bridged the gap between home and school by inviting parents into her classroom and collaborating with them to immerse children in a rich literacy environment involving both French and their home languages.

Section 4. Practice Meets Theory: Voices of Teachers and Students

In the Preface to this book, I noted that although much of the analytic focus is on *theoretical* concepts, my interest starts and ends with what happens between teachers and students in classrooms. In this final section, my goal is to illustrate very concretely how theoretical constructs and instructional practices are infused within each other. I draw primarily on two projects in which I participated during the past 20 years to highlight the classroom reality and the instructional implications of the theoretical constructs that have been discussed in the preceding pages. I have emphasised consistently that these theoretical concepts were derived from instructional practice and, once articulated, they serve to validate and extend the impact of instructional practices in an ongoing two-way dialogue.

The two projects from which I draw are the *Multiliteracies Project* (Cummins & Early, 2011; Cummins *et al.*, 2005) and *Songide'ewin: Aboriginal Narratives* (Cummins *et al.*, 2015; Montero, *et al.*, 2013). The Multiliteracies project ran from 2002 to 2006 and involved collaborative research with teachers primarily in the Vancouver and Toronto areas. We explored what pedagogical options emerged when 'literacy' was conceived as 'multiple', reflecting both the new literacies ushered in by technological change and the multilingual literacies practiced by the majority of the world's population who use two or more languages in their daily lives. In this section, I draw specifically on the instructional practice of Lisa Leoni who encouraged her students to use their full multilingual repertoire to engage with learning. Three of the students (Kanta, Madiha and Sulmana) whose creative work and reflections are profiled were in Lisa's Grade 7/8 classroom during the 2003/2004 academic year. The following year, Madiha and Tomer were members of Lisa's ESL class. In both contexts, students carried out projects using their home languages together with English. The title pages of two of the dual language identity texts created by these students are shown in Figure 11.8.

The *Songide'ewin: Aboriginal Narratives* project took place in the context of a Native Studies programme that operated in Sir John A. Macdonald Secondary School in Hamilton Ontario. The programme functioned as part of the regular school day and offered credit courses related to Indigenous issues and realities that were open to all students in Grades 9 through 12. *Songide'ewin* is an Ojibwe word meaning *strength of the heart* and it expresses the identity-affirming process and outcomes of the visual art and poetry project undertaken between 2010 and 2013 by students in the Native Arts and Culture course at the school.

The project was initiated by Dr Kristiina Montero of Wilfred Laurier University in Waterloo Ontario, in collaboration with First Nations elders and secondary school students, together with their teachers, as a means of

Figure 11.8 Dual language books created by students in Lisa Leoni's class (http://multiliteracies.ca/index.php/folio/viewProject/8)

bringing First Nations youth and non-Indigenous preservice teachers together to learn about each other in a non-hierarchical manner. Students and teacher education candidates worked with Ojibwe elder and artist Rene Meshake to create visual and literary identity texts that communicated messages about Indigenous identity through multimodal images, colours, symbols, song, and language. For example, in their paintings and in the poetry they wrote in response to the paintings, students explored symbols such as the eagle, bear, turtle, wolf, drum, and eagle feather that connected them to the land, sacred teachings, and worldviews.

More than 75 identity texts were created by students, teachers, and preservice teachers (Figure 11.9). This creative work was exhibited in three Ontario art galleries between May 2012 and May 2013. A short video of the exhibit opening at the Art Gallery of Hamilton (April 12, 2013) can be viewed at https://www.youtube.com/watch?v=Tk5tTtVM2jQ. Video-recorded interviews with participants in the project were conducted by Kristiina Montero and Jim Cummins with the assistance of Thomas Cummins and Enamul Huque.

In the following sections, the identity texts and students' reflections on these texts, together with teacher perspectives, that emerged from these two projects are viewed through the lens of the theoretical constructs and evidence-based instructional responses outlined in Figure 5.1 and Table 6.2. Several of the examples reflect multiple dimensions of teachers' instructional practices (e.g. scaffolding, engaging students' multilingual repertoires, connecting with students' lives, and affirming identity) but for purposes of illustration I have highlighted just one theoretical construct in relation to each example. The perspectives of Lisa

Figure 11.9 Rene Meshake with paintings created by First Nations youth in the Songide'ewin project. Photo credit, Jim Cummins. Reprinted with permission of Rene Meshake.

Leoni and her students were recorded at various stages of the project, in interviews and recorded conversation, as well as during a panel presentation at the Ontario Teachers of English as a Second Language (TESL) conference in October 2005. The quotations are extracted from Leoni *et al.*, 2011: 48–53).

Multiliteracies Project Teacher Perspectives

Educator role definitions

As noted in Chapter 5, educator role definitions refer to the mindset of expectations, assumptions, and goals that educators bring to the task of teaching multilingual students. This concept was very much in evidence in the description of Sylvie's orientation to teaching and to the languages of minoritised students outlined previously in this chapter (Mary & Young, 2021). Lisa Leoni expressed her philosophy of teaching as follows:

> My overarching goal as a teacher is to uncover all that is unknown to me about my students—linguistically and culturally, and especially to understand the community they are part of (their parents, their friends, their faith) and the list goes on. So, when a student enters my class, I want to discover all that I can about that student as a learner and as a person.

Identity negotiation/affirmation

Lisa highlighted on multiple occasions the importance of linking instruction to students' emerging identities and particularly the powerful role that identity texts could play in this process.

The way I see it everything has to relate to the identity of the students; children have to see themselves in every aspect of their work at school.

What I love about using identity texts as a teaching strategy is that it validates students' cultural and linguistic identities. They also help connect what students are learning in the class to their prior lived experiences and when these connections happen, learning becomes real for them because they are using their language and culture for purposes that have relevance for them. Most importantly, they end up owning the work that they produce.

Teaching for crosslinguistic transfer

As noted in preceding chapters, there is overwhelming research evidence supporting the interdependence hypothesis and the importance of teaching for crosslinguistic transfer. As Lisa points out, crosslinguistic transfer is likely to occur to some extent even when this process is not facilitated by the teacher, but when teachers encourage students to use their L1 as a resource for learning, the process becomes efficient rather than haphazard.

Whether students are given the opportunity or not, it's been clear to me that students learning an additional language use their first language to help them make sense not only of grammatical structures or concepts represented by vocabulary but also of the world around them. ... Opportunities like writing a dual language book bring out the inner voice of students and make visible to the teacher what is usually invisible.

When Tomer entered my class last year, a lot of the work he produced was in Hebrew. Why? Because that is where his knowledge was encoded, and I wanted to make sure that Tomer was an active member and participant in my class.

Multiliteracies Project Student Perspectives

Scaffold instruction by engaging multilingual repertoires

Students' reflections repeatedly highlighted the important role that their home languages played in transferring knowledge from one language to the other and scaffolding their learning of English and other academic content. The comments below also point to the impact of Lisa's crosslinguistic pedagogy on their awareness of how language works, their literacy engagement, the importance of connecting instruction to students' lives, and affirming their identities.

Tomer. With *Tom Goes to Kentucky* it was easier to begin it in Hebrew and then translate it to English and the other thing that made it easier was that I chose the topic. Because I love horses, when I'm writing about horses it makes me want to continue to do it and do it faster.

I think using your first language is so helpful because when you don't understand something after you've just come here it is like beginning as a baby. You don't know English and you need to learn it all from the beginning; but if you already have it in another language then it is easier, you can translate it, and you can do it in your language too, then it is easier to understand the second language.

It helps when you want to understand something but you can't and so you try to understand it in the first language, and it's coming really slow and you try to translate it into English, and then slowly you can get it and you can begin to ask questions, and then you don't need any more the first language.

It makes it more faster to be able to use both languages instead of just breaking your head to think of the word in English when you already know the word in the other language so it makes it faster and easier to understand.

Develop language awareness and reinforce academic language

Kanta. My first language is Punjabi, my second language is Urdu, and my third language is English. ... It helped me a lot to be able to write it in two languages and especially for Madiha who was just beginning to learn English because the structure of the two languages is so different. So, if you want to say something in Urdu it might take just three words but in English to say the same thing, you'd have to use more words. So, for Madiha it helped the differences between the two languages become clear.

When I came here, I was forced to speak English; I wasn't allowed to speak Urdu. So, the teacher at first she gave me a colouring book and a big package of colours. From that experience of being forced to use English only, I did learn English pretty fast and it was a good thing to learn English but my English writing structure was really poor because I couldn't see the difference between Urdu and English and the process of writing them. So in one way it helped me learn English faster but for Madiha who got a chance to use both English and Urdu it helped her see the differences between the two languages and her writing in English improved a lot more and better than mine did.

Affirm identity

The impact of creating dual language identity texts was powerfully expressed by Madiha, Sulmana and Kanta.

Madiha. I am proud of *The New Country* because it is our story. Nobody else has written that story. And when we showed it to Ms. Leoni she said it was really good. She said 'It's about your home country, and family, and Canada, it's all attached, that's so good.' I like that because it means she cares about our family and our country, not just Canada. Because she cares about us, that makes us want to do more work. My parents were really happy to see that I was writing in both Urdu and English; my mother was happy because she knows that not everyone has that chance.

Sulmana. When I told my parents about the book, they were really surprised to hear that their daughter could actually write in both languages and they were really happy to know that I as a normal girl who had been in Canada for the last 3 years actually got an opportunity to write a book in English and Urdu because when you are living in Canada you don't often get a chance to write something in Urdu or your first language.

When my grandma came here last Sunday and I told her about the book, first of all, she couldn't believe it and then I said, 'Wait grandma, I'll show you proof'. And I showed her the package Sarah [Cohen] gave us [to come to the TESL conference]. She was so surprised and so happy that her granddaughter is so popular, that her books are all around Canada and after she saw the whole thing she was like 'Wow, you're great', and she started kissing me.

Kanta. How it helped me was when I came here in Grade 4, the teachers didn't know what I was capable of. I was given a pack of crayons and a colouring book and told to get on colouring with it. And after I felt so bad about that—I'm capable of doing much more than just that. I have my own inner skills to show the world than just colouring, and I felt that those skills of mine are important also. So, when we started writing the book [The New Country], I could actually show the world that I am something instead of just colouring. And that's how it helped me, and it made me so proud of myself that I am actually capable of doing something, and here today [at the Ontario TESL conference] I *am* actually doing something. I'm not just a colouring person—I can show you that I am something.

Promote literacy engagement

Obviously, writing dual language books is an excellent example of literacy engagement but the affirmation that students experienced from their teacher, parents, and classmates as a result of their book reinforced their motivation to read and write more in both languages. Sulmana expresses this clearly.

Sulmana. When we were working on *The New Country*, I felt really good and I wanted to write more stories afterward. When I was doing it, I was really happy. It was fun to be able to write in both languages and to work on a project with my friends and I really liked having the chance to write in both languages and to improve my Urdu. It was my first experience translating English to Urdu, so we worked together because I had forgotten many of the words in the last three years, so my vocabulary improved a lot too. I had to ask my Mom a lot of words when we were writing it in Urdu but also before that, when I realised that we were going to be writing it in both languages I went home from that day and started reading more books in Urdu at home because I hadn't been doing that so much, so I had forgotten some words and I wanted my writing to make sense.

Songide'ewin Project Student Perspectives

The following reflections come from two of the students involved in this project who co-authored the paper *Activist Literacies: Validating Aboriginality Through Visual and Literary Identity Texts* (Montero et al., 2013). The insights of Adam Marsh and Cassandra Bice-Zaugg highlight how the identity texts created by First Nations students have played a significant role in dissipating the colonising and exclusionary forces at play in the lives of their authors.

Identity texts as decolonising pedagogy

Adam. I grew up in Toronto all my life. I was raised by my mother's [white] family. I knew nothing about my [First Nations] culture. I knew I was First Nations. I knew I was Native. Coming to this school and the amazing Native program here has helped me find who I am. (Montero et al., 2013: 80).

When I was making the painting, I thought a lot about myself. I have a lot of self-identity problems. ... I put a lot of that into this painting. [It] has changed my life pretty much. How I look at everything now and how I think of things—[I have] a different perspective.

This painting is spiritual and emotional for me. There is so much spirituality in my painting—the colour purple represents my spirituality. The eagle—it is the highest-flying bird, and we use its feathers during our ceremonies. I think the eagle might be my spiritual guide, totem animal, clan animal, and spiritual helper. I think the eagle might be mine because there is so much in my life that has to do with the eagle. It is always there to help me. So, there is a lot of spirituality with the eagle on the painting. (Montero et al., 2013: 83-84).

Adam also highlighted the contrast between the Native Studies programme he was attending and his previous educational experiences. In the two high schools and three elementary schools he attended in Toronto, Aboriginal culture was completely absent. Instruction in these schools was about Canada, not the people who were here first. By contrast, the Native Studies programme put Aboriginal people first. His overall experience in the programme enabled him to find himself, and he unconsciously expressed a lot of his identity in the painting (foregrounded in Figure 11.10; see Montero et al., 2013: 83).

Cassandra. It was an amazing process to see and feel all of these powerful emotions through the painting. I had to dig deep and work through the emotions and feelings I was experiencing. I know that those around me had to do their own work around the effects of Residential Schools, drugs and alcohol, and identity issues. How do you put all those things together? It was really difficult. However, *the process helped me develop whom I thought I was born to be.* I was able to verbalize that if I am able to say "*I*

Figure 11.10 Display of students' art and poetry from the Songide'ewin exhibit at the Art Gallery of Hamilton. Photo credit M. Kristiina Montero; reprinted with permission of M. Kristiina Montero.

know who I am," then my kids will be able to do the same, as will their children, their children's children, and so on and so forth. I am comforted to think that if I know who I am and find strength in my First Nations identity, I will help my future generations stay away from drugs and alcohol, for example. If I hadn't created this poem and written down my experiences, then I don't know that I would be able to ensure a solid future for my successive generations. (Montero *et al.*, 2013: 85-86; emphasis original).

In discussing the Songide'ewin project with Kristiina Montero and Jim Cummins (videorecording, June 12, 2012), Cassandra highlighted the identity transformation that she had experienced since attending the Native Studies programme. She felt that she had learned more in the few months she was in the programme than in her entire previous educational career. In contrast to her previous school experiences that were unconnected to her life and identity, the Native Studies programme had enabled her to actually truly learn stuff. It had created a sense of home, stability, and community. All of the identity-affirming interactions that took place with teachers and classmates added building blocks to the person she might become. For Cassandra, her experience in the programme had given her the fundamentals to figure out who she was and where she came from, and, most importantly, who she's going to be and who her children are going to be, all of which constitutes her identity. When asked if any of her previous educational experiences had connected with her life and identity, she emphatically responded, *Never—never, ever, ever, ever.*

The four authors of the *Activist Literacies* paper (Montero *et al.*, 2013) reflected on their experience of being involved in the project, or in my case, being an observer from the sidelines. I reproduce below part of what Cassandra said and my own reflections as an outside observer of the project.

> **Cassandra.** This experience gave me a gift of poetry. I started to develop a passion for poetry during this project. I didn't know I had this passion. Since this project I have written and shared many pieces of poetry. ... Participating in this project was like hearing a collective voice telling me: 'We are proud of you. We care about you. You have a future.' Being able to express my thoughts about who I am as an Anishinaabekwe (an Ojibwe woman) made me feel like I belonged and was connected to a larger community (Montero *et al.*, 2013: 88).

> **Jim.** As I listened to Rene, Adam, Cassandra, and their classmates in the Native Studies program talk with insight and passion about their paintings and poems, and later read through the transcripts, I was profoundly moved. Their creative work certainly connected with and rooted itself in the oppression their communities have endured over centuries at the hands of the Canadian government, with the collusion of Canadians more generally, but the themes that they articulated were not ones of oppression and racism but of emergence, regeneration, and empowerment, understood as the collaborative creation of power. Power was being created in an additive way as students interacted with Elders; it grew within students as their high school studies enabled and encouraged them to view their histories, experiences and the wider society through an Aboriginal lens; their identity texts, understood as both process and product, not only expressed their identities, these texts enabled their identities to be projected into new social spheres (art galleries, university classrooms), and in the process they acted as a catalyst for the re-creation of students' identities. Their private voices, in the past frequently expressed only as whispers, have gone public. Just as the *Idle No More* movement of Aboriginal resistance to Canadian government policies has occupied public spaces during the past year, the identity texts created in the context of the Native Studies program illustrate how Aboriginal voices can make themselves heard once again in Canadian classrooms. During the past 30 years, I have frequently reacted with disgust as Canadian politicians wrap themselves in the cloak of 'multiculturalism' and, in the process, erase the ugly history of racism against Aboriginal peoples and other groups that is intrinsic to the Canadian narrative. Schools have a major role to play in uncovering and exposing the hypocrisies of official discourses and injecting issues of power and identity back into the core of education. Educators and policymakers might do well to listen to Cassandra as she says: *Take away identity and what do you have? If you have a student that doesn't know who they are, do you think they care about what goes on in the classroom?* (Montero *et al.*, 2013: 89–90).

Concluding Thoughts: Beyond Panaceas and Scapegoats

The insights of teachers and students outlined in this chapter illustrate and illuminate intersecting facets of the theoretical framework discussed in previous chapters. These insights highlight the centrality of creating educational spaces and orchestrating teacher-student interactions that enable minoritised students to use language powerfully across a range of genres and registers to express and extend their emerging identities. There isn't just one instructional panacea or 'magic bullet' that will make this happen. All of the evidence-based instructional responses discussed in Chapter 6 (e.g. Table 6.2) need to be mobilised to create interpersonal spaces that will promote collaborative relations of power in the classroom.

Translanguaging pedagogy that engages students' multilingual repertoires is one important component of an effective and empowering instructional response. But it's not the whole story. Within the context of the theoretical framework elaborated in Chapters 5 and 6, translanguaging pedagogy can clearly play a role in decolonising curriculum and validating students' varieties of home and school languages. As illustrated in this chapter, engaging students' multilingual repertoires can also serve to scaffold students' access to instruction in the dominant school language. However, there are numerous additional and equally important instructional strategies for scaffolding instruction and decolonising curriculum that go beyond translanguaging (e.g. Montero *et al.*, 2013). In order to reverse underachievement among minoritised students, teachers need to implement a range of instructional approaches that scaffold meaning, reinforce knowledge of academic language across the curriculum, promote sustained literacy engagement, connect with students' lives, and affirm identities.

A danger in the current academic discourse that centers on translanguaging is that this component gets foregrounded and other components, equally significant in reversing underachievement, fade into the background. García and colleagues (e.g. García, 2017) have integrated translanguaging with transformative or critical pedagogy but they say little about more general ways of scaffolding instruction, reinforcing knowledge of academic language, or promoting literacy engagement. Thus, there is a danger that translanguaging gets positioned as a panacea – a universal remedy for underachievement among minoritised students. Unfortunately, the causes of underachievement are rooted in a complex matrix of power relations that are likely to frustrate one-dimensional solutions.

The potential positive impact of translanguaging pedagogy is also likely to be undermined by associating it with the profoundly counter-intuitive and evidence-free proposition that 'a language is not something that a person speaks' (Otheguy *et al.*, 2015: 256). When Kanta informs us that her first language is Punjabi, her second language is Urdu, and her third language is English, she is presumably claiming that she *speaks* these languages. The rhetorical contortions required to convince Kanta that she is experiencing false consciousness when she thinks she *speaks* three different languages seem pointless.

Likewise, teachers may be puzzled when they are informed that the languages they teach exist in the social realm but have no reality within the individual's cognitive apparatus or architecture. Teachers spend long hours in the classroom working hard to enable students to incorporate these languages into their cognitive apparatus. The response of most of the teachers I have worked with, and learned from, over the past 40 years to the claim that people don't speak languages would likely be: 'OK, whatever. What are the implications of this for my teaching?' The short answer to this question is *that there are no implications of the claim that languages have no cognitive or linguistic reality for what goes on in the classroom.* Even if the dubious claim that people do not speak languages were valid, it would not change the fact that languages have experiential, material, *and cognitive* reality for individuals. Just ask anybody who has struggled to learn a language whether this process has cognitive reality, and the response will be 100% affirmative. As discussed in Chapter 10, the fact that there are no differences in the instructional implications of Unitary Translanguaging Theory (UTT) (which denies the cognitive reality of languages) and Crosslinguistic Translanguaging Theory (CTT) (which acknowledges that people *do* speak languages) suggests that teachers can safely ignore this theoretical dispute.

What is less easy for educators to ignore are the claims that UTT theorists make about academic language and additive bilingualism. Flores (2020: 22) has claimed that 'academic language is a raciolinguistic ideology that frames racialized students as linguistically deficient and in need of remediation'. UTT advocates have also undermined the legitimacy of 'additive bilingualism', characterising it as 'monoglossic' and hence implicated in pedagogies of language separation. Some have gone further by framing additive approaches to bilingualism (presumably including those advocated by Bartlett & García [2012]) as permeated by discourses of appropriateness rooted in raciolinguistic ideologies (Flores & Rosa, 2015).

I have argued that these accusations are without merit. They confound particular theoretical constructs with problematic instructional practices despite the fact that there is no logical or empirical connection between the two. None of the critics of 'academic language' has disputed the fact that there are differences in the *relative frequency* with which certain discourse structures, grammatical constructions, and specialised vocabulary are employed in everyday face-to-face contexts as compared to academic contexts. Furthermore, by making the construct of 'academic language' the *scapegoat* for problematic instructional practices, they take the focus away from problematic instruction and demonise *all* attempts to develop students' knowledge of academic language. If 'academic language' is a raciolinguistic ideology and reinforcing academic language across the curriculum invariably involves molding minoritised students into 'white speaking subjects' (Flores & Rosa, 2015: 157), then it is not at all clear how teachers should engage with curriculum expectations that require them to expand students' reading and writing skills and enable them to use an increasing range of academic registers in effective and powerful ways.

I find much more persuasive the argument advanced by Delpit (1988, 1995) that schools should teach racialised students the linguistic 'codes of power' in a way that recognises the arbitrariness of these codes and valorizes students' own languages and language varieties. This involves saturating the dominant discourse with new meanings and transforming it so that students can see themselves within it and use it for powerful social purposes. First Nations students, Adam and Cassandra, have eloquently and powerfully expressed the profound impact of this transformation on student identities.

The scapegoating of the constructs of 'additive bilingualism' and 'additive approaches to bilingualism' is similarly spurious and instructionally counter-productive. The construct simply references educators' commitment to support minoritised students in developing literacy in their home language together with the school language. It says *nothing* about how languages are processed cognitively. In many sociopolitical contexts that are highly assimilationist and often xenophobic, teachers who adopt an additive orientation to children's home languages are actively challenging coercive relations of power that permeate the wider educational and societal discourse. In the French context, for example, Sylvie highlighted the struggle against skeptical school inspectors and other teachers that was required for her 'to go against the flow' and validate students' languages and cultures in her classroom (Mary & Young, 2021). For more than 40 years, this type of orientation to children's bilingualism has been characterised in the research literature as an additive approach. I find it both embarrassing and offensive to see the additive approaches of teachers such as Sylvie, Lisa Leoni, and thousands of others misconstrued, without qualification or nuance, as rooted in raciolinguistic ideologies.

I think as researchers we can do better. There is a need not only for more constructive and generous dialogue among researchers, but also an opening up of two-way dialogue between educators and researchers where researchers listen more and respect the role of educators as knowledge generators.

Notes

(1) Back in March 2006 after an International Schools conference in Geneva, I had the opportunity to observe elementary (Grade 5) and secondary (Grades 8/9) students at La Chataigneraie campus of the Geneva International School translate poems and

stories into their home languages that they had written initially in English. Students then read these texts aloud to the other students in the class. I described this experience in a Foreword I wrote for Maurice Carder's (2007) book *Bilingualism in International Schools: A Model for Enriching Language Education*:

> This was a new initiative for the teachers and one that produced surprising results and reactions among all involved. Students quickly overcame their initial ambivalence at the suggestion that they bring their home languages into the English-medium classroom. Despite some initial groans, most of them quickly produced home language equivalents of the poems or passages they had written initially in English. Other students (and their teachers) listened intently, appreciating this new dimension of their friends who had previously presented themselves in the classroom only in English, their second or third language. Some students had not developed literacy in their home language and so could not write their poems in that language, but they were able to translate them orally from the English written version. Facets of identity, previously shrouded, flashed spontaneously onto the classroom stage.
>
> I can only describe my own impressions of these events: for the teachers, surprise and delight that something they had not tried before had worked so well, a realisation that their students had talents and experiences beyond what they might typically reveal through English. For the students, initial shyness at revealing their private selves to their classmates and their teacher gave way to quiet satisfaction that they *could* express complex ideas and feelings through their home languages as well as through English; satisfaction also that their identities as bilinguals and multilinguals had been acknowledged and affirmed and that they had risen to the cognitive and linguistic challenge of imaginatively linking their two languages. (Cummins, 2007c: xi)

Appendix 11.1: A Sampling of Crosslinguistic/Translanguaging Instructional Initiatives and Identity Texts Implemented in Canadian and International Contexts 2000–2020

This annotated listing excludes the projects and publications discussed in more detail in previous chapters. The projects and publications are organised according to geographic region. The list does not pretend to be complete or comprehensive, but it provides at least a starting point for further exploration of translanguaging/crosslinguistic pedagogy as it is evolving through the creative initiatives of teachers and researchers. I have not annotated publications associated with the CUNY-NYSIEB project because this pioneering project is well known and easily accessible at https://www.cuny-nysieb.org/. Similarly, there is a wealth of instructional resources and project descriptions available through the European Centre for Modern Languages (ECML) (https://www.ecml.at/). For example, the project *Teaching the School Language in a Context of Diversity* highlights language diversity as a resource and provides many tools to support teachers in changing from a monolingual to a plurilingual mindset (https://maledive.ecml.at/Home/Projectdetails/tabid/3481/Default.aspx). Particularly useful in times of educational disruption is the *Treasure Chest of Resources*

for Learners, Parents and Teachers in Times of Covid-19 (https://www.
ecml.at/Resources/TreasureChestofResources/tabid/4397/language/en-GB/
Default.aspx).

Canada

The ÉLODiL project

Éveil au Langage et Ouverture à la Diversité Linguistique—Awakening
to Language and Opening up to Linguistic Diversity (https://www.elodil.
umontreal.ca/) developed a variety of classroom activities to promote students' awareness of language and appreciation of linguistic diversity. This
ongoing project was undertaken initially in Montreal (Dr Françoise
Armand, Université de Montréal) and Vancouver (Dr Diane Dagenais,
Simon Fraser University) (e.g. Armand & Dagenais, 2012) and is currently
also active in Ontario (Lory, 2021). The *ÉLODiL* website includes several
pedagogical guides focusing on intercultural education and linguistic
diversity, family stories as a resource for learning to write, and plurilingual drama activities (Armand *et al.*, 2013).

The Multiliteracies Pedagogy project

Initiated in 2003 by Dr Heather Lotherington of York University in
Toronto, this project involved a range of collaborations between educators
in Joyce Public School and researchers at York University to explore how
the concept of plurilingualism could be translated into pedagogical design.
The professional learning community at Joyce Public School worked with
students on a variety of multilingual and multimodal projects including
rewriting traditional stories from a critical perspective using their
multilingual linguistic repertoires (Lotherington, 2011; Lotherington &
Paige, 2017).

I am plurilingual! Je suis plurilingue!

This resource was created by Dr Gail Prasad as a companion to her
2015 doctoral dissertation on children's plurilingualism in English- and
French-medium schools. In addition to a description of the research and
its outcomes, the site (https://www.iamplurilingual.com) showcases an
extensive sampling of the plurilingual multimodal texts created by students and teachers in schools in Toronto (Canada), Montpellier (France)
and Sète (France) (Prasad, 2016).

Family Treasures and Grandma's Soup

This dual language book project was initiated by Dr Hetty Roessingh
at the University of Calgary in collaboration the Almadina Language
Charter Academy. Its goal was to enable Kindergarten and grade 1 students to create dual language books to enhance their early literacy development (Roessingh, 2011, 2020).

Scribjab

At Simon Fraser University, Dr Diane Dagenais and Dr Kelleen Toohey have collaborated for many years with educators in the implementation of projects focused on developing students' awareness of language and promoting their multilingual and multiliteracy skills (see, for example, Marshall and Toohey, 2012). The website *ScribJab* (www.scribjab.com) emerged from this work which is described as follows on the website: '*ScribJab* is a web site and iPad application for children (age 10-13) to read and create digital stories (text, illustrations and audio recordings) in multiple languages (English, French and other non-official languages). *ScribJab* creates a space for children to communicate about their stories, and come to an enhanced appreciation of their own multilingual resources'. Dagenais *et al.* (2017) provide a detailed account of the origins and impact of *Scribjab*.

Global Storybooks Project

Developed through the initiative of Dr Bonny Norton of the University of British Colombia, Global Storybooks is a free multilingual literacy resource for children and youth worldwide (https://globalstorybooks.net/). Students and teachers can read, download, and listen to a wide variety of illustrated stories from the African Storybook and other open sites (Norton & Tembe, 2020).

Me Mapping Project

This project, initiated by Antoinette Gagné and colleagues at the Ontario Institute for Studies in Education at the University of Toronto, provides a series of videos focusing on English language learners' identities as well as their experiences and perspectives on the world around them. Students talk about their linguistic repertoire, important milestones in their lives, their experiences at school, and their hopes and aspirations for their future. (https://sites.google.com/view/memapping/home?authuser=0).

Other translanguaging/crosslinguistic pedagogy projects

Other projects implemented by Canadian educators and researchers include Cummins and Persad (2014), Kapoyannis (2019), Ntelioglou *et al.* (2014), Stille and Prasad (2015) and Van Viegen Stille *et al.* (2016). Coelho (2012, Chapter 7) also provides a useful review of Canadian projects that 'make space for community languages' within the school.

Europe

Two projects carried out in France (*Comparons Nos Langues* [Auger, 2008] and the *Didenheim Project* [Hélot & Young, 2006]) have been described in Chapter 11. The *L'Altroparlante* project carried out in Italy (Carbonara & Scibetta, 2020) has also been described in this chapter. A useful listing of other European projects is provided in Kuyumjian (2020: 87-88). Recent European research on translanguaging and/or identity texts includes Straszer (2018) and Veum *et al.* (2020).

Finally, one of the most enlightened and useful official government documents that I have read related to linguistic diversity in education was produced in September 2020 by the Icelandic Ministry of Education, Science, and Culture (Peskova *et al.*, 2020). Entitled *Guidelines for the Support of Mother Tongues and Active Plurilingualism in Schools and Afterschool Programs*, the 'guidelines discuss the importance of supporting the active plurilingualism of children and youth in preschools, compulsory schools, afterschool programs and in upper secondary schools, developing co-operation with parents and strengthening communication with children in their daily work' (2020: 5).

The Language Friendly Schools (LFS) Project

This project was started by Ellen-Rose Kambel of the RUTU Foundation in The Netherlands and Emmanuelle Le Pichon Vorstman formerly of the University of Utrecht and currently at the University of Toronto. The project's website describes its rationale as follows:

> Within a Language Friendly School, everyone welcomes and values all languages spoken by the students, the parents and the school stakeholders. ... Language Friendly Schools are schools that have developed a language plan involving all members of the school: students, teachers and staff. It is a plan that is adapted to the school's own needs and aims at creating an inclusive and language friendly learning environment for all students. (http://languagefriendlyschool.org)

Currently nine schools in The Netherlands and one in Canada have applied and been accepted into the LFS community. Numerous other schools are in the process of developing and implementing their 'language-friendly' policies and instructional initiatives according to the broad guidelines suggested by the LFS project.

The Language Friendly Schools project was selected in 2020 by the HundrED organisation (hundred.org) and the Swedish Cultural Foundation as one of the 10 most significant innovations in bilingual/multilingual education implemented internationally between 2003 and 2019 (see https://hundred.org/en/collections/bilingual-education). For further information see Gärkman *et al.* (2020), Kambel and Le Pichon (2020), Le Pichon (2020), and Le Pichon *et al.* (2020).

International School of The Hague (ISH)

Spearheaded by English-as-an-additional-language (EAL) teachers, Mindy McCracken and Lara Rikers, and amplified by the technological expertise of EAL teacher and Language of the Month Leader, Amy Kuong, the ISH has explored multilingual pedagogies across the curriculum over the past decade. Translanguaging instructional practice is mostly aligned with the original Welsh model (e.g. Williams, 2000) insofar as class assignments are largely split into input and output flows (e.g. students carry out research in L1 and present findings in L2; they draft their writing in L1 and write the final version in L2). Under these circumstances, the L1 acts as a bridge to stronger L2 development (personal communication, Mindy McCracken, May 31, 2020). This work is briefly described in McCracken *et al.* (2018, 2020) and Martin and McCracken (2018). A sense of what ISH teachers have accomplished can be gauged from the following video: https://drive.google.com/file/d/1bEiAaZL2Cd22Oroyuh jg7ReINay51rKS/view?usp=sharing

Interlingual teaching

This term was coined by EAL teacher and consultant, Eithne Gallagher, to refer to the multilingual instructional practices she initiated in Marymount International School in Rome, Italy (Gallagher, 2008, 2011, 2020). The meaning of the term is largely equivalent to translanguaging or crosslinguistic pedagogy. An identity text fairy tale entitled *The Power of Friendship* created by students in her class can be viewed at http://eithne-gallagher.net/resources.htm. Gallagher has also authored a young children's book series entitled *The Glitterings* (Gallagher, 2015; Gallagher & Walker, 2015) which follows the adventures of four polyglot creatures who love languages and are curious about all the different languages coming from planet Earth (see video entitled *Multilingual Storytelling with the Glitterings* at: https://www.youtube.com/watch?v=O-yoa_lR0Mc).

The EDINA project

This project, whose full name is *Education of International Newly Arrived Migrant Pupils*, was initiated by Emmanuelle le Pichon-Vorstman and Venhar Sariaslan working with policymakers, schools, and researchers from Finland, Belgium and the Netherlands (https://edinaplatform. eu/). The project developed a variety of tools to support educators working with newly arrived students with respect to reception, observation, differentiation, assessment and intercultural communication.

Identity texts as a catalyst for identity reconstruction among newcomer students

This impressive project documents the innovative practices of the author, at the time a practising teacher of newcomer students in northeastern France, that pushed the boundaries of what was considered effective and acceptable instructional practice within the highly assimilationist French educational system (Kádas, 2017; Pickel, 2021; Pickel & Hélot, 2014). The project documents the process of identity reconstruction among newcomer students that resulted from the creation of multimodal and multilingual identity texts that were displayed in a public exhibition in one of the prominent art galleries in the students' hometown of Mulhouse. The impact of the project on the students was so profound that one of them joked to another, 'You're going to tell this to your grandchildren' (Pickel, 2021).

Les Sacs d'histoires

This 14-minute film documents a home-school literacy partnership implemented in 2007 by educators in Geneva (Elisabeth Zurbriggen, Paulette Magnenat, and Pascale Sonney) (https://edu.ge.ch/site/archiprod/les-sacs-dhistoires/). The school, which served a highly diverse student population, bought bright orange backpacks for children in the initial grades of primary school and children brought home books in French and their home languages to read with their parents. In addition to the books, the backpacks contained an audio CD with the books read in multiple languages, a game, a glossary of words that appeared in the book, and a surprise). Parents helped create the home language versions of the books by translating and pasting the home language text below the French text.

Similar projects were carried out by educators in several Toronto-area school districts during the 1980s, but to my knowledge, were never documented. Projects such as this are exactly what the research on print access and literacy engagement (see Chapter 6) suggests should be happening in *all* schools serving multilingual and socially disadvantaged children. Case studies of young children from various multilingual backgrounds carried out by British researcher Raymonde Sneddon (2008: 71) indicated numerous positive outcomes associated with children learning to read in their home languages as well as in English: 'The study highlights the positive impact on children's confidence, on their personal identity as bilinguals in a multicultural British society, on their achievement in English literacy as well as the involvement of their parents in their schools'.

India

Trilingual identity text created by Indigenous/Tribal village community

Bapujee Biswabandan's doctoral dissertation (University of Toronto, 2020) explored how mother-tongue multilingual education could be implemented in contexts where multiple languages are represented in the community. Biswabandan worked collaboratively over a period of almost one year with teachers, parents, community members, and a local NGO in a remote Indian village, culminating in the creation and publication of a multilingual children's story book written by 40 parents, many of whom would be considered 'non-literate' by conventional standards. The stories were written in Ho, Santali, and Odia and reflected parents' own cultures and experiences. The project demonstrated that the multilingual repertoires of parents can be used as a powerful resource for implementing multilingual education in linguistically diverse Indigenous contexts. The fact that most parents had experienced very limited educational opportunities and consequently had developed minimal formal literacy skills was not an impediment to their active engagement in creating a multilingual story book based on their cultural realities and experiences. Video documentation of mother-tongue based multilingual education in India can be accessed at the following site: https://www.youtube.com/results?search_query=bapujee+biswabandan+odisha

Biswabandan's (2020) work with Indigenous/Tribal communities in India illustrates how researchers can challenge coercive relations of power by injecting new perspectives into community or classroom discourses. Similar parental and/or community identity text writing projects have been described by Taylor (2011) and Eccles *et al.* (1994) (see Cummins, 2001a: 229-230, for a description of the *Hmong Parent Education Project* conducted by Eccles and colleagues).

Japan

Creating a multilingual ethos in a Japanese elementary school

Japanese researchers, Junko Majima and Chiho Sakurai (2021) report on a project where they have worked for more than a decade with a highly diverse primary school in Osaka. Over the course of this period, the school instituted a range of initiatives aimed primarily at Chinese-speaking students in the school to foster inclusion and bilingual development. To my knowledge, this is the only documentation of this orientation in the Japanese context, which has remained steadfastly assimilationist and monolingual in pedagogical policies and practices.

Among the initiatives undertaken by the school are the employment of a Chinese full-time teacher in 2012, and 'pull-out' classes for Chinese students, where the native Chinese teacher sometimes uses Chinese for instruction and promotes awareness of the two languages. The Chinese teacher also facilitated better communication with parents of the Chinese students. The linguistic ecology of the school was transformed as a result of the display of multilingual signs and posters, bilingual presentations at graduation ceremonies, and explicit affirmation of students' bilingualism by the teachers. Longitudinal analysis of quantitative data showed that students who had developed Chinese reading skills in addition to conversational and listening skills performed significantly better in Japanese reading than those who had attained conversational and/or listening Chinese skills but not literate Chinese skills, a pattern of findings that supports the interdependence hypothesis.

Mexico

Decolonizing Primary English Language Teaching

This is the title of a book written by Mario E. López-Gopar (2016) a university professor and teacher educator at the University of Oaxaca.

López-Gopar documented the ways in which Indigenous teacher education candidates, whose focus was English language teaching, used multilingual identity texts to create decolonising spaces in schools and classrooms. In the Foreword to the book (Cummins, 2016: xiv), I noted that the decolonising pedagogy intuitively constructed and implemented by Mario and *La Banda* of student teachers elevated Indigenous languages to the same status as Spanish and English: 'The liberation of voice that emerged in the resulting interpersonal spaces resulted in languages, previously dormant and fearful, "flying across the room"'. The compelling narrative of this project illustrates how translanguaging and identity texts can combine to create empowering spaces for both teachers and students. López-Gopar *et al.* expressed the outcomes of the project as follows:

> The student teachers also validate their students' multilingual identities, resist the 'native speaker' versus 'non-native speaker' dichotomy, confront the hegemony of Spanish over Indigenous languages, and attribute an international importance to their formation as English teachers. (López-Gopar *et al.*, 2011: 241)

United Kingdom

Multilingual Digital Storytelling (MDST)

Jim Anderson and Vicky Macleroy (2016) working out of Goldsmiths, University of London, documented the outcomes of a five-year multilingual digital storytelling project (2012-2017) involving seven community-operated complementary schools, six mainstream schools, and three overseas schools in Algeria, Palestine and Taiwan. The project included both primary and secondary level students who were studying a variety of languages: Arabic, Chinese, Croatian, English, English as an additional or foreign language, French, German and Greek. Critical ethnography, linked to ecological, collaborative, and multimodal perspectives, was chosen as the central methodological approach to data gathering and interpretation.

With respect to outcomes of the project, the authors identified a variety of concrete claims for which they found evidence in their data. These claims coalesced around students' active engagement with the MDST activities, enthusiasm for using the full range of their plurilingual skills, willingness to employ translanguaging as a scaffold to support task completion, affirmation of the identities of students who spoke community languages with family members, increased parental involvement with students' learning, and increases in metalinguistic awareness. Macleroy (2021) discusses how the shared multilingual interpersonal spaces created by digital storytelling enabled students to push identity boundaries and to reposition themselves in relation to their own languages and cultures and those of others with whom they communicated. They developed what Macleroy termed 'competences of complexity' in relation to their own identities, the identities of others, and the communities to which they belonged.

The nature of the project did not enable the researchers to investigate the extent to which there might have been positive impacts on students' overall educational achievement. However, they suggest that it would be beneficial in future projects of this kind to add an e-portfolio component to the MDST activities. This would enable students to reflect actively on their intercultural exchanges and multilingual digital projects while, at the same time, enabling researchers to capture process data throughout the course of the project activities. Further information on this project is available on the project website: https://goldsmithsmdst.wordpress.com/

United States

Early Authors Program (EAP)

This project was initiated by Ryerson University (Toronto) professor Dr. Judith Bernhard during a study leave in Florida in 2003-2004. The EAP was a large-scale, early literacy programme implemented in Miami-Dade County that involved 32 child-care centers, 800 families and 1,000 children, who with their teachers and parents produced more than 3,000 books in English, Spanish and Haitian-Creole. The EAP was designed in collaboration with Alma Flor Ada and Isabel Campoy, based on principles articulated in their book, *Authors in the Classroom* (2003). This innovative family literacy project engaged parents and children in joint literacy activities such as writing and illustrating dual language identity texts that were based on events in the children's lives, children's interests, and family history (Bernhard *et al.*, 2006).

The evaluation of the project involved 1000 children randomly chosen from the 32 child-care centers who were compared with a control group of children who did not experience the intervention. The results of the project were summarised as follows in the Research Synthesis report published by the National Academies of Sciences, Engineering and Medicine (NASEM):

> The children in the experimental group showed significant growth in language expression and comprehension, and while the intervention did not reduce their initial developmental lag, they did not fall further behind, as did the control group students. The intervention group students started and remained 2 months behind the national norms in language skills for their age group, while the control group had fallen behind by more than 5 months by the end of the study period. Most important, the children who participated in the intervention activities gained in literacy engagement and in their self-esteem. (NASEM, 2017: 195)

This project highlights once again the importance of 'literacy saturation' (Wylie & Thompson, 2003) at the preschool level as well as literacy-related initiatives that involve parents as partners in their children's education.

Developing critical multilingual language awareness (CMLA) through the prism of children's plurilingualism

The power of collaborative research with educators to generate knowledge is vividly illustrated in the inspirational project conducted by Gail Prasad (in close collaboration with teachers and school leaders) that was carried out over several years in a public elementary school in the midwestern United States (Prasad & Lory, 2020). The school principal invited Prasad in January 2016 to work with teachers and other school staff to explore instructional options for building on students' home languages as a means of connecting curriculum to students' lives and fostering understanding and respect for cultural and linguistic diversity. At the time of the project, the school enrollment was 454 students, 30% of whom reported speaking 23 different home languages.

Drawing on the metaphor of students' plurilingualism as a prism (Prasad, 2016), Prasad worked with teachers to design the instructional approach according to five principles, which are paraphrased below based on Prasad and Lory (2020: 805-806):

(1) Teachers and students draw on the diverse language ecology of their school community to integrate a focus on language across the school curriculum.
(2) Parents, families and community members are invited to contribute their language and cultural expertise to help students develop language awareness and forge linkages between the language and literacy practices in which they engage in home, school and community contexts.
(3) Students from diverse language, cultural, and social backgrounds work collaboratively on multilingual activities and projects.
(4) Teachers promote students' critical awareness of language and how it is used in different contexts and for different purposes, by actively engaging students in comparing different languages, how they function, and how concepts and linguistic patterns can be transferred across languages.
(5) Students produce and publish collaborative, critical and creative multilingual inquiry-based projects, which are often shared with multiple audiences beyond their classroom through the use of technology.

Prasad and Lory (2020) describe three cycles through which the project progressed from January 2016 through the end of the 2018 school year. As a result of positive responses from students, families, and teachers to the initial collaboration (January–June 2016), the principal hired a teacher, designated as a 'multilingual educator', to work with teachers across the entire school (K–5) to design and implement collaborative multilingual content-based literacy projects. During the second cycle (September 2016–June 2017), kindergarten through third-grade classes produced 17 multilingual class books related to content areas such as science and social studies. Prasad and Lory describe one outcome of this process:

> Following this second cycle, the school received the highest rating across the district for families' sense of belonging within their school as reported by the annual school district parent survey. The principal attributed this positive outcome in large part to the work that teachers were doing to engage students and their families in collaborative multilingual projects. (Prasad & Lory, 2020: 808)

During the third cycle, the principal increased the multilingual educator's teaching allocation to enable her and Prasad to work together to design and teach a weekly 30-minute class from kindergarten to fifth grade. The focus was on developing students' critical multilingual language awareness and supporting teachers to enable students to create whole-class multilingual books.

Prasad and Lory (2020) describe a variety of other positive outcomes of the project related to students' attention to linguistic diversity and their openness towards different languages and language users as well as impact in the broader community (e.g. the local public library included students' multilingual books in its circulating library collection). According to Prasad and Lory, these impacts illustrate how design-based research can interrupt the historical marginalisation of linguistically and culturally minoritised students and their families. They conclude with a message to researchers which aligns closely with the orientation to collaborative knowledge building and theory generation that I have tried to infuse in this book:

> As such, we call for more researchers to share the responsibility for supporting teachers and students through applied empirical classroom-based research that documents and analyzes complex languaging practices in classrooms and supports LCC [linguistic and cultural collaboration] in schools. (Prasad & Lory, 2020: 816)

About the Author

Autobiographical Reflections

As this book neared completion, several people suggested that it would be useful to provide additional background information so that readers could locate the research and theory discussed in the book within my own personal narrative life trajectory. I have decided to situate myself within the book in three different ways. First, I provide a 'standard' third-person biographical statement similar to the many I have submitted over the past 45 years to edited books and academic conferences. Next, I list some of the research projects and publications that I consider have made significant contributions to language policies, instructional practice, and educational theory. Finally, I reproduce an introductory statement that I wrote (along with the other three authors, M. Kristiina Montero, Cassandra Bice-Zaugg and *Makwa Oshkwenh*-Adam Cyril John Marsh), as part of the paper entitled *Activist Literacies: Validating Aboriginality Through Visual and Literary Identity Texts* (Montero *et al.*, 2013).

Biographical Statement

Jim Cummins is a Professor Emeritus at the Ontario Institute for Studies in Education of the University of Toronto. His research focuses on literacy development in educational contexts characterised by linguistic diversity. In numerous articles and books, he has explored the nature of language proficiency and its relationship to literacy development with particular emphasis on the intersections of societal power relations, teacher-student identity negotiation, and literacy attainment. Over the past 25 years, his major focus has been on working actively with teachers to identify ways of increasing the literacy engagement and academic success of learners in multilingual school contexts.

Dr Cummins is a recipient of the International Reading Association's Albert J. Harris award (1979). He is also a recipient of the Teachers of English to Speakers of Other Languages (TESOL) International Association, President's Award (2018) and the California Association for Bilingual Education Legacy Award (2021). He holds honorary doctorates from the Bank Street College of Education, New York City (1997), Hedmark University College, Norway (2014), University of Athens, Greece (2017) and University of the Aegean, Rhodes, Greece (2017).

Contributions of Personal Significance

A consistent theme that stands out for me when I look back at the research and scholarly writing that I have produced is my focus on searching for theoretical coherence in the empirical evidence. As noted in Chapter 2, the threshold hypothesis was proposed as a way of resolving the apparent contradiction between earlier research that associated bilingualism with cognitive and academic difficulties and the more recent research that pointed in the opposite direction. The interdependence hypothesis was likewise formulated to partially explain why a home-school language switch could result in very different academic outcomes in subtractive sociolinguistic contexts involving 'submersion' in a dominant language as compared to additive contexts such as Canadian French immersion programmes.

However, one major large-scale national study of bilingual and L2 immersion programmes appeared inconsistent with the emerging research data. John Macnamara's (1966) book *Bilingualism and Primary Education: A Study of Irish Experience* claimed to show that Irish pupils instructed primarily through Irish (their L2) showed significant delays in both their English reading comprehension skills and in their ability to solve mathematical word problems. My critique of Macnamara's study showed, in fact, that there was no difference in the English achievement of Irish primary school pupils who were instructed primarily through Irish in comparison to Irish pupils instructed primarily through English. Additionally, Macnamara's claim that instruction through a weaker language caused delays in problem arithmetic confounded the effects of teaching through a weaker language with the effects of *testing* through a weaker language (Cummins, 1977, 1978b). Thus, there was no contradiction between Macnamara's findings and those that, at the time, were emerging from French immersion programmes.

The reanalysis I was able to carry out on the Wright and Ramsey (1970; Ramsey & Wright, 1974) findings regarding the impact of age on arrival on immigrant students' learning of English (described in Chapter 3) served a similar function in resolving apparent inconsistencies between their conclusions and those of Skutnabb-Kangas and Toukomaa (1976) who reported that Finnish immigrant students who arrived in Sweden at ages 9-10, after they had attained initial literacy in Finnish, performed better in both languages over the long-term than their peers who had arrived at earlier ages. The reanalysis (Cummins, 1981c) also highlighted for the first time the relatively lengthy academic catch-up trajectory (typically at least 5-7 years) experienced by many immigrant-background students. This pattern of findings pointed to the need to distinguish between the language skills involved in carrying out school-based academic tasks and those involved in everyday communication. The findings also highlighted the need to provide ongoing instructional support for language learners even after they appeared to be relatively fluent in conversational L2 skills.

The search for theoretical coherence also fueled my attempts to integrate psychoeducational constructs such as the *common underlying proficiency* (see Chapter 4) with the coercive sociopolitical realities experienced by minoritised and racialised students and communities in countries around the world. It became clear to me in the early 1980s that psychoeducational theoretical ideas, although an important part of the puzzle, were limited in their ability to account for patterns of underachievement. Obviously, the operation of coercive power relationships was evident both in the international and domestic arenas. This is illustrated, for example, in the international arena by the US-backed overthrow of the democratically elected Allende government in Chile in 1973, resulting in the torture and death of tens of thousands of people. Domestically, coercive power relations in the educational arena were brutally illustrated in the psychological and physical torture of Canadian Indigenous students in residential schools operated by religious groups, termed 'cultural genocide' by the Truth and Reconciliation Commission of Canada (2015). However, prior to the 1980s, 'mainstream' educational research and theory almost totally ignored the ways in which societal power relations impacted schooling, with the result that school curricula, teacher education, and instruction itself were sanitised to reinforce the multiple mythologies of virtue that are the foundation of nations.

As outlined in Chapter 5, beginning with my 1986 paper in the Harvard Educational Review entitled *Empowering Minority Students: A Framework for Intervention*, I attempted to draw lines of causality between societal power relations, ranging from coercive to collaborative, and both the structures of schooling and the ways in which teachers orchestrated patterns of identity negotiation between themselves and their students. The goal of this analysis was to identify ways in which teachers could challenge the operation of coercive relations of power and promote collaborative relations of power. The definition of *empowerment* as 'the collaborative creation of power' expressed the ways in which societal power relations were infused in patterns of teacher-student identity negotiation. The teacher's role in this process was lucidly expressed by California high school students, Adriana and Rosalba Jasso (1995:255): 'We had a teacher who believed in us; he didn't hide our power; he advertised it'.

Finally, the research I have carried out over the past 25 years has primarily involved working collaboratively with educators of multilingual students whose instructional practice has been focused on creating classroom spaces where students can use their entire multilingual repertoire and

cultural knowledge to express and 'advertise' the intellectual and imaginative power they carry within themselves. I feel very fortunate to have had
the opportunity to learn from these teachers and their students.

Personal statement from the Montero *et al.* (2013) 'Activist Literacies' paper written 'to provide you, the reader, with sufficient identity markers so you may situate us within the work' (2013: 74)

My name is Jim Cummins. Like many Canadians, I was born and grew
up outside of Canada, in my case, Ireland. I left Ireland to pursue Ph.D.
studies at the University of Alberta in Edmonton in the early 1970s. I spent
two years back in Dublin in the mid-1970s before coming back to Canada
as an immigrant. The collective history within which my own identity is
embedded involves a continuous struggle for independence and self-deter-
mination against an oppressive colonial power. Independence was achieved
in the early 1900s but at a cost. The famine of the mid-1800s reduced the
Irish population from eight million to four million through death and emi-
gration; the Irish language all but disappeared and is still only a shadow of
its former presence despite intensive efforts at revitalization. Initially, my
academic work proceeded in isolation from this collective cultural inheri-
tance. I carried out research on the effects of bilingualism and bilingual
education focusing on the cognitive aspects of these processes. It was only
in the 1980s when I became involved in the ongoing debates on bilingual
education for Latino/Latina students in the United States that I began to
realize that societal power relations were fundamental to everything that
goes on in schools. Underachievement among socially marginalized groups
who had been and still were subject to intensive racism was largely a result
of the fact that schools reflected and transmitted this racism directly to
students and communities. It follows that 'instructional effectiveness'
requires that schools actively challenge the operation of coercive relations
of power. Yet, this perspective is totally absent from the mainstream 'educational reform' or 'school improvement' literature. It is almost as though
words like 'power' and 'identity' have been blacklisted and 'invisibilized'
by policymakers. When Kristiina [Montero] first showed me the art and
literature created by students in the Native Studies program, they spoke to
me not only as works of extraordinary insight and beauty, but also as a
powerful and eloquent repudiation of the shallowness of educational policymaking in many parts of the world. I feel grateful and privileged to be
connected to this project in a very minor way (Montero *et al.*, 2013: 75–76).

References

Abu-Rabia, S. (2005) Social aspects and reading, writing, and working memory skills in Arabic, Hebrew, English, and Circassian: Quadrilingual case of Circassians. *Language, Culture and Curriculum* 18, 27–58.

Abu-Rabia, S. and Siegel, L.S. (2003) Reading skills in three orthographies: The case of trilingual Arabic–Hebrew–English-speaking Arab children. *Reading and Writing: An Interdisciplinary Journal* 16, 611–634.

Abutalebi, J. (2008) Neural aspects of second language representation and language control. *Acta Psychologica* 128, 466–478. doi:10.1016/j.actpsy.2008.03.014

Ada, A.F. (1988a) The Pajaro Valley experience: Working with Spanish-speaking parents to develop children's reading and writing skills in the home through the use of children's literature. In T. Skutnabb-Kangas and J. Cummins (eds) *Minority Education: From Shame to Struggle* (pp. 223–238). Clevedon: Multilingual Matters.

Ada, A.F. (1988b) Creative reading: A relevant methodology for language minority children. In L.M. Malave (ed.) *NABE '87. Theory, Research and Application: Selected papers* (pp. 97–112). Buffalo: State University of New York.

Ada, A.F. and Campoy, I. (2003) *Authors in the Classroom: A Transformative Education Process*. Boston: Allyn and Bacon.

Adatia, S. (2019) *La richesse de la diversité – The richness of diversity* [video file]. Retrieved from https://youtu.be/V6ewEZlBFyQ

Aguila, V. (2010) Schooling English learners: Contexts and challenges. In California Department of Education (2010) *Improving Education for English Learners: Research-Based Approaches* (pp. 1–18). Sacramento: California Department of Education.

Adesope, O.O., Lavin, T., Thompson, T. and Ungerleider, C. (2010) A systematic review and meta-analysis of the cognitive correlates of bilingualism. *Review of Educational Research* 80, 207–245.

Agirdag, O. (2010) Exploring bilingualism in a monolingual school system: Insights from Turkish and native students from Belgian schools. *British Journal of Sociology of Education* 31 (3), 307–321. doi:10.1080/01425691003700540

Agirdag, O. and Vanlaar, G. (2016) Does more exposure to the language of instruction lead to higher academic achievement? A cross-national examination. *International Journal of Bilingualism*. doi:10.1177/1367006916658711.

Alfaro, C. and Bartolomé, L. (2017) Preparing ideologically clear bilingual teachers honoring working-class non-standard language use in the bilingual education classroom. *Issues in Teacher Education* 26 (2), 11–34.

Alisaari, J., Jäppinen, E., Kekki, N., Kivimäki, R., Kivipelto, S., Kuusento, K., Lehtinen, E., Raunio, A., Repo, E., Sissonen, S., Tyrer, M. and Vigren, H. (eds) (2020) *Kielestä Koppi – Oppimateriaali Kielitietoiseen Perusopetukseen (Focus on Language – A Study Book for Language Sensitive Basic Education)*. Turku, Finland: University of Turku.

Alladi, D.M., Bak, T.H., Duggirala, V., Surampudi, B., Shailaja, M., Shukla, A.K., Chaudhuri, J.R. and Kaul, S.D. (2013) Bilingualism delays age at onset of dementia, independent of education and immigration status. *Neurology* 1938–1944. doi:10.1212/01.wnl.0000436620.33155.a4

Allington, R.L. and McGill-Franzen, A. (2017) Summer reading loss is the basis of almost all the rich/poor reading gap. In R. Horowitz and S.J. Samuels (eds) *The Achievement Gap in Reading: Complex Causes, Persistent Issues, and Possible Solutions* (pp. 170–184). New York: Routledge.

Allington, R.L. and McGill-Franzen, A. (2018) Summer reading loss. In R.L. Allington and A. McGill-Franzen (eds) *Summer Reading: Closing the Rich/Poor Reading Achievement Gap* (2nd edn) (pp. 1–21). New York: Teachers College Press.

Anderson, J. and Macleroy, V. (2016) *Multilingual Digital Storytelling: Engaging Creatively and Critically with Literacy*. London and New York: Routledge.

Anstrom, K., DiCerbo, P., Butler, F., Katz, A., Millet, J. and Rivera, C. (2010) *A Review of the Literature on Academic English: Implications for K-12 English Language Learners*. Arlington, VA: The George Washington University Center for Equity and Excellence in Education.

Antoniou, M. (2019) The advantages of bilingualism debate. *Annual Review of Linguistics* 5 (1), 395–415. Retrieved from https://www.annualreviews.org/doi/10.1146/annurev-linguistics-011718-011820.

Ardasheva, Y., Tretter, T.R., and Kinny, M. (2012) English language learners and academic achievement: Revisiting the threshold hypothesis. *Language Learning* 62 (3), 769–812. doi:10.1111/j.1467-9922.2011.00652.x.

Armand, F. and Dagenais, D. (2012) S'ouvrir à la langue de l'autre et à la diversité linguistique [Becoming aware of others' languages and of linguistic diversity]. *Education Canada*, 52 (1). Retrieved from http://www.cea-ace.ca/education-canada/article/s'ouvrir-à-la-langue-del'autre-et-à-la-diversité-linguistique

Armand, F., Lory, M.-P. and Rousseau, C. (2013) 'Les histoires, ça montre les personnes dedans, les feelings. Pas possible si pas de théâtre' *(Tahina). Revue de linguistique et de didactique des langue* 48, 37–55.

Armand, F. and Maraillet, É. (2013) Éducation interculturelle et diversité linguistique. Montréal : Université de Montréal, Elodil (Éveil au Langage et Ouverture à la Diversité Linguistique). http://www.elodil.umontreal.ca/guides/education-interculturelle-et-diversite-linguistique/

Astington, J.W. and Olson, D.R. (1990) Metacognitive and metalinguistic language: Learning to talk about thought. *Applied Psychology* 39, 77–87. doi:10.1111/j.1464-0597.1990.tb01038.x

Au, K.H. (1979) Using the experience-text-relationship method with minority children. *Reading Teacher* 32 (6), 677–679.

Auerbach, E. (1993) Reexamining English only in the ESL classroom. *TESOL Quarterly* 27, 9–32.

Auerbach, E. (2016) Reflections on 'Reexamining English only in the ESL classroom.' *TESOL Quarterly* 50 (4), 936–939. doi: 10.1002/tesq.310

Auger, N. (2004) Comparons nos langues, démarche d'apprentissage du français auprès d'enfants nouvellement arrivés. Montpellier: Centre régional de documentation péda-gogique. Retrieved from: https://assets.vlor.be/www.vlor.be/attachment/Livret%20-%20ComparonsNosLangues.pdf

Auger, N. (2008) Comparing our languages: A tool for maintaining individual multilin-gualism. *Synergies Sud-Est Européen* 1, 93–99. Retrieved from: http://gerflint.fr/Base/SE-europe/auger.pdf

Auger, N. (2014) Exploring the use of migrant languages to support learning in mainstream classrooms in France. In D. Little, C. Leung and P. Van Avermaet (eds) *Managing Diversity in Education: Languages, Policies, Pedagogies* (pp. 223–242). Bristol, UK: Multilingual Matters.

August, D. and Hakuta, K. (1997) *Improving Schooling for Language-Minority Children: A Research Agenda*. Washington, DC: National Research Council.

August, D. and Shanahan, T. (eds) (2006) *Developing Literacy in Second-Language Learners. Report of the National Literacy Panel on Language-Minority Children and Youth*. Mahwah, NJ: Lawrence Erlbaum Associates Publishers.

August, D. and Shanahan, T. (eds) (2008a) *Developing Reading and Writing in Second-Language Learners: Lessons from the Report of the National Literacy Panel on Language-Minority Children and Youth*. Mahwah, NJ: Lawrence Erlbaum.

August, D. and Shanahan, T. (2008b) Introduction and methodology. In D. August and T. Shanahan (eds) *Developing Reading and Writing in Second-Language Learners: Lessons from the Report of the National Literacy Panel on Language-Minority Children and Youth* (pp. 1–17). Mahwah, NJ: Lawrence Erlbaum.

August, D. and Shanahan, T. (2010) Effective English literacy instruction for English learners. In California Department of Education (2010). *Improving Education for English Learners: Research-Based Approaches* (pp. 209–249). Sacramento: California Department of Education.

August, D., Beck, I.L., Calderon, M., Francis, D.J., Lesaux, N.K. and Shanahan, T. (2008) Instruction and professional development. In D. August and T. Shanahan (eds) *Developing Reading and Writing in Second-Language Learners: Lessons from the Report of the National Literacy Panel on Language-Minority Children and Youth* (pp. 131–250). Mahwah, NJ: Lawrence Erlbaum.

Aukerman, M. (2007) Rethinking the conversational/academic language proficiency distinction in early literacy instruction. *Reading Teacher* 60, 626–635. doi:10.1598/RT.60.7.3.

Avineri, N. and Johnson, E.J. (2015) Invited Forum: Bridging the 'Language Gap'. *Journal of Linguistic Anthropology* 25 (1) 66–86.

Bahry, S. and Zholdoshalieva, R. (2012) Educational and linguistic equity for Yughur and Kyrgyz minorities in northwest China: Disadvantages of dominant-language submersion and mother-tongue education. In A.S. Yeung, C.F.K. Lee and E.L. Brown (eds) *International Advances in Education: Global Initiatives for Equity and Social Justice, Volume 7: Communication and Language* (pp. 25–53). Charlotte, NC: IAP.

Bailey, A. (2007) Introduction: Teaching and assessing students learning English in school. In A. Bailey (ed.) *The Language Demands of School: Putting Academic English to the Test* (pp. 1–26). New Haven, CT: Yale University Press.

Baker, C. (2001) *Foundations of Bilingual Education and Bilingualism* (3rd edn). Clevedon: Multilingual Matters.

Baker, C. (2011) *Foundations of Bilingual Education and Bilingualism* (5th edn). Bristol: Multilingual Matters.

Baker, C. and Hornberger, N.H. (2001) *An Introductory Reader to the Writings of Jim Cummins*. Clevedon: Multilingual Matters.

Baker, C. and Wright, W. (2017) *Foundations of Bilingual Education and Bilingualism* (6th edn). Bristol: Multilingual Matters.

Baker, K.A. and de Kanter, A.A. (1981) *Effectiveness of Bilingual Education: A Review of the Literature*. Washington, DC: U.S. Department of Education.

Ballinger, S., Lau, S.M.C. and Quevillon Lacasse, C. (2020) Cross-linguistic pedagogy: Harnessing transfer in the classroom. *The Canadian Modern Language Review* 76 (4), 265–277.

Ballinger, S., Lyster, R., Sterzuk, A. and Genesee, F. (2017) Context-appropriate crosslinguistic pedagogy: Considering the role of language status in immersion education. *Journal of Immersion and Content-Based Language Education* 5 (1) 30–57. doi 10.1075/jicb.5.1.02bal

Banks, J.A. (2016) Multicultural education: Characteristics and goals. In J.A. Banks and C.A.M. Banks (eds) *Multicultural Education: Issues and Perspectives* (9th edn) (pp. 2–23). Hoboken, NJ: John Wiley and Sons.

Bankston, C.L. and Zhou, M. (1995) Effects of achievement of Vietnamese youths in New Orleans. *Sociology of Education* 68, 1–17.

Barac, R. and Bialystok, E. (2011) Cognitive development of bilingual children. *Language Teaching* 44 (1), 36–54.

Barr, C.D., Uccelli, P. and Phillips Galloway, E. (2019) Specifying the academic language skills that support text understanding in the middle grades: The design and validation of the core academic language skills construct and instrument. *Language Learning* 69, 978–1021.

Bartlett, F.C. (1932) *Remembering: A Study in Experimental and Social Psychology*, Cambridge, UK: Cambridge University Press.

Bartlett, L. and García, O. (2011) *Additive Schooling in Subtractive Times: Bilingual Education and Dominican Immigrant Youth in the Heights*. Nashville, TN: Vanderbilt University Press.

Bartlett, L. and Koyama, J. (2014) Immigrants and education. In M. Bigelow and J. Ennser-Kananen (eds) *The Routledge Handbook of Educational Linguistics* (pp. 237–251). London and New York: Routledge.

Battiste, M. (2013) *Decolonizing Education: Nourishing the Learning Spirit*. Saskatoon, Canada: Purich Publishing.

Beacco, J.-C., Byram, M., Cavalli, M., Coste, D., Cuenat, M.E., Gouiller, F. and Panthier, J. (2016) *Guide for the Development and Implementation of Curricula for Plurilingual and Intercultural Education*. Strasbourg, France: Council of Europe.

Beacco, J.-C., Krumm, H.-J., Little, D. and Thalgott, P. (2017) *The Linguistic Integration of Adult Migrants: Some Lessons from Research*. Berlin: Walter de Gruyter.

Beauboeuf-Lafontant, T. and Smith Augustine, D. (eds) (1996) *Facing Racism in Education*. 2nd edn. Reprint Series No. 28, Harvard Educational Review. Cambridge, MA: Harvard Educational Review.

Benson, C. (2019) Learners' own languages as key to achieving Sustainable Development Goal Four and beyond. In I. Idiazabal and M. Pérez-Caurel (eds) *Linguistic Diversity, Minority Languages and Sustainable Development /Diversidad Lingüística, Lenguas Minorizadas y Desarrollo Sostenible/Diversité Linguistique, Langues Minoritaires et Développement Durable* (pp. 116–132). Bilbao: Servicio de Publicaciones de la Universidad del País Vasco.

Benson, C. (2021) MLE implementation in Ethiopia and Mozambique: How the above-below-side framework shakes out in two multilingual contexts. In C. Benson and K. Kosonen (eds) *Language Issues in Comparative Education II* (pp. 57–81). Leiden: Brill Sense.

Benson, C., Heugh, K., Bogale, B. and Gebre Yohannes, M.A. (2012) Multilingual education in Ethiopian primary schools. In T. Skutnabb-Kangas and K.Heugh (eds) *Multilingual Education and Sustainable Diversity Work: From Periphery to Center* (pp. 32–61). New York and London: Routledge.

Benson, C. and Kosonen, K. (eds) (2021) *Language Issues in Comparative Education II*. Leiden: Brill Sense.

Berliner, D.C. (2009) *Poverty and Potential: Out-of-School Factors and School Success*. Boulder, CO and Tempe, AZ: Education and the Public Interest Center and Education Policy Research Unit. Retrieved from https://eric.ed.gov/?id=ED507359

Bernhard, J.K., Cummins, J., Campoy, F.I., Ada, A.F., Winsler, A. and Bleiker, C. (2006) Identity texts and literacy development among preschool English language learners: Enhancing learning opportunities for children at risk for learning disabilities. *Teachers College Record* 108 (11), 2380–2405.

Berthele, R. and Lambelet, A. (eds) (2018) *Heritage and School Language Literacy Development in Migrant Children: Interdepedence or Independence?* Bristol, UK: Multilingual Matters.

Berthele, R. and Vanhove, J. (2020) What would disprove interdependence? Lessons learned from a study on biliteracy in Portuguese heritage language speakers in Switzerland. *International Journal of Bilingual Education and Bilingualism* 23 (5), 550–566. doi:10.1080/13670050.2017.1385590

Beykont, Z.F. (1994) *Academic Progress of a Nondominant Group: A Longitudinal Study of Puerto Ricans in New York City's Late-Exit Bilingual Programs.* Unpublished doctoral dissertation, Harvard University.

Bhatnager, J. (1980) Linguistic behavior and adjustment of immigrant children in French and English schools in Montreal. *International Journal of Applied Psychology* 29, 141–158.

Bhatt, R.M. and Bolonyai, A. (2019) On the theoretical and empirical bases of translanguaging. *Working Papers in Urban Language & Literacies.* Paper 254, 1–25.

Bhattacharya, J., Quiroga, J. and Olsen, L. (2007) *Bridging Multiple Worlds: Creating Affirming Environments for Young People to Thrive.* Oakland, CA: California Tomorrow.

Bialystok, E. (2020a) Bilingual effects on cognition in children. *Oxford Research Encyclopedias: Education.* doi:10.1093/acrefore/9780190264093.013.962

Bialystok, E. (2020b) Null results in bilingualism research: What they tell us and what they don't. *Journal of Multilingual Theories and Practices* 1 (1), 8–22. https://doi.org/10.1558/jmtp.17104

Bialystok, E. and Craik, F.I.M. (2010) Cognitive and linguistic processing in the bilingual mind. *Current Directions in Psychological Science* 19 (1), 19–23.

Biber, D. (1986) Spoken and written textual dimensions in English: Resolving the contradictory findings. *Language* 62, 384–414.

Biber, D., Conrad, S. and Reppen, R. (1998) *Corpus Linguistics: Investigating Language Structure and Use.* Cambridge: Cambridge University Press.

Biber, D., Johansson, S., Leech, G., Conrad, S. and Finegan, E. (1999) *Longman Grammar of Spoken and Written English.* Edinburgh Gate: Pearson Education.

Blankstein, A. and Noguera, P. (eds) (2016) *Excellence through Equity: Five Principles of Courageous Leadership to Guide Achievement for Every Student.* Alexandria, VA: ASCD.

Boykin, A.W. and Noguera, P. (2011) *Creating the Opportunity to Learn: Moving from Research to Practice to Close the Achievement Gap.* Alexandria, VA: ASCD.

Bransford, J.D., Brown, A.L. and Cocking, R.R. (2000) *How People Learn: Brain, Mind, Experience, and School.* Washington, DC: National Academy Press.

Brevik, L.M., Olsen, R.V. and Hellekjær, G.O. (2016) The complexity of second language reading: Investigating the L1-L2 relationship. *Reading in a Foreign Language* 28 (2), 161–182.

Britt, M.A., Richter, T. and Rouet, J.-F. (2014) Scientific literacy: The role of goal-directed reading and evaluation in understanding scientific information. *Educational Psychologist* 49 (2), 104–122. doi:10.1080/00461520.2014.916217

Broome, Y. (2004) Reading English in multilingual South African primary schools. *International Journal of Bilingual Education and Bilingualism* 7, 506–528.

Brozo, W., Shiel, G. and Topping, K. (2007) Engagement in reading: Lessons learned from three PISA countries. *Journal of Adolescent and Adult Literacy* 51, 304–315.

Bruner, J.S. (1975) Language as an instrument of thought. In A. Davies (ed.) *Problems of Language and Learning* (pp. 61–88). London: Heinemann.

Buchweitz, A. and Prat, C. (2013) The bilingual brain: Flexibility and control in the human cortex. *Physics of Life Reviews* 10, 428–443. doi:10.1016/j.plrev.2013.07.020

Bunch, G.C. (2013) Pedagogical language knowledge: Preparing mainstream teachers for English learners in the new standards era. *Review of Research in Education* 37, 298–341.

Bunch, G.C. (2014) The language of ideas and the language of display: Reconceptualizing 'Academic Language' in linguistically diverse classrooms, *International Multilingual Research Journal* 8 (1), 70–86. doi:10.1080/19313152.2014.852431

Bunch, G.C., Walqui, A. and Pearson, P.D. (2014) Complex text and new common standards in the United States: Pedagogical implications for English Learners. *TESOL Quarterly* 48 (3), 533–559.

Butler, Y.G. and Hakuta, K. (2004) Bilingualism and second language acquisition. In T.K. Bhatia and W.C. Ritchie (eds) *The Handbook of Bilingualism* (pp. 114–144). Malden, MA: Blackwell.

Cain, K., Oakhill, J. and Bryant, P. (2004) Children's reading comprehension ability: Concurrent prediction by working memory, verbal ability, and component skills. *Journal of Educational Psychology* 96 (1), 231–242.

California Department of Education (2010) *Improving Education for English Learners: Research-Based Approaches.* Sacramento: California Department of Education.

Callahan, R., Wilkinson, L. and Muller, C. (2010) Academic achievement and course taking among language minority youth in U.S. schools: Effects of ESL placement. *Educational Evaluation and Policy Analysis* 32 (1), 84–117. doi:10.3102/016237 3709359805

Canagarajah, A.S. (2006) TESOL at forty: What are the issues? *TESOL Quarterly* 40 (1), 9–34.

Canale, M. (1984) On some theoretical frameworks for language proficiency. In C. Rivera (ed.) *Language Proficiency and Academic Achievement* (pp. 28–40). Clevedon: Multilingual Matters.

Candelier, M., Camilleri-Grima, A., Castellotti, V., De Pietro, J.-F., Lörincz, I., Meissner, F.-J., Schröder-Sura, A. and Noguerol, A. (2007) *A Travers les Langues et les Cultures.* Strasbourg: Conseil de l'Europe.

Carbonara, V. and Scibetta, A. (2020a) *Imparare Attraverso le Lingue: Il Translanguaging come Pratica Didattica.* Rome: Carocci Editore.

Carbonara, V. and Scibetta, A. (2020b) Integrating translanguaging pedagogy into Italian primary schools: implications for language practices and children's empowerment. *International Journal of Bilingual Education and Bilingualism.* Published online 5 April. doi:10.1080/13670050.2020.1742648

Carnine, D.W., Silbert, J., Kame'enui, E.J. and Tarver, S.G. (2003) *Direct Instruction Reading* (4th edn). Upper Saddle River, NJ: Pearson Education.

Carder, M. (2007) *Bilingualism in International Schools: A Model for Enriching Language Education.* Clevedon: Multilingual Matters.

Carter, P.L. and Welner, K.G. (2013) *Closing the Opportunity Gap: What America Must Do to Give Every Child an Even Chance.* New York, NY: Oxford University Press.

Carver, R.P. (2000) *The Causes of High and Low Reading Achievement.* Mahwah, NJ: Lawrence Erlbaum Associates.

Casanave, C.P. and Schecter, S.R. (eds) (1997) *On Becoming a Language Educator: Personal Essays on Professional Development.* Mahwah, NJ: Lawrence Erlbaum Associates.

Cashion, M. and Eagan, R. (1990) Spontaneous reading and writing in English by students in total French immersion: Summary of final report. *English Quarterly* 22 (1–2), 30–44.

Celic, C. and Seltzer, K. (2013) *Translanguaging: A CUNY-NYSIEB Guide for Educators.* New York, NY: CUNY-NYSIEB, The Graduate Center, The City University of New York. Retrieved from https://www.cuny-nysieb.org/translanguaging-resources/trans languaging-guides/

Cenoz, J. (2013a) Defining multilingualism. *Annual Review of Applied Linguistics* 33, 3–18. doi:10.1017/S026719051300007X

Cenoz, J. (2013b) The influence of bilingualism on third language acquisition: Focus on multilingualism. *Language Teaching* 46, 71–86.

Cenoz, J., and Gorter, D. (2011) Focus on multilingualism: A study of trilingual writing. *The Modern Language Journal* 95, 356–369.

Cenoz, J. and Gorter, D. (2013) Towards a plurilingual approach in English language teaching: Softening the boundaries between languages. *TESOL Quarterly* 47, 591–599. doi: 10.1002/tesq.121

Cenoz, J. and Gorter, D. (2014) Focus on multilingualism as an approach in educational contexts. In A. Creese and A. Blackledge (eds) *Heteroglossia as Practice and Pedagogy* (pp. 239–254). Berlin, Germany: Springer.

Cenoz, J. and Santos, A. (2020) Implementing pedagogical translanguaging in trilingual schools. *System*, doi:10.1016/j.system.2020.102273

Chamberlain, C. and Mayberry, R.I. (2008) ASL syntactic and narrative comprehension in good and poor readers: Bilingual-bimodal evidence for the linguistic basis of reading. *Applied Psycholinguistics* 29, 367–388.

Chen, S., Lawrence, J.F., Zhou, J., Min, L. and Snow, C.E. (2018) The efficacy of a school-based book-reading intervention on vocabulary development of young Uyghur children: A randomized controlled trial. *Early Childhood Research Quarterly* 44, 206–219.

Cheung, A.C.K. and Slavin, R.E. (2012) Effective reading programs for Spanish-dominant English language learners (Ells) in the elementary grades: A synthesis of research. *Review of Educational Research* 82 (4), 351–395. doi:10.3102/0034654312465472.

Chomsky, N. (1987) The manufacture of consent. In J. Peck (ed.) *The Chomsky Reader* (pp. 121–136). New York: Pantheon Books.

Chow, P. and Cummins, J. (2003) Valuing multilingual and multicultural approaches to learning. In S.R. Schecter and J. Cummins (eds) *Multilingual Education in Practice: Using Diversity as a Resource* (pp. 32–61). Portsmouth, NH: Heinemann.

Christensen, G. and Segeritz, M. (2008) An international perspective on student achievement. In Bertelsmann Stiftung (ed.) *Immigrant Students Can Succeed: Lessons from Around the Globe* (pp. 11–33). Gütersloh: Bertelsmann Stiftung.

Christensen, G. and Stanat, P. (2007, September) *Language Policies and Practices for Helping Immigrant Second-Generation Students Succeed.* The Transatlantic Task Force on Immigration and Integration convened by the Migration Policy Institute and Bertlesmann Stiftung. Retrieved from http://www.migrationinformation.org/transatlantic/

Chuang, H.-K., Malatesha, J. and Dixon, L.Q. (2012) Cross-Language transfer of reading ability: Evidence from Taiwanese ninth-grade adolescents. *Journal of Literacy Research* 44 (1), 97–119. doi: 10.1177/1086296X11431157

Chumak-Horbatsch, R. (2012) *Linguistically Appropriate Practice: A Guide for Working with Young Immigrant Children.* Toronto: University of Toronto Press.

Chumak-Horbatsch, R. (2019) *Using Linguistically Appropriate Practice: A Guide for Teaching in Multilingual Classrooms.* Bristol: Multilingual Matters.

Chumak-Horbatsch, R., Adatia, S. and Quintal, S. (2020) Home languages in the French-language classroom? But of course! *Réflections* 39 (1), 2020.

Clarke, M.A. (1990) Some cautionary observations on liberation education. *Language Arts* 67 (4), 388–398.

Cline, T. and Frederickson, N. (eds) (1996) *Curriculum Related Assessment: Cummins and Bilingual Children.* Clevedon: Multilingual Matters.

Clines, F.X. (1981) Reagan defends cuts in budget and asks for help from mayors. *New York Times*, 3 March, Retrieved from www.nytimes.com/1981/03/03/us/reagan-defends-cuts-in-budget-and-asks-for-help-of-mayors.html

Cobo-Lewis, A., Eilers, R.E., Pearson, B.Z. and Umbel, V.C. (2002a) Interdependence of Spanish and English knowledge in language and literacy among bilingual children. In D.K. Oller and R.E. Eilers (eds) *Language and Literacy in Bilingual Children* (pp. 118–132). Clevedon, UK: Multilingual Matters.

Cobo-Lewis, A., Pearson, B.Z., Eilers, R.E. and Umbel, V.C. (2002b) Effects of bilingualism and bilingual education on oral and written English skills: A multifactor study of standardized test outcomes. In D.K. Oller and R.E. Eilers (eds) *Language and Literacy in Bilingual Children* (pp. 64–97). Clevedon: Multilingual Matters.

Coelho, E. (2004) *Adding English: A Guide to Teaching in Multilingual Classrooms.* Toronto: Pippin Publishing Corporation.

Coelho, E. (2012) *Language and Learning in Multilingual Classrooms: A Practical Approach*. Bristol: Multilingual Matters.

Cohen, S.L. (2011) Making room for identity in second language writing: The promise and possibilities of dual language identity texts. *Writing & Pedagogy* 3 (1), 217–239.

Cohen, S.L. and Leoni, L. (2012) Expanding the voices of literacy. In A. Honigsfeld and A. Cohan (eds) *Breaking the Mold of Education for Culturally and Linguistically Diverse Students: Innovative and Successful Practices for the 21st Century* (pp. 163–172). New York: Rowman & Littlefield Publishers Inc.

Collier, V. P. (1987) Age and rate of acquisition of second language for academic purposes. *TESOL Quarterly* 21, 617–641.

Collins, M.F. (2005) ESL preschoolers' English vocabulary acquisition from storybook reading. *Reading Research Quarterly* 40, 406–408.

Cook, V. (1992) Evidence for multi-competence. *Language Learning* 42, 557–591.

Cook, V. (1995) Multi-competence and learning of many languages. *Language, Culture and Curriculum* 8, 93–98.

Cook, V. (2007) The goals of ELT: Reproducing native-speakers or promoting multicompetence among second language users? In J. Cummins and C. Davison (eds) *International Handbook of English Language Education, Volume 1* (pp. 237–248). Norwell, MA: Springer.

Cook, V. (2016) Premises of multi-competence. In V. Cook and Li Wei (eds) *The Cambridge Handbook of Linguistic Multi-Competence* (pp. 1–25). Cambridge: Cambridge University Press.

Corson, D. (1995) *Using English Words*. New York: Kluwer.

Corson, D. (1997) The learning and use of academic English words. *Language Learning* 47 (4), 671–718.

Coste, D., Moore, D. and Zarate, G. (2009) *Plurilingual and Pluricultural Competence. Studies towards a Common European Framework of Reference for Language Learning and Teaching*. Strasbourg, France: Council of Europe Publishing. First published in French, 1997.

Council of Europe. (2001) *Common European Framework of Reference for Languages: Learning, Teaching, Assessment*. Strasbourg, France: Council of Europe Publishing. Retrieved from https://www.coe.int/en/web/common-european-framework-reference-languages/home

Council of Europe. (2020) *Common European Framework of Reference for Languages: Learning, Teaching, Assessment. Companion Volume*. Strasbourg, France: Council of Europe Publishing. Retrieved from https://www.coe.int/en/web/common-european-framework-reference-languages/home

Council of Great City Schools (2014) *A Framework for Raising Expectations and Instructional Rigor for ELLs*. Washington, DC: Council of Great City Schools.

Creese, A. and Blackledge, A. (2010) Translanguaging in the bilingual classroom: A pedagogy for learning and teaching? *The Modern Language Journal* 94 (1), 103–115.

Creese, A. and Blackledge, A. (eds) (2014) *Heteroglossia as Practice and Pedagogy*. Berlin: Springer.

Cucchiara, M. (2019) Language of learning: Content-rich texts build knowledge and skills. *The Learning Professional* 40 (2), 32–36.

Cummins, J.P. (1974) Bilingualism and Cognitive Representation. Unpublished doctoral dissertation, Department of Educational Psychology, University of Alberta.

Cummins, J. (1976) The influence of bilingualism on cognitive growth: A synthesis of research findings and explanatory hypotheses. *Working Papers on Bilingualism* 9, 1–43.

Cummins, J. (1977) Immersion education in Ireland: A critical review of Macnamara's findings. *Working Papers on Bilingualism* 13, 121–129.

Cummins, J. (1978a) Educational implications of mother tongue maintenance for minority language groups. *Canadian Modern Language Review* 34, 395–416.

Cummins, J. (1978b) Immersion programmes: The Irish experience. *International Review of Education* 24, 273–282.

Cummins, J. (1979a) Linguistic interdependence and the educational development of bilingual children. *Review of Educational Research* 49, 222–251.

Cummins, J. (1979b) Cognitive/academic language proficiency, linguistic interdependence, the optimum age question and some other matters. *Working Papers on Bilingualism* 19, 197–205. (ERIC document # ED184334).

Cummins, J. (1980a) The cross-lingual dimensions of language proficiency: Implications for bilingual education and the optimal age issue. *TESOL Quarterly* 14, 175–187.

Cummins, J. (1980b) Psychological assessment of immigrant children: Logic or intuition? *Journal of Multilingual and Multicultural Development* 1, 97–111.

Cummins, J. (1980c) The entry and exit fallacy in bilingual education. *NABE Journal* 4, 25–60.

Cummins, J. (1980d) The construct of language proficiency in bilingual education. In J.E. Alatis (ed.) *Current Issues in Bilingual Education. Georgetown University Round Table on Languages and Linguistics* (pp. 81–103). Washington, D.C.: Georgetown University Press.

Cummins, J. (1981a) Four misconceptions about language proficiency in bilingual education. *NABE Journal* 5, 31–45.

Cummins, J. (1981b) The role of primary language development in promoting educational success for language minority students. In California State Department of Education (ed.) *Schooling and Language Minority Students: A Theoretical Framework* (pp. 3–49). Los Angeles: Evaluation, Dissemination and Assessment Center, California State University.

Cummins, J. (1981c) Age on arrival and immigrant second language learning in Canada. A reassessment. *Applied Linguistics* 2 (2), 132–149.

Cummins, J. (1982) Interdependence and cultural ambivalence: Regarding the pedagogical rationale for bilingual education. Rosslyn, Virginia: National Clearinghouse for Bilingual Education.

Cummins, J. (1983) *Heritage Language Education: A Literature Review.* Toronto: Ministry of Education. (ERIC # ED233588)

Cummins, J. (1984a) *Bilingualism and Special Education: Issues in Assessment and Pedagogy.* Clevedon: Multilingual Matters.

Cummins, J. (1984b) Wanted: A theoretical framework for relating language proficiency to academic achievement among bilingual students. In C. Rivera (ed.) *Language Proficiency and Academic Achievement* (pp. 2–19). Clevedon: Multilingual Matters.

Cummins, J. (1984c) Language proficiency and academic achievement revisited: A response. In C. Rivera (ed.) *Language Proficiency and Academic Achievement* (pp. 71–76). Clevedon: Multilingual Matters.

Cummins, J. (1986) Empowering minority students: A framework for intervention. *Harvard Educational Review* 56, 18–36.

Cummins, J. (1989) *Empowering Minority Students.* Sacramento: California Association for Bilingual Education.

Cummins, J. (1990) Empowering minority students: An analysis of the bilingual education debate. *Estudios Fronterizos* 8, 15–35.

Cummins, J. (1991) Interdependence of first- and second-language proficiency in bilingual children. In E. Bialystok (ed.) *Language Processing in Bilingual Children* (pp. 70–89). Cambridge: Cambridge University Press.

Cummins, J. (1993) Negotiating identities in the ESL classroom: The 1992 Ian Gertsbain Memorial Lecture. *Contact* 19 (1), 30–32.

Cummins, J. (1994a) Semilingualism. In R.R. Asher (ed.) *International Encyclopedia of Language and Linguistics* (2nd edn) (pp. 3812–3814). Oxford: Elsevier Science Ltd.

Cummins, J. (1994b) From coercive to collaborative relations of power in the teaching of literacy. In B.M. Ferdman, R.-M Weber and A. Ramirez (eds) *Literacy Across Languages and Cultures* (pp. 295–331). Albany, NY: SUNY Press.

Cummins, J. (1996) *Negotiating Identities: Education for Empowerment in a Diverse Society* (1st edn). Los Angeles: California Association for Bilingual Education.

Cummins, J. (1997a) Echoes from the past: Stepping stones towards a personal critical literacy. In C.P. Casanave and S.R. Schecter (eds) *On Becoming a Language Educator: Personal Essays on Professional Development* (pp. 57–68). Mahwah, NJ: Lawrence Erlbaum Associates.

Cummins, J. (1997b) Educational attainment of minority students: A framework for intervention based on the constructs of identity and empowerment. In A. Sjögren (ed.) *Language and Environment* (pp. 89–101). Stockholm: Mangkulturellt Centrum.

Cummins, J. (2000) *Language, Power and Pedagogy: Bilingual Children in the Crossfire.* Clevedon: Multilingual Matters.

Cummins, J. (2001a) *Negotiating Identities: Education for Empowerment in a Diverse Society* (2nd edn). Los Angeles: California Association for Bilingual Education.

Cummins, J. (2001b) Assessment options for bilingual learners. In J.V. Tinajero and S. Hurley (eds) *Literacy Assessment of Bilingual Learners* (pp. 115–129). Boston: Allyn and Bacon.

Cummins, J. (2003) Foreword. In N.H. Hornberger (ed.) *Continua of Biliteracy: An Ecological Framework for Educational, Policy, Research, and Practice in Multilingual Settings* (pp. vii–xi). Clevedon: Multilingual Matters.

Cummins, J. (2004a) Multiliteracies pedagogy and the role of identity texts. In K. Leithwood, P. McAdie, N. Bascia and A. Rodigue (eds) *Teaching for Deep Understanding: Towards the Ontario Curriculum that We Need* (pp. 68–74). Toronto: Ontario Institute for Studies in Education of the University of Toronto and the Elementary Federation of Teachers of Ontario.

Cummins, J. (2004b) Review of D.K. Oller and R.E. Eilers (eds) *Language and Literacy in Bilingual Children.* Clevedon, UK: Multilingual Matters, 2002. *Journal of Child Language* 31 (2), 424–429.

Cummins, J. (2007a) Rethinking monolingual instructional strategies in multilingual classrooms. *The Canadian Journal of Applied Linguistics* 10, 221–240.

Cummins, J. (2007b) Pedagogies for the poor? Re-aligning reading instruction for low-income students with scientifically based reading research. *Educational Researcher* 36, 564–572.

Cummins, J. (2007c) Foreword. In M. Carder, *Bilingualism in International Schools: A Model for Enriching Language Education* (pp. viii–xi). Clevedon, UK: Multilingual Matters.

Cummins, J. (2008a) BICS and CALP: Empirical and theoretical status of the distinction. In B. Street and N. H. Hornberger (eds) *Encyclopedia of Language and Education, 2nd Edition, Volume 2: Literacy* (pp. 71–83). New York: Springer Science + Business Media LLC.

Cummins, J. (2008b) Review of *Where Immigrant Students Succeed: A Comparative Review of Performance and Engagement in PISA 2003* (Petra Stanat and Gayle Christensen, eds, 2006). *Curriculum Inquiry* 38 (4), 493–499.

Cummins, J. (2008c) Total immersion or bilingual education? Findings of international research on promoting immigrant children's achievement in the primary school. In J. Ramseger and M. Wagener (eds) *Chancenungleichheit in der Grundschule: Ursachen und Wege aus der Krise* (pp. 45–56). Wiesbaden: VS Verlag fur Sozialwissenschaften/Springer Science + Business Media.

Cummins, J. (2009a) Transformative multiliteracies pedagogy: School-based strategies for closing the achievement gap. *Multiple Voices for Ethnically Diverse Exceptional Learners* 11, 38–56.

Cummins, J. (2009b) Literacy and English-language learners: A shifting landscape for students, teachers, researchers, and policy makers. Review of D. August and T. Shanahan (eds) *Developing Reading and Writing in Second-Language Learners: Lessons from the Report of the National Literacy Panel on Language-Minority Children and Youth.* New York: Routledge, 2008. *Educational Researcher* 38 382–384.

Cummins, J. (2013) BICS and CALP: Empirical support, theoretical status, and policy implications of a controversial distinction. In M. Hawkins (ed.) *Framing Languages and Literacies: Socially Situated Views and Perspectives* (pp. 10–23). New York: Routledge.

Cummins, J. (2014a) Rethinking pedagogical assumptions in Canadian French immersion programs. *Journal of Immersion and Content-Based Education* 2 (1), 3–22.

Cummins, J. (2014b) To what extent are Canadian second language policies evidence-based? Reflections on the intersections of research and policy. *Frontiers in Psychology* 5, 1–10. Article 358. doi:10.3389/fpsyg.2014.00358

Cummins, J. (2015) Literacy policy and curriculum. In J. Rowsell and K. Pahl (eds) *Handbook of Literacy Studies* (pp. 231–248). London: Routledge.

Cummins, J. (2016) Reflections on: Cummins, J. (1980) The cross-lingual dimensions of language proficiency: Implications for bilingual education and the optimal age issue. *TESOL Quarterly* 50 (4), 940–944. doi: 10.1002/tesq.339

Cummins, J. (2017a) Teaching for transfer in multilingual educational contexts. In O. García and A. Lin (eds) *Bilingual Education: Encyclopedia of Language and Education* (3rd edn) (pp. 103–115). New York: Springer Science + Business Media LLC.

Cummins, J. (2017b) Teaching minoritized students: Are additive approaches legitimate? *Harvard Education Review* 87 (3), 404–425.

Cummins, J. (2017c) BICS and CALP: Empirical and theoretical status of the distinction. In B. Street and S. May (eds) *Literacies and Language Education: Encyclopedia of Language and Education, 3rd Edition* (pp. 59–71). New York: Springer Science + Business Media LLC.

Cummins, J. (2018) Urban multilingualism and educational achievement: Identifying and implementing evidence-based strategies for school improvement. In P. Van Avermaet, S. Slembrouck, K. Van Gorp, S. Sierens and K. Maryns (eds) *The Multilingual Edge of Education* (pp. 67–90). London: Palgrave Macmillan.

Cummins, J. (2019) Should schools undermine or sustain multilingualism? An analysis of theory, research, and pedagogical practice. *Sustainable Multilingualism* 15, 1–26. Available at: http://uki.vdu.lt/sm/index.php/sm and https://content.sciendo.com/view/journals/sm

Cummins, J. (2020) Dialogue/Response—Engaging translanguaging pedagogies in language classrooms. In S.M.C. Lau and S. Van Viegen (eds) *Plurilingual Pedagogies: Critical and Creative Endeavors for Equitable Language in Education* (pp. 205–212). Cham, Switzerland: Springer Nature.

Cummins, J. (2021) Translanguaging: A critical analysis of theoretical claims. In P. Juvonen and M. Källkvist (eds) *Pedagogical Translanguaging: Theoretical, Methodological and Empirical Perspectives* (pp. 7–36). Bristol: Multilingual Matters.

Cummins, J. (in press) Teachers as knowledge-generators and agents of language policy: Research, theory, and ideology in plurilingual pedagogies. In E. Piccardo, A. Germain-Rutherford and G. Lawrence (eds) *Routledge Handbook of Plurilingual Education*. New York: Routledge.

Cummins, J., Bismilla, V., Chow, P., Cohen, S., Giampapa, F., Leoni, L., Sandhu, P. and Sastri, P. (2005) Affirming identity in multilingual classrooms. *Educational Leadership* 63 (1), 38–43.

Cummins, J., Brown, K. and Sayers, D. (2007) *Literacy, Technology, and Diversity: Teaching for Success in Changing Times.* Boston: Pearson Education.

Cummins, J. and Cameron, L. (1994) The ESL student IS the mainstream: The marginalization of diversity in current Canadian educational debates. *English Quarterly* 26 (3), 30–33.

Cummins, J. and Danesi, M. (1990) *Heritage Languages: The Development and Denial of Canada's Linguistic Resources*. Toronto: Our Schools/Our Selves and Garamond Press.

Cummins, J. and Das, J.P. (1977) Cognitive processing and reading difficulties. *Alberta Journal of Educational Research* 23, 245–256.

Cummins, J. and Early, M. (2011) (eds) *Identity Texts: The Collaborative Creation of Power in Multilingual Schools*. Stoke-on-Trent: Trentham Books.

Cummins, J. and Early, M. (2015) *Big Ideas for Expanding Minds: Teaching English Language Learners across the Curriculum*. Toronto: Rubicon Press/Pearson Canada.

Cummins, J., Hu, S., Markus, P. and Montero, M.K. (2015) Identity texts and academic achievement: Connecting the dots in multilingual school contexts. *TESOL Quarterly* 49 (3), 555–581.

Cummins, J., Mirza, R. and Stille, S. (2012) English language learners in Canadian schools: Emerging directions for school-based policies. *TESL Canada Journal* 29 (6), 25–48.

Cummins, J. and Persad, R. (2014) Teaching through a multilingual lens: The evolution of EAL policy and practice in Canada. *Education Matters* 2 (1). Available at: http://em.synergiesprairies.ca/index.php/em/issue/view/7

Cummins, J. and Sayers, D. (1995). *Brave New Schools: Challenging Cultural Illiteracy through Global Learning Networks*. New York: St. Martin's Press

Cummins, J. and Swain, M. (1983) Analysis-by-rhetoric: Reading the text or the reader's own projections? A reply to Edelsky et al. *Applied Linguistics* 4 (1), 23–41.

Cummins, J., Swain, M., Nakajima, K., Handscombe, J., Green, D. and Tran, C. (1984) Linguistic interdependence among Japanese and Vietnamese immigrant students. In C. Rivera (ed.) *Communicative Competence Approaches to Language Proficiency Assessment: Research and Application* (pp. 60–81). Clevedon: Multilingual Matters.

Cunningham, A.E. and Stanovich, K.E. (1997) Early reading acquisition and its relation to reading experience and ability 10 years later. *Developmental Psychology* 33, 934–945.

CUNY-New York State Initiative on Emergent Bilinguals (2021) *Translanguaging and Transformative Teaching for Emergent Bilingual Students: Lessons from the CUNY-NYSIEB Project*. London and New York: Routledge.

Dagenais, D., Toohey, K., Bennett Fox, A. and Singh, A. (2017) Multilingual and multimodal composition at school: ScribJab in action. *Language and Education* 31 (3), 263–282.

Daller, M. and Ongun, Z. (2018) The Threshold Hypothesis revisited: Bilingual lexical knowledge and non-verbal IQ development. *International Journal of Bilingualism* 22 (6) 675–694. doi:10.1177/1367006917690835

Darling-Hammond, L. (2010) *The Flat World and Education: How America's Commitment to Equity Will Determine Our Future*. New York, NY: Teachers College Press.

Darvin, R. and Norton, B. (2014) Transnational identity and migrant language learners: The promise of digital storytelling. *Education Matters* 2 (1), 55–66.

de Bot, K., Verspoor, M. and Lowie, W. (2007) A dynamic systems theory approach to second language acquisition. *Bilingualism, Language and Cognition* 10, 7–21. Retrieved from http://www.rug.nl/staff/c.l.j.de.bot/DeBotetal2007-Bilingualism.pdf

DeFazio, A.J. (1997) Language awareness at The International High School. In L. Van Lier and D. Corson (eds) *Knowledge about Language. Encyclopedia of Language and Education* (pp. 99–107). Dordrecht: Kluwer Academic Publishers, Inc.

Dei, G.S. (1996) *Anti-Racism Education: Theory and Practice*. Halifax: Fernwood Publishers.

Delpit, L.D. (1988) The silenced dialogue: Power and pedagogy in educating other people's children. *Harvard Educational Review* 58, 280–298.

Delpit, L. (1995) *Other People's Children: Cultural Conflict in the Classroom*. New York: The New Press.

Delpit, L. and Dowdy, J.K. (2002) *The Skin that We Speak: Thoughts on Language and Culture in the Classroom*. New York, NY: The New Press.

Demie, F. (2013) English as an additional language: How long does it take to acquire English fluency? *Language and Education* 27 (1), 59–69.

Demie, F. (2018) English language proficiency and attainment of EAL (English as second language) pupils in England. *Journal of Multilingual and Multicultural Development* 39 (7), 641–653. doi:10.1080/01434632.2017.1420658

Denos, C., Toohey, K., Neilson, K. and Waterstone, B. (eds) (2009) *Collaborative Research in Multilingual Classrooms*. Bristol: Multilingual Matters.

DevTech Systems Inc. (1996) *A Descriptive Study of the ESEA Title VII Educational Services Provided for Secondary School Limited English Proficient Students: Final Report*. Washington, DC: National Clearinghouse for Bilingual Education.

Diaz, R.M. (1983) Thought and two languages: The impact of bilingualism on cognitive development. *Review of Research in Education* 10, 23–54.

Diaz-Rico, L.T. and Weed, K.Z. (2002) *The Crosscultural, Language, and Academic Development Handbook: A Complete K-12 Reference Guide* (2nd edn). Boston: Allyn and Bacon.

DiCerbo, P.A., Anstrom, K.A. Baker, L.L. and Rivera, C. (2014) A review of the literature on teaching academic English to English language learners. *Review of Educational Research* 84 (3), 446–482.

Dolson, D. (1985) The effects of Spanish home language use on the scholastic performance of Hispanic pupils. *Journal of Multilingual and Multicultural Development* 6, 135–156.

Dolson, D. and Burnham-Massey, L. (2011) *Redesigning English-Medium Classrooms: Using Research to Enhance English Learner Achievement*. Covina, CA: California Association for Bilingual Education.

Donaldson, M. (1978) *Children's Minds*. Glasgow: Collins.

Dressler, C. and Kamil, M. (2006) First- and second-language literacy. In D. August and T. Shanahan (eds) *Developing Literacy in Second-Language Learners. Report of the National Literacy Panel on Language-Minority Children and Youth* (pp. 197–238). Mahwah, NJ: Lawrence Erlbaum Associates Publishers.

Duarte, J. and Günther-van der Meij, M. (2018) A holistic model for multilingualism in education. *EuroAmerican Journal of Applied Linguistics and Languages* 5 (2), 24–43. Retrieved from doi:10.21283/2376905X.9.153

Duarte, J. and Günther-van der Meij, M.T. (2020) 'We learn together'—Translanguaging within a holistic approach towards multilingualism in education. In J.A. Panagiotopoulou, L. Rosen and J. Strzykala (eds) *Inclusion, Education and Translanguaging: How to Promote Social Justice in (Teacher) Education?* (pp. 125–144). Wiesbaden: Springer Fachmedien.

Duke, N. (2000) For the rich it's richer: Print experiences and environments offered to children in very low and very high-socioeconomic status first-grade classrooms. *American Educational Research Journal* 37 (2), 441–478.

Duncan-Andrade, J.M.R. and Morrell, E. (2008) *The Art of Critical Pedagogy: Possibilities for Moving from Theory to Practice in Urban Schools*. New York: Peter Lang.

Dutro, S. and Kinsella, K. (2010) English language development: Issues and implementation in kindergarten through grade 5. In California Department of Education (2010). *Improving Education for English Learners: Research-Based Approaches* (pp. 151–207). Sacramento: California Department of Education.

Duursma, E., Romero-Contreras, S., Szuber, A., Proctor, C.P., Snow, C., August, D. and Calderón, M. (2007) The role of home literacy and language environment on bilinguals' English and Spanish vocabulary development. *Applied Psycholinguistics* 28, 171–190. doi:10.1017/S0142716407070099.

Eccles, F., Kirton, E. and Xiong, B. (1994) *The Family Connection: Hmong Parent Education Project.* Merced, CA: Merced County Office of Education.

Echevarria, J. and Short, D. (2010) Programs and practices for effective sheltered content instruction. In California Department of Education (2010) *Improving Education for English Learners: Research-Based Approaches* (pp. 251–321). Sacramento: California Department of Education.

Edele, A. and Stanat, P. (2016) The role of first-language listening comprehension in second-language reading comprehension. *Journal of Educational Psychology* 108 (2), 163–180.

Edelsky, C. (1990) *With Literacy and Justice for All: Rethinking the Social in Language and Education.* London: The Falmer Press.

Edelsky, C., Hudelson, S., Flores, B., Barkin, F., Altweger, B. and Jilbert, K. (1983) Semilingualism and language deficit. *Applied Linguistics* 4, 1–22.

Edwards, J. (2012) *Multilingualism: Understanding Linguistic Diversity.* London: Continuum.

Ehri, L.C., Nunes, S., Stahl, S. and Willows, D. (2001) Systematic phonics instruction helps students learn to read: Evidence from the National Reading Panel's meta-analysis. *Review of Educational Research* 71, 393–447.

Elley, W.B. (1991) Acquiring literacy in a second language: The effect of book-based programs. *Language Learning* 41, 375–411.

Elley, W.B. (2001) Guest editor's introduction. *International Journal of Educational Research* 35, 127–135.

Elley, W.B. and Mangubhai, F. (1983) The impact of reading on second language learning. *Reading Research Quarterly* 19, 53–67.

Englander, K. and Corcoran, J.N. (2019) *English for Research Publication Purposes: Critical Plurilingual Pedagogies.* Abingdon: Routledge.

Escamilla, K., Hopewell, S., Butvilofsky, S., Sparrow, W., Soltero-González, L., Ruiz-Figueroa, O. and Escamilla, M. (2014) *Biliteracy from the Start: Literacy Squared in Action.* Philadelphia, PA: Caslon.

Espinosa, C. and Herrera, L. (2016) Reclaiming bilingualism: Translanguaging in a science class. In O. García and T. Kleyn (eds) *Translanguaging with Multilingual Students: Learning from Classroom Moments* (pp. 160–178). New York, NY: Routledge.

Esser, H. (2006) *Migration, Language, and Integration.* AKI Research Review 4. Berlin: Programme on Intercultural Conflicts and Societal Integration (AKI), Social Science Research Center. Retrieved from https://bibliothek.wzb.eu/pdf/2006/iv06-akibi-lanz4b.pdf

Faltis, C. (1989) Code-switching and bilingual schooling: An examination of Jacobson's new concurrent approach. *Journal of Multilingual and Multicultural Development* 10 (2), 117–127.

Faltis, C. (2014) Acquiring academic language practices in prison in Aztlán: Fake it until you make it, *International Multilingual Research Journal* 8 (1), 56–69. doi: 10.1080/19313152.2014.852429.

Faltis, C.J. and Hudelson, S.J. (1998) *Bilingual Education in Elementary and Secondary School Communities: Toward Understanding and Caring.* Boston: Allyn and Bacon.

Fanon, F. (1967) *Black Skin: White Masks.* New York: Grove Press.

Faas, D. (2014) Germany after the 'PISA Shock': Revisiting national, European and multicultural values in curriculum and policy discourses. In D. Little, C. Leung and P. Van Avermaet (eds) *Managing Diversity in Education* (pp. 43–56). Bristol: Multilingual Matters.

Ferrón, M.A. (2012) *Educational Effects of Implementing a K-12 Dual Language Instruction Program in a Community with a High Percentage of Hispanics and Hispanic English Language Learners*. Executive Summary, Unpublished doctoral dissertation, The University of Texas at Brownsville and Texas Southmost College.

Fish, S., Hoffmeister, R.H. and Thrasher, M. (2005) Knowledge of rare vocabulary in ASL and its relationship to vocabulary knowledge in English in Deaf children. Paper presented to the IASCL conference, Berlin.

Fitzgerald, J. (1995) English-as-a-second-language learners' cognitive reading processes: A review of research in the United States. *Review of Educational Research* 65, 145–190.

Flores, N. (2013) The unexamined relationship between neoliberalism and plurilingualism: A cautionary tale. *TESOL Quarterly* 47 (3), 500–520.

Flores, N.L. (2019) Translanguaging into raciolinguistic ideologies: A personal reflection on the legacy of Ofelia García. *Journal of Multilingual Education Research* 9, Article 5. See https://fordham.bepress.com/jmer/vol9/iss1/5

Flores, N. (2020) From academic language to language architecture: Challenging raciolinguistic ideologies in research and practice. *Theory into Practice* 59 (1), 22–31. doi:10.1080/00405841.2019.1665411.

Flores, N. and Rosa, J. (2015) Undoing appropriateness: Raciolinguistic ideologies and language diversity in education. *Harvard Educational Review* 85, 149–171.

Flores, N. and Schissel, J.L. (2014) Dynamic bilingualism as the norm: Envisioning a heteroglossic approach to standards-based reform. *TESOL Quarterly* 48 (3), 454–479.

Foorman, B.R., Koon, S., Petscher, Y., Mitchell, A. and Truckenmiller, A. (2015) Examining general and specific factors in the dimensionality of oral language and reading in 4th–10th grades. *Journal of Education Psychology* 107, 884–899. https://doi.org/10.1037/edu0000026

Fordham, S. (1990) Racelessness as a factor in Black students' school success: Pragmatic strategy or pyrrhic victory? In N.M. Hidalgo, C.L. McDowell and E.V. Siddle (eds) *Facing Racism in Education* (Reprint series No. 21) (pp. 232–262). Cambridge MA: Harvard Educational Review.

Foucault, M. (1984) *The Foucault Reader*. London: Penguin Random House.

Francis, D., Lesaux, N. and August, D. (2006) Language of instruction. In D. August and T. Shanahan (eds) *Developing Literacy in Second-Language Learners. Report of the National Literacy Panel on Language-Minority Children and Youth* (pp. 365–413). Mahwah, NJ: Lawrence Erlbaum Associates Publishers.

Frederickson, J. (1995) (ed.) *Reclaiming Our Voices: Bilingual Education, Critical Pedagogy and Praxis*. Ontario, CA: California Association for Bilingual Education.

Freire, P. (1970/1981) *Pedagogy of the Oppressed*. New York: Continuum.

Galante, A. (2020) Plurilingual and pluricultural competence (PPC) scale: The inseparability of language and culture. *International Journal of Multilingualism*. See https://doi.org/10.1080/14790718.2020.1753747

Gallagher, E. (2008) *Equal Rights to the Curriculum: Many Languages, One Message*. Clevedon: Multilingual Matters.

Gallagher, E. (2011) Weaving other languages and cultures into the curriculum in international primary schools. In J. Cummins and M. Early (eds) *Identity Texts: The Collaborative Creation of Power in Multilingual Schools* (pp. 76–81). Stoke-on-Trent: Trentham Books.

Gallagher, E. (2015) *The Glitterlings*. Oxford: Oxford International Early Years, Oxford University Press.

Gallagher, E. (2020) Languages matter. *EAL Journal* Autumn 2020, Issue number 13, 26–28.

Gallagher, E. and Walker, M. (2015) *The Glitterlings: Teacher Resource Book*. Oxford: Oxford International Early Years, Oxford University Press.

Galtung, J. (1980) *The True Worlds. A Transnational Perspective*. New York: The Free Press.

Gamse, B.C., Jacob, R.T., Horst, M., Boulay, B., Unlu, F. *et al.* (2008) *Reading First Impact Study Final Report (NCEE 2009-4038)*, Washington, DC: National Center for Education Evaluation and Regional Assistance, Institute of Education Sciences, US Department of Education.

Gándara, P. (1999) *Review of Research on Instruction of Limited English Proficient Students: A Report to the California Legislature*. Santa Barbara: University of California, Linguistic Minority Research Institute.

Gándara, P. (2013) Meeting the needs of language minorities. In P.L. Carter and K.G. Welner (eds) *Closing the Opportunity Gap: What America Must Do to Give Every Child an Even Chance* (pp. 156–168). New York: Oxford University Press.

Garan, E.M. (2001) What does the report of the National Reading Panel really tell us about teaching phonics? *Language Arts* 79 (1), 61–70.

Garbe, C., Lafontaine, D., Persson, U-B, Shiel, G. and Valtin, R. (2016) *Literacy in Sweden: Country Report, Children and Adolescents*. European Literacy Policy Network (ELINET). Retrieved from http://www.elinet.eu/fileadmin/ELINET/Redaktion/user_upload/Sweden_Long_Report.pdf

García, O. (2007) Foreword. Intervening discourses, representations and conceptualizations of language. In S. Makoni and A. Pennycook (eds) *Disinventing and Reconstituting Languages* (pp. xi-xv). Clevedon: Multilingual Matters.

García, O. (2009) *Bilingual Education in the 21st Century. A Global Perspective*. Boston: Basil Blackwell.

García, O. (2013) Theorizing translanguaging for educators. In C. Celic and K. Seltzer, *Translanguaging: A CUNY-NYSIEB Guide for Educators* (pp. 1–6). New York, NY: CUNY-NYSIEB, The Graduate Center, The City University of New York. Retrieved from https://www.cuny-nysieb.org/translanguaging-resources/translanguaging-guides/

García, O. (2014) Countering the dual: Transglossia, dynamic bilingualism and translanguaging in education. In R. Rubdy and L. Alsagoff (eds) *The Global-Local Interface and Hybridity: Exploring Language and Identity* (pp. 100–118). Bristol: Multilingual Matters.

García, O. (2017) Critical multilingual language awareness and teacher education. In J. Cenoz, D. Gorter and S. May (eds) *Language Awareness and Multilingualism, Encyclopedia of Language and Education* (pp. 263–280). doi 10.1007/978-3-319-022 40-6_30

García, O. (2018) The multiplicities of multilingual interaction. *International Journal of Bilingual Education and Bilingualism* (21) 7, 881–891 doi:10.1080/13670050.2018.1 474851

García, O. (2019) From translanguaging to translingual activism. In D. Macedo (ed.) *Decolonizing Foreign Language Education: The Misteaching of English and Other Colonial Languages* (pp. 152–168). New York: Routledge.

García, O. (2020) Singularity, complexities and contradictions: A commentary about translanguaging, social justice, and education. In J.A. Panagiotopoulou, L. Rosen and J. Strzykala (eds) *Inclusion, Education and Translanguaging: How to Promote Social Justice in (Teacher) Education?* (pp. 11–22). Wiesbaden: Springer Fachmedien.

García, O. and Woodley, H.H. (2015) Bilingual education. In M. Bigelow and J. Ensser-Kananen (eds) *The Routledge Handbook of Educational Linguistics* (pp. 132–144). London and New York: Routledge.

García, O., Ibarra Johnson, S., and Seltzer, K. (2016) *The Translanguaging Classroom: Leveraging Student Bilingualism for Learning*. Philadelphia, PA: Caslon.

García, O. and Kleifgen, J.A. (2019) Translanguaging and literacies. *Reading Research Quarterly*. Published online, 12 November. doi:10.1002/rrq.286

García, O. and Kleyn, T. (eds) (2016) *Translanguaging with Multilingual Students: Learning from Classroom Moments*. New York and London: Routledge.

García, O. and Lin, A.M.Y. (2017) Translanguaging in bilingual education. In O. García and A.M.Y. Lin (eds) *Bilingual and Multilingual Education (Encyclopedia of Language and Education, Vol. 5)* (pp. 117–130). Dordrecht: Springer.

García, O. and Li Wei (2014) *Translanguaging: Language, Bilingualism and Education.* New York: Palgrave Macmillan.

García, O. and Otheguy, R. (2014) Spanish and Hispanic bilingualism. In M. Lacorte (ed.) *The Routledge Handbook of Hispanic Applied Linguistics* (pp. 639–658). New York, NY: Routledge.

García, O. and Otheguy, R. (2020) Plurilingualism and translanguaging: Commonalities and divergences. *International Journal of Bilingual Education and Bilingualism* 23 (1), 17–35. doi:10.1080/13670050.2019.1598932

García, O. and Sylvan, C.E. (2011) Pedagogies and practices in multilingual classrooms: Singularities in pluralities. *Modern Language Journal* 95 (3), 385–400. doi: 10.1111/j.1540-4781.2011.01208.x0026-7902/11/385–400

García, O. and Solorza, C.R. (2020) Academic language and the minoritization of U.S. bilingual Latinx students. *Language and Education.* doi:10.1080/09500782.2020.1825476

Gärkman, H., Katija, A. and Christopher, P. (2020) *Spotlight: Bilingual Education.* HundrED Research Report #012. Retrieved from https://hundred.org/en/collections/bilingual-education

Gay, G. (2010) *Culturally Responsive Teaching.* New York, NY: Teachers College Press.

Gee, J.P. (1990) *Social Linguistics and Literacies: Ideologies in Discourses.* New York: Falmer Press.

Gee, J.P. (1999) Critical issues: Reading and the new literacy studies – Reframing the National Academy of Sciences report on reading, *Journal of Literacy Research* 31 (3), 355–374.

Gee, J.P. (2000) The limits of reframing: A response to Professor Snow. *Journal of Literacy Research* 32 (1), 121–130.

Gee, J.P. (2001) Identity as an analytic lens for research in education. In W.G. Secada (ed.) *Review of Research in Education* 25 (pp. 99–125). Washington DC: American Educational Research Association.

Gee, J.P. (2004) *Situated Language and Learning: A Critique of Traditional Schooling.* London, UK: Routledge.

Genesee, F. (1984) On Cummins' theoretical framework. In C. Rivera (ed.) *Language Proficiency and Academic Achievement* (pp. 20–27). Clevedon: Multilingual Matters.

Genesee, F., Geva, E., Dressler, C. and Kamil, M.L. (2006a) Synthesis: Cross-linguistic relationships in working memory, phonological processes, and oral language. In D. August and T. Shanahan (eds) *Developing Literacy in Second-Language Learners: A Report of the National Literacy Panel on Language-Minority Children and Youth* (pp. 153–174). Mahwah, NJ: Lawrence Erlbaum.

Genesee, F., Lindholm-Leary, K., Saunders, W.M. and Christian, D. (eds) (2006) *Educating English Language Learners: A Synthesis of Research Evidence.* New York: Cambridge University Press.

Geva, E. and Ryan, E.B. (1993) Linguistic and cognitive correlates of academic skills in first and second language. *Language Learning* 43, 5–42.

Geva, E. (2014) Introduction. The cross-language transfer journey – a guide to the perplexed. *Written Language and Literacy* 17 (1), 1–15. doi:10.1075/wll.17.1.01gev

Giampapa, F. (2010) Multiliteracies, pedagogy and identities: teacher and student voices from a Toronto Elementary School. *Canadian Journal of Education* 33 (2), 407–431.

Giampapa, F. and Sandhu, P. (2011) 'We're just like real authors': The power of dual language identity texts in a multilingual school. In J. Cummins and M. Early (eds) *Identity Texts: The Collaborative Creation of Power in Multilingual Schools* (pp. 82–87). Stoke-on-Trent: Trentham Books.

Gibbons, P. (1991) *Learning to Learn in a Second Language*. Newtown, Australia: Primary English Teaching Association.

Gibbons, P. (2007) Mediating academic language learning through classroom discourse. In J. Cummins and C. Davison (eds) *International Handbook of English Language Teaching* (pp. 701–718). New York: Springer Science + Business Media LLC.

Gibbons, P. (2009) *English Learners, Academic Literacy, and Thinking: Learning in the Challenge Zone*. Portsmouth, NH: Heinemann.

Gibbons, P. (2015) *Scaffolding Language, Scaffolding Learning*. Portsmouth, NH: Heinemann.

Gibbons, P. (2017) Foreword. In M. Gottlieb and M. Castro (eds) *Language Power: Key Uses for Accessing Content* (pp. xiii-xiv). Thousand Oaks, CA: Corwin.

Gögolin, I. (2005) Bilingual education: The German experience and debate. In J. Söhn (ed.) *The Effectiveness of Bilingual School Programs for Immigrant Children*. AKI Research Review 2 (pp. 133–145). Berlin: Programme on Intercultural Conflicts and Societal Integration (AKI), Social Science Research Centre. PID: https://nbn-resolving.org/urn:nbn:de:0168-ssoar-110296. Retrieved from http://www.ssoar.info/ssoar/handle/document/11029

Goldenberg, C. (2008, Summer) Teaching English language learners: What the research does—and does not—say. *American Educator* 8–23, 41–44. Retrieved from https://www.aft.org/sites/default/files/periodicals/goldenberg.pdf

Goldenberg, C., Rueda, R. and August, D. (2006) Sociocultural influences on the literacy attainment of language-minority children and youth. In D. August and T. Shanahan (eds) *Developing Literacy in Second-Language Learners: Report of the National Literacy Panel on Language-Minority Children And Youth* (pp. 269–318). Mahwah, NJ: Lawrence Erlbaum.

Goldstein, D. (2020) An old and contested solution to boost reading scores: Phonics. *New York Times*, 15 February. Retrieved from https://www.nytimes.com/2020/02/15/us/reading-phonics.html?action=click&module=Top Stories&pgtype=Homepage

González, N., Moll, L. and Amanti, C. (2005) *Funds of Knowledge: Theorizing Practices in Households, Communities, and Classrooms*. Mahwah, NJ: Lawrence Erlbaum.

Goodrich, J.M., Lonigan, C.J. and Farver, J.M. (2013) Do early literacy skills in children's first language promote development of skills in their second language? An experimental evaluation of transfer. *Journal of Educational Psychology* 105 (2), 414–426. doi:10.1037/a0031780

Goodrich, J.M., Lonigan, C.J., Kleuver, C.G. and Farver, J.M. (2016) Development and transfer of vocabulary knowledge in Spanish-speaking language minority preschool children. *Journal of Child Language* 43, 969–992. doi:10.1017/S030500091500032X

Gottlieb, M. and Castro, M. (2017) *Language Power: Key Uses for Accessing Content*. Thousand Oaks, CA: Corwin.

Grabe, W. (2004) Research on teaching reading. *Annual Review of Applied Linguistics* 24, 44–69. doi:10.1017/S0267190504000030

Graham, B. (2020) *Living and Learning in a Yolŋu World: Recollections and Reflections*. Available from bethgraham@netspace.net.au.

Graham, S. and Herbert, M. (2010) *Writing to Read: Evidence for How Writing Can Improve Reading*. New York: Carnegie Corporation.

Greene, J. (1998) *A Meta-Analysis of the Effectiveness of Bilingual Education*. Claremont, CA: Tomas Rivera Policy Institute.

Grey, S., Sanz, C., Morgan-Short, K. and Ullman, M.T. (2018) Bilingual and monolingual adults learning an additional language: ERPs reveal differences in syntactic processing. *Bilingualism: Language and Cognition* 21 (5), 970–994. doi:10.1017/S1366728917000426

Grin, F. (2018) On some fashionable terms in multilingualism research: Critical assessment and implications for language policy. In P.A. Kraus and F. Grin (eds) *The Politics of*

Multilingualism: Europeanisation, Globalization and Linguistic Governance (pp. 247–273). Amsterdam: John Benjamins Publishing Company.

Grosjean, F. (1982) *Life with Two Languages: An Introduction to Bilingualism.* Cambridge, MA: Harvard University Press.

Grosjean, F. (1989) Neurolinguistics, beware! The bilingual is not two monolinguals in one person. *Brain and Language* 36, 3–15.

Groth-Marnat, G. (2003) *Handbook of Psychological Assessment.* (4th ed). New York: John Wiley and Sons, Inc.

Gullifer, J.W., Kroll, J.F. and Dussias, P.E. (2013) When language switching has no apparent cost: Lexical access in sentence context. *Frontiers in Psychology* 4.

Guthrie, J.T. (2004) Teaching for literacy engagement. *Journal of Literacy Research* 36 (1), 1–30.

Guthrie, J.T., Schafer, W.D. and Huang, C.-W. (2001) Benefits of opportunity to read and balanced instruction on the NAEP. *The Journal of Educational Research* 94 (3), 145–162.

Hafiz, F. and Tudor, I. (1989) Extensive reading and the development of reading skills. *English Language Teaching Journal* 43, 4–11.

Hakuta, K. (1985) Cognitive development in English instruction. In National Clearinghouse for Bilingual Education (ed.) *Issues in English Language Development* (pp. 63–67). Rosslyn VA: InterAmerica Research Associates Inc.

Hakuta, K. (1987) Degree of bilingualism and cognitive ability in mainland Puerto Rican children. *Child Development* 58, 1372–1388.

Hammine, M. (2019) Our way of multilingualism: Translanguaging to break a chain of colonialism. In C.A. Seals and V.L. Olsen-Reeder (eds) *Embracing Multilingualism across Educational Contexts* (pp. 100–125). Wellington, New Zealand: Victoria University Press.

Haneda, M. (2014) From academic language to academic communication: Building on English learners' resources. *Linguistics and Education* 26, 126–135.

Hanford, E. (2018) Hard words: Why American kids aren't being taught to read (podcast and article). Retrieved from https://www.apmreports.org/story/2018/09/10/hard-words-why-american-kids-arent-being-taught-to-read

Harris, S. (1990) *Two Way Aboriginal Schooling: Education and Cultural Survival.* Canberra: Aboriginal Studies Press.

Haver, J.J. (2018) *Vindicated: Closing the Hispanic Achievement Gap through English Immersion.* Lanham, MD: Rowman and Littlefield.

Heath, S.B. (1982) What no bedtime story means: Narrative skills at home and school. *Language in Society* 11, 49–77.

Hélot, C., Frijns, C., VanGorp, K. and Sierens, S. (eds) (2018) *Language Awareness in Multilingual Classrooms in Europe: From Theory to Practice.* Amsterdam: de Gruyter Mouton Publishers.

Hélot, C. and Young, A. (2006) Imagining multilingual education in France: A language and cultural awareness project at primary level. In O. García, T. Skutnabb-Kangas and M.E. Torres-Guzmán (eds) *Imagining Multilingual Schools: Languages in Education and Glocalization* (pp. 69–91). Clevedon: Multilingual Matters. Accessible from http://christinehelot.u-strasbg.fr/wpcontent/uploads/2013/02/2006-Imagining-Mult-educ-in-France.pdf

Heppt, B., Sofie Henschel, S. and Haagb, N. (2016) Everyday and academic language comprehension: Investigating their relationships with school success and challenges for language minority learners. *Learning and Individual Differences* 47, 244–251. doi:10.1016/j.lindif.2016.01.004

Herdina, P. and Jessner. U. (2002) *A Dynamic Model of Multilingualism: Changing the Psycholinguistic Perspective.* Clevedon: Multilingual Matters.

Hermans, D., Knoors, H., Ormel, E. and Verhoeven, L. (2008) The relationship between the reading and signing skills of deaf children in bilingual education programs. *Journal of Deaf Studies and Deaf Education* 13, 518–530.

Hermans, D., Ormel, E. and Knoors, H. (2010) On the relation between the signing and reading skills of deaf bilinguals. *International Journal of Bilingual Education and Bilingualism* 13, 187–199.

Hernandez-Chavez, E., Burt, M. and Dulay, H. (1978) Language dominance and proficiency testing: Some general considerations. *NABE Journal* 3, 41–54.

Heugh, K. (2011a) Theory and practice – language education models in Africa: Research, design, decision-making and outcomes. In A. Ouane and C. Glanz (eds) *Optimising Learning, Education and Publishing in Africa: The Language Factor. A Review and Analysis of Theory and Practice in Mother-Tongue and Bilingual Education in Sub-Saharan Africa* (pp. 105–158). Hamburg, Germany and Tunis Belvédère, Tunisia: UNESCO Institute for Lifelong Learning and the Association for the Development of Education in Africa/African Development Bank.

Heugh, K. (2011b) Cost implications of the provision of mother-tongue and strong bilingual models of education in Africa. In A. Ouane and C. Glanz (eds) *Optimising Learning, Education and Publishing in Africa: The Language Factor. A Review and Analysis of Theory and Practice in Mother-Tongue and Bilingual Education in Sub-Saharan Africa* (pp. 253–289). Hamburg, Germany and Tunis Belvédère, Tunisia: UNESCO Institute for Lifelong Learning and the Association for the Development of Education in Africa/African Development Bank.

Heugh, K., Benson, C., Bogale, B. and Gebre Yohannes, M. (2012) Implications for multilingual education: Student achievement in different models of education in Ethiopia. In T. Skutnabb-Kangas and K. Heugh (eds) *Multilingual Education and Sustainable Diversity Work: From Periphery to Centre* (pp. 239–262). New York and London: Routledge.

Heyman, A. (1973) *Invandrarbam: Slutrapport.* Stockholm: Stockholms Invandramamd.

Hidalgo, N.M., McDowell, C.L. and Siddle, E.V. (eds) (1990) *Facing Racism in Education.* Reprint Series No. 21, Harvard Educational Review. Cambridge, MA: Harvard Educational Review.

Hiebert, E.H. and Martin, L.A. (2010) Opportunity to read: A critical but neglected construct in reading instruction In E.H. Hiebert (ed.) *Reading More, Reading Better* (pp. 3–29). New York, NY: Guilford.

Hiebert, E.H. and Mesmer, H.A.E. (2013) Upping the ante of text complexity in the common core state standards: examining its potential impact on young readers. *Educational Researcher* 42 (1), 44–51. doi:10.3102/0013189X12459802

Hoffmeister, R.J. and Caldwell-Harris, C.L. (2014) Acquiring English as a second language via print: The task for deaf children. *Cognition* 132, 229–242. doi.org/10.1016/j.cognition.2014.03.014

Hoffmeister, R.J., de Villiers, P., Engen, E. and Topol, D. (1998) English reading achievement and ASL skills in deaf students. *Proceedings of the 21st Annual Boston University Conference on Language Development.* Brookline, MA: Cascadilla Press.

Hopewell, S. (2011) Leveraging bilingualism to accelerate English reading comprehension. *International Journal of Bilingual Education and Bilingualism* 14 (5), 603–620.

Hornberger, N.H. (1989) Continua of biliteracy. *Review of Educational Research* 59, 271–296.

Hornberger, N.H. (2003) (ed.) *Continua of Biliteracy: An Ecological Framework for Educational Policy, Research, and Practice in Multilingual Settings.* Clevedon: Multilingual Matters.

Hornberger, N.H. and Link, H. (2012) Translanguaging and transnational literacies in multilingual classrooms: A biliteracy lens. *International Journal of Bilingual Education and Bilingualism* 15 (3), 261–278

House of Commons Education Committee (2014) *Underachievement in Education by White Working Class Children. First Report of Session 2014–15.* London: The Stationery Office Limited.

Hulstijn, J.H. (2011) Language proficiency in native and nonnative speakers: An agenda for research and suggestions for second-language assessment. *Language Assessment Quarterly* 8, 229–249. doi:10.1080/15434303.2011.565844

Hulstijn, J.H. (2015) *Language Proficiency in Native and Non-Native Speakers: Theory and Research*. Amsterdam: John Benjamins.

Hulstijn, J.H. (2019) An individual-differences framework for comparing nonnative with native speakers: Perspectives from BLC Theory. *Language Learning* 69, 157–183. doi:10.1111/lang.12317

Hwang, J.K., Mancilla-Martinez, J., Brown, J. McClain, J. Oh, M.H. and Flores, I. (2020) Spanish-speaking English learners' English language and literacy skills: The predictive role of conceptually scored vocabulary. *Applied Psycholinguistics* 41, 1–24.

Isola, R.R. and Cummins, J. (2020) *Transforming Sanchez School: Shared Leadership, Equity, and Evidence*. Philadelphia, PA: Caslon Publishing.

Jacobson, R. (1981) The implementation of a bilingual instructional model: The new concurrent approach. In R.V. Padilla (ed.) *Ethnoperspectives in Bilingual Education Research, Vol. 3*. (pp. 14–29). Ypsilanti, MI: Eastern Michigan University.

James, Z. (2021) Stakeholder perspectives on medium of instruction policy in Ethiopia. In C. Benson and K. Kosonen (eds) *Language Issues in Comparative Education II* (pp. 146–162). Leiden: Brill Sense.

Janks, H. (2010) *Literacy and Power*. London and New York: Routledge.

Janks, H. (2014) *Doing Critical Literacy: Texts and Activities for Students and Teachers*. New York and London: Routledge.

Jaspers, J. (2018) The transformative limits of translanguaging. *Language and Communication* 58, 1–10.

Jasso, A. and Jasso, R. (1995) Critical pedagogy: Not a method, but a way of life. In J. Frederickson (ed.) *Reclaiming our Voices: Bilingual Education, Critical Pedagogy and Praxis* (pp. 253–259). Ontario, CA: California Association for Bilingual Education.

Jensen, B. and Thompson, G. A. (2020) Equity in teaching academic language: An interdisciplinary approach. *Theory into Practice* 59 (1), 1–7. doi:10.1080/00405841.2019.1665417

Jeon, E.H. and Yamashita, J. (2014) L2 reading comprehension and its correlates: A meta-analysis. *Language Learning* 64 (1), 160–212.

Jessner, U. (2006) *Linguistic Awareness in Multilinguals: English as a Third Language*. Edinburgh: Edinburgh University Press.

Jessner, U. (2008) Multicompetence approaches to language proficiency development in multilingual education. In J. Cummins and N.H. Hornberger (eds) *Encyclopedia of Language and Education. Vol. 5: Bilingual Education* (2nd edn) (pp. 91–113). New York: Springer.

Jezer-Morton, K. (2020) Canada's 'founding mothers' of French Immersion. *The Canadian Encyclopedia*. Published online 9 January. Retrieved from: https://www.thecanadianencyclopedia.ca/en/article/canada-s-founding-mothers-of-french-immersion-olga-melikoff-murielle-parkes-and-valerie-neale

Jiménez, R.T., David, S., Fagan, K., Risko, V.J., Pacheco, M., Pray, L. and Gonzales, M. (2015) Using translation to drive conceptual development for students becoming literate in English as an additional language. *Research in the Teaching of English* 49 (3), 248–271.

Kádas, T. (2017) *L'intégration des élèves nouvellement arrivés en France dans l'espace scolaire français: langues, représentations, identités en contexte*. [The integration of newcomer students into the French education system: Languages, social representations and identities in context] Unpublished doctoral dissertation. University of Strasbourg, Strasbourg.

Kalan, A. (2016) *Who's Afraid of Multilingual Education? Conversations with Tove Skutnabb-Kangas, Jim Cummins, Ajit Mohanty and Stephen Bahry about the Iranian Context and Beyond*. Bristol: Multilingual Matters.

Kalantzis, M., Cope, B. and Slade, D. (1989) *Minority Languages and Dominant Culture: Issues of Education, Assessment and Social Equity.* London: Falmer Press.

Kambel, E.-R. and Le Pichon, E. (2020) Kieliystävällinen koulu [Language friendly school]. In J. Alisaari, E. Jäppinen, N. Kekki, R. Kivimäki, S. Kivipelto, K. Kuusento, E. Lehtinen, A. Raunio, E. Repo, S. Sissonen, M. Tyrer and H. Vigren (eds) *Kielestä koppi – Oppimateriaali kielitietoiseen perusopetukseen* [Catch the language – A studybook for language sensitive basic education] (pp. 293 – 298). Turku, Finland: University of Turku.

Kapoyannis, T. (2019) Literacy engagement in multilingual and multicultural learning spaces. *TESL Canada Journal* 36 (2), 1–25. doi:10.18806/tesl.v36i2.1298

Katzman, L.I., Gruner Gandhi, A., Harbour, W.S. and LaRock, J.D. (eds) (2005) *Special Education for a New Century.* Reprint Series No. 41, Harvard Educational Review. Cambridge, MA: Harvard Educational Review.

Kaufman, A.S., Raiford, S.E., and Coalson, D.L. (2016) *Intelligent Testing with the WISC-V.* Hoboken, NJ: Wiley.

Kecskés, I. and Papp, T. (2000) *Foreign Language and Mother Tongue.* Mahwah, NJ: Lawrence Erlbaum Associates.

Kieffer, M.J., Petscher, Y., Proctor, C.P. and Silverman, R.D. (2016) Is the whole greater than the sum of its parts? Modeling the contributions of language comprehension skills to reading comprehension in the upper elementary grades. *Scientific Studies of Reading* 20, 436–454. doi:10.1080/10888438.2016.1214591

Kirwan, D. (2014) From English language support to plurilingual awareness. In D. Little, C. Leung and P. Van Avermaet (eds) *Managing Diversity in Education: Languages, Policies, Pedagogies* (pp. 189–203). Bristol: Multilingual Matters.

Kirwin, D. (2020) Converting plurilingual skills into educational capital. *Learn: Journal of the Irish Learning Support Association* 41, 35–55.

Klesmer, H. (1994) Assessment and teacher perceptions of ESL student achievement. *English Quarterly* 26 (3), 8–11.

Kleyn, T. and García, O. (2019) Translanguaging as an act of transformation: Restructuring teaching and learning for emergent bilingual students. In L.C. de Oliveira (ed.) *The Handbook of TESOL in K-12* (pp. 69–82). New York: John Wiley and Sons Ltd.

Koda, K. (2008) Impacts of prior literacy experience on second-language learning to read. In K. Koda and A.M. Zehler (eds) *Learning to Read across Languages: Cross-Linguistic Relationships in First- and Second-Language Literacy Development* (pp. 68–96). New York, NY: Routledge.

Kolers, P.A. (1968) Bilingualism and information processing. *Scientific American* 2018 (3), 78–89.

Komesaroff, L. (2008) *Disabling Pedagogy: Power, Politics, and Deaf Education.* Washington, DC: Gallaudet University Press.

Kozol, J. (2005) *The Shame of the Nation: The Restoration of Apartheid Schooling in America.* New York, NY: Crown Publishers.

Krashen, S.D. (2004a) *The Power of Reading: Insights from the Research* (2nd edn). Portsmouth, NH: Heinemann.

Krashen, S.D. (2004b) False claims about literacy development. *Educational Leadership* 61 (6), 18–21.

Kroll, J. and Bialystok, E. (2013) Understanding the consequences of bilingualism for language processing and cognition. *Journal of Cognitive Psychology* 25 (5), 497–514.

Kroll, J.F., Bobb, S.C. and Hoshino, N. (2014) Two languages in mind: Bilingualism as a tool to investigate language, cognition, and the brain. *Current Directions in Psychological Science* 23 (3), 159–163.

Kubota, R. (2020) Promoting and problematizing multi/plural approaches in language pedagogy. In S.M.C. Lau and S. Van Viegen (eds) *Plurilingual Pedagogies: Critical and*

Creative Endeavors for Equitable Language in Education (pp. 303–322). Cham, Switzerland: Springer Nature.

Kuyumjian, N.M.M. (2020) *Langue et Socialisation: l'Impact des Activités Inter-culturelles en Contexte Scolaire Multilingue.* Doctoral thesis, l'Université Paul-Valéry Montpellier III.

Labov, W. (1969) *A Study of Non-Standard English.* Washington, DC: Center for Applied Linguistics. Retrieved from https://files.eric.ed.gov/fulltext/ED024053.pdf

Labov, W. (1972) *Language in the Inner City.* Philadelphia: University of Pennsylvania Press.

Ladson-Billings, G. (1994) *The Dreamkeepers: Successful Teachers of African American Children.* San Francisco: Jossey-Bass Publishers.

Ladson-Billings, G. (1995) Toward a theory of culturally relevant pedagogy. *American Educational Research Journal* 32, 465–491.

Lambert, W.E. (1974) Culture and language as factors in learning and education. In F.E. Aboud and R.D. Meade (eds) *Cultural Factors in Learning and Education. Proceedings of the Fifth Western Washington Symposium on Learning* (pp. 99–122). Bellingham, WA: Western Washington University.

Lambert, W.E. (1975) Culture and language as factors in learning and education. In A. Wolfgang (ed.) *Education of Immigrant Students: Issues and Answers* (pp. 55–83). Toronto: Ontario Institute for Studies in Education.

Lambert, W. E. (1984) An overview of issues in immersion education. In California State Department of Education (ed.) *Studies on Immersion Education: A Collection for United States Educators* (pp. 8–30). Sacramento: California State Department of Education.

Lambert, W.E. and Tucker, G.R. (1972) *Bilingual Education of Children: The St. Lambert Experiment.* Rowley, MA: Newbury House.

Lau, S.M.C. and Van Viegen, S. (2020a) Plurilingual pedagogies: An introduction. In S.M.C. Lau and S. Van Viegen (eds) *Plurilingual Pedagogies: Critical and Creative Endeavors for Equitable Language in Education* (pp. 3–22). Cham, Switzerland: Springer Nature.

Lau, S.M.C. and Van Viegen, S. (eds) (2020b) *Plurilingual Pedagogies: Critical and Creative Endeavors for Equitable Language in Education.* Cham, Switzerland: Springer Nature.

Lechner, S. and Siemund, P. (2014) Double threshold in bi-and multilingual contexts: Preconditions for higher academic attainment in English as an additional language. *Frontiers in Psychology* 5, 546, 1–8.

Lee, M. (1985) *Letters to Marcia: A Teacher's Guide to Anti-Racist Education.* Toronto: Cross Cultural Communication Centre.

Leoni, L., Cohen, S., Cummins, J., Bismilla, V., Bajwa, M., Hanif, S., Khalid, K. and Shahar, T. (2011) 'I'm not just a coloring person': Teacher and student perspectives on identity text construction. In J. Cummins and M. Early (eds) *Identity Texts: The Collaborative Creation of Power in Multilingual Schools* (pp. 45–57). Stoke-on-Trent: Trentham Books.

Le Pichon, E. (2020) Digital literacies and language friendly pedagogies: Where are we now? *School Education Gateway.* Retrieved from: https://www.schooleducationgate-way.eu/en/pub/viewpoints/experts/digital-literacies-pedagogies.htm

Le Pichon, E., Siarova, H. and Szonyi, E. (2020) *The Future of Language Education in Europe: Case-Studies of Innovative Practices.* NESET II report, Luxembourg: Publications Office of the European Union. https://nesetweb.eu/en/resources/library/the-future-of-language-education-in-europe-case-studies-of-innovative-practices/

Leung, C. and Valdés, G. (2019) Translanguaging and the transdisciplinary framework for language teaching and learning in a multilingual world. *The Modern Language Journal* 103 (2), 348–370. doi:10.1111/modl.12568

Lewis, K. and Davies, I. (2018) Understanding media opinion on bilingual education in the United States. *Journal of Social Science Education* 17 (4), 40–67. doi:10.4119/UNIBI/jsse-v17-i3-1096

Lewis, G., Jones, B. and Baker, C. (2012a) Translanguaging: Origins and development from school to street and beyond. *Educational Research and Evaluation* 18 (7), 641–654. doi:10.1080/13803611.2012.718488

Lewis, G., Jones, B. and Baker, C. (2012b) Translanguaging: Developing its conceptualisation and contextualisation. *Educational Research and Evaluation* 18 (7), 655–670. doi:10.1080/13803611.2012.718490

Levin, T. and Shohamy, E. (2008) Achievement of immigrant students in mathematics and academic Hebrew in Israeli school: A large-scale evaluation study. *Studies in Educational Evaluation* 34, 1–14.

Liddicoat, A. and Heugh, K. (2015) Educational equity for linguistically marginalised students. In M. Bigelow and J. Ennser-Kananen (eds) *The Routledge Handbook of Educational Linguistics* (pp. 79–91). London and New York: Routledge.

Lin, A.M.Y. (1996) Bilingualism or linguistic segregation? Symbolic domination, resistance, and code-switching in Hong Kong schools. *Linguistics and Education* 8, 49–84.

Lin, A.M.Y. (1997) Bilingual education in Hong Kong. In J. Cummins and D. Corson (eds) *Bilingual Education. Vol. 5 Encyclopedia of Language and Education* (pp. 281–289). Dordrecht: Kluwer Academic Publishers.

Lin, A.M.Y., Wu, Y. and Lemke, J.L. (2020) 'It takes a village to research a village': Conversations between Angel Lin and Jay Lemke on contemporary issues in translanguaging. In S.M.C. Lau and S. van Viegen (eds) *Plurilingual Pedagogies* (pp. 47–74). Cham: Springer.

Lindholm-Leary, K.J. and Borsato, G. (2006) Academic achievement. In F. Genesee, K. Lindholm-Leary, W. Saunders and D. Christian (eds) *Educating English Language Learners: A Synthesis of Research Evidence* (pp. 176–222). New York, NY: Cambridge University Press.

Lindsay, J. (2010) *Children's Access to Print Material and Education-Related Outcomes: Findings from a Meta-analytic Review.* Naperville, IL: Learning Point Associates.

Lindsay, J.J. (2018) Interventions that increase children's access to print material and improve their reading proficiencies. In R.L. Allington and A. McGill-Franzen (eds) *Summer Reading: Closing the Rich/Poor Reading Achievement Gap* (pp. 41–58). New York: Teachers College Press.

Lindsey, K.A., Manis, F.R. and Bailey, C.E. (2003) Prediction of first-grade reading in Spanish-speaking English-language learners. *Journal of Educational Psychology* 95, 482–494. doi:10.1037/0022-0663.95.3.482

Lippi-Green, R. (1997/2012) *English with an Accent: Language, Ideology and Discrimination in the United States.* New York: Routledge.

Little, D. (2005) The Common European Framework and the European Language Portfolio: Involving learners and their judgements in the assessment process. *Language Testing* 22 (3), 321–336. doi:10.1191/0265532205lt311oa

Little, D. (2010) The linguistic and educational integration of children and adolescents from migrant backgrounds. Strasbourg: Council of Europe. Retrieved from https://rm.coe.int/CoERMPublicCommonSearchServices/DisplayDCTMContent?documentId=09000016805a0d1b

Little, D. and Kirwin, D. (2018) Translanguaging as a key to educational success: The experience of one Irish primary school. In P. Van Avermaet, S. Slembrouck, K. Van Gorp, S. Sierens and K. Maryns (eds) *The Multilingual Edge of Education* (pp. 313–339). London: Palgrave Macmillan.

Little, D. and Kirwin, D. (2019) *Engaging with Linguistic Diversity.* London: Bloomsbury Academic.

Loewus, L. (2019) National reading scores are down. What does it mean? *Education Week*, October 30. Retrieved from https://www.edweek.org/teaching-learning/national-reading-scores-are-down-what-does-it-mean/2019/10

López-Gopar, M. E. (2016) *Decolonizing Primary English Language Teaching.* Bristol: Multilingual Matters.

López-Gopar, M.E., Clemente, Á. And Sughrua, W. (2011) Co-Creating identities through bilingual identity texts and dialogical ethnography. *Writing & Pedagogy* 3 (1), 241–264.

Lory, M.-P. (2021) A non-traditional approach to listening to students' voices. In L. Mary, A-B. Krüger and A.S. Young (eds) *Migration, Multilingualism and Education: Critical Perspectives on Inclusion* (pp. 220–221). Bristol: Multilingual Matters.

Lotherington, H. (2011) *Pedagogy of Multiliteracies: Rewriting Goldilocks*. New York: Routledge.

Lotherington, H. and Paige, C. (eds) (2017) *Teaching Young Learners in a Superdiverse World: Multimodal Approaches and Perspectives*. New York: Routledge.

Lucas, T., Henze, R. and Donato, R. (1990) Promoting the success of Latino language-minority students: An exploratory study of six high schools. *Harvard Educational Review* 60 (3), 315–340.

Lucas, T. and Katz, A. (1994) Reframing the debate: The roles of native languages in English-only programs for language minority students. *TESOL Quarterly* 28, 537–562.

Lyster, R. (2019) Translanguaging in immersion: Cognitive support or social prestige? 75 (4), 340–352.

Lyster, R., Collins, L. and Ballinger, S. (2009) Linking languages through a bilingual read-aloud project. *Language Awareness* 18 (3–4), 366–383. doi:10.1080/096584109031 97322

Macedo, D.P. (1994) *Literacies of Power: What Americans Are Not Allowed to Know*. Boulder, CO: Westview Press.

Macedo, D. (ed.) (2019) *Decolonizing Foreign Language Education: The Misteaching of English and Other Colonial Languages*. New York: Routledge.

Macnamara, J. (1966) *Bilingualism and Primary Education*. Edinburgh: Edinburgh University Press.

MacSwan, J. (1999) *A Minimalist Approach to Intrasentential Code Switching*. New York, NY: Garland Press.

MacSwan, J. (2000) The Threshold Hypothesis, semilingualism, and other contributions to a deficit view of linguistic minorities. *Hispanic Journal of Behavioral Sciences* 20 (1), 3–45.

MacSwan, J. (2017) A multilingual perspective on translanguaging. *American Educational Research Journal* 54 (1), 167–201. doi:10.3102/0002831216683935

MacSwan, J. (2020) Translanguaging, language ontology and civil rights. *World Englishes*. 1–13. Published online 16 March. doi:10.1111/weng.12464

MacSwan, J. and Rolstad, K. (2003) Linguistic diversity, schooling, and social class: Rethinking our conception of language proficiency in language minority education. In C.B. Paulston and R. Tucker (eds) *Sociolinguistics: The Essential Readings* (pp. 329–340). Oxford: Blackwell.

Macleroy, V. (2021) Framing critical perspectives on migration, fairness and belonging through the lens of young people's multilingual digital stories. In L. Mary, A-B. Krüger, and A.S. Young (eds) *Migration, Multilingualism and Education: Critical Perspectives on Inclusion* (pp. 202–220). Bristol: Multilingual Matters.

Majima, J. and Sakurai, C. (2021) A longitudinal study of emergent bilinguals among Chinese pupils at a Japanese Public School: A focus on language policies and inclusion. In L. Mary, A-B. Krüger and A.S. Young (eds) *Migration, Multilingualism and Education: Critical Perspectives on Inclusion* (pp. 93–110). Bristol: Multilingual Matters.

Makalela, L. (2018) Teaching African languages the *Ubuntu* way: The effects of translanguaging among pre-service teachers in South Africa. In P. Van Avermaet, S. Slembrouck, K. Van Gorp, S. Sierens and K. Maryns (eds) *The Multilingual Edge of Education* (pp. 261–282). London: Palgrave Macmillan.

Makoni, S. and Pennycook, A.D. (2005) Disinventing and (re)constituting languages. *Critical Inquiry in Language Studies: An International Journal* 2 (3), 137–156.

Makoni, S. and Pennycook, A.D. (2007a) Disinventing and reconstituting languages. In S. Makoni and A. Pennycook (eds) *Disinventing and Reconstituting Languages* (pp. 1–41). Clevedon: Multilingual Matters.

Makoni, S. and Pennycook, A.D. (eds) (2007b) *Disinventing and Reconstituting Languages*. Clevedon: Multilingual Matters.

Mancilla-Martinez, J. and Lesaux, N.K. (2011) The gap between Spanish speakers' word reading and word knowledge: A longitudinal study. *Child Development* 82 (5), 1544–1560.

Mangubhai, F. (2001) Book floods and comprehensible input floods: Providing ideal conditions for second language acquisition. *International Journal of Educational Research 35*, 147–156.

Manyak, P.C. (2004) 'What did she say?' Translation in a primary-grade English immersion class. *Multicultural Perspectives* 6, 12–18.

Mariani, L. (1997) Teacher support and teacher challenge in promoting learner autonomy. *Perspectives*, 23 (2). Retrieved from http://www.learningpaths.org/papers/papersupport.htm

Markus, P., Westernoff, F. and Jones-Vo, S. (2021) *Powerful Practices for Supporting English Learners*. San Francisco, CA: Corwin Press.

Marshall, E. and Toohey, K. (2010) Representing family: Community funds of knowledge, bilingualism, and multimodality. *Harvard Educational Review* 80 (2), 221–241.

Martin, K.M., Aponte, H.J. and García, O. (2019) Countering raciolinguistic ideologies: the role of translanguaging in educating bilingual children. *Cahiers Internationaux de Sociolinguistique* 16 (2), 19–41.

Martin, J. and McCracken, M. (2018) Finding Young EAL learners' voices: Using Google Translate in class, May 21. [The EAL Journal Blog Post]. See: https://ealjournal.org/2018/05/21/finding-young-eal-learners-voices-using-google-translate-in-class/

Martin-Jones, M. and Romaine, S. (1986) Semilingualism: A half-baked theory of communicative competence. *Applied Linguistics 7*, 26–38.

Mary, L., Krüger, A.-B. and Young, A.S. (eds) (2021) *Migration, Multilingualism and Education: Critical Perspectives on Inclusion*. Bristol: Multilingual Matters.

Mary, L. and Young, A.S. (2017) From silencing to translanguaging: Turning the tide to support emergent bilinguals in transition from home to pre-school. In B.A. Paulsrud, J. Rosén, B. Straszer and Å. Wedin (eds) *New Perspectives on Translanguaging and Education* (pp. 108–128). Bristol: Multilingual Matters.

Mary, L. and Young, A.S. (2021) 'To make headway you have to go against the flow': Resisting dominant discourses and supporting emergent bilinguals in a multilingual pre-school in France. In L. Mary, A-B. Krüger and A.S. Young. (eds) *Migration, Multilingualism and Education: Critical Perspectives on Inclusion*. Bristol: Multilingual Matters.

Massaro, D.W. (2015) Two different communication genres and implications for vocabulary development and learning to read. *Journal of Literacy Research* 47 (4) 505–527. doi:10.1177/1086296X15627528

May, S. (2011) The disciplinary constraints of SLA and TESOL: Additive bilingualism and second language acquisition, teaching and learning. *Linguistics and Education* 22 (3), 233–247. doi:10.1016/j.linged.2011.02.001

May, S. (2014) Disciplinary divides, knowledge construction, and the multilingual turn. In S. May (ed.) *The Multilingual Turn: Implications for SLA, TESOL and Bilingual Education* (pp. 7–31). New York: Routledge.

McCollum, P. (1999) Learning to value English: Cultural capital in a two-way bilingual program. *Bilingual Research Journal* 23 (2 and 3), 113–134.

McCracken, M., Rikers, L. and Cummins, J. (2020) Developing a multilingual ethos to foster student and teacher agency. *International Schools Magazine* 22.

McCracken, M., Rikers, L., Tee, S. and van Eerdewijk, J. (2018) Bringing Identity Language into our school. *International Schools Magazine* 20 (3), 31–33.

McField, G. and McField, D. (2014) The consistent outcome of bilingual education programs: A meta-analyses of meta-analyses. In G. McField (ed.) *The Miseducation of English Learners* (pp. 267–297). Charlotte, NC: Information Age Publishing.

McGill-Franzen, A.M., Lanford, C. and Adams, E. (2002) Learning to be literate: A comparison of five urban early childhood programs. *Journal of Educational Psychology* 94 (3), 443–464.

McQuillan, J. and Tse, L. (1996) Does research matter? An analysis of media opinion on bilingual education, McQuillan 1984–1994. *Bilingual Research Journal* 20 (1), 1–27.

Melby-Lervåg, M. and Lervåg, A. (2011) Cross-linguistic transfer of oral language, decoding, phonological awareness and reading comprehension: A meta-analysis of the correlational evidence. *Journal of Research in Reading* 34, 114–135.

Menéndez, B. (2010) Cross-modal bilingualism: language contact as evidence of linguistic transfer in sign bilingual education. *International Journal of Bilingual Education and Bilingualism* 13, 201–223.

Menken, K., Funk, A. and Kleyn, T. (2011) Teachers at the epicenter: Engagement and resistance in a biliteracy program for 'Long-Term English Language Learners' in the U.S. In C. Hélot and M. Ó Laoire (eds) *Language Policy for the Multilingual Classroom: Pedagogy of the Possible* (pp. 81–106). Bristol: Multilingual Matters.

Menken, K. and Sánchez, M.T.M. (2019) Translanguaging in English-only schools: From pedagogy to stance in the disruption of monolingual policies and practices. *TESOL Quarterly* 53 (3), 741–767.

Mertin, P. (2018) *Translanguaging in the Secondary School*. Woodbridge: John Catt Publishers.

Messick, S. (1987) *Validity*. Research Report, Educational Testing Service, Princeton, New Jersey.

Messick, S. (1994) The interplay of evidence and consequences in the validation of performance assessments. *Educational Researcher* 23, 13–23.

Minami, M. and Kennedy, B.P. (eds) (1991) *Language Issues in Literacy and Bilingual/Multicultural Education*. Reprint Series No. 22, Harvard Educational Review. Cambridge, MA: Harvard Educational Review.

Mohanty, A.K. (2018) *The Multilingual Reality: Living with Languages*. Bristol: Multilingual Matters.

Moll, L.C., Amanti, C., Neff, D. and Gonzalez, N. (1992) Funds of knowledge for teaching: Using a qualitative approach to connect homes and classrooms. *Theory into Practice* 31 (2), 132–141.

Mol, S.E. and Bus, A. (2011) To read or not to read: A meta-analysis of print exposure from infancy to early adulthood. *Psychological Bulletin* 137 (2), 267–296.

Molyneux, P., Scull, J. and Aliania, R. (2016) Bilingual education in a community language: lessons from a longitudinal study. *Language and Education* 30 (4), 337–360. doi:10.1080/09500782.2015.1114630

Monsrud, M.-B., Rydland, V., Geva, E., Thurmann-Moe, A.-C. and Halaas Lyster, S.-A. (2019) The advantages of jointly considering first and second language vocabulary skills among emergent bilingual children. *International Journal of Bilingual Education and Bilingualism*. doi: 10.1080/13670050.2019.1624685

Montero, M.K., Bice-Zaugg, C., Marsh, A.C.J. and Cummins, J. (2013) Activist literacies: Validating Aboriginality through visual and literary identity texts. *Journal of Language and Literacy Education* 9 (1), 73–94. Available at http://jolle.coe.uga.edu/wp-content/uploads/2013/06/Validating-Aboriginality.pdf

Moore, D., Lau, S.M.C. and Van Viegen, S. (2020) Mise en écho des perspectives on plurilingual competence and pluralistic pedagogies: A conversation with Danièle Moore. In S.M.C. Lau and S. Van Viegen (eds) *Plurilingual Pedagogies: Critical and Creative*

Endeavors for Equitable Language in Education (pp. 23–46). Cham, Switzerland: Springer Nature.

Motha, S. (2006) Decolonizing ESOL: Negotiating linguistic power in U.S. public school classrooms. *Critical Inquiry in Language Studies: An International Journal* 3 (2 and 3), 75–100.

Mougeon, R. and Canale, M. (1978–79) Maintenance of French in Ontario: Is education in French enough? *Interchange* 9, 30–39.

Muñoz-Sandoval, A., Cummins, J., Alvarado, C.G. and Ruef, M. (1998) *The Bilingual Verbal Abilities Tests.* Itasca, IL: Riverside Publishing.

Nagy, W. and Townsend, D. (2012) Words as tools: Learning academic vocabulary as language acquisition. *Reading Research Quarterly* 47, 91–108. doi:10.1002/RRQ.011

Nakanishi, T. (2015) A meta-analysis of extensive reading research. *TESOL Quarterly* 49, 6–37.

Naqvi, R., Carey, J., Cummins, J. and Brooks, A. (2015) The role of identity narratives in overcoming barriers to parental engagement. *TESOL in Context* 25 (1), 16–33.

Naqvi, R., Thorne, K., Pfitscher, C., Nordstokke, D. and McKeough, A. (2013) Reading dual language books: Improving early literacy skills in linguistically diverse classrooms. *Journal of Early Childhood Research* 11 (1), 3–15. doi:0.1177/1476718X 12449453

National Academies of Sciences, Engineering and Medicine (NASEM) (2017) *Promoting the Educational Success of Children and Youth Learning English: Promising Futures.* Washington, DC: The National Academies Press. doi:10.17226/24677.

National Reading Panel (2000) *Teaching Children to Read: An Evidence-Based Assessment of the Scientific Research Literature on Reading and its Implications for Reading Instruction.* Washington, DC: National Institute of Child Health and Human Development.

Neuman, S.B. (1999) Books make a difference: A study of access to literacy. *Reading Research Quarterly* 34 (3), 286–311.

Neuman, S.B. and Celano, D. (2001) Access to print in low-income and middle-income communities: An ecological study of four neighbourhoods. *Reading Research Quarterly* 36, 8–26.

New London Group (1996) A pedagogy of multiliteracies: Designing social futures. *Harvard Educational Review* 66, 60–92.

New York State Bilingual Common Core Initiative. (2013) NYS Bilingual Common Core Initiative: Theoretical Foundations. Albany, NY: New York State Department of Education. Retrieved from http://www.engageny.org/sites/default/files/resource/attachments/nysbcci-theoretical-foundations.pdf

Niederberger, N. (2008) Does the knowledge of a natural sign language facilitate Deaf children's learning to read and write? Insights from French Sign Language and written French data. In C. Plaza Pust and E. Moralez-Lopez (eds) *Sign Bilingualism: Language Development, Interaction, and Maintenance in Sign Language Contact Situations* (pp. 39–50). Amsterdam and Philadelphia, PA: John Benjamins.

Niederberger, N. and Prinz, P. (2005) La connaissance d'une langue des signes peut-elle faciliter l'apprentissage de l'écrit chez l'enfant sourd? (Does the knowledge of a natural sign language facilitate deaf children's learning to read and write?). *Enfance* 4, 285–297.

Nieminen, L. and Ullakonoja, R. (2017) The development of Russian heritage pupils' writing proficiency in Finnish and Russian. In R. Berthele and A. Lambelet (eds) *Heritage and School Language Literacy Development in Migrant Children: Interdepedence or Independence?* (pp. 161–187). Bristol: Multilingual Matters.

Nieto, S. and Bode, P. (2018) *Affirming Diversity: The Sociopolitical Context of Multicultural Education.* 7th ed. Boston: Pearson.

Ní Ríordáin, M. and O'Donoghue, J. (2009) The relationship between performance on mathematical word problems and language proficiency for students learning through the medium of Irish. *Educational Studies in Mathematics* 71, 43–64. doi:10.1007/s10649-008-9158-9

Noguera, P.A. (2003) *City Schools and the American Dream: Reclaiming the Promise of Public Education*. New York, NY: Teachers College Press.

Norton B. (2013) *Identity and Language Learning: Extending the Conversation* (2nd edn). Bristol: Multilingual Matters.

Norton, B. and Tembe, J. (2020) Teaching multilingual literacy in Ugandan classrooms: The promise of the African Storybook. *Applied Linguistics Review*. Ahead of print. doi:10.1515/applirev-2020-2006

Norton Peirce, B. (1995) Social identity, investment, and language learning. *TESOL Quarterly* 29 (1), 9–31. doi:10.2307/3587803

Ntelioglou, B.Y., Fannin, J., Montanera, M. and Cummins, J. (2014) A multilingual and multimodal approach to literacy teaching and learning in urban education: A collaborative inquiry project in an inner-city elementary school. *Frontiers in Psychology* 5, 1–10. doi:10.3389/fpsyg.2014.00533.

Nurmela, I., Awasthi, L.D. and Skutnabb-Kangas, T. (2012) Enhancing quality education for all in Nepal through indigenised MLE: The challenge to teach in over a hundred languages. In T. Skutnabb-Kangas and K. Heugh (eds) *Multilingual Education and Sustainable Diversity Work: From Periphery to Centre* (pp. 151–177). New York and London: Routledge.

Nusche, D. (2009) *What Works in Migrant Education? A Review of Evidence and Policy Options*. OECD Education Working Papers, No. 22, OECD Publishing. doi:10.1787/227131784531.

Ó Duibhir, P. (2018) *Immersion Education: Lessons from a Minority Language Context*. Bristol: Multilingual Matters.

OECD (2004) *Messages from PISA 2000*. Paris: OECD.

OECD (2010a) *PISA 2009 Results: Learning to Learn—Student Engagement, Strategies and Practices (Volume III)*. Paris: OECD. Retrieved from http://www.oecd.org/dataoecd/11/17/48852630.pdf

OECD (2010b) *Strong Performers and Successful Reformers in Education: Lessons from PISA for the United States*. Paris: OECD. Retrieved from http://www.oecd.org/dataoecd/32/50/46623978.pdf

OECD (2010c) *Closing the Gap for Immigrant Students: Policies, Practice and Performance*. OECD Reviews of Migrant Education. Paris: OECD.

OECD (2010d) *PISA 2009 Results: Overcoming Social Background – Equity in Learning Opportunities and Outcomes (Volume II)*. Paris: OECD. Retrieved from http://www.oecd.org/pisa/pisaproducts/48852584.pdf

OECD (2012) *Untapped Skills: Realising the Potential of Immigrant Students*. Paris: OECD. Retrieved from http://www.oecd.org/edu/Untapped%20Skills.pdf (2015) *Helping Immigrant Students Succeed at School – and Beyond*. Paris: OECD. Retrieved from https://www.oecd.org/education/Helping-immigrant-students-to-succeed-at-school-and-beyond.pdf

OECD (2016) *PISA 2015. Results in Focus*. Paris: OECD. Retrieved from https://www.oecd.org/pisa/pisa-2015-results-in-focus.pdf

Office of the Inspector General (2006) *The Reading First program's Grant Application Process. Final Inspection Report* (Report No. ED-OIG/I13-F0017). Washington, DC: U.S. Department of Education.

Ogbu, J.U. (1978) *Minority Education and Caste*. New York: Academic Press.

Ogbu, J.U. (1992) Understanding cultural diversity and learning. *Educational Researcher* 21 (8), 5–14 and 24.

Oller, J.W. (1978) The language factor in the evaluation of bilingual education. In J.E. Alatis (ed.) *International Dimensions of Bilingual Education. Georgetown University Round Table on Languages and Linguistics* (pp. 410–422). Washington, D.C: Georgetown University Press.

Oller, J.W. (1980) A language factor deeper than speech: More data and theory for bilingual assessment. In J.E. Alatis (ed.) *Current Issues in Bilingual Education. Georgetown University Round Table on Languages and Linguistics* (pp. 14–30). Washington, D.C.: Georgetown University Press.

Olsen, L. (2010) *Reparable Harm: Fulfilling the Unkept Promise of Educational Opportunity for California's Long Term English Learners.* Long Beach, CA: Californians Together.

Ordonez, C.L., Carlo, M., Snow, C. and McLaughlin, B. (2002) Depth and breadth of vocabulary in two languages: Which vocabulary skills transfer? *Journal of Educational Psychology* 94, 719–728. doi:10.1037/0022-0663.94.4.719.

Ormel, E. (2008) *Visual Word Recognition in Bilingual Deaf Children.* Unpublished doctoral dissertation, University of Nijmegen, The Netherlands.

Otheguy, R., García, O. and Reid, W. (2015) Clarifying translanguaging and deconstructing named languages: A perspective from linguistics. *Applied Linguistics Review* 6 (3), 281–307. doi:10.1515/applirev-2015-0014

Otheguy, R., García, O. and Reid, W. (2019) A translanguaging view of the linguistic system of bilinguals. *Applied Linguistics Review* 10 (4), 625–651.

Paap, K.R. and Greenberg, Z.I. (2013) There is no coherent evidence for a bilingual advantage in executive processing. *Cognitive Psychology* 66 (2), 232–258.

Padden, C. and Ramsey, C. (1998) Reading ability in signing deaf children. *Topics in Language Disorders* 18, 30–46.

Pahl, K. and Rowsell, J. (2005) *Understanding Literacy Education: Using New Literacy Studies in the Classroom.* San Francisco: SAGE.

Panagiotopoulou, J.A., Rosen, L. and Strzykala, J. (2020) *Inclusion, Education and Translanguaging: How to Promote Social Justice in (Teacher) Education?* Wiesbaden: Springer Fachmedien.

Palmer, D. and Martínez, R.A. (2013) Teacher agency in bilingual spaces: A fresh look at preparing teachers to educate Latina/o bilingual children. *Review of Research in Education* 37, 269–297. doi:10.3102/0091732X12463556

Paris, D. (2012) Culturally sustaining pedagogy: A needed change in stance, terminology, and practice. *Educational Researcher* 41 (3), 93–97. doi:10.3102/0013189X 12441244

Paris, D. and Alim, H.S. (2017) *Culturally Sustaining Pedagogies: Teaching and Learning for Justice in a Changing World.* New York, NY: Teacher's College Press.

Parrish, T. et al. (2006) *Effects of the Implementation of Proposition 227 on the Education of English Learners, K–12: Findings from a Five-year Evaluation (Final Report).* Palo Alto and San Francisco: American Institutes for Research and WestEd.

Paulsrud, B., Rosén, J., Straszer, B. and Wedin, Å. (eds) (2017) *New Perspectives on Translanguaging and Education.* Bristol: Multilingual Matters.

Paulston, C.B. (1975) Ethnic-relations and bilingual education: Accounting for contradictory data. *Working Papers in Bilingualism* 6, 1–44. Retrieved from: https://files.eric. ed.gov/fulltext/ED125253.pdf

Paulston, C.B. (1982) *Swedish Research and Debate about Bilingualism.* Stockholm: Swedish National Board of Education.

Peal, E. and Lambert, W.E. (1962) The relationship of bilingualism to intelligence. *Psychological Monographs* 76 (27), 1–23.

Pearson, P.D. (2004) The reading wars. *Educational Policy* 18, 216–252.

Peskova, R.E., Honkowicz-Bukowska, D., Jónsdóttir, F.B., Gunnþórsdóttir, H., Jónsdóttir, K.L.S., Ólafsdóttir, S. (2020) *Guidelines for the Support of Mother Tongues and Active Plurilingualism in Schools and Afterschool Programs.* Reykjavík: Ministry of Education, Science and Culture. Retrieved from http://www.modurmal. com/guidelines-for-the-support-of-mother-tongues-and-active-plurilingualism/.

Petrovic, J.E. and Olmstead, S. (2001) Review: Cummins, language, power, and pedagogy. *Bilingual Research Journal* 25 (3), 405–412.

Phillips Galloway, E. and Uccelli, P. (2019a) Beyond reading comprehension: exploring the additional contribution of Core Academic Language Skills to early adolescents' written summaries. *Reading and Writing* 32, 729–759. doi:10.1007/s11145-018-9880-3

Phillips Galloway, E. and Uccelli, P. (2019b) Examining developmental relations between core academic language skills and reading comprehension for English learners and their peers. *Journal of Educational Psychology* 111, 15–31. doi:10.1037/edu0000276

Phillips Galloway, E., Uccelli, P., Aguilar, G. and Barr, C.D. (2020) Exploring the cross-linguistic contribution of Spanish and English academic language skills to English text comprehension for middle-grade dual language learners. *AERA Open* 6 (1), 1–20. doi:10.1177/2332858419892575

Phillipson, R. (1992) *Linguistic Imperialism*. Oxford: Oxford University Press.

Piccardo, E. (2013) Plurilingualism and curriculum design: Towards a synergic vision. *TESOL Quarterly* 47 (3), 600–614.

Piccardo, E. (2016) Plurilingualism: Vision, conceptualization, and practices. In P. Trifonas and T. Aravossitas (eds) *Handbook of Research and Practice in Heritage Language Education* (pp. 1–17). New York, NY: Springer Science + Business Media LLC. doi:10.1007/978-3-319-38893-9_47-1

Piccardo, E. and North, B. (2020) The dynamic nature of plurilingualism: Creating and validating CEFR descriptors for mediation, plurilingualism and pluricultural competence. In S.M.C. Lau and S. Van Viegen (eds) *Plurilingual Pedagogies: Critical and Creative Endeavors for Equitable Language in Education* (pp. 279–301). Cham, Switzerland: Springer Nature.

Pickel, T.K. (2021) 'Spaces of power, spaces of resistance': Identity negotiation through autobiography with newcomer immigrant students. In L. Mary, A-B. Krüger and A.S. Young. (eds) *Migration, Multilingualism and Education: Critical Perspectives on Inclusion* (pp. 185–200). Bristol: Multilingual Matters.

Pickel, T. and Hélot, C. (2014) 'Because it is my life, and I'm the one who makes choices'. Newcomers in the French education system and career guidance: What about their plurilingual competence? In P. Grommes and A. Hu (eds) *Plurilingual Education: Policies – Practice – Language Development* (pp. 161–117). Hamburg: John Benjamins.

Pike, L. (1979) *An Analysis of Alternative Item Formats for testing English as a Foreign Language*. TOEFL Research Reports No. 2. Princeton, NJ: Educational Testing Service.

Plüddemann, P. (2015) Unlocking the grid: language-in-education policy realisation in post-apartheid South Africa. *Language and Education* 29 (3), 186–199.

Porter, R.P. (1990) *Forked Tongue: The Politics of Bilingual Education*. New York: Basic Books.

Portes, A. and Rumbaut, R.G. (2001) *Legacies: The Story of the Immigrant Second Generation*. Berkeley: University of California Press.

Prada, J. and T. Nikula, T. (2018) Introduction to the special issue: On the transgressive nature of translanguaging pedagogies. *EuroAmerican Journal of Applied Linguistics and Languages* 5 (2), 1–7. doi:10.21283/2376905x.9.166

Prasad, G. (2016) Beyond the mirror towards a plurilingual prism: Exploring the creation of plurilingual 'identity texts' in English and French classrooms in Toronto and Montpellier. *Intercultural Education* 26 (6), 497–514. doi:10.1080/14675986.2015.1109775

Prasad, G. and Lory, M.-P. (2020) Linguistic and cultural collaboration in schools: Reconciling majority and minoritized language users. *TESOL Quarterly* 54 (4), 797–822.

Prax-Dubois, P. and Hélot, C. (2020) Translanguaging in multilingual pre-primary classrooms in La Réunion: Reflecting on inclusion and social justice in a French postcolonial context. In J.A. Panagiotopoulou, L. Rosen and J. Strzykala (eds) *Inclusion, Education and Translanguaging: How to Promote Social Justice in (Teacher) Education?* (pp. 41–61). Wiesbaden: Springer Fachmedien.

Pressley, M., Duke, N.K. and Boling, E.C. (2004) The educational science and scientifically based instruction we need: Lessons from reading research and policy making. *Harvard Educational Review* 74, 30–61.

Prevoo, M.J.L., Malda, M., Emmen, R,A.G., Yeniad, N. and Mesman, J. (2015) A context-dependent view on the linguistic interdependence hypothesis: Language use and SES as potential moderators. *Language Learning* 65 (2), 449–469. doi:10.1111/lang.12099

Prevoo, M.J.L., Malda, M., Mesman, J. and van Ijzendoorn, M.H. (2016) Within- and cross-language relations between oral language proficiency and school outcomes in bilingual children with an immigrant background: A meta-analytical study. *Review of Educational Research* 86 (1), 237–276. doi:10.3102/0034654315584685.

Prinz, P. and Strong, M. (1998) ASL proficiency and English literacy within a bilingual deaf education model of instruction. *Topics in Language Disorders* 18 (4), 47–60.

Proctor, C.P., August, D., Snow, C. and Barr, C.D. (2010) The interdependence continuum: A perspective on the nature of Spanish–English bilingual reading comprehension. *Bilingual Research Journal* 33, 5–20.

Proctor, C.P., Harring, J.R. and Silverman, R.D. (2017) Linguistic interdependence between Spanish language and English language and reading: A longitudinal exploration from second through fifth grade. *Bilingual Research Journal* 40, 372–391. doi:10.1080/15235882.2017.1383949

Qian, D. (2002) Investigating the relationship between vocabulary knowledge and academic reading performance: An assessment perspective. *Language Learning* 52, 513–536.

Ramanathan, V. and Morgan, B. (2007) TESOL and policy enactments: Perspectives from practice. *TESOL Quarterly* 41 (3), 447–463.

Ramirez, J.D. (1992) Executive summary. *Bilingual Research Journal* 16, 1–62.

Ramirez, L.L. (2012) Teaching our tongues: Student-run language classes as a celebration of linguistic and cultural diversity in schools. In A. Honigsfeld and A. Cohan (eds) *Breaking the Mold of Education for Culturally and Linguistically Diverse Students: Innovative and Successful Practices for the 21st Century* (pp. 199–206). New York: Rowman & Littlefield Publishers Inc.

Ramphal, D.K. (1983) *An Analysis of Reading Instruction of West Indian Creole-Speaking Students*. Unpublished doctoral dissertation, University of Toronto.

Ramsey, C.A. and Wright, E.N. (1974) Age and second language learning. *The Journal of Social Psychology* 94, 115–121.

Ravitch, D. (2013) *Reign of Error: The Hoax of the Privatization Movement and the Danger to America's Public schools*. New York: Alfred A. Knopf.

Reid, D.K., Hresko, W.P. and Hammill, D.D. (2001) *Test of Early Reading Ability* (3rd edn). Austin, TX: Pro-Ed.

Relyea, J.E. and Amendum, S.J. (2020) English reading growth in Spanish-speaking bilingual students: Moderating effect of English proficiency on cross-linguistic influence. *Child Development* 91 (4), 1150–1165. doi:10.1111/cdev.13288

Reyes, M.L. (2001) Unleashing possibilities: Biliteracy in the primary grades. In M.L. Reyes and J. Halcón (eds) *The Best for Our Children: Critical Perspectives on Literacy for Latino Students* (pp. 96–121). New York: Teachers College Press.

Richardson, E. (2014) When language is and not the issue: The case of 'AAVE' literacy research, teaching, and Labov's prescription for social (in)equality. In M. Bigelow and J. Ennser-Kananen (eds) *The Routledge Handbook of Educational Linguistics* (pp. 185–194). London and New York: Routledge.

Riches, C. and Genesee, F. (2006) Literacy: Crosslinguistic and crossmodal issues. In F. Genesee, K. Lindholm-Leary, W.M. Saunders and D. Christian (eds) *Educating English Language Learners: A Synthesis of Research Evidence* (pp. 64–108). New York, NY: Cambridge University Press.

Rivera, C. (ed.) (1984) *Language Proficiency and Academic Achievement*. Clevedon: Multilingual Matters.

Roberts, T. (2008) Home storybook reading in primary or second language with preschool children: Evidence of equal effectiveness for second language vocabulary acquisition. *Reading Research Quarterly* 43 (2), 103–130.

Roessingh, H. (2011) Family Treasures: A dual language book project for negotiating language, literacy culture and identity. *Canadian Modern Language Review* 67 (1), 123–148.

Roessingh, H. (2020) Culturally responsive pedagogy and academic vocabulary teaching and learning: An integrated approach in the elementary classroom. *TESL Canada Journal* 37 (1). doi:10.18806/tesl.v37i1.1334

Rolstad, K. (2014) Rethinking language at school. *International Multilingual Research Journal* 8 (1), 1–8. doi:10.1080/19313152.2014.852423

Rolstad, K. (2017) Second language instructional competence. *International Journal of Bilingual Education and Bilingualism* 20 (5), 497–509, doi:10.1080/13670050.2015.1 057101

Rolstad, K., Mahoney, K. and Glass, G.V. (2005) The big picture: A meta-analysis of program effectiveness research on English language learners. *Educational Policy* 19 (4), 572–594.

Rossell, C.H. and Baker, K. (1996) The effectiveness of bilingual education. *Research in the Teaching of English* 30, 7–74.

Rossell, C.H. and Kuder, J. (2005) Meta-Murky: A rebuttal to recent meta-analyses of bilingual education. In J. Söhn (ed.) *The Effectiveness of Bilingual School Programs for Immigrant Children*. AKI Research Review 2 (pp. 43–76). Berlin: Programme on Intercultural Conflicts and Societal Integration (AKI), Social Science Research Center. PID: https://nbn-resolving.org/urn:nbn:de:0168-ssoar-110296. Retrieved from http://www.ssoar.info/ssoar/handle/document/11029

Rothstein, R. (2004) *Class and Schools: Using Social, Economic, and Educational Reform to Close the Black-White Achievement Gap*. Washington, DC: Economic Policy Institute.

Ruiz, R. (1991) The empowerment of language minority students. In C. Sleeter (ed.) *Empowerment through Multicultural Education*. Albany, NY: SUNY Press.

Salaün, M. (2013) *Décoloniser L'école? Hawaii, Nouvelle-Calédonie. Expériences Contemporaines*. Rennes: Presses Universitaires de Rennes.

Sastri, P., Chau, M. and Chow, P. (2010) Infusing Aboriginal content and students' home languages into the school curriculum. *The Teaching Librarian* 18 (3), 32–34.

Saunders, W.M. and O'Brien, G. (2006) Oral language. In F. Genesee, K. Lindholm-Leary, W.M. Saunders and D. Christian (eds) *Educating English Language Learners: A Synthesis of Research Evidence* (pp. 14–63). New York, NY: Cambridge University Press.

Scarcella, R. (2003) *Academic English: A Conceptual Framework*. Santa Barbara: The University of California Linguistic Minority Research Institute Technical Report 2003-1.

Schecter, S.R. and Cummins, J. (eds) (2003) *Multilingual Education in Practice: Using Diversity as a Resource*. Portsmouth, NH: Heinemann.

Schissel, J.L., Leung, C. and Chalhoub-Deville, M. (2019) The construct of multilingualism in language testing. *Language Assessment Quarterly* 16 (4–5), 373–378, doi:10.1 080/15434303.2019.1680679

Schissel, J.L., Leung, C., López-Gopar, M. and Davis, J.R. (2018) Multilingual learners in language assessment: Assessment design for linguistically diverse communities. *Language and Education* 32 (2), 167–182. doi:10.1080/09500782.2018.1429463

Schleppegrell, M.J. (2004) *The Language of Schooling. A Functional Linguistics Perspective*. Mahwah, NJ: Lawrence Erlbaum.

Schlesinger, A.J. (1991) *The Disuniting of America*. New York: W.W. Norton.

Schoonen, R., Hulstijn, J. and Bossers, B. (1998) Metacognitive and language-specific knowledge in native and foreign language reading comprehension: An empirical study among Dutch students in grades 6, 8 and 10. *Language Learning* 48, 71–106.

Scribner, S. and Cole, M. (1978) Literacy without schooling: Testing for intellectual effects. *Harvard Educational Review* 48, 448–461.

Seltzer, K. (2019) Reconceptualizing 'home' and 'school' language: Taking a critical translingual approach in the English classroom. *TESOL Quarterly* 53 (4), 986–1007. doi:10.1002/tesq.530

Shanahan, T. and Beck, I. (2006) Effective literacy teaching for English-language learners. In D. August and T. Shanahan (eds) *Developing Literacy in Second-Language Learners: Report of the National Literacy Panel on Language-Minority Children and Youth* (pp. 415–488). Mahwah, NJ: Lawrence Erlbaum.

Shohamy, E. (2006) *Language Policy: Hidden Agendas and New Approaches.* New York, NY: Routledge.

Shohamy, E. (2011) Assessing multilingual competencies: Adopting construct valid assessment policies. *The Modern Language Journal* 95, 417–429. doi:10.1111/j.1540-4781.2011.01210.x

Shuy, R.W (1978) Problems in assessing language ability in bilingual education programs. In H. Lafontaine, B. Persky and L. Golubchick (eds) *Bilingual Education* (pp. 376–380). Wayne, NJ: Avery Publishing Group Inc.

Sierens, S., Slembrouck, S., Van Gorp, K., Agirdag, O. and Van Avermaet, P. (2019) Linguistic interdependence of receptive vocabulary skills in emergent bilingual preschool children: Exploring a factor-dependent approach. *Applied Psycholinguistics* 40, 1269–1297. doi:10.1017/S0142716419000250

Sierens, S. and Van Avermaet, P. (2014) Language diversity in education. In D. Little, C. Leung and P. Van Avermaet (eds) *Managing Diversity in Education* (pp. 204–222). Bristol: Multilingual Matters.

Sierens, S., Van Gorp, K. Slembrouck, S. and Van Avermaet, P. (2020) The strength of cross-language interdependence for listening comprehension proficiency in Turkish–Dutch emergent bilinguals: Testing three hypotheses. *Language Learning.* Ahead of print. doi:10.1111/lang.12441

Singleton, J.L., Morgan, D., DiGello, E., Wiles, J. and Rivers, R. (2004) Vocabulary use by low, moderate, and high ASL-proficient writers compared to hearing ESL and monolingual speakers. *Journal of Deaf Studies and Deaf Education* 9 (1), 86–103.

Singleton, J., Supalla, S., Litchfield, S. and Schley, S. (1998) From sign to word: considering modality constraints in ASL/English bilingual education. *Topics in Language Disorders* 18 (4), 16–30.

Skourtou, E., Kourtis-Kazoullis, V. and Cummins, J. (2006) Designing virtual learning environments for academic language development. In J. Weiss, J. Nolan, J. Hunsinger and P. Trifonas (eds) *The International Handbook of Virtual Learning Environments* (pp. 441–467). New York: Springer.

Skutnabb-Kangas, T. (1975) *Om tvåspråkighet och skolframgång* (On bilingualism and school achievement). Åbo: Svenska Litteratursällskapet i Finland, Nämnd för samhällsforskning, Forskningsrapport nr 20.

Skutnabb-Kangas, T. (2000) *Linguistic Genocide in Education – or Worldwide Diversity and Human Rights?* Mahwah, NJ and London, UK: Lawrence Erlbaum Associates.

Skutnabb-Kangas, T. (2009) Multilingual education for global justice: Issues, approaches, opportunities. In T. Skutnabb-Kangas, R. Phillipson, A.K. Mohanty and M. Panda (eds) *Social Justice through Multilingual Education* (pp. 36–62). Bristol: Multilingual Matters.

Skutnabb-Kangas, T. (2015) Linguicism. *The Encyclopedia of Applied Linguistics.* Malden, MA: Blackwell. Published Online: 19 June. doi:10.1002/9781405198431.wbeal1460.

Skutnabb-Kangas, T. and Cummins, J. (eds) (1988) *Minority Education: From Shame to Struggle.* Clevedon: Multilingual Matters.

Skutnabb-Kangas, T. and Heugh, K. (2012) Notes on terminology. In T. Skutnabb-Kangas and K. Heugh (eds) *Multilingual Education and Sustainable Diversity Work: From Periphery to Centre* (pp. xv–xvii). New York and London: Routledge.

Skutnabb-Kangas, T. and McCarty, T.L. (2008) Key concepts in bilingual education: Ideological, historical, espistemological, and empirical foundations. In J. Cummins and N.H. Hornberger (eds) *Encyclopedia of Language and Education, 2nd Edition, Volume 5: Bilingual Education* (pp. 3–18). New York: Springer Science + Business Media LLC.

Skutnabb-Kangas, T., Phillipson, R. and Dunbar, R. (2019) *Is Nunavut Education Criminally Inadequate? An Analysis of Current Policies for Inuktut and English in Education, International and National Law, Linguistic and Cultural Genocide and Crimes Against Humanity*. Report prepared for Nunavut Tunngavik.

Skutnabb-Kangas, T. and Toukomaa, P. (1976) *Teaching Migrant Children's Mother Tongue and Learning the Language of the Host Country in the Context of the Socio-Cultural Situation of the Migrant Family*. Helsinki: The Finnish National Commission for UNESCO.

Slavin, R.E. and Cheung, A. (2005) A synthesis of research on language of reading instruction. *Review of Educational Research* 75, 247–284.

Slavin, R.E., Madden, N.A., Dolan, L.J. and Wasik, B.A. (1996) *Every Child, Every School: Success for All*. Newbury Park, CA: Corbin.

Slembrouck, S. and Rosiers, K. (2018) Translanguaging: A matter of sociolinguistics, pedagogics, and interaction? In P. Van Avermaet, S. Slembrouck, K. Van Gorp, S. Sierens and K. Maryns (eds) *The Multilingual Edge of Education* (pp. 165–187). London: Palgrave Macmillan.

Slembrouck, S., Van Avermaet, P. and Van Gorp, K. (2018) Strategies of multilingualism in education for minority children. In P. Van Avermaet, S. Slembrouck, K. Van Gorp, S. Sierens and K. Maryns (eds) *The Multilingual Edge of Education* (pp. 9–39). London: Palgrave Macmillan.

Smith, F. (1988) *Joining the Literacy Club: Further Essays into Education*. Portsmouth, NH: Heinemann Educational Books, Inc.

Sneddon, R. (2008) Young bilingual children learning to read with dual language books. *English Teaching: Practice and Critique* 7 (2), 71–84.

Snoddon, K. and Weber, J. (eds) (2021) *Critical Perspectives on Plurilingualism in Deaf Education*. Bristol: Multilingual Matters.

Snow, C.E. (2000) On the limits of reframing: Rereading the National Academy of Sciences report on reading. *Journal of Literacy Research* 32 (1), 113–120.

Snow, C.E. (2006) Cross-cutting themes and future research directions. In D. August and T. Shanahan (eds) *Developing Literacy in Second-Language Learners: Report of the National Literacy Panel on Language-Minority Children and Youth* (pp. 631–651). Mahwah, NJ: Lawrence Erlbaum.

Snow, C.E. (2010) Academic language and the challenge of reading for learning about science. *Science* 328, 450–452. doi:10.1126/science.1182597

Snow, C.E., Burns, M.S. and Griffin, P. (eds) (1998) *Preventing Reading Difficulties in Young Children*. Washington, DC: National Academy Press.

Snow, C.E. and Hoefnagel-Höhle, M. (1979) Individual differences in second-language ability: A factor-analytic study. *Langugage and Speech* 22 (2), 151–162.

Snow, C.E. and Uccelli, P. (2009) The challenge of academic language. In D.R. Olson and N. Torrance (eds) *The Cambridge Handbook of Literacy* (pp. 112–133). Cambridge: Cambridge University Press. doi:10.1017/CBO9780511609664.008

Snow, M.A. and Katz, A. (2010) English language development. Foundations and implementation in kindergarten through grade five. In California Department of Education (2010) *Improving Education for English Learners: Research-Based Approaches* (pp. 83–149). Sacramento: California Department of Education.

Soltero-González, L., Sparrow, W., Butvilofsky, S., Escamilla, K. and Hopewell, S. (2016) Effects of a paired literacy program on emerging bilingual children's biliteracy outcomes in third grade. *Journal of Literacy Research* 1–25. doi:10.1177/1086296X16653842

Sparks, R.L., Patton, J., Ganschow, L., Humbach, N., and Javorsky, J. (2008) Early first-language reading and spelling skills predict later second-language reading and spelling skills. *Journal of Educational Psychology* 100, 162–174. doi:10.1037/00 22-0663.100.1.162

Sparks, R., Patton, J., Ganschow, L. and Humbach, N. (2009) Long-term crosslinguistic transfer of skills from L1 to L2. *Language Learning* 59, 203–243.

Sparks, R.L., Patton, J. and Murdoch, A. (2014) Early reading success and its relationship to reading achievement and reading volume: Replication of '10 years later'. *Reading and Writing* 27, 189–211. doi:10.1007/s11145-013-9439-2

Sparrow, W., Butvilofsky, S., Escamilla, K., Hopewell, S. and Tolento, T. (2014) Examining the longitudinal biliterate trajectory of emerging bilingual learners in a paired literacy instructional model. *Bilingual Research Journal* 37 (1), 24–42. doi:10.1080/15235882. 2014.893271

Spiro, J. and Crisfield, E. (2018) *Linguistic and Cultural Innovation in Schools: The Languages Challenge*. Cham, Switzerland: Palgrave Macmillan.

Spolsky, B. (1984) A note on the dangers of terminological innovation. In C. Rivera (ed.) *Language Proficiency and Academic Achievement* (pp. 41–43). Clevedon: Multilingual Matters.

Stanat, P. and Christensen, G. (2006) *Where Immigrant Students Succeed: A Comparative review of Performance and Engagement in PISA 2003*. Paris: Organisation for Economic Cooperation and Development.

Stanovich, K. (2000) *Progress in Understanding Reading. Scientific Foundations and New Frontiers*. New York, NY: Guildford Press.

Starfield, S. (1994) Language, cognition, and ESL literacy. Cummins, EAP, and academic literacy. *TESOL Quarterly* 28 (1), 176–179.

Staring, F. and Broughton, A. (2020) *Education Begins with Language: Thematic Report From A Programme of Seminars With Peer Learning to Support the Implementation of the Council Recommendation on A Comprehensive Approach to the Teaching and Learning of Languages*. Brussels: European Commission.

Steele, C.M. (1997) A threat in the air: How stereotypes shape intellectual identity and performance. *American Psychologist* 52 (6), 613–629.

Stille, S. and Prasad, G. (2015) 'Imaginings': Reflections on plurilingual students' creative multimodal works. *TESOL Quarterly* 49 (3), 608–621.

Strang, R. (1945) Variability in reading scores on a given level of intelligence test scores. *Journal of Educational Research* 38, 440–44

Straszer, B. (2018) Linguistic schoolscaping and the visibility of languages in the linguistic landscape of a minority language pre-school in Sweden. *EAL Journal* 8, 26–28.

Street, B. (1984) *Literacy in Theory and Practice*. New York: Cambridge University Press.

Strong, M. and Prinz, P. (1997) A study of the relationship between American Sign Language and English literacy. *Journal of Deaf Studies and Deaf Education* 2, 37–46.

Sullivan, A. and Brown, M. (2013) *Social Inequalities in Cognitive Scores at Age 16: The Role of Reading*. London: Centre for Longitudinal Studies, Institute of Education, University of London. Retrieved from www.cls.ioe.ac.uk

Swain, M. (2006) Languaging, agency and collaboration in advanced second language learning. In H. Byrnes (ed.) *Advanced Language Learning: The Contribution of Halliday and Vygotsky*. London: Continuum.

Swain, M., Kinnear, P. and Steinman, L. (2011) *Sociocultural Theory in Second Language Education: An Introduction through Narratives* (1st edn). Bristol: Multicultural Matters.

Swain, M. and Lapkin, S. (2013) A Vygotskian sociocultural perspective on immersion education: The L1/L2 debate. *Journal of Immersion and Content-Based Language Education* 1 (1), 101–129. doi:10.1075/jicb.1.1.05swa

Swain, M., Lapkin, S., Rowen, N. and Hart, D. (1991) The role of mother tongue literacy in third language learning. In S.P. Norris and L.M. Phillips (eds) *Foundations of Literacy Policy in Canada* (pp. 185–206). Calgary, AB: Detselig Enterprises.

Swanson, H.L., Rosston, K., Gerber, M. and Solari, E. (2008) Influence of oral language and phonological processing on children's bilingual reading. *Journal of School Psychology* 46, 413–429. doi:10.1016/j.jsp.2007.07.002.

Swanwick, R. (2017a) Translanguaging, learning and teaching in deaf education. *International Journal of Multilingualism* 14 (3), 233–249.

Swanwick, R. (2017b) *Languages and Languaging in Deaf Education: A Framework for Pedagogy.* Oxford: Oxford University Press.

Sweller, J., van Merriënboer, J.J.G. and Paas, F. (2019) Cognitive architecture and instructional design: 20 years later. *Educational Psychology Review* 31, 261–292. doi:10.1007/s10648-019-09465-5

Taylor, S.K. (2011) Identity texts as decolonized writing: Beyond the Cowboys and Indians meta-narrative. *Writing & Pedagogy* 3 (1), 289–304.

Taylor, S.K. (2014) From 'monolingual' multilingual classrooms to 'multilingual' multilingual classrooms: Managing cultural and linguistic diversity in the Nepali educational system. In D. Little, C. Leung and P. Van Avermaet (eds) *Managing Diversity in Education* (pp. 257–272). Bristol: Multilingual Matters.

Tamati, S.T. (2011) The trans-acquisitional approach: A bridge to English in kura kaupapa Māori. *Pacific-Asian Education* 23 (1), 91–102.

Tamati, S.T. (2016) Transacquisition Pedagogy for Bilingual Education: A Study in Kura Kaupapa Māori Schools. Doctoral dissertation submitted to the University of Auckland.

TESOL (1997) *ESL Standards for Pre-K-12 Students.* Alexandria, VA: TESOL, Inc.

The Guardian, May 6, 2014. OECD and Pisa tests are damaging education worldwide – academics. Retrieved from: https://www.theguardian.com/education/2014/may/06/oecd-pisa-tests-damaging-education-academics

Thomas, W.P. and Collier, V.P. (1997) *School Effectiveness for Language Minority Students.* Washington, DC: National Clearinghouse for English Language Acquisition. Retrieved from: http://www.ncela.gwu.edu/files/rcd/BE020890/School_effectiveness_for_langu.pdf

Thompson, K.D. (2015) English Learners' time to reclassification: An analysis. *Educational Policy* 31 (3), 330–363. doi:10.1177/0895904815598394

Thordardottir, E. (2011) The relationship between bilingual exposure and vocabulary development. *International Journal of Bilingualism* 15, 426–445.

Thorndike, R.L. (1973) *Reading Comprehension Education in 15 Countries.* Stockholm, Sweden: Almquist and Wiksell.

Tizard, J., Schofield, W.N. and Hewison, J. (1982) Collaboration between teachers and parents in assisting children's reading. *British Journal of Educational Psychology* 52, 1–15.

Toohey, K., Manyak, P. and Day, E. (2007) ESL learners in the early school years: Identity and mediated classroom practices. In J. Cummins and C. Davison (eds) *International Handbook of English Language Teaching* (pp. 625–638). New York, NY: Springer Science.

Troike, R. (1984) SCALP: Social and cultural aspects of language proficiency. In C. Rivera (ed.) *Language Proficiency and Academic Achievement.* Clevedon: Multilingual Matters.

Truth and Reconciliation Commission of Canada (2015) *Canada's Residential Schools: The History, Part 1 Origins to 1939. The Final Report of the Truth and Reconciliation Commission of Canada, Volume 1.* Retrieved from: http://nctr.ca/assets/reports/Final%20Reports/Volume_1_History_Part_1_English_Web.pdf

Tsokalidou, R. and Skourtou, E. (2020) Translanguaging as a culturally sustaining pedagogical approach: Bi/multilingual educators' perspectives. In J.A. Panagiotopoulou,

L. Rosen and J. Strzykala (eds) *Inclusion, Education and Translanguaging: How to Promote Social Justice in (Teacher) Education?* (pp. 219–235). Wiesbaden: Springer Fachmedien.

Uccelli, P., Barr, C.D., Dobbs, C.L., Phillips Galloway, E., Meneses, A. and Sanchez, E. (2015a) Core academic language skills: An expanded operational construct and a novel instrument to chart school-relevant language proficiency in pre-adolescent and adolescent learners. *Applied Psycholinguistics* 36, 1077–1109. doi:10.1017/S014271641400006X.

Uccelli, P., Phillips Galloway, E., Barr, C., Meneses, A. and Dobbs, C. (2015b) Beyond vocabulary: Exploring cross-disciplinary academic-language proficiency and its association with reading comprehension. *Reading Research Quarterly* 50, 337–356. doi:10.1002/rrq.104

Uccelli, P. and Phillips Galloway, E. (2018) What educators need to know about academic language: Insights from recent research. In C.T. Adger, C.E. Snow and D. Christian (eds) *What Teachers Need to Know about Language* (2nd edn) (pp. 62–74). Bristol: Multilingual Matters.

Uccelli, P., Phillips Galloway, E., Aguilar, G. and Allen, M. (2020) Amplifying and affirming students voices through CALS-informed instruction. *Theory into Practice* 59 (1), 75–88. doi:10.1080/00405841.2019.1665413

Usborne, E., Caouette, J., Qumaaluk, Q. and Taylor, D.M. (2009) Bilingual education in an Aboriginal context: Examining the transfer of language skills from Inuktitut to English or French. *International Journal of Bilingual Education and Bilingualism* 12 (6), 667–684.

UNESCO (1953) *The Use of Vernacular Languages in Education.* Monographs on Fundamental Education, VIII. Paris: UNESCO.

United States v. State of Texas (1981) Civil action #5281 (Bilingual Education). Memorandum Opinion.

U.S. Commission on Civil Rights (1973) *Teachers and Students: Differences in Teacher Interaction with Mexican-American and Anglo students.* Washington, D.C.: U.S. Government Printing Office.

Valdés, G. (1997) Dual-language immersion programs: A cautionary note concerning the education of language-minority *students. Harvard Education Review* 67 (3), 391–429.

Valdés, G. (2001) Heritage language students: Profiles and possibilities. In J. Kreeft Peyton, D. Ranard and S. McGinnis (eds) *Heritage Languages in America: Preserving a National Resource* (pp. 37–80). Washington, DC: Center for Applied Linguistics.

Valdés, G. (2004) Between support and marginalisation: The development of academic language in linguistic minority children. *International Journal of Bilingualism and Bilingual Education* 7, 102–132. doi:10.1080/13670050408667804.

Valdés, G. (2017) Entry visa denied: The construction of symbolic language borders in educational settings. In O. García, N. Flores and M. Spotti (eds) *The Oxford Handbook of Language and Society* (pp. 321–348). Oxford: Oxford University Press.

Valdés, G. (2020) (Mis)educating the children of Mexican-origin people in the United States: The challenge of internal language borders. *Intercultural Education*, doi: 10.1080/14675986.2020.179412

Valencia, R. (1997) Conceptionalizing the notion of deficit thinking. In R. Valencia (ed.) *The Evolution of Deficit Thinking: Educational Thought and Practice* (pp. 1–12). London: The Falmer Press.

Valentino, R.A. and Reardon, S.F. (2015) Effectiveness of four instructional programs designed to serve English Learners: Variation by ethnicity and initial English proficiency. *Educational Evaluation and Policy Analysis* 20, 1–26. doi:10.3102/016237 3715573310

Van Avermaet, P., Slembrouck, S., Van Gorp, K., Sierens, S. and Maryns, K (eds) (2018) *The Multilingual Edge of Education.* London: Palgrave Macmillan.

Vanhove, J. and Berthele, R. (2018) Testing the interdependence of languages (HELASCOT Project). In R. Berthele and A. Lambelet (eds) *Heritage and School Language Literacy Development in Migrant Children: Interdepedence or Independence?* (pp. 97–118). Bristol: Multilingual Matters.

Van Viegen Stille, S., Bethke, R., Bradley-Brown, J., Giberson, J. and Hall, G. (2016) Broadening educational practice to include translanguaging: An outcome of educator inquiry into multilingual students' learning needs. *The Canadian Modern Language Review* 72 (4), 480–503.

Verhoeven, L. (1991a) Acquistion of biliteracy. In J.H. Hulsijn and J.F. Matter (eds) *Reading in Two Languages* (pp. 61–74). Amsterdam: AILA.

Verhoeven, L. (1991b) Predicting minority children's bilingual proficiency: Child, family, and institutional factors. *Language Learning* 41, 205–233.

Veum, A., Hogga Siljan, H. and Maagerø, E. (2020) Who am I? How newly arrived immigrant students construct themselves through multimodal texts. *Scandinavian Journal of Educational Research* 1–16. doi:10.1080/00313831.2020.1788147

Vincent, C. (1996) *Singing to a Star: The School Meanings of Second Generation Salvadorean Students*. Doctoral dissertation, George Mason University, Fairfax, VA.

Volante, L., Klinger, D., Bilgili, Ö. and Siegel, M. (2017) Making sense of the performance (dis)advantage for immigrant students across Canada. *Canadian Journal of Education/ Revue canadienne de l'éducation* 40 (3), 229–361.

Volodina, A., Weinert, S. and Mursin, K. (2020) Development of academic vocabulary across primary school age: Differential growth and influential factors for German monolinguals and language minority learners. *Developmental Psychology* 56 (5), 922–936. doi:10.1037/dev0000910

von der Mühlen, S., Richter, T., Schmid, S., Schmidt, E.M. and Berthold, K. (2016) Judging the plausibility of arguments in scientific texts: a student–scientist comparison. *Thinking and Reasoning* 22 (2), 221–249. doi:10.1080/13546783.2015.1127289

Vygotsky, L.S. (1935/1997) The question of multilingual children. In L.S. Vygotsky (ed.) *The Collected Works of L.S. Vygotsky. Vol. 4* (pp. 253–259). New York, NY: Plenum Press.

Vygotsky, L.S. (2000) *Thought and Language* (A. Kozulin, Trans.). Cambridge, MA: MIT Press.

Wagner, S. and Grenier, P. (1991) *Analphabétisme de Minorité et Alphabeéisme d'Affirmation Nationale à Propos de l'Ontario Français. Volume I: Synthèse Théoretique et Historique*. Toronto: Ministère de l'Education.

Wald, B. (1984) A sociolinguistic perspective on -' current framework for relating language proficiency to academic achievement. In C. Rivera (ed.) *Language Proficiency and Academic Achievement* (pp. 55–70). Clevedon, UK: Multilingual Matters.

Walker, D. (2014) *A Pedagogy of Powerful Communication: Youth Radio and Radio Arts in the Multilingual Classroom*. New York: Peter Lang.

Walton, F. and O'Leary, D. (2015) *Siviumut: Towards the Future Together. Inuit Women Education Leaders in Nunavut and Nunavik*. Toronto, ON: Women's Press and Canadian Scholars Press.

Weber, J.-J. (2014) *Flexible Multilingual Education: Putting Children's Needs First*. Bristol: Multilingual Matters.

Weber, J.-J. (2015) *Language Racism*. London: Palgrave MacMillan.

Wedin, Å. (ed.) (2017) *Språklig Mångfald i Klassrummet (Linguistic Diversity in the Classroom)*. Stockholm: Lärarförlaget.

Weiss, L.G., Saklofske, D.H., Holdnack, J.A. and Prifitera, A. (2016) WISC-V: Advances in the assessment of intelligence. In L.G. Weiss, D.H. Saklofske, J.A. Holdnack and A. Prifitera (eds) *WISC-V Assessment and Interpretation: Scientist–Practitioner Perspectives*. New York: Academic Press.

Wells, G. (1981) *Learning through Interaction: The Study of Language Development*. Cambridge: Cambridge University Press.

Wickström, M. (2015) Making the case for the mother tongue: Ethnic activism and the emergence of a new policy discourse on the teaching of non-Swedish mother tongues in Sweden in the 1960s and 1970s. In M. Halonen, P. Ihalainen and T. Saarinen (eds) *Language Policies in Finland and Sweden: Interdisciplinary and Multi-Sited Comparisons* (pp. 171–195). Bristol: Multilingual Matters.

WIDA Consortium (2012) *Amplification of the English Language Development Standards.* Madison: Board of Regents of the University of Wisconsin System. Retrieved from http://www.wida.us/standards/eld.aspx

Wiley, T.G. (1996) *Literacy and Language Diversity in the United States.* Washington, DC: Center for Applied Linguistics and Delta Systems.

Wiley, T.G. and Rolstad, K. (2014) The common core state standards and the great divide. *International Multilingual Research Journal* 8 (1), 38–55. doi:10.1080/19313152.20 14.852428.

Williams, C. (1994) Arfarniad o ddulliau dysgu ac addysgu yng nghyd-destun addysg uwchradd ddwyieithog [An evaluation of teaching and learning methods in the context of bilingual secondary education] (Unpublished PhD thesis). University of Wales, Bangor, UK.

Williams, C. (1996) Secondary education: Teaching in the bilingual situation. In C. Williams, G. Lewis and C. Baker (eds) *The Language Policy: Taking Stock* (pp. 39–78). Llangefni, UK: CAI.

Williams, C. (2000) Welsh-medium and bilingual teaching in the further education sector. *International Journal of Bilingual Education and Bilingualism* 3 (2), 129–148.

Wilson, K. and Devereux, L. (2014) Scaffolding theory: High challenge, high support in academic language and learning (ALL) contexts. *Journal of Academic Language & Learning* 8 (3), A91-A100.

Wink, J. (2010) *Critical Pedagogy: Notes from the Real World.* 4th ed. New York: Longman, 2010.

Wong Fillmore, L. (1982) Language minority students and school participation: What kind of English is needed? *Journal of Education* 164 (2), 143–156. doi:10.1177/002205748216400204

Wong Fillmore, L. (1991) When learning a second language means losing the first. *Early Childhood Research Quarterly* 6, 323–346.

Wong Fillmore, L. (2000) Loss of family language: Should educators be concerned? *Theory into Practice* 39 (4), 203–210.

Wong Fillmore, L. (2009) English language development: Acquiring the language needed for literacy and learning. Retrieved from http://assets.pearsonschool.com/asset_mgr/versions/2011-11/810BE0C344E9450E567F7A8877946BDB.pdf

Wong Fillmore, L. (2014) English language learners at the crossroads of educational reform. *TESOL Quarterly*, 48 (3), 624–632.

Wong Fillmore, L. and Fillmore, C.J. (2012) What does text complexity mean for English learners and language minority students? Stanford University Understanding Language project. Retrieved from http://ell.stanford.edu/papers/language

Wong Fillmore, L. and Snow, C.E. (2018) What teachers need to know about language. In C.T. Adger, C.E. Snow and D. Christian (eds) *What Teachers Need to Know about Language* (2nd edn, p. 8–51). Bristol: Multilingual Matters.

Wright, E.N. and Ramsey, C. (1970) Students of non-Canadian origin: Age on arrival, academic achievement and ability. Research report #88, Toronto Board of Education.

Wylie, C. Hodgen, E. Ferral, H. and Thompson, J. (2006) *Contributions of Early Childhood Education to Age-14 Performance. Evidence from the Longitudinal 'Competent Children, Competent Learners' Study.* Wellington, New Zealand: Ministry of Education.

Wylie, C. and Thompson, J. (2003) The long-term contribution of early childhood education to children's performance – evidence from New Zealand. *International Journal of Early Years Education* 11 (1), 69–78. doi:10.1080/0966976032000066109

Yong, E. (2016, February 10) The bitter fight over the benefits of bilingualism. *The Atlantic*. Retrieved from: http://www.theatlantic.com/science/archive/2016/02/thebattleoverbilingualism/462114/

Zanger, V.V. (1994) 'Not joined in': The social context of English literacy development for Hispanic youth. In B.M. Ferdman, R.-M. Weber and A. Ramirez (eds) *Literacy across Languages and Cultures* (pp. 171–198). Albany, NY: SUNY Press.

Zentella, A.C. (2015) Books as the magic bullet. *Journal of Linguistic Anthropology* 25 (1), 75–77.

Zwiers, J. (2008) *Building Academic Language: Essential Practices for Content Classrooms*. Grades 5–12. San Francisco, CA: Jossey-Bass.

Index

Academic Expertise framework 74–76
Academic support programme (ASP)
52–54
Accent 8, 39, 45–46
Actuality implies possibility 309–310,
333
Additive approaches to bilingualism
129, 275, 283–285, 304, 355–356
Additive bilingualism xxxv–xxxvi, xi,
18, 101, 129, 131, 236, 266–269, 272,
275, 277–283, 285, 288, 301–302, 304,
306, 311, 355–356
Additive bilingual programmes xxiii,
69, 101, 145, 283, 302
Additive contexts and home
environment 14, 94–95, 369
American Sign Language (ASL) 29, 32,
220, 222–223, 225
Antiracist education 67, 82, 110,
207, 237
Aotearoa/ New Zealand 91, 123, 190,
233–234
Australia/Australian 61, 84, 90–91, 95,
249, 259
Autonomous minorities 64
Autonomous orientation to language/
literacy 153, 172–173, 175, 178,
195, 202

Banking education 62, 77
Banyan tree 234
Basic language cognition (BLC) 46, 58,
180, 186–188, 207
Bicultural ambivalence 61–64
Bilingual cognitive advantage/benefits
13, 15–17

Caste minorities 61, 64
Challenge zone framework 52, 58

Codeswitching xxxv, xi, 146, 230, 235,
269, 271–272, 274, 322–323
Coercive relations of power xxxv,
xxxix, xi, 3–4, 7, 10, 61, 70–74, 81,
83, 86, 114, 150, 162, 204, 259, 278,
284, 297, 302, 356, 363, 370–371
Cognitive engagement 74–76
Collaborative relations of power xvi,
61, 71–72, 77, 82, 354, 370
Common European Framework for
Languages (CEFR) 295
Common underlying conceptual base
30, 217
Common underlying proficiency (CUP)
xxxix, xi, 9, 27–30, 33, 52, 129, 134,
144, 209, 217, 220, 226, 229–230,
232–234, 236–241, 248, 263, 267, 271,
279, 281, 286–287, 299, 302, 370
Common underlying reservoir of
literacy abilities 30, 241
Comparons Nos Langues project
328, 359
Comprehensible input 75
Connect instruction to students' lives
111, 115, 205, 283, 311, 348
Consequential validity xxxiv, xxxix, 52,
56, 129–130, 135, 141–142, 145–146,
149–151, 159. 168, 171, 185–186, 192,
201–202, 231, 237–238, 248, 272–273,
286, 303, 311
Context-embedded 50, 55, 200
Context-reduced 50, 53, 55
Continua of bi/multiliteracy 289, 291,
299–300
Conversational fluency 8, 10, 12, 21, 38,
43, 45–47, 54–55, 57–58, 130, 139,
152, 180, 189, 201
Conversational language 46, 48, 130,
180, 192, 200, 216

413